Moving Forward, Looking Back

THE UNIVERSITY
WINCHESTER

Moving Forward, Looking Back

**The European Avant-garde and the Invention of
Film Culture, 1919-1939**

Malte Hagener

Amsterdam University Press

Front cover illustration: photo taken during the shooting of BERLIN, DIE SINFO-
  NIE DER GROSSSTADT, GER 1927, Walter Ruttmann. Courtesy of the Deutsche
  Kinemathek – Museum für Film und Fernsehen

Cover design: Kok Korpershoek, Amsterdam
Lay-out: JAPES, Amsterdam

ISBN   978 90 5356 960 3 (paperback)
ISBN   978 90 5356 961 0 (hardcover)
NUR   674

© Malte Hagener / Amsterdam University Press 2007

Table of Contents

Acknowledgements

A book is always a long and winding endeavour to which many people contribute, a lot of them in ways not intended and often even unconsciously. So this list invariably contains names of people who never meant to participate in the creation of this book and who might even be surprised to find their names here. Of course, mistakes, omissions and faults are completely my own. Meanwhile, I am more than happy to point out the support of a number of friends, acquaintances and colleagues.

The basic framework, organisationally, intellectually and financially has been provided by the Universiteit van Amsterdam and the project » Cinema/Media Europe «, which gave me the opportunity to research and write this book, so my first bow has to go to those who made it possible to participate in this project. I have shared many hours and thoughts with my colleagues Marijke de Valck, Floris Paalman and Ward Rennen in classes and libraries, but also in our offices, first in the Vendelstraat and later in the Turfdraagsterpad. However, this project was all the more extraordinary because many other members from all corners of Europe made our meetings and activities so rewarding and stimulating. Thanks also to Melis Behlil, Yesim Burul, Tarja Laine, Gerwin van der Pol, and Eleftheria Thanouli who contributed to our common effort of rethinking European cinema. However, the largest debt I owe is to Drehli Robnik. He showed up one day at the Ph.D. seminar and has become, along with Gabu Heindl, a good friend ever since.

A number of colleagues and friends in Amsterdam have been helpful in various ways, either listening to my half-baked ideas over dinner, sharing film experiences, taking the time to read earlier drafts of chapters, or just helping out when it was most necessary: Ivo Blom, Karel Dibbets, Charles Forceville, Julia Nordergraaf, Martina Roepke, Wim Staat, Wanda Strauven, Arnth van Tuinen, and Reimer van Tuinen. As part of the Amsterdam School of Cultural Analysis, I was lucky to be supported by Eloe Kingma and Hent de Vries. The first scholars to seriously involve themselves in the ideas raised in this book were on my Ph.D. committee and so thanks to Jeroen Boomgaard, Ian Christie, Vinzenz Hediger, Jan Simons, and Frank van Vree.

A number of invitations allowed me to develop and test out ideas that have helped to shape this book. The first crucial presentation was given at New York University in February 2002 where Elena Gorfinkel and Charles Leary organised what turned out to be the first in a series of get-togethers focused on the idea of Cinephilia. At the conference I met Federico Windhausen, a fellow spirit of the avant-garde, while Bill Simon guided me to some references that I would not have been aware of otherwise. In New York, Steven Aldridge and Suzy Beemer provided not only food and shelter, but also stimulating talks and friendship. The series of conferences continued in 2003 in Amsterdam and in 2004 in London where Jenna Pei-Suin Ng and David Forgacs rose to the occasion. At all three conferences, a group of young scholars combined two virtues: a congenial and friendly atmosphere and excellent scholarship. Thanks to the organisers and everybody present on these occasions.

Since 2002, I have been a regular at the Gradisca Spring School in the Friaul region of Italy, an initiative that is focussed on the coming of sound to European cinema. Leonardo Quaresima and his team have established an extraordinary event in a small town between Venice, Istria and the Alps, which unites academic rigour, an impeccable organisation with Italian style, good food and a stimulating atmosphere. In this extraordinary atmosphere, I have met many exceptional scholars who helped me in various ways, among them mention has to go to Nataša Ďurovičová, Charles O'Brien, Francesco Pitassio, Davide Pozzi and Laura Vichi as well as the amazing staff of the Magis Spring School. In Gradisca, I also first met Petr Szczepanik who became a friend when he joined me in Thuringia where the short distance between Jena and Weimar allowed us to see each other more often than we would have otherwise been able to on our trajectories between Amsterdam, Berlin, Brno, Prague and other places.

Other occasions and invitations also helped me to shape my thoughts and words: Jan Distelmeyer and Erika Wottrich organised a conference on Tobis in 2002 in Hamburg, which was overseen by Hans-Michael Bock who, years before, had been instrumental in my first serious contact with film history. In Coimbra, Paulo Granja – with whom I share many interests – hosted a congress on the European film club movement where Christel Henry contributed valuable information, while Patricia Pascoal and Pedro Teixeira offered lodging along the way. In Jena, where I am currently based, I was lucky to be able to present part of my research and received reactions from Michael Barchet and Karl Sierek, which have found their way into this work.

Tim Bergfelder not only gave valuable advice at a crucial point, he was also one of the first who encouraged me to seriously venture into film studies when I was as an undergraduate in Norwich. Andrew Higson, another Norwich regular, helped me to track down Jamie Sexton whose work on the British film societies is a model of thorough and meticulous scholarship. Michael Wedel and Johann N. Schmidt were much more than partners on an editing project that offered stimulating ideas and texts along the way. Milena Gregor helped with access to Esfir Shub's films, while Martin Barnier, Francesco Bono and Sofia Rossholm shared their ideas on the coming of sound.

A number of friends were not involved directly with the creation of this work, yet their support nevertheless was instrumental in my efforts. Christiane Kühl and Chris Kondek saved the day by providing English versions of Benjamin texts during a period when time was especially short, while Ulrike Kassun und Peter Crisp often provided welcome digressions away from my work. Vinzenz Hediger and Alexandra Schneider are esteemed colleagues and good friends of equal measure. In Hamburg, Ronald Hoffmann, David Kleingers, and Kurt Rehkopf; in Bonn, Tasja Frenzel and Carsten Schinko; and in Dresden, Jürgen Müller deserve honourable mention. Robin Curtis, Jeanpaul Goergen, Irmbert Schenk, Thomas Tode, and William Uricchio also gave support along the way.

Finally, I have to thank two people to whom I am indebted in many more ways than I can ever express here. Thomas Elsaesser not only gave me the opportunity to work in the Cinema/Media Europe project and supervised the work on which this book is based, he is also a model of scholarship and engaged teaching. Without his intellectual rigour and sharp intelligence, without his film-historical knowledge and keen interest, this project in its present form would have been unthinkable. Marjan Parvand saved me more than once when I was stuck; her criticism is as sharp as her support is undivided, her energy is as constant as her love is inspiring. It is to her that I dedicate this book.

Malte Hagener
Jena, March 2007

Introduction
Avant-garde Culture and Technological Transformations

The technical revolutions are the cracks of artistic development
where the tendencies become visible, exposed so to speak.
In each new technical revolution the tendency turns from
a hidden element of art as if it's on its own into a manifest element.
And finally, here we are with film.
Walter Benjamin (1927)[1]

The title of this book – *Moving Forward, Looking Back* – points towards three crucial issues that I will discuss at length in the chapters that follow. Firstly, it takes its cue from two metaphorically condensed images related to the avant-garde: Walter Benjamin's angel of history (inspired by Paul Klee's painting *Angelus novus*) and Niklas Luhmann's oarsmen who are focussed on the place they are coming from.[2] Besides developing these condensed signs that have given me my title, I am deeply indebted to both theoreticians to whose writings I have returned time and again in my study of the avant-garde. Moreover, both allegorical configurations share some common ground: the figures are facing backwards and can only see where they are coming from, they are driven inexorably towards an invisible future (paradoxically, or even vainly for Luhmann, and tragically for Benjamin) and they can only make sense of their actions in retrospect. Therefore, their intentions, their operations and the results thereof diverge wildly in the case of the avant-garde. It is this gap between direction of movement and direction of observation that is characteristic of the avant-garde and that will figure prominently in the following pages.

Secondly, these figurative metaphors condense a crucial issue for the avant-garde, which is central to the argument I put forward: the avant-garde was mentally fixed on an ever-invisible future that was continually eluding its grasp. The avant-garde was working towards a time that it had already anticipated, a future seemingly so imminent that it was only a matter of *how* to achieve it, not *whether* it could be achieved. This strange logic is somehow comparable to the *futur antérieur* and was at the same time focussed on the past and on the future: the avant-garde rebelled against prior historical styles, against the traditional networks and institutions of the art system; it attempted to do away with everything that came before it in one *tabula rasa*-gesture and not that infrequently this conflict with the past proved to be so strong and pervasive that the avant-garde exhausted itself in an ostentatious rebellion against the past. The avant-garde thrived on a future that was ultimately unattainable, and if it could be reached at all, it would have meant the end of the avant-garde since it would have fulfilled its purpose: the avant-garde could never exist for a moment in the present. It is this strange and paradoxical structure, caught between past and future that we will encounter on many occasions when examining the avant-garde.

And thirdly, *Moving Forward, Looking Back* also succinctly sums up the stance that this work as a whole takes: it is simultaneously a film-historical work in the traditional sense – it takes the film avant-garde as its object and sketches its development in a novel version – and a meta-historical work since it also details how the avant-garde contributed to the writing and rewriting of film history. Moving forward, looking back is thus the mode in which the avant-garde functioned (or rather: had to function), but also the mode that this work takes up in redrawing the map that emerges as the sum of the activities of the interwar avant-garde in Europe. However, before delving into the details of the avant-garde, I want to turn to Walter Benjamin for some important insights into the relationship between technological developments, artistic production and socio-political transformations.[3]

Any production, including artistic production, occupies a certain position in relation to the means of production that it needs and uses. This position might be affirmative, critical or negotiating between these poles with denial being the most extreme form of affirmation. The avant-garde – if we take it to be radically different from previous artistic styles or schools that merely followed one another in a succession of changing fashions – is characterised by the way it positioned itself differently within social, economic and cultural force fields.[4] In his text » The Author as Producer « (» Der Autor als Produzent «) Benjamin astutely outlined the relationship between avant-garde artist and the means of production. Using the example of Sergei Tretiakov as the » operating author « in contrast to the merely » informing author «, Benjamin concedes that the operating author is not only *avant-gardistic* in his basic convictions as expressed in his artistic output, but also in his attitude towards the means of production as expressed in all of his activities, beyond the artefact of the finished work. The foremost task of the artist – Benjamin's » author « is just shorthand for the artist in general – is not only to produce works that are groundbreaking and revolutionary, but also to create a novel position in relation to the means of production: » ...to supply a production apparatus without trying, within the limits of the possible, to change it, is a highly disputable activity even when the material supplied appears to be of a revolutionary nature. «[5] Without the apparatus of production and distribution, even the avant-garde artist is unable to launch his/her work in the public sphere, but at the same time s/he is obliged to change the very institution that is necessary for its own dissemination. The avant-garde has to aim for the restructuring of the very preconditions of its own existence – this paradox is at the centre of the cultural-aesthetic movement. For Benjamin, a critical stance alone does not suffice. As a negative example, Benjamin refers to the journalistic report. A characteristic genre of the *Neue Sachlichkeit* (New Sobriety), the report was boosted enormously by the rise of two new media: illustrated press and radio. In Benjamin's view, it ultimately only succeeded in producing picturesque images of poverty that soothed the antagonism and brutality inherent in social-economic relations between the rich and the poor. Benjamin's argument against these fashionable images of misery culminates in the call for the author as photographer and vice versa to break down the boundaries and specialisations erected between supposedly different activities:

> [I]ntellectual production cannot become politically useful until the separate spheres of competence to which, according to the bourgeois view, the process of intellectual production owes its order, have been surmounted; more precisely, the barriers of competence must be broken down by each of the productive forces they were created to separate, acting in concert [6]

The first step of avant-garde (or as Benjamin would have it: revolutionary) activity is to break down those specialisations and separations that bourgeois society has erected: between different art forms, between art and life, between theory and practice, between producer and consumer, between artist and audience. The avant-garde has to work on two fronts: it has to produce art, but, equally important, it also has to work towards a transformation within the means of production. As a model, Benjamin points to Brecht's epic theatre that he characterises as a » dramatic laboratory « – the key task for artists is to determine his/her place in relation to the means of production and to integrate the resulting realisation in his/her artistic production. The idea of art as a laboratory is one key to understanding the avant-garde. In this perspective the artist becomes a scientist and engineer setting up parameters and experiments for testing out results: the work of art becomes a test arrangement, not unlike in a scientific series of experiments.

The avant-garde occupied the position of a minesweeper in relation to the culture at large: it tested territory, marked out dangerous spots and cleared the way for the larger cohorts of mainstream culture to follow. The positioning of the avant-garde vis-à-vis these broader cultural trends is as interdependent as it is paradoxical: mainstream culture needs the avant-garde as a pathfinder and scout to explore unknown regions while the avant-garde in turn simultaneously needed the mainstream as an opposition to distinguish itself from, but also as a mass movement to follow. To claim a position ahead of the majority only makes sense if someone was there to follow (at least potentially). Yet, if the majority suddenly caught up, the avant-garde would lose its self-proclaimed status and be swallowed up. The movement was trapped between two poles, either it would lose contact with the mainstream and become obscure and esoteric or it would move too slowly for the culture at large and become stale and dated – both dangers would mean the end of the movement. The danger of falling into the trap of complacency and smugness has been astutely observed by a young Lotte Eisner who, in 1928, was just earning her first experiences at the trade magazine *Film-Kurier*:

> If the avant-garde is no longer the privilege of the truly brave pioneers, the danger might occur that it becomes a common basis for the slowly moving masses. ... The avant-garde needs to sound out its own rows; it must free itself from those, who may harm it. ... The avant-garde has to be aware of remaining avant-garde. It has to know its friends and accept criticism from its own. Otherwise it will become, despite its name, yesterday's news.[7]

The situation was never static, but the avant-garde was operating in a dynamic environment of push-and-pull between the avant-garde and mainstream, which almost invariably led to a cyclical rise and fall of the avant-garde.

The avant-garde has traditionally been the domain of art history and, to a lesser extent, of literary studies. If we follow Benjamin's lead and consider the avant-garde in relation to new media, another look at the film avant-garde should yield interesting results in many respects. The avant-garde has been seen as a cross-media initiative that occupied many different cultural (plat) forms. They consisted of a network of key players (André Breton, Sergei Tretiakov, Tristan Tzara, Bertolt Brecht…) who set up shop in a handful of key places (Zurich, Paris, Moscow, Berlin, London, Amsterdam/Rotterdam) and they communicated via a handful of key network nodes (little magazines, exhibitions, congresses). In film, the avant-garde achieved neither the same strength nor purity as it did in literature, performance, and the visual arts. Yet, by moving film from a marginal position to the centre, by taking Benjamin seriously, I hope to not only contribute to film studies, but also open up a new perspective on the avant-garde as a broader phenomenon.

The film avant-garde, when compared to its siblings in the other arts, was confronted with special problems: It had to gain access to the means of production, which proved cumbersome, difficult and expensive, especially after the introduction of sound. The film avant-garde – and that is part of its special position compared to its manifestations in other art forms – could neither draw a binary opposition between itself and commercial mass culture nor between itself and mainstream bourgeois art, two strategies often employed by the avant-garde in other art forms. On the one hand, it needed an established apparatus of production, distribution and exhibition in order to find a public and for that reason the film avant-garde had to compromise to a certain extent with the mainstream forces of institutionalised cinema. In literature and the visual arts it was relatively easy to bypass the traditional ways of reaching a public by publishing a magazine or staging an exhibition whereas in film the construction of an alternative system of production, distribution and exhibition required enormous amounts of time and energy – and compared to film industry institutions it always remained rudimentary.[8] On the other hand, film was not yet established as an accepted art form and many active on the fringes of the avant-garde were striving to secure film a place in the pantheon of accepted art forms rather than trying to get rid of art altogether. This » impurity « is characteristic of the film avant-garde which could never disentangle itself completely from the typical bourgeois position as it hoped to elevate film to an accepted art form.

The film avant-garde had to engage in various tasks on different fronts: on the one side, it was confronted with technological modernisation as it occupied a new medium while, on another side, it could not cut itself completely off from the social and cultural modernity of life styles and consumerism because of cinema's involvement with popular culture. Unlike the high modernism that possibly found its strongest expressions in the radical abstractions of Malevich and Mondrian, in the nonsensical attacks on reason in Dadaist performances and Surrealist *écriture automatique* or in the complicated style experiments of Joyce and Pound, the film avant-garde could not escape the triangulation of modernism (artistic style), modernity (lifestyle and consumer culture) and modernisation (technology).[9] Whereas the other arts often took the latter two as material, they nevertheless largely withdrew into intellectual realms of complexity and abstraction. The film avant-garde, by contrast, not only negotiated » the modern « as a topic of representation, it also had to cope with it in terms of production, distribution and exhibition. The cinema had to find its place in a field that was thoroughly structured by modern technology.

For Benjamin, the technological breaking points, the moments of extreme transformation brought the political and social issues of art to the fore. It is at times of intense change that the most urgent issues become most visible, but the development is technological before it trickles down into the culture at large: » …the most important, elementary progressions of art are neither new content nor new form – the revolution of technology precedes both. «[10] Yet, the specific employment of technology in art is neither a given nor determined by the technology itself. The use of technology is the result of a complex process of discussion, negotiation, subjugation, resistance and appropriation. Technology, culture and society cannot be considered as separate entities. This book deals with the European cinematic avant-garde, its dynamics and networks, its discourses and practices, its self-understanding during the period between 1919 and 1939 and its subsequent historiography. My approach is partly inspired by Walter Benjamin, yet my own position is also determined by my own historical *situat-*

edness, which diverges from Benjamin's contemporary observer status. When Andreas Huyssen re-evaluated the canonical avant-garde of the interwar period from the vantage point of the post-modern in the 1980s he argued that

> conformism would eventually overpower the tradition of avantgardism, both in advanced capitalist societies and, more recently, in East European societies as well. ... In most academic criticism the avantgarde has been ossified into an elite enterprise beyond politics and beyond everyday life, though their transformation was once a central project of the historical avantgarde.[11]

Since Huyssen wrote this the situation has changed considerably as the bipolarity of Cold War politics has given way to a new post-Wall complexity, but the concentration on the aesthetic features of the avant-garde at the expense of its transformative energies in political, social and cultural issues has persisted. From the current vantage point more than fifteen years after the fall of the Wall, I believe it is possible to cast a glance back at the avant-garde of the first decades of the Twentieth Century which has since its inception been thoroughly canonised as historical.[12] By adapting a perspective that might be loosely called » post-ideological « the avant-garde will look considerably different and this change of focus will hopefully yield interesting results. Specifically, I want to address how the avant-garde associated itself with film and how the cinema engaged with everyday life, mainstream institutions such as government agencies or the electric industry and technical innovations such as sound, what political objectives can be gleaned from their activities and what strategic alliances they adopted. For the most part I will focus on ephemeral instances such as exhibitions and screenings, discussions and teaching, financing and commissions, networking and self-promotion, not as a context for the films, but as an integral part of what the avant-garde conceived as their project of transforming life and art by breaking down the barriers conventionally and separating them, while not obscuring their differences. In a move comparable to the Hegelian gesture of *sublation* (» *Aufhebung* «), the aim of this study is to understand the totality of avant-garde activities in the field of cinema as a series of discourses, by examining the paradoxical temporal, topological and geographical construction of this avant-garde in relation to European interwar society and to a major change in media technology – the coming of sound. The aim is to reconsider the arrival of sound in European cinema from the perspective of the avant-garde and of industry, which will, I hope, not only encourage scholars to take another look at this particular chapter of film history, but help re-assess the role of the avant-garde in this (and perhaps other) modern media transformations in more general terms.

Novel technological developments like photography and film not only add new formats to the existing ensemble of the arts, but these reproductive media have far-reaching influences in the reconfiguring of the field at every level. For Benjamin these developments had pervasive implications. One such consequence was that the avant-garde – by (self-)definition in the forefront of artistic development – had to adopt the most advanced media in order to fulfil its mission of engendering social, political, economic and cultural transformations. The key idea of the avant-garde – its self-proclaimed goal – was the reconfiguration of the cultural sphere and by extension, the change of the political, social and economic foundations. Breaking down the barriers between art and society, between culture and politics, between theory and practice, overcoming these (artificially erected) boundaries was *the* crucial element in the program of the avant-garde. Thus, the self-definition of any member of the avant-garde could not be limited to that of an artist, instead they saw themselves as propagandists and preachers, as engineers and scientists, as politicians and practical jokers and as magicians and muggers. Their activities were happening within an environment characterised by a number of media considered to be new in the 1920s. Film, radio, the gramophone, illustrated press and sound film all opened up new spaces and public spheres that the avant-garde attempted to claim and occupy. It is on this playing field, shaped by a media-savvy public, a jagged landscape of technology, and new media with new techniques that the manoeuvres and negotiations, the attacks and withdrawals of a dynamic avant-garde were taking place.

1 Reframing the Historical Avant-garde – Media, Historiography and Method

[N]o other single factor has influenced the emergence of the new
avantgarde art as much as technology, which not only fueled
the artists' imagination ..., but penetrated to the core of the work itself.
The invasion of the very fabric of the art object by technology
and what one may loosely call the technological imagination
can best be grasped in artistic practices such as collages,
assemblages, montage and photomontage; it finds its ultimate
fulfillment in photography and film, art forms which can not only
be reproduced, but are in fact designed for mechanical reproducibility.

Andreas Huyssen (1980)[1]

Four Layers and Three Frames

The avant-garde has often been conceptualised either as a movement or as a network – both metaphors point to its dynamic and malleable nature. Flow and change are defining characteristics of a phenomenon that had taken up the cause of transforming and revolutionising life and art. The energy thus generated within avant-garde circles did not circulate completely without channels or river beds, the flow did not run from a central summit down an evenly shaped cone in all directions with equal force. The avant-garde formed (semi-)permanent connections and it had nodes through which much of the current was channelled. These networks and nodes can be detected on different levels, which should not be thought of hierarchically, but rather rhizomatically. The layers are not vertically subordinated to one another, but they are horizontally connected in a variety of fashions: overlapping with one another, complementing or contradicting each other or clicking into each other in various manners. None of those layers predetermines the other, but they all influence each other as they are interrelated in a variety of ways. The model of layers and frames attempts to construct a mental map that does not concede privilege to any of these levels.

Even though the tiers are not hierarchically stacked on top of each other, they can be identified and described. The first layer relates to physical, geographical and topological location and movement and is provided by the cities of modernism. My concentration on Berlin, Paris, London, Amsterdam, and Moscow with glances to Brussels, La Sarraz, Magnigotorsk, Stuttgart and some other places reflects the cultural logic of the network of modernist art. Rather than developing evenly in major cities across Europe, the avant-garde emerged in several places more or less simultaneously. These places subsequently became centres of gravity and attracted energy, activists and followers on an international level. Paris in the 1920s was not only a home to avant-garde filmmakers, activists and theoreticians from all over France, but also from Spain and Italy, from Great Britain and Germany, from Brazil and Romania. Berlin was a similar meeting point for Germans, Austrians and Hungarians, but also for Scandinavians, Russians, as well as for Czech and Polish citizens. When Scotsman John Grierson turned London into a centre of innovative filmmaking in the 1930s, the cast of characters was similarly international, with activists from places as far as the United States, Brazil and New Zealand. At least for a relatively small group of activists the cities that I concentrate on were forming a global network not altogether different from the one that Saskia Sassen has more recently diagnosed for the global financial system that spans across New York, London and Tokyo.[2] An artist would often move through different milieus that might shift from time to time from one place to another. To give one example: After leaving his hometown of Lund in Sweden, Viking Eggeling first mingled with the cubists in Paris, during World War One he was part of the cosmopolitan artist-intellectual scene in Zurich and Ascona and after the war until his untimely death in 1924 he was part of the emergent German film avant-garde and worked closely with Hans Richter, both in Berlin and at Richter's family home in Forst (Lausitz).[3] This » city « level belongs to a general history of the avant-garde and I will not delve too deeply into the social, political, cultural and economic reasons for the attraction of these cities as this would exceed the frame of my study.[4]

At the second level, the channels of transmission and network nodes are provided by institutions: organisations, associations, clubs and various support structures. The ciné-clubs and specialised film theatres, the film societies and audience organisations, the various (inter-)national affiliations and links came into existence with the explicit purpose of making contacts and personal acquaintances more permanent and stable. A cinema specialising in avant-garde film gathers an audience that exceeds the small and necessarily limited circle of friendship and acquaintance. Also located on this level are such industry departments as the Tobis company, which experimented with sound between 1928 and 1930, Grierson's different state-sponsored film units or Ufa's *Kulturfilmabteilung*. These film production institutions did not belong to the avant-garde proper, but existed in close proximity and in constant exchange with it. These efforts amount to an attempt at forming an alternative network different from that of the commercial film industry. In a systemic logic this level helps to stabilise otherwise highly susceptible structures. By having organisations for screening, distribution or production one acquires a higher degree of security in planning – a film club with regular screenings and annual subscription provides an audience that does not have to be mobilised anew for every screening. I will discuss the networks of audience organisations in detail in chapter three.

The next level could be said to be made up of the events that these semi-permanent networks of the second level created: the screenings and discussions, the meetings and exhibitions – only by achieving a certain regularity on this more fleeting level could one move to the level of a permanent organisation: a ciné-club that does not meet on a regular basis ceases to exist, a specialised cinema that shows conventional fare loses its distinguishing mark in comparison to normal cinemas. Yet again, since the avant-garde by definition constantly had to reinvent itself, it often oscillated between the fleeting and ephemeral event (often guerrilla style) and the stable, but also more staid organisation with its bureaucracy and almost unavoidable conservatism. Also included on the third level are such singular events as the festival in La Sarraz (even though the participants believed it was the beginning of a more stable and ongoing series), the Stuttgart exhibition (which toured different cities, but in retrospect it only amounted to a series of local events) or the music festival in Baden-Baden in the years leading up to the introduction of sound. I will concentrate on these events – fragments of a practice that attempted to achieve regularity and stability, but also constantly broke away from permanence and finality – in chapter four.

The fourth level can be conceptualised as the elements that circulated inside these networks: the lectures and personal appearances, the visits and travels, but also the commissions and films in which certain elements, key players, ideas, and conceptions took shape, fell apart and reconfigured constantly (even though the network is the flow and vice versa – we have to be wary with the notion that there is a network separate from the substance flowing inside the vessels).

These four levels do not necessarily encompass all of the possible interests in the avant-garde. One could, for example, discuss the biography of the key players not in terms of the auteur theory, but as attractors and dynamic structures inter-connecting the different layers. My interest in these semi-successful and unstable attempts at network building, in these rhizomes of the avant-garde is archaeological. When reviewing the events and institutions one can reconstruct how the players involved in the avant-garde conceptualised the development of the movement and intended to sustain it. These four layers will be overlaid and complemented with three frames of reference, one temporal (the historical period under investigation), one geographical (the spatial extension of the layers), and one conceptual (the tools and methods employed in this work).

1.1   The Temporal Frame: Historiography and the Coming of Sound Film

> *The period of the transition to sound film offers*
> *a splendid example of historical overdetermination.*
> Alan Williams (1992)[5]

The first wave of the cinematic avant-garde emerged in the 1920s and had its peak around 1930. The time period under investigation is thus framed by two World Wars and these two decades are marked in the middle by the introduction of synchronised sound to the cinema. Sound film and the intricate history of its introduction between (roughly) 1927 and 1932 will provide a temporal frame for this study. This media transition has been examined from a variety of perspectives: the technology, the systems of synchronisation and the film industry,[6] the international traffic of money, know-how and patents,[7] the shift in Hollywood from silent to sound[8] and the introduction of sound film in different European countries.[9] In contrast, the continuities and ruptures of the avant-garde across this historical divide have occupied a marginal place in film history: What was the fate of the film avant-garde during the coming of sound, what were the dominant opinions, how did production, distribution and exhibition react to the technological restructuring? These and other questions will be addressed in the following chapters.

The traditional story of the film avant-garde and the coming of sound is worn-out and staid. It is normally told along these lines: The devastation of World War One was hardly over when young and progressive artists in different parts of Europe challenged traditional norms in a project that evolved into the European film avant-garde in the course of the 1920s. Aesthetically explorative, politically confrontational and internationally minded, this group of creative individuals forged continually closer ties until, all of a sudden, the introduction of sound destroyed cosmopolitanism, aroused nationalism, and brought the hopeful bloom to a sudden end. It is along these lines that the story of the classic avant-garde in film is normally told. Let it suffice to invoke just one example to stand in for countless other text books and historical overviews:

> [T]his experimental phase ended with the coming of sound. … [T]he termination was also informed by the anti-realist agendas common to all the avant-gardes, with sound representing a decisively realist › supplement ‹ to the image. … The search for cinematic › specificity ‹ was polemical and separatist on the one hand – against theatrical and narrative models – synthesising and hybridising on the other, with models from painting and music.[10]

In this brief extract there are a number of unspoken, half-spoken and outspoken assumptions which are at least debatable to me: To start with, sound is seen as intrinsically and by definition a realist supplement to the image (does this imply that the image is non-realist? Or is the image » less realistic « than sound?). Secondly, the film avant-garde is pictured as inherently anti-realist, and ambivalently poised between drawing on other arts and defining itself in contrast to them. Thirdly, the alleged turn to realism is bound up (causally?) with the introduction of sound. The discussion around cinema as an art form, my fourth objection, is limited to an early phase in which abstraction provided the guiding concept whereas the Soviet contribution is absent as well as the emerging documentary after 1930. And the last point of criticism to the standard version concerns the limiting way in which the avant-garde is defined: negatively, as based on experimentation and antagonism to certain concepts of the industry (separation of the film from the life of the spectator, individual reception). Interpreting the introduction of sound as the sole, or at least the main reason for the downfall of the avant-garde implicitly advocates a technological determinism in which a new medium is defined *a priori* in a deterministic fashion as shaped by its technological set-up, not by its social and cultural usage and utility. Sound film is by no means inherently realistic – even if it has often been employed that way.

Traditional accounts retrospectively purify the avant-garde in an act of reductionism that limits its scope to abstract moving shapes and formal experiments, to *cinéma pur* and *absoluter Film*.[11] Yet, filmmakers and activists had over the course of the 1920s slowly moved towards hybrid forms in which realist depictions were juxtaposed with unusual perspectives and innovative or conflicting editing patterns. In the traditional view, the influence of the Soviet montage school – which had its breakthrough in Western Europe with the celebrated presentation of Sergei Eisenstein's BRONENOSEZ » POTEMKIN « (SU 1925, › Battleship Potemkin ‹) in April 1926 in Berlin – is often absent. The Soviet Union as a shorthand for radically different cultural and artistic activities and output in the way it was received outside the Soviet Union – highly selective and idiosyncratic – will form the vanishing point for many of the activities and players discussed here as the communist country offered in the 1920s a very different model of cinema culture and of society at large.[12]

The introduction of sound in the United States was considerably different from the transition in Europe. It has been argued that » sound as sound, as a material and as a set of technical procedures, was inserted into the already constituted system of the classical Hollywood style «[13]. David Bordwell, Janet Staiger and Kristin Thompson propose in their monumental *Classical Hollywood Cinema* that sound caused little trouble and even less change for an already established system. Unlike in Europe, the production methods and the industrial balance of power in the US was not fundamentally shaken by the coming of sound. Most certainly, a normative power was inherent in the introduction of sound in both America and Europe, leading to a greater standardisation. Therefore, the coming of sound can be seen as an important step in the shift of control from exhibitors to manufacturers of motion pictures: » The coming of synchronized recorded sound to world cinema essentially completes the mechanization of the medium. And with full mechanization comes the most pervasive, general change brought about by the conversion to sound: increased standardization. «[14] Shooting practices and local exhibition specificities, projection speed and musical accompaniment – all had to yield to the overwhelming power that the introduction of sound carried with it like a gigantic tidal wave. For the avant-garde this meant that it not only had to deal with the new medium of sound cinema, but it moreover had – if it wanted to be more than an alternative aesthetics, but revolutionise the cinema in all its aspects – to take account of a situation that was in turmoil and undergoing a gigantic transformation between 1928 and 1932. It is exactly this time period in which the most fascinating experiments and the most intense efforts at building an alternative network culminated.

1.2 The Geographical Frame: Europe and the Cities of Modernism

> *The media is vital to the argument that modern nations are imagined*
> *communities. But contemporary media activity is also clearly one of the*
> *main ways in which transnational cultural connections are established.*
> Andrew Higson (2000)[15]

Besides the temporal frame just sketched, this study also constitutes a spatial field: geographically, it will take » Europe « as its frame of reference. Europe allows me to get away from a reliance on two traditional and narrow frames of reference: the biographical and the national. Employing the framework of » the national « in cinema studies has increasingly been questioned in the past ten to fifteen years. The discourse on the nation and cinema can be roughly divided into three phases.[16] Until well into the 1970s, sometimes as late as the early 1980s, the term » national cinema « has been employed in an unproblematic manner, in accordance with » nation «, » national culture « and all other derivative thereof which were largely considered as givens. Since the 1980s, a body of material has been produced in a second wave dealing with the » national « in film studies in more refined and sophisticated ways. Most studies from the second stage of the discussion dealt with questions of European national cinemas, especially with England as a focus of interest. In the 1990s, in a third phase, the emphasis has increasingly shifted to » minor «, » marginal « or » subaltern « national cinemas and complicated earlier modernist approaches to European national cinemas, pointing out the necessarily hybrid or multiple character of any national cinema culture. One could also speak of a shift of focus from a classic-realist mode in which representations were taken directly and at face value to a modernist approach complicating matters but firmly from within a European perspective using most often the theories of Benedict Anderson, Anthony Smith and Eric Hobsbawm,[17] while the third phase coincides with the fragmenting trajectories and lines of flights elaborated in post-modern, postcolonial and poststructuralist theories discernible in the work of, amongst many others, Homi Bhabha and Edward Said.[18]

No matter how diverse opinions may be, one thing seems to be certain: to talk of a national cinema always constructs an imaginary coherence. The problems involved in this act of boundary drawing have been pointed out in recent work in film studies that took the historical and political studies mentioned above into account.[19] Referring to European cinema is not done with the aim of substituting a » bad « object (the national) with a » good « one (Europe), but it will focus on the practice at a specific historical moment which was characterised by its European scope. The film avant-garde as conceptualised in this study is characterised in the actual and factual exchange of ideas, practitioners, and films. The issue of nation is not central to these questions because the question of why and how the state (as a political and juridical entity) and the nation (as an imagined community) intervened in these exchanges is not pertinent. Rather, I am interested in how the concept » Europe « has been mobilised in different projects and to different aims. The nation-state in various political and organisational forms returns with a vengeance in the 1930s when many avant-garde filmmakers turned to the state for financial and organisational support, although mostly indirectly through government agencies or political parties. In some countries, the nation-state also played a key role in the self-historicising of the avant-garde when offshoots of the movement founded the first film archives and film museums financed by governments.

The pronounced internationalism of the avant-garde movement actually requires a European framework. When Louis Delluc screened DAS CABINET DES DR. CALIGARI (GER 1919/20, Robert Wiene, › The Cabinet of Dr. Caligari ‹) at the cinema *Colisée* in Paris on 14 November 1921 it was not only a partisan action in aesthetic terms, but it was first and foremost a political provocation. Just as Fernand Léger had consciously sought the confrontation with the anti-German establishment the year before when he insisted on including German (expressionist) artists in the reopened *Salon des Indépendents*, Delluc's internationalism saw cinema not only as a new emerging art form, but also as a social and political force with a wide-ranging impact. Under the banner of aesthetic innovation (and officially announced as a benefit screening for the Spanish Red Cross) Delluc included a film from Germany into a French cinema programme, at that time an enemy whose products were despised and prohibited. Effectively, this event broke the French boycott as the successful reception of DAS CABINET DES DR. CALIGARI brought other German films into French cinemas.[20] Similarly, when Eisenstein's POTEMKIN hit Berlin's screens in early 1926 it was an event that immediately had European repercussions. Seen from the perspective of the avant-garde, the national was a frame to overcome and get rid of.

If the national is the Scylla of studying the film avant-garde, then the biographical is its Charybdis. Biography provides the easiest ready-made frame of reference available for aesthetic study. A biography supplies a clear structure (chronology, organic development, physical coherence) and tends towards isolating works of art from their context in which they were first produced and received. In focusing on stylistic analyses of isolated artefacts one misunderstands the avant-garde, which is striving towards a media concept which has to be grasped in its totality before contemplating isolated elements. My interest therefore focuses on the strategic manoeuvring, the political and social interventions (intra-filmic and, equally important, extra-filmic), the networking and publishing efforts, and the discursive regimes established, modified and rejected. I doubt that the most fruitful way of doing historiographical work in the arts is to put the durable and material work of art above more fleeting and ephemeral activity, to put the seeming consistency of the biography above the more unstable networks and connections. For reasons of convenience, tradition, institutional ramifications and support mechanisms the study of the film avant-garde has focused on either of the two sides – the national or the biographical. I will downplay both structures in the following chapters and instead concentrate on institutions, events, networks and discourses.

While Europe is the geographical frame of this work in a wider sense, the following pages focus on a number of cities as the hubs of activity. This study concentrates on events and institutions in Western Europe with Paris, Berlin, London and Amsterdam as its main centres (marginally other places such as Switzerland and Belgium will also be featured) and the Soviet Union as its vanishing point. Even though comparable activities took place in Lisbon and Prague, in Stockholm and Ljubljana, in Warsaw and Rome, the most influential activities happened around the cities first mentioned – they were the major nodes in the network that made up the European avant-garde of the interwar period. To get an understanding of the interconnected nature of the avant-garde, of its internal functioning and of the wider patterns of emergence it is paramount to reconstruct this core network around which other activities wrapped themselves. Malcolm Bradbury has described these cities of modernism as » generative environments of the new arts, focal points of intellectual community, indeed of intellectual conflict and tension. «[21] He goes on to argue that these cities were not only cosmopolitan spaces of communication, but also the topic of artistic activity, a metaphor as well as a place. The city was both a cause and an effect of the modern world as much as the avant-garde: both were results of the fundamental social, political, economic, psychic and economical transformations, but both also contributed to them. Bradbury isolates the novel as the quintessential artistic form of the city. While the connection between the city and the novel is certainly crucial, I would contend that the cinema, and especially the city symphony, provides the ultimate metaphor of and for the modern life in the city.

1.3   The Conceptual Frame: Crisis, Archaeology and Systems

A consistently archaeological approach not only has to widen
the range of questions deemed relevant, but also to change
the starting-point of the questions and to put into doubt
one's own historiographic premises; for example
by including discontinuities, the so-called dead ends
and the possibility of an amazing otherness of the past.
Thomas Elsaesser (2002)[22]

The historiographical model employed here testifies to a number of influences. The first theoretical frame was provided by the New Film History that emerged in the 1980s and added methodological rigour to traditionalist, non-theoretical history and fact-finding missions.[23] The move away from the film as text and an increased attention towards the cinema as a social, economic, political and cultural institution is my key influence from the New Film History.[24] A second inspiration has been Michel Foucault's conception of history as archaeology and genealogy. The third theorist to be reckoned with is Niklas Luhmann and his version of systems theory, which helped me to rethink the interactions, co-optations and dependencies of the avant-garde within a public media arena. Wherever possible, I have harked back to the writings of the activists from the 1920s and 1930s as many of the tools for the understanding of the film avant-garde have been developed by the people involved in these activities.

In terms of historiography the period of the introduction of sound can be seen as a prime example of a » crisis-model of historiography «[25] which involves a triple focus: on indexicality, on economic factors and on political issues. In theoretical and aesthetic terms, the coming of sound resulted in a » crisis of indexicality « – the (representational) film image now had to cope with an addition that was perceived by some observers to heighten realism, yet that also opened up a gap between the visible body on the screen and the audible sound from the loudspeakers. Not only does the film image originate at the back of the architectural space of the cinema while sound comes from behind the screen in front of the spectators, but sight and sound are also inscribed and worked upon with different technological processes on different apparatuses. The simultaneity and synchronicity between image and sound perceived by the spectator is therefore in technological terms an arbitrary relation and was seen as such from the very start. Sound film did not only have aesthetic repercussions, its economic ramifications challenged the existing order of the institution cinema. The gigantic costs involved in wiring production facilities and cinemas in a relatively short time around 1930 caused a gigantic upheaval in economic terms. This economic-institutional crisis was deepened by the first global depression following the US stock market crash of October 1929. The third crisis is cultural and political in nature: The introduction of sound not only brought noise and music to the film, but also language. In the silent era, inter-titles were easy to replace, thus adapting a film for a different market was fairly easy and relatively unproblematic. With sound the different methods of translation all became problematic: subtitles made the otherness of a language omnipresent in visual as well as in aural terms while it was perceived by contemporaries as a step back towards the inter-titles of the silent era that had just been left behind. Dubbing coupled a visible human body with an audible voice not connected to the body, thus destroying the assumed unity of sight and sound that many thought was the main achievement of sound film.[26] In some countries (e.g., Czechoslovakia, Italy) this resulted in an extreme, sometimes even violent reaction against dialogue spoken in a foreign language. This triple crisis – of indexicality, the economic-institutional base of the film industry, and the national – highlights problems and contradictions because the ensuing upheaval questioned many elements of the institution cinema.

In my discussions of the contemporary discourses I have been influenced by the concept of archaeology as elaborated by Michel Foucault.[27] In a number of studies on prison and surveillance,[28] on the organisation of knowledge and the construction of categories,[29] on the » invention « of insanity in the age of reason,[30] and on the medical gaze,[31] Foucault has exemplified his historiographical practice on specific objects. He has pioneered a method of understanding specific practices as discourses that perform at least two intimately related functions: these practices as discourses play a central part in the constitution of society and they regulate exclusion and inclusion. For Foucault the acts of discursive demarcation are the basis for analysing how power, language and society interact at specific moments in the creation of specific historical configuration. Foucault's theory is useful in understanding discursive operations as historical practices that are being operated in order to produce hierarchical divisions.

Within media history, the concept of archaeology has gained ground in the last ten years developing its own methodology.[32] Wolfgang Ernst has likened the archaeological method to the cold and emotionless gaze of a machine that first and foremost registers without interpreting. He has juxtaposed it to the hermeneutic gaze, which always already sees something else behind every text or object. Whereas hermeneutics attempt to fit everything in an already known horizon of expectation, the aim of media archaeology is » ...primarily to describe the artefact in its *givenness* – in other words: as a *datum*, as data – i.e., letting it stand as a monument instead of (just as historians tend to operate) transforming it into a document or an illustration of an underlying history. «[33] The method of media archaeology consists first of all of an act of » forgetting « everything that has come after the fact in an attempt to understand a period on its own terms. By going back in time and trying to understand what was meant by a specific practice, by attempting to see historical facts as monuments of a past practice, archaeology tries to reconstruct this practice.

By returning to a specific sub-genre of film studies, the study of early cinema, Thomas Elsaesser has opened a new perspective on today's media. In Elsaesser's archaeology, early cinema functions as a possible blueprint for the restructured field of new media, but also for the possible development of film and media studies into new media studies. The attention given to moments of transitions and change, possibility and utopia has influenced my model. Elsaesser provides a number of parameters and paradigms with an agenda for future research and a renewed media history: The refusal to search for beginnings amounts to a renewal of history, questioning the already-said at the level of existence gives new perspectives on well-known facts, an attention to the dead-ends and failures of media history opens up a space of possible futures that were imaginable at a certain point in time, and a heightened awareness for the absence of evidence as the evidence of a past presence opens history up to a wider perspective.[34]

Finally, Niklas Luhmann has developed a useful method of conceptualising the relationship of different systems to each other that does not revert to simplistic notions of influence, to folk psychology or to direct cause-effect schemata.[35] In his branch of systems theory, a system is characterised by its complete closure to the outside; the basic distinction runs between the system itself and the environment because this distinction creates the system in the first place, it brings it into existence. A system can observe the environment only according to the terms of its own operation: » Self-referential systems do not possess any other way of contact with the environment than self-contact. «[36] Thus, the economic system, which operates under the basic distinction of paying or not paying (having money or not, trading or not) assesses everything according to this code and logic, including those operations that involve entities outside its boundaries. Every system translates outside events into its own frequency because this is the only way that a system is able to understand what is going on in the environment. Thus, communication and interaction are always self-reflexive, necessarily indirect and distorted by the translation from one code to another. Communication that is meaningful in one system might be just white noise when picked up by another. To take the systems theory idea into my field of study: The systemic logic and functioning of the film industry and the avant-garde were separate from each other (even though neither of them achieved full autonomy) and one system was basically not visible to the other system as they worked under different operational premises. For the film industry the avant-garde did not exist as a stable entity because everything outside the industry is perceived as environment; the same holds true vice versa for the avant-garde. Moreover, the industry and the avant-garde were both incapable of understanding the other system according to the basic codes on which they were operating, but translated their operations into their own frequency. These translations of signals and codes make misunderstanding, or rather: distortion and white noise, inevitable.

1.4   The Corpus: Defining the Avant-garde

> [The historiography of artistic modernism] has typically formalized
> the work of early twentieth-century European movements in ways that
> decontextualize the works and diminish access to their historical significance.
> For decades the analysis and evaluation of these movements has subjected
> them to normative procedures that sidestepped political issues and guaranteed
> their conformity to the separation of art and pointed social purpose ....
> This work has been disproportionately aestheticized in such a way that the losses
> for cultural history exceed the gains for art's formal and craft history.
> Stephen C. Foster (1998)[37]

There is certainly no shortage of books on the film avant-garde: There are histories of film theory which provide ample space for the contribution of the avant-garde[38], very detailed historical studies of specific groups which were active in producing, exhibiting, publishing and teaching avant-garde cinema,[39] reprints of magazines dealing with avant-garde film[40] and studies of specific movements,[41] national cinematographies[42] or *auteurs* of this period,[43] not to mention those books that gave a general overview of avant-garde, independent and experimental film.[44] These studies all have their historical and analytical use value and if I depart from them it is with a measure of respect for the achievements of those pioneers who came before. Where I intend to diverge from these studies is, very broadly speaking, in the way in which they dissect and isolate a specific person, oeuvre or facet without taking into account or reflecting the *dispositifs*, discourses, networks, systems, levels of self-reference or structuring absences that I consider to be much more crucial shaping factors than the biography or the nation-state. I believe that the works of avant-garde art can only be understood adequately if analysed in its context of production, distribution and consumption, if scrutinised dialectically, and thus brought to another level of generality.

Especially interesting and fascinating are those instances that transgress or blow up conventional categories into which retrospective thinking had squeezed the avant-garde. To give an example: instead of concentrating on Hans Richter as an artist in the conventional sense (producing works that are aesthetically explorative and that can be hermeneutically analysed), he can be rethought as an activist on many different fronts. Richter organised exhibitions, programmed a cinema for an artistic-industrial exhibition and founded film so-cieties, lectured and wrote, published and networked, not to mention the many different film forms in which he worked (advertisement, industrial film, compi-lation film, experimental short). These fields are disparate in some senses, but they also belong together. They are part of a whole discourse which can only be discerned when practice is taken as seriously as the material results of the work. Other key figures that will feature centrally in this study are Béla Balázs, Ger-maine Dulac, Sergei Eisenstein, Joris Ivens, László Moholy-Nagy, Walter Rutt-mann and Dziga Vertov, to mention only the most famous ones. These agents adhered to an ideal of totality at a time before the functional differentiation of the film industry and after the introduction of sound did away with these con-ceptions of wholeness.

In analysing the Dutch *Filmliga*, Tom Gunning has argued for a wide perspec-tive in the study of the film avant-garde. Traditional approaches have concen-trated on films and theoretical texts in keeping with traditional thinking, which was based on the analysis of texts (herein of course following structuralist ter-minology in which film counts as a text too). Gunning argues for the inclusion of facets, which are more ephemeral and harder to detect: institutions and pro-gramming, distribution, publication and debate.[45] He argues that films and printed texts in the magazine *Filmliga* form only the most visible trace of a net-work consisting of a group of people in several Dutch cities meeting in order to watch films and discuss them afterwards. Retrospective analyses very often ne-glect the social practices because material results (films, books) are much easier to get a hold of and analyse. Moreover, film studies are not well equipped meth-odologically to deal with social practice because the genealogy in (hermeneuti-

cally inflected) humanities provide an orientation towards audio-visual artefacts or written texts. Furthermore, theory formation is normally considered retrospectively: histories of film theory are written afterwards on the basis of the
important canonised texts (mostly from canonised writers). For contemporary
observers in the 1920s and 1930s, the situation was much more difficult: For
them, film theory, or rather, attempts at theory formation, were much more a
process than a result, more a snapshot than a monolith, whereas later critics
and historians look at those texts that have for various reasons stood the test of
time. What I will attempt here is to give the theorisation some of its procedural
nature back. Theory is a process, not a product.

As I have just laid out, the object to be reconstructed in the following pages is
not without its vicissitudes. It may start with a simple question that raises complicated problems: Does one speak of avant-garde in the singular or in the plu-
ral? The avant-garde as a unified movement perhaps never existed, but a loose
structure, which saw itself as belonging together, can be detected. Avant-garde
was a common name both as a self-description and also as a name given by
others during the period under consideration.[46] When I examine the activities
of the avant-garde I am not primarily interested in the aesthetic style of their
films or the underlying philosophy. Therefore, I am not interested in questions
such as whether BALLET MECHANIQUE (FR 1924, Fernand Léger / Dudley Murphy) is Dada, Surrealist or Constructivist, as this would mean a departure from
the archaeological method. The different strands of the avant-garde had very
strong personal, intellectual and organisational continuity and categorisation or
compartmentalisation was a very unimportant factor at the time. Sometimes,
when it is necessary to differentiate Constructivism from Expressionism, I will
distinguish different trends, but on the whole the proximity of the different
movements is stronger than their differences.

The complete scope of the specific » practice « of the avant-garde is important
for a thorough understanding and this will be the focus of my study: In lecturing and writing, the avant-garde formulated some of their ideas (though these
texts certainly form no simple description of their ideas and convictions), production, distribution, and exhibition show attempts at putting these ideas into
practice. In teaching and in building institutions, we can recognise the attempt
of constructing structures that are independent of individual actors and that
will be self-sustaining over time. Their activities formed a discourse and they
attempted to create a system of their own, yet they never achieved operational
closure to the environment in a Luhmannian sense. A concentration on the films
alone results in a duplication of the limits of traditional film history because the
end product often camouflages the work and negotiations that led to the finished artefact. Examining a film that originates with the avant-garde under

purely aesthetic principles misconceives the movement's ideas about the transformation of film culture.

My turn from the work of art to the network of art, from hermeneutics to discourse and from biography to systems theory does not imply a disregard for the artefacts and their possible resonances in aesthetic analyses which are often exquisite and multi-layered, but I am pursuing a different path of understanding this movement. Every step, be it the making of a film, the founding of a ciné-club or the publication of an article, can be seen as a systemic operation focussed on the survival, nourishment and expansion of the avant-garde. By adopting an archaeological gaze couched in a logic of systems theory I hope to shed new light on well known, forgotten and unknown facets of the network that constituted the European film avant-garde. The practice under examination brought forth works of art that are neither by-products nor objects waiting for exegesis, but elements of a system that I want to reconstruct. In my opinion, many of the activities, filmmaking or not, aimed at creating a *Medienverbund* (media offensive) in an ensemble of different media, an audience capable of growing and a changed production situation working together to create a new art for new statements in a new public sphere.

Ultimately, the avant-garde was as much a symptom of modernity – being unthinkable without the widespread technological, social, political, economic and cultural changes that are united under this banner – as a cause that contributed to the uncertainty that many felt when confronted by a radically transformed environment. The avant-garde itself acted as a half-transparent mirror that on the one hand reflected modernity in all its deeply felt ambivalence, yet on the other hand it also gave an interpretation of the human condition under changed circumstances. Not coincidentally, the city symphony became the most celebrated genre of the avant-garde and something of a fad in the late 1920s as it provided a *mise-en-abyme* and allegory of the conditions that had brought the avant-garde movement into existence. The city viewed through the lens of the technologically most advanced medium focused on contradictions inherent in the avant-garde. The city as an allegory and shorthand of modern life with all its social and economic factors that contributed to it became the most decisive factor in avant-garde activity. The avant-garde with all its critical and affirmative potential is as divided at heart as modernity – while it aimed ultimately at » solving « the problems of modernity, it was itself » part of the problem «. It is only in this dialectical nature that one can understand the avant-garde, its triumphs and defeats which are often to be found in the same instance and which we should rather see in an inclusive » as-well-as « logic instead of in an exclusive » either-or « dichotomy.

This is an archaeological work in the sense that I have gathered a number of well-known and less well-known facts in order to understand the specific prac-

tice of a group at a specific moment in history. I have attempted to let the historical documents talk back as monuments from a distant past on their own
terms. By developing a logic out of the practice of the avant-garde I hope to
avoid the problematic nature of hermeneutics in which a horizon of expectation
puts everything into perspective before the elements are allowed » to speak for
themselves «. For my purposes I have gathered, summarised and analysed material that has become available in the last ten to 15 years. As I had to create my
own object in the first place, I had to fight with an instability of what I was
dealing with. As a result, I have attempted to construct a frame of reference
and a number of ideas for the study of the avant-garde cinema between 1919
and 1939 and the transformations of a technological medium. I hope that some
of the ideas put forward on the following pages will give rise to renewed attention to the avant-garde and will bring forth novel research and revisionist historiography.

1.5   The Avant-garde as Angel of History: Theses on the Interwar Film Avant-garde

> [U]pheavals such as the coming of recorded sound intensify
> and help direct the progress of trends already in place.
> In continental Europe, for example, these included the weakening
> and fragmentation of the post war avant-garde movements.
>
> Alan Williams (1992)[47]

I will subsequently present four theses that will occupy a central position in one
of the four following chapters. Yet, by its dialectical and networked nature, the
other three ideas will also simultaneously be present, perhaps less visible and
worked out within the text. The co-presence of these four points is also a sign of
the interconnected and indivisible nature of the different elements that constitute the avant-garde.

1. In 1929, after the successes of the *Werkbund*-exhibition in Stuttgart and the
meeting in La Sarraz,[48] with a boom in audience organisations and an upsurge
in publishing and writing, the avant-garde seemed to be on the verge of a
breakthrough to a mass movement. Yet, the opposite was the case: the avant-
garde fell apart and petered out. One could formulate the first thesis as: Why
did the avant-garde not stay together firmly and build on what had been
achieved by 1929? I will argue that a number of aporias riddled the avant-garde
and with the introduction of sound film these internal contradictions became
increasingly points of conflict. Groups that had been kept together before by a

vague opposition to the commercial feature film or to narrative cinema broke apart. One of the important tasks of the avant-garde was to raise these aporias to the level of consciousness. As the fault lines were being realised, different people took different approaches to these problems and consequently went in different directions. Yet, it was paramount that these issues of in/dependence, abstraction/realism, communism/fascism, and commercialism/elitism were addressed properly and thoroughly. The post-war avant-garde turned to these forerunners, yet in a highly selective fashion: they were looking for heroic and spiritual forefathers in order to build a genealogy justifying their actions. In a way, my *four aporias* point out one central problem of any alternative political or social movement aimed at change (and thus still valid for the post-war avant-garde): What is the role of art in society and how can culture engender change while operating in an environment that it wants to transform? The aporias of the avant-garde will be the focus of the following chapter and I will illustrate them by a rereading of contemporary debates. Also pertinent to this issue is the question of self-definition, of what avant-garde was meant to be and the self-positioning of the artists.

2. The second thesis aims at restructuring and reconfiguring the history of the European cinema in the interwar period. It is my contention that sound film had a decisive effect on the avant-garde, but that it is insufficient to argue that sound brought about the downfall of the avant-garde. In aesthetic terms, sound film proved to be a welcome addition to the avant-garde as many early sound films were made in a context that was clearly influenced by the avant-garde. Here are some examples of early sound films that belong to a combined history of the avant-garde and the mainstream that put sound to innovative use: MELODIE DER WELT (GER 1928/29, Walter Ruttmann, › Melody of the World ‹), ALLES DREHT SICH, ALLES BEWEGT SICH (GER 1929, Hans Richter, › Everything turns, everything moves ‹), SOUS LES TOITS DE PARIS (FR 1929/30, René Clair, › Under the roofs of Paris ‹), LE MILLION (FR 1930, René Clair, › The Million ‹), DAS LIED VOM LEBEN (GER 1930, Alexis Granowsky, › The Song of life ‹), M (GER 1930-31, Fritz Lang), PHILIPS RADIO (NL 1931, Joris Ivens), ENTUZIAZM: SINFONIJA DON-BASSA (SU 1930, Dziga Vertov, › Enthusiasm: Donbass Symphony ‹), KUHLE WAMPE, ODER WEM GEHÖRT DIE WELT (GER 1932, Slatan Dudow, › Kuhle Wampe, or to whom belongs the world? ‹), DEZERTIR (SU 1933, Vsevolod Pudovkin, › Deserter ‹), and the sound films of Oskar Fischinger or Len Lye. One could also point to Richter's work in advertising in Switzerland or the films produced as part of the film department of the Bata shoe company in Zlín (Czechoslovakia).[49] Besides these films, many of the central figures of the avant-garde had interesting ideas on the employment of sound and did not reject the new technology outright. Some of the reasons for the restructuring and func-

tional differentiation of the field (terms I find more productive than » destruction « or » downfall «) are connected to the introduction of sound, but should be
framed in a slightly more complicated fashion. Sound film did in fact act as an
engine and catalyst that restructured cinema culture in total. Yet, this is often
very hard to distinguish from effects brought about by reactions to the beginning global economic downturn following on the heels of the October 1929 Wall
Street crash. It could be argued that the decisive factor for the decline or restructuring of the avant-garde was not the aesthetic implications of the sound film,
but the economic results, i.e., higher production costs and extra investments in
wiring cinemas for sound. Yet again, films continued to be made that were innovative and initiatives continued to be active after the introduction of sound
for longer periods of time.

The avant-garde, through its *strategic convergence*, had reached a critical mass
by 1929 and the ensuing *functional differentiation* has been understood by many
as a demise. On the one hand, the avant-garde did not manage to engender
change in a way that many of its adherents were hoping for. On the other hand,
one can also describe the development that set in around 1929 as the ultimate
triumph of the film avant-garde: It did not bring about a transformation of the
kind it had hoped for (i.e., a revolution), but it had a considerable impact in a lot
of different areas. The avant-garde could be held responsible for the naturalisa-
tion of the documentary as a genre and for the foundation of film archives in
different countries, for large-scale government support for cinema in virtually
all European countries, for the establishment of film theory as a field of its own,
and for the emergence of art house cinemas. The cultural acceptance of cinema
as an artistic form and cultural force leads us invariably back to the avant-garde
and its wide-ranging activities. Thus, what counts as a defeat from one perspective, can be rephrased as a success story when using a different focus. It is this
change of perspective that this study proposes and I will focus on the strategic
convergence and functional differentiation in my chapter on the film societies.
This movement was intimately connected with the avant-garde and provided a
platform for the films and ideas developed within a smaller circles of activists. I
will attempt to lay out how the different strands converged briefly and then
diverged again.

3. My third thesis is involved with the understanding of the avant-garde as a
movement. The avant-garde aimed at a *Aufhebung (sublation) of life and art* in a
Hegelian sense – the ultimate task was to break down the barriers between art
and life in order to achieve a different world in which art would occupy a different (social/economic/cultural) position. It is my contention that in order to
understand this utopian nature of the avant-garde it is necessary to see the activities as not just limited to filmmaking, but that they were attempting to re-

structure the cinema as an institution and to produce a veritable discourse on the cinema. The writings and publications, the activities in teaching and lecturing, the foundation of ciné-clubs and international networks are not secondary activities that were undertaken in order to heighten the visibility and effect of the films, but they have to be considered as part and parcel of the avant-garde. By restructuring the institution cinema, from the production process to the screening context, from the film script to the spectator's head, the activists wanted to gain access to the means of production and transform the medium from within. Only by writing and talking about film differently did it make sense to make different films, only by changing film education would a new generation emerge that would look differently upon the cinema. I emphasise this approach to cinema as discourse (different from aesthetic or industrial approaches) in chapter four, which deals with the development of theory, criticism and publishing, with the constitution of networks in which teaching and event culture played a key role that is still being undervalued.

4. My final and fourth point is that the avant-garde was bound to fail because of a *paradoxical temporal construction* that was inscribed into its very conception. In its original meaning in military jargon the avant-garde has an advance function in spatial terms. The transposition of the term to arts and culture transposed the spatial dimension into time. Avant-garde art is ahead in temporal terms; it is experimenting with forms and topics that will only later become acceptable to the mainstream. By projecting all hope into the future, by promising an amazing time ahead, the avant-garde is directed into the future. The avant-garde can never be a reform movement – it is by definition revolutionary. At the same time that the promise of the avant-garde is futuristic (it is therefore no coincidence that the first true avant-garde movement called itself » Futurism «), its reference to art is steeped in the past. Many of the activities emerge from a deep-seated discontent with the *status quo*: the avant-garde rebels against traditional art and the way that traditional art is presented, discussed and received. This results in a temporal double bind – rebelling against the past while promising the future – which creates an insolvable riddle that haunted the avant-garde all through its existence and makes it a movement that cyclically rises and falls. The avant-garde is constantly proclaiming that it is already operating in the future and a standstill would mean that it would be assed by. A permanent state of avant-garde-ness would be as much a paradox as a permanent revolution (or, for that matter, an » institutionalised revolution « like the Mexican). This cyclical nature is as inevitable as the temporal construction of looking into the past while being fixed on the future. This temporal paradox managed to play itself out everywhere, from the NEP period in the Soviet Union to the political infighting around 1930 in Europe. As already mentioned, the Soviet Union strongly pre-

sents this paradoxical temporal construction and therefore chapter five, the » Vanishing Point Soviet Union «, will concentrate on this structure. The Soviet Union proclaimed itself as the first state to have achieved a future, which would sooner or later be the destiny of every other society.

My final chapter on two simultaneously very different and very similar films, John Grierson's DRIFTERS (GB 1929) and Walter Ruttmann's MELODIE DER WELT (GER 1929), which share more than their year of production, will attempt to illustrate the deeply paradoxical nature of the avant-garde. Both films participate in strategies developed within avant-garde films while also drawing on other filmmaking traditions. Yet, both films have to be situated in a number of different contexts in order to fully understand their potential as well as their impact. These contextual factors will reflect back on the films and demonstrate how a specific film form (the documentary) could emerge from the encounter of certain stylistic features with an organisational model borrowed from the media strategies of the avant-garde, yet with a radically new support system in the service of the nation-state. The final chapter will thus return to the films from which I departed in the main body of this work. This symbolic return to the material with a renewed agenda in mind will, I hope, demonstrate that the approach proposed here does not necessarily lead away from the films, but that it also opens a fresh perspective on otherwise well-known classics.

All four theses just outlined come together in an internal tension that is difficult to overcome: the aporias are internal contradictions without any easy solution; the convergence and differentiation are movement in opposing directions whereas it is hard to exactly pinpoint the moment of transformation; the sublation of art and life was a utopian aspiration that proved to be impossible to achieve in practice; and finally the temporal paradox literally illustrates my title » Moving Forward, Looking Back « which I understand as a subterranean motto of the avant-garde. The movement in two directions at the same time, a productive, albeit insurmountable internal contradiction, a dialectic tension that generated energy, yet also proved disastrous. Curiously enough, this paradox has also been played out famously by two thinkers who are strange bedfellows indeed. Niklas Luhmann has argued that avant-garde art is often only understandable when you have internalised in a preceding step the autonomy of art as a self-enclosed sub-system of society. After having observed this, Luhmann quite typically slips from his cold and somewhat technocratic prose to a sudden flash of aphorism and metaphor: » What is paradoxically called avant-garde, has pushed this backward-looking mode of determination to extremes – like rowing oarsmen who only see where they are coming from while they have turned their backs to the goal of their journey. «[50] The avant-garde looked in the opposite direction in which it was moving; it attempted to overtake the present by being transfixed by the future, which had not yet been achieved. Walter Benjamin has seen a very similar construction at work in his description of the angel of history:

> His face is turned toward the past. Where we perceive a chain of events, he sees one single catastrophe which keeps piling wreckage upon wreckage and hurls it in front of his feet. The angel would like to stay, awaken the dead, and make whole what has been smashed. But a storm is blowing from Paradise; it has got caught in his wings with such violence that the angel can no longer close them. This storm irresistibly propels him into the future to which his back is turned, while the pile of debris before him grows skyward. This storm is what we call progress.[51]

Not coincidentally, Benjamin borrows this materialist-religious image from a painting he had bought from Paul Klee, an avant-garde artist who was a founding member of the *Bauhaus* collective. Both Benjamin and Klee could have recognised themselves in the description of the angel of history. The avant-garde as angel of history is being blown and driven by progress (or, as one might have it: modernisation) relentlessly into a future that it cannot see. The only way that the avant-garde can heal past wounds is by promising, or giving an advance on the future that it never can fully redeem. Thus, at heart, the avant-garde is a tragic movement because it faced the shambles and fragments of history, but the avant-garde could not change the past, as much as it wanted to. The course into the future is determined by a merciless storm – in Benjamin's image, facing the past therefore does not mean being backwards in historical terms, but the avant-garde is the only group that truly tried to figure out how to make sense of the past in a way that would make it productive for the future. A crucial difference between Luhmann's and Benjamin's conceptions of history thus remains: while in Luhmann's image the movement is active (rowing), Benjamin's angel of history is passive (being driven by the storm of progress). For Luhmann, the avant-garde wants to achieve the future while for Benjamin it wants to heal the past. What appears to be absent in both descriptions is the present.

2 The Dialectics of Self-Conception – Film Avant-garde and Industry Around 1930

The new thing here is that these points emerge in their full importance;
that the author, for their sake, takes temporary leave of his oeuvre
and, like an engineer starting to drill for oil in the desert, takes up
his activity at precisely calculated places in the desert of contemporary life.
Here these points are situated in the theatre, the anecdote, and radio;
others will be tackled at a later stage.
Walter Benjamin (1930)[1]

The avant-garde was – by the mid- to late-1920s – theoretically and practically well on its way toward a *Medienverbund* which can be conceptualised as a media offensive in keeping with the avant-garde motto of converting art into life and life into art.[2] There was no doubt that producing ground-breaking and innovative films was simply not enough, and that a concerted effort of publication, distribution, production, teaching, lecturing, exhibiting and networking was needed in order to create and win over a public toward their aims. One of the problems at the time was, as we shall see, that whereas there was a widespread consensus that a *Medienverbund* was necessary, neither the means for achieving it nor the function to which such a public should be put were clear to anybody at the time. Besides, the coming of sound fundamentally changed the production process and accelerated tendencies already underway, such as the convergence of the avant-garde with the industry. Classically, this has been interpreted as selling-out or as a breakdown, yet within the logic of a constructivist avant-garde[3] it is necessary to leave the path of self-expression and move towards mass-producible and mass-consumable forms to create a new aesthetics: typography and photography, advertisement and propaganda, industry and commerce. Furthermore, the film avant-garde was never completely sealed off from the industry as both co-existed in an interdependency of master and slave, of parasite and host. Although antagonistically poised against each other, both needed the other: the avant-garde relied on the industry for technological support and commissions while the industry needed the avant-garde for innovation and the development of new prototypes. Or, to stay within the military terminology that the avant-garde was so fond of: the avant-garde literally acted as the spearhead of cinema culture. Being small, mobile and versatile, the avant-garde was a minesweeper and bridge-builder and it could test out terrain and seek the safest route. Mainstream filmmakers at large often followed the routes pioneered by the avant-garde. Not surprisingly, not every stretch of land marked out by the avant-garde proved to be useful to the industry and often when some of these adventurous trailblazers returned from a fascinating detour that ultimately led to a dead-end, they discovered that the caravan of mainstream film culture had passed them by and they were suddenly in the *arrière-garde*. However, while it worked in the service of the commercial film industry, the avant-garde also attempted to change the means of production on which it partly relied. This was the balancing act that the filmmaker-as-producer in Benjamin's sense had to perform on a tightrope.

The avant-garde acted as a kind of *Research & Development* department and had a much broader impact than they or anybody else actually realised at the time. The avant-garde developed tools, strategies and models that became common currency in the film culture in general and persisted on into the post-war period. Moreover, one of the main contributions of the avant-garde was that it brought a number of aporias inherent in film culture into focus. Those contradictions showed the fissures and tensions that riddled a larger part of cinema culture and the problems that had to be addressed. Even though the avant-garde itself was not really able to solve these problems, it developed methods and suggested answers that would later contribute to quite different questions. In a way, the avant-garde posed the right questions and recognised the key problems, but did not manage to resolve them in a way that they would directly profit from these solutions. In the late 1920s, as the avant-garde was extending its network, some people realised the mutual dependence of the avant-garde and the industry:

> Hopefully it will be possible to combine the goals of society with those of the industry. Otherwise, what is the use of modernity, if it is only a toy for fiddlers. Film production today must be won for tomorrow's film. ... Therefore, film production companies from all over the world are equally interested in the avant-garde of the experimenters and fiddlers. Those with insight know this. And now they have to be encouraged to recognise the avant-garde as their creative task force. Moreover, the technicians and the theorists should realise that they are workers in today's film industry, and that as soon as their attempts and experiences show any practical results should be incorporated into present-day film production.[4]

Ernst Jäger's call for a dialectic relationship between the avant-garde and the industry would certainly not have satisfied a cultural critic like Benjamin: Jäger, editor-in-chief of the largest German film trade paper *Film-Kurier*, saw himself as a spokesman for the industry, possibly more forward-thinking than most of his colleagues, but nevertheless steeped in a logic of functional utilitarianism. In general, the *Film-Kurier* followed a similar logic as the largest German studio

Ufa: The German film industry was the only serious challenge to Hollywood's domination of the world market where German films would once again achieve international recognition. The avant-garde was only interesting insofar as they could contribute to this goal. Experiments should yield prototypes, which then in turn would contribute to the well being of the industry. Even though Benjamin was also critical of the avant-garde, his criticism originated from a revolutionary stance: its aim had to be radical change and therefore many experiments for him were not fierce enough or simply stuck in a bourgeois ideology of art. The avant-garde was operating between these two poles – providing prototypes for the industry at large, on the one hand, and contributing towards revolutionary activities, on the other – during this time when many different factions were interested in its development.

It is doubtful whether the avant-garde could have really found practical solutions to the problems they addressed, even more so than the doubts about whether this was even their aim. If we conceptualise the avant-garde within a cyclical model, it tries out new directions that were either ignored or followed. If it were ignored, this kind of movement characterised by constant movement would come to a standstill because nobody was following it; if they were followed, then the avant-garde would be seen as passé. By definition, the avant-garde must be constantly in motion and changing shape in order to discover new spaces – the coming of sound certainly meant great changes, but to claim that it meant the end of the avant-garde ignores many of the continuities (personal, institutional, stylistically) that crossed the line from silent to sound film. Moreover, it implies a static image of the avant-garde to claim that the movement came to an end with the coming of sound. I believe that one can only properly understand the avant-garde when considering it in its dynamic and ever-changing forms. The avant-garde did not fall with the coming of sound, it restructured and diversified itself in the early 1930s – and sound film was just one factor (more or less indirectly) in this development. Also crucial were the worldwide economic crisis, the growing political polarisation, and a certain momentum, which had brought many strands into congruence around, 1929 and that afterwards drove them apart again.

2.1 Aporias of the Avant-garde

> *...an experimental approach can only be found*
> *in the new possibility of the advertising film.*
> *Indeed, the advertising film provides an economic*
> *basis for all pioneer work at the moment.*
> Oswald Blakeston (1931)[5]

> *[O]ne day somebody should figure out how much*
> *› experimental ‹ work has been done in commercials*
> *that would not have been done without them.*
> Hans Richter (1949)[6]

As I have argued in chapter one, the coming of sound should not be seen as a radical break or moment of decline, but rather as a catalyst which made visible a number of internal contradictions in the self-organisation of the avant-garde. These aporias were exposed when synchronised sound changed the production process, the exhibition patterns and the financial basis of filmmaking fundamentally and when – almost simultaneously – the economic crisis altered the balance of power between producers and distributors, between patent holders and cinema owners. What I want to consider here are the internal contradictions of and the tensions within the avant-garde if viewed as a unified movement in the 1920s (and the contemporaries at the time considered the avant-garde at least to a certain degree as such). I will consider issues of independence (in terms of money and organisation), of commercialism (in terms of audience address), of abstraction (film style), and of politics (the idea of progress). I will furthermore ponder the various attempts at defining avant-garde and avant-garde cinema because the concept is rather fleeting and amorphous, which takes on new shapes and guises along the way. An important element for a reconsideration of the avant-garde in relation to the industry will be constructivism because the film avant-garde had to engage directly with a technical and reproductive medium.

The first and probably most obvious problem faced by the avant-garde was the independence and/or dependence of the filmmaker. Filmmakers are dependent in a number of ways on a variety of factors, which are beyond their control: Financially, a filmmaker is limited by monetary resources. While any writer, painter or other artist can represent wildly extravagant set pieces such as an elaborate battle sequence, fantastic imagery or strange effects in his/her work, a filmmaker faces many limitations concerning financial, organisational and technical resources. Even the most basic equipment necessary to shoot a film demands a considerable investment and film material is also very costly. Thus, no filmmaker was financially independent, no matter if he or she was commercially minded or took an avant-garde stance.[7] Film, like architecture, is a medium that requires huge investments, thus limiting the possibility of true independence in a monetary way.[8] Once a film was produced despite pecuniary difficulties the real difficulties began: the film still needed distribution and exhibition possibilities in order to reach an audience. Since the avant-garde organised these sectors also on the basis of a cottage industry the reach of these films was limited. The economic aspect of filmmaking could be a possible reason for the abstract films of the early 1920s as the production process was artisanal (and thus in keeping with the romantic ideals of originality and creation) and no sets or co-workers were necessary. These formal experiments offered at least the possibility of a partial independence from some of the industry's constraints. Contrary to traditional arguments which either argue that abstract films were the furthest removed from realist depiction or purport that the move towards anti-realistic representation followed, in the logic of modernism, the lead of painting, one could argue that an even more important reason for this tendency was the anti-industrial vein inherent in this kind of film. Abstract or, as they were known in Germany at the time, » absolute « films did away with actors and props, sets and costumes. At any rate, the autonomy of the avant-garde filmmaker regarding the means of production was a debated issue as this basic tenet of other arts was barely attainable for the large-scale film apparatus.

As a general consequence of the economic frame, hardly any of the avant-garde films of the 1920s and 1930s (or of any other period for that matter) are independent in the sense that they were produced without any outside interference in the form of a commission, a patron or a helping hand by a studio. This could take very different forms as I will briefly outline in connection to Walter Ruttmann, Hans Richter, Joris Ivens, three filmmaker-activists who played a central role in the avant-garde, and Oskar Fischinger and Alexander Hackenschmied[9], two slightly more marginal activists that by virtue of their later activities in the United States connect the historical film avant-garde in interwar Europe to the US post-World War Two scene. All five filmmakers made a considerable number of advertising films (in which a client finances a film that presents a certain product as being useful or desirable) such as DER ZWEI-GROSCHEN-ZAUBER (GER 1929, Hans Richter, › The Two-Penny Magic ‹) for a newspaper, DAS WUNDER (GER 1922, Walter Ruttmann, › The Miracle ‹) for liquor, DAS WIEDERGEFUNDENE PARADIES (GER 1925, Walter Ruttmann, › Paradise Regained ‹) for flowers, PHILIPS RADIO (NL 1931, Joris Ivens) for the electric company or SILNICE ZPÍVÁ (CZ 1937, Alexander Hackenschmied et al., › The Highway Sings ‹) for Bata tyres. They also worked for exhibitions and initiatives in the public sector that formed parts of larger media offensives, especially in connection with reformist social and architectural ideas: Ruttmann made DER

AUFSTIEG for the public health exhibition *GeSoLei* (GER 1926, › The Ascent ‹); Richter was in charge of promotional films for the exhibition BAUEN UND WOH-NEN (GER 1928, › Building and Dwelling ‹) and DIE NEUE WOHNUNG (CH 1930, › New Living ‹) commissioned by the Schweizer Werkbund[10] while Joris Ivens made WIJ BOUWEN (NL 1929, › We Are Building ‹) and newsreels for various left-wing organisations. They also worked for commercial film productions: Ruttmann made BERLIN, DIE SINFONIE DER GROSSSTADT (GER 1926/27, › Berlin, Symphony of a Big City ‹) as a » quota-quickie « for Fox[11], Richter shot two experimental sound films in collaboration with Tobis, VORMITTAGS-SPUK (GER 1927/28, › Ghosts before Breakfast ‹) and ALLES DREHT SICH, ALLES BEWEGT SICH (GER 1929, › Everything Turns, Everything Revolves ‹). They contributed openers and sequences for regular commercial programs – Richter's INFLATION (GER 1928) and RENNSYMPHONIE (GER 1928, › Race Symphony ‹) were meant as introductions for regular commercial films while Ruttmann's » falcon dream «- sequence was part of Fritz Lang's DIE NIBELUNGEN (GER 1922-24) – and films poised between commercials and industrial films: the films for electric and chemical companies by Ivens (PHILIPS RADIO, NL 1931; CREOSOTE, NL 1931) and Richter (EUROPA RADIO, NL 1931 and HALLO EVERYBODY, NL 1933) and Ruttmann's MELODIE DER WELT (GER 1928/29, › Melody of the World ‹) commissioned by Tobis and Hapag. Even the earliest experiments in abstract film (*absoluter Film*) were supported by Ufa (Richter and Eggeling[12]) and by Emelka (Ruttmann[13]). And Ivens' first steps would have been unthinkable without his father's business where he could experiment with and use a variety of different technologies for film production. Oskar Fischinger who took up and continued some abstract tendencies developed in the first half of the 1920s, in the late decade worked for the *Kulturfilmabteilung* of the Ufa (SCHÖPFERIN NATUR, GER 1927, › Creatress Nature ‹), contributed special effects to Fritz Lang's DIE FRAU IM MOND (GER 1928–29, › The Woman in the Moon ‹) collaborated with Ernö Metzner on DEIN SCHICKSAL (GER 1928, › Your Destiny ‹), a film supporting the social democratic party, and he also made several advertising films.[14] Alexander Hackenschmied, retrospectively normally seen as the central proponent of the Prague film avant-garde, started his active film involvement in 1929: he published photographs and wrote about film for the fashionable society weekly *Pestrý týden* (» Colourful Week «) and *Národni osvobození* (› National Liberation ‹) and he was hired as an artistic consultant for Gustav Machatý's EROTIKON (CZ 1929). In the following years Hackenschmied made two » independent « films, BEZÚL ELNÁ PROCHÁZKA (CZ 1930, › Aimless Walk ‹) and NA PRAŽSKÉM HRAD (CZ 1932, › Prague Castle ‹), while also pursuing a career in the film industry as a visual consultant. In the mid-1920s, Hackenschmied worked mainly for the publicity department of the shoe manufacturer Bata in Zlín where a thoroughly modern city had been constructed.[15] This list is far from exhaustive. The closer one studies the production history of the avant-garde, the clearer the interrelatedness and entangled co-existence with state institutions and industry becomes.

While industry commissions proved to be the most important source for the avant-garde, there were older models to turn to like the private patronage typical of art in the pre-modern period. Tom Gunning has pointed out the irony that the film allegedly shot at the festival of La Sarraz in 1929 by the participants – LA GUERRE ENTRE LE FILM INDÉPÉNDANT ET LE FILM INDUSTRIEL / TEMPÊTE SUR LA SARRAZ (CH 1929, › The War between Independent and Commercial Film ‹ / › The Storming of La Sarraz ‹) – featured Hélène de Mandrot as the embodiment of independent cinema.[16] De Mandrot was a wealthy art patron who had invited the filmmaking activists to her castle and basically financed the meeting (just as she had supported the progressive architects the year before when she hosted the *CIAM – Congres International des Architectes Modernes*). The film shot at La Sarraz thus mirrored and allegorised the strange dependence of the avant-garde on private patrons – a model of art production, which had basically vanished into obscurity with the rise of the bourgeoisie in the 18th century (introducing the capitalist market model in the realms of art).[17] The avant-garde faced the problem of who would pay for their films: the state, private patrons or the public? Or could a market be created for these films to support regular production, no matter how small? There are some isolated cases and thus exceptions that prove the rule in which private patrons financed films like the Vicomte de Noailles who paid the bills for Man Ray's LES MYSTÈRES DU CHÂTEAU DE DÉ (FR 1929, › The Mystery of the Chateau of the Dice ‹), Luis Buñuel's and Salvador Dalí's L'ÂGE D'OR (FR 1930, › The Golden Age ‹), and Jean Cocteau's LE SANG D'UN POÈTE (FR 1930, › The Blood of a Poet ‹), the rich Parisian jeweller Leon Rosenthal who sponsored ROMANCE SENTIMENTALE (FR 1929, Grigorij Alexandrov, › Sentimental Romance ‹) in order to entertain his mistress Mara Gris or the Comte Etienne de Beaumont who financed some of Henri Chomette's films in the mid-1920s. Now, while private financing hardly seems like an option given the resulting dependence on the benevolence of rich art patrons hardly bent on revolution, the film shot at La Sarraz ironically could only have been made in this specific situation and therefore allegorically commented on the situation of the avant-garde vis-à-vis commissions. Some months earlier, in May 1929, Walter Ruttmann had already considered this problem. Under the title » Der isolierte Künstler « (» The Isolated Artist «) he had published thoughts on this conundrum:

> It might be possible to reach the reconciliation and equilibrium between art and commerce through an exterior power: for example, through patronage or the state. Patrons, however, only exist in fairy tales or to promote a diva and the state seems – at least in capitalistic countries – to neglect the problem. What we are left with is art's own initiative. But who represents film as art? The possibility to build unions among

those who want art and consider art to be important exists in France, perhaps also in Holland and some other places. It is called › avant-garde ‹, its existence has been recognised and, to a certain extent, it has evolved into a reliable source because avant-garde has delivered proof for a recognised demand. ... This foreign success cannot be imitated in Germany. ... Therefore, we can only hope for a personality, flexible enough, to con and swindle his way into the opponent's headquarters and convince him.[18]

This text, written and published just before La Sarraz, demonstrates how aware a key player such as Ruttmann was of the contradictions inherent in the avant-garde. Ruttmann dismisses the state as a potential partner – actually, it was the state in various countries that supported the 1920s avant-garde in the decade to come, not only in terms of personnel, but also in continuing their program and aesthetic innovations. Ruttmann put some hope into audience organisations like the Dutch *Filmliga* and the French ciné-clubs (which he saw as the germ for a market for avant-garde films), but ultimately saw no chance for a similar advance in Germany. Ruttmann left unanswered who the » opponent « really was – and thus in whose headquarters the » flexible personality « should advance. Ruttmann's paradoxical statement of » conning one's way into the enemy headquarters « eventually acquired a new urgency upon his return to Germany in 1933 and his willingness to take on commissions from the Nazis, including propaganda films for rearmament and the helping hand he lent Leni Riefenstahl in the making of Triumph des Willens (GER 1934/35, › Triumph of the Will ‹).

In fact, this question of funding and (in)dependence was one of the main topics at two crucial international meetings in La Sarraz 1929 and at the succeeding meeting in Brussels 1930:

> One question in particular fueled the discussions and led to the taking of opposite positions: the definition itself of › independent cinema ‹; the majority of participants – among whom were Moussinac, Richter, Balázs, Ruttmann, and Eisenstein – realised the illusory character of absolute independence and understood the phrase as a cinema free of the industry's rules.[19]

While acknowledging the impossibility of achieving independence in its » purest « sense, this formulation reveals another set of problems: If one understands independence as the freedom from the laws of the industry, then the question is: which laws of which industry? As I will argue, the film industry had very different interests than the electrical industry and even within the film industry, the exhibition outlets had a very distinct position from, say, the producers or the hardware manufacturers. These were indeed some of the fault lines and predetermined breaking points that would structure the debates and positions of the 1930s; whether to look for independence in the service of the state or of a political party, whether to move into industrial filmmaking or to concentrate on advertising. A similar case of this recognition, albeit with a different solution, can be found in a statement made by director Victor Trivas in 1931, himself a frequent border crosser between avant-garde and commercial cinema:

> I cannot imagine an independent cinema. Film is an industrial product that has to find its way to consumers. Films are made for them – and thus films have to be above all accessible to the masses. If they are not, the goal is lost both socially and commercially. The director has to be willing to find a true connection between himself and the audience. Devastating dependencies are those that are valid for everyone...[20]

Trivas' polemic was directed against Ufa's influence in Germany which, in his opinion, forced all of its artists into the same straitjacket which then only generated mediocre results, which is similar to populist criticism of Hollywood's film factories. Yet, even Ufa was far from monolithic as the *Kulturfilmabteilung* supported many experiments and even became a (temporary) home to a number of avant-garde activists. One has to, however, distinguish different factions within the industry as much as within the avant-garde.

These considerations and debates gave rise to the idea of an experimental film studio or film laboratory, which was hotly debated in Germany in 1928/29. Not coincidentally, Moritz Seeler named his experimental production company, founded in the key year of 1929, *Studio 1929*, paying homage to both the ongoing debate in Germany and the Parisian cinema *Studio 28*. As is well known, this experimental company only made one film, although a highly influential one: MENSCHEN AM SONNTAG (GER 1929, Robert Siodmak et al., › People on Sunday ‹).[21] The studio that activists rallied around was expected to focus research on the survival of art, education, culture and industry and provide a steady and reliable base for experiments. Since the cinema was increasingly viewed as a crucial element in the construction of national identity both internally and externally, as a decisive industrial factor and as an independent form of expression more and more voices supported an experimental studio. Whereas a widespread agreement existed concerning the necessity of such an institution the crucial question was, again, who would finance this facility and, perhaps even more importantly, who would control it. The usual suspects named in this discussion were the state and the industry, but the unresolved question haunting the arguments remained the dependency of the experiment on the financing body. The state or the industry would only pay if they could expect something in return for their investments.[22] In this discussion, Hans Richter took a partisan position when he objected to the term » experiment « in relation to the avant-garde. Richter connected » experiments « with commercial productions characterised by internally unconnected elements. For Richter it was important to start with a new conception of cinema and discover new techniques from this perspective, rather than try novel tricks and techniques without an underlying theory. The balance between industry and avant-garde that he addresses in this respect needs a studio in which new work is fostered, but according to a specific plan.[23]

Another possible solution to this impasse could have been for the avant-garde to claim a non-professional status. By claiming amateur status one could have opted for a certain naïveté that would be understood as less a proclamation of modesty and more as an avant-garde statement of radical difference. By occupying a non-professional position one could implicitly open up the field of filmmaking to anyone with a camera. The production of films was not limited anymore to professionals and the industry, everybody could participate. A number of companies introduced affordable and portable cameras in the course of the 1920s, which made filmmaking equipment available to a wider circle. A whole system of amateur initiatives with clubs, magazines and institutions soon emerged.[24] Yet, on the whole, there was very little contact between the avant-garde and the amateur movement who could have been natural partners.[25] In general, the question of in/dependence proved to be a constant bone of contention, and yet, one that offered no simple solution.

A similar case was the question of which (part of the) audience should be addressed with what means. The main opponent of the avant-garde was not the industry *per se*, but the *film* industry with its unabashed *commercialism*. In the manifestoes and position papers, the film industry was often attacked for their bold market-orientation. The avant-garde by contrast often faced the opposing charge of *elitism*, of producing elitist art that was beyond ordinary people's understanding. This second aporia can be detected in the manifesto of the Dutch *Filmliga* stating that they were against *cinema* and in favour of *film*: » Once in a hundred times we see: the film. For the rest we see: cinema. «.[26] They equated cinema with kitsch, Hollywood, formulaic filmmaking, and sentimentalism whereas film pointed towards the discourse around medium specificity. Film denotes, they thought, the essence of the medium towards which the avant-garde strived (even though they never agreed on what that would be). Many of the film societies with their publications and events originally aimed at developing that aspect of film that turned it into art without thinking too much about representations of reality or abstraction, about political and social change or revolution. This impetus against mass culture reveals a current, which was more interested in elevating film to the level of the established arts and thus adhering more closely to the bourgeois and romantic conception of art rather than revolutionising the institution art. The Dutch *Filmliga*, the London Film Society and the Parisian cinephile community – many successful initiatives in this sector modelled itself on the theatre, literature, music, and the visual arts rather than approaching cinema as a mass medium. A tension can be found here between attempts to lift film up to the status of accepted art forms and the counter impulse from avant-garde circles that opposed the traditional institutions of high culture: museums, theatres, galleries, concert halls, literary clubs, etc. This tension between revolutionising cinema by breaking down all of the traditional categories of art or elevating it to the » respected circles « persisted throughout the 1920s and 1930s.

Or, to put it in socio-historical terms: Because film was a latecomer to the stage of art it was undecided whether it should try to leapfrog its way right into the avant-garde movements of Dada and Surrealism (thereby skipping the period of bourgeois art in which a market and a public of (dis)interested citizens would purchase and collect art) or whether to rush quickly through that period. In fact, traces of both models co-existed in the period under investigation. Moreover, an anti-industrial (and thus anti-modern) streak runs through the film avant-garde's activities; in its opposition to assembly line filmmaking, the activists found themselves in a contradictory position vis-à-vis a thoroughly modern machine that produced social fantasies such as Hollywood, Paris-Joinville or Ufa-Babelsberg. Thus, some avant-garde groups such as the Surrealists wholeheartedly embraced serial dramas and crime films and opposed the lofty idealism of the commercial art cinema or serious attempts of identifying an artistic essence of film. The clash between Antonin Artaud (supported by the Surrealist group) and Germaine Dulac over LA COQUILLE ET LE CLERGYMAN (FR 1927) was partly based on the divergent definitions of avant-garde cinema.[27]

Yet, some avant-garde activists tried to overcome this simplistic dichotomy by differentiating even within the film industry between projects that were acceptable and those considered to be running against all principles of the avant-garde. Germaine Dulac who not only alternated experiments in *cinéma pur* with serials and commercial features, but also spent her whole career on the interstices of the industry and the avant-garde made a distinction in order to break down the crude dichotomy:

> The film industry is producing commercial films, i.e., films intended to reach a wide audience, and market-oriented films. Market-oriented films are willing to make any concession necessary and pursue purely financial ends; commercial films use expressions and techniques in the best way possible and it is among these that one occasionally finds interesting works, without ignoring the necessary profits. In this case, we have a union of industry and art.
>
> From commercial cinema emerges the total work, the balanced film for which the industry and the avant-garde work in two divided camps. In general, the industry is not interesed in the artistic elements while the avant-garde cares about nothing else. This results in antagonism. Avant-garde and commercial cinema, or art and film industry, form an inseperable whole. But the avant-garde – without which there would

be no development in film – has against itself the majority of the public and all producers.[28]

By breaking open this binary distinction between art and industry and by introducing »*films commerciaux*« as a third term, Dulac found a pragmatic in-be-
tween-space, the liminal space where the film industry joined hands with some
of the experimental attempts first attempted in avant-garde circles. It is via the
transitional space of »commercial cinema« as described by Dulac, in some
sense congruent with commercial art cinema, that innovation seeped into the
mainstream. When conceived as a cyclical model, the avant-garde would lead
the way with experiments – some of which were subsequently accepted in commercial art cinema of which only some in turn would enter the mainstream.
These features that found their way to a broader public gradually became unac-
ceptable to the avant-garde, so novel ways had to continue to be invented.
However, I do not want to imply an overly simplistic model of trickling down
or innovation and implementation – instead, I would conceptualise the relationship that follows a logic that emerges from system's theory. One could conceptualise mainstream, art cinema and experimental films as three interconnected
systems in which particular elements of the output of one system is absorbed by
another system and translated to its own frequency. As some devices are re-
worked, recycled and employed in commercial cinema this is picked up again
by the avant-garde which then discards these features altogether as they receive
them back from its arch enemy. Thus, certain techniques that might have been
characteristic of the avant-garde in the mid-1920s were picked up by the industry, changed and recycled and were sometimes then even fed back to the avant-
garde. A similar idea was advanced in the German trade press in mid-1928:

> It sounds like a paradox, but experiments are deals. ... If you find something that is
> worth a risk, then push it through. In the long run, valuable inspirations have always
> been successful. Improvement is only possible by trying out new ways. Film as an art
> for the masses can easily run into the danger of solidifying.[29]

This mutual dependency, this dialectical relationship between the avant-garde
and the film industry is crucial to an understanding of the dynamic attraction
and repulsion between the two entities which are in fact not clearly distinguish-
able and their relationship is not reducible to a binary opposition.

Mainstream filmmaking, not in Dulac's sense of a third term (commercial cinema), but a market-driven industry, is almost by definition populist: It has to
create its own audience since cinema competes on an open market of various
forms of entertainment without, as a rule of thumb, any support mechanisms
from state governments or private patrons.[30] Commercial cinema is therefore
mostly conservative in its formal aspects, sentimental in content and traditional

in the social norms depicted; at least, this was the opinion (and the polemic formulation) of the avant-garde. An early form of resistance against the overwhelming normative framework of the commercial industry and probably the
most radical break with the representational paradigm was, for many activists,
abstraction. The models were often borrowed from painting as in the early work
of Hans Richter, Viking Eggeling, Henri Chomette, Man Ray, Walter Ruttmann,
among others. Later developments leaned toward political radicalisation, but
one avant-garde streak in the 1930s combined music with abstract moving
shapes and colours, exemplified by the work of Oskar Fischinger and Len Lye.
Opposition to the industry was not directed against the industry as such, but
against the commercialism and the general public of the film industry. The competition with mass media was something that accepted art forms (literature,
visual art) only had to deal with to a limited degree, thus, the film avant-garde
had no model to imitate. Of course, the film avant-garde was to a certain extent
aware of its inherent elitism which frowned upon mass taste and mass-produced distraction.

In 1931, Joris Ivens discussed the documentary film as an avant-garde film, as
the last stand of the avant-garde against the supreme film industry, to retain the
typical military terminology of so many of these writings. Ivens starts off by
claiming that » the documentary film is the only means that remains for the
avant-garde filmmaker to stand up to the film industry «.[31] He clearly distinguishes between commissioned films for the (non-film) industry and work
within the film industry. While the former only deals with one person (or one
entity such as a board of directors) who is normally not an expert on questions
of film, the latter amounts, in Ivens' opinion, to a sell-out as one is caught in a
system that thrives on selling the same sentimental stories to the audience, trying to keep their common taste at a low level. There is of course a big difference
in terms of usage between a commissioned industrial film and a commercial
feature, which Ivens hints at, but fails to make explicit. The key difference is the
way the spectator is addressed – or what has been theorised in relation to commercial cinema, on the one hand, as the operations of paratexts[32] and, on the
other, as spectatorship.[33] While a commercial feature needed to draw an audience based on its story, stars, spectacle values, narrative engine or any other
» unique selling point « that could help to market a film, a commissioned industrial film was normally shown to audiences interested in a company or a certain
technology. These spectators were much more open to experimental formats as
their main incentive for watching a film was not entertainment. Thus, different
forms of address or a stronger emphasis on information were accepted in these
circles more readily than in the commercial circuit where big investments
needed big cash returns which consequently creates a climate disinclined to innovation. But the creation and durable existence of this spectator base who ac-

cepted different forms of address did not work in the long term; this was precisely the incentive of the various film societies that failed in their attempt to fundamentally alter cinema culture, but which nevertheless managed to build up an alternative and long-running distribution and exhibition circuit.[34]

The way the spectator is addressed – whether aiming for a large mainstream audience or limiting the discourse to a select group – had direct effects on the style of the films. Another factor, the question of the essence of cinema, which was high on the discursive agenda in the 1920s, also contributed to my third aporia, which directly relates to the films themselves. As critics and theorists discussed cinema as an art form they often hit upon the dichotomy between *realism* and *abstraction* in film. When the first serious discussions regarding film appeared they mostly stated that film had to move away from theatre, that it should not copy reality because – as the argument went – a camera is a mechanical tool for the photographic recording and reproduction of reality. Thus, a film that revealed outside reality in a documentary manner did not qualify as art because it was fabricated by a machine that reproduced optical effects of reality in a mechanical fashion. And the definition of art at that time implied that the outside world had to be filtered through human subjectivity in order to present an idiosyncratic or subjective interpretation of reality. Therefore, the early avant-garde currents such as Expressionism, Impressionism or even the Soviet Montage school distorted and stylised ordinary reality in order to adhere to the standards of art as a singular and subjective vision of outside reality. The most extreme experiments in this direction were the early abstract works of Walter Ruttmann, Hans Richter and Viking Eggeling. They had eliminated reference to outside reality as much as possible. No trace of the photographic index in a Peircian sense can be found in these plays of shape, plane, size, direction and (not to be forgotten) colour.[35] This was also in tune with theories of the cinema advanced at the time: both Béla Balázs and Rudolf Arnheim attempted to single out those elements of the cinema that converted it into an art. Both stressed capacities that were inherently anti-realist, both saw the artistic capacities of cinema beyond its indexical nature.[36]

Yet, the » *absoluter Film* « only blossomed very briefly. After two matinees on 3 and 10 May in 1925, the zenith of the absolute film had already been reached.[37] Even though the term continued to float around in discussions for a while, the only other major event under this banner brought together light projections by Ludwig Hirschfeld-Mack (DREITEILIGE FARBENSONATINE, GER 1925 and REFLEKTORISCHE FARBENSPIELE, GER 1925) with films by Hans Richter (FILM IST RHYTHMUS, i.e. RHYTHMUS 23, GER 1923-1925),[38] Viking Eggeling (SYMPHONIE DIAGONALE, GER 1923-1924), Walter Ruttmann (OPUS 2, GER 1921; OPUS 3, GER 1924; OPUS 4, GER 1925), Fernand Leger and Dudley Murphy (IMAGES MOBILES, i.e. BALLET MECANIQUE, FR 1924) and René Clair (ENTR'ACTE, FR

1924). The term persisted in the German context for a while and by 1928 it had become an issue of polemics. While Hans Richter was instrumental in founding the *Gesellschaft » Neuer Film «*[39] which aimed at promoting an alternative kind of cinema, Walter Ruttmann – himself a pioneer of abstract movement with his series OPUS I-IV (GER 1919-1925) who had turned with BERLIN. DIE SINFONIE DER GROSSSTADT (GER 1926/27) away from pure abstraction – at exactly the same time wrote an article on, as he called it, the » absolute fashion «:

> It was inevitable: The › absolute ‹ film is now in fashion. Years ago when I presented the first examples, it was welcomed fanatically by some, mildly frowned upon by others. The low tide of film production is the reason why absolute film is now propagated as the Holy Bible. Its diffuse character is helpful for its propaganda.
>
> What is an absolute film? A film where one does not have to rely on the way the film is made for it to develop into art, but a film where the theory and the idea of film as an autonomous art is the most important – a priori: › *Only* in this way are films aesthetic laws. ‹
>
> It would certainly be delightful if the artist were to supersede the *routiniers*. But is it good for film when its artistic cleansing is forced upon it too eagerly? Is film actually understood, if one's goal is absolute music? Should films be shown in poorly attended cinemas? Become *virginised* for a small community of the aesthetically high-demanding people concerned only with its structural pureness?
>
> When it [the absolute film, MH] becomes self-sufficient and a goal in itself, it begins to lean toward the storerooms of *l'art pour l'art*. It is from here that film has just liberated us.[40]

Hans Richter presented the first program of the *Gesellschaft » Neuer Film «*, including Richter's own FILMSTUDIE (GER 1928) on 15 January 1928 in a private house and one month later, on 19 February, in a cinema on Kurfürstendamm. Since Ruttmann's article was published between these two screenings, it does not appear far-fetched to see the text as an attack on Richter and his activities. Ironically, Ruttmann had been scolded by Kracauer and others for the lack of social relevance and political responsibility of his BERLIN-film[41], which had premiered some months earlier in September 1927. Taking up this charge, Ruttmann now railed against Richter, whose approach was at this point much more abstract than Ruttmann's, even though their development was actually not that different. Between the lines (» poorly attended concert halls «), Ruttmann was possibly poking fun at Richter's engagement with the *Deutsche Kammermusiktage* in Baden-Baden, a festival devoted to » new music « which had begun screening films with modern scores and experiments in synchronisation in 1927.[42] Richter had been commissioned in 1928 to make a film for which Paul Hindemith, the artistic director of the festival, composed the music. Perhaps most importantly, Ruttmann dispensed with the notion of autonomous film art:

He objected to the idea that theory should be the overriding or prefiguring practice. A theory should develop from a practice, not the other way around. The
attraction of cinema is precisely that it could free art from the *l'art pour l'art* and
give it a new chance to engage with social reality – Ruttmann poised the cinema
as part of modernity against film art as part of high modernism.

Implicitly (and sometimes even explicitly), the thrust of the avant-garde was
anti-narrative. Many films that were shown within the context of the film societies that were considered avant-garde were non-narrative. The dominant form
of commercial cinema displayed a regime of heavily formalised narrative schemata centred on characters. This became the major point of attack on the film
industry as this became clear in Tom Gunning's formulation of the program of
the Dutch *Filmliga*:

> The *Filmliga* was not only established to show films not usually screened elsewhere,
> but also to discover and teach new ways of film spectatorship. Essentially, this meant
> an undermining of the dominance of narrative. The Liga did program a number of
> narrative films, but it also started a frontal attack on the hegemony of the narrative
> film as it is represented in the classical Hollywood feature film. It offered a variety of
> alternatives. The abstract films, the heavily political but often not very psychological
> Soviet films, the absurdist mixture of dadaist and surrealist films, the visual associa-
> tion and the symbolism of the French Impressionists, the dynamic images of every-
> day life in the city symphonies and other documentaries – in all of these forms one
> searched for organisational principles that were far from the conventional stories,
> which focused on well-rounded characters. New film forms required new audiences
> and the Filmliga's programs had to break with old film spectatorship habits in order
> to create a new appreciation for film art.[43]

The question of narrative, which was bound up in the opposition to the mainstream film industry, proved to be a point of contestation in this discussion
around realism and abstraction. Yet, when looking at the films screened at the
Film und Foto-exhibition in Stuttgart in 1929 which were meant to give an overview of the development in the first decade of the avant-garde one discovers
narrative films nowadays considered classics of the silent cinema like THE CIR-
CUS (US 1926-28, Charlie Chaplin) and VARIETÉ (GER 1925, E.A. Dupont), but
also films like the Zille adaptation DIE VERRUFENEN (GER 1925, Gerhard Lamprecht), or the Cecil B. DeMille production CHICAGO (US 1927, Frank Urson),
both films nowadays largely forgotten.[44] The rhetorical purity of the manifestoes and theoretical treatises was not always matched by the programs, which
were far more varied than one would assume from studying the founding documents of these organisations.

From the mid-1920s onwards, in the context of the *Neue Sachlichkeit* (new sobriety) or of political movements, outside reality was able to regain its higher

status among avant-garde filmmakers.[45] Tom Gunning has argued that the op-position between realism and abstraction is more an academic differentiation that does not do justice to the filmmakers and activists of the 1920s and 1930s:

> Here we see a theoretical opposition whereas in practice different film styles form a dialectic relation instead of excluding each other. This can in part be explained by the fact that these seemingly mutually exclusive techniques were both opposed to the commercial feature film.[46]

Yet, if we replace the abstraction vs. realism opposition with the opposition of both to the commercial feature film we return to our second aporia of commer-cialism/elitism. It should be kept in mind though that these oppositions were mainly mobilised in order to construct a common enemy to hold together an alliance that was highly diverse and at the same time striving in very different directions. If we consider, for example, the microscopic films of J.C. Mol (they were included in several programs of the *Filmliga* for their qualities as » absolute films « and also screened at the *FiFo*-programme in Stuttgart) we see a scientific impulse to depict phenomena that are too small for the normal eye. The same holds true for Jean Painlevé's work, a scientist » discovered « and hailed by the surrealists.[47] This attempt to construct a new kind of visuality in order to make processes undetectable to the human eye visible, links Mol and Painlevé's films with the New Vision as proposed by Moholy-Nagy.[48] A similar convergence of scientific and aesthetic functions of reproductive media was predicted by Wal-ter Benjamin: » To demonstrate the identity of the artistic and scientific uses of photography which heretofore usually were separated will be one of the revolu-tionary functions of the film. «[49] Yet, this striving to render visible the invisible is very different from an artistic urge for self-expression and more comparable to a disinterested observer who is attempting to maintain one's pure neutrality.

John Grierson is an important figure in tracing back of some of the shifts that occurred simultaneously with, yet independently of, the introduction of sound in the context of the avant-garde.[50] Grierson, trained as a social scientist, had developed an interest in the cinema as a mass medium while doing research in the United States from 1924 to 1927. After returning to England, he was hired as head of the newly formed Empire Marketing Film Board where he was able to put some of his ideas into practice. Part of the energy generated in the various alternative cinema activities in England flowed into the so-called » Documen-tary Film Movement « led by Grierson whose ideas represent a transition from the avant-garde ethos of the late 1920s to other forms of filmmaking outside the film industry in the 1930s. In fact, Grierson's school could be considered an on-going effort to bridge the gap between art and life through filmmaking and, equally important, through distribution and exhibition (a lot of energy was put into these two sectors, yet they are often forgotten in accounts of the movements). In the 1970s, Grierson was often attacked for being a naive realist, yet his theory, which rested upon sociological theories of mass communication and German idealist philosophy, aimed to make visible the reality of human relations which, according to this approach, can only be accessed through empirical reality. Grierson argued that » the principal function of the documentary film [w]as that of representing the interdependence and evolution of social relations in a dramatic, descriptive and symbolic way. «[51] Grierson was obsessed by modernisation and its effects on society, yet he was less a modernist in the sense that it is normally applied to artists of this particular period.[52]

Another important facet of this debate re-emerges around Soviet cinema: the montage films of Vertov, Eisenstein, Pudovkin, Dovshenko and others made a lasting impact in Western Europe in the second half of the 1920s. Yet, these foreign successes in Berlin, Amsterdam, Paris and London happened paradoxically at a time when their particular style of filmmaking was already on the retreat. Starting in 1928 with the end of the New Economic Policy (NEP), Stalinist doctrines were slowly but steadily altering the course of the Soviet cinema. What had dominated (at least in artistic terms) the Soviet cinema of the 1920s, namely a materialist film style based on ideas of collage, construction, juxtaposition and dialectical participation of the spectator in the reception process, gave way to Socialist Realism which can be conceptualised in two contradictory fashions. The Soviet cinema of the 1930s moved towards character development modelled on realist novels, identification through empathy, invisible editing according to Hollywood orthodoxy, and a spectator-film relation based upon interest in the unfolding narrative. » Formalism «, » cosmopolitanism «, » intellectualism « (as it was labelled by Stalinist functionaries purging the industry). In short, abstraction was driven back in favour of a more realist engagement with the outside world (not so much as it was, but rather as it was being anticipated). This shift in the Soviet cinema seemed to happen parallel to developments in other European countries – in the commercial industry as well as in the avant-garde. The move to Socialist Realism also meant a return to commercial and populist forms of filmmaking in which audience identification was becoming increasingly important, replacing issues such as medium specificity or abstraction. But, Socialist Realism can also be conceptualised in a very different manner: Soviet cinema from the 1930s was able to solve some of the problems of the avant-garde by becoming thoroughly integrated into the Stalinist scheme of society. While the 1920s presented a full-fledged utopian cinema (showing the world in the future according to the ardent followers of communism), the 1930s became dystopian in the way that art normatively dictated what a good Communist was. As art was now integrated into life and society (as official doctrine), it was argued that art had a direct influence on the functioning of social relations. Thus, a critical portrayal of social problems became potentially an act of sabotage because of art's direct influence on society. The price that the avant-garde had to pay in the Soviet Union for gaining influence, for being reintegrated into daily life was that they were made directly responsible for their representations.[53]

When members of the avant-garde met in 1930 in Brussels for their second congress, a year after the high spirits of La Sarraz, the shaky alliance of filmmakers disintegrated over *politics (communism / fascism)*. This is the fourth and final point in which contradictory opinions haunt the avant-garde. At the meeting in Brussels, Spanish and Italian delegates blocked a resolution that made the main goal of avant-garde film the fight against fascism. Thus, it became clear they were in the camp of the fascists, *Falangistas* and followers of Mussolini respectively. Many other participants were considered left wing and saw the opposition to fascism as their most important task. Yet, even within the group of left-wing filmmakers, which might appear homogeneous at first glance, many rifts persisted, most of which related to the differences between the Social Democrats and Communists: While the Social Democrats had a reformist approach to society and also sought alliances with bourgeois groups to further their cause, the Communists had a revolutionary attitude and opposed any appeasing motion that could endanger their mission. While Social Democrats strove for change via reform, the Communists saw violent revolution as the only path to real change. Anything that diminished the tension between the classes was deemed counter-revolutionary to the Communists. That is why they opposed reforms proposed by the Social Democrats because reforms only postponed revolution by giving the workers a share of petit bourgeois complacency and an illusionary sense of influence. The doctrine of a » class against class « conflict was especially adhered to by the European communists until the mid-1930s, as dictated by Moscow. Actually, the last gasps of the avant-garde of the interwar period (but also probably one of its most successful episodes) happened to be the filmmaking during the Spanish civil war and the *front populaire* era in France (1936-1938) which came about as the Communist strategy had changed to forging alliances with all of the opponents of rampant fascism.[54]

As a consequence, films calling for social reforms were opposed by the Communists until the mid-1930s. Thus, an initiative like the British state-funded Film Units (Empire Marketing Board, 1927-33; General Post Office, 1933-39; Crown Film, 1939-45) stood diametrically opposed to radical left-wing ideas. When the state (or institutions closely linked to the state) directly or indirectly financed a project, the filmmaker was consequently dependent on an allegiance to a system that the Communists aimed to topple. Famous debates like the legal conflict between Brecht and Eisler on the one side, and Balázs, Pabst and Nebenzal on the other, over the control of DIE 3-GROSCHEN-OPER (GER 1930, › The Three-Penny-Opera ‹) should be read in the context of this conflict. It replays the division within the left around the question of ownership and copyright. Brecht's aim was to radicalise social conflicts – he consciously occupied a position that the production team around Pabst and Nebenzal could not share. Since the film was produced within a framework of a capitalist free market, the production company needed the cash return while Brecht, on the other hand, wanted to radically undermine this production model.[55] The same could be said of Eisenstein's failed attempts to make a film in the United States that lived up to his expectations of revolutionary filmmaking. His rift with another famous left-wing writer, activist and agitator, Upton Sinclair, in the making of QUE VIVA MEXICO (US 1930-32) also shows the problematic nature of these types of pacts. Sinclair raised money from the US left in order to finance Eisenstein's venture. However, because a variety of circumstantial, personal – Sinclair's lack of experience in film production, Eisenstein's undisciplined shooting style, natural catastrophes and rainy seasons as well as political reasons – Eisenstein's clashes with Sinclair's brother-in-law Hunter Kimbrough, who came along to Mexico as production manager and watchdog, Stalin's telegram to Sinclair – saw the ill-fated project turn to shambles.[56] For similar reasons, the infamous » Aragon-affair « within Surrealist circles was driven by incompatible political and cultural agendas; it eventually led to the » resignation « of such devoted Bretonian followers as Luis Buñuel or Pierre Unik (both of whom subsequently worked together on TIERRA SIN PAN).[57] Interestingly, a key figure in the Aragon affair was Georges Sadoul who had accompanied Aragon on his trip to Kharkov for the Second International Conference of Proletarian and Revolutionary Writers. Sadoul, in turn, became one of the key figures in 1930s French film culture as well as in the post-war institutionalisation of film studies in French universities.

The avant-garde of the 1920s and 1930s was constantly shaken by these four aporias, which it could address dialectically, although they proved to be insurmountable obstacles. Many of the activists involved were aware of the problems and fault lines, but were unable to overcome them. In the contemporary writings and discussions at the time, these points were addressed repeatedly without arriving at any practicable solutions. It was the search for medium specificity inspired by avant-garde groups in the traditional arts and a vague opposition to the commercial film industry, which united the players until roughly 1930. When sound film was introduced and with fascism on the rise in various European countries, and as the economy spiralled downward at the beginning Depression, the contradictions around independence, elitism, abstraction, and politics were brought into the open. What had appeared for several years as a flourishing and oppositional force to be reckoned with, lost some of its momentum in the 1930s. Even though film societies were certainly as numerous as in the 1920s and alternative films continued to be made, the notion of altering cinema culture in a short period of time was lost. The energy that had gravitated towards avant-garde cinema went elsewhere. Even though the cinema continued to played an important role in revolutionary activities, it now became subordinated to other concerns. Another fundamental problem in the self-consciousness of the avant-garde was the model of production and reception that the players involved would adhere to. My four aporias are certainly not the only possibility of delineating the fault lines inside the avant-garde. One way of reconfiguring them would be to address them as problems of funding and finance (in/dependence), aesthetics and style (abstraction/realism), address and audience (elitism/populism) and politics and power (communism/fascism). This underlines some of the crucial areas in which the avant-garde was actively searching for a solution, a dialectical synthesis so to speak of the two antithetical terms.

2.2   Machine Aesthetics or Self-Expression: Constructivism or Expressionism

> *Since production (productive design) mainly serves*
> *the progress of mankind, we must try to expand*
> *the means of production (the apparatus) – onto fields*
> *until now only used for reproduction – into productive fields.*
> László Moholy-Nagy (1922)[58]

The avant-garde as a movement is often related to the wider currents of modernism, which implies following the logic of separating the work of art from the network and institution of art. It attempted to create objects in a realm completely detached from their space of production and consumption, quite contrary to avant-garde's original impetus to reconcile art and life.[59] Thus, modernism in this sense was opposed to realism in a diametrical way and effectively excluding some of the currents of the avant-garde of the 1920s and most of the activities in the 1930s as it tried to render visible the world in new ways (Ivens's 1930s work, Grierson's school, the New Deal filmmakers, the films of the *front populaire*, but also Leni Riefenstahl). I will instead follow Thomas Elsaesser who has distinguished three forms of » the modern «:

> the › modernism ‹ of an artistic avant-garde; the › modernisation ‹, as it affects labour and work, with Fordist production-line techniques replacing the workshop and the craft practices when sound was introduced; and third › modernity ‹ as a particular attitude to life, in Western societies usually associated with increased leisure time and new patterns of consumption. What makes these distinctions so tricky, but also

crucial is that in the domain of cinema, it is not always obvious that one can play off
› modernism ‹ (in the sense of an artistic avant-garde) against the different forms of
› modernisation ‹ (in technology, industry and science) and › modernity ‹ (in lifestyles,
fashion and sexual mores) seeing how parts of the filmic avant-garde accommodated
itself to the forced modernisation undertaken by the new industrial power that was
Nazi Germany in the mid-1930s...[60]

The modern is part of wider social, technological, political and cultural shifts,
but in cinema it is especially hard to tell apart the overlapping frames of modernism, modernity and modernisation. In Bill Nichols' view, modernism is Habermas' » unfinished project « that could still be taken up while I would argue
that its emergence is as much as its incompleteness a retrospective » invention of
a tradition « by those involved in the movement and its subsequent historiography.

Instead, I propose an alternative distinction that seems helpful in reconsider-
ing avant-garde practice around the coming of sound: namely something between an expressionist (expressive) and a constructivist (functionalist) avant-
garde. While the former *subjectivised* experience, that strives towards the expression of interior states and phenomena at the level below or beyond consciousness, the latter worked within an industrial framework, attempting to rationa-
lise and modularise cultural production as part of the wider economic context.
Surrealists are by extension also expressionists in this heuristic scheme as they
wanted to give form to interior and irrational (or more precisely, pre-rational)
processes, thoughts, instincts and feelings. The constructivists, on the other
hand, were thoroughly modern (in all of the three senses just outlined) in their
cooperation with the industry, in their employment of radical new technologies
of production, multiplication and diffusion and finally in their fascination for
cars and aeroplanes, for innovative machines and for the velocity of the new.[61]
Even the production process for the two avant-gardes was thoroughly different:
Surrealists and Expressionists not only adhered to a romantic ideal of singular
creation and of personal (self-)sacrifice, but they also produced their works in a
traditional and artisanal way that often disregarded new technologies. The Constructivists on the other hand relied on technological tools, industrial reproduction and professional expertise. In this respect, an anecdote recounted by Hans
Schoots in his seminal biography of Joris Ivens is quite telling: In the autumn of
1927, Ivens, a young enthusiast involved in Amsterdam's *Filmliga* and working
in his father's photographic business, but completely unknown as a filmmaker,
paid a visit to Walter Ruttmann in Berlin. Ruttmann was more than 10 years
older than Ivens and at the peak of his career; apart from Sergei Eisenstein,
possibly the most celebrated avant-garde filmmaker at that historical moment.
Ivens, born into a family of photography professionals and a graduate from the

technical university in Berlin, reports: » From our perspective in faraway Holland, Ruttmann was an artistic giant, but when I saw him at close hand, wres-
tling with an old, poorly equipped camera, and limited by a lack of craftsmanship, I realized that from a technical point of view I was more than his
equal. «.[62] In fact, while Ruttmann would always wrestle with the conflicting
expressionist and constructivist paradigms, Ivens was squarely on the side of
constructivism. Ruttmann's artistic ego was schooled in painting – just as Hans
Richter and Viking Eggeling, the champions of filmic abstraction in the 1920s,
had been – while Ivens' mind had the fine-tuning of an engineer. His background in his father's photography business and his studies at a technical university had given him a thoroughly different notion of the role and function of
the artist.

The extension of this parallel to production forms and artistic self-definition is
crucial because here lies the more useful dimension of this distinction. While
Ruttmann always struggled with his self-definition as an artist and his dependency on various sources, Ivens in 1931 made his claim on the » avant-garde
documentary «. Ivens shifted from artistic self-expression to a more political domain: whereas in the 1920s, abstraction was seen as a radical weapon in itself, in
the 1930s a new urgency drove filmmakers towards documentaries and, generally speaking, a more direct depiction of reality with the aim of changing it. In
his article, Ivens commences by stating that » [t]he sound film is the starting
point for all future possibilities of radio and television «[63] – sound film was
there to stay – end of discussion. He went on to argue in favour of commissioned films. In fact, Ivens saw industrial commissions as escape out of the impasse that had opened up for filmmakers with the introduction of sound:

> Because the documentary film mainly thrives on commissions – and for industries
> there is no better way of advertising – the documentary filmmaker only has to deal
> with one man: a businessman, an outsider in the field of filmmaking. Therefore, it is
> in the interest of that director to make a good film using truth and the documentary's
> character as the sole criterion. Should he work for the film industry, however, he has
> to deal with a board, artists, and censorship. He is no longer independent, he is
> bound; he is more or less a slave. To break free from this slavery, he has to be abso-
> lutely sure of the production and also be able to convince his spectator, whether it
> concerns someone from the industry or not.[64]

Invoking Hegel's dialectic of master and slave, Ivens' commentary is very telling for an avant-garde filmmaker with respect to comparing the film industry to
slavery whereas, for him, a commissioned film was freedom. This is a clear echo
of the 1920s stance: the film industry is the enemy which unites the avant-garde.

For constructivists the autonomy of art was a bourgeois illusion that was
merely perpetuating the limiting and enclosing of art in clearly circumscribed

places in society, in ghettos like museums or galleries. It was the constructivist ethos that tried to transpose the machine aesthetics and industrial forms into mass culture and everyday life, but also into museum culture and the art world. Constructivists believed that artists should leave the bourgeois and isolated sphere of so called » autonomous art « and enter design and advertising, newspapers and media in order to reach a broader public. Thus, the industry and avant-garde were not necessarily antagonistically poised against each other in constructivist thinking. Instead, artists more or less affiliated to this approach (*Bauhaus* teachers such as Walter Gropius, László Moholy-Nagy and Oskar Schlemmer, architects J.J.P. Oud, Mart Stam, and Cornelis van Eesteren, photographers Piet Zwart and Paul Schuitema, graphic artists George Grosz and John Heartfield, to name but a few) entered the public sphere with commercial works, breaking open the ghetto of art where provocations and innovations were accepted and tolerated to a certain degree. This » lethal embrace « of tolerance towards innovation in the art system defused even potentially provocative positions as the impact as well as the audience were minimised by the limits imposed within the system. By actively addressing the mass-mediated audience, the constructivists tried to break open the system, to rebuild the public, to educate the masses, to create a » new vision « (Moholy-Nagy), a » new typography « (Tschichold), a » new architecture « (Le Corbusier) with the ultimate goal of creating the » new man «.[65] Seen in this light, the industry was actually a partner of the avant-garde, albeit a difficult one, probably not a friend, but also not an enemy. For constructivists, art played an important role in reshaping society and on the way to creating the » new man «. The self-awareness of the artist had to shift accordingly from a romantic notion of the individual genius to the technician engineering a new society in his laboratory of art.[66]

The industry, on the other hand, also had good reasons to work with avant-garde artists. At various times, even the film industry employed avant-garde artists in considerable numbers. In the early- to mid-1920s, Ufa supported a number of experimental approaches to filmmaking in the *Kulturfilmabteilung* and under production head Erich Pommer the company also integrated a degree of experimentation in their films. DAS CABINET DES DR. CALIGARI and other films in the early 1920s had been successful at home and abroad. During the introduction of sound, Tobis had filmmakers such as Walter Ruttmann, Hans Richter, Alexis Granowsky, René Clair and his brother Henri Chomette under contract.[67] These companies were using the avant-garde as an outsourced *Research & Development* department because film studios normally did not invest in units working on new aesthetic developments (as opposed to technical innovations). As soon as these new techniques were either ready to go into mass production or had proven to be uninteresting, the film industry disposed of the artists again. For advertising, with its constant hunger for new sensations, the appeal of the avant-garde was more logical: avant-garde art, advertising and fashion always had close ties and continue to attract each other. For the avant-garde, the industry assignments fulfilled three purposes: Firstly, these works provided a material support in terms of income. Secondly, they also potentially opened up the limited audience that the institution of art had to offer to a wider public in which mass-produced commodities circulated. And thirdly, these assignments also gave the artists the opportunity to engage in new experiments because equipment was often provided that was otherwise outside their reach.

Constructivist thinking opposed the traditional role of the artist as original genius as much as the traditional role of the craftsman. Whereas the romantic notion of the genius contains the idea of the lonely searching soul being misunderstood by contemporaries, the notion of the craftsman implies a mastery of material and also a guild-like organisation. The guild's main function is to keep outsiders out – and thus implicitly to keep the balance between the number of artists and the commissions without an intervening market regulating supply and demand. While the metaphor of the craftsman suggests a functionalist relationship to the objects created (which might have been attractive to constructivist thinking), the disinterestedness of the craftsman in political and social terms was certainly a negative connotation that overshadowed its positive aspects. The Dutch photographer Paul Schuitema recognised these problems inherent in the various self-images of the artist and instead devised his own role as a fighter. In this view, art becomes a practice and weapon which had to be continually resharpened in order to win the battle:

> It is naive to believe that it is enough to be just a proletarian to deal with weapons in the class struggle. Class-conscious proletarian struggle means exercise and eventually mastery of the weapons in class struggle. The training of the proletarian photo-correspondent must primarily be related to operating his camera and only subsequently to the study of seduction. No romanticism, no art, rather objective, openly seductive propaganda: tactically aimed towards class struggle, technically aimed at the job.[68]

Echoes of Ivens' comments on Ruttmann can be heard in Schuitema's position. Technical mastery and constant practice are of equal importance; the question of commissions and the publication or genre are not even considered, unless they are in relation to the audience which is addressed by the revolutionary propaganda. In this connection, it is important to note that Schuitema and Piet Zwart, a typographer with similar political ideas, both worked extensively in advertising for industrial products. Both also joined the activist group *Opbouw*, dominated by architects such as Van Eesteren, Oud and Stam, who had pioneered new ways of building using pre-fabricated parts and functionalist styles. This active role within the production process that was often pioneered by architects was also taken up by photographers, typographers, writers, and as we shall see, avant-garde filmmakers. Thus, advertising was an easy way into the industry: » Advertising offered them [Schuitema and Zwart] the opportunity to play an active role in the production process ... and to present their theories about contemporary forms of production to a wide audience by using ultra-modern production facilities. «[69] This engagement in commercial assignments was not limited to Western Europe as Lev Manovich has observed: » [A]lready in the 1920s, left avant-garde artists, both in Europe and in Soviet Russia worked for commercial industries on publicity and advertising campaigns. «[70] In the 1920s, it was the Soviet Union which provided the vanishing point for the avant-garde; as political and other tensions rose towards the outbreak of World War II, the United States joined the Soviet Union as another vanishing point.[71] These young and dynamic societies each offered a different utopia based on restructuring social relations beyond class affiliation and family pedigree.

Besides the idea of the fighter, the times also offered another metaphor for the artist to use as a self-image – given the fact that the innate genius of romanticism and the craftsman of the Gothic period were dated concepts that had to be refuted. The engineer was certainly a key metaphor for cultural activism in the interwar period. In a text written in 1930, Ruttmann hinted at this engineering model by introducing the metaphor of a laboratory that was also used by Joris Ivens in a similar context:

> What is surprising about the film industry is that when it is compared to other industries and production fields it never had a laboratory. ... And still the laboratory could have been the nutrition necessary to develop and strengthen it. ... Not to improve and develop the apparatus would have been the task of this laboratory. ... Instead, here experimental departments should be created to prove the range of possibilities ... within film as a form of expression.[72]

The figure of the engineer represented ideas of progress and rational production, of non-individual authorship and social progress without falling into the traps of traditional bourgeois notions of autonomous art and individual genius.[73] But this interest in the engineer as a symbol of the time was not limited to the avant-garde at the *Bauhaus* or similar circles across Europe. As Thomas Elsaesser has pointed out, the engineer also haunts the commercial feature film of the Weimar cinema in various ways because he occupies a crucial mediating position between different discourses:

> ... the figure of the engineer [is] positioned ambiguously between both the worker and the boss, but also between the inventor and those that commercialise an invention. The reason the engineer seems so crucial is because he has to mediate between two sets of binary oppositions, that of the class discourse ..., but also of the discourse of science and technology. ... On the side of science is the figure of the professor or inventor – selfless, absent-minded, beneficial in his quest for pure knowledge. On the

other side is the businessman: unscrupulous and megalomaniac, who stops at nothing in order to steal, sabotage or keep for himself the work that by rights belongs to others. The business man or financier is thus the one who applies science, who makes technological progress and productivity possible, but he is invariably seen as the villain. Here we have, in some sense, the romantic anti-capitalist, anti-technology vision intact, except that both sides need the engineer – the inventor in order to rescue him from his other-worldliness, and the businessman because only the engineer can make the invention › work ‹. The engineer's job is therefore to help materialise the immaterial (pure disembodied thought) and to moralise the material (pure inert matter). These oppositions and the mediating function of the engineer stand in glaring contrast to the actual relations affecting the processes of technology and invention.[74]

What seems to be at issue in the trope of the engineer and the metaphor of engineering as cultural production is not some internal quarrel among the avant-garde, but rather the rhetorical domination of a discourse about technical progress, social engineering, and the future organisation of society that played a role in public life. The mass media was competing with the avant-garde over questions regarding the development of society and culture. Not coincidentally then, the avant-garde directly or indirectly found themselves in such movements as fascism, Grierson's filmmaking unit, Roosevelt's cultural initiatives and the French *front populaire* – all movements designed to find a path to the future organisation of society. A more useful division to describe some aspects of the changes between the 1920s and the 1930s would thus be to replace the binary opposition of abstraction vs. realism with the transformation from the laboratory (research pure and simple, not necessarily determined by its use value) to engineering (applied science).

Constructivists had declared their goal as wanting to leave the isolated corner of elitist art: As a result, both the Soviet Union and later the United States with their grand projects, utopian visions and social experiments became the main destinations for avant-garde artists since here ideas were put into practice.[75] Here, the conflicts between the industry and the art world seemed to subside for a while as both the communist functionaries, and after 1933, Roosevelt's New Deal administration actively participated and supported artistic and cultural production. Lev Manovich has drawn similar parallels between the constructivist German and Russian avant-garde of the 1920s, on the one hand, and contemporary new media, on the other: » [A]ctive participation of the European avant-garde artists in building American techno-society, whether through cinema (in Hollywood), architecture or design, can be understood as an equivalent of the Russian artists' collaboration with the new Revolutionary state. «[76] Ivens and Piscator, Brecht and Moholy-Nagy, Eisenstein and Vertov, Richter and Buñuel all found themselves either in the United States or in the Soviet Union by

1940 – the aporias of the avant-garde had now settled into the bipolar division of the globe that would determine the course of history for the next 50 years.

2.3   Self-propaganda or Revolutionary Agitation: Organising Visual Facts

> *The designer is not sketching, but organising the optical factors.*
> *His work is not like handicraft; it is limited to taking notes,*
> *building groups and technical organization.*
> Paul Schuitema (1930)[77]

I have so far avoided the question of what I mean by avant-garde as it is a historically malleable and complicated concept. Like most writers on the topic, I am indebted to one of the key theoretical studies of the avant-garde and its historiography, namely Peter Bürger's *Theory of the Avant-garde*. Bürger sees the avant-garde as a reaction to the social isolation of artistic practice within the » institution art «. After aestheticism (*l'art pour l'art*) had turned art's lack of influence on politics and society into its program, the avant-gardes began to radically question the basic assumptions of the production, dissemination and presentation of art in modern society. In Bürger's view, the avant-garde is determined by its resistance and opposition to traditional notions and concepts of the institution art: » The avant-garde is opposed to both the apparatus of distribution to which the work of art is subjected and the concept of autonomy which describes the status of art in bourgeois society. «[78] Now, Bürger's focus is on Dada and Surrealism, especially in its forms as literature and visual art, while film complicates the picture. Bürger's historical reasoning works for traditional arts with a long prehistory of emancipation from economic dependency (to the point of an independence without impact) while modern media like photography and film experienced a much shorter evolution and occupied a very different position in the 1920s. Moreover, while financing was often a factor of little importance to writers or painters, it was the crucial element in artistic production for the modern mass media. While Bürger's central contention that the avant-garde is inherently different from a new style or aesthetic school remains valid for the cinema, the shift from literature and visual arts to reproductive media requires a new perspective.

For traditional historians of the film avant-garde, the avant-garde movement had basically ceased to exist by 1930. However, if the avant-garde had not fallen apart by 1930, as I concede, what would have happened to it instead? After abstraction had exhausted itself as a rallying point, and as the film societies began to unite a variety of people with very different ideas about the cinema (which was revealed with the coming of sound) different paths were followed. Grierson's school sought the patronage of the state as did the New Deal film-makers in the United States. Meanwhile, political activists like Ivens were financed by various international left-wing organisations while he also filmed in the Soviet Union. Ruttmann and Riefenstahl chose to accept commissions from the Nazi party, Hans Richter mainly worked in advertising and on industrial films, returned to painting and made a living as a teacher. At the same time, Soviet cinema changed course from a concentration on montage and juxtaposition of images to Socialist Realism. In fact, all of these avant-garde currents in the 1920s were, by the 1930s, able to reach an audience much greater than the one they had ever addressed before.

Given the wide variety of films that are now regarded as avant-garde classics, how can we construct a somewhat coherent corpus of the avant-garde? For example, where do we draw the line between commercial art films and avant-garde films? Art cinema was produced in Germany in the wake of the success of DAS CABINET DES DR. CALIGARI (GER 1919/20, Robert Wiene) which had garnered considerable success abroad. The German industry realised that expressionism as a label could sell a German product abroad and at home because it fit into preconceived conceptions of art, on the one hand, and of German-ness, on the other. Throughout the 1920s, art cinema tried to draw a larger domestic audience by including stars and spectacles, by using popular narratives while simultaneously constructing an artistically valued alternative to Hollywood through brand name artists (directors), complicated and nested narratives and the use of cultural capital from the literary sphere.[79] Famous examples of this trend culminating in the mid-1920s include Fritz Lang's DIE NIBELUNGEN (GER 1922-24) and METROPOLIS (GER 1925/26), F.W. Murnau's FAUST (GER 1926) and DER LETZTE MANN (GER 1924, ›The Last Laugh‹), as well as E.A. Dupont's VARIETÉ (GER 1925). Yet, these films were actually produced within the film industry that the avant-garde was so opposed to in rhetorical terms. The European situation might have been special because of the existence of a commercial art cinema relatively open to innovation, while also addressing a mass audience that allowed for a certain measure of moderation between the radical experiments of the avant-garde and the formulaic films of the film industry.[80] As Charles Boost has remarked in a brief history of the institutions of the film avant-garde, it was in fact commercial art films that contributed some of the key works to the history of the avant-garde:

> ... despite the enthusiasm and activity of an inventive avant-garde, the big and lasting impulses in the process that led to the recognition of film as art came from assignments made with private subsidies or in industrial context. Three films have played a dominant role in showing the cinema-going public, including critics and theoreticians, the possibilities and potentials of the new medium in the period 1920-1930.

Das Cabinet des Dr. Caligari, Potemkin as well as La Passion de Jeanne d'Arc were in their own time and have since remained eye-opening, shocking films that did not fit into the frame of film productions up till then. They created revolutions in spectatorship, shook existing definitions and in a short period of time (the time of release) clarified a lot of what was only vaguely understood or otherwise confirmed what had only been a vague thought until then.[81]

Three commercial art films provided the model and impulse for much of the activity in avant-garde circles. It is therefore much too easy to draw a line between » good « artists and the » bad « industry. In technological as well as in economic terms, there was no clear demarcation between the two. However, it is important to note that avant-garde artists were employed from the early 1920s onwards to provide special services such as Ruttmann's dream of the falcon sequence for Lang's Die Nibelungen. Ruttmann may have considered this a commercial assignment where he could make enough money to finance his own » private « experiments. Nevertheless, when we look at Ruttmann's career and survey his methods, it fits his overall trajectory of someone working on the margins, but always keen on finding a wider audience.

Thomas Elsaesser has suggested an alternative definition for the Dada film, which can be usefully extended to include avant-garde cinema:

> What Dada was in regard to cinema was not a specific film, but the performance, not a specific set of techniques or textual organization, but the spectacle. One might argue that in order for a film to have been Dada it need not be made by a Dadaist, or conversely, that there were no Dada films outside the events in which they figured.[82]

Dada film should thus not be defined by the form or content of the films, but rather by the relationship between film and spectator. Maybe this could be used to describe the interwar film avant-garde as a whole – avant-garde film is defined by a peculiar and specific kind of spectatorship, by the way the relationship of film and audience is constructed, by the framing of the cinematic event. In this respect, avant-garde also points back to early cinema in how the spectator became a part of the performance.[83]

The avant-garde was a small and endangered species and every new film was seen as a triumph for the movement. The avant-garde films which are canonised as such are always primarily advertising films for the avant-garde itself. Since avant-garde as an idea is characterised by a self-reflexive modernism it is very much determined by its opposition to institutions and traditions, it is always context-dependent, namely dependent upon the specific antagonism exhibited in the works. Thus, the avant-garde could only function by continuously promoting itself as new and innovative and as being against traditional institutions. The avant-garde was constantly » preaching to the converted «, making films for avant-garde film societies that were already won over by the concept that would then eternally be replicated in the films. The avant-garde had no choice but to continue to innovate – what was a novelty one day already appeared trite and old the next. Avant-garde is a » movement « in the literal sense of the term: it is directed against stasis and formulaic solutions, it is in constant flux and transformation. It is, therefore, quite difficult to see what a » success « could have been for the avant-garde because if they found themselves attuned with a mass audience they could no longer be considered to be in the forefront which, of course, would force them to break new ground again. An avant-garde is most successful when it is caught up in the mainstream, while simultaneously ceasing to exist – the ultimate success of the avant-garde is therefore to make itself redundant. The avant-garde can only succeed in » failure «, in becoming conventionalised, superfluous and thus pointless, i.e., no longer avant-garde.

Addressing this specific dialectic Andor Kraszna-Krausz has pointed out why Germany and Russia were especially fruitful countries for avant-garde activities (one could add the Netherlands to the list as well). As we have just outlined, a certain movement was necessary in order to break new ground not just on the side of the avant-garde, but also in the industry because the avant-garde could only claim to be a trailblazer if some of their innovations were incorporated into the broader circles of (film) culture. To claim to be in the forefront without any tangible results or followers would be senseless and esoteric. Therefore, a dynamic interchange between various groups in the cinema was necessary for an avant-garde to be successful:

> While in America a too vehement film industry suppresses a too weak Avantgarde and in France a too vehement Avantgarde overpowers a too weak industry; in Germany – and it is similar in Russia – a mid-heavy industry seems to mix with a mid-heavy Avantgarde. … The German Avantgarde has found also new contents [sic] for new technics [sic], while the French had been forced to discover new technics [sic], without their contents ever turning up. The French waited for tasks that never came. They practiced for a work which they had expected in vain.[84]

Kraszna-Krausz wrote this on the occasion of a review of the Stuttgart film program, the first comprehensive retrospective of 1920s avant-garde cinema. It offers a specific balance between the avant-garde and the industry that would yield the optimum results: » One saw that the Avantgarde could claim more right of existence if it was connected with a whole army behind it – practically or theoretically. « The vanguard must have connections with the army and the other way around, only then can both profit from the dynamic relationship that is ever changing and never static.

When we turn from the film industry in the narrow sense to the industry in the general sense a certain reframing around the concept of propaganda is nec-

essary. In the 1920s and 1930s, the term » propaganda « was not limited to political agitation (although it could mean that too), but also referred to any film
that forcefully made a point and to convince the spectators of something. It
should furthermore be understood that our contemporary demarcations that
distinguish documentary from industrial film or advertisement from political
propaganda were not common currency circa 1930. Thus, different genres and
film styles converge under the term propaganda: advertising and industrial
films, political films and committed documentaries, commissioned work and
filmmaking in the service of the state. A catalogue accompanying an exhibition
of photo montages in 1930 stated: » The most important use of photomontage is
in propaganda, in commercial as well as political contexts. «[85] It is exactly this
varied usage that is interesting in relation to the avant-garde: As classificatory
schemes differ historically, today's terminology also denotes different things.
Implicitly then, the ideas at the time regarding propaganda were very different.
If propaganda could mean product promotion as well as political persuasion,
social reform as well as revolutionary agitation then there was no contradiction
between working for the industry and working for different political or social
causes.

Most avant-garde films that are canonised as such are predominantly determined by their formal(ist) innovations and by their relation to the film industry,
to traditional film formats and genres, to conventional models of story telling.
Most avant-garde films are therefore characterised by their opposition and ne-
gativity. A rather lengthy list comprises the type of films that Ivens made in a
couple of years:

> Even in his early years he was already using every form and type of filmmaking in-
> cluding feature film and newsreel. Within four years, between 1927 and 1931, he had
> worked on: science films ...; home-movies ...; feature films ...; newsreel ...; social repor-
> tage ...; company films ... and many other commissioned films ...; even animated films
> ...; aesthetic form and movement studies ...; poetic nature recordings ...; subjective
> films ...; political pamphlets ...; film sketches ...; and abstract art .... He also worked
> on contrasting aspects: microshots as well as panoramic shots from an airplane; ex-
> pressionist influences derived from vitalism as well as the abstract › absolute ‹ film;
> the feature film as well as the newsreel; assignments for a trade union or for umbrella
> organizations of the communist party, as well as assignments for large capitalist en-
> terprises; subjective imagery as well as scientific imagery; formal aesthetics as well as
> social reportage; animation as well as news pictures. He boasted a many-sided and
> inspired start like nobody else. In essence, all of the elements of his later work were
> present at the start. «[86]

This list creates an individual artistic sensibility where everything was already
in place in the early days of his career, thus, reversing chronology and, teleolo-

gically speaking, seeing early films with eyes that are already aware of the entire career. What I propose instead is rather the inverse: In an archaeological fashion I am trying to observe something else in the avant-garde, by forgetting later developments that in the above account become the line of flight for everything Ivens made early in his career. Such an auteur perspective is rather misleading as one always invariably ends up with retrospective explanations, which construct an imaginary coherence across a diverse body of work. In fact, I would argue that these films were animated by a belief in the function and impact of film as a medium (not necessarily as an art form). I also think that they had a certain effect in mind for the spectators, which gives them a coherence quite different from an auteuristic subjectivity.

And finally, we must also look at the self-referentiality of the avant-garde. Tom Gunning has argued that Joris Ivens' DE BRUG (NL 1928) » shows that it is impossible to disentangle the visual experience of a modern structure from the object itself. «[87] Thus, if the modern structure is inseparable from its visual experience, then the avant-garde film must reveal the structure of the objects portrayed in its films. Because cinema itself is as inseparably a part of this modern world as these objects (cities, bridges, ocean liners, department stores, etc.) any of these films is at least implicitly a film about cinema itself and about the specific » new vision « that is characteristic of it. The epitome of this self-advertisement of cinema as a modern structure rendering the modern structure visible (and not just making films about it, but mirroring its very relations to itself) is surely Dziga Vertov's CELOVEK S KINOAPPARATOM (SU 1929, › The Man with the Movie Camera ‹). The works of Ivens or Ruttmann, Richter or Cavalcanti between 1928 and 1932 also circled around these topics and can thus be seen as the biggest campaign in favour of cinema ever conducted. The same spirit of modernity that gave birth to the Eiffel tower also gave birth to cinema: Avant-garde films that attempted to bring film into its own often used this structure as their subject, thereby creating a *mise-en-abyme* in which the cinema could talk to itself and about itself.[88]

2.4 Conclusion

> [B]y incorporating technology into art, the avantgarde liberated technology
> from its instrumental aspects and thus undermined both bourgeois notions of
> technology as progress and art as › natural ‹, › autonomous ‹, and › organic ‹.
>
> Andreas Huyssen (1980)[89]

Most theories dealing with the artistic avant-garde have referred either to literature or to the visual arts as either an implicit or explicit model.[90] The main fea-

ture of the avant-garde has been seen as the attempt to break down the barriers
between art and life – in both directions, thus making art an integral part of life
and including real life in art. In this process, both parts of the equation are effectively cancelled out, as their distinction vanishes and we are unable to differentiate between them. However, both concepts in this synthesis are also simultaneously redeemed and retained on a different level. It is this Hegelian
dialectic of *Aufhebung* (sublation) that the avant-garde was aiming for, but never
truly achieved.

In thinking about the film avant-garde one encounters several problems,
which have not been thoroughly examined thus far: The definition of what constitutes an avant-garde film is not clear at all. What distinguishes an avant-
garde film from a commercial art film is often very hard to point out. Moreover,
what has retrospectively often been labelled as documentary, advertisement, industrial film or *Kulturfilm* might, in the logic of the day, actually be an avant-
garde film. Even though every categorisation always presupposes an exclusion-
ary and an inclusionary gesture,[91] the issue with respect to the film avant-garde
seems especially significant and difficult to resolve. In keeping with avant-
garde logic, every new film of theirs also questioned the traditional boundaries
erected rhetorically between various film styles. By including the scientific films
of J.C. Mol or Jean Painlevé the avant-garde emphasised different aspects of
these films. By praising Louis Feuillade's serials, the surrealists consciously pro-
voked the bourgeois tastemakers. Here lies the true purpose of the avant-garde:
to constantly question boundaries and limits, including their own, and thereby
radically undermine even their own *raison d'être*. If the avant-garde were to stop
doing this, it would lose its momentum and thus never succeed in the traditional sense of institutionalisation or system stabilisation. That some films produced within the avant-garde circles of the interwar period are now canonised
in museums and *cinémathèques* around the world is simultaneously the triumph
and the defeat of the avant-garde and further underscores the dialectic at the
heart of this movement. The avant-garde's goal was radical change, yet only
succeeded in entering those institutions of mainstream culture that they ab-
horred, fought and detested.

As I have argued, a number of aporias riddled the film avant-garde and the
different actions and manifestations fluctuated between the various positions
making the avant-garde at best an unstable configuration. Retrospectively, abstraction has proven to be the most crucial factor in deciding which films were
to enter the canon of the avant-garde – as (high) » modernism « began to replace
avant-garde as the guiding term for the art historical studies focusing on the
first half of the Twentieth Century. Since the visual arts of the 1920s tended
towards abstraction, their model has been transferred to film without too much
discussion. In effect this shift of focus from transformation as a social force to

abstraction as a formal category has effectively meant a *depolitisation* of the avant-garde. Consequently, topics like (political) engagement or realism (which were at the time much hotter issues than the question of abstraction, which was already an outdated concept by 1928) proved to be conspicuously absent from canonical accounts (1960s to 1980s) of the interwar avant-garde manifestations. The four aporias I have elaborated upon in this chapter: independence/dependence, abstraction/realism, commercial/elitist, communist/fascist could also be reconfigured as problems of funding, aesthetics, address (audience) and politics.[92]

3   Strategic Convergence and Functional Differentiation – The Film Societies and Ciné-Clubs of the 1920s and 30s

> *Of course the organisation of work is much more troublesome*
> *than the (artistic) work itself, i.e., we increasingly*
> *considered the organisation an indispensable part of artistic work.*
> *This was only possible because the work as a whole was political.*
> Bertolt Brecht, Slatan Dudow et al. (1931/32)[1]

Film clubs, film societies and ciné-clubs have not been high on the agenda of film historians. While, generally speaking, production has always generated more research than distribution and exhibition, circulation has largely been left on the margins. Ciné-clubs and film societies have either been dealt with in biographical works or in regional studies that concentrated on a specific city (and often a specific screening space or institutional context). Both approaches to these alternative outlets, on the one hand, neglect the national and international exchange of the initiatives; on the other, it has limited the scope to specific constellations thus never reaching a comparatistic perspective. In order to contextualise artistic practice and to arrive at an archaeology of the avant-garde, this chapter examines the nexus of film societies, their activities and publications, their programming policies and networking efforts.

What could be called » the first wave of cinephilia «[2] includes not only the films that have claims to fame, but, more importantly, activities in the cinema sector beyond the commercial and industrial structures in a wide sense (exhibition, publishing, public debate, distribution). This chapter is confined mainly to key activities in Britain, the Netherlands, Belgium, Germany, Switzerland and France in the 1920s and 1930s. This limitation is not only dictated by the practicability of access to material, but – as will emerge later in this chapter – it follows the pattern of closest cooperation and the most intense activities. Film societies were typical in large metropolitan centres, which had a large enough density of artists and intellectuals interested in the novel and innovative use of film. Even though there were similar efforts in » marginal « places like Portugal, Poland or Denmark, these were not as continuous, as broad or as closely interrelated as the phenomena that I am dealing with here. I will argue that the practically simultaneous growth of film clubs in several European cultural centres was far from coincidental and was intertwined with a technological shift, i.e., the coming of sound, but also with changes in the public sphere, a reconfigured film industry and a generally transformed political landscape. Far from disappearing without a trace or failing in its goals, as traditional historiography would have it, the ciné-clubs had a strong impact over the long term. In the course of the 1930s, the activities led to (self-) employment in various educational, governmental and filmmaking bodies, but more importantly, also in film archives.

Film societies can be defined as social organisms that provide a framework for viewing and discussing films, for developing theories and for distributing and making films.[3] This chapter roughly follows a chronological itinerary from the first efforts after World War One to the emerging mass movement of the late 1920s. The programming policy as well as the manifestoes and programs are artefacts that constitute an alternative and oppositional practice. The boom around 1930 can be conceptualised as a strategic convergence – different groups united for some time under the avant-garde banner. In the second part of the chapter, the development in the 1930s will be sketched, especially in respect to how cinema came to occupy a different position for the nation-state and how archives were instituted. The key concept for the development after the coming of sound will be functional differentiation. The coming of sound thus functions as a conceptual relay since the transition brought contradictions into the open and forced the avant-garde to reconsider and reconfigure their activities.

While the main cities in Europe were Amsterdam, Berlin, Brussels, London, and Paris, I decided to leave out two other territories important to alternative film culture in this chapter: the Soviet Union and the United States, the two » big others « in the eyes of Western Europe. While I will deal with the Soviet Union in a separate chapter, the United States deserves its own study and will not be dealt with in this book in any great detail, even though it will crop up occasionally.[4] Furthermore, as bourgeois art never gained a strong (public) footing with state support and elite backing, the avant-garde in the US had a different relationship to mass culture and technology. For that reason, an inclusion of the Unites States would alter the perspective considerably. An appreciative nod should go to avant-garde developments in Japan, which to some extent paralleled those in Europe and the United States, but also diverged considerably and have been the topic of some accessible studies recently.[5]

Most of the details that are generally known about the 1920s and 1930s and the activities of the film societies, ciné-clubs, Filmligas, Filmverbände we owe to the people who were actually involved in the initiatives. The few people who started the film clubs and then became important figures in filmmaking, film publishing, film theory and film archives were also the ones who wrote down their stories. In fact, the pioneers of the 1920s have not only written their own histories, but moreover, they penned the first important books on film theory and history and they also founded archives and university courses. A fairly small group of mobile and ambitious activists, practitioners and theoreticians, first made history and later wrote it down, created the first canon in the film societies and subsequently determined which films were written about and preserved. They practically predetermined what later generations were able to watch, read and think about. Their merits notwithstanding, it is surprising how unquestioned this pioneer generation was (and still is) taken at face value in their memories and mythologies.

3.1   Emergence

There are dozens of millions who love cinema,
from every country, from every class, from the most
intellectual to those with only the most basic culture.
Charles de Vesme (1920)[6]

When thinking about the beginnings of film societies one encounters problems involving definitions and dates well-known to the historian of early cinema in relation to the » emergence of cinema «. Thomas Elsaesser has described the problems inherent in any definition of the origins of cinema:

> While considering what cinema really is, some things that appear self-evident have to be questioned. Is cinema any series of photographs that contain movement, or pictures, sketched or photographed, and mechanically driven, thereby creating the impression of continuous movement? ... Is it the projected picture or the exhibition of living pictures in front of a paying audience? ... There are ... at least ... two dozens ... candidates.[7]

In this vein we should pause for a moment and reconsider what type of object we are dealing with here. What constitutes a ciné-club? Does it exclusively show films or formulate an anti-establishment stance? Is it imperative that it works on a subscription basis or that it invites practitioners for debates? Is it a necessary condition that its main goal be to foster aesthetic connoisseurship or that it have an explicitly political agenda? This is similar to the problem of the origin and birth of cinema. We should be wary of locating foundational moments that can be charged with historical significance and instead question the parameters that guide these decisions.

Despite these cautionary remarks, one has to start in Paris because the city almost certainly remains the capital of cinephilia and cinema culture to this day.[8] This chapter will use developments in the French capital as its launching pad. There are always several events one could point to and choosing one is probably as arbitrary as choosing another when locating the origin of a practice that had many forerunners in theatre clubs and artists' societies, in associations for workers' cultural education and other gatherings devoted to the aesthetic and cultural appreciation of the cinema. Nevertheless, the screening at the Parisian cinema *La Pépinière* on 12 June 1920, organised and conducted by Louis Delluc, Georges Denola and Charles de Vesme and devoted to the work of French animator Emile Cohl, has often been cited as the significant starting point.[9] This event evolved into a movement and the formation of the *Ciné-Club de France* can be traced back to this screening. The event took place in Paris and was co-organised by Louis Delluc, one of the key figure in Parisian intellectual cinema culture of the early 1920s.[10] It was in the spring of 1921, that the Italian-born critic Ricciotto Canudo followed suit with another influential film society, the *Club des Amis du Septième Art (CASA)* – the origin of the phrase » Seventh Art « can be found in Canudo's writings and activities. *CASA* was mainly frequented by members of the avant-garde such as Germaine Dulac, Marcel L'Herbier, Alberto Cavalcanti, Jean Epstein, Léon Moussinac, Blaise Cendrars, Jean Cocteau, Robert Mallet-Stevens, Fernand Léger, Jaque Catelain, Harry Baur, and Gaston Modot. While Delluc was a theatre critic and writer, Canudo had moved among numerous circles of the European avant-garde (primarily visual arts) before turning to cinema. While Delluc's *conférences* and published texts regarded film as a democratic mass art, Canudo's *CASA* was more high-brow and frequented mostly intellectuals.[11] In early 1925, the organisations founded by Delluc and Canudo merged after the deaths of both Canudo and Delluc (Canudo in 1923, Delluc in 1924). This merger resulted in the first nation-wide organisation of its type, linking different film clubs into the *Ciné-Clubs de France*, which later came under the directorship of Léon Moussinac, Jacques Feyder and Germaine Dulac.[12] The seeds for a strategic convergence in the late 1920s were sown early on when high-brow modernists, cinephiles who had a lot of confidence in film's potential as mass art[13], political activists on both ends of the spectrum (although mainly left-wing), anarchists and pacifists, technological visionaries of romantic inclination (i.e., F.W. Murnau or Abel Gance) and others rallied around various avant-garde concepts. In the years leading up to the introduction of sound, the avant-garde was able to integrate various groups as part of an (apparently) common cause. It is also interesting to note that these activists were simultaneously filmmakers, writers, and activists-organisers, which remains a crucial element of this first wave. Cinema was not yet fully functionally differentiated and these players easily crossed lines between various factions, segments and functions.[14]

The number of ciné-clubs in Paris quickly rose in the course of the 1920s, and the first ciné-club outside Paris was probably founded in 1925 in Montpellier.[15] Ciné-clubs were often instigated by journals or the other way round; already in this nascent form, the alternative networks were characterised by an approach that incorporated different media and a variety of formats (screenings, conferences, magazines, leaflets). Contrary to commercial cinemas, which sold a film on the strength of a star or a story, the ciné-clubs aimed at gathering a number of subscribers in order to have a core audience for each screening. Magazines, leaflets, discussions and other supplements formed part of the media strategy followed by the avant-garde. Other activities such as exhibitions soon followed. While Canudo's club had already been active within the high modernist and intellectually highbrow *Salon d'Automne* for some years, 1924 saw a first major exhibition on the cinema, *L'Art dans le cinéma français*, at the *Musée Galliera*.[16]

In the mid-1920s the ciné-clubs were joined by cinemas specialising in avant-garde and film art while also constructing a repertory of classics. Three Parisian places deserve mention as legendary screening spaces: the *Théâtre du Vieux Colombier*, *Studio des Ursulines* and *Studio 28*. The *Théâtre du Vieux Colombier* opened on 14 November 1924 with a program of André Sauvage's mountain-climbing documentary LA TRAVERSÉ DU GRÉPON / L'ASCENSION DU GRÉPON (FR 1923), Marcel Silver's experimental L'HORLOGE (FR 1924) and Charlie Chaplin's short SUNNYSIDE (US 1921). This mixture of repertory classics, non-fiction and experimental work, in a more narrow sense, was typical for avant-garde clubs as well as cinemas of the 1920s. The format mixing of scientific, educational and aesthetic styles resulted in broader programs than retrospectives of the avant-garde that focused on formal innovations. The *Vieux Colombier* was run by Jean Tédesco who had taken over the editorship of the cinephile magazine *Cinéa* in 1924 after Louis Delluc had died. The second important cinema, the *Studio des Ursulines*, directed by Armand Tallier, opened on 21 January 1926 in Montparnasse and its initial program consisted of a mixture of repertory, experimental, and accessible art cinema: MIMOSA LA DERNIÈRE GRISETTE (FR 1906, Leonce Perret), a re-edited version of ENTR'ACTE (FR 1924, René Clair / Francis Picabia) and FREUDLOSE GASSE (GER 1925, G.W. Pabst, › Joyless Street ‹). The third important cinema for avant-garde and repertory purposes was *Studio 28* under the directorship of Jean Mauclaire, which borrowed its name from the year it opened.[17] Not coincidentally, these three names allude to other arts, in this case to painting and theatre, a strategy typical of later art house cinemas and video shops with a more ambitious selection calling themselves Theatre, Studio or Gallery. The French film clubs leaned towards debate and were quite communicative, with discussions often occurring after screenings. Ian Christie has pointed out that the French started theorising the medium's specificity (*photogénie* was the key term), but also built a whole system around it: » They [the French avant-garde] spawned a support system of film clubs, specialized cinemas, and magazines, all devoted to the promotion of film as modern art; and this network soon spread beyond France, creating a sympathetic context for innovative work from elsewhere «.[18] The motive of the network is crucial to my approach as film was re-invented as a discursive medium by the avant-garde and paralleled a diversification into different fields. To give but one example: Jean Tédesco at the *Théâtre du Vieux Colombier* not only worked in exhibition and publishing (the journal *Cinéa*), but he also went into film production himself. He commissioned Jean Epstein with a film illustrating the concept of PHOTOGÉNIES (FR 1924), compiled from outtakes and non-fiction material. Tédesco subsequently became the in-house producer for Epstein as he financed SIX ET DEMI-ONZE (FR 1927), LA GLACE À TROIS FACE (FR 1927), and LA CHUTE DE LA MAISON USHER (FR 1928). Moreover, he improvised a studio on the roof of his cinema where Renoir shot LA PETITE MARCHANDE D'ALLUMETTES (FR 1927/28). Tédesco, as an avant-garde activist, did not limit himself to programming and running a cinema; his approach to film was much broader and encompassed different segments of a *Medienverbund* such as production and publishing.

In England, the situation was different and it took longer before cinema found broader support. Film critic Ivor Montagu travelled to Paris in 1925 to find out more about how to start, program, and run a film club. Montagu had met the actor Hugh Miller on the return journey from a field trip to Berlin where he had reported for *The Times* on German film while Miller was doing some acting in various German studios. It was during a voyage between these two European production centres that the idea for an alternative exhibition organisation in Britain was first formulated.[19] The explicit model was the British Stage Society, which was instrumental in bringing Ibsen, Strindberg, Shaw, Cocteau, Pirandello and other modern authors to the attention of a wider audience in England; the original name was going to be *Independent Film Theatre Ltd*, but it was subsequently changed. An assorted circle of people interested in film art gathered in London in 1925 to form the *Film Society*, including critics Iris Barry and Walter Mycroft, Lord Sidney Bernstein, a » socialist millionaire «, and director Adrian Brunel. Founding members included H.G. Wells, G.B. Shaw, J.M. Keynes and many more lending their names for cultural capital and respectability. The British *Film Society*, compared to its continental relatives, was relatively highbrow and bourgeois; it modelled itself on a theatre society and boasted famous writers – the explicit model was first and foremost literature and theatre. Despite these highbrow credentials (or maybe because of them?), the organisation did not find any cooperation within the film industry. Adrian Brunel fell from grace with the film industry because of his involvement with the *Film Society*; he had to resign from the council in order to get his industry job back, » as my employers insisted that my association with the Society would damage the prestige of the films I made for them «.[20] On the whole, the British film industry was opposed to the idea of a film society as they considered alternative activities as interference in their business. Part of the reason for this strong antagonism might have been the explicit aim of the Film Society, which was to transform cinema, whereas in other countries the target group was less explicitly the industry and more the intellectual tastemakers.

Indeed, the founding manifesto of the *Film Society* explicitly vowed to change the film industry from within; yet, compared to more radical battle cries from Germany or the Netherlands it is rather tame:

> The Film Society has been founded in the belief that there are in this country a large number of people who regard the cinema with the liveliest interest, and who would welcome an opportunity seldom afforded the general public of witnessing films of intrinsic merit, whether new or old... It is felt to be of the utmost importance that films of the type proposed should be available to the Press, and to the film trade itself, including present and (what is more important) future British film producers, editors, cameramen, titling experts and actors... It is important that films of this type should not only be shown under the best conditions of the most actively minded people both inside and outside the film world, but that they should, from time to time, be revived. This will be done. In this way standards of taste and of executive ability may be raised and a critical tradition established. This cannot but affect future productions...[21]

Despite tensions between *Film Society* and the film industry and despite the fact that we tend to think nowadays of clear-cut distinctions between the industry and the artistic side, most of the key figures involved in the founding of the society also had close links with the industry: Miller was an actor in commercial productions, Brunel was a successful commercial director who also tried his hand at experimentation, but he was certainly not on the same level as Eisenstein, Ruttmann or Man Ray. Bernstein made his money as an exhibitor and distributor who backed the film society through his involvement in the industry as the owner of the Granada cinema chain, which showed quality film programs. Even the critics who one would suspect would side with the artists had a lot of cross-over potential: Barry who moved in circles with T.S. Eliot, Wyndham Lewis, Herbert Read, W.B. Yeats, and Ezra Pound at that time, had gotten her start working in the film industry by reporting for *The Spectator* on trade shows for Bernstein's cinema chain. Later in New York, she established close ties with Hollywood in order to fill the archive at the newly founded film department of the *Museum of Modern Art* (*MOMA*). Some time later, Montagu and Brunel created a small company for the retitling of foreign films into English that were shown at the *Film Society*. This company became the entry point for young enthusiasts into film making, many of which later became associated with the British Documentary Film Movement.[22] But not all of them joined the Grierson circle: Montagu worked with Michael Balcon and Alfred Hitchcock, was active in left-wing film activities in the 1930s and founded a society of film technicians. The combination of such diverse activities is unthinkable nowadays, so Montagu has been described as » one of a rare species in that he was a cinema intellectual and a producer working in the orthodox commercial feature industry. «[23] However, the movement of these people back and forth between industry and writing, between publishing, distribution and promotion was not really that » rare «, and much more typical of that period than we are accustomed to think. The opposition between art and business is foremost a rhetorical device used to create a common enemy and banner under which people could be gathered who otherwise had a very different outlook (in terms of politics, culture, organisation). The British situation was special insofar as a high-brow organisation monopolised avant-garde cinema for a relatively long time. The convergence in this case was between different cultural agents that occupied key positions in literature, the theatre, the film industry or journalism – different segments of society took an active interest in the cinema and formed an elite network through the London Film Society. Only with the founding of left-leaning screening clubs and production cooperatives such as the workers' film societies around 1930 did a more political streak enter the film avant-garde in the British context.

In Amsterdam, legend has it that a scandalous and overcrowded screening of Pudovkin's MATJ (SU 1926, › Mother ‹) organised by the artist's society *De Kring* in May 1927 led to the formation of the *Filmliga*. The film was temporarily shut down by the police, with people fleeing through the windows until Amsterdam's mayor was finally awakened late that night only to decide that the screening could continue.[24] While this is not entirely wrong in factual terms, it contains a measure of legend-building that is typical for autobiographically tainted storytelling. The original plan behind screening MATJ originated with a film distributor who had purchased Pudovkin's film, but was not able to screen it because censorship prohibited its screening. This businessman was Ed. Pelster, member of the of the trade organisation *Nederlandsche Bioscoop-Bond* (NBB) and later also of the *Filmliga*, but he remained an outsider to the circle that included Joris Ivens, Menno ter Braak and Henrik Scholte. With press screenings he mobilised journalists who in turn organised this closed screening for the artistic society. About a year later, the film satisfied the censors and it went into » ordinary « commercial distribution with some success. On the one hand, the *Filmliga* had vowed to help films get screened that would otherwise not be able to find an audience. However, the *Filmliga* could not help MOTHER get a distributor since there was already a distributor waiting to bring the film into the cinemas before and after the incident. The real problem here (as was quite often the case in the interwar period) was censorship, but even here it is not very clear in which direction the support went. It was actually Pudovkin's film that gave the *Filmliga* a publicity push because newspapers all over the country reported on the MOTHER incident and on the new society that was established as a reaction to the events. On the other hand, the *Filmliga* did help the commercial distributor when the film got its normal cinema release over a year later. It is a well-known fact that a scandal is the best thing that can happen to a work of art. In fact, the *Filmliga* was not able to screen MOTHER when it came out because the distributor (even though he was a member of the *Filmliga*) preferred renting the film to commercial cinemas.

The first manifesto of the Dutch *Filmliga* pitted cinema against film, kitsch against art: » Once in a hundred times we see: the film. For the rest we see: cinema. «[25] The *Filmliga* activists clearly distinguished between the good object film and the bad object cinema. This stance is echoed in serious film criticism, various archives, and in theoretical works: It is only the film that counts here, not the cinematic experience, the architecture, social activity, sound accompaniment, viewing habits or any multitude of other factors relevant to the film experience. This framework of cinema going as an activity only became important in the 1990s when the influence of cultural studies, new film history and media archaeology began to influence film studies. Even in the 1920s, the simplictic dualism of commercialism vs. art, kitsch vs. culture, avant-garde vs. industry was never pure and a rather crude construction. To give some examples: The Soviet trade agencies trying to sell revolutionary films in Western Europe preferred to make a deal with commercial distributors (as foreign currency was badly needed) than with a film society which normally paid less. When Eisenstein visited the Netherlands in 1930, he spent much more time with the association of commercial distributors than with the *Filmliga* (much to the dismay of the *Filmliga*). And, to cross the Channel for an additional example, when PoTEMKIN first came to England it was not at the request of the *Film Society*, but was arranged by the Film Booking Offices, a commercial company which had a contract with the Soviet trade delegation in Berlin.[26]

The history of audience organisations in Germany testifies to the heavily politicised public sphere of the Weimar Republic. Initiatives for alternative exhibition (mainly ambulant cinemas) existed in Germany from the early 1920s onwards. The travelling projections were organised by political groups such as Willi Münzenberg's *Internationale Arbeiterhilfe* (IAH) and other grassroots organisations.[27] The IAH was founded in 1921 when a famine struck parts of the Soviet Union and Münzenberg was asked to organise a world-wide aid program for the inhabitants of the affected regions. Unlike the German communist party the KPD, which only started their film activities around 1930, the IAH was active in film work from its inception and toured with film programs to local chapters. In the winter of 1924/25, a tour of three Soviet non-fiction films (on child care for orphans, on the winter help activities of the IAH for the Soviet population and on Lenin's funeral) occurred mainly in medium-sized towns in southwestern Germany.[28] Production and distribution were later organised through Münzenberg's company *Prometheus*. Attempting to construct an alternative to the large media conglomerates, Münzenberg consciously emulated the model of the national-conservative media entrepreneur Hugenberg.[29]

Social democratic and union organisations – who were in direct competition for working-class support with the communists for most of the 1920s – also arranged cinema events. Yet, unlike film societies and like many of the IAH activities, these were not audience organisations, but rather politically motivated screening events for an audience of party members. Film societies typically emerged from a group of people interested in a different kind or use of film. In 1922, the Social Democratic Party SPD and the trade union *Allgemeiner Deutscher Gewerkschaftsbund* (ADGB) founded the *Volksfilmbühne*,[30] and its own » Film- und Lichtspieldienst « for the production and distribution of films.[31] Their two productions, DIE SCHMIEDE (GER 1924, Martin Berger) and FREIES VOLK (DE 1925, Martin Berger), stimulated public controversies but were financially not successful.[32] These early initiatives were top-down insofar as members of left-wing parties got involved in cultural film work in order to mobilise members for political action, either for singular events or for a regular audience organisation. In this respect, they represent marginal cases of film societies, which are normally defined as audience associations that emerge from grassroots activities.

The situation in Germany was different from that in France, the Netherlands or England as politisation was much stronger while the » cinephile « or » essentialist « leanings of the Parisian or Amsterdam cineaste apparently were much weaker in Berlin, Hamburg, Breslau, Stuttgart or Frankfurt. The politically motivated screening clubs only emerged in England and the Netherlands in circa 1930 (workers' film society, *Vereeniging voor Volkscultuur*), while they precede the aesthetically oriented organisations in Germany. However, the ideas and local initiatives for film clubs with an artistically oriented agenda could already be detected in the first half of the 1920s. An editorial in the liberal trade journal *Film-Kurier* in May 1923 called for a » Film-Liga «, a society for screening artistically ambitious films, in order to convince opponents of film – (» Film-Gegner «, a term later used by Hans Richter) – of the value of certain films. Gerhart Hauptmann, an intellectual and artist with an outspoken interest in the cinema, is proposed as a public figure head. The whole idea was, in a spirit of reform and education (of the masses), to promote alternative cinema, but it always appeared somewhat condescending towards » uneducated people «:

> The quintessence of propaganda must culminate in this claim: Support the audience as a whole in raising its expectations and go to the cinema often, then the kitsch will slowly disappear. In the end, the audience always gets what it desires.[33]

Nevertheless, it took until the late-1920s for such a society to be realised. Until that time, alternative cinema culture was largely dependent on circles close to the communist party. The proximity of the *Prometheus* to the communist party KPD made their entry into regular cinemas difficult as some 90% of cinemas were controlled by major cinema chains affiliated with Ufa or the Hollywood majors. These cinemas often refused to rent their halls to the communist party or to cultural organisations affiliated with the KPD. Therefore, many of these cinema events that had (party-)political ramifications took place either in communal spaces with antiquated equipment or in open-air screenings, contexts that tended to support a distracted manner of reception and spectatorship not favourable to the avant-garde's aesthetic experiments. In fact, these activities tended to show non-fiction material and agit-prop films with some Soviet montage films mixed in. In these circles, the experimental films from Germany or France were practically never screened.[34] It was not until the late-1920s that these efforts would give rise to an audience organisation with a broader base.

A decisive moment in the slowly emerging field of alternative cinema culture in Germany was the matinee of » *Der absolute Film* « on 3 and 10 May 1925. It was shown again because of the enthusiasm expressed during the first screening when many people had to be turned away.[35] The event at the Berlin cinema *Ufa-Theater am Kurfürstendamm* was organised by the *Novembergruppe*, an aesthetically minded association of artists with avant-garde leanings, in cooperation with Ufa.[36] While the communist-oriented *Volksfilmverband* was intertwined with the political side of the avant-garde, this event highlights the desire of the avant-garde to be recognised as » legitimate « (i.e., bourgeois) art. Tellingly, the screening neither took place in a working-class neighbourhood nor in the old centre of Berlin, but in the bourgeois and commercial centre of the new West. At the same time, this occasion emphasised the links between artistic innovations and the industry and the proximity of the avant-garde to the emerging documentary film. In fact, it was Dr. Edgar Beyfuß, dramaturg of the Ufa-*Kulturfilmabteilung* (department of educational and documentary films), who introduced the screening. The *Kulturfilmabteilung* could be described as Ufa's *Research & Development* department, which developed innovative trick effects, camera equipment, shooting techniques and technical inventions. Here, Eggeling and Richter were able to conduct their first experiments and gain some support for the still miniscule avant-garde cinema movement. The year before (1924) Beyfuß had together with A. Kossowsky published a book about the emerging field[37] in which documentary, experimentation, education and activism overlapped. The *Kulturfilmabteilung* and initiatives in the same field (cinemas in Germany invariably started their programs with short educational films in order to obtain tax breaks) proved to be not only influenced by and influential for many of the early avant-garde activists, but also gave many of them a chance to try their hand at filmmaking or offered a safe haven and steady source of income for an otherwise unpredictable future.

The *Gesellschaft Neuer Film* (GNF) was connected to the important matinee » Der absolute Film « and in some respects a continuation of the aesthetic style with Hans Richter as its driving force. The » society new film « presented radical films and was officially founded on 15 January 1928 in Berlin by Hans Richter, Guido Bagier, Karl Freund and Frank Warschauer.[38] The society only organised two events in Berlin, one privately in West Berlin (» *in einem Privathaus des Berliner Westens* «) on 15 January 1928 with the premiere of Richter's own FILMSTUDIE (GER 1926, at this occasion still called » Rhythmus «), Alberto Cavalcanti's LA P'TITE LILI (FR 1927/28) and Henri Chomette's JEUX DES REFLETS ET LE LA VITESSE (FR 1925) accompanied by Guido Bagier on the piano.[39] The other screening took place on 19 February 1928 at the commercial cinema *U.T. Kurfürstendamm* where a similar program – films by Richter, Beaumont (Henri Chomette's patron, i.e., most probably again JEUX DES REFLETS ET LE LA VITESSE), Cavalcanti, Eggeling and Man Ray – were shown to an invited audience.[40] Hans Richter himself later commented on this initiative:

> Everywhere in Europe people were becoming very conscious of the film avant-garde. ... Between Paris, Holland, and Berlin an international exchange of films, people and articles was taking place. Since all of my films were screened at the › Studio des Ursulines ‹, and also shown in Holland, I felt included, but also responsible for doing something about our European movement in Germany. ... Thus, we [Karl Freund, Guido Bagier and me] in 1926-27 established the society › Neuer Film ‹.[41]

This film program was subsequently also screened in Frankfurt[42], and possibly in other provincial cities as well. Hans Richter provided his personal contacts for international links: the Dutch *Filmliga* mentions the *GNF* in their report on their international network and their first year of activities.[43] The *Gesellschaft* » *Neuer Film* « did not survive for very long. Some months later the news media was speculating whether the GNF had disbanded: Meanwhile, Guido Bagier had returned to his involvement with sound cinema and accepted a job at Tobis[44] while Karl Freund was working in England.[45] An interview in *Close Up* Freund hints at possible tensions within the society regarding the question of abstraction and realism when asked about the society » that you founded for the absolute film in Berlin «:

> There was not sufficient support; we had to give up the performances. Myself, I am a purist, I am not so sure that I like all these absolute films, so many of them are drawing. Film is celluloid coated with silver emulsion, and should be used to record light and shade. I think of all the experimenters I prefer Man Ray.[46]

In effect, Hans Richter seems to have been the driving force from the beginning, but with the inactivity of his co-founders and a general uncertainty about their direction, Richter did not act more decisively on behalf of this film society.

On 13 January 1928, the *Volksfilmverband für Filmkunst* (VFV – People's Film Association for Film Art) was officially established in Berlin, trying to bind together antagonistic forces across the left-wing spectrum: communists, anarchists and left-wing social democrats united under the symbolic intellectual head of Heinrich Mann who functioned as the first president of the organisation. The actual day-to-day business was taken care of by Rudolf Schwarzkopf while Franz Höllering (editor-in-chief of the illustrated left-wing *Arbeiter-Illustrierte-Zeitung*) edited the monthly magazine *Film und Volk*. The VFV assembled an honorary council made up of intellectuals and artists to support and broaden the activities of the society.[47] It pronounced itself as a non-partisan organisation, although their founding manifesto signed by Mann is quite outspoken in political terms:

> We neither want nor demand high-flown experiments. We do not have an education-craze steeped in aesthetics and literature. We know that cinema primarily wants and ought to be a place of relaxation and entertainment. But we think, that entertainment does not mean › trash ‹, that relaxation is not the same as › intellectual poverty ‹.
>
> Our fight is directed against artistic trash, intellectual poverty and not the least also against the political and social reaction, that all too often puts its stamp on today's film production. Our fight has as its aim to make film what it could and should be: a means to disseminate knowledge, enlightenment and education, thoughts, ideas – means for understanding among the people and for reconciliation – a lively factor of everyday life as well as of intellectual and artistic life.[48]

The German context is thus markedly different from the French discourse, which revolved around concepts such as *photogénie* and *cinéphilie*. It is also different from the tendency of the Dutch *Filmliga* towards abstraction; the vast majority of German initiatives were heavily politicised. It should be borne in mind, however, that the VFV, even though it called itself variably » left-wing « or » liberal « was initially not connected to party politics – even it later increasingly followed the communist party.[49] Two factors may have contributed to this: First, Germany's young republic was highly politicised, especially in its later years; and second, Germany's film market provided the fiercest resistance against American imports with Ufa leading the way. Germany had a strong homegrown film industry and was the most important European market. Here the cinema was caught between such issues as foreign policy and national policy, quotas and contingents, national self-assertion and international power, the desire to be entertained and the will to be educated. Nevertheless, the *Volksfilmverband* marked a clear break with earlier initiatives as intellectuals now joined

forces with party functionaries, artists stood shoulder to shoulder with union-
ists and political, cultural and aesthetic concerns all merged. This strategic convergence seemed to provide a counterweight to the power of the large corporations from Berlin-Babelsberg to Hollywood. However, this instant of utopian
possibility which offered the various groups a common aim and strategy was
short-lived.

As the *Gesellschaft Neuer Film* was founded two days after the *Volksfilmverband*
and as the board of the former is hardly ever mentioned in the magazine of the
latter, *Film und Volk*[50], it is possible that Richter's initiative was, in some respects, a reaction to the VFV. Moreover, Walter Ruttmann ranted against Richter's new film society. Ruttmann made fun of its » absolute fashion «. And indeed, Ruttmann's name can be found among the honorary council members of
the VFV, while I found no hint that any of the activists involved in the GNF
were ever closely connected to the VFV. Testifying to a rift within the avant-
garde between those who would put politics above aesthetics and those for
whom aesthetic innovation came before political activity, this incident demonstrates that the superficial unity of the avant-garde presented during occasions
such as the La Sarraz meeting or the Stuttgart exhibition were already nothing
but an illusion in order to forge an alliance at that time prior to the coming of
sound. This construction has often been reiterated in gestures of retrospective
reasoning.[51]

One lesson is that the emergence of film societies, despite the nationally diverse contexts, and the whole opposition of art to industry was to a large extent
done for publicity and necessary for the avant-garde to mobilise a public. Some
segments of the audience were easier to motivate when forced up against a
common enemy. It was more the opposition (to commercial cinema culture, to
narrative film, to apolitical and bourgeois stories) than a common aim that united the activists of the ciné-clubs for some years. Even though most of the films
screened in the film societies were also playing in commercial cinemas, even
though a lot of the people active in these initiatives worked in and for the industry, even though the film societies could not function without organisational
structures similar to those of the industry, they continued to employ the dichotomy to stake out a position. The avant-garde thrived on an imaginary opposition that ultimately proved to also be one of the reasons for its downfall when
the internal divisions became obvious for the first time. The glue that held the
film societies together was a vague and sometimes even populist aversion to a
certain kind of commercial cinema. Nevertheless, this antipathy was strong
enough to create a climate in which many people believed that the cinema was
a factor to be reckoned with in drastic and radical socio-political transformations. It was this utopian aspiration that contributed to the strategic convergence of different groups.

3.2 Screening Practice

> *The Society is under no illusions. It is well aware*
> *that Caligari's do not grow on raspberry bushes,*
> *and that it cannot, in a season, expect to provide*
> *its members with an unbroken succession of masterpieces.*
> The Film Society (1925)[52]

The screening practice at the Parisian ciné-clubs and specialised theatres was initially more inspired by notions of film history and classics than animated by any ideas of abstract or experimental work. On the one hand, very few avant-garde films were made by the first half of the 1920s (the first wave of films now canonised as part of the classical avant-garde was made circa 1924), on the other, the notion of film art had to be worked through and established. For that reason, the early programs of the French outlets for alternative cinema consisted of Chaplin and Griffith, Feuillade and Sjöström, Stiller and Lang – it was primarily an historical orientation that contributed to the emergence of alternative screening outlets.[53] The ciné-clubs on the whole remained high-brow and elitist. With the notable exception of Moussinac's *Les amis de Spartacus* in 1928, most of the events were made by and for a bourgeois intellectual public. The rhetoric of the clubs claiming that transforming the audience's taste would necessarily lead to a change in film production was therefore not utterly convincing as they invariably reached only a small segment of the audience (that would often not attend the cinema otherwise). The charge of elitism remained a perennial problem of the avant-garde as their audience was a segment that did not need to be won over – more often than not, avant-garde audience organisations were preaching to the converted. Another problem was the import restrictions and quotas enacted by the French government to protect the domestic film industry: In 1928, quotas endangered the Parisian specialised cinemas because foreign films could no longer be exhibited and cinemas united to demand exemptions from this law.[54]

The *Film Society* in London, probably the longest-living audience organisation in interwar Europe, was active for 14 years (1925–39) with some eight events annually (only six performances during the last two seasons), showing approximately 500 short and feature-length films in a total of 108 performances. The first 4 seasons were presented at the New Gallery, the screenings then moved to the Tivoli in 1929, and in 1935 back to the New Gallery after 6 seasons for the last 4 seasons.[55] The successive moves testify to its growing popularity in 1929 (the auditorium of the Tivoli was considerably larger) and the subsequent decline of spectator numbers thereafter. Of the films screened by the *Film Society*, 23% were British, 20% came from France and Germany, 15% were American, and 7.5% were Soviet. Slightly more than half of the films were silents (263), the other half sound (237); the majority of the films had not been shown before in England (312 films), while many shorts (137) were revivals, mostly comedy classics (Chaplin, slapstick). Sound obviously did not lead to the downfall of the society as enough films could be found during the 1930s that were suitable for screening. The Film Society was ultimately a bourgeois club as the membership fee (twenty-five shillings per season) was too high for most workers.[56] The first program in October 1925 demonstrates the variety of *Film Society* interests: The mix of films was typical for the audience organisations of the time, ranging from commercial art cinema with Paul Leni's WACHSFIGURENKABINETT (GER 1923) – often presented as reprises, thus pointing toward the construction of a canon of classical works and the repertory cinema movement – to abstract films with Walter Ruttmann's LICHTSPIELOPUS 2, 3, 4 (GER 1919-25), from the ever-popular Chaplin (CHAMPION CHARLIE, US 1916) and local heroes (Adrian Brunel's TYPICAL BUDGET, GB 1925) to pre-war Westerns (HOW BRONCHO BILLY LEFT BEAR COUNTRY, US 1912). Whereas some of the radical manifestoes read as if purely abstract, » absolute « films were the sole diet, in fact the programs were very mixed to cater to an audience of similar diversified tastes.

It is only in retrospective that the film societies and the avant-garde have been purified and reduced to a handful of formal experiments. Whereas today's list of avant-garde classics is short and could be squeezed into 3 or 4 evenings of film screenings (and indeed often is at cinémathèques and film museums), the film societies presented programs that took place regularly (once per month) for years. Thus, it was necessary to resort to » commercial art cinema «[57], old Chaplin films, as well as documentary, scientific or educational films. Film societies basically had three programming options: Meet at irregular intervals (whenever new films were available) or resort to older films that had been shown before. The third option, the programming policy of the Dutch *Filmliga*, was a didactic approach to programming, screening bits and pieces from older films to demonstrate specific points. While the first option almost invariably led to a process of disintegration, the second was the most common option, with the side effect of blurring the initial opposition to ordinary cinema culture. This tendency led to an overlap with commercial cinemas and finally to art cinemas which snatched the more lucrative films from the screening clubs. The *Filmliga* option was only possible if there was a strong board that pursued its own agenda.

The Dutch *Filmliga* had perhaps one of the most severe regulatory boards of directors among the international film societies: Older, pre-war films were combined with avant-garde classics, but also with quality art films to prove the superiority of abstract film art. The main proponent of this educational programming policy was probably Menno ter Braak who published a book of his theoretical convictions regarding film theory entitled » Militant Cinema «.[58] The main asset of the *Filmliga* was the sheer variety of films. The aim of this policy was manifold: On the one hand, spectators would learn to recognise the » superior quality « of avant-garde cinema; for that reason sequences from commercial feature films were sometimes shown, discussed and commented upon.[59] Comparing and contrasting were according to Gunning the key features of the *Filmliga* programming. Furthermore, Amsterdam presented many films that have become classics of art cinema: F.W. Murnau's Nosferatu (GER 1921), C.T. Dreyer's La Passion de Jeanne d'Arc (FR 1928), and the Russian montage films.

The German context was characterised by political struggles, but also by friction with the commercial film industry. The first event organised by the *Volksfilmverband* quickly ran into difficulties when the film industry put pressure on the director of their meeting place, the Berlin cinema Capitol, to resign (which he did not) in order to stop the VFV's first event,[60] which, on 26 February, 1928, boasted two programmatic addresses by Heinrich Mann and Béla Balázs,[61] a montage of snippets from newsreels and features entitled Was wir wollen – Was wir nicht wollen (GER 1928, Béla Balázs, Albrecht Viktor Blum). A short film by Ernst Angel and Albrecht Viktor Blum, Zeitbericht – Zeitgesicht (GER 1928), was censored and thus not shown.[62] The main feature of the evening was Vsevolod Pudovkin's Konec Sankt-Peterburga (SU 1926).[63] The initial plan called for regional variety, with the German capital as its figurehead. In Berlin, a cinema should be acquired for premieres already before autumn of 1928, a plan that did not come to fruition.[64] Some reports written by Rudolf Schwarzkopf, secretary of the German *Volksfilmverband*, bear further witness to the difficulties faced by this film society. An event in the spring of 1928, only shortly after the founding of the organisation, was scheduled to feature G.W. Pabst speaking on censorship followed by a screening of his Die Liebe der Jeanne Ney (GER 1927). However, the film industry blocked the screening of the film which was not yet » *abgespielt* «, i.e., it was still being shown in a considerable number of commercial cinemas. Even though Pabst supported the screening of his film and gave a lecture, the organisers were not able to obtain the film and had to show another feature instead. Quite ironically, Pabst some years later ended up in court to argue over the adaptation of Die 3-Groschen-Oper (GER 1930), more or less on the opposite side of this debate. Because the film producers and distributors owned the rights to the films, even the directors were powerless against the producer's copyright. This incident also demonstrated that the industry perceived the film societies as a threat to their domination of the film market. After this experience, the organisers changed their tactics, neither the press nor the industry were informed about the screening of Eisenstein's Oktjabr' (SU 1927) in order to avoid » unpleasant and harmful polemics. ... Generally speaking, we want to advertise and work quietly in the future and approach the public only once our preparations have proceeded far enough. «[65] The industry lobby proved to be very strong in Germany, and so the *Volksfilmverband* decided to build an organisation more or less secretly before confronting the powerful industrialists again. Distributors, producers and cinema owners all attempted to block the society's activities. The society publicly complained about (politically motivated) unfair pricing and other behaviour by various cinema owners in medium-sized German cities, which forced the VFV to turn to multi-purpose spaces in pubs, restaurants or union halls.[66]

Wherever possible, the *Volksfilmverband* requested that artists and technicians involved in the production give an introduction to their films. Moreover, the didactic technique of showing extracts from various films appears to have been widespread. The difference is crucial: while screening films in their entirety meant focusing on the aesthetic value of the work as a whole, the presentation of clips put the focus emphatically on education because these aspects needed presentations and explanations, both regarding their placement within the wider context of the film and the question of why they had been selected for the screening. A typical program would look like this: » Well-chosen and edited clips «[67] from three films directed by Vsevolod Pudovkin, MATJ (SU 1926), KONEC SANKT-PETERSBURGA (SU 1926), POTOMOK CINGIS-HANA (SU 1928), and parts of ZEMLJA W PLENU (SU 1928, Fedor Ozep). Pudovkin attended the screening, as did Ozep, MATJ actress Vera Baranovskaia and cameraman Anatoli Golownja. Less than three weeks later, the same organisation presented a program of educational and scientific films (*Kulturfilme*) at the same cinema, selected and introduced by Dr. Edgar Beyfuß who worked for the Ufa at the time, » to give the public an insight into the varied materials of film production «.[68] The main feature, the three-part DIE WUNDER DES FILMS (GER 1928, Edgar Beyfuß) shows: first how travelogues are made; second, the problems of making animal documentaries; and third, showing trick techniques used in educational cinema. Aesthetic appreciation and artistic innovation were second after the educational impetus of the film programs. The politically motivated institutions, often aimed at the working class, in particular gravitated toward a didactic and educational approach. The implicit model here is cinema as educational tool, even if the avant-garde considered these two elements as inseparably intertwined. The aesthetically motivated societies, by contrast, usually drew a bourgeois audience and were oriented towards the artistic value of works of art and their model was the gallery or the museum. Consequently, the film was either a tool for understanding the world in a different manner or an end in itself as art appreciation.

3.3 Peak Years 1928-1931

> *May the dear God give the unfaithful a sign and*
> *the › Camera ‹ a whole-page advertisement in his heaven,*
> *so that the public may come in masses.*
> Rudolf Arnheim (1928)[69]

While the film society movement evolved slowly but steadily over the 1920s, there was a sudden boom in film societies between 1928 and 1931, followed by a slow tapering off of activities, interest, and attendance over the course of the 1930s. Despite much activity and countless screenings, a steep drop in visibility and public interest occurred in the early 1930s which continued, albeit at a slower pace, throughout the 1930s. After observing the peak years, I will then turn in the next sections to sectors such as archiving and film in national life where some of the avant-garde energy migrated to and proliferated over the course of the 1930s. In keeping with the metaphor of the network, my focus will be on the flow and distribution of energy: around 1929-30 the film avant-garde generated support, interest and, from those who felt threatened by changes in the status quo, outright hostility. For a brief moment the cinema became the rallying point for circles interested in political, social and cultural transformations through modern media.

The boom in film societies was again led by France, with Léon Moussinac's organisation *Les amis de Spartacus*, which was only active for eight months from March to November 1928. The organisation managed to gather an impressive number of members, something between 8,000 and 80,000 across France. Moussinac himself reports 20,000 subscribers in the capital alone.[70] The club was able to achieve its explosive growth because of a clear profile – *Les amis de Spartacus* concentrated on exhibiting Soviet films prohibited by French censorship – and good promotion work with press screenings and publicity. Even though their agenda was political and revolutionary, their approach was democratic (i.e., decidedly anti-elitist) and they wanted to show » all films, new or old, censored or not, expressing beauty or technical, artistic, ideological or educational truths «.[71] The subscription price was five francs per month and the first screening occurred on 12 April 1928 with the documentary LA VIE SOUS-MARINE (FR 1927, Jean Painlevé) and Sergei Eisenstein's BRONENOSEZ » POTEMKIN « (SU 1925).[72] In hindsight there is disagreement about whether the club's activities were discontinued for political (anti-communist) or for economic reasons (pressure from cinema owners and film distributors who feared the competition). In any case, Paris' infamous chief of police, Jean Chiappe, banned further activities. Economic and political fears both possibly contributed to the mounting pressure on the decision makers that eventually led to the closure of *Les amis de Spartacus*.

At the time, conservative politicians were worried about communist activities, which were being forcefully combated in France and the film industry also feared that a new competitor might become a genuine threat. Similar incidents of exhibitors putting pressure on film societies were noted in Berlin and Zurich. The industry seems to have grown wary and anxious of alternative cinema circuits by the end of the 1920s in France, Germany, Switzerland, the Netherlands and England. As long as the film societies remained small circles of artists and intellectuals they did not pose any danger politically or economically, but when they were on the verge of a mass movement, the conservative powers grew anxious.

One of the clearest signs of success for the movement – the installation of permanent exhibition outlets and specialised cinemas in Paris, London, Amsterdam, Berlin and other places – illustrates the flip side of success: how a movement was partly destroyed by its own achievements. The three Parisian pioneers, *Vieux Colombier*, *Studio des Ursulines* and *Studio 28*, proved to be so successful that they opened second houses for outsourcing their programs – like Jean Tédesco did when he repeated the programs from the *Vieux Colombier* at the *Pavillon du cinéma* from early 1927 to the summer of 1928[73] – or they convinced outsiders to start their own repertory cinemas like the *Ciné-Latin*, the *Salle des Agriculteurs*, *L'Oeil de Paris* or the *Studio Diamant*. Contrary to Richard Abel's claim that » [o]f the specialized cinemas, only two survived beyond 1930 «[74], a second boom of repertory cinemas is detectable in the early 1930s. Indeed, there was a short drop in specialised cinemas in early 1930, however already later that year, in October 1930, the new *Studio de Paris* opened in Montparnasse with a repertory program.[75] A change in legislation allowed the presentation of foreign films outside the strict quota laws if no more than five Parisian and provincial cinemas were screening the particular film, and thus avantgarde cinemas again thrived in the early 1930s. This led to another crisis in the winter of 1932, when no less than 17 cinemas were screening films under the label » avant-garde «. Most of these cinemas screened original (sound) versions of foreign films and foreshadowed today's practice in which some Parisian cinemas present original versions, while the others are dubbed in French.[76] By early 1933, a number of those specialised exhibition outlets had already closed down due to lack of suitable films and overscreening.[77]

England had a veritable boom of film societies in 1929: The *Film Society* of London moved in November 1929 from the New Gallery, an auditorium counting 1,400 seats, to the Tivoli, which seated 2,000-3,000 spectators, because the number of members had increased dramatically and could not be accommodated by the original venue. Societies in Edinburgh, Yorkshire, and Glasgow were also founded that same year. On the local level, there were a number of other film societies at the time.[78] On 28 October 1929, the *London Workers' Film*

Society was founded in London, with its first screening presenting Victor Turin's TURKSIB (SU 1929); the English version was translated and prepared by John Grierson, a pivotal figure in the worlds of avant-garde, documentary and political lobbying work.[79] The organisation quickly spread throughout the country with local chapters in Liverpool, Manchester, Edinburgh and other places. In fact, a *Federation of Workers' Film Societies* was set up simultaneously with the London chapter, so a nation-wide network was conceptualised from the very beginning. The Federation also offered advice on how to establish and run one's own society, it provided films and legal assistance. The *Film Society* was considered too bourgeois, stuffy and politically conservative by contemporary left-wing activists because it attracted mainly affluent intellectuals and wealthy liberals. Moreover, the membership fee was too high and thus excluded most workers. As a result, the *Film Society* had an exclusively bourgeois-intellectual membership base, a fact not lost on contemporary observers. When workers' clubs wanted to screen Soviet revolutionary cinema, they were prohibited from doing so, however, the *Film Society* got permission as the censorship board considered the audience less dangerous and less inclined to be overwhelmed by revolutionary messages.[80] This fairly straight and incisive division between an aesthetically minded and bourgeois *Film Society* preoccupied with film as art and a politically oriented *Workers' Film Society* interested in film as a political weapon was most visible in England. Perhaps it is this strong demarcation line that led Peter Wollen to propose the, in my opinion, problematic notions of » two avant-gardes «, one formalist-aestheticist and one political-radical.[81] This distinction could possibly be argued for England, but it breaks down when transferred to France, the Netherlands, Germany or the Soviet Union. Even in England, an individual like Ivor Montagu could easily cross the lines between aesthetic and political transformation, further undermining this distinction.

The *Workers' Film Society* was closely related to worker's associations and party politics, similar to the situation in Germany.[82] Indeed, the Federation and its activities could have been modelled on the *VFV* and the French equivalent *Les amis de Spartacus*. In September 1930, chapters were active in London, Bradford, Edinburgh, Glasgow, Manchester/Salford, Cardiff and Liverpool. As class divisions and censorship were especially strong in England, the society ran into constant trouble in the renting of cinemas as well as the booking of films. Like *Les amis de Spartacus* a film club geared towards a working-class audience was deemed much more dangerous than a bourgeois association primarily interested in film art. Another initiative was the *Progressive Film Institute* which was a commercial organisation interested in political cinema. The *PFI* was not a film society in the strictest sense (it was not an audience institution soliciting for members), but rather a company active in the alternative sector which ventured into production and developed a distribution organisation in the 1930s, parallel to *Kino*, a commercial distributor specialising in Soviet films and working almost exclusively in 16mm. The *PFI* was mainly aimed at the *Film Society* and the *British Film Institute* which was beginning to co-opt much of the energy by the early to mid-1930s[83] while the London *Film Society* had coagulated into a wholly bourgeois club for screening » quality art « film. The *PFI* also ventured into production and is in some respects more related to the cinema practice of Münzenberg's media empire or the French *front populaire* than to the film club movement of the 1920s. The board of directors consisted mainly of left-wing activists.[84]

Whereas the British situation was characterised by divisions into many different groups and interests, the Netherlands, in contrast, showed a more unified image with the *Filmliga* giving a framework and context to most alternative cinema events. In fact, this had its advantages – being able to work from a steady base with at least some security provided by the institution – but also its drawbacks – the opinion of the Amsterdam board clashed on numerous occasions with local chapters who were less » pure « and more inclined towards » quality entertainment « or » art cinema «. The screening context of the *Filmliga* was modelled on a science laboratory with the films serving as the experiments. While in France, a passionate cinephilia provided space for subjective and irrational affection, the *Filmliga* was very sober in its chosen objects of worship. Menno ter Braak as the ideological head of the *Filmliga* and as the most outspoken and rhetorically versed proponent of formal experiments and abstractions, influenced the screening policy considerably. By 1929, the *Filmliga* had grown into a nationwide organisation with nine departments in different cities, touring that year with eight large film programs from city to city, publishing a monthly film magazine, and inviting famous guests from abroad. In 1929 and 1930 the guests included: René Clair, Jean Mauclair of *Studio 28* in Paris, Sergei Eisenstein, Hans Richter, and Charles Dekeukelaire.

Audience organisations, specialised cinemas, distribution circuits, publication to support various activities, meetings and conferences among the key players – showed that there was a veritable network to support the avant-garde in place. On 9 November 1929, the Filmliga opened a cinema of their own in Amsterdam, *De Uitkijk*, which was modelled after the three Parisian precursors, the *Vieux Colombier*, the *Studio des Ursulines* and *Studio 28*. For the *De Uitkijk*'s opening show, Joris Ivens' short film HEIEN (NL 1929) was followed by Carl Theodor Dreyer's LA PASSION DE JEANNE D'ARC (FR 1928). The cinema *Die Kamera* was opened in Berlin on the boulevard Unter den Linden the same year, to become the fifth art house or avant-garde theatre in Europe.[85] For a while, the *Kamera* was partly state-funded with subsidies from the city, the radio association and the cultural ministry, but the ambitious financing evaporated in the wake of the economic crisis in 1932.[86]

In Germany, the *Volksfilmverband* evolved quickly into a mass organisation. In March 1928, one month after its official inauguration, the association already boasted more than 30 payment offices in Berlin alone where members could acquire tickets or the magazine *Film und Volk*. Chapters of the society were active in Hamburg and Frankfurt[87] while in Dresden, Leipzig and Breslau (today: Wrocław) they were in the process of being founded. The organisation concentrated on recruiting members in large companies among the working class where sympathisers were installed as go-betweens to actively promote the membership enrolment. This method was similar to political party work or trade union activities, again pointing out the proximity of the initiatives in Germany to party politics. The *VFV* also planned open-air screenings in the boroughs of Wedding and Friedrichshain, traditional working class areas in Berlin.[88]

By the end of 1929, the *Volksfilmverband für Filmkunst* boasted impressive numbers: it had evolved into 14 groups in Berlin (with 62 payment offices) and 33 in other cities. Six thousand members were listed for Berlin, 1500 in Hamburg, 3000 in Breslau and there were chapters in Dresden, Leipzig, Munich, Nürnberg, Erfurt, Chemnitz, Offenbach, Frankfurt and other cities.[89] In November 1929, a report stated that the *VFV* had organised 730 film evenings during the year in various parts of the country and that 32 film programs were at that time on tour through various cities and regions throughout Germany. While initial plans had called for it running its own cinemas, just like the *Filmliga* did in Amsterdam with *De Uitkijk*, the trajectory and aims changed:

> No high profile production plans
> but rather transformation
> towards practical plans,
> Strengthening work amongst working film friends
> Active fight against reactionary film and film trash that today is in great demand.[90]

This shift away from the initial drive towards vertical integration and toward a more direct political engagement with the film industry characterises the development of the *VFV* during the few years of its existence. The cinema was increasingly functionalised in the political battles of the late Weimar Republic. The publication organ of the institution was a monthly magazine entitled *Film und Volk* which only survived two years before fusing with the left-wing theatre magazine *Arbeiterbühne* in 1930, becoming *Arbeiterbühne und Film*; publication of this new magazine quickly ceased a year later in 1931 due to economic problems. In 1931, the *VFV* joined the communist *Interessensgemeinschaft für Arbeiterkultur* (*IfA* – Interest group for workers' culture), a cultural umbrella organisation under the direct influence of the KPD, thus giving up its independent status. It appears as if the bigger organisation *IfA* swallowed up the *VFV*, due possibly to in-fighting within the communist party about the general strategies advanced by the *ComIntern*. Some local chapters of the *VFV* were active even after the official merger such as the group led by Willi Bredel in Hamburg, while Friedrich Wolf kept a communist-oriented film society going until the winter of 1932-33 in Stuttgart when he had to flee Germany and went to Moscow in exile.

Attempts to stimulate grass-roots activities (discussions of films, amateur film production) came fairly late in Germany and their success has to be gauged ambivalently. The *Volksfilmverband* was, on the one hand, very successful as it built upon a solid organisational base within the communist party and its numerous affiliations and association in its vicinity. On the other hand, its proximity to party politics also proved to be a problem as the *VFV* was far too entangled in ideological battles to be able to create any real group feeling beyond its political objectives such as the *Filmliga* in the Netherlands. For example, the *VFV* agitated against LOHNBUCHHALTER KREMKE (GER 1930, Marie Harder) and other films produced by the social democrats instead of trying to integrate all reform-oriented left-wing forces. The *VFV* thus strictly followed the course laid out by the communist international, which had, in the early 1930s identified the social democrats as its main enemy and competitor. Likewise, the social democrats, led by their newspaper *Vorwärts*, agitated against the *Volksfilmverband*, arguing that it was a communist organisation disguised as an apolitical cultural institution.[91] The direction within the organisation appears initially to have been contradictory. In the same issue of the magazine *Film und Volk* of March/April 1928, two articles argued contrary views vis-à-vis the social democrats. Arthur Hollitscher described the evolution of the *VFV* as he fulminated against the social democrats and trade unions when he recalls meetings with them: » ... we even had occasionally consultations with representatives of trade unions and educational committee members from the social democratic party – however soon everything sunk into conscious lethargic sleep... «[92]. In the same issue, Heinrich Mann, the president of the society, took a different stance and argued in favour of a popular front in the cinema sector:

> The › Volksverband für Filmkunst ‹ is left, but neutral in terms of party politics. It wants to form a popular front against bad, untruthful and reactionary films. This movement includes all of the progressive elements no matter to which political party they belong.[93]

This tension between a popular front and the conscious intensification of the conflict between communists and social democrats characterised the organisation in its few years of existence. Even a liberal trade paper like the *Film-Kurier* voiced its scepticism of the *VFV* as either a front for the communists or run by untalented and embittered screenwriters eager to take revenge on their more successful colleagues.[94]

The most important association besides the political initiatives was the *Deutsche Liga für den unabhängigen Film* (» German League for Independent Film «) that rallied on behalf of independent and censored films. The association was founded on 14 May 1930 by Hans Richter, Mies van der Rohe, Asta Nielsen, Lotte Reiniger, Walter Ruttmann, Hans Feld and Paul Hindemith among others.[95] On the surface, its ideas were quite similar to that of the *Volksfilmverband*, but it was further removed from party politics and run by artists and intellectuals (with a socialist, communist or broadly liberal orientation nevertheless). It associated itself with the ideas that emerged during the La Sarraz meeting, where the establishment of a transnational network of film clubs was planned, turning the *Deutsche Liga* effectively into the German branch of the La Sarraz network and presenting film programs in some German cities. At least six German cities had local groups: Berlin, Munich, Frankfurt, Stuttgart, Essen and Hannover.[96] The first trace of activities can be found in Munich where the institution of a local chapter was formed on 22 May 1930 with a lecture by Hans Richter and the screening of short films.[97] The first public activity in Berlin took place on 16 November 1930, some five months later and more than a year after La Sarraz, at the *Rote Mühle* in Berlin-Halensee.[98] While the *VFV* concentrated its activities on the Eastern boroughs with a largely working class population (Neukölln, Wedding, Kreuzberg, Friedrichshain), the *Deutsche Liga* chose the rather ritzy and bourgeois Berlin West. After a programmatic statement by Richter where he asked the audience to support the production of a different kind of film, the main part of the evening was devoted to talks by Bertolt Brecht, Kurt Weill and their lawyer Otto Joseph about the 3-Groschen-Oper. In the second half of this first event, Man Ray's L'Etoile de mer (FR 1928) and three acts of Dovzenko's Zemlja (SU 1930, Earth) were screened. The *Deutsche Liga* was more aesthically oriented than the *VFV*, which had a clear political agenda – Man Ray's surrealist film would not have interested the communist-oriented association and, meanwhile, Dovzenko was probably the least (openly) political filmmaker among the Soviet innovators. Further events were announced: a debate between Richter and Asta Nielsen on the role of acting and montage in cinema and the screening of Mehanika golovnogo mozga (SU 1925, Vsevolod Pudovkin). However, even if the society did have a broad aesthetic orientation, political issues still managed to intervene, as is already visible in Brecht and Weill's battle against the production company Nero over the ownership of a mass-produced cultural commodity, the film based on Brecht and Weill's play. On the other side of the rift we find not the captains of industry, but two intellectuals and film artists who were also considered left-wing: the scriptwriter Belá Balázs and the director G.W. Pabst.[99] The association had segments in

other places as well; Liga programs were seen in Frankfurt am Main and Breslau (today: Wrocław). Thomas Tode claims that the *Liga* developed towards a
vertical integration: » On a limited level in developed into a critical organisation
of spectators with intelligent programs and a modest distribution system of league films «[100], yet few traces of the activities of the association outside Berlin
remain.

All of these developments in the various centres across Western Europe reveal factors that deserve attention. For instance, the films had to be available,
there had to be a chance to watch older films in order for a film culture to
evolve. Unlike books, which are more easily accessible, mobile and reproduci-
ble, film in its material form as a conveyor of visual information was quite im-
practical. A film was expensive to reproduce and transport and it was easily
prone to damage. For big commercial films with dozens or even hundreds of
existing copies, this potential threat was minimal, however, for an avant-garde
film with only one or two existing copies the possibility of damage and destruction was a serious issue. The proliferation of Soviet trade agencies, backlists of
distributors and directors travelling with their personal print of a film led to the
increased visibility and circulation of film art, which acquired its critical mass in
1929. The late 1920s was a time of ever-increasing mobility in most sectors of
society; for the film societies it meant that distribution of films increased and
that a number of filmmakers could travel to major cities, lecture, present films,
take part in promotional activities and maybe even shoot films abroad. The
apotheosis of these grand tours is Sergei Eisenstein's extended voyage to
Europe and the US in the early 1930s. The Soviet film had enjoyed unprece-
dented success throughout Western Europe in the second half of the 1920s and
was a decisive influence on the initiatives mentioned here. During these years,
international exchange and travel allowed a small group of famous avant-garde
filmmakers (one could even speak of a star system here) to make and present
films basically where they wanted. Invariably, they were asked to do industrial
films on various symbols of modernisation (travel, technology, medicine, modern factories).

Another sign of the growing success and proliferation of bottom-up screening
organisations can be seen in the various manuals and how-to-guides to filmmaking. In one of the central organs of the film avant-garde, *Close Up*, Winifred
Bryher ran a loose series of articles giving hints and ideas on how one could
improve the standard of local cinema programs, start a film society, obtain
films, attract like-minded cinéphiles, and in general, support independent cinema.[101] In Germany, the bottom-up theatre society *Volksbühne* published a man-
ual on running a film club.[102] Moreover, in many of the avant-garde forums and
magazines one can find distributors' advertisements , but also more ads placed

by hardware manufacturers of projectors and cameras, as the film societies were discovered as a niche market that eventually became quite large by 1930.

Even though I have concentrated on » the cities of modernism « with the nodes Amsterdam/Rotterdam, Berlin, London, and Paris, a couple of other places also deserve mention because similar patterns of emergence and development can also be found here. I have concentrated on a Western European context because the activities here were the most intense, co-operation was strongest and the core of the European film avant-garde of the 1920s operated within the major metropolitan centres of Paris, Berlin, London, and Amsterdam/Rotterdam. Thus, passing over more peripheral places should not imply that they do not have significance, it just means that for reasons of space and time, I have limited myself to central nodes. In fact, the periphery experienced a similar development to the ones sketched here, although on the whole less intensely.

Belgium followed the examples set in the French periphery and its network became part of the French circles. The critic Albert Valentin founded a ciné-club in 1926 in Brussels at the *Palais des beaux-arts*,[103] and the directorship was assumed by Carl Vincent in the following year.[104] Elsewhere in Belgium, at Ostende, a » club du cinéma « was founded in 1928, which pioneered late night screenings from 11 at night to half past twelve with films by Louis Delluc, Lupu Pick, Man Ray, Robert Wiene, Alberto Cavalcanti, René Clair and Marcel L'Herbier.[105] These clubs became part of a nationwide network that also spawned Liège, Antwerp, Ghent and Leuven – the Belgium network was modelled on and was closely connected to France's network.[106] This national association, the *Club du Cinéma*, which managed to survive well into the 1930s was biased towards the artistic-aesthetic aspect of the avant-garde[107] although the socialists also took an active interest in cinema matters, especially in the course of the 1930s.[108]

In Switzerland, alternative distribution and exhibition came somewhat later, at a time when other societies could already look back upon several years of activities. The *Werkbund* exhibition *Film und Foto* travelled after its show in Stuttgart to Zurich where it was shown from late August until late September 1929, however, the film program curated by Hans Richter was not screened.[109] In Geneva, the *Ciné-Club de Genève*, started operation in 1928. Its monthly meetings supplemented by the magazine *Ciné* were oriented towards French avant-garde cinema, but it found its public forum in the English-language magazine *Close Up*, which was published in Switzerland as well. The Geneva club's inauguration occurred on 14 March 1928 with Man Ray's EMAK BAKIA (FR 1927) and Jean Epstein's LA GLACE À TROIS FACE (FR 1927). On 18 April, Alberto Cavalcanti was the guest of honour while on 2 May films by Germaine Dulac were screened. The club became part of the French-language network that also spread to Belgium.[110] The Eidgenössische Technische Hochschule (ETH – Poly-technic university) in Zurich had already established a film office (Filmstelle) in 1922 that screened films and offered lectures and courses on cinema, although within a framework of educational and technical questions – initially, aesthetic or social considerations played a minor role. In 1932, the film office instigated a successful regular film program which eventually proved too time consuming and work intensive; for that reason it was turned over in 1933 to the *Schweizer Werkbund* (SWB), which had organised the Zurich stay of the *FiFo*-exhibition in 1929, and had also commissioned Hans Richter for a project on reformist mod-ern architecture with DIE NEUE WOHNUNG (CH 1930).[111] By 1930, they had al-ready invited Hans Richter for a presentation and a lecture and then continued with regular programs, sometimes with guests like László Moholy-Nagy, until the group ceased activity after 36 film programs in 1935. This close connection between education (university), professional design (Werkbund) and humanist engagement is typical for the reformist wing of alternative cinema culture.

A workers' film society, *Foreningen for Filmskultur* (» Association for Film Cul-ture «), was founded in Denmark in 1930[112] and an *Associação dos Amigos do Cin-ema* (» Association of the friends of the cinema «) existed in Porto from the sec-ond half of the 1920s onwards.[113] The Portuguese membership association for film enthusiasts handed out an annual prize, ran a library, was involved in pub-lication and production, but it is unclear if it also screened films regularly. It may have been an exceptional film club insofar as it was not based on exhibition practice. The further development in Portugal in the 1930s was more in the sec-tor of amateur film societies; thus, oriented towards solving technical problems instead of developing screening practice and aesthetic capabilities of judgment. Film societies in the more traditional sense in Portugal only emerged in the 1940s.

Poland had two artists' associations promoting artistic film in the 1930s: *Stow-arzyszenie Milosnikow filmu Artystycznego* (*START* – Society of the Devotees of the Artistic Film) from 1930 to 1935 and after 1937 the *Spoldzielna Autorow Filmo-wych* (Co-Operative of Film Authors). The former included directors Aleksan-der Ford and Wanda Jakubowska, but also film historian Jerzy Toeplitz and rallied around the slogan » the struggle for films for the public good « while the latter incorporated Stefan and Franciszka Themerson who made some note-worthy avant-garde films.[114] However, Poland did not have any real film socie-ties until after World War Two.[115] Czechoslovakia had a very active and cross-media avant-garde in the interwar period that gathered around the key figure of Karel Teige who promoted the cause of » poetism « (a mixture of constructivism and lyricism). A short-lived film society was founded in 1927 and around this time production was started. Svatoplup Innemann, Alexander Hackenschmied, Otakar Vávra, Jan Kučera, František Burian, Jiři Lehovec and Karel and Irene

Dodal formed the core of an active avant-garde that produced everything from architectural studies to advertising.[116] These activists organised » weeks of avant-garde film « in the early 1930s and produced works on a more steady basis. In the mid-1930s, most of the people in this circle moved to Zlín, an industrial city designed and built by and for the shoe company Bata where they formed a film department that produced experimental advertising films.[117] In keeping with the spirit of the time, the films promoted the shoes and the city (much like Philips and Eindhoven or later Volkswagen and Wolfsburg) which both stood for the relentless modernising drive that had also taken hold in Czechoslovakia.[118]

If we look at the ciné-club movement in purely quantitative terms, and if we compare their size, number or frequency of activities alone, then the peak of the film society movement is some time between 1930 and 1935. This clearly shows that it was not sound film that brought down the European avant-garde as has so often been stated. The strategic convergence of several interest and lobby groups during the 1920s was mirrored by the functional differentiation on the other side of the divide, although many new groups were founded after 1930 and many continued their activities long after.

3.4   Institutionalisation and Functional Differentiation in the 1930s

> There is always, in such movements, a moment when
> the original tension of the secret society must either explode
> in a matter-of-fact, profane struggle for power and domination,
> or decay as a public demonstration and be transformed.
> Walter Benjamin (1929)[119]

By the mid- to late 1930s many film clubs had vanished, transformed into political, governmental, educational or archival institutions or developed into amateur organisations largely devoid of a wider social and political agenda, let alone revolutionary fervour. The people and institutions who had been active in different sectors of the cinema – film societies like *Filmliga* had effectively ventured into distribution and production – before the 1930s, saw a growing sense of divergence and disintegration, which might be described in a more productive fashion as functional differentiation. Many film societies limited themselves to monthly or bi-monthly screening forums having foregone the dynamic drive for change that had propelled these movements into the forefront of aesthetic development in the late 1920s. Art house cinemas evolved out of this functional differentiation on the side of exhibition.[120] Meanwhile, archives were the result of the preservational impulse, publishing and teaching stemmed from the reform-oriented side of the activities, and curating activities and meetings galvanised into film festivals, which were also born in the 1930s. One of the three Parisian art cinemas of those years, the *Vieux Colombier*, closed down in 1934 when Tédesco turned solely to production. Likewise, the *Film Society* of London went into decline and lost much of its critical momentum in the course of the 1930s, before ceasing all operations with the outbreak of World War Two.

After a couple of years with seemingly unrestricted growth, the avant-garde not only reached a critical mass in 1929-30, it also showed its first symptoms of fatigue. Even among circles not unsympathetic to the avant-garde in general such as the German trade paper *Film-Kurier* harsh criticism of the snobbish attitude and lack of popular support arose:

> It is alarming that our avant-garde is obviously driven by inbred ideas. The strong talents are missing, the schools blossoming. One steals it from the other. That carousels circle, guys linger on fair grounds – how often has the eye seen this. What detours, what formal baggage is created for nothing. ... A couple of experiments are squeezed out for the initiated, the best educated. The *Snobgarde* films.[121]

Even though this might not be a representative opinion, similar voices criticising the formulaic and repetitive film format can also be found in the avant-garde organ *Close Up*. An article by Robert Herring in May 1929 pokes fun at some of the typical stylistic features of the avant-garde that had rapidly become clichés. Herring advises the aspiring amateur to travel to Paris, shoot on the Metro and under the Eiffel Tower, » show that you know BERLIN « and add a measure of water and traffic in order to make a successful avant-garde film.[122]

In England, the success of various societies seduced commercial cinemas into screening an alternative program occasionally, regularly or exclusively. A number of modernist high-brow and avant-garde magazines such as *Film Art* or *World Film News* note the stability of the alternative film audience. *Cinema Quarterly* assessed the situation in 1932:

> The comparative success of such films as LE MILLION, MÄDCHEN IN UNIFORM, and KAMERADSCHAFT, despite their foreign dialogue and lack of organised publicity, has proven beyond doubt that there is an intelligent cinema audience sufficiently large to support films of the highest artistic standard...[123]

These films, which would have been the standard fare of film societies in the 1920s, were now ending up on commercial screens. Obviously, this was stealing business from the audience organisations whose original impetus was to screen films that did not stand a chance otherwise. The success of the film societies resulted in a larger audience, which in turn led to their demise as commercial cinemas at least in part took over their film selection. The British magazine also lists many film societies being active across Great Britain, which often linked up with educational institutions (Oxford University, Eton College), but also sub-standard film societies more oriented towards practical work than screening practice. Thus, commercial art films with some audience potential drifted toward normal cinemas while some of the bottom-up film societies turned to amateur work instead.[124] The first larger meetings of amateurs took place in the late 1920s at the » National Convention of Amateur Cinematograph Societies « in October 1929 in London, for instance.[125]

For programming purposes, the main problems of the film clubs after 1930 were how to deal with sound films. The introduction of sound had intensified the capitalisation of the film industry. As an effect, smaller companies ceased to exist or merged with larger corporations, of which France is a particularly good example.[126] Film production became more costly and consequently, films had to recoup more money per release. Film societies and alternative screening spaces often could not compete anymore with commercial exhibitors. Those films that had in the past guaranteed the survival of the organisations now went to commercial art cinemas that became increasingly professionalised. Film societies needed one or two » hits « per season to generate publicity and new members, now they turned into a second- or even third-run-house because the most interesting films were confiscated by other bigger players. An attempt to counteract this growing commercialisation of the alternative sector was the founding of an international office for the distribution of films by the *Filmliga*.[127]

The introduction of sound had similar repercussions for production. Filmmakers associated with the avant-garde made sound films but they were often commercial and produced by large companies: René Clair made films for the multinational syndicate Tobis, Fritz Lang and G.W. Pabst worked for Seymour Nebenzal's Nero-Film, while another champion of the 1920s, Abel Gance, fell into obscurity. These larger companies had a clear distribution priority to large metropolitan cinemas and nationwide cinema chains. Meanwhile, film societies ended up at the bottom of the receiving end when it came to specific films. Other former protagonists of the avant-garde turned increasingly towards industrial films such as Walter Ruttmann, Hans Richter and Joris Ivens who made films for Hapag, Philips, Creosoot and the German steel industry. These producers also had their agendas and only gave films to ciné-clubs once they had fulfilled their purpose. As a result, the programs often resorted to silent film, whereas normal cinemas had already switched over to sound film – a strange detail as something from the past was placed in a context that claimed to be in the forefront of aesthetic and technological development. Production costs rose with the new equipment, so that producers were less likely to take risks by financing experimental films. Moreover, wiring cinemas for sound required considerable investments. Sound film was not the cause *per se*, but the catalyst that introduced new methods of management and organisation within the industry. These developments, in turn, helped transform the avant-garde and its exhibition wing. However, film societies' demand for sound film technology was soon satisfied. An ad placed in the British magazine *Cinema Quarterly* aimed at film clubs and educational institutions reads:

> Film Societies, Schools, Clubs and Study Groups!
> Western Electric offer you a trouble free hiring service providing – for a moderate inclusive fee – portable sound equipment – suitable for audiences of up to 600 people – services of an operator and, if required, a programme of films, entertainment, travel, scientific, educational, etc. The equipment can be erected in any hall at short notice...[128]

One problem for the film societies was that they were discovered as a niche market. Commercial suppliers took away that business from the screening clubs, which had previously guaranteed their success and visibility, leaving the initiatives with the harder-to-market stuff. The same could also be said of the commercial art houses that were emerging everywhere across Europe from the second half of the 1920s onwards. There was a lot of change among the cinemas which occasionally or regularly screened different kinds of films, but in the larger cities commentators were pretty certain that one or more repertory theatres could be supported on a regular and commercial basis by a local audience.[129]

3.4.1 Film and National Life

> *Just as one will come together, in order to organize the joint*
> *export of German film fabrications to foreign countries,*
> *the crucial companies will also cooperate in financing film experiments.*
> *These experiments will serve the production as a whole and*
> *will be under the control of the industry.*
> Ernst Jäger (1927)[130]

There were already calls in the second half of the 1920s for a national effort to coordinate experimental film work. Ernst Jäger's statement quoted above reflects this combination that conventionally aimed at integrating the avant-garde into the wider context of film culture. To call for the state to support film appeared to be a natural, given the fact that the state heavily regulated the cinema via censorship, import quotas, taxes, building and fire regulations and other laws. The leading spokesmen of the film industry therefore believed that the state also had an obligation to help the cinema. There were various appeals for state-supported institutions such as a film laboratory, a film school, a state cinema, and academic research.[131] Whereas radical theorists like Walter Benjamin would have disagreed and argued instead for a radicalisation of the avant-garde in order to engender transformations, many observers wanted to integrate the fledging movement into mainstream film culture. The effect could have been twofold: first, the experimental impulses could have been harnessed and second, this new construction could have been used to promote ideas such as nationalism, which was on the rise everywhere in Europe after 1929.

As the energy of the film societies functionally differentiated the movement also lost its revolutionary momentum, while other groups and sectors followed the film societies and embraced film because the importance of cinema had been made. New groups now » discovered « film as a medium for building, sustaining, influencing, and manipulating a or *the* public. Political parties and governments became major motion picture producers as they began to realise the value of film. This shift can be seen across a variety of countries in different configurations. John Grierson established the Empire Marketing Board (EMB) and the General Post Office (GPO) Film Units in England, two governmental agencies that were active across vast fields of production, distribution, exhibition and marketing. The situation in Nazi Germany was in some respect comparable to that in the Soviet Union where the state became increasingly involved in production. In Italy, the *Istituto Luce* and the production company *Cines*, and the involvement of Benito Mussolini's son Vittorio, gathered much energy and momentum. State efforts involved in cinema in democratic systems include the French *front populaire*, which was quite active in filmmaking and Roosevelt's New Deal as part of the larger programs to employ artists and creative personnel. The last occasion to generate a vigorous response from filmmakers was the Spanish Civil War, which attracted artists and activists from many countries who came to defend the Republic. Of course, many of these films were openly political and therefore also intensified differing political meanings within the film societies, which had previously been glossed over by a vague allusion to film art or independence, to *absoluter Film* or *cinéma pure*. These movements happened as a result of larger tectonic shifts in the political landscape: a growing polarisation moved the majority either towards the political left or to the right, a growing social division and political tension was intensified by the crisis following the stock exchange crash of 1929, and a general search for alternative social and ideological models to deal with the critical situation turned to ever more radical solutions.

The Empire Film Board and General Post Office Film Unit are nowadays mainly remembered for their innovative films. In fact, the two Griersonian institutions' main aims – if we can judge them by their statutes and other written documents – were to bring films to people changing the way audiences typically view a film. The main tasks and activities involved the organisation of film presentations and the building and maintenance of a distribution network; while film production was more of a supplement. The reason for this is easy to

see as different kinds of films were needed for various alternative screening circuits aimed at social reform and adult education. Seen from this perspective,
Grierson's governmental film institutions learned from the film clubs: One of
the main reasons they lost their inertia and dynamism was their inability to
screen enough films during the arrival of sound. Grierson had learned his lesson and his celebrated films, it could be argued, were made to overcome the
shortage of screenable films. As Ian Aitken writes: » [T]he documentary film
movement did not only consist of a collection of films. It was also established to
service a campaign for political and cultural reform, and it utilized film, written
material, speeches, lectures, and other means of persuasion to that end. «[132]
Grierson's film units were first and foremost a headquarters for publicity campaigns, which tried to create a *Medienverbund* in which the films were an important element, but not an end in themselves. However, the documentary film
movement was not the only initiative in Britain that continued the work that
began with the *Film Society.*

The *British Film Institute* (*BFI*) was founded with a semi-official status in October 1932 (officially in autumn 1933) based on a government report *The Film in
National Life.*[133] Its aim was to further cooperation between the film industry
(» those who make, distribute, exhibit films «) and » all who are interested in the
artistic, educational and cultural possibilities of films «. In the beginning, the *BFI*
was mainly occupied with educational films financed with the help of a special
cinema tax.[134] The film archive *National Film Library* was established by the *BFI*
in 1935. Some of the free floating energy of the late 1920s was channelled into
this project, some of which survived in the film magazines of the 1930s (*Cinema
Quarterly* and *Sight and Sound,* both published from 1932 onwards; *Film Art* was
first published in 1933). The rest of the energy was absorbed by what came to be
known as the Documentary Film Movement of John Grierson. Ivor Montagu, a
key *Film Society* figure, has argued along similar lines when he described the
final days of that institution: » The banner has passed to the BFI, the NFA, the
BFFS, Film Festivals that milk not mainly USA and Europe but the wider world,
the NFT and the commercial theatres for specialised audiences. «[135] This shift to
acronyms is only the most visible sign of a growing institutionalisation that had
tamed the transformative energy of the film avant-garde.

A similar configuration in which the state used the cinema for its own purposes can be found in the debate that surrounded the establishment of the *Swedish Film Association* in 1933. In fact, the state had heeded the call of the avant-
garde that Ruttmann and others had uttered, but it responded in unexpected
ways to the avant-garde. In a way, the reaction of the state was similar to that of
the industry: they only devoured those parts of the avant-garde that it considered useful and left the rest to decay. Certainly, by being digested, the avant-

garde had some influence, but never in the direct way that they themselves had envisioned. The Swedish professional society focused on

> a didactical documentary discourse. In short, the ideas behind the Film Association were to » artistically, culturally and technically promote cinema in Sweden. « As an academic undertaking it sought to promulgate a new national film culture, not only in terms of refined production guidelines, but also as to cultivate public taste and, via publications, inform on cinematic matters. ... With the task to increase the cultural prestige of cinema, it addressed all kinds of filmic issues: from film aesthetics and manuscript contests to state funding of production and film theoretical specula-tions.[136]

This event was followed by a public debate about the role and function of the cinema in the life of the nation, which continued throughout the 1930s. One should keep in mind that these state activities occurred regardless of the politi-cal organisation: from the communist Soviet Union through social democratic Sweden, the reformist United States and England on down to fascist Germany and Italy. Most of the topics, aims, discourses and interests had only arisen in the (imaginary) realm of the film societies only a few years earlier; with the coming of sound the nation-state finally became interested in cinema as a med-ium in its own right. In this respect, the coming of sound would not only mark the final stage of the shift of control from the exhibitor to the producer, but it also marked the completion of the phase in which the nation-state would gra-dually occupy and use film as a means of propaganda and self-promotion. Thus, from the battlefield of World War One and the founding of the Ufa one could see a line developing that stretched to the emerging state institutions that were concerned with cinema as we have already seen in Sweden or in England.

In 1928, the most important German trade paper, the *Film-Kurier*, reserved a whole page to request that the state fund a number of initiatives important to the (liberal) forces within the film industry. Besides the traditional call for tax breaks, the rest of the appeal is rather unusual and could have been copied right out of an avant-garde magazine. The *Film-Kurier* requests that the state support experimental film and film music studios as well as schools for film and for film music, more attention be paid to cinema in universities, a film museum and an archive and payment for film music.[137] This devotion to experimentation, on the one hand, while safeguarding the future (schools) and the past (archive, museum) are avant-garde typical issues, but that these calls arose from an in-dustry forum illustrates how some of these ideas had become common currency in circa 1930. In fact, vocational training, a devotion to experimental work, sup-porting film in the service of the nation and a serious commitment to historicity went hand in hand at the time when sound was just being introduced.

These transformations were not lost on the avant-garde activists. Iris Barry, one of the hidden protagonists in the transfiguration of the avant-garde movement into filmmaking in the service of the nation-state and the archive-historicist impulse, was travelling across Europe in 1935 in order to acquire films for the MOMA archive when she reported on Leni Riefenstahl's TRIUMPH DES WILLENS (GER 1934/35):

> Elsewhere, an entirely new and significant tendency is apparent in an attempt to record out-standing national events by means of film. ... The use of film for such purposes is new. ... Lately, the British Government has been the producer of a number of lively » shorts « dealing specifically with its own activities in the domestic realm of communication – radio, post-office, weather bureau, and the like. Technically, it is these which have the most likeness to the new kind of German films of which I speak, though the latter take a much larger canvas. The mass meeting of the Nazi Party at Nürnberg in the autumn of 1934 was not merely filmed, the whole meeting was organized in such a way that a direct and living record of the celebration could be made. Camera emplacements had been carefully worked out and installed, a battery of cameras was trained on the gathering so as to provide close shots, long shots, travelling shots – and so that the speeches and other sounds might be properly recorded. THE TRIUMPH OF THE WILL, as this full-length picture made for domestic consumption only is called, proved one of the most brilliantly assembled and edited films imaginable: it enables a remote member of the general public to participate as at first hand in the meeting.[138]

Barry not only makes the connection between the Griersonian school and filmmaking in Nazi Germany in terms of support mechanisms, but also stylistically. The participatory dimension of the state-sponsored cinema of the 1930s could also be an avant-garde legacy as the destruction of barriers between film and spectator, between producer and consumer had been high on the agenda of the alternative movements of the previous decade. That this participation of the spectator in the events on the screen would take such a turn as in the case of Riefenstahl was certainly not foreseeable by the avant-garde activists.

3.4.2 Archiving and Historicity

[The state] could, for example, start by building a film archive.
It would thus establish the means to keep those important films
accessible, which failed to be complete successful. If a homeland is ever
established for these orphans, the interested public would gather
around them and if the archive was connected to the possibility
of screening the films, this would be the second important step
and would mean the establishment of a state cinema.
Walter Ruttmann (1928)[139]

The idea of film preservation and the creation of a film archive are nearly as old as film itself. The first calls for a film archive, » *Une nouvelle source de l'histoire* « and » *La photographie animée, ce qu'elle est, ce qu'elle doit être* «, were written by the Polish photographer Boleslaw Matuszewski and sent to French institutions in 1898. However, he had arrived too early and at the time his calls went unheeded.[140] Closer to my purpose here, Louis Delluc as one of the » founding fathers « of the film avant-garde had by the early 1920s already called for a » library or repertory of significant films …, not only to preserve but to promulgate the idea of cinema art and to educate cinema audiences in order to support further innovations and the cinema's eventual achievements «.[141] The construction of a canon of important works, the consciousness for film history, the attempt to guarantee access to this history and the integration of these concerns into a transformed cinema culture – all these issues were important elements of avant-garde film culture. The programming of older films has been a staple of film societies as their initial impetus partly resulted from the desire to re-watch specific films. The forms that it took – homages, reveries or negative re-evaluations – differed widely. Sometimes it was done solemnly with the desire to watch films that one had missed, demanding in turn a second- and third-run market: » One often wants to see films one has missed. It is never possible. After a year or two they are as dead as a doornail. Some enterprising person might pull strings so that the best survived, and more than that, are shown. «[142] Yet, a media event was sometimes very consciously created, for example in the efforts by Robert Aron (initially the driving force behind the La Sarraz meeting) and Jean Georges Auriol to bring Georges Méliès back into public consciousness.[143] A special issue of their magazine *La revue du cinéma* in October 1929 included original texts, scenarios, reprints and a critical essay by Paul Gilson that was supplemented by a screening of eight Méliès-films at the Salle Pleyel, co-organised by *Studio 28*, and the papers *L'ami du peuple* and *Figaro*.[144] Despite the different forms that these early film historical events took, a consciousness for the history of the cinema was typical of the avant-garde, which ultimately resulted in film collections and written film histories. The first ones to venture into these areas were veterans from the ciné-clubs in the 1930s who were influenced by concerns advanced in avant-garde circles in the 1920s.

For the archiving movement, the coming of sound proved to be a crucial moment. One fundamental change brought about by this media change was the sudden devaluation of silent films. Within the course of six months the film stock – the » library « or » archive « as proponents of cultural conservation would have it or the » backlist « as the US studios call their older products – was considered worthless. It led to the wholesale destruction of film material – in economic terms it appeared pointless to waste money on storing objects that did no longer have any exchange value – and also opened the way for collectors to acquire many old films that had been unattainable before. When the swift shift to sound film became obvious in Europe in 1930, all of the producers and distributors followed suit, quickly selling off their remaining silent films to far-off regions in South America or China, which were a couple of years behind in respect to the transition to sound.[145] This devaluation of silent film also triggered the archival movement begun by several young enthusiasts who had been members of different ciné-clubs and grown up within the circles of alternative film culture. The impulse for restructuring cinema culture gave way to attention being paid to those » orphans « who were now homeless – as the state had not yet responded to Ruttmann's call for an archival movement that had already begun as a private enterprise by a select few.

In the course of the 1930s, one aspect of the film society movement became the first generation of archivists: Iris Barry had been an important figure in the London *Film Society* until she departed for New York in 1930 after her divorce from Alan Porter and after having been sacked by the *Daily Mail*. [146] Some months earlier, in the summer of 1929, the first director of the Museum of Modern Art, Alfred H. Barr, Jr., had been commissioned to draw up a plan for the new institution by its trustees. His plan included departments of commercial and industrial art, theatre design, film, photography, as well as painting and sculpture. However, because of the depression, MOMA started out collecting only paintings and sculpture, the most established arts and thus easier to convince private patrons (on which MOMA had to rely as a privately financed institution). Iris Barry worked as a freelance writer until 1932 when she became the » film librarian « at the MOMA. In a pamphlet written in 1932 entitled *The Public as Artist*, Barr again called for the inclusion of film in the museum's collection. Barry started her job at MOMA, establishing relationships with Hollywood through the backing of John Hay Whitney as the first important step to acquiring the necessary material for the archives. Tellingly, Barry did not start by approaching the avant-garde, even though that was her background. She recognised the limitations inherent in the film societies and she knew that she only had a long-term chance if she could muster big industry support in Hollywood. The Film Library was founded in 1935 (which later turned into the Department of film, which remains its name to this day) and its cinema was established in 1939 and has not stopped since.

We should not forget that it was also Iris Barry who preserved some of the avant-garde spirit and built bridges that helped exiles as different as Luis Buñuel and Siegfried Kracauer during the war. Her support perhaps saved Buñuel from obscurity on the margins of the 1920s surrealist movement and who seemed to vanish into thin air after having collaborated on two films with Salvador Dalí. The same could be said about Kracauer: Without his seminal study *From Caligari to Hitler* which he could not have written without the support of Barry, he might have ended up as a film critic who would nowadays only be remembered by experts (such as Hans Feld or Willy Haas). There is also a third important person whom she helped and whose life she possibly gave a new direction: In 1936, Barry went to Europe and visited Eisenstein in Moscow while he was working on BEZIN LUG (SU 1936). Barry convinced Eisenstein's assistant Jay Leyda (who had been in Moscow for three years) to come with her to MOMA as her new assistant. What goes around comes around: Buñuel, Kracauer, Leyda – three key figures of the avant-garde, film historiography, and film theory were all helped at crucial moments by Iris Barry who herself had gotten her film education at the London *Film Society*. The circles of the avant-garde filmmaking and screening clubs had a lasting influence that outlived their actual period of operation because the energy generated spilled over into different projects in different locations.

In Paris, Henri Langlois, slightly younger than the pioneer generation (born in Smyrna, today Izmir, in 1912), and in François Truffaut's words » perhaps the most gifted of film lovers «[147], was a pivotal figure in the institutionalisation of film archives in the period of the 1930s to the 1960s.[148] In Langlois' and Georges Franju's ciné-club *Cercle du Cinéma*, discussions were not allowed after screenings – as they attempted to create a different kind of ciné-club. They combined the idea of a film club that exhibited films with the idea of an archive that stored films to create the *Cinémathèque*.[149] Actually, the money for the first prints they bought came from Paul-August Harlé, publisher of the trade weekly *La Cinématographie Française*, but also financially involved in printing businesses and poster design. Moreover, Harlé convinced Alexandre Kamenka, president of Albatros Films, to deposit his films with Langlois and Franju, among them many » commercial « art film classics of the 1920s such as LE BRASIER ARDENT (FR 1923, Ivan Mosjoukine / Alexandre Volkoff), FEU MATHIAS PASCAL (FR 1924, Marcel L'Herbier), CARMEN (FR 1926, Jacques Feyder), UN CHAPEAU DE PAILLE D'ITALIE (FR 1927, René Clair) and LES NOUVEAUX MESSIEURS (FR 1928, Jacques Feyder).[150] Harlé made a lot of connections in the industry until he fell from grace with Langlois, himself a legendary » difficult « character. The introduction of sound proved to be the key moment for Langlois, already an avid film lover by then, inspiring him to pursue his lifetime project of film archiving and presenting:

> The triumph of the sound film only a year after A Girl in Every Port [i.e., 1928/1929] was to prove the determining event in Langlois's career. Not because he rejected sound ... but because he soon realized that it was to endanger the survival of decades of silent masterpieces. ... The revolution of the talkies was imposed, as Langlois said, by box-office receipts, against the conservative filmmakers and critics. For the first time in the history of cinema, they began to cherish its past and tried to safeguard it.[151]

Critics and filmmakers were often the conservative ones in regards to technical developments and, not necessarily the industry, which followed the money trail wherever it led. The industry remains first and foremost disinterested in the aesthetic, social, or political value of changes regarding the production and exhibition of films. An industry organised according to capitalist principles followed the audience; and if the audience wanted something new the industry would provide it.

Industry connections were vital for a film archive to get the ball rolling and while the ciné-clubs provided the basis for the selection criteria, the industry link remained crucial, for Barry as well as for Langlois. While the avant-garde classics were easily acquired through personal acquaintance, the larger productions proved more difficult to obtain. In fact, the archives pioneer generation realised from the very start that it either needed government support (as in England, Sweden and Germany) or direct industry support (as in the US and France) because otherwise these films would have been just too expensive and impossible to obtain. One of the key problems of the film societies had been the availability of films – their purchase had often been blocked by commercial distributors or producers – the archivists had surely learned their lessons and started building up their archives by using connections to the industry. In the period 1936–38, Germaine Dulac was given this task since she was influential in the French film industry as the director of the newsreel and documentary department at Gaumont.[152]

Whereas the *Cinémathèque Française* was a private initiative, in Britain, collecting and archiving film and related cinematic material fell within the domain of the newly founded *British Film Institute*. The state took a lively interest in film matters in England: The various educational activities in the context of the London *Film Society* led to the foundation of the *BFI* and subsequently to the *National Film Archive*. Ivor Montagu himself later became a member of the *BFI* Film Archive Selection Committee. Despite the many differences, veterans from the film club movement played an important role here as well. Olwen Vaughan, the daughter of the founder of the Merseyside Film Society, rose up within the circles of the ciné-club movement to reign over the *BFI*, establishing the film archive, and hiring Ernest Lindgren as its first curator. Lindgren became Langlois's chief nemesis in the post-war period and emerged as the epitome of the archivists who refused to screen in order to preserve while for Langlois archiving meant screening films from the archive. Even though this distinction between Lindgren and Langlois has been exaggerated, an archive always has to deal with the dialectics of archiving and presentation.

In Germany, as in England or Sweden, it was the nation-state that established a film archive. On the first anniversary of the Nazi's ascension to power, the *Reichsfilmkammer* (film chamber) donated a number of films to the future film archive. The foundation of this institution was further propagated under the auspices of Dr. Seeger (head censor) by ministerial bureaucrat Dr. Böttger within Goebbels' Ministry of Enlightenment and Propaganda. Four days before the official founding, with Hitler present, Böttger was replaced by Frank Hensel, an Nazi film activist from prior to 1933.[153] Hensel had produced propaganda films such as Ein Feiertag in Hessen-Nassau / Hitlers braune Soldaten kommen (GER 1931) or Hitlers Kampf um Deutschland (GER 1932). Thus, even in Nazi Germany the archival impulse was connected to non-mainstream or » alternative film culture « of the 1920s and early 1930s. For the national socialists, the archive was a perfect match between the preservatory impulse and nationalism as it facilitated a rewriting of history through the command of audiovisual documents.[154]

Since I seem to be mainly dealing with men, a brief remark on the role of women: Germaine Dulac must be counted as one of the film avant-garde's pivotal figures , but less oriented towards propagating her own personality and work, preferring to be a go-between, organiser, and enabler. [155] Women were also crucial in the early years of the archive movement. Dulac had to occupy one of the two positions that the informal networks of the avant-garde had left to women: she served as a » maternal « background presence, a caretaker eclipsed by the men. In this position, Dulac was comparable to Iris Barry in New York or Olwen Vaughan in London – in some ways, Mary Meerson inherited Dulac's role in Paris as the stable assistant to Henri Langlois's flamboyance and extravagance, along with Lotte Eisner and Marie Epstein. In London at the *BFI*,Vaughan operated behind the figure of Ernest Lindgren, while Barry moved in the shadow of *MOMA*'s founding director Alfred Barr. The other possible position for women was that as objects that were traded between the men. An example of this is how a woman like Gala moved from Paul Eluard to Salvador Dalí, Pera Attaschewa was the partner of both Hans Richter and Sergei Eisenstein, Erna Niemeyer who had studied at the Bauhaus Weimar in the early 1920s, worked with Viking Eggeling and subsequently married Hans Richter and later, surrealist writer Philippe Soupault. Her own photography (as Ré Soupault) has only recently been rediscovered.[156] Apart from the motherly and older helpers and the muses to be traded as objects there was little space for women's roles in the avant-garde circles between such flamboyant self-promoters as Hans Richter, László Moholy-Nagy, Walter Ruttmann, Joris Ivens or Sergei Eisenstein.

Once the archives had been established, international exchange was necessary. The idea for an international network of alternative cinema institutions is certainly as old as the first film societies; these groups were international from the very beginning, albeit in a chaotic, personal and unsystematic way. Films, texts, discourses and ideas were traded and exchanged internationally from the mid-1920s onwards. At La Sarraz in 1929, an international league for independent film was founded and some years later an international federation active in the business of conserving and collecting old films was proposed by Germaine Dulac who urged Georges Franju and Henri Langlois to institutionalise their international contacts with the archives in London and New York, which were at the time directed by Olwen Vaughan and Iris Barry respectively. While travelling in Europe in the mid-1930s, Iris Barry also stopped in Berlin where she reported favourably on the *Reichsfilmarchiv* and in Paris where she met with Henri Langlois, a meeting that led to the founding of the international network of film archives (FIAF).

However, the idea of history was not limited to the preservational impulse and the archival movement, but even the films themselves also increasingly dealt with the historicity of the film material and of the scenes and events represented in film. By in 1928, Ufa had already produced a film that summarised and historicised the career of popular actress Henny Porten, HENNY PORTEN – LEBEN UND LAUFBAHN EINER FILMKÜNSTLERIN (GER 1928, Oskar Kalbus). A year later a compilation of love cinematic scenes followed, RUND UM DIE LIEBE (GER 1929, Oskar Kalbus). Both films were screened and discussed in avant-garde circles as the concept of compiling of *Querschnitt* related to aesthetic ideas such as collage or re-montage.[157] Another example of this trend is the trajectory of Germaine Dulac. Ever since the late 1910s, Dulac had always oscillated between openly experimental and more mainstream work. Her work in the 1930s opened up the avant-garde further to industrial films, but also to questions regarding film and history. In fact, her last major project was a compilation film titled LE CINÉMA AU SERVICE DE L'HISTOIRE (FR 1935). Dulac had been in charge of the newsreel FRANCE-ACTUALITÉS since 1932 and a critic praised her work: » It is thanks to her that the programs of France-Actualités are characterised by such objectivity, such honesty and such lucky choices that we have already noted. «[158] In LE CINÉMA AU SERVICE DE L'HISTOIRE, Dulac provides a history of the near-past (since World War One) from archival material and gives a sketch of the state of the world.[159] This found-footage history film has its equivalent in the Soviet compilation film as developed by Esfir Shub who made a trilogy based on archival material, sketching Russian and Soviet history from the end of the 19th Century to the beginning of the Five-Year Plan.[160]

3.5 Conclusion

> *The avant-garde film is not solely for the entertainment of the masses. It is at the same time more egotistical and more altruistic. Egotistical because it is the personal expression of a pure idea; altruistic in its exclusive endeavors for the development of the medium. The real avant-garde film possesses the fundamental trait of containing under a sometimes-opaque surface the germ of inventions that will lead the film on its way to its future form. The avant-garde is born of both the criticism of the present and the anticipation of the future.*
>
> Germaine Dulac (1932)[161]

In this chapter I have looked at the film society movement in detail. The ciné-clubs and audience organisations were part and parcel of the historical film avant-garde of the interwar period. The ciné-clubs cannot be separated from the avant-garde and vice versa – these were closely connected initiatives pointed in the same direction. Yet, we should not make the mistake of placing these attempts in a binary opposition to the industry even though at that time this opposition was sometimes mobilised for a distinctive rhetorical function, i. e., to create a common enemy. Instead, we must look closely at the dialectical interplay between avant-garde and industry. And, despite the disappearance of many ciné-clubs activities in the course of the 1930s, they created something more durable than mere ephemeral events. What was at stake was not only a new public, but a new way of viewing films and a new way of thinking about film. In the increasing activities of the late 1920s, the avant-garde was capable of generating energy and providing a cause to rally around. It is this strategic convergence that characterises the rise of the film societies – strategic in the sense that the various groups all saw cinema to varying degrees as a functional medium that could be fitted into their own schemes. At the time few people realised that the various groups involved in avant-garde activities would move in such very different directions over the course of the 1930s.

It was not so much the altered situation after 1929 – sound film and economic crisis – that brought about the decline of the film societies, but it was this new situation that made the internal contradictions of the earlier strategic convergence more visible. The complete independence often proclaimed as a goal was illusory and only a few of the canonised classics were actually made independently. The relationship with the industry (Tobis, Ufa, Deutsche Universal, Gau-mont-Franco-Film-Aubert, Hapag), with hardware manufacturers and electronics companies (Siemens & Halske, Philips, AEG, Bata, Shell) with state agencies that were becoming increasingly important in the 1930s (Grierson's film units in Britain, the increasingly firm grip of the Nazi party on filmmaking in Germany, the French popular front in the period 1936-38, Soviet state productions, New Deal filmmaking in the United States), political positions had to be reconsidered after its peak in 1929. It turned out that the avant-garde and the film societies as a movement were not able to reconcile their divergent meanings and positions. The vast, trans-European network at first attempted to seriously theorise film and its foundations. The energy did not evaporate or vanish later, but merely got transformed in accordance with the laws of thermodynamics: nothing was lost. The functional differentiation filtered the energy into the archives, cinema in the service of the nation-state and the documentary as a genre – these were all results of the ciné-club and the avant-garde movement of the 1920s as the energy was recycled and preserved in new forms. Some other examples of the migrating energy in the networks of the film avant-garde – publishing, theorising, and teaching – will be addressed in the following chapter.

4   Mapping a Totality of Networks, Nodes and Flows – Discourses as Practice

Avant-garde means intellectual curiosity in a field
where one can still make countless passionate discoveries
René Clair (1927)[1]

This chapter will deal with a variety of practices: publishing and theorisation, teaching and event culture, and last but not least, one major part of this chapter will be devoted to an exploration of the various attempts by the avant-garde to overcome the increasingly limited screening situation of the traditional *dispositif* of the cinema. In all of these practices we can recognise how the avant-garde worked toward a reintegration of art into life: art's function should be different from the cult status of pre-modern art and from the bourgeois autonomous art of the modern period. The different examples discussed here show the avant-garde on its way to becoming total cinema: by writing differently about the cinema, the avant-garde hoped to influence and change spectators, by venturing into teaching, the aim was to transform a future generation of practitioners and theoreticians, by organising events the avant-garde wanted to create moments of qualitative transformations, and all of these measures culminated in an effort to create an immersive cinema experience as a possible utopia of spectatorship, reception and exhibition. This utopian promise that encompasses technology, film style and spectatorship shows avant-garde ideals at their most obvious: cinema was more than just the films projected. The hope was to overcome any distinction separating screen and auditorium, life and art, theory and practice, film and spectator. Thus, the last part of this chapter on the immersive film experience tries to map the utopian aspirations towards a totality as a spatial installation. The attempts of breaking open the codified, distanced and sanitised way of film reception astutely demonstrate how the avant-garde wanted to liberate the cinema from its two gaolers: mass entertainment on the one side and bourgeois art on the other.

4.1   Publishing as Discourse Formation: Magazines and Books

A few years ago books on the cinema were almost as scarce
as intelligent films. Today the number can fill a shelf or two…
Herbert Read (1932)[2]

One of the key nodes for the avant-garde in general, not just for film, was the magazine, or as it is sometimes called, » the little magazine «. These publication organs were established among networks of acquaintances and friends, came out irregularly, often did not survive more than a couple of numbers and were produced in an amateur or artisanal style.[3] In fact, their mode of production is similar to the films produced in a comparable fashion in networks of relations and on the surface all too often appear to be » poor « and » imperfect « compared to the » polished « and outwardly » perfect « commercial products.[4] The avant-garde approached the arts not as distinct disciplines but as a large field that could not be divided into sharply delineated entities. In their intermedia orientation many of the general magazines (i.e., not specialised in film) dealt with the cinema as well as with literature, the visual arts, theatre, performance, dance, architecture and other issues of relevance. The magazines were decidedly transdisciplinary and convincingly internationalist – articles were often published in their original language with – or without – accompanying translation. The magazines as well as the key players involved in the movements formed connections between the key places: they were conduits for communication in which positions could be outlined and work could be published. The magazines provided the basis for inclusion and exclusion (of persons, topics, positions) and guaranteed a measure of exchange that transcended the limited level of friendship and acquaintance.

The number of general magazines, often short-lived, but often remaining influential until the present day, that were published in those crucial years between 1919 and 1939, especially in the period from the mid-1920s to the mid-1930s is very hard to estimate. A handful of them reached prominent status. One general magazine also interested in film was *G. Material zur elementaren Gestaltung*. G stands for *Gestaltung* and the publication consisted of a total of six issues that appeared from July 1923 to 1926 under the editorship of Hans Richter and supported by, among others, Theo van Doesburg, Werner Graeff, El Lissitzky and Mies van der Rohe. All of the artist-activists involved were crucial figures in the exchange between places (Doesburg between the Netherlands and Germany, El Lissitzky between the Soviet Union and Germany), between art forms (architecture, film, visual arts, all of them also produced texts of » theory «) and between styles (Dada, Constructivism, Surrealism). G was mainly the product of the meeting of the Russian and the German Constructivists while *i10*, under the directorship of Arthur Lehning – who in the 1920s commuted between the » cities of modernism « Amsterdam, Rotterdam, Paris and Berlin – was more closely connected to the Dutch scene, which was particularly strong on architecture. *i10* had sections on architecture (edited by J.J.P. Oud) and on photography and film (edited by László Moholy-Nagy). The magazine appeared in the period from January 1927 to June 1929, following in the footsteps of *De Stijl*, albeit in a more radical fashion while lobbying for a revolutionary integration of art and life.[5]

In France, besides André Breton's *La Révolution Surréaliste* (1924-29), the literary journal *transition* and the magazine *documents*, which in some respects was a successor to Breton's magazine were published in Paris. *Documents* came out in 1929-30 with Georges Bataille and Carl Einstein as the key figures and with a strong focus on ethnography.[6] Sometimes magazines exhausted their energy in a very short period of time, publishing only a few issues. Germaine Dulac herself published only one issue of her magazine *Schémas* in 1927, which included texts by Dulac and Hans Richter defending abstraction, which were confronted with essays by Henri Fescourt and Jean-Louis Bouquet in support of narrative film.[7] Some magazines were supported by influential institutions such as *Die Form* which was published by the *Werkbund* or the magazine *Bauhaus* connected to the design and architecture school in Weimar and Dessau. In Frankfurt, architecture, design, photography and film were discussed in *Das neue Frankfurt* that was published from 1925 to 1932. Other magazines catered to a specific (national) audience such as the Hungarian exile magazine *Ma* (› Today ‹, 1918-25, published in Vienna).

These general and transdisciplinary magazines created a transgeneric and transdisciplinary communication platform for political, social and cultural revolutionaries and had complimentary journals devoted to cinema. Publishing activity, especially between 1927 and 1933, was enormous and the quality as well as quantity of film magazines only reached a similar level again in the 1960s. The English-language magazine *Close Up* that exhibited its outspoken internationalism by including texts in French and German came out from July 1927 to December 1933 in Switzerland and it was probably the single most important film journal in the interbellum. In the 1930s, a number of British magazines continued the serious discussion of film: *Cinema Quarterly* was published from 1932 to 1935 and was followed by *World Film News* (1936-38) – the first three numbers of the latter were edited by Hans Feld, formerly editor-in-chief at the most important German trade paper *Film-Kurier*. The editorship was then taken over by Marion A. Grierson, John Grierson's sister who was also working in the circles of the documentary film movement. The founder of the documentary film movement was a regular contributor to the magazine as well as other activists involved in it. While *Cinema Quarterly* was published in close proximity to the British documentarists with many collaborators writing articles, *Film Art* (the first issue was called *Film*) which was published from 1933 to 1937 was more oriented towards formal experiment and saw itself as a successor to *Close Up*, which had ceased publication shortly before *Film Art* started to appear. If we look at the multitude of » little magazines « on cinema, the large number of active film societies – in autumn 1934 the British *Cinema Quarterly* remarked that » the film societies movement is growing rapidly throughout the country «[8] – as well as the relatively stable number of films produced we can see that the avant-garde did not cease to exist in the 1930s. Publication activities should not be limited to magazines alone: the *Film Society* of London produced detailed notes accompanying the programmed films that were handed out for the monthly screening.[9] Unlike the avant-garde magazines and in keeping with the spirit of the London *Film Society* these texts were situating films historically and aesthetically, but they were not radical battle cries for change.[10]

In Germany, the left-wing *Volksfilmverband* published its magazine *Film und Volk* from February 1928 until March 1930; after the audience organisation fused with a theatre organisation the organ of the new Communist oriented organisation was called *Arbeiterbühne und Film*, published in 1930/31. Otherwise, the German film discourse settled into several different organs; one forum for a serious discussion of the cinema were the quality dailies, mostly liberal in outlook like the *Frankfurter Zeitung* or the *Vossische Zeitung*. The *Frankfurter Zeitung* boasted two prominent critics, Siegfried Kracauer and Bernhard Diebold, a Swiss citizen who championed abstract cinema supporting Walt(h)er Ruttmann and Oskar Fischinger. Even the trade press clearly aligned to the film industry (with the two important dailies *Film-Kurier* and *Lichtbild-Bühne*) often ran articles on the avant-garde or by activists and in general showed a keen interest in the developments beyond the industry proper. The fact that publications nominally devoted to an audience of people active in the film industry were interested in avant-garde affairs testifies to the crossover potentialities of the movement around 1930. Finally, a number of general left-leaning magazines like *Die Weltbühne* (Hans Siemsen and Rudolf Arnheim being the key writers on the cinema) or *Der Querschnitt* published reviews as well as longer pieces on the cinema.

The Dutch *Filmliga* published a monthly journal from 1927 to 1931, which not only ran texts in Dutch, but also exhibited its internationalism like *Close Up* with a multilingual quality publishing articles in English, French and German. France boasted several magazines devoted to film within an intellectual and artistic context: *Cinéa – Ciné pour tous*, the single most important French film magazine, emerged in late 1923 when Jean Tédesco took over editorship of *Cinéa* (1921-23) from the then recently deceased Louis Delluc and merged it with its rival *Ciné pour tous* (1919-23) ran by Pierre Henri. It not only brought together critics and filmmakers, theoreticians and practitioners, but it also lobbied for a repertory cinema and argued in general for a film avant-garde. In the late 1920s, Jean-Georges Auriol published the glossy and elitist magazine *La Revue du cinéma* (1928-31), which echoed Léon Moussinac's call for a different cinema in both aesthetic and social terms. Other influential specialised film magazines were the popular stars-and-genres oriented *Cinémagazine* (from 1921 onwards) on which Robert Florey served as Hollywood correspondent, himself the director of some experimental short in the late 1920s such as THE LIFE AND DEATH OF 9413 – A HOLLYWOOD EXTRA (US 1927), and *Photo-Ciné* (1927, edited by Jean Dréville). Apart from these journals, there were a number of publications that were either connected to the film industry (like the most important French trade paper *Cinématographie française*) or to the popular press (*Ciné-Miroir*, *Cinémonde* or *Pour Vous*) plus flourishing publication activity in newspapers and general magazines that were all concerned with avant-garde issues.[11]

While the magazines (and to a certain extent, newspapers reporting on film) provided active networks and platforms for debates, the more extended pieces started to appear in book form by the mid-1920s. An incomplete list of books published in those years shall suffice to substantiate the thesis that those names and titles staked the premiere claim for the demarcation of the evolving field of film theory and history. The books published in this period can be grouped in several waves, which allow us to understand the shifting ideas, fashions and alliances. Serious publishing began in the mid-1920s and the decade from 1925 to 1935 was only surpassed in quality and quantity of publication in the 1960s.

In the mid-1920s, many of the debates and networks were still characterised by their national scope – consequently, the books primarily addressed a national audience and national preoccupations. It was only in the second half of the 1920s that a truly European network and discourse emerged from the overlap and fusion of erstwhile separate institutions. Therefore, the first wave of books published around 1925 was still characterised by a largely separated audience. Three very different books came out in German in 1924-25 which all revolved around the question of film's role within a wider social and cultural context. While Belá Balázs in *Der sichtbare Mensch* saw the cinema as a pacemaker on the way to a visual society that would overcome many of the problems of human language, Edgar Beyfuss and A. Kossowsky gathered a large number of contributors in their *Kulturfilmbuch* – an anthology that conceptualised the cinema as occupying a position between education, science and national culture. Finally, Willi Münzenberg's pamphlet *Erobert den Film!* put the cinema in the camp of overthrowing the existing order and creating a new communist world.[12] As different as these three approaches were, they all shared a discontent with the status quo and attempted to open up a future for the cinema different from the situation as it was. The positions were markedly diverse: Balázs wrote as a critic, but since he was also active as a screenwriter he occupied a position on the fringes of the industry. Beyfuss by contrast was one of the crucial instigators and film production innovators (he was employed by Ufa) and a bridge-builder between the industry and the avant-garde, while Münzenberg ran an international conglomerate of communist media outlets. The fact that all of them were able to occupy multiple positions – scriptwriter and critic (later also teacher and director), producer and lecturer, head of a publishing house and propagandist – testifies to the flexible nature of film culture during this period. This was the climate from which the avant-garde was able to emerge.

The first wave of serious cinema writing in France appeared around the same time: three influential books were published in French in 1925. Georges Michel Coissac's *Histoire du cinématographie* was mainly a history of the technological and industrial development of the film whereas Léon Moussinac's *Naissance du cinéma* argued from an avant-garde position in which film's potential as art was based on plastic and rhythmic elements. Furthermore, Moussinac summed up the evolution of the cinema through various stages in different nations. The third, Henri Fescourt's and Jean-Louis Bouquet's *L'Idée et l'écran*, conceptualised cinema as a popular art of storytelling that was possibly in need of some refining of its style and method, but should not revert to abstraction or pure rhythm. These three books illustrate the major positions of the French discourse in the first half of the 1920s between the drive towards abstraction and the attempt to create an innovative narrative and popular cinema. In a somewhat similar vein British film critic and founding member of the *Film Society* of London Iris Barry wrote about the cinema as a popular art form in *Let's Go to the Pictures* (1926).[13]

This initial wave of books attempted, on the one hand, to sum up the evolution of the cinema over the first 30 years while, on the other hand, they wanted to point the way in which cinema should and could be advancing. Apart from Moussinac and Münzenberg's treatises this first round of serious publications on the cinema was characterised by cautionary works that attempted to elevate the cinema into the canon of the established arts. It is safe to conclude that in around 1925 the avant-garde was still a miniscule movement that had not yet realised its radical potential. But this would shortly change because a few years later the impact of the Soviet cinema left not only a strong impression on filmmaking and criticism, but a number of books attested to the influence that Eisenstein & Co. had on Western European film in the second half of the 1920s. In France, Pierre Marchand and René Weinstein reported on *L'art dans la Russie nouvelle: Le cinéma (1917-1926)* (1927) while Léon Moussinac explained *Le cinéma soviétique* (1928). German critic Alfred Kerr celebrated *Russische Filmkunst* (1927) while the Anglo-Swiss POOL collective published Winifred Bryher's report on *Film Problems of Soviet Russia* (1929).[14] These books were reactions to the sudden and unexpected appearance of the Soviet montage cinema. While the books published in around 1925 were mostly still defined by national culture and language, the Soviet cinema created a point of convergence for the various schools and styles. The wave of Soviet films stimulated a certain synchronicity in the major avant-garde centres of Western Europe. Moreover, the » *Russenfilme* « carried the dynamic promise that film could and would be an agent for social, political and cultural change – the cinema took on a new urgency and significance for many observers. Even though these films were often hindered by censorship and seldom seen by large audiences, their discursive promise and battle cry was heard widely. The art and culture of the young and revolutionary country was an avant-garde promise merely by the fact of its sheer existence. Or, to most conservative oberservers, it signalled the threat of imminent revolution.[15]

Just as the film societies and ciné-clubs peaked around 1930, a number of important books came out in these crucial years when the avant-garde seemed on the verge of a mass movement breakthrough. Accompanying the *Werkbund* exhibition » Film und Foto «, in itself an international affair, were two books, one on cinema, Hans Richter's *Filmgegner von heute – Filmfreunde von morgen* (1929); and the other on photography, Werner Graeff's *Es kommt der neue Photograph!* (1929). These two books formulated an alternative aesthetic and the social use of audiovisual media supported by many examples. These two books, along with the touring exhibition and the film programs, formed a veritable media offensive. Two other radical books were also published in 1929: Léon Moussinac's *Panoramique du cinéma* lobbied for – among other things – the foundation of an international library and cinémathèque to preserve the heritage of cinema; in the most important Dutch book on film theory prior to World War Two, *Cinema Militans*, Menno ter Braak argued for a cinema built on the parameters of rhythm and form. Only a year later, Paul Rotha of the London *Film Society* joined ranks with *The Film Till Now* (1930), which proved to be an influential film history well into the postwar era.[16] One can already sense a decisive shift from the immediate pre-1930 years when the radical transformation of cinema appeared imminent to contemporary observers while Rotha's book was one of the first concise histories of the cinema, testifying to the sense that the past was gaining ground on the future. A similar development took place in all of the avant-garde centres: Guido Bagier wrote on *Der kommende Film* in 1928, looking optimistically forward to sound cinema while Rudolf Arnheim's swan song for silent cinema *Film als Kunst* (1932) only a few years later cast a nostalgic glance back on that era. Béla Balázs' *Der Geist des Films* came out in 1930, while C.A. Lejeune's cautious collection *Cinema* was published in 1931, and Ilja Ehrenburg's influential novel *Die Traumfabrik* was translated into German in 1931. While these works in some respects still illustrate the period's enthusiasm and high hopes, they nevertheless also already display the fault lines along which the avant-garde began to diverge.[17] Some writers (Ehrenburg, Moussinac, Richter) believed in the revolutionary capacities of the cinema while others (ter Braak, Arnheim) were ultimately more interested in the formal parameters of film. However, for a short instant these preoccupations overlapped and the intersection of these two sectors formed the avant-garde. Lejeune worked as a film critic for British mainstream newspapers and argued in favour of an ambitious art cinema. Bagier was a protagonist for the introduction of sound in Germany supported by large capital interests (Siemens & Halske, AEG), but he also gave commissions for early sound films to Walter Ruttmann and founded a ciné-club with Hans Richter.

Nonetheless, possibly the most lasting impression was made by the many translations of Russian theory that were circulating during this time: a German edition of Pudovkin's *Filmregie und Filmmanuskript* became available in 1928 and an English one of *On Film Technique* in 1929 (the expanded version was translated by Montagu as *Film Technique and Film Acting* in 1933-35) and the release of Sergei Eisenstein's STAROE I NOVOE (SU 1926-29, › The Old and the New ‹) was accompanied by a German book, to mention only a few of the book-length studies.[18] The reception of Soviet theory is in many respects characterised by an » *Ungleichzeitigkeit* «, to borrow a term from Ernst Bloch, a seemingly temporal synchronicity which nevertheless testifies to an uneven development, to different states that coexisted at the same time. Dziga Vertov provides a good example of this paradox of temporality: Vertov was a pioneer of revolutionary filmmaking and groundbreaking theory in the early-1920s Soviet Union, but he only became known in the West in 1929 when he travelled extensively through Western Europe, giving lectures in major filmmaking and avant-garde centres and translations of his texts were published in important magazines. The reception of Soviet theory in the West was decidedly different from the Soviet reception because Vertov was being read there at a time when he was under attack from the increasingly conservative Soviet *nomenklatura*, but also from the young Turks of *Novy Lef*. This inverse perspective explains some of the peculiarities of the Western European reception. On the whole, one can read the development of the avant-garde via the publications: from their humble beginnings to an explosion of different magazines, the peak of which was reached when numerous translations of Soviet directors appeared circa 1930. After 1930, the stream became wider, but also steadier and calmer: whereas prior to film's radical novelty, the promise of its possibilities created a revolutionary furore. The 1930s showed a functional differentiation in which the amateur movement, the documentary movement, political filmmaking and other movements departed and the crossover potential that had pushed the avant-garde forward receded into the background.

4.2 Teaching

> *[The intention of the Bauhaus] is the intellectual and technical*
> *education of creative human beings for creative work,*
> *especially for building and fulfilling practical or experimental work,*
> *especially for building houses inside and out, as well as*
> *for the development of models for industry and handicraft.*
> Bauhaus (1926)[19]

Teaching film is a topic that has thus far not garnered much interest in film history. Certain institutions have produced brochures, books or texts on their own histories, but they are mostly self-celebratory and often produced on the occasion of anniversaries. Despite this neglect in film studies, I believe that teaching and vocational training formed an integral element of the avant-garde conception of restructuring the cinema: By creating a new generation of practitioners they would guarantee the sustained activities of the institutions and networks, by passing on ideas, the avant-garde strived for proliferation via the teacher. Quite logically, teaching should not be seen as a lesser job accepted only to increase one's status or to earn a living, but as an attempt to stabilise and sustain an alternative network of film culture. Teaching logically occupies a central position in this pursuit. Moreover, teaching also requires an active reflection on the practice that would otherwise often go unquestioned; thus, teaching reinforces the tendency to theorise and reflect upon the practices already inherent to the avant-garde. Teaching always presupposes a certain measure of self-reflexivity. In a systemic logic, teaching can be seen as a step towards the self-reflexive autopoeisis of the system. The constructive reproduction of the avant-garde position achieved through teaching could lead to the stabilisation and autonomy of the system. The more people were drawn to avant-garde convictions, the more support could be expected for the network of films, magazines, screening clubs and cinemas. Not coincidentally, it was in the Soviet Union that the first film school was founded – the avant-garde spirit of the revolutionary country was sure that the education of a new generation was of paramount importance in the construction of a communist reality.[20] Teaching in the Soviet Union not only began earlier and was undertaken in a more intensive manner than in other countries, it was also the most experimental in form: traditional hierarchies were toppled, conservative teaching methods were discarded and radical forms were put to the test. Teaching methods modelled on project work or workshop situation fit in especially well within the avant-garde conceptions of overcoming distinctions between theory and practice.

In France, (cycles of) lectures were a mainstay of the flourishing scene of ciné-clubs that developed at first in Paris and later spread throughout the country.

While the orientation of many of the societies was not teaching per se, conferences (i.e., extended introductions to films or evaluations afterwards) soon
evolved into lecture cycles that could be classified as attempts to systematise
and mediate ideas and conceptions about cinema. The first major series of lectures was held in conjunction with the exhibition » L'Exposition de l'art dans le
cinéma français « at the *Musée Galliera* in May and June of 1924, while a second
series was held in October 1924. Talks were given by central figures of the
avant-garde scene such as Léon Moussinac, Marcel L'Herbier, Jaque Catelain,
Robert Mallet-Stevens, Jean Epstein and others.[21] A year later, the new *Ciné-
club de France* organised a lecture cycle at the recently opened *Théâtre du Vieux
Colombier* from 28 November 1925 to 20 February 1926, with a similar cast of
speakers: Jean Epstein, Jean Tédesco, Germaine Dulac and Marcel L'Herbier.[22]
Contrary to commercial cinema which sold the cinema experience as such, the
avant-garde created a whole system with magazines and lectures forming an
integral part of a new kind of cinema. However, with the possible exception of
Moussinac's *Les Amis de Spartacus*, the French institutions were not radical in
their teaching methods. Lectures and other formats of frontal teaching rein-
forced the hierarchy between teacher and student and a situation in which
knowledge originates form a figure of authority, which was contrary to avant-
garde ideals.

Within the circles of the European avant-garde of the 1920s, the *Bauhaus* was
probably the institution that went the furthest towards the realisation of crucial
avant-garde ideals: breaking down the distinction between life and art (working
and living spaces merged in Gropius' building in Dessau), tearing down the
separation between the arts, overcoming the limitations of the studio, putting
ideas into practice (in Gropius' settlement Dessau-Törten and his *Arbeitsamt* as
well as in Hannes Meyer's *Laubenganghäuser*) and linking the production of art-
work and craft work with teaching and debating, theorising and publishing
(*Bauhaus-Bücher*). In the *Bauhaus*, this impulse of turning an aesthetic revolution
into a social revolution was strong, however, in retrospect it was only really
utopian in the few years of the Weimar Republic when a relative stability (1924-
29) allowed it to prosper in Dessau. The dual teaching system of combining
craftsmanship and art that was intended to overcome the distinctions between
theory and practice, creativity and technique, and form and content.[23] In this
respect, the *Bauhaus* was one of the few attempts for the realisation of avant-
garde ideas during a certain period of time, in a specific place and with a relatively stable group of people. Crucially, the *Bauhaus* adopted the metaphor of
the laboratory in which teaching (and research) was an integral part of cultural
development.

Talking more specifically about film, László Moholy-Nagy was the key figure
who worked in both photography and cinema at the *Bauhaus*. Originally hired

in March 1922 as the successor of Johannes Itten, Moholy-Nagy was to give the general introductory course (» Vorkurs «) and become director of the metal workshop. He later began teaching photography and was also responsible for the film activities at the *Bauhaus*. Yet, practical film work only happened periodically because the *Bauhaus* never managed to establish a veritable film workshop, which is one of the reasons why Moholy-Nagy moved to Berlin in 1928 to pursue filmmaking.[24] Film activities took place within the context of the institution at irregular intervals, for example, the screening of a film program upon the occasion of the opening of the famous Gropius building in Dessau. This new complex of connected buildings had an auditorium equipped for cinema and the program consisted of documentary and educational films.[25]

Moholy-Nagy's influential treatise on painting, photography and film was published at the *Bauhaus* in its celebrated series of books.[26] In 1930, two years after Moholy-Nagy had departed from the *Bauhaus*, then-director Hannes Meyer reported to the mayor of Dessau that he had secured Dziga Vertov and Hans Richter as teachers.[27] However, before the course even started that same year, the institution had to abandon Dessau for political reasons because the Nazis became part of Dessau's city government and cancelled the financial and organisational support which led to Meyer's resigning as director. The *Bauhaus* was continued by Mies van der Rohe in Berlin with a strong focus on architecture, which meant that regular work in the Bauhaus on cinema did not materialise.

In the mid-1920s, while still at the *Bauhaus*, Moholy-Nagy was still hoping the film industry would sponsor an experimental film school:

> My and our investment will find its structure in ideas, suggestions, plans, › manuscripts ‹, theories. It shall be the issue of the others, let us say of the industry, to invest on the other side: namely by making the means accessible where one can expect something. To expect that is the task of the sustaining factors and where evidence has already been produced, there remains no challenge.[28]

The turn from the utopian attempt to reconcile art and life towards a more functionalist and pragmatic approach is apparent in the transition from the *Bauhaus'* initial dogma of a » Synthese von Kunst und Handwerk am Bau « (1919, » The synthesis of art and handicraft in building «) to the new slogan » Kunst und Technik – eine neue Einheit « (1923, » Art and technology – a new unity «). On the one hand, this turn illustrates a new realism which no longer hoped for an esoteric new human being and clearly accepted the facts, but on the other, it also ran the risk of falling victim to an ideology of pure efficiency devoid of utopian expectations. One possible solution was to view functionalism not as the soulless dictatorship of efficiency, but to reconfigure functionalism as including the human emotional and affective aspects of the individual.[29]

For an understanding of the avant-garde it is crucial to see that teaching comprised a major part of their total strategy. Moholy-Nagy traversed all of the traditional borders between the arts: he worked in painting and photography, film and sculpture, typography and graphic design, scenography and shop window and exhibition design. However, and maybe above all, he was a theoretician and a teacher who in true avant-garde fashion never separated artistic production from vocational work or theorising. He taught all of his life at various institutions, most famously at the *Bauhaus*, but also in England and the United States:

> In 1929, he asked those responsible in the government and the community to withdraw from painting academies and instead establish › light studios ‹ where teachers and students could learn to examine and master the – in his opinion – most modern design form of design of its time. Eight years later in exile in London, he returned to this suggestion. Meanwhile, the name for the teaching facility, the › Academy of Light ‹, had become much more ambitious. In 1939, he finally introduced a mandatory class › Light Atelier ‹ for his students at the › School of Design ‹ in Chicago which he had established.[30]

Moholy-Nagy called on the state to establish studios, schools or workshops for educational and experimental purposes – the question of in/dependence was not only hotly debated within film circles, but formed a key issue for the constructivist avant-garde as a whole which aimed at a transformation of life and art and tried to address a wider public by going into sectors of industrial design. Thus, the problem arose to whom the avant-garde should turn as a sponsor and source of income.

Important teaching activities often took place within the framework of film societies. In November-December of 1929, Sergei Eisenstein and Hans Richter gave a three-week course at the Film Society Study Group, a subdivision of the London *Film Society*. Hans Richter has retrospectively remembered this workshop:

> Ivor Montagu, the nephew of the director of the Bank of England, who had also been at the La Sarraz meeting, invited Eisenstein to give lectures at the Film Society that Montagu led. (He asked me to do a workshop there.) In the meantime, Montagu attempted to set up a Hollywood engagement for Eisenstein, thereby providing him with adequate production possibilities outside the Soviet Union. The speeches were attended enthusiastically by those who later rose to fame in British film production circles especially in the field of documentary productions.[31]

Eisenstein lectured in English, while Richter shot a short film with the students, EVERYDAY (GB 1929/1975), which, however, was only completed in the 1970s. Among the participants at the workshop were later prominent figures of the

British documentary movement such as Basil Wright, Mark Segal, Lionel Britton, Michael Hankinson and Len Lye. Six lectures were given by Eisenstein from 19 to 29 November 1929 on the following topics: script technique, montage and rapid editing, conflict and resolution, first form of expression: psychology, second form of expression: montage, third form of expression: allegory.[32] In Britain, vocational activity and filmmaking were perhaps as closely intertwined as it was in the Soviet Union. John Grierson, for example, did not operate his film units with the ambition of becoming a » director « or even an » artist « in the conventional sense. He wanted to firmly establish film as a medium of persuasion and reform, run a state-sponsored agency and offer training to young activists. In fact, a contemporary observer like the *émigré* photographer Wolfgang Suschitzky remembers Grierson and Rotha not so much as filmmakers, but primarily as teachers:

> Both wanted to teach, I believe. Grierson was an academic and surrounded himself with people from Cambridge and Oxford. He had little knowledge of film and learned all he knew about film through practical work. ... Grierson and Rotha wanted to enlighten the people in this country about poverty, medicine and health. Rotha wrote several books. ... He was a film theorist. For example, he wrote about Russian films that were totally unknown here in England because they were censored. Still, we had the possibility to see some films by Vertov, Pudovkin and Eisenstein in private screenings. There was a film club and a movie theatre on Regent Street that showed imported Russian films.[33]

When John Grierson set up his film unit, one of his first activities was to introduce regular screenings of films made outside of the Empire Marketing Board. On the one hand, this helped Grierson to shape his ideas of how propaganda was dealt with in other countries, on the other, it also provided illustrative material for the aspiring filmmakers in Grierson's unit. Grierson himself described these viewing sessions:

> [W]e must have seen every propaganda film in existence between Moscow and Washington. We certainly prepared the first surveys of the propaganda and educational services of the principal Governments. We ran, too, a school of cinema where all the films we thought had a bearing on our problem were brought together and demonstrated in whole or part, for the instruction of Whitehall.... We had all the documentaries and epics worth a damn; though, in calculation of our audience, we had perforce to change a few endings and consider some of the close-ups among the less forceful arguments.[34]

The films being screened resemble a typical film society program: a handful of the German and French avant-garde and abstract classics (Walter Ruttmann,

Alberto Cavalcanti) were mixed in with many of the Soviet montage films plus Robert Flaherty's films, which were especially significant for Grierson.

In Germany, the left-wing *Volksfilmverband* organised several courses on film topics: the first issue of the society's new organ, *Film und Volk*, announced a film course by Béla Balázs that was accompanied by screenings and ran over several Sundays.[35] The theatre innovator Erwin Piscator had pioneered the use of projected film in his theatre shows in the 1920s[36], on which George Grosz, Curt Oertel, Walter Ruttmann, Leo Lania, Svend Noldan, László Moholy-Nagy, Albrecht Viktor Blum and others collaborated.[37] In 1929, he initiated a school for theatre and film in Berlin with the intention of educating a new generation of theatre workers while at the same time acting as a laboratory for his many theatre projects. With the introduction of sound film, Piscator saw an increased influence of the theatre on the cinema. László Moholy-Nagy, Béla Balázs, Carl Oertel, Guttmann, Hanns Eisler, Leo Lania were the teachers of the film section.[38] Many other avant-garde activists were also active educators. In Paris, Germaine Dulac taught film at the *Ecole Technique de Photographie et de Cinématographie* in the 1930s.[39]

Despite these crucial teaching activities in France, Germany, England, the Netherlands and other Western countries the hotbed of teaching was the Soviet Union in terms of both intensity and innovation. Vance Kepley has examined the workshop of Lev Kuleshov in more detail which was characterised by three interrelated aspects: » an interest in the precision of science ... the social influence of modern industrial practice ... [and] the tradition of pragmatism in pedagogy «.[40] In fact, education was a crucial factor after the Bolsheviks seized power because they realised that the future of the revolution depended on a re-education of both an elite who would lead the country, and the masses who worked on the farms and factories who would ensure the Soviet Union's progress. Thus, while cinema played a central role in the education of the masses who were partly analphabetic, it also introduced novel methods of persuasion. Filmmaking, however, would be advanced by educating a new generation of practitioners who would carry on the task of creating a truly Soviet cinema. From this perspective, cinema first and foremost has an instructional value that in turn gives rise to its social use value. Aesthetic experiments are, in this perspective, neither an end in themselves nor a category of appreciation, but only necessary insofar as the new times required a new style for creating a new man. Not surprisingly then, many of the most valued Soviet filmmakers (including Kuleshov, Eisenstein, Pudovkin and Vertov) devoted considerable parts of their careers to teaching and developing the State Film Institute (the first of its kind) – an activity that would be quite unthinkable in Hollywood in any period of its history. In Hollywood, most directors only start teaching, if ever at all, after they retire from active filmmaking. In traditional historiography teaching has often been interpreted as a retreat from the heavily policed public sphere of the Stalinist 1930s. Yet, this is hardly convincing since it remains doubtful whether the education of the next generation for the state would have been seen as a less political activity than the actual making of films. If those activists denounced as » formalists « were considered completely unreliable (i.e., if indeed that was the reason why the directors were » not allowed « to make films anymore), one would have hardly trusted them to educate the next generation of filmmakers. I prefer to believe that the more experimental work of the 1920s was seen in the following decade as a necessary yet passing phase and that those in the forefront of the 1920s developments remained useful, however in other functions. Thus, education served as a suitable field for this first wave of innovators of the Soviet cinema as they could communicate the revolutionary fervour of the first decade of Soviet cinema to students.

The Moscow-based State Film Institute (GTK) has often been called the first film school in the world. Even though there were simultaneous activities in Petrograd, these proved to be rather short-lived courses while the State Film Institute had a lasting influence on further developments in the teaching of film. It was founded in 1919 when the authorities realised that the majority of the experts of Tsarist cinema had fled the country and that specialists were badly needed in all technical aspects of filmmaking. In an effort to make the education of those specialists efficient and centralised, Vladimir Gardin was appointed to develop such a film school, which started classes in the summer of 1919.[41] Despite the revolutionary utopianism of the early Soviet Union, the atmosphere at the State Film Institute has been characterised as a » spirit of pragmatism «[42]. While this may be true, the attention to project work, problem solving and hands-on learning also corresponded with avant-garde ideals of the artist-engineer. Over the course of the 1920s, the improvised vocational school developed into an established institute of higher education (the Soviet version of a university). Simultaneously, the emphasis of teaching shifted from hands-on project work to a more formalised and abstract academic training. Estimates as to the success of this undertaking vary widely. Some have lauded the installation of the school and its innovative approaches to teaching while others have pointed out the practical problems resulting from a lack of funds and experience.[43]

A crucial element in the early years of the school was Kuleshov's workshop which was active from 1922 to 1926. In these courses Kuleshov tried to break with old teaching methods:

> In Kuleshov's application of project teaching, research and training went hand-in-hand. There was no scholastic tradition to be passed on but a new field, cinema, to be explored by teacher and student alike. ... Classes ignored most tried academic rituals. ... No formal grades were ever issued. ... A sense of shared responsibility governed the classes.[44]

Kuleshov and his students started staging » films without film «, turning necessity into advantage as no film material was available at the time and the workshop was attempting to emulate editing and rapid scene transition on a theatre stage. These productions can be seen as » a scientific inquiry into the nature of cinema ... as a de facto laboratory: [Pudovkin] consciously imitated the rituals and rhetoric of science to justify his theoretical claims. «[45] The » films without film « also followed the wider cultural logic of the Soviet Union before the first Five-Year-Plan came into effect: the arts were able to open upon a utopian field on which the hope of future development could be projected. The reality was so shockingly desolate that it could not serve as a measuring stick anyway, wildly futuristic ideas could be tried out. Just as architects were drawing up plans that would never be realised, Kuleshov's workshop staged films that were never (meant to be) shot. The strategy discernible in the Soviet film school serves to illustrate the multi-level approach that the avant-garde took: making different films was just one element, the main purpose was to make films differently – to restructure the institution cinema, especially the relationship between spectator and film.

The State Film Institute was founded as a *tekhnikum*, a practical school for vocational training organised around workshops and practical work. Within the four-year teaching period, students worked closely with mentors – most of the big names of Soviet cinema at one time or another taught at the school – and were also involved in production work outside the school context. While this scheme grew partly out of necessity, it also illustrates an approach to cinema that combines intellectual development with practical work. After several restructuring efforts in the 1920s under the direct influence of Lunarcharski, the school became more of an academic institute, but what remained from the initial spirit was the proximity of filmmakers to the institute. In 1932, Eisenstein was added as a permanent member to the school's faculty and he brought many collaborators with him like Esfir Shub who led the editing section in Eisenstein's directing classes. At the same time that it was recognised that film required a wide context the film archive was established. The GTK founded its *cinémathèque* in 1931, starting with a collection of 500 Soviet and foreign films. In 1932, an » Office for the History of Soviet Film « was founded. Finally in 1934, Nikolai Lebedev, a film historian, was appointed the head of the institution, marking the increased status of history, archive and canon in the Soviet context – but also remaining in tune with developments in other countries. It was this functional differentiation into film history, vocational film education, archiving, screening alternative films and cinema in the service of the national interest that is characteristic of the 1930s.[46]

4.3   Event Culture: Exhibitions, Conferences, Festival

> ... *at La Sarraz, it was the weapons that were in question,*
> *quick and meticulous, a general mobilization of all industrious units,*
> *preparations of plans for the campaign aimed at securing*
> *the artistic film's place in the sun and providing audiences*
> *in obscure cinemas at least one meal per week.*
> Freddy Chevalley (1929)[47]

While the formation of a steady base of subscribing supporters and regular screening activities was instrumental for the creation of an alternative cinema culture, another necessary activity for the construction of an international network was the organisation of events which could unite many different kinds of activists while also mobilising an audience and creating a public sphere. These events can be seen as trial runs for a different kind of cinema culture: as long as the film societies, with their local constituencies, their logistic, financial and organisational limitations in the procurement of films and guests and their relatively long breaks between activities could at best achieve a limited success, special events were organised to create temporary utopias. The meeting in La Sarraz (and to a lesser degree, the exhibition in Stuttgart) in particular can be seen as trial runs for an avant-garde future in which films were integrated into life and the avant-garde would have broad base of international support. Some of these events were planned and executed by the film industry and they offered the avant-garde a sidebar or a specific section where they could gather within a larger context, sometimes – as in the cases of the events in Stuttgart or La Sarraz – they were specifically organised by and for the avant-garde. The events I will discuss here were even more trans-national than the film clubs because they were intended for international audiences and their event character motivated many key figures of the film avant-garde to participate.

One of the first formats used besides screening clubs were exhibitions, which had an important function as they could draw together more energy at a specific place and for a limited period of time than could be generated in (ir)regular weekly or monthly activities. Exhibitions were nodes that focused energy, crossroads where biographical, stylistic and national paths crossed as well as showcases in which a wider public was addressed than that those who normally attended the film societies. Moreover, exhibitions lent important support for the legitimisation of film as an accepted art form. By emulating strategies typical of the visual arts, cinema attempted to increase its status as an art form. Not surprisingly, France with its intellectual and artistic scene, was the pacemaker as far as exhibitions were concerned. The ciné-club run by Ricciotto Canudo, *Club des amis du septième art* (*CASA*), was frequented by artists and intellectuals. This

organisation was able to include film programs and lectures on film in the pres-
tigous *Salon d'Automne*, an annual visual arts exhibition. For three years, from
1921 to 1924, the film program ran back to back with the exhibition and film
fragments often accompanied the lectures, making this event a pioneer in early
teaching activity as well. The increasing convergence of various ciné-clubs and
the generally favourable devotion to the cinema among Parisian intellectual circles led to the » Exposition de l'art dans le cinéma français «, a major exhibition
on cinema that ran from May through October 1924 at the *Musée Galliera*.[48]

The situation in Germany was markedly different: while in France the avant-
garde movement clearly emerged from the ranks of intellectuals and artists in
both literature and the visual arts, the proximity of the avant-garde and the
industry in Germany was much closer than in other countries. In retrospect, it
is difficult to judge whether this was a cause or an effect of the way the German
avant-garde oriented itself towards constructivism, just as French filmmaking
was inspired by concepts such as *photogénie* and lyrical or musical analogies.[49]
Exhibitions in Germany were characterised by a relatively strong film industry
presence (compared to France) that occasionally crossed over into avant-garde
circles. One regular event was the *Funkausstellung* (radio communication exhibition) which took place annually in Berlin from 1924 onwards. At the 5th edition
in 1928, the year in which the first experimental television transmission was
presented, the premiere of Ruttmann's early experimental sound film
DEUTSCHE WELLE – TÖNENDER RUNDFUNK (GER 1928) took place within the
context of the exhibition. The film was a cross-section of images from German
cities explaining how the new radio system worked. The *Funkaustellung* in general was intended to the convergence of radio, television, and (sound) film, but
because it was a consumer-oriented show it was dominated by the industry.[50]

A big event that in some ways foreshadowed later developments was the
Kino- und Photoausstellung (Kipho) in Berlin, from 25 September to 5 October
1925. The exhibition mixed technical, economic, social, educational and artistic
concerns and proved to be a huge audience success, drawing approximately
100,000 spectators. The exhibition itself shows a mixed approach similar to the
concept of the *Funkausstellung* (a consumer show that basically served as a
ready-made showcase for the industry's new products) and more artistically
minded conferences. The *Kipho* was characterised by conflicting interests and
unsuccessful meetings, which made it a singular event because it ultimately
lacked a clear focus. It attempted to cater to both the industry and the masses
and it was interested in artistic and educational as well as economic and cultural matters. Even though it drew an enormous number of visitors, the conference
nevertheless had a focus that was just too wide and thus it never led to a follow
up.

Probably the most famous avant-garde aspect of this event is Guido Seeber's short propaganda KIPHO-FILM for the exhibition which was screened as a trailer in regular cinemas. This film can be considered a milestone of the avant-garde as it symptomatically condenses many of the then crucial discourses in an allegory of its production. The film marked the beginning of co-operation between the avant-garde and the industry in a playful manner. The film also inaugurated the trend where avant-garde films advertised public events, such as the film that promoted the touring health exhibition *GeSoLei* (*Gesundheitspflege, Soziale Fürsorge, Leibesübungen*) put together by the Dresden Hygienemuseum, which had commissioned Walter Ruttmann's DER AUFSTIEG (GER 1926). There was also Hans Richter's film for the Swiss Werkbund which was made to support their exhibition DIE NEUE WOHNUNG (CH 1930).[51] Even though Seeber is a marginal figure in the avant-garde, the KIPHO FILM, which appeared at the beginning of avant-garde filmmaking in Germany, demonstrates the inextricable close proximity of the avant-garde to the industry. The film introduces an early trailer format using famous images combined with surprising tricks and montages: scenes from DAS CABINET DES DR. CALIGARI (GER 1919/20, Robert Wiene), WEGE ZU KRAFT UND SCHÖNHEIT (GER 1924/25, Wilhelm Prager), and DIE NIBELUNGEN (GER 1922-24, Fritz Lang) are combined in a splitscreen with a caricature of DER LETZTE MANN (GER 1924, F.W. Murnau) and Ottomar Anschütz' pre-cinematic device *Schnellseher*. At first, the screen was split kaleidoscopically into five fields with rapidly changing motifs showing scenes of film production: decorations being built, film being dried on gigantic drums, a gramophone playing during the shooting in the studio. Then a title announces » *Du musst...* « followed by a shot of Caligari outside his tent on a fairground as a barker, then the title » *...zur Kipho* « and another film clip showing the audience entering Caligari's tent. This short film satirises the famous modern campaign for the film on its initial cinema release in 1920 which had as its tag line » *Du musst ... Caligari werden* « (» You must become Caligari «). The KIPHO trailer evokes the transformative power of cinema not only in a highly self-reflexive way by using the paradigmatic status of certain scenes to present an image of the industry that produces these commodities. The short film also comments on the (alleged) origins of the cinema as a fairground attraction and ironically conjures up film's quasi-mystical power to transform itself while also exposing the steps in the production chain that are normally hidden from view and invisible in the finished product. The audience is invited into the tent (i.e., the exhibition) and there gains an exclusive behind-the-scenes view of filmmaking, which is the promise of this short film. The first section of the trailer shows the process of production in an almost constructivist fashion – prefiguring in some ways Dziga Vertov's later CELOVEK S KINOAPPARATOM (SU 1929)[52] – while the second section winks ironically at the overall impression that the finished film presents:

cinema is simultaneously an industrial product that consists of a number of separate steps in a production chain that can be isolated conceptually and visually, but it also overwhelms us like a magic trick, enchanting and fascinating
us just like the fairground crowd is lured into the tent and then hypnotised by
cinema's spec(tac)ular power. With cinema – the KIPHO-FILM seems to say – one
can have one's cake and eat it too. Cinema perfectly integrates the rational and
industrial product with irrational and hypnotising forces. In this way, the short
film echoes avant-garde preoccupations with the exploration of the fundamental basic tenets of the medium. Not coincidentally, Hans Richter included Seeber's film in his programmatic retrospective on the occasion of the 1929 *FiFo*
exhibition in Stuttgart.

Besides, the inclusion of scenes from DAS CABINET DES DR. CALIGARI was
anything but coincidental as the paradigmatic status of the film for the avant-
garde is hard to over-estimate and the same allegorical shortcut between mysti-
cal powers and modern technology mediated by avant-garde style is already
exhibited in CALIGARI itself.[53] Part of the success of the film relies on its power
to speak on multiple levels to multiple audiences: by borrowing visual tropes
and techniques from the visual arts, it promised to give an educated audience a
cinematic experience that would be elevated to the status of art. Meanwhile, by
borrowing motifs and narrative tricks from genres as sensationalist as the detective and fantasy genres, it offered a mass audience the thrills that had become
associated with the popular medium. To spectators outside Germany it provided an acceptable image of the erstwhile enemy, filtered through distorted
shapes and convoluted plots that satisfied assumptions people had about the
brooding and gloomy Germans.[54] It was not lost on contemporary observers
that this kind of film had transformed from a style in an art-historical sense to a
style of modernity, typical of fashion and advertising in only five years. Rudolf
Arnheim, upon the occasion of a revival of CALIGARI in October 1925 (possibly
on the occasion of the *Kipho*), remarked that the tag line » *Du musst Caligari werden* « (» You have to become Caligari «) only conjured up associations with the
cigarette advertising slogan » *Du darfst nur Walasco rauchen!* «[55] (» You may only
smoke Walasco! «). The cinema as medium and cultural force cannot be isolated
from the popular culture at large – therefore, style is always also fashion and
design. Seeber's trailer knowingly alluded to this multiplicity of levels on which
the avant-garde was operating.

The *Internationale Tentoonstelling op filmgebied* (› International Exhibition on
Film «), a conference similar to the *Kipho* was organised by the film industry
and the specialised press from 14 April to 15 May 1928 in Den Haag: with of
sound film presentations by Küchenmeister and Tri-Ergon.[56] Part of this fair
was an international conference on educational cinema, the *Internationale Leer-
film Conferentie.*[57] Maybe these events are best characterised as experimental ve-

nues for the exploration of how regular events could best deal with cinema. Andor Kraszna-Krausz has criticised these early attempts at exhibiting films for their concentration on the economic side of cinema: » the principal mistake of all such attempts was that they had tried to show the commercial side before all and left the nucleus of the craft in the shadows of the background. «[58] At least three models seem to overlap in these early exhibition formats pointing simultaneously forward and backward in time: First, these conferences copied World Fair formulas which lured a mass audience with their modern technological wonders. Second, these events catered to a trade fair audience mostly interested in the business aspects. Third, we have the film festivals that began to be developed as regular events in the course of the 1930s. It took several years until the various formats were established. The avant-garde contributed to the developments of the functional differentiation of the World Fair and the amusement park, the trade fair and the film festival, different formats that are still with us today.

Another important event that served as a forum for the presentation of experiments in the combining of image and music was the music festival *Festspiele Deutsche Kammermusik*. The director, experimental composer Paul Hindemith, had moved the festival from Donaueschingen to Baden-Baden. For a couple of seasons during this annual event, the film avant-garde rubbed shoulders with experimental composers, but they also found a ready-made audience that was accustomed to experimentation and innovative approaches, more open than an ordinary cinema audience. It was especially the years leading up to the introduction of sound film that cooperation intensified and every year experiments combining experimental films with experimental music were presented at the festival to a public interested in » new music «. The collaboration between avant-garde filmmakers and musicians began seriously in 1927 from 15 to 17 July. That year the festival presented one of Walter Ruttmann's Opus films with music by Hanns Eisler for two clarinets, trumpet and a string trio. The same film was presented twice with the same score: once played by a live orchestra present in the auditorium (synchronised with the support of Carl Robert Blum's *Musiksynchronometer*) and once with a light-sound copy from Tri-Ergon. Other films screened were Felix the Cat at the Circus (US 1926) with music by Paul Hindemith specifically composed for the Welte organ, an instrument often used in cinemas (also synchronised by Carl Robert Blum's *Musiksynchronometer*) and Sprechender Film (GER 1927, Guido Bagier).[59]

It was during the music festival in Baden-Baden in 1928 and 1929 that Hans Richter began working with Paul Hindemith.[60] Richter was commissioned to make a film in 1927 and he chose Hindemith to compose the music for his film. Thus, this film is also a commissioned work, but not in the service of the industry, but for an art market, much like today's *documenta* or *Biennale*. The festival in Baden-Baden was at the time interested in mechanical music, in film and in radio – a veritable *Medienverbund* was in the making which crossed the boundaries between the industry and the avant-garde. The lesson offered by these collaborations was not lost on the artists involved: by collaborating with composers, by getting used to the radio, by coping with mechanical devices (Blum's *Musiksynchronometer*) and with filmic synchronisation (Tobis was heavily involved in this) and by working with the film industry they transformed implicit hierarchies and categories and standard working procedures.

Hindemith wanted to develop original music for the mechanical organs and pianos that were in most of the large cinemas (Welte-Kinoorgeln). He was against traditional instruments or traditional tunes (from operetta, songs, etc.), but instead wanted to have mechanical music to accompany mechanical films. To that end, he used Carl Robert Blum's *Musiksynchronometer*, a machine used to synchronise the speed of the film with the speed of a musical notation scroll used to cue the musicians. Edmund Meisel had used this chronometer for his work on Ruttmann's BERLIN and Eisenstein's POTEMKIN. Darius Milhaud also worked with this device when he wrote music to accompany newsreels for the festival edition of 1928.[61] The film that Richter made for the festival in 1928, VORMITTAGSSPUK, is normally deemed important because it marks the shift for Richter from abstract to concrete representations and forms, the step from pure formal experiments to surrealism and a more immediate political engagement. In another perspective, this film could also be seen as a shift from a precarious independence to an engagement with the industry.

In 1929, Tobis produced the entire film program for the Baden-Baden festival which was to become a legendary event thanks to the premiere of Bertolt Brecht's and Kurt Weill's *Lindberghflug*.[62] With the introduction of sound imminent in the German cinemas, this move garnered much attention and the publicity gained for a festival that had for years catered only to a small, select audience of new music lovers was considerable.[63] Tobis's intentions, which had developed a hardware system, but desperately needed software (due to a » patents war « the American films could not be used) are easy to explain: Because they did not have an R&D department they employed avant-garde artists because commercial film personnel had no feel for experimentation. Richter claimed that it was » especially remarkable that the German sound film company Tobis has, on the occasion of the music festival at Baden-Baden on 25 July, prepared a number of sound films that deal with sound film as an artistic problem. «[64] Besides Richter's VORMITTAGSSPUK (GER 1927-28), Richter's ALLES DREHT SICH, ALLES BEWEGT SICH (GER 1929) with music by Walter Gronostay premiered at the 1929 festival.[65] Moreover, Alberto Cavalcanti's LA P'TITE LILLI (FR 1927-28) with music by Darius Milhaud was also screened. Collaborations that began here resulted in longer collaborations. Richter and Milhaud later worked together for Philips on HALLO EVERYBODY (NL 1933) and for Central-film in Zürich on DIE EROBERUNG DES HIMMELS (CH 1938), Gronostay and Richter for Philips as well on EUROPA RADIO (NL 1931). The festival actually took place between the Stuttgart exhibition and the La Sarraz meeting, so a line could be drawn between the three events of that summer. In fact, in his book on the Stuttgart exhibition *Filmgegner von heute – Filmfreunde von morgen* Richter claimed that film composers wished that sound would eventually find its place within the machinery of cinema: »Sound can be noise, tone or speech – however, it only becomes sensible in film, if it has its own place in an artistic master plan.«[66] This might hint at conceptions of *Medienverbund* much more than *Gesamtkunstwerk*, a constructivist and piecemeal approach to the components that operate independently towards a common goal rather than an overarching scheme of romantic wholeness in which everything is subjected to one big totality. It was less a total vision of one concept subordinating everything than an organisation of independent networks working towards a common goal, each keeping their (relative) autonomy.

The first comprehensive retrospective of the 1920s avant-garde took place as early as 1929. The exhibition organised by the *Werkbund* in Stuttgart on film and photography with its film program curated by Hans Richter and featuring an appearance by Dziga Vertov can be seen – along with La Sarraz – as the apotheosis of the avant-garde, but it must also be considered the turning point when development went in a different direction. The two most decisive events both took place in the summer of 1929, less than 300 km apart (Stuttgart and La Sarraz) and temporally within three months (mid-June and early September respectively). The *Werkbund* exhibition »Film und Foto« in the summer of 1929 in Stuttgart was an epoch-making event. There had been a number of earlier exhibitions on cinema and modern photography, but the *FiFo* was the first to concentrate on the artistic and cultural side of the medium, not being (co-)organised by the industry.[67] The 1925 Berlin-*Kipho*, for example, addressed film as art, but it was largely an exhibition dominated (and organised) by the industry, and thus still had the character of a trade fair. Moreover, Stuttgart had the advantage of timing because by the end of the 1920s the *Neue Sachlichkeit* trend had become accepted at least by a part of the general public, and so the exhibition was also a place to collect material from Germany and abroad, much of which was seen here for the first time together and contextualised, effectively turning the photography exhibition into a retrospective. The announcements for the *FiFo* in the specialised press from early 1929 onwards verify much interest in the event, in Germany, but more importantly, all over Europe. Famous names curated national sections – El Lissitzky, the tireless propagandist of Soviet revolutionary art and culture, coordinated the Russian section while Piet

Zwart was in charge of the Dutch contribution – and many groups and institutions were prepared well in advance of the opening.[68]

The photography exhibition at the *Neue Städtische Ausstellungshalle* ran from 18 May to 7 July 1929.[69] The exhibition took up thirteen rooms and was intended to offer an overview of contemporary trends in photography. László Moholy-Nagy accepted the task of curating the first room which was designed to present an overview of the development of photography up to the 1920s. The remaining twelve rooms were organised by nationality. Unlike earlier photographic exhibitions, the *FiFo* had installed a jury with no professional photographers in order to break away from the household names found in industrial photography.[70] The film section consisted of 15-film programs curated by Hans Richter and shown from 13 to 26 June 1929 at the Königsbau-Lichtspiele in Stuttgart.[71] The films were selected according to three focal points: 1. Master works of cinematic production; 2. Advances of the avant-garde; 3. Soviet features and documentaries.[72] Two of the most striking features of Richter's film program were the inclusion of CHICAGO (US 1927, Frank Urson), a Cecil B. DeMille production that is today largely forgotten, and the absence of Luis Buñuel's and Salvador Dalí's UN CHIEN ANDALOU (FR 1928) which was not being screened. Considering how well connected Richter was and how carefully chosen the program was, it is hard to believe that it could have been an oversight. Jan-Christopher Horak has argued that the film lacked a concept of film language (as developed by Richter) and was excluded for that reason.[73]

Dziga Vertov participated as the Soviet delegate. The only other lecture or conference apart from the opening night (with addresses by Geheimrat Dr. Peter Bruckmann, Heilbronn, Hans Richter on behalf of the film avant-garde and Friedrich Kurt, Stuttgart, on behalf of the *Werkbund*[74]) was given by Dr. Edgar Beyfuss of the Ufa-*Kulturfilmabteilung*, a fixture in German avant-garde circles who had already participated in the organisation of the matinee » Der absolute Film « in 1925. Even though Beyfuss was well-established within these circles, it is still interesting that Beyfuss was chosen over the likes of René Clair, Walter Ruttmann, Alberto Cavalcanti or some of the other protagonists in the European avant-garde movement. A possible explanation would be to point out Richter's tireless self-promotion as an artist, theoretician and organiser (appearing in Stuttgart as filmmaker, curator, *conférencier* and author of the quasi-catalogue *Filmgegner von heute – Filmfreunde von morgen*) which would preclude the inclusion of too many other big names. However, observed from a different perspective, Beyfuss' importance, at least in the German context, remains under-estimated. His central position is underscored by the significance of Ufa's support of the avant-garde. After all, it was Ufa that helped out Richter and Eggeling in 1920 in designing a short animation sequence (and thus started the brief blossoming of *absoluter Film* in Germany), it was Beyfuss who first screened Hans

Richter's films in a cinema in Germany when he presented the matinee *Der absolute Film* in 1925 (with Beyfuss as a *conférencier*). One can also speculate that Beyfuss had a hand in Richter's commission for INFLATION (GER 1928) as the opener to the Ufa production DIE DAME MIT DER MASKE (GER 1928, Wilhelm Thiele). Besides underlining the often-overlooked importance of Ufa to the German avant-garde (Walter Ruttmann had also received early, crucial assignments from Ufa such as the » dream of the falcon « sequence in Fritz Lang's DIE NIBE-LUNGEN, GER 1922-24), it is possible (but speculative) that Richter was merely repaying a favour. Beyfuss (in his capacity as a Ufa employee) should be considered a hidden protagonist of the avant-garde: his film WUNDER DES FILMS was also included in the Stuttgart program. Moreover, Beyfuss' lecture was presented in conjunction with an avant-garde program that introduced a selection of now-classic works by Eggeling, Richter, Ruttmann, Clair, Cavalcanti, Chomette, Man Ray and others.[75] Whatever Beyfuss' real function may have been, the fact that he was chosen over an avant-garde artist must be considered crucial and has until now been overlooked.

When the *FiFo* conference opened in Stuttgart, other cities lined up to host the exhibition after Stuttgart. A travelling exhibition of the photo section, smaller than the original Stuttgart collection, was subsequently exhibited in Zürich, Danzig, Vienna, Munich, Tokyo, Osaka and Berlin, often accompanied by film screenings.[76] In Berlin, the lack of space meant that only half of the already small show was exhibited.[77] The exhibition opened on 19 October 1929 in the courtyard of the former *Kunstgewerbemuseum* (today: *Martin-Gropius-Bau*) and ran for one month until 19 November.[78] A film program was quickly assembled to be presented in five matinees consisting of mostly new material at the *Capitol* and a programme of classics at the repertory cinema, the *Kamera*.[79] By changing from a singular event into a travelling exhibition the *FiFo* attempted to overcome the limitations of a spatially and temporally circumscribed situation characteristic of an event. On the one hand, this attempt failed because the exhibition was rather the crowning achievement of a development than the launching pad for future activities. Genealogically, it arose at the same time as film festivals and film exhibitions. Triumph and defeat were, as is so often the case with the dialectics of the avant-garde, two sides of the same coin.

La Sarraz rightfully occupies a central position among the European avant-garde of the interwar period for a couple of reasons: It was the only time that so many of the movement's protagonists were assembled in one place at one time[80]. In terms of timing, La Sarraz came at exactly the right moment in early September 1929. Many key figures were present either in Stuttgart or in La Sarraz or both: Ruttmann, Richter, Balázs, Moussinac, Eisenstein, Vertov and Cavalcanti. During the La Sarraz meeting films were shown, one film was actually shot there, lectures were given, and discussions were held. Like Stuttgart, it was an event from which the industry was conspicuously absent.[81] But in the long run this proved to be a problem since the avant-garde needed the industry as much as the other way around. Nevertheless, many contemporaries thought the transnational avant-garde was on the verge of its breakthrough, even if La Sarraz marked the peak of the 1920s developments, which all went in a very different direction in the 1930s.[82] Some problems and fissures became more obvious in La Sarraz: Hans Richter objected to the fact that G.W. Pabst had been invited (he declined the invitation) because Richter thought Pabst worked for the industry and was not a true independent filmmaker. This, in turn, was used against Richter in an article on La Sarraz published in *Close Up* (their not-so-secret champion was Pabst), which accused Richter of unnecessarily limiting the avant-garde to abstract cinema.[83] Again, the implicit aporias of the avant-garde came to the fore and showed that the superficial unity was nothing but self-deception. Even at the critical *Congres International du Cinéma Indépendent* (CICI) the glue that held the avant-garde together showed its weaknesses and fissures, many of which were already apparent to the keener observers.

In 1930 things had already begun to change: The successor to La Sarraz was a conference in Brussels (*2e Congres International du Cinéma Indépendent et Moderne – CICIM*) which took place from 27 November to 2 December 1930 at the Palais des Beaux Arts.[84] Following the high hopes and the enthusiasm of the previous year in Stuttgart and La Sarraz, the Brussels meeting was at the time often perceived to be a failure.[85] The films screened in Brussels attest to the trouble the avant-garde had in securing commissions for sound films. Among those present were Robert Aron, Jean Painlevé and Gustave Cauvin from Paris, Carl Vincent from Brussels, Hans Richter from Berlin, Jiminez Caballero from Spain, Kenneth MacPherson presenting BORDERLINE, and Helene de Mandrot, the host of the first congress at La Sarraz.[86] Of the approximately two dozen films shown on this occasion only three were sound films: King Vidor's HALLELUJAH (US 1929) and THUNDER (US 1929), a tribute to the recently deceased Lon Chaney, neither of which were shown in their entirety, but only as excerpts. Walter Ruttmann's MELODIE DER WELT (GER 1928/29), the only sound film available that could qualify as avant-garde, was screened in its entirety. However, in subsequent years, interesting experimental work with sound film emerged from the avant-garde. Thus, it was neither sound film nor the economic grip of the industry that prevented the development of the avant-garde. The first plans for a third conference in Berlin for May 1932 were already being made a few weeks after the conference in Brussels, but the plan never materialised.[87]

Issues other than sound also came compellingly to the fore . The delegates in Brussels dissolved the League of Independent Cinema, which had been established only a year earlier at La Sarraz and founded a new organisation, the *As-*

sociation des artistes et écrivains révolutionnaires (AEAR), the main goal of which was to resist the rising tide of fascism in Europe. The Italian (Enrico Prampolino) and Spanish (Juan Piqueraz) delegates objected , as they had moved into the camps of Mussolini and the Falangista respectively. This political rift became an obviously unbridgeable one and the conflict only intensified during the course of the 1930s. The dissent between left-wing and right-wing activists was not the only rift; more subtle differences arose within the political left: The affair around the 3-GROSCHEN-OPER (which premiered on 19 February 1931) with Bertolt Brecht and Kurt Weill on one side, and Belá Balázs, G.W. Pabst and producer Nebenzal on the other was a symptom of mutating political alliances. These opponents in court had only shortly before been struggling for similar goals in the 1920s. Another classic case was the public and heated debate where Sergei Eisenstein accused Béla Bálasz of valuing the individual shot more than the montage and of adhering to an overtly traditional aesthetic conception of realism. They were basically on the same side politically as communist party members.[88] For a loosely constructivist avant-garde like the Soviet filmmakers the value of art was in the combination of elements, in the construction and montage of sections of film – and not in the elements themselves which were only building blocks. Another classic example is the debate between Siegfried Kracauer and Walter Ruttmann. Even though Ruttmann was one of the most successful filmmakers in the second half of the 1920s Kracauer continually scolded him for his lack of political engagement, for his reliance on formal relations instead of looking at social dependencies and for his general disinterestedness.[89] Kracauer makes his point perhaps most forcefully in his comparison of Vertov and Ruttmann:

> While Ruttmann's associations are purely formal – he seems to be satisfied with superficial and unclear links in his sound films – through montage Wertow gains meaning and connection between the pieces of reality. Ruttmann puts them side-by-side without explaining them; Wertow interprets by representing.[90]

Politically, institutionally and aesthetically alliances that once seemed promising and rich began to seem suddenly very unstable.[91]

However, on another note, the Brussels meeting can be viewed as a point of divergence but this was not at all obvious to contemporaries because they were naturally looking for details that were already familiar to them. When comparing the films that were screened in Brussels to those shown at La Sarraz there was a tendency to shift away from formal experimentation and towards a greater engagement with the social or political context.[92] Brussels also continued the convergence of the avant-garde and the industry on several levels: Hans Richter, for example, worked mainly on industry commissions in the 1930s, particularly promotional films, while his rival and companion Walter Ruttmann continued his work in Nazi Germany. Some filmmakers like Joris Ivens and Henri Storck turned to radical and independent films that were largely free of formal experiments and modelled on agit-prop works. Germaine Dulac, pioneer of the French avant-garde in the early 1920s, had found employment within the French industry and attended the Brussels conference to recruit avant-garde activists to work for her in the industry:

> The presence of Germaine Dulac, director of one of the largest French production houses, Gaumont-Franco-Film-Aubert (GFFA), who supported the 1930s generation of cineastes, was emblematic of the confluence with the commercial cinema. It was at Brussels effectively that she hired Vigo for directing Taris (1931) as well as Henri Storck, chosen as assistant by Pierre Billon at the Studio Buttes-Chaumont. [93]

Dulac's itinerary and movements between avant-garde and the industry demonstrates how unstable the categories and labels were: Even today, Dulac is still mainly remembered for her most experimental works, La souriante Madame Beudet (FR 1923) and La coquille et le clergyman (FR 1927), which achieved notoriety when the surrealists disrupted the premiere. But again, she theorised and taught, she made commercial and industrial films, she was in charge of the French society of ciné-clubs and she recruited avant-garde filmmakers to work for the industry.

4.4   The Myth of Total Cinema

> *The most modern have already threatened to project*
> *reflective games in the sky, instead of painting or drawing.*
> *This light cone is perhaps a graphic page*
> *from the future book of art history.*
> Rudolf Arnheim (1927)[94]

The dream of total cinema is an old one – complete immersion was dreamed up long before cinema came into existence and some have searched for the roots of cinema in the dream of submersion in another reality.[95] In his article » *Le mythe du cinéma total* « André Bazin has reflected on this myth of the origin of cinema. For Bazin, cinema was conceived mentally – » invented « as an idea so to speak – long before it came into existence as a technological fact, yet in practice the cinema remains but a shadow of what it was meant to be. Bazin dreams of a total cinema:

> It is the myth of an all-encompassing realism, a recreation of the world according to its own image, an image that would feel neither the ballast of free interpretation of an artist nor the unidirectionality of time. And even if film in its early years did not have

all capacities of the eventual total film, it was against its will and only because his fairies were technically not capable of giving this, even had they wanted to.[96]

For Bazin, the silence of the silent cinema was only a coincidence and every addition (sound, colour, widescreen) was a step towards the realisation of what cinema was meant to be. Hyperbolically, Bazin concludes his short essay with the declaration that the cinema has not been invented yet: » *Le cinéma n'est pas encore inventé!* « Despite its problematic technological determinism and teleological nature, it is interesting to note how this origin myth, which is also a myth of imperfection (the cinema is not fulfilling its promise), is reiterated and played out in the various advances made by avant-garde filmmakers. The avant-garde ideal of transforming life and integrating it into art meant that the film avant-garde often imagined overcoming the limiting dimensions of the theatre because cinema as a social event with all its rituals and expectations ultimately reduced the impact of the medium. The auditorium's architecture eliminated any possibility for interaction or participation, while the style of films in terms of narrative and editing reduced the spectator to a passive receiver of audio-visual cues, while the promotion of the cinema experience focused on maintaining the status quo. Blowing up the cinema or taking film out of the cinema and into the streets promised to interpellate and assault, to encounter and confuse people everywhere. For those reasons, many avant-garde activists preferred total immersion inside the cinema theatre or total projection everywhere outside. There are thus two strands in the avant-garde dream of total cinema: either the cinema itself would expand spatially and technologically in order to make the experience in the auditorium overwhelming and breathtaking or the cinema would be thrust into the life and daily routines of the people, abandoning the auditorium to encounter spectators outside engaged in their daily routines. Both strategies ultimately (and teleologically) culminated in the utopian idea of the convergence of life and art: either cinema would become lifelike and impossible to distinguish from our perception of reality or cinema would be found everywhere, again making it indistinguishable from our environment. By pointing out a genealogy of total and expanded cinema I want to show how the film avant-garde of the 1920s and 1930s was engaged in those dreams of complete immersion.

Perhaps the most consistent experimenter in the direction of wanting to destroy the traditional *dispositif* of cinema, but also the most contradictory figure on the margins of the avant-garde and art film is Abel Gance. He often publicly played up the image of the misunderstood artist and genius ruined by the evil forces of the film industry. In fact, there is another side to Gance that is equally important: the technician, the engineer, the *bricoleur*. In this perspective, his patents, technological developments and inventions become an integral and perhaps even the most decisive aspects of his cinema. Gance imagined and tried to create an expansive cinema in the sense that the avant-garde of the 1960s conceived it: to overwhelm and envelop, surround and enchant in visual as well as audio terms. This overwhelming cinema was to be achieved not via narrative, image and sound alone; it would require a transformation, in effect a magnification of the cinematic apparatus. His ideas of poly-visions, experiments with wide-screen, enhanced depth of image, multiple projections and surround sound began in the 1920s and lasted for the duration of his career until the post-war era.

Gance has always been a contradictory and controversial figure and remains so: On the one hand, Gance saw himself as an industrial designer of mass communication, on the other, he played up the image of the misunderstood artist. After his initial successes with J'ACCUSE (FR 1918) and LA ROUE (FR 1920-22), Gance spent a considerable amount of time researching what he called » visual language «. His proposal of seeing film as a modern form of visual hieroglyphs relates, on the one hand, to the research that was being done on Russian Constructivism and into the laws and rules of visual communication. On the other hand, it points toward the future, toward concepts from film theory such as Christian Metz' attempt to formulate film as a language system. Attempts at developing a universal language were also a mainstay of the avant-garde in the first decades of the Twentieth Century. This was true in painting (Vasily Kandinsky, Paul Klee), in literature (Khlebnikov, Hugo Ball, Kurt Schwitters, James Joyce) and in film (Hans Richter, Viking Eggeling). But, even within the popular film world, this was a hot topic of debate as has been demonstrated by Miriam Hansen.[97] The result of Gance's experiments was his monumental NAPOLÉON (FR 1925-27) which is overflowing with visual tropes. The film, with its superimpositions, mobile shots, awkward camera angles and, of course, with the famous triple screen employed at climactic moments, could be called » an encyclopaedia of optical effects «. In various ways, Gance tried to expand and exceed the limits of the conventional frame, addressing the spectator in new and unexpected ways; or, as Gance himself put it: » From that time onwards I had understood the necessity to surpass the ordinary limits of the screen. The silent cinema had reached the extreme limits of its capabilities. On my part, I had attempted to surpass them. ... The triptych had the advantage of enriching the alphabet. «[98] Gance saw the limitations of the silent cinema in the rigid frames of recording and projection, which he tried to overcome, but he always remained within the confines of the metaphor of a cinematic language.

For NAPOLÉON he devised, developed and put into practice a system of three overlapping images side-by-side that were shot simultaneously and projected synchronously on screen. Gance's system was complicated and cumbersome and only a few cinemas in major cities were able to project these films in the correct format. In Paris, one of the leading avant-garde theatres permanently installed an apparatus for screening triptych films after the success of Abel Gance's NAPOLÉON, which, to my knowledge, is a unique case:

> The real *raison d'être* of Studio 28 was as a *laboratory of film*, it does not have an ani-
> mated orchestra with ascending movements, only one thing is important: the *photo-*
> *graphic projection booth* and the *screen* which is one piece, nine meters wide and forms
> one vast frescoed mural in the front of the auditorium. Studio 28 is the only space in
> Paris where a triptych projection is permanently installed and all research about this
> invention is done by the inventor himself: Abel Gance.[99]

The author of this piece was none other than Jean Mauclaire, himself a protago-
nist of the Parisian avant-garde scene as the owner and programmer at *Studio 28*. Mauclaire also held the exclusive distribution rights to Abel Gance's triptych films. By converting his cinema to the triptych format he was attempting to support the search for a cinematic essence, which culminated in the orchestration of images. Invariably, the idea of the laboratory returns, with the artist-di-
rector as the engineer – only here the laboratory space moves from the film studio to the cinema.

The triptych technique was also used for films which were not specifically made for this *dispositif* as if to demonstrate the universal nature of the technology: J.C. Mol's UIT HET RIJK DER KRISTALLEN (NL 1927) was shown on the tri-
ple screen at *Studio 28* in February 1928.[100] Again, this demonstrates how much the film avant-garde is a phenomenon that was active across a broad field and was not limited to just producing experimental films. The activities of the avant-
garde were also evident in exhibitions, teaching, publishing, writing and the curating of exhibitions. Mauclaire even went so far as to claim that this new triple image would do away with the typical musical accompaniment. In *Studio 28*, the experiment was extended to sound accompaniment as the live orchestra was replaced by mechanical music thanks to the triptych's overwhelming presence:

> The possibilities of the triptych are even more broad, permitting the orchestration of
> images, the triptych will kill the orchestra. We are also employing *mechanical music*, a
> necessary concession for the preparation of too brusque a transition. But one not-so-
> distant day the auditoria will possess nothing but *a screen and a booth*. Cinema suffices
> on its own. The cinema is a force that will make fun of its adversaries.[101]

Mauclaire argued, not unlike the formalist theories of Arnheim and others, for a cinema that was characterised not by its realistic features and life-likeness, but by those characteristics that lent the cinema a life of its own. Indeed, Mauclaire believed that the orchestration of images could be replaced with the orchestration of sound.

Gance's NAPOLEON was one of the outstanding successes, which was capable of crossing over from a limited avant-garde public to a general audience like DAS CABINET DES DR. CALIGARI (GER 1919/20, Robert Wiene), BERLIN, DIE SINFONIE DER GROSSSTADT (GER 1926/27, Walter Ruttmann) or LA PASSION DE JEANNE D'ARC (FR 1928, Carl Theodor Dreyer). Alexander Dovzhenko, during his visit to Berlin,[102] was taken by Hans Richter to watch the film which Richter compared favourably to Fritz Lang's METROPOLIS (GER 1925-26): » We visited together the premiere of Abel Gance's NAPOLEON at the Ufa-Palast am Zoo. As depressing and stupid the monstrous METROPOLIS had seemed at the same place before, as great and intelligent NAPOLEON revealed itself to be. «[103] As Richter remembered , Dovzenko's enthusiasm culminated in his ideas for a different kind of cinematic *dispositif*, when upon leaving the cinema, the Soviet director exclaimed:

> What I want to do? A film about snow and ice, but not only projected on three screens in the front, but projected everywhere. On the ceiling, the sides and even behind the viewer. He should freeze with the hero and warm up with him at the fire, while outside the hungry wolves draw increasingly small circles around us. The frozen fish we rip with our teeth and the frozen faces are rubbed in the snow. The viewer shakes, freezes, awakens and almost frozen considers himself the hero.[104]

Dovzenko was already imagining IMAX in the late 1920s, envisioning today's » experience economy « with its shopping malls, theme parks and amusement rides. His synaesthetic totality went beyond representation in the traditional sense and envisioned the cinema as the simulation of a different world.

After the laboriously long work Gance put in on NAPOLÉON, he toyed with various projects, but it was not until the middle of 1929 that he again turned towards a subject that gripped his imagination. He opted for LA FIN DU MONDE, based on a » rather quaint and tedious novel «[105] by the French astronomer Camille Flammarion about the last days on earth just before a comet destroys all life on the planet. The book has been described as a mixture of heavy-handed symbolism, spiritual theories, scientific speculation and Christian eschatology. Besides the scope of the project, critics have speculated that there might have been a political reason for Gance's choice: the film prominently features an institution modelled on the League of Nations, which Gance supported. In the film, it is an international institution that saves the day for humanity that has otherwise turned to sectarianism and spirituality. Here was a project, which might be able to demonstrate the necessity and positive effects of such institutions, which were often seen as powerless constructions by contemporaries in which endless discussion would lead to no visible results.[106]

This film was Gance's first sound film and because he had no previous experience with the new technology he turned for technical support to Walter

Ruttmann who had just finished his first sound film, MELODIE DER WELT (GER 1928/29). Ruttmann is in many respects a figure similar to Abel Gance, always struggling with his self-definition as an artist, poised between constructivism and a romantic cult of creative genius, and in political terms equally difficult to pin down. Both were at the forefront of the emerging avant-garde in 1927, after NAPOLÉON and BERLIN had received enthusiastic reviews. After the introduction of sound, both experienced a sudden loss of reputation to which their joint project contributed. The production of LA FIN DU MONDE (FR 1930) proved disastrous: Despite an unusually large budget, the film soon ran into financial difficulties; sound technology was only in the process of being introduced at the time in France, thus problems had to be solved on a pragmatic day-by-day basis. The film was finished without Gance's presence and the reception was devastating. Supporters of Abel Gance like film historian Kevin Brownlow know the reasons for his downfall: His is the classic case of a filmmaker's career cut short by sound film as Gance's reputation never returned to its original stature in the 1920s, never fully recovering from the failure of LA FIN DU MONDE. Here was a highly original genius destroyed by a combination of careless and greedy producers with flawed technology that the artist was forced to use because of the follies of an uneducated audience.

However, the background to LA FIN DU MONDE can also be told in another way: what could have attracted Gance to this project apart from the grandiose scope of the project? Was it the chance to do for sound what NAPOLEON had done for visuals – to present a kaleidoscopic encyclopaedia of every imaginable sound effect? The triptych was meant to enrich the visual possibilities of the silent film via its construction, while LA FIN DU MONDE developed what Gance has termed » *perspective sonore* «. This surround sound system *avant la lettre* was developed for LA FIN DU MONDE and its technological achievements were conceived to contribute to the success of the film. Just prior to production, Gance applied for a patent for » perspectival sound « on 13 August 1929. Loudspeakers were placed in various locations in the cinema, not just behind the screen as was usual, but also along the sides of the auditorium, on the ceiling and the floor. In this manner the space would become truly three-dimensional and the film would extend beyond the flat, two-dimensional surface of the screen. In this vein, Gance had also experimented with various systems of enhanced depth in film, early forms of three-dimensional cinema. Gance saw the cinema as a medium that should allow the audience to immerse themselves, via the story telling, the choice of prototypical story and last but not least by its technological effects.

The sound system in 1929 was not ready to be marketed yet because it had not undergone a testing phase, which ultimately contributed to the failure of the film. The problems with Gance's plans were not new. Even the projection of the NAPOLÉON triptychs proved difficult in practice; very few big city cinemas could screen them. But NAPOLÉON could still function as an ordinary film with-out the tryptich effect. The contribution of the triptychs to the impact of the film has in retrospect possibly been overestimated. The problem of LA FIN DU MONDE was that, unlike his earlier historical film, many scenes simply did not work without the surround feeling that Gance had envisioned. The film is lar-gely a montage of reactions to the imminent destruction of the earth; the tedious string of scenes lacking narrative coherence only becomes comprehensible with the effect of the surround sound system. Thus, LA FIN DU MONDE should not be judged by standards normally applied to ordinary narrative films, it should be seen instead as a promotional film demonstrating the capacities of the new sys-tem. Gance continued his experiments with *Polyvision* and *écrans variables* into the 1950s when Hollywood had adapted a tamed version of his triptychs in their various wide-screen formats.[107]

This dream of immersion was meant to render the cinema invisible by extra-polation: the cinematic apparatus would expand into the auditorium space and become so realistic that the representation would overshadow the technology behind it. This utopian possibility has been developed and extended in amuse-ment parks and gaming arcades, but most importantly by the IMAX company, which might locate its genealogy in the avant-garde.[108]

But, there was another total cinema tendency among the avant-garde that wanted to abolish cinema altogether or at least to transform it beyond recogni-tion. Film was to be taken to the streets and shops, to private homes and public events – or projection would eliminate representational reality and be limited to only forms, lines and colours. Indeed, the first daylight film projectors that were able to bring films outside the cinema were developed and installed in the 1920s in department stores, museums and exhibition spaces. Besides these commer-cial applications, the avant-garde activists also devised alternative methods of taking film out of the cinema and into other walks of life. Implicitly, this concep-tion also refers back to the relationship between the auditorium space and the screen space as two of the most crucial variables of the cinema as *dispositif*.[109]

The attempt to bring cinema out of the auditorium space helped focus many tendencies of » pre-cinematic films «, films that were not quite films yet or films that were imagined, but not produced such as the futurist colour music of Carlo Carrà and Arnoldo Ginna in Italy (1910-1912), Duncan Grant's *Abstract Kinetic Painting with Collages* (1914), a scroll to be moved synchronically through a light box to a Bach piece, or the serial paintings *Rythme coloré* of Leopold Survage in France (1912/13). Avant-garde ideas of how to overcome traditional bourgeois distinctions between art forms (especially between music and visual art) mixed with *fin-de-siècle* conceptions of a synaesthetic *Gesamtkunstwerk* that united all of the arts in one single form.

The music analogy implies a similar conception of expanded cinema. Viking Eggeling, shortly before his death, imagined » a system for the projection of light onto the clouds at night, based on the still-to-be-developed theory of › Eidodynamics ‹. «[110] Here, the cinema intersects with much larger trends of spatial-movement art – the abstract films of Richter, Eggeling and Ruttmann are in this perspective much less singular events; rather, they evolve out of a tradition of revolutionary visual arts, sculpture, music and architecture. The central and common element unifying these trends is the concentration on light as the main medium of new art.[111] Not coincidentally, all three filmmakers had their own very strong ideas about musical accompaniment to their films (or silence as in the case of Eggeling). Ruttmann collaborated with composer Max Butting on scores for his films while Oskar Fischinger started off with musical pieces, which he would then visually illustrate. Eggeling wanted a complete suppression of sound (another strong idea about the relationship between visual and aural elements in the cinema). Meanwhile, Richter in 1928 and 1929 collaborated intensely with different modern composers in his commissions from the Baden-Baden music festival. Thus, while it is possible for the film avant-garde to argue that » independent experiments … before 1925 are few and far between «,[112] this neglects the larger context in which the attempts with scroll paintings and coloured projection, movable stages and light sculptures, serial painting and musical visualisations contextualise the » absolute films «.

In his early years, Oskar Fischinger collaborated with composer and musician Alexander Laszlo. Laszlo had written a treatise on coloured light music.[113] This combination of music and sound in a performance was part of a trend which resulted in countless public shows and written reactions throughout the 19th century and well into the 20th.[114] Laszlo toured successfully throughout Germany with a light organ and films prepared by Fischinger in the mid-1920s. Fischinger continued experimenting with multiple projections and combinations of abstract moving colours and shapes with static slides accompanied either by music specifically composed by Erich Korngold or a percussion group.[115] Fischinger continued his experiments well into the 1950s:

> Later, when Fischinger was disillusioned with the film industry because of the Hollywood studios' refusal to give him creative control, he hoped to strike gold by inventing a Lumigraph, a piano that projected colours onto a screen. He imagined that every good bourgeois home would like a Lumigraph next to the piano.[116]

The post-World War Two avant-garde would take up this challenge, albeit without truly acknowledging the debt to these early innovators.

Many of these devices and experiments are now largely forgotten. For instance, the trials at the *Bauhaus* where ideas about overcoming traditional boundaries between the various art forms was one of the driving forces behind this endeavour. The *Bauhaus* teachers Kurt Schwerdtfeger (*Farbenlichtspiel*, GER 1921-23) and Ludwig Hirschfeld-Mack (*Reflektorische Farbenspiele*, GER 1921-23) worked on similar ideas of projecting (coloured) light in conjunction with musical and stage experiments. Both presented performances as part of the matinee *Der absolute Film* in Berlin in 1925. In a similar way, ENTR'ACTE (FR 1924) was originally conceived as an intermission during Francis Picabia's avant-garde ballet *Ballet Suédois* presenting *Relâche* in Paris[117] while Erwin Piscator regularly used projection technology as part of his theatre productions.[118] These films were prepared by protagonists from the German avant-garde movements like Albrecht Viktor Blum, George Grosz, Leo Lania, Svend Noldan and others.[119] There are more examples in the 1920s of multimedia events that combined stage and film.[120] One of the more obvious problems of these projections was the fleeting nature of a complicated set-up that was put together for one show and then dismantled. By contrast, film is a relatively stable technology: even decades later one can still revive and project a film (as long as it has not suffered too much from poor storage).

Probably one of the most famous apparatuses devised to » explode « cinema was Moholy-Nagy's kinetic sculpture » light-space-modulator « (» *kinetische Skulptur Licht-Raum-Modulator* «), immortalised in his film LICHTSPIEL SCHWARZ-WEISS-GRAU (GER 1931/32). Its construction comes out of a tradition that attempted to create a composite art from music, light, colour and movement in a three-dimensional space.[121] The development of the » light-space-modulator « was greatly aided in terms of financing and technology by one of the leading German manufacturers of electronic equipment and technology, *AEG* (*Allgemeine Elektrizitäts Gesellschaft*, established in 1883). This company was interested in a device that projected mobile advertisements from moving vehicles such as trains, cars and buses. The underlying idea was to make advertisements mobile, to use the city as a projection screen, to use those objects or vehicles already moving through the city as projection booths. While traversing streets and squares, the moving projector on a bus, car or tram would project images or slogans on objects, buildings and people. Moholy-Nagy combined two important strands here: on the one hand, the fascination for the city as the *locus classicus* of modernity and modernism, the city as cause and effect of the fundamental transformations brought about in perception and experience. On the other hand, we have the idea of expanding and destroying cinema that is clearly visible in the classical avant-garde, but that only received more notice after World War Two when Gene Youngblood coined the term » expanded cinema «[122] and experiments at Knokke and elsewhere introduced a wider public to these ideas. Moholy-Nagy's film LICHTSPIEL SCHWARZ-WEISS-GRAU (GER 1931/32) is considered the first demonstration of this machine, a trial run of a propaganda machine that was not intended for cinema in the ordinary sense.

Seen in this light, a film normally referred to as an avant-garde classic acquires a wholly new genealogy and is inserted into the lineage of the industrial film or the documentary when we view the result as documenting light and shadow.[123] Moholy-Nagy's interest in light as a medium of expression is complemented by his choice of subject matter in his other films which deal with the city and the living conditions of various groups of people: IMPRESSIONEN VOM ALTEN MARSEILLER HAFEN (GER 1929), BERLINER STILLLEBEN (GER 1930), and GROSSSTADTZIGEUNER (GER 1932).

Architecture was only added later on, but similarly mirrored Moholy-Nagy's concerns with living conditions and constructivist preoccupations with social engineering: ARCHITEKTURKONGRESS ATHEN (GER 1933) and NEW ARCHITECTURE AT THE LONDON ZOO (GB 1936).[124]

I will now return to my opening point about expanded cinema *avant la lettre*. For Bazin, the inventors and industrialists who capitalised on the new medium – the Edisons and Lumières –belong to the sidelines of film and cinema history. Those who matter are the fanatics who gave everything to achieve the myth of total cinema:

> The fanatics, the madmen, the selfless pioneers who were, like Bernard Palissy, capable of burning their furniture to film a couple of seconds of flickering images are neither industrialists nor scholars, but possessed by the images of their fantasy. Film was born from the convergence of their obsession, from a myth, the myth of *total cinema*.[125]

It is those » men obsessed by their own imaginings « that we find in the circles of the avant-garde, stubbornly following this Bazinian myth which proved unattainable, but whose pursuit brought about some of the most interesting examples of avant-garde activity. Even much later, these ideas survived underground and only resurfaced at certain points in history. Not coincidentally, Alexander Hackenschmied/Hammid, one of the key figures in the Czech avant-garde in the 1930s worked with Francis Thompson on several early IMAX films in the 1960s such as To BE ALIVE! (1964), To THE FAIR (1965), WE ARE YOUNG / NOUS SOMMES JEUNES (1967) or US (1968), which were made for Expos or other events.[126]

4.5   Conclusion

> *The concurrence of institution and content reveals the*
> *social irrelevance as a characteristic feature of art in*
> *bourgeois societies and challenges the claims of self-criticism within art.*
> *The historical avant-garde movement has achieved this self-criticism.*
> Peter Bürger (1974)[127]

My discussion of several facets of the avant-garde – publishing, teaching, exhibitions, and the utopia of a cinema expanded beyond the limits of the screen and reaching into the lives of the spectators – basically focused on three branches: first, to show how the avant-garde was a broad cultural and political movement that was much more than a handful of » masterworks « or » classics « characterised by formal experimentation. Avant-garde culture also encompassed exhibitions and publishing, teaching, theorising and activism of various approaches. Secondly, this wide field cannot be merely characterised as a context or as an ancillary or secondary activity in support of film, because the strategy of the avant-garde was geared towards a total restructuring of cinema as an institution. For that reason the avant-garde formed media strategies that were meant to transform the social and political order. Thirdly, from an archaeological perspective, the attempts at overcoming the standard relationships of cinema, the traditional *dispositif* aptly demonstrates the far-sighted nature of the avant-garde: what was at stake was not an experimental technique or a formal innovation, but the cinema in its totality. Looked at from a contemporary perspective, they were indeed *our* avant-garde.

5 Vanishing Point Soviet Union – Soviet Cinema and the West between Innovation and Repression

*In those first decades after the October Revolution we can already
recognize the roots of cold war – the bipolar division of the territories
of the globe and the frantic competition between the two systems.
The New Deal legislation itself, along with the construction of
comparable welfare systems in Western Europe, might be cast as a
response to the threat conjured up by the Soviet experience, that is,
to the increasing power of workers' movement both at home and abroad.*
Michael Hardt & Antonio Negri (2000)[1]

In the 1920s, the young and dynamic society of the Soviet Union appealed to avant-garde sensibilities everywhere. In the field of cinema, the Soviet Union did not only produce innovative and lasting works of art – retrospectively, often collectively grouped in formalist terms as » montage cinema « or more politically minded called » revolutionary cinema « –, but, more importantly for my purposes here, it also attempted to change cinema as an institution: its mode of production, exhibition and the reception process, as well as film criticism and censorship, acting style, exhibition practice and many other things. What was at stake in the Soviet Union was not just another style or school of filmmaking, but the attempt to build a radically different cinema from that in the capitalist states. The Soviet experiment did, to many curious and well-meaning observers in Western countries, adhere to avant-garde ideals of breaking down the barrier that separated art and life, theory and practice, thinking and doing. It was after the premiere of Eisenstein's BRONENOSEZ » POTEMKIN « (SU 1925, › Battleship Potemkin ‹) in Berlin that the Soviet montage cinema started its triumphal march across Europe. Before that, the Soviet filmmakers had sharpened their eyes, intellect and scissors on Western film – the technique of *remontage* with which Western films had been adapted for Soviet audiences fit perfectly well into the notions of reshaping the cinematic discourse. For some years, until roughly 1929-30 the » Russenfilme «, as they came to be known in Germany which was the main conduit of exchange between Western Europe and the Soviet Union, carried the brightly burning torch of hope and the future before the introduction of sound cast long shadows across the vast landscape of Soviet cinema. At the same time, the restructuring introduced by the Stalinist administration, industrially manifested in the first Five-Year-Plan (1928-32), which suc-

ceeded the NEP phase of a limited market economy and culturally represented
by the rising dogma of Socialist Realism, changed the self-organisation of the
film industry, altered the governing aesthetic assumptions and generally led to
an increasing restriction of freedoms. The dominant cultural movement shifted
from avant-garde and wide-ranging experiments to academic and formal Social
Realism – this is how the traditional story goes. Some years later, the Soviet
Union, for many emigrants as well as for Soviet citizens, turned from an imaginary and metaphorical vanishing point, from a hopeful beacon guiding the
path into a brighter future, to a vanishing point in a literal sense when many
artists and intellectuals perished in the Stalinist purges of the mid-1930s. It is
this development that I will present in more detail on the following pages.

The archaeology of the European avant-garde would be incomplete without a
chapter on the interaction between the Soviet Union and the West. Soviet cinema thus occupies a special place: It can be seen as encapsulating the other developments *in nuce*. The Soviet cinema experience partly acts as an allegory for
the European avant-garde , which ventured out on their labyrinthine journeys
from hopeful beginnings to war, extermination, and exile. While I will flesh out
the general trajectory sketched above, I will also propose a parallel reading
stressing the utopian aspects of the avant-garde that had to remain unfulfilled,
but that turned out to be important but seemed to many like an elusive goal in
the mid-1920s. The subtext of this chapter will thus deal with the paradoxical
temporal structures inherent in the cultural logic of the avant-garde. At the time
of the coming of sound the discrepancy between the proclaimed utopian situation hailed in the avant-garde classics and the harsh reality manifest in the desolate state of the Soviet cities and countryside became too wide, thus art and
reality had to converge again. The ensuing changes incorporated the avant-
garde idea of transforming life into art and art into life, only in a very different
way from the Constructivists. While in the 1920s, artists strove to be » engineers
of material reality «, in the 1930s they were asked (or rather: ordered) to become
» engineers of human souls « (Stalin).[2] Or, to put it differently: The avant-garde,
in its concentration on the material basis of creation (abstraction, isolating elements and elemental building blocks, modularisation, recombination), in fact
supported what they most vehemently rejected: an increased autonomy for art.
In Marxist logic, the constructivist avant-garde was tampering with the super-
structure which was determined by the basis anyway. The avant-garde art of the
1920s thus seemed completely useless (in social-revolutionary terms) to orthodox Marxists looking back at the earlier phase from the 1930s. Therefore, constructivism and montage cinema were denounced as formalism and academic
art, in other words anti-Soviet. This outward pressure was echoed by an internal contradiction as the avant-garde had in general opposed the autonomy of
bourgeois art. In the course of the 1920s, constructivism seemed to increasingly

lose its status as an agent for change. The true calling of art in orthodox Marxism was to change the consciousness of the people, which in turn would change the foundation of society (paired with the transformations of their lives by Soviet culture). To accommodate an avant-garde in the sense that it was used in the 1920s meant to accommodate bourgeois art in the long run (because any avant-garde that is successful will eventually eliminate itself) which was unthinkable in a » classless « society like the Soviet Union. It is not the coming of sound that shattered the accomplishments of the avant-garde, but the changed social, cultural, technological and economic context that acted as a catalyst for the dramatic restructurings of the networks of the avant-garde.

A disclaimer is necessary at this point: I am not concerned here with Soviet cinema *per se*, but rather with the questions of interdependence, projection, overlap, influence, resonance, retrospection and historiography. I will try to give an overview of how the Soviet cinema developed over a period of a few years, from a utopia and eventually into a dystopia. This is neither an industry study nor an account of the aesthetic developments of a specific national cinema (there are many accounts easily available that I have benefited from using), but rather an inquiry into » the imaginary dimension of the Soviet cinema « – its circulation abroad, in the form of films, persons, ideas, discourses, but also the circulation and influence of other cinemas in the Soviet Union. In this vein I will examine the origins of the Soviet cinema from the refashioning of Griffith, Lang and Lubitsch, I will look at the reception of some classics of the Soviet cinema of the 1920s, I will deal with the travels of the luminaries Eisenstein, Vertov, Pudovkin in the West, I will examine how the cult of personality was reintroduced into a constructivist avant-garde, I will try to understand the logic behind attracting Western filmmakers like Ivens, Ruttmann, Piscator or Richter and I will look at exile in the Soviet Union during which many people were killed in the purges and who had only just escaped Hitler's deadly grip shortly before. I will also consider how the avant-garde practices of combining filmmaking with vocational training and theorisation, and exhibitions with network building and publishing were adapted or innovated upon in the Soviet Union.

5.1   The Avant-Garde in the Soviet Context

> *Part of the Soviet experiment years ago, as Eisenstein explained it to me,*
> *was to abolish art because it was useless. Of course, that theory is not*
> *easily put into practice as this apparent uselessness is the chief virtue of art.*
> Josef von Sternberg (1965)[3]

Even when considering the imaginary dimension of the Soviet cinema it is important to understand the self-organisation of the film industry (or the organisation from above through state intervention). Around 1920, the Soviet film administration faced two interrelated problems simultaneously. The first issue was how to restart the cinema sector as everything from production to exhibition had broken down after the war, two revolutions, a civil war, famine and general disorder. The second difficulty was how to create a *new* kind of cinema – and what kind of new cinema. The conflict that resulted from these interrelated problems was probably inevitable and could be summed up in the dramatic question of whether it was more important to have a functioning economy at the expense of a traditional aesthetic or whether it was more important for a new aesthetic to be developed which would then also create its own form of organisation. Basically, this dilemma was as unsolvable as the chicken-or-egg question because both are two sides of the same coin. This dialectical tension returns and haunts the filmmaking practice as well as the theoretical debates[4] in many respects. This includes the discussion around the dearth of suitable scenarios (unsuitable in terms of commercial potential or ideological content?) as well as the question of the acted or the non-acted film[5] (and non-fiction vs. documentary) to the debate about Sovkino's production policy (orientation towards export or home market?) and the question of entertainment or enlightenment (what is the function of cinema?). At the heart of this problem were issues regarding dependency and the political agenda, which were what the Western avant-garde encountered: How can an avant-garde film be made in a context that is not (yet) ready to follow the avant-garde? Is it possible to make a critical film while legitimising the very structures that one is working against because the film is financed, distributed or screened by the very circles the avant-garde is struggling against? How can one work in the very art system one ultimately wants to destroy?

One of the first activities of the new Soviet government in October 1918 was to equip an *agit train* that was sent to the civil war front lines. The agit-prop combined new methods of persuasion with economic necessity. The goal was to have a self-contained unit of cultural and artistic workers who responded directly to situations encountered on the front. The train » contained a printing-plant equipped for the publication of newspapers and leaflets, a theatre company prepared to write as well as to perform plays, and a film-crew, headed by the young veteran of both newsreel and studio work, Edward Tisse. «[6] Later, film studios were included on these trains, creating self-contained and independent cultural-political units that were meant to break down the distinction between production and reception by directly interacting with the audience. Films and screenings were continually altered in this feedback loop of responding to immediate circumstances. This integration of the filmmaking process was typical of an avant-garde ethos in which art and life were to be integrated.

The Bolshevik government took control of the cinema directly after the Revolution; in January 1918, a Division of Photography and Cinema was formed as part of the Commissariat of Enlightenment and, in April 1918, foreign trade was monopolised.[7] One of the first measures was to send film trader Jacques Roberto Cibrario in New York to acquire cameras, lighting equipment and film stock. After he embezzled one million dollars for the purchase of equipment, a substantial part of the Soviet Union's modest foreign capital, the Soviet Union resorted to a economic system that was completely closed to the outside world.[8] The » Cibrario affair «, as it became known, might have taught Soviet authorities that poor self-sufficiency with limited resources was preferable to a dependency on wealthy capitalist trade. From 1924 onwards, the acquisition of foreign films was restricted to the two largest companies, Sovkino and Mezhrabpom', also the two main producers of commercial film fare throughout the 1920s. Both were heavily attacked in the intellectual film press of the time for their production of genre films and sentimental tearjerkers. While Sovkino was liquidated in 1930, Mezhrabpom', which remained essential for the trade, projections, and translations between the Soviet Union and the West, was able to survive into the mid-1930s. While filmmakers were also attacked for their unpopular films and experimentation (Vertov, Eisenstein and others), Sovkino and Mezhrabpom' came under fire for their » commercialism «, again illustrating the tension between an economically self-sufficient cinema sector and a revolutionary art that broke with older models and formulas. Neither the » studio solution « (making genre films, only now with communists as heroes and capitalists as villains) nor the » avant-garde solution « (making films that only a few intellectuals would appreciate) proved acceptable in the Soviet Union. Intellectuals and functionaries either turned up their noses at the reactionary trash that contaminated audiences or the masses simply stayed away from obscure and esoteric film experiments. Traditional and experimental film style managed to survive side by side for some time, but tension increased as the various factions fought fiercely over the course that Soviet cinema should take.

In the early years, economic problems prevented the Soviet film industry from producing enough films to satisfy demand. The reality for audiences in Soviet cinemas after the Revolution therefore consisted mainly of German films;

in the early 1920s, approximately 80-90% of films in Soviet cinemas were of German origin.[9] From approximately 1922 onwards, US films were increasingly screened as the German market had been opened up to Hollywood imports. Germany continued to be the main conduit for both film imports and exports.[10] In the 1920s, the Soviet government demanded economic independence for the film industry, however, the money necessary for reopening theatres or for rebuilding studios had to be acquired on the foreign market. Indeed, even though imported foreign films were considered to be problematic in terms of ideology, they were guaranteed moneymakers as Soviet audiences loved Charlie Chaplin, Douglas Fairbanks, Mary Pickford, and especially the German action star Harry Piel. On average, a foreign film made ten times more money than a Soviet film at the box office.[11] Soviet officials only tolerated foreign films as long as the domestic film industry could not meet the demand. Throughout the 1920s, the number of Soviet films steadily rose and by the end of the first Five-Year-Plan (1928-32) foreign films had disappeared altogether. Thus, the goal of autonomy was achieved, but only after returning to a limited market economy during the transitional period of the New Economic Policy (NEP), yet another paradoxical split that the industry had to deal with.[12]

It has to be remembered that the Soviet cinema until 1928 was largely free of state intervention in economic terms. The distribution and exhibition sector was dominated by commercial production, both foreign and Soviet. The New Economic Policy forced artists, entrepreneurs, and institutional personnel alike to follow strict commercial rules.[13] It was only in 1927 that the government began to change the economic and political system for the film and cinema industry. The transformation of the film sector occurred slowly beginning in 1928, until the increasingly repressive policy culminated in the Stalinist purges of 1936-38.[14] The majority of famous Soviet films were indeed made at a time when a shift in policy was imminent during the second half of the 1920s. The relative instability of the transitional situation and the openness of an unknown future contributed to the innovative rush of Soviet cinema. The avant-garde is by definition a transitory and fleeting phenomenon that is characterised by flux and constant movement, and it has thus historically flourished in periods of uncertainty, crisis, upheaval and transition.

The NEP phase of the mid-1920s meant that the film industry returned temporarily to a market economy. The Soviet Union – which saw itself striding ahead of the capitalist countries in their march towards socialism – experienced tension between economic necessity and artistic integrity. The discussions of the mid-1920s accused films of either being laden with » commercialism « (a large part of the genre production of Mezhrabpom' and Sovkino) or with » leftist deviation « (later termed » formalism «; initially Dziga Vertov was the target, later also Sergei Eisenstein and others). In fact, it was only with the advent of Socialist Realism that a dialectical synthesis presented a solution for the conflicting positions – albeit a cruel one that most of the avant-garde activists from the 1920s were not willing to embrace. In this perspective, Socialist Realism was a logical outcome of the tensions and paradoxes that Soviet cinema was unable to overcome in its first 15 years of existence.

Traditional film history tells the story of Soviet cinema as a Phoenix-like rise from the ashes of war and civil unrest with the subsequent terrible oppressiveness of the Stalinist bureaucracy. While I do not want to deny the validity of such a perspective in absolute terms (for many well-meaning observers as well as for filmmakers directly involved, it must have appeared this way), I want to propose a slightly different view. Socialist Realism, which was introduced in the 1930s, did in fact solve problems that the canonical avant-garde had compellingly addressed, but were unable to resolve. The avant-garde contribution consisted of pointing out a number of paradoxes (in/dependence of art, commercialism or elitism, socialism or fascism, abstraction or realism).[15] The avant-garde promised a remedy to the modern fragmentation by reuniting art and life, yet it proved unable to fulfil that promise. Indeed, the Soviet solution was not particularly untypical if one considers the answers to the challenges that the 1920s avant-garde faced in the 1930s in places like Europe and the United States. In this way, the Stalinist cinema of the 1930s (and art under Stalin in general) took a similar path to the British documentary movement, to the French *front populaire* and the fascist avant-gardes in Germany, Portugal and Italy. The specific contribution of the » realist « developments in the 1930s was to offer another way out of the impasses exposed by the avant-garde. While the avant-garde of the 1920s rebelled against the romantic cult of the genius, it nevertheless sustained another myth: that of individual creation. In the 1930s, this was replaced by the myth of the absolute artist and leader who rules everything and everybody, be it Stalin, Mussolini or Hitler. It is important to remember that this kind of realism was markedly different from the » critical realism « that flourished especially in literature and painting in the second half of the 19th century (Gustave Flaubert, Honoré de Balzac, Emile Zola, Charles Dickens, George Eliot, Anton Chechov, Gustave Courbet, Adolph Menzel). At least in the countries under totalitarian rule, the Fascist and Socialist Realism did not function as criticism of the status quo, but it was a *utopian realism* that promised the beauty and perfection of the future that society was in the process of achieving (or had already achieved).

The Soviet Union was a focus of interest everywhere in the West as it attempted to create an entirely new state and an entirely new society. The country was run in an avant-garde spirit in the way the governing group treated the country as one big laboratory with millions of inhabitants. The new state was not only a staging ground in socio-economic and organisational terms where state-of-the-art theories could be put into practice. The realm of culture and art in fact formed a synecdoche or metonymy for the whole country. The most advanced art of the most advanced country – so it appeared to many sympathetic observers – was by definition the avant-garde of the avant-garde. Not only did the arts reflect the state of things – all canonised classics dealt explicitly with the situation leading up to the revolution, with the revolution or with life since – but they also worked within a context that was markedly different from that of filmmakers in the West. In fact, the contradictory situation of the NEP in the mid-1920s, a communist state reverting to a market economy, heightened the importance of culture as hopes and dreams for achieving a final and happy stage of communism had to be postponed into the future. Peter Kenez has described this contradictory situation:

> On the one hand, the Bolsheviks had far-reaching ambitions in remaking society and man, and on the other they did not possess the means to assert their will in the existing society. Their reach exceeded their grasp. Bolshevik utopianism was born out of weakness: It makes little sense to develop modest plans at a time when they lacked the tools for accomplishing even these; they felt free to allow their imagination to roam. As a result, they disliked gradualist, ameliorist methods, and instead were attracted to all sorts of ephemeral schemes. Many of the unusual features of Soviet life in the period can be explained by keeping in mind the contradiction between great ambition and limited means.[16]

As a result of the NEP and the general economic situation, the promised paradise had to be found in spheres other than daily life, which meant there had been little change since the Revolution (and if any, the people were actually a little worse off). In general, the arts and culture became an arena in which the government hoped to quickly achieve its utopian ideal, which remained unattainable in daily life. Culture was the sector where progress appeared most visible, thus making it the ideal showcase both for the population at home and to observers in capitalist countries in order to demonstrate the achievements of the revolution even if they were only imaginary at this point. Quite logically, this discrepancy between illusionary self-image and harsh reality could only be upheld for a limited period of time and soon the internal contradiction between the two became too strong. With Socialist Realism and the Stalinist purges in the 1930s, this dislocation of the self-image in Soviet cinema was shifted to another plane as it approached the level of daily life again, albeit in a brutal and utterly cynical fashion.

   In fact, right after the revolution, the country had been violently thrown backwards through a period of destruction that resulted in a total collapse of the major industries, shortages of food, failures of the communication networks and in general a setback to earlier times. The avant-garde drew its energy from this period: because nothing worked, everything became possible; the present reality offered nothing, so there was no measuring stick against which projections into the future could be compared. This spirit would be re-evoked retrospectively in Victor Skhlovski's description in 1927 of freedom triumphing over necessity:

> In those days socialism was considered to be an advance. The air of liberty and not necessity, a paradox premonition of the future were at that time a substitute for the fat, the wooden logs. This was the general atmosphere. ... We flew on an iron wrecking ball from the past into the future – and gravity no longer existed, just like Jules Verne's ball.[17]

Flying on a wrecking ball from the past to the future: This is the paradoxical temporal construction that characterises the avant-garde. While being steeped in the past against which they aimed their artistic rebellion , the avant-garde nevertheless remained totally focused on the future. But what is missing from this view is the present. This co-existence of past and future has also been remarked upon by Janina Urussowa as a typical feature of the post-revolutionary decade: » The simultaneous presence of past and future in the homeless everyday life of young Soviet society was characteristic of the first post-revolutionary decade. «[18] Typical artistic activity consisted of devising new architectural and city plans that would never be put into practice. A classic example is Vladimir Tatlin's monument to the Third International that was constructed as a model and displayed all around the country, but was never built. The Kuleshov workshop staged » films without film « in the same spirit.[19] Similar moments of » utopian possibility « or » dream architecture « can be found in Eisenstein's film architecture devised for his unrealised *Glass House* project,[20] and outside of the Soviet Union, in Mies van der Rohe's Turmhaus at Berlin's Friedrichstraße (and in many avant-garde ideas from the 1920s that were not realised), and even in Abel Gance's cinema exploding installation pieces Napoléon (FR 1925-27) and La Fin du monde (FR 1930). This de-valuation of the past in favour of a future that is nonetheless unattainable is a crucial characteristic of the avant-garde.

5.2 The Birth of Montage Cinema from the Spirit of Re-editing

> *The basic technical contribution of Kuleshov ... was the discovery*
> *that there were, inherent in a single piece of unedited film two strengths:*
> *its own, and the strength of its relation to other pieces of film.*
> Jay Leyda (1960)[21]

In the first years after the Revolution, the young Soviet Union produced almost no feature films, concentrating instead on two other forms of filmmaking which are treated marginally in classic film histories: re-montage and non-fiction. In this section, I will deal with the re-editing of existing films while in the following section I will treat the categorisation of Soviet films in relation to the fiction / non-fiction divide in more detail. Interestingly, the two most famous film-makers who took up film right after the Revolution (and before the triumvirate of Sergei Eisenstein, Vsevolod Pudovkin, and Alexander Dovshenko rose to prominence) could be seen as embodiments of these two larger trends in the Soviet cinema of the interwar period: Lev Kuleshov is known for his montage experiments, most famously the formulation of the proverbial »Kuleshov effect«, while Dziga Vertov represents the category-exploding non-fiction productions that characterise the first fifteen years of Soviet cinema. Without wanting to personify these larger trends while attempting to undermine the overriding *auteur* theory of art history, the oeuvre of these two celebrated directors contributes to a genealogy of re-editing and non-fiction.

As mentioned earlier, in the early years of the Soviet Union most films exhibited were of foreign origin, either German or American. Yet, these films were often shown in different versions from the original as the film committee had already in early 1919 founded a section for the re-montage of foreign films (and of films produced under the Tsar), a practice common during the entire existence of the Soviet Union.[22] A good many filmmakers sharpened their eyes and scissors on these transformations, the most famous were Lev Kuleshov, Sergei Eisenstein and Esfir Shub. First, excessively violent or overtly sexual scenes were cut and discarded, not unlike censorship in Western countries. More importantly though, far-reaching changes were made when films were converted ideologically: whole sequences were edited differently, titles were changed, shots were removed and so on to give a film a different political thrust. The classic example of the »bolshevikation« of Western films is the transformation of DR. MABUSE, DER SPIELER (GER 1921/22, Fritz Lang) into THE GILDED ROT (SU 1924, Eisenstein/Shub).[23] The Soviet montage school is unthinkable without this practice of creating new meaning by cutting, repositioning or exchanging shots.

This practice fitted on several levels into the logic of the avant-garde: In terms of formal technique, a re-montage was akin to collage because the creative act consisted of cutting up, isolating elements, destroying an old context and creating a new one when re-combining the pre-existing elements in a different form. Re-montage could also be related to the Dadaesque technique of destroying an ordered bourgeois universe and creating non-sense (or anti-sense); the title THE GILDED ROT could have easily been invented for a Zürich Dada soirée or for a meeting of the Parisian surrealists. Moreover, an element of abstraction can be found in this strategy as the narrative – which traditionally takes centre-stage – recedes into the background and fresh meaning is created from existing material in a new assembly. It is on these three levels – collage technique, destroying order, and abstraction from a narrative universe – that the Soviet cinema aligned itself with avant-garde preoccupations in a more general way. In fact, the practice of reverse engineering (i.e., taking something apart in order to understand its function) is typical of a constructivist ethos: isolate the element, examine how energy is generated through the sequence, contrast and alternation of these pieces, and put the elements back together again. The modular approach of constructing from a limited number of existing entities, proved to be crucial to the Soviet avant-garde.

This technique was widespread. Practically all foreign films were re-edited and, as Yuri Tsivian reports, these specialists and cinephiles *avant la lettre* developed an extraordinary pride and confidence in their work:

> They were connoisseurs: no one in the film industry (or outside it) knew Western cinema better than the re-editors; they were experts: few filmmakers compared to them in mastering the technique of editing ...; they were arrogant: they believed they could improve Griffith! And despite being badgered by film critics, they were proud of their profession! «[24]

However, not only aspiring filmmakers used this training, it also directly fed into the education of a future generation of film practitioners. Georgii and Sergei Vasiliev, later famous filmmakers in their own right, put together an educational film from existing material, AZBUKA KINOMONTAZHA (SU 1926, › The ABC of Film Editing ‹), that illustrated the practice of re-editing. Sergei Vasiliev also published a book under this title in 1929 and the film was used in class at the Film Institute in Moscow, the first film school anywhere in the world. The avant-garde cannot be characterised solely by a specific aesthetic program or an innovative formal gadget, but only by its overall approach to filmmaking which aimed at overcoming the barriers separating life and art. Thus, teaching, theorising, screening films, editing journals are not secondary or ancillary activities, but are as crucial to the overall conception of the avant-garde as filmmaking.

The reversal of hierarchies – related to the theory of re-montage – was another factor important for the emergence of the Soviet cinema. One can point out the inversion of the traditional evaluation of the arts, most famously encapsulated in Lenin's legendary claim for film as » the most important of the arts «, one is reminded of eccentricity and the carnivalesque in FEKS (factory of the eccentric actor)[25], one can refer to the significance of the circus, highly valued by Eisenstein, and of the music hall which featured prominently for the futurists[26] or one can indicate the notion of » *ostranie* « (making strange) developed by the Russian formalists. The reversal of hierarchy, the inversion of centre and periphery adheres to an avant-garde practice of breaking down traditional barriers and evaluations, of toppling traditional value judgements, of overcoming stale and fixed rankings. Undermining and turning around the narrative, making a film state something unintended as in the re-montage is akin to this reversal of established hierarchies.

The organisation of labour followed a typical communist model: the collective or the reliance on a small and stable group. One thinks here of the FEKS collective, of Eisenstein and his assistants (they called themselves » the iron five «), of Kuleshov's workshop, of Dziga Vertov's Cinema-Eye group, of the Proletkult collective and many more.[27] While, on the one hand, this was meant to limit the level of alienation from work diagnosed in orthodox Marxism for workers in Fordist factories, these small groups of highly skilled specialists are also reminiscent of engineering teams in research departments. The Soviets were fascinated by modern industrial production in which labour was organised according to abstract models of flow and efficiency. In the desire for renewal and restructuring, these examples are not only novel models for organising labour processes, but also early teaching activities. Thus, the collective was not only a work collective compatible with communist society, but it moreover led to a dissemination of knowledge and abilities that were in traditional film cultures heavily policed by specialists' associations. The pedagogical impetus of the avant-garde has traditionally been neglected, but I believe that education is a crucial element in any attempt at restructuring the power relations in the cinema.

5.3 Exploding Categories, Toppling Hierarchies

The re-organisation of the world according to aesthetic principles
has been proposed several times in the West and even attempted,
however it is in Russia that it has truly succeeded for the first time.
Boris Groys (1988)[28]

The films that were being made initially in the period of war, civil unrest and the immediate aftermath of the Revolution were mostly non-fiction films, yet they quickly became a curious mixture of fiction and non-fiction. This distinction only played a subordinate role in these years: the Soviet Union, caught in a process of realising a future that was already known (through Marxist orthodoxy) distinguished more between accomplished goals and future aims, than between fact and fiction. After an initial phase of experimentation, the focus shifted to more concrete goals of persuasion, but also to entertainment. Discussions centred on questions such as the acted or non-acted film, a distinction similar to the line between fiction and non-fiction, but with a somewhat different focus.[29] As Denise Youngblood argues, even within avant-garde circles this tension persisted:

> [F]rom the beginning, the artistic left in cinema was more diverse than it has been portrayed. It was divided into those who supported fiction films with weakly developed narratives and those – the most radical – who rejected the fiction film altogether, advocating the nonfiction film in its place. While the importance of the former faction would persist, the influence of the latter had all but ended by 1924 as revolutionary romanticism was eschewed by young film activists more intent on rebuilding a shattered industry than indulging in sloganeering and the writing of aesthetic platforms.[30]

Applying these distinctions to some of the Soviet classics, it is indeed very hard to classify them: BRONENOSEZ » POTEMKIN « (1925, Sergei Eisenstein, › Battleship Potemkin ‹) uses many elements from documentary film and it was meant to reenact an incident from the pre-revolutionary days. The expensive films – one is tempted to say: blockbusters – commissioned for the tenth anniversary of the Revolution in October 1927, OKTJABR' (Sergei Eisenstein, › Ten Days That Shook the World ‹ / › October ‹), KONEC SANKT-PETERSBURGA (Vsevolod Pudovkin, › The End of St. Petersburg ‹), ODINNADCATYJ HRONIKA (Dziga Vertov, › The Eleventh Year ‹), VELIKIJ PUT' (Esfir Shub, › The Great Way ‹), and MOSKVA V OKTJABRE (Boris Barnet, › Moscow in October ‹), make use of real locations and actors, of newsreel footage and re-enactment.[31] These films could be integrated into many different film histories. They are commissioned films when one concentrates on the question of what the government wanted to achieve and whom

they chose for the task. They are examples of film propaganda when the emphasis was on the formal structure that was intended to persuade the spectator.
They belong to the history of documentary in the way these films have been
used later as reservoirs of footage depicting the revolution – the staged scenes
of the storming of the Winter Palace in Eisenstein's and Pudovkin's films are
now considered non-fiction material in contemporary TV documentaries about
the history of the Russian revolution. They are arguably heritage films in the
way that a not too distant past was idealised and an » imaginary community «[32]
was constructed around the represented events. These films are also docu-dra-
mas in the way some of them mix historical footage and re-enactment while
also, last but not least, being early examples of cinematic events. But, it is important to see that these distinctions did not seem to exist at the time for the
filmmakers, but that they were only later introduced as rigid demarcations between different genres of film.[33]

Esfir Shub is a key example of tearing down traditional categories; her trilogy
of Russian history 1896-1928 – comprising PADENIE DINASTII ROMANOVYH (SU
1927, › The Fall of the Romanoff Dynasty ‹) during the years 1912-17, VELIKIJ
PUT' (SU 1927, › The Great Way ‹) on the post-revolutionary decade 1917-27,
ROSSIJA NIKOLAJA II I LEV TOLSTOJ (SU 1928, › Czar Nikolaus II and Leo Tolstoi ‹) on two key figures of the epoch 1897-1912 – can be understood as an
extended historical essay. Rewriting recent history in ideological terms became
an important facet of Soviet filmmaking, but also of the avant-garde in the
West. Historiography, albeit in an altered form, could be seen as a key element
for the early avant-gardists, together with their didactic impact.[34] Indeed, this
might fruitfully direct us away from a purely formalist understanding of the
avant-garde. To make historical films while also changing the idea of history
amounted to nothing less than to a whole reinterpretation of the texture of the
world. Vertov in the mid-1920s was in this respect probably more important
than Eisenstein who only moved centre-stage after the success of his films
abroad:

> Vertov's influence went beyond documentary. Many observers felt that he influenced
> fiction films for the 1920s, in that his work and polemics helped to turn them away
> from earlier artificialities. Thus he may have strengthened the Soviet fiction film,
> though he scarcely intended to do so. There may also be a Vertov influence in the use
> of climactic actuality sequences in a number of fiction films – as in Kuleshov's cele-
> brated satire THE EXTRAORDINARY ADVENTURES OF MR. WEST IN THE LAND OF THE
> BOLSHEVIKS (NEOBYCHAINIYE PRIKLUCHENIYA MISTERA VESTA V STRANYE BOLSHEVI-
> KOV, 1924) and in Ermler's FRAGMENT OF AN EMPIRE (OBLOMOK IMPERII, 1929). Both
> end with tours of restored and rebuilt Moscow.
> The work of Dziga Vertov and of those he influenced had unquestionable propagan-
> da values for the Soviet government in the early and middle 1920s. Yet Vertov

thought of himself not as a propagandist, but as a reporter: his mission was to get out the news. Conflict – or potential conflict – between the obligations of a journalist and the demands of doctrine was not yet sensed as a problem in the early Vertov days. This happy moment passed quickly.[35]

But for a short moment before the documentary had coagulated into a form of filmmaking with its own rules, conventions, methods and standards[36], many forms of filmmaking could freely mix and mingle. To claim Vertov (or Shub, Turin, or Kalatozonov, for that matter) as a documentary filmmaker is retrospective reasoning, which disregards the specific historical situation in which these films were produced.

Just consider the variety of projects that Dziga Vertov was involved in before 1925: he oversaw the KINONEDELIA newsreel (SU 1918/19, 43 instalments), a rather traditional collection of informational reports, and the KINOPRAVDA newsreels (1922-25, 23 instalments), a far more experimental approach to the cinematic news format, he made compilation films and the canonised avant-garde classic KINOGLAZ (SU 1920), he worked on » cinema advertisements «, an early kind of commercial in the service of state institutions, he developed plans for the » Cinema Eye « project and a » Radiopravda « while also collaborating on animation films.[37] While he directed his avant-garde energy into many projects, they were all linked to emerging Soviet state agencies. Thus, from another perspective Vertov could also be seen less as an auteur of documentaries (his usual film-historical status), but as a maker of commissioned films. Annette Michelson has pointed out this other side of Vertov, the filmmaker in the service of others:

> The entire production of the group of *kinoki*, organized and administered by Vertov as chairman of their executive Council of Three between 1924 and 1934 … was commissioned by specific agencies for specific ends. Thus, FORWARD, SOVIET! (1925) had been commissioned by the Moscow Soviet as a demonstration of the progress made during the immediately post-Revolutionary construction of the new administrative capital of the socialist state; ONE-SIXTH OF THE WORLD (1926) was commissioned by Gostorg, the Bureau of Foreign Trade; THE ELEVENTH YEAR (1928) was a tenth-anniversary celebration of the advances in hydroelectric power; and ENTHUSIASM (1930) … celebrated the Stakhanovite acceleration of mining and agriculture in the Don Basin. THE MAN WITH THE MOVIE CAMERA (1929) stands alone as Vertov's wholly autonomous metacinematic celebration of filmmaking as a mode of production .... THREE SONGS OF LENIN [was] commissioned for the tenth anniversary of Lenin's death (and it was, of course, one of several such commissions)...[38]

One should add, however, that CELOVEK S KINOAPPARATOM was produced by VUFKU, the Ukrainian state trust for film, and thus Michelson's label of

» autonomous « appears problematic even for this avant-garde classic. The phenomenon of the avant-garde making commissioned or industrial films is not
limited to the Soviet Union as I have elaborated above.[39] Indeed, when thinking
about the celebrities of the interwar avant-garde, none of them – including Eisenstein, Richter, Ivens, Ruttmann and Buñuel – has more than one or two independently produced films to their credit. An ongoing dilemma for the avant-
garde, in a practical filmmaking sense as well as in theoretical discussions, is the
dependency on others for their filmmaking. Since no network of independent
outlets (film societies, *cinémas d'art et d'essai*, art houses, worker's clubs) tight
enough for the sustained support of independent filmmakers existed,[40] the
question persisted of where to look for support: the industry, the state or
wealthy patrons.

The Soviet filmmakers largely worked with support from the state as the Soviet Union appeared to be a radical new attempt to free itself from the conservatism of the established bourgeois nations. Therefore, no matter how much these
films might defy categorisation, they still share one important element: they
were all directly or (slightly) indirectly made in the service of the state. As Peter
Kenez has argued:

> Between 1925 and 1929, the studios made 413 films. ... [W]ith only a few exceptions,
> the films were made in order to serve the interests of the state. Some were made to
> popularize sports or the state lottery, or to help the fight against venereal disease, but
> the great majority were political. Even in these relatively liberal days, the Soviet re-
> gime rarely and barely tolerated a film that was made either › only ‹ to entertain or to
> give nothing but aesthetic pleasure.[41]

The Soviet Union, reminiscent of Ruttmann's call for the state as a sponsor of a
new film form,[42] put this specific form of support into practice. But the filmmakers paid a price for this dependency on the state: An existing institution
(the Soviet state) had no interest in abolishing itself, which was ultimately the
goal of the avant-garde. The avant-garde wanted to render art superfluous because life had changed to such a degree that the distinction between life and art
was meaningless. In systemic logic, an existing system (like the totality of state
institutions concerned with cinema) always works towards stabilisation and not
towards destroying itself. For a while, during the 1920s, the development of
avant-garde films made sense within the existing institutions (because radical
changes had to be instituted and propagated), but in the long run this could not
last and film style soon coagulated into Socialist Realism. Therefore, after the
revolutionary drive for novelty weakened in the course of the 1920s, the Soviet
authorities in the 1930s could neither tolerate an autonomous sphere for art nor
a privately funded film sector – the avant-garde working on the project of abol-

ishing art ultimately had to clash with the new leaders of the state who were also the new leaders of the art form.

5.4 Time and History: The Temporal Framework of the Avant-Garde

> *Any examination of a given epic form is concerned*
> *with the relationship of this form to historiography.*
> Walter Benjamin (1936)[43]

The avant-garde was characterised by an unconditional sense of utopianism that was directed solely at the future. Nevertheless, the avant-garde was caught up in a special kind of temporal relation which is deeply paradoxical at heart. By taking a closer look at Esfir Shub's trilogy of Soviet history, I want to approach this sense of a limitless future that could not exist without the past, and did away with the present. The energy of the avant-garde's utopianism was derived in no small measure from an overwhelming sense of being steeped in the past. While the avant-garde constantly claimed that it was winning the future, it needed the past as a dead horse for flogging.

When Esfir Shub began work on the film that would become the first part in the trilogy of Soviet history, Padenie dinastii Romanovyh (SU 1927), she realised that hardly any film documentation of the revolution existed in the Soviet Union. In their desperate lack of *valuta*, old film had been either reused or sold to the West. Shub started tracking down and collecting film stock in various places in the Soviet Union, but also pushed Sovkino to acquire material abroad. The Russian trade organisation Amtorg was even asked to acquire film stock in the United States for Shub, material that had been sent there as part of the workers' international relief. According to legend, Shub viewed about one million metres of film for the trilogy – only 6,000 metres were used, less than one percent.[44] In her autobiography she reports on her research trips in words that echo the archivist's labour of unearthing forgotten treasures. In Leningrad she discovered that

> all the valuable negatives and positives of war-time and pre-revolutionary newsreels were kept in a damp cellar ... The cans were coated with rust. In many places the dampness had caused the emulsion to come away from the celluloid base. Many shots that appeared on the lists had disappeared altogether. Not one metre of negative or positive on the February Revolution had been preserved, and I was even shown a document that declared that no film of that event could be found in Leningrad.[45]

Shub took on the task of the archivist cum found-footage filmmaker: tracking down material, following the most obscure traces, preserving and identifying the findings, and finally arranging everything in a new order, be it an archival catalogue or a film. Similar to makers of cross-section films like Walter Ruttmann and Albrecht Viktor Blum, Germaine Dulac and Edgar Beyfuss, the objective of her search was for the right shot.[46] Not unlike today's found-footage filmmakers who scan archives or flea-markets, attics or cellars, Shub went to extraordinary lengths to secure the material she needed for her project.

VELIKIJ PUT' (THE GREAT WAY), the second part of Shub's trilogy dealing with the post-revolutionary decade, was one of several state commissions on the occasion of the tenth anniversary of the October Revolution. Shub completely abstained from shooting new material while Eisenstein and Pudovkin were competing with elaborate re-stagings of the historical events culminating in the storming of the winter palace. They were effectively creating Spielbergian versions of history in which the construction of a certain (hi)story overrides all other concerns. Today's documentaries about the Russian revolution are unthinkable without these staged shots of the event which have long ago turned into real documentary footage of the event. Vertov and Shub, by contrast, concentrated on the technical and economic achievements of the Soviet Union in their typical montage structures – Vertov full of optical tricks and fast cutting, Shub slower in pace and giving the image and the single shot more scope.

In contrast to Eisenstein and Pudovkin, Shub maintained that any kind of real, historical material was preferable to a recreation of that same event, no matter how much » better « or more » realistic « the recreated material might be. Shub's argument in favour of her method was that the » non-acted « film (the term used in the Soviet Union at the time) was superior to the acted film because in retrospect we observe films differently. While » acted films « get weaker with age, her work would only increase in value as it utilised real film material:

> We think that in our epoch we can film only newsreel and thus preserve our epoch for a future generation. Only that. This means that we want to film the here and now, contemporary people, contemporary events. It does not worry us in the least whether Rykov or Lenin act well in front of the camera or whether this is a played moment. What is important to us is that the camera has filmed both Lenin and Dybenko even if they do not know how to show themselves off in front of the camera because it is this moment that characterises them most of all.
>
> Why does Dybenko not approach you in an abstract fashion? Because it is him and not someone portraying Dybenko. It does not worry us that here is a played moment. Let us talk about non-played cinema. Let it have its played moments. But what is the difference if you look, for example, at a remarkable played film made three years ago? You will not be able to watch it because it has become quite simply indigestible.

When you look at a non-played film this does not happen: it survives, it is interesting because it is a small fragment of the life that has really passed.[47]

Shub's text is mainly directed against Eisenstein's and Pudovkin's films that restaged the revolution and chose the same actor to play Lenin, mainly because of a striking facial and physical resemblance, even though his acting was rather clumsy. Whereas staging and the use of actors offer the opportunity of retrospectively altering what has happened and thus gives one almost boundless opportunities of how it will appear, using archival material means limiting oneself to existing shots. Yet again, the films Shub created are in no way neutral depictions of a time past, but they were very partial and present a strong version of history.

Shub's work should be seen in the context of debates that occurred in contemporary intellectual film magazines. The key discussion concerning the work of Esfir Shub took place in the magazine *Lef*, succeeded by *Novij Lef*, dominated by left-wing activists like Sergei Tretiakov, Viktor Shklovski and Osip Brik (also Shub's husband). *Lef* developed the concept of a » factory of facts «. Directed not only against the dream factory of Hollywood or Babelsberg, but also against Kozinzev's and Trauberg's factory of the eccentric actor FEKS as well as Eisenstein's factory of attractions, the factory of facts (or in poststructuralist fashion » fact-ory «) was meant to accompany the re-structuring measures put into practice in the Soviet Union in the 1920s. But the factory of facts was not meant to simply show the empirical evidence of the changes in the economic or social sector, but instead was meant to » organise life «, as it was called. » To organise life « meant that art played a crucial role in the building of the new society as the revolution had broken down the boundaries between art and life – the aim of all avant-garde activity. Art was now part of the new Soviet reality and thus participated actively in the transformation of the country, and did not just represent the change.[48] In this sense, many avant-garde activists felt that the Soviet Union had reached a stage that Western art forms could not compete with – art and life had a much stronger link in the Soviet Union than in Western Europe. Vertov, in an article published in *Pravda* in July 1926, argued against big fiction film studios and asked for a centralised film factory of facts: » Every non-played film in one place with a film laboratory. With an archive of non-played films. «[49] However, some time later Vertov fell from grace with the theoreticians of the avant-garde for his alleged lack of » radicalism «.

In 1927, a discussion in the pages of *Lef* played Shub off not against Eisenstein or Pudovkin (for the intellectual radicals of *Lef* that would have meant flogging already dead horses), but against the other Soviet innovator of the non-acted film: Dziga Vertov. The *Lef* authors went even further than Vertov because they valued the idea of the fact more than the creative montage. They attempted to eradicate authorship and the showmanship of brilliant editing by resorting to non-authored images or at least images not produced for the specific purpose for which they were used because at bottom the debate revolved around the question of how to write history.

If one makes a distinction between creating new images, on the one hand, and storing, sorting and manipulating them, on the other, then even Dziga Vertov's CELOVEK S KINOAPPARATOM (1929) consists of newly shot material. Shub was even more radical, as she reused only old material. Shub criticised Vertov for manufacturing facts and for staging and shooting his non-fiction material. Her avant-garde credentials went so far as to override the concerns of authorship and intentionality appreciated in the avant-garde movement of the cine-eyes which still believed in a collective *auteur*:

> The studio must ... remove its Futuristic sign and become simply a factory for non-played cinema where people could work on editing newsreels, films of the history of the Revolution made from newsreel footage, where scientific production films and general cultural films could be made as a counterweight to played entertainment films.[50]

The » kinoki «-group around Vertov was an important source of innovation for non-fiction filmmaking after the revolution, but by the second half of the 1920s this group had become the focus of criticism. The larger shift from an emphasis on rapid montage and the manipulative power of images to a valorisation of the long shot and a rather encyclopaedic style of editing is visible in the Shub vs. Vertov debate. It was not only the bravado editing that they criticised, but also Vertov's manner of filmmaking. As Victor Shklovsky wrote:

> I think that newsreel material is in Vertov's treatment deprived of its soul – its documentary quality. A newsreel needs titles and date. ... Dziga Vertov cuts up newsreels. In this sense his work is not artistically progressive. In essence he is behaving like those of our directors whose graves will be decorated with monuments, who cut up newsreels in order to use bits in their own films. These directors are turning our film libraries into piles of broken film.[51]

Not only does Shlovsky accuse Vertov of staging films and distorting reality, he moreover scolds him for destroying film, and for endangering the heritage of Soviet history. To Shklovsky, the preservation of the archive was more important than Vertov's films. Ultimately, as the debates within film circles became fiercer in the second half of the 1920s, the charge amounted to a wilful destruction of the heritage of the revolution, to a distortion of history as seen from the viewpoint of Marxist materialist history.

Mikhail Iampolski has examined the conception of history inherent in the compilation films of Esfir Shub. As we have seen, the film archive not only became a place for the preservation of film, but as the stored material provided an unauthored view of the past, the archive became the bearer of history. Ideally, a film of this kind should consist of many shots from all kinds of different sources. The document, the single shot was the basic building block in this conception of filmmaking: » The document not only became alienated from the director, it became a *document from the past*. «[52] The idea was to store the present day reality – the building of the new communist world – for the future in a temporal paradox typical of the avant-garde as a whole. The recorded material, the shot as document and monument became a view of the past for a future which was certain and imminent according to the laws of materialist history, but not yet fully achieved. The *Lef* activists evaluated the raw material higher than any rhetorical structure – the document was eternal, the film was fleeting and the archive was the place from which films were born and to which they returned: » In so far as the material was understood as raw material for permanent re-combination, the film archive became an endless and inexhaustible source for the future filmmaker. «[53] As a consequence, montage became practically indistinguishable from cataloguing. Shub's films do in fact contain long sequence where one gets the impression that every scene of » soldiers leaving for the front « or » workers in a factory « that she found, was included in the film. They sometimes look like catalogues of what was available at the time. This should not only present a direct view of reality, but it should also guard against the dangers of authored and virtuoso combinations. The underlying idea was to solve the paradox of the avant-garde that wanted to do away with artistic subjectivity (the romantic notion of the genius) theoretically, yet it only replaced it with another kind of genius as exhibited in the breathtaking montage sequences. Furthermore, an archaeological gaze is manifest in the films of Shub, which first and foremost treated single elements as monuments that keep their strangeness and distance as they were not inserted into a master plan. The shot is able to maintain some of its autonomy even though a different pattern may overlay the single element to a certain extent.

The final sequences of THE GREAT WAY demonstrate this paradoxical temporal construction. Children of different ethnic backgrounds are shown, underscoring the idea that the Soviet Union covering » one sixth of the earth « included all kinds of different people – communism as a universal hope for mankind. These children vowed to finish the work begun by their fathers. The final title declares » On this great way we will, following Iljitsch's legacy, build our new world «. The past is being evoked for a future to be won and achieved. Vladimir Iljitsch Lenin, metonymically standing in for the preceding generation that carried out the Revolution, has begun the revolutionary work and the children will fulfil this task. The past is modelled to promise a bright future, the present is already a past as it is just one step on the way to the future. This temporality was typical of the phase of the New Economic Policy that characterised the 1920s. As I have argued, culture became a crucial sector in this phase because the achievements of communism were most visible here, both inside and outside the country. While the economy went back to a model of capitalism, the arts exhibited the achievements and, more importantly, what the purpose of the fundamental transformations were. The promises were huge, the present situation was gloomy and cinema had the function of redeeming this advance on the future that had been handed out.

This, I maintain, is also the core dilemma of the avant-garde, not only in the Soviet Union, but anywhere where artists occupy this position. It's very name, avant-garde, already announces that it is ahead of the rest, striding forward and leading the mainstream. The avant-garde carries within itself the promise of a future better than the past or the present. Yet again, most of the iconoclastic energy of the avant-garde is directed against traditional bourgeois art, against its conventions of individual creation and individual reception and against its places of worships like museums or theatres. The avant-garde, while wanting to achieve the future, has its eyes firmly fixed on the past. This precarious and even tragic situation is succinctly summed up in Benjamin's angel of history who is eternally focused on wounds and catastrophes that the past has inflicted, which it wants to heal, but this is relentlessly pushed forward into the future.[54]

5.5   Berlin as the Gateway to the West

> *The peak output of the Russian film industry is more*
> *conveniently observed in Berlin than in Moscow.*
> Walter Benjamin (1927)[55]

In the course of the 1920s, the one-way-street of Western films coming to the Soviet Union developed into a policy of exchange. The conduit through which the vast majority of the Soviet films would reach Western screens was certainly Berlin; in fact, Germany was the first country to officially recognise the Soviet Union after the Revolution. Germany and the Soviet Union had already signed a trade agreement in April 1918, in the wake of the Brest-Litovsk Treaty, a contract followed by many close collaborations. One of the first Soviet films seen by a foreign audience documented the famine of 1921, GOLOD... GOLOD... GOLOD (SU 1921, Vladimir Gardin / Vsevolod Pudovkin); it was shown on 26 March 1922 in Berlin[56] and also that same year in Louis Delluc's ciné-club in Paris.[57] Based on this success, the *IAH*, closely linked to the communist party and to the Communist International (ComIntern), toured with programs of mostly non-fiction films to worker's clubs and union societies around Germany. These films were shown for humanitarian and political purposes – to rally support for the Soviet Union – and money was collected for hunger relief and to support the struggling state of the workers and peasants. The response to these films demonstrated the interest that Western audiences had for what was going on inside the Soviet Union, but they did not yet exhibit a radical new approach to filmmaking. The films were documents of the Soviet crisis and their aim was direct and immediate – to raise money for the starving workers and peasants. At this early stage of interchange, films were meant to evoke workers' solidarity in Germany and other countries for their Soviet comrades. The medium of film was largely chosen because it was easier to reach workers in the cinema than via publications or lectures. Nevertheless, film was not the only means for targeting workers' solidarity. The *IAH* arguably conceived and executed a veritable media campaign which in style was akin to the avant-garde idea of a united media front. Another important element of this relief effort was a media offensive that also included the magazine *Arbeiter-Illustrierte Zeitung* (originally titled *Sowjetrussland im Bild* until 1921).[58]

In September 1922, POLIKUSHKA (SU 1919/20, Alexander Sanin) was the first Soviet fiction film to be distributed commercially abroad.[59] This film, based on a story by Leo Tolstoy, fit into the preconceived ideas of the Russian cinema with its story of oppression in rural, Tsarist Russia. The ensuing pattern of distribution shows a peak of interest and popularity around 1930. From 1922 to 1925 two or three Soviet films annually found their way to German screens. 1926 brought the breakthrough with seven films, it was 13 in 1927, 12 in 1928 and 1929, 13 in 1930, eight in 1931 and 13 in 1932.[60] A combination of factors made Berlin important as the interface and channel through which many interchanges between the Soviet Union and the West took place. Germany had a geographical advantage as the most immediate access point. Furthermore, Germany had early on recognised the Soviet Union and their main trading partners were each other. Culturally, both countries had a long history of exchange and co-operation. In economic terms, this exchange was a crucial factor for the regeneration of the Soviet industry. Kristin Thompson has argued: » [I]f we take 1924 as the year when the Soviet cinema's recovery finally took hold, it becomes apparent that German-Soviet dealings played an extensive rôle in it. «[61] In the winter of 1925-26 *Prometheus* was founded as a daughter company of the *IAH*, a new distribution company specialised in Soviet films, which would later also venture into production.[62]

It is important to remember that the *IAH* was not a German organisation, but an international organisation (in its operations rather comparable to today's international NGOs) that had its headquarters in Germany. The *IAH* resulted from a change in policy in 1921 of the ComIntern, which reverted to a united front and support of the struggling Soviet Union – instead of trying to foment immediate revolutions in other countries. In fact, as the German communist party followed an anti-ComIntern strategy for some years in the mid-1920s, membership in the *IAH* lagged far behind that of other countries – in 1926, there were 1.25 million members in England, 600,000 in Japan, but only 25,000 in Germany.[63] The figurehead of the *IAH*, Willi Münzenberg, was able to build up a veritable media empire, possibly the most important alternative attempt at challenging the European media conglomerates. The various affiliations, *Weltfilm* and *Prometheus*, *VFV* and *IAH*, *Aufbau* and *Mezhrabpom'*, all worked together not towards creating revenue (the profits were channelled either into enlarging the companies or into workers' relief in the Soviet Union and elsewhere), but towards achieving change. While the set-up and internal organisation of the *IAH* mirrored that of the existing industry,[64] its aim did not: the commercial film industry strove towards a maximisation of profits while Münzenberg's aim was a communist revolution, to overthrow the existing economic and social system. In this way, Münzenberg shared avant-garde ideas in that he tried to topple the existing order of the film industry (and of society). It was the German-Soviet joint-venture *Mezhrabpom-Rus'* (*Mezhrabpom'* is the Russian acronym for » International Workers' Relief «) that succeeded in building up a vertical integrated structure while also keeping up its transnational network between the Soviet Union and Germany:

> Mezhrabpom-Rus' plowed some of its profits back into activities which contributed to the agitational and educational roles the government had mandated for Soviet cinema. It funded an › agit-steamer ‹ which carried cinema and other cultural activities into the countryside as part of the government's effort to reach remote areas of the USSR. It also used profits from its popular entertainment films to produce several agitational works.[65]

Mezhrabpom-Rus' (after the old *Rus'* management had been bought out in 1926 and the company was renamed *Mezhrabpomfil'm*) had a decisive advantage over other Soviet companies in the mixed economy of the NEP years: it was sufficiently capitalised because its capital sources were in hard Western currencies. All of the other film enterprises (*Sovkino*, *Sevzapkino* etc.) lacked sufficient funds for increasing production as a large part of their technical equipment and film stock had to be imported from abroad. But this joint venture was not just making a lot of interesting films since the financial situation was considerably better here, it was also co-producing films and setting up a pattern of exchange with the West.

Mezhrabpom' was producing a mixture of revolutionary works and genre films. It had its first successes with the science fiction drama AELITA (SU 1924, Iakov Protazanov), the family melodrama MEDWESHJA SWADBA (SU 1925, Konstantin Eggert, › The Bear's Wedding ‹) and the adventure serial MISS MEND.

PRIKLJUCENIJA TREH REPORTEROV (SU 1926, Fedor Ozep / Boris Barnet), but it also produced some of those films that are now considered classics of the Soviet cinema, like KONEZ SANT-PETERSBURGA (SU 1927, Vsevolod Pudovkin) and TRI PESNI O LENINE (SU 1933, Dziga Vertov). Another important contribution to the alternative cinema culture of the interwar period were the international co-productions such as FALSCHMÜNZER / SALAMANDRA (GER/SU 1929, Grigori Roschal) and DER LEBENDE LEICHNAM / SHIWOI TRUP (GER/SU 1929, Fedor Ozep).[66] This inauguration of co-productions between Germany and Soviet Russia was revived after the introduction of sound with Pudovkin's DEZERTIR, yet cut short in January 1933 when Hitler came to power. Other projects from this production line include failed films such as the unfinished METALL (GER/SU 1930-32, Hans Richter)[67] and VOSSTANIE RYBAKOV / DER AUFSTAND DER FISCHER (SU/GER, 1931-34, Erwin Piscator).

It might appear like anecdotal history, but it is arguably of allegorical significance that the film most often singled out as a precursor of » the golden age « of Soviet cinematography had as its topic the relationship between the West and the Soviet Union. NEOBYCHAINIYE PRIKLUCHENIYA MISTERA VESTA V STRANYE BOLSHEVIKOV (1924, Lev Kuleshov) participates in an imaginary dialogue via the cinema.[68] In Kuleshov's film, the Western, crime film, and chase sequences take turns with the *éducation idéologique* of an American capitalist who is on a business trip in Moscow. The textbook capitalist is turned into a textbook communist during his adventures and experiences. [69] In fact, many of the Soviet avant-garde activists were fervent admirers of all things American as America stood for progress and new developments. And even though the US and the Soviet Union were diametrically opposed ideologically, in many respects they were both young countries characterised by an extraordinary dynamic development in the 1920s centred on industrialisation and automation and they both provided models to which other countries turned. Despite all their differences, there was also a good deal of attraction between the Soviet Union and the United States. Not coincidentally, many filmmakers in the Soviet Union preferred Hollywood over Berlin or Paris for inspiration. Indeed, Kuleshov the most » Hollywoodised « of the Soviet *auteurs*, acknowledged his debt to the US cinema, even if that was an influence completely inflected by his avant-garde position:

> If he [Kuleshov, MH] looked to the conventions of Hollywood commercial cinema, he did so out of self-consciously modernist motives. If he raided capitalist cinema for models, he was also selecting out properties that he could apply to Soviet definitions of modernity in the arts. Whatever his debt to the Americans, his ideas also conformed to the program of the Russian avant-garde, specifically to ... the Constructivist ethos.[70]

As Kepley suggests, Kuleshov's modernism was in the spirit of the constructivist avant-garde treating the artist as a precision engineer who fabricated functional and streamlined objects far removed from a romantic ideal of individuality, genius and authorship. What attracted Kuleshov to the Hollywood cinema was its efficiency of narrative form, the energies it was able to generate, and its streamlined narrative process which proved to be highly popular in the Soviet Union as well as in all other countries that Hollywood films reached. Choosing the US cinema as its (formal) model was also a polemical choice since it meant rejecting the laborious and slow Russian dramas which had been produced in pre-revolutionary times and continued to be made in the first half of the 1920s with few changes. More often than not, modernism as a cultural and artistic movement and the modernisation of work and private life, of production methods and leisure time proved to be natural allies.

If one has to single out one specific event as a point of crystallisation, there is little doubt which moment to choose. POTEMKIN had its premiere in Berlin only three days after its first official screening in Moscow. On 18 January 1926 it opened in two cinemas in Moscow's centre and on 21 January it was shown in Berlin at the *Großes Schauspielhaus* at a closed memorial meeting for Lenin who had died on 21 January two years earlier.[71] The reception in the Soviet Union was mixed: while some observers hailed the film as a new achievement, others, especially fellow filmmakers, found fault with Eisenstein's film. The fate of POTEMKIN shows a pattern that does not seem altogether untypical of innovative films that only get real recognition after achieving success abroad.[72] When the German board of film censors prohibited public screenings of Eisenstein's film, *Prometheus*, Münzenberg's distribution and production company which owned the foreign rights to the film, called theatre director Erwin Piscator and theatre critic Alfred Kerr as witnesses with views the liberal intellectual establishment would listen to. On 10 April, the German supreme board of film censorship (*Filmoberprüfstelle*) approved the film with some cuts and regular screenings started despite strong protests from the political right on 29 April 1926 at the Apollo Theatre on the Friedrichstraße where it enjoyed a long and triumphant run. A variety of reasons contributed to the success of the film: a heavily politicised public sphere followed by intense interest in the developments inside the Soviet Union, the fights over censorship and cuts of the film created the hype necessary for a media event, and Edmund Meisel's score heightened its dramatic appeal. Meisel's music combined the routine of cinema accompaniment with some of Eisenstein's ideas and a tamed modernism in music and noise.[73] Finally, throughout the summer, bans in specific territories (the provincial states of Württemberg, Bavaria, Hesse and Thuringia) and temporarily on a nationwide level ensured that the film remained a hot topic of discussion and contributed in no small measure to the enormous success of the film. Even though from the first premiere version (1,740 m) more than 400 metres were cut in subsequent years (1,353 m – the version that was in circulation when the Nazis came to power in January 1933), the film made its impact and soon moved on to other countries: » [T]he explosive combination of POTEMKIN and Berlin in the 1920s had put both Eisenstein and Soviet film on the world cultural map. «[74] POTEMKIN was subsequently sold to 36 countries and it continued to be the only solidly canonised classics of the Soviet cinema of the 1920s.[75]

The British reception was similar to the German one in terms of censor reaction, however, the public's enthusiasm was nowhere near that of the Berlin frenzy. In fact, it took 3 years until the first closed screening of POTEMKIN took place at the Tivoli Palace in London's Strand organised and attended by the London *Film Society* on 10 November 1929. The reaction was somewhat cool, but Britain had already received its share of Soviet revolutionary cinema, thus the film was not a complete novelty. POTEMKIN had made its imaginary impact in Britain because the ban and public debate was widely discussed in public while the cinematographic void had been filled by other Soviet films. Moreover, British censorship was very severe, so Soviet films with revolutionary content were – if at all – only screened in closed film society circles. Most of the films considered classics in retrospect did not make it to regular cinema screenings.[76] POTEMKIN remained banned in Britain until after World War Two, just as it was in France. However, in France it was seen by many people in ciné-clubs and the French premiere was considerably earlier than the English: it was shown in Paris on 18 November 1926 at the *Ciné-Club de France*. In France, the line ran between the ciné-clubs which were often able to screen those films and the ordinary cinemas which only played the Soviet genre productions. Hardly any of the classic revolutionary films passed the censors for public exhibition and only Moussinac's *Amis de Spartacus*, Canudo's *Club des amis de septième art*, and the *Ciné-Club de France*, and a few communist party organisations and occasionally *Studio 28* were able to show Soviet films with revolutionary content.[77] The impact of the Soviet cinema was thus largely » imaginary « because most people only heard and read about the allegedly sensational films as they were unable to see them in the cinema.

POTEMKIN divided public opinion throughout Western Europe: the film was screened in Vienna, Geneva, and Stockholm, but it remained banned in Italy, Spain, Belgium, Denmark, Norway and the Baltic Republics.[78] The impact of Soviet films can hardly be overestimated and their influence can be seen in many classics of the transitional period: René Clair's SOUS LES TOITS DE PARIS (FR 1930) was influenced by Abram Rooms TRET'JA MESCANSKAJA (SU 1927, › Bed and Sofa ‹ / › Third Meshchanskaia Street ‹), Josef von Sternberg's SHANGHAI EXPRESS (US 1932) by Leonid Trauberg's GOLUBOJ EKSPRESS (SU 1929, › The Blue Express ‹) and Bunuel's LAS HURDAS / TIERRA SIN PAN (ES 1932) is indebted to SoL' SVANETII (SU 1930, Michail Kalatoznov). Moreover, without POTEMKIN and the impact of Soviet montage the whole British school of documentary would have been unthinkable. When Grierson's DRIFTERS premiered at the *Film Society* in London, it did so alongside Eisenstein's POTEMKIN; Grierson himself worked on adapting that classic for an English audience (translating titles, preparing it for censorship). Grierson was also instrumental in starting the Workers' Film Society which had as the main attraction on its first day of screening Victor Turin's TURKSIB. Just like Eisenstein's film, the English version was put together by Grierson.[79]

However, the proliferation and influence of Soviet films in the West was no one-way street. Whereas the early 1920s Soviet audiences saw mainly entertainment films from Germany and the US, in the latter half of the decade it was also art and avant-garde films that found an interested audience in the Soviet Union's big urban centres. According to Léon Moussinac who travelled frequently to the Soviet Union, the Soviet public (at least in the big cities) had by 1928 seen the films of Louis Delluc, Jean Epstein, René Clair, Abel Gance, Marcel L'Herbier, Germaine Dulac, Alberto Cavalcanti, Walter Ruttmann and Hans Richter.[80] Jay Leyda reported that the filmmakers in the Soviet Union were familiar with the work of Abel Gance, D.W. Griffith, James Cruze, Fritz Lang, G.W. Pabst, F. W. Murnau, Ernst Lubitsch and Richard Oswald. In 1927, Ilja Ehrenburg brought several avant-garde films from Paris for a screening to the Soviet Union.[81] And stylistic developments also ran on parallel tracks like when Vertov after a screening of René Clair's PARIS QUI DORT (FR 1923/24) confided in his diary how he so much wanted to make a similar film in technical terms.[82] The Soviet Union participated in the international network of alternative screenings, however, because the situation was different (and even though NEP did create a sort of market situation, it was still considerably different from a capitalist economy), these events took place in political or social organisations within close proximity to the state.

5.6 Publication and Travelling: Translations and the Grand Tour

Along with the Constructivists, Eisenstein developed a kinetic art,
not as an aesthetic experiment or exciting spectacle of interest in itself,
but from a › passionate desire to incite the spectator to action ‹
Standish Lawder (1975)[83]

Not soon after the first films of the montage school made their way to the West, the makers followed suit. Again, Berlin was the gateway and network node for cultural, economic and geographical reasons. The itinerary was almost invariably the same: from Moscow they went to Berlin and from there to other German cities (Frankfurt, Stuttgart, Hamburg) and then to other European avant-garde centres – Paris, London, Amsterdam and Rotterdam. The celebrated innovators visited mainly those metropolitan centres where production and exhibition in the alternative sector took place on a broader level. Thus, Spain and Portugal were not part of the itineraries and neither were Scandinavia or the Balkans, only the central European space demarcated in the Northwest by London, in the Southwest by Paris, with Berlin as both the imaginary and actual turnstile. Only Eisenstein and his close collaborators Alexandrov and Tissé spent any time exploring rural France and subsequently also crossed the Atlantic to the United States (and Mexico). These trips have been well researched and discussed, but always from a biographical angle and never in a synthesising fashion where the ant-like paths become visible in a comparative perspective.

Vsevolod Pudovkin paid several visits to Western Europe in the decisive years between 1927 and 1932. [84] In January 1927 Pudovkin travelled to Berlin for 2 weeks in order to attend the international premiere of MATJ. He returned to Berlin for the premiere of KONEC SANKT-PETERSBURGA on 5 November 1928, this time he stayed longer to work on a film: in the winter of 1928-29 Pudovkin played the leading role in DER LEBENDE LEICHNAM / SHIWOI TRUP (GER/SU 1928/29, Fedor Ozep), a German-Russian co-production between *Mezhrabpom'* and *Prometheus*. Filming took place in Berlin and Pudovkin took advantage of his extended stay in Germany to travel to the Netherlands for two days to visit the *Filmliga* for a screening of MATJ on 10 January.[85] On this occasion, Pudovkin invited Ivens to the Soviet Union to make a film there.[86] Pudovkin also travelled to London for three days upon invitation of Ivor Montagu for another screening of MATJ and a talk at the *Film Society* of London on 3 February 1929. During the same period, the German edition *Filmregie und Filmmanuskript* was published (late 1928). Despite his shooting schedule and his travels outside Germany, he found the time to lecture on film: On 13 January, Pudovkin was present at a matinee with Soviet films at the *Tauentzien-Palast* organised by the *Volksfilmverband* where KONEC SANKT-PETERSBURGA was screened.[87] This marketing opportunity was not lost on his contemporaries: The *Lichtbild-Bühne*, a trade paper which ran its own publishing house which published Pudovkin's book, reported at length on the lectures and activities of the Soviet director and published large ads alongside the articles.[88] On 29 February 1929, after nearly four months abroad, he returned to Moscow. In late May 1931, Pudovkin travelled to Germany for a third time, again to make a film, only this time not as an actor, but as a director of DEZERTIR, the story of a strike of dock workers in Hamburg. Pudovkin stayed to do research in Germany until 26 June 1931. Upon his return to the Soviet Union, he continued to work on the script until Hitler's ascent to power made shooting in Hamburg impossible and as a result the film was entirely produced in the Soviet Union.

The decisive year for the European avant-garde and the moment of its highest convergence of the various developments was certainly 1929: Dziga Vertov's first trip to Western Europe as a filmmaker of reputation was an extended voyage from early May to early August 1929 presenting CELOVEK S KINOAPPARATOM (SU 1929), planned and organised with the support of El Lissitzky and his German wife Sophie Küppers who probably also had a hand in the translation of Vertov's Russian texts for the various lectures he gave. He attended the screenings at the *Werkbund* exhibition *Film und Foto* in Stuttgart and was invited to La Sarraz as the Soviet delegate, however, he was forced to return to the Ukraine before the meeting.[89] It is worth recounting this trip in more detail because it illustrates typical stations and institutions: On 3 and 4 June he was at the Planetarium in Hanover, on 9 June he presented a film at the Phoebus-Palast in Berlin,[90], the following day at the Bauhaus in Dessau, and on 11 June at the Museum Folkwang in Essen. He visited the *Film und Foto* exhibition in Stuttgart where he gave a lecture on 16 June, on 23 June Vertov was at the association » Das Neue Frankfurt « in Frankfurt am Main,[91], on 29 and 30 June at the Bayerische Landesfilmbühne in Munich[92] and finally on 2 July, the tour ended at the Marmorhaus in Berlin. Conspicuously, it was only in Berlin that he appeared twice at (nominally) commercial venues, all of the other occasions were in the context of the film society and avant-garde movement (*Bauhaus, FiFo* exhibition, *Das neue Frankfurt*).[93] Vertov moved on to France where he was featured on 23 July 1929 at *Studio 28*. In Paris he stayed with his younger brother Boris Kaufman who was just about to start his celebrated co-operation with Jean Vigo on APROPOS DE NICE (FR 1929/30), ZERO DE CONDUITE (FR 1933), and L'ATALANTE (FR 1933/34).[94] Not only did he present films and give lectures, he also made production plans: Vertov was invited to make films on the building of new cities (in Frankfurt), on travel between Europe and the United States (in Hanover), and on medicine (in Zurich; the offer came from Lazare Wechsler and the film was later shot by Eisenstein, Alexandrov and Tissé as FRAUENNOT – FRAUENGLÜCK in late-1929). Vertov also planned to go to La Sarraz, but the Soviet authorities called him back for an assignment for a sound film about the industrial region of the Donbass (in the Ukraine).

When the film was finished he toured for seven months from June to December with ENTUZIAZM: SINFONIJA DONBASSA (SU 1930) in 1931.[95] The tour started as usual in Berlin, moved on to several German cities (Hannover, Hamburg), to Switzerland, London, Paris and finally the Netherlands from where he returned via Berlin to Moscow.[96] Even on a trip lasting six months, he seldom left the already well-trodden paths. During his second extended European journey, Vertov also visited London for the first time from 10 until 23 November where he presented ENTUZIAZM. Vertov was present at the screenings of his own films at the London *Film Society*, as Thorold Dickinson reports:

> When Vertov attended the presentation of his first sound film, ENTHUSIASM, to the Film Society of London on November 15, 1931, he insisted on controlling the sound projection. During the rehearsal he kept it at a normal level, but at the performance flanked on either side by the sound manager of the Tivoli Theatre and an officer of the Society, he raised the volume at the climaxes to earsplitting level. Begged to desist, he refused and finished the performance, fighting for possession of the instrument of control, while the building seemed to tremble with the flood of noise coming from behind the screen.[97]

It was also in London that Charlie Chaplin watched ENTUZIAZM at the private screening rooms of United Artists in Wardour Street on 17 November 1931 and wrote Vertov a note afterwards: » Never had I known that these mechanical sounds could be arranged to sound so beautiful. I regard it as one of the most exhilarating symphonies I have heard. Mr. Dziga Vertov is a musician. The professors should learn from him, not quarrel with him. Congratulations. «[98] On the same voyage Vertov paid his only visit to the *Filmliga*, and on 9 and 10 December gave lectures in Rotterdam and Amsterdam.[99]

Sergei Eisenstein's trips were reminiscent of Pudovkin's and Vertov's journeys. Eisenstein arrived in Berlin on 26 March 1926 (accompanied by his cameraman Eduard Tisse).[100] Initially, the purpose of the trip was to learn about technology and the German industry and to try out equipment – a research trip, in other words. During his stay in Berlin, Eisenstein witnessed the censorship debate concerning POTEMKIN after the German Board of Film Censors (*Filmprüfstelle*) had prohibited public exhibition of the film. He visited the major studios and saw Lang working on METROPOLIS[101] and Murnau making FAUST. Eisenstein and Tisse attempted to stick around for the premiere of their films, extending their trip beyond their planned length, but on the order of Sovkino they finally returned to the Soviet Union on 26 April 1926, three days before the international premiere of POTEMKIN.[102] This relatively unknown journey was followed three years later by an extended voyage, which lasted for three years and took Eisenstein and his collaborators throughout Western Europe, to the United States and Mexico. In the meantime, Eisenstein had become an international celebrity partly through screenings of his films in the West, partly because of the many visitors that came to Moscow where Western intellectuals invariably sought out Eisenstein because of his command of languages, his classic education and his wit and irony. In 1927-28 Eisenstein met Léon Moussinac, Edmund Meisel, Käthe Kollwitz, Diego Riviera, Sinclair Lewis, Le Corbusier, Valeska Gert, Stefan Zweig, Joseph Schenck, John Dos Passos and many more who visited the Soviet Union.[103]

The most famous trip was also the longest and possibly the biggest failure in terms of projects that fell through: the grand tour Eisenstein made with Tisse and Alexandrov in the key year of 1929. Their assignment was » to learn from the West and to teach the West «. Jay Leyda has summed up the manifold reasons for this trip:

> In August 1929, three months before the release of OLD AND NEW, the Eisenstein group left the Soviet Union for a stay abroad of undetermined length. By now there was an accumulation of reasons for the trip: a study of sound-film techniques in European studios was possibly the primary reason, and the one usually advanced, but there was also the hope of working for the world's best-equipped film industry, Hollywood; Eisenstein had received many invitations to go there, the latest being from Joseph Schenck who visited Moscow in the summer of 1928; a trip to America was looked upon as a deserved vacation for a group that had worked so continuously without leave. A more pressing reason was connected with Eisenstein's project to film *Capital*: he felt that he could not honestly undertake such a task without seeing the capitalist world at its zenith ....[104]

In the late Summer of 1929, on 19 August, Eisenstein, Tisse, and Alexandrov boarded a train to Berlin where they attended the German premiere of STAROE I NOVOE / GENERAL'NAJA LINIJA (SU 1926-29, › The Old and the New / The General Line ‹)[105] and then moved on to Switzerland for the La Sarraz meeting in early September 1929, the moment when many biographies, activities, discourses and trajectory overlapped before all taking on their own directions. Eisenstein was the undisputed star of the La Sarraz meeting, especially after the Swiss police had heightened the suspense by first refusing them entry because they feared that the three communist troublemakers would incite a revolution. The following months in Europe took them on a zigzag route. Soon after the conference, on 19 September, Eisenstein went back in Berlin for meetings, talks, plans and lectures. Tisse and Alexandrov stayed behind in Zürich for a while to shoot FRAUENNOT – FRAUENGLÜCK, a film about a woman's right to family planning produced by the Polish émigré Lazare Wechsler.[106] In November 1929, the trio travelled from Berlin to London upon the invitation of the London *Film Society* where POTEMKIN was shown on 10 November 1929, alongside Grierson's DRIFTERS. The Soviet group went to Paris on 29 November, but was already back in London on 3 December where Eisenstein participated in Hans Richter's course on filmmaking – the material was later edited together by Richter into the film EVERYDAY, in which Eisenstein can be seen as an English policeman. Many of the later protagonists of the British documentary film movement and feature film participated in the workshop: Grierson, Basil Wright, Thorold Dickinson, Anthony Asquith, Ian Dalrymple and Herbert Marshall. Eisenstein stayed for a couple of weeks, leaving London (after visits to Windsor and Oxford) in late December 1929. For Christmas and New Years he was back in Paris and then visited the Netherlands as a guest of honour at the *Filmliga* from 14 to 20 January[107] until he returned to Paris in February 1930.[108]

In Paris, the next job was to raise money for shooting ROMANCE SENTIMEN-TALE (FR 1930), which was financed by the millionaire Leonard Rosenthal to indulge his mistress Mara Gris. Many more offers reached Eisenstein, among them such curiosities as making a long advertising film for Nestlé's condensed milk (on the strength of the milk sequence in THE OLD AND THE NEW) or shooting an anniversary film on Simon Bolivar commissioned by the Venezuelan government.[109] Interestingly, it was not the European film industry which was interested in hiring the young Soviet director, with most of the assignments coming either from private patrons, companies outside of the film business, state institutions or organisations involved with reformist social change. Besides a multitude of anecdotes, Eisenstein became the centre of a dispute when a screening at the Sorbonne got cancelled (he gave an inflammatory speech instead)[110] and his visa was not prolonged. He was still able to meet with influential artists and intellectuals like Abel Gance, James Joyce, Gertrude Stein, André Malraux, Joris Ivens, Germaine Krull, Eli Lotar, André Kertesz and others. Eisenstein was even approached to collaborate with Fyodor Chaliapin on DON QUIXOTE, a project Walter Ruttmann was also associated with and that finally ended up being directed by G.W. Pabst in 1932-33. Eisenstein left France on 6 May 1930 on a ship appropriately named *Europa*. Two years later, in May 1932, he was back in the Soviet Union after several unsuccessful projects at Paramount and the disastrous Mexican adventure QUE VIVA MEXICO! financed by Upton Sinclair.[111] He returned via New York, on the same *Europa* to Cherbourg, then on to Hamburg where he hoped in vain to receive his Mexican material. On the train to Moscow, Eisenstein met Bertolt Brecht and Slatan Dudow, on their way to the Soviet premiere of KUHLE WAMPE.

The final missing name in the traditional pantheon of great Soviet directors is Alexander Dovshenko who spent some time in Warsaw and Berlin at the Ukrainian embassies (possibly as a spy and rabble-rouser) in the early 1920s. His only trip as a filmmaker to the West in the period under consideration took place in the second half of 1930. Dovzhenko left the Soviet Union on 19 June 1930 and visited major European film production centres in Poland, Czechoslovakia, Germany, France and Great Britain: »During his trip he met the French director Abel Gance, H.G. Wells, Albert Einstein and other celebrated artists and intellectuals. ... He undertook the trip with the primary purpose of investigating new trends in film-making, especially the rise of sound film.«[112] Director Boris Barnet also spent two and a half months in Germany and France in 1933. His film OKRAINA (SU 1933, OUTSKIRTS) was presented at a closed screening in Paris attended by Victor Trivas, Jacques Feyder, Joris Ivens, Ilja Ehrenburg, Isaac Babel and others.[113]

Having recounted the main itineraries, at least five reasons for these trips can be named: First, the Soviet industry's impoverishment meant that filmmakers had to look abroad for innovations of technology as well as technique. Not coincidentally, Eisenstein visited the sets of METROPOLIS and FAUST on his first Berlin trip, the two most advanced special effects spectacles of the German art cinema of the 1920s, while doing research in Hollywood on his second trip. The Soviet film industry was characterised by a lack of film stock, by insufficient lighting gear and a general dearth of modern equipment. Second, the chance to make films abroad was seductive in terms of the means available even to an independent production. Pudovkin certainly took advantage of the possibility of shooting abroad, but so did Eisenstein and his entourage, even though their extended trip of 1929–1931 marks the climax as well as the end of this period. Third, this also proved to be interesting to Soviet authorities because they might raise badly needed foreign currency this way. The fourth reason – and visible in the case of Eisenstein's stay in Mexico – was the beginning Stalinization at home, both aesthetically and organisationally. After the restructuring had set in around 1928, it became increasingly difficult for independent minds to execute their projects. The criticism levelled against OKTJABR' is a case in point here; the climate in the Soviet Union was slowly changing, so journeys also became a welcome opportunity to get away from a difficult situation at home, which to some observers might have appeared at the time as a passing interlude. The changes in aesthetic policy and organisational structure made it more difficult for the innovators of the mid-1920s to realise their projects that were used to working in relative freedom. Paradoxically, the craze for Soviet films in Western Europe was peaking at a moment when the climate in the Soviet Union was radically changing. While troubles were intensifying at home, hopes were high in Western Europe – a further temporal paradox. The fifth and final reason is possibly less personal for the filmmakers and shows that the Soviet Union also had an interest in these trips. These luminaries also toured the big cities of Western Europe as goodwill ambassadors and as activists for the Soviet cause. In the long run, the Soviet Union had an interest in either spreading its cause or at least establishing political, economic and cultural ties and relationships.[114] Germany was an important trading partner while also – as many believed in the late 1920s – the next country that would see a communist revolution. Thus, the trips were also meant as propaganda for the revolutionary cause.

As influential as the tours of Soviet filmmakers in the West were, they were possibly equalled or even surpassed in effect by the many Western translations of Russian texts published in journals, magazines and books . The distinction between theory and practice did not exist for the avant-garde, so it was only logical for Pudovkin, Eisenstein, Vertov and others to make not only films but also publish related articles. In the West they were eagerly read as testimonies and manuals to aid in the understanding of the Soviet cinema. Pudovkin's volumes on » The Film Scenario « and on the » Film Director and Film Material «, written during the production of MATJ and published in 1926, were already enormously successful in the Soviet Union.[115] They were quickly translated into German and only a little later into English by Ivor Montagu who underlined the importance of these texts:

> [T]he most influential of all the things in all cinema, English and American, even the commercial cinema, I dare say, was the Pudovkin book that I translated. ... That Pudovkin book was so simple, no Eisenstein book could have had the same influence. What is in it was pinched either from Kuleshov who taught it directly to him or from Eisenstein, but he translated it as the simple, idealist and poetic-minded person that he was, into simple language that everybody could understand, and anybody even the simplest amateur can get ideas from Pudovkin.[116]

Beginning in 1928 with the travel activities, there is a marked increase of articles translated from the Russian to be found in Western magazines and newspapers. These texts, often coinciding with a lecture series, were published in widely diverse organs, from communist party newspapers (*L'Humanite*) to established trade papers (*Filmkurier, Lichtbildbühne*), from left-wing intellectual magazines (*Die Weltbühne*) to specialised avant-garde film journals (*Filmliga, Film und Volk, La revue du cinéma, Close Up*). It is apparent from this variety of publications how widespread interest in the cinema was and how central the Soviet cinema stood from 1926 until 1930.

In fact, translations became a two-way road, a dialogue of a sort that contributed to the sense of a network in the process of transforming cinema as such. Publishing boomed even prior to film production's more experimental development. In some respects, magazines paved the way for the later creative outburst in filmmaking. The energy devoted to theorising some of the crucial issues connected to cinema was necessary to open up the path that would be taken from the mid-1920s onwards. With the exception of France, no other country could boast a livelier publication and magazine scene than the Soviet Union. Publishing can be seen as an avant-garde activity because it can lead the way for filmmaking or for trying out ideas and positions since the avant-garde is always as much about possibility as about reality. This avant-garde function was due to accessibility (it was easier for young Turks to publish an article or even start a magazine than make a film) and to a lack of funds for making films because very few films were actually made in the Soviet Union at the time. Like Kuleshov's » films without film « and imaginary architecture, little magazines opened up a space of possibility as well as a space for unexpected encounters and juxtapositions – just like their Western equivalents *i10, transitions, de stijl, Die Form, G* or *documents*. It also reflected the situation in the decade after the Revolution when a public discussion about the means and methods of the Soviet cinema was still possible. It was in this turbulent period of cinema that publication did not follow film-making, but actually often led the way. In the decade between 1922 and 1932, 173 books on film were published;[117] even though most of these titles were biographies of foreign stars or accompanied popular releases, many of them were serious attempts at theorising cinema. In the Soviet Union, twisted temporalities were not unusual: filmmakers celebrated abroad came under fire at home while films that had not even been made yet were reviewed and discussed and– just as Soviet cineastes wrote about sound film before they had even seen, let alone made, a sound film.

5.7 Allegories of the Heavy Industry: The Battle with Sound

> *Our cherished dreams of a sound cinema are being realised.*
> Sergei Eisenstein, Grigori Alexandrov, Vsevolod Pudovkin (1928)

Discussions regarding film form and style and the problems involved in financing and organising Soviet cinema began to re-surface after a brief period of exaltation in the mid-1920s that followed the relative stabilisation of the cinema sector. The industrial restructuring began seriously in March 1928 with the Party conference on cinema, which resulted in the first Five-Year-Plan (which lasted until 1933) on cinema.[118] Slowly the (limited) free-market situation of the NEP was converted to one of state control. Big institutions were liquidated or purged like Sovkino in June 1930, which was subsequently restructured and reborn as Soiuzkino with Boris Shumyatsky as chairman.[119] The government organisation culminated in 1935 when the All-Union Creative Conference on Cinematographic Affairs derided Eisenstein[120], when a film festival was held in Moscow and when Shumyatsky went on a long research trip to Europe and the US with some of his most dedicated and politically reliable co-workers. Upon his return he decided to build a Soviet Hollywood on the Krim, which was scheduled to produce some 700 films annually. At the same time, entertainment was pushed back to make room for more obvious propaganda. But the megalomaniacal plans for the Soviet Hollywood did not materialise as Shumyatsky fell from grace with Stalin (and was eventually killed in the purges of 1938). One of the final steps away from the heyday of the 1920s was the liquidation of the *Mezrabpom'* in early 1936. The period from 1928 to the mid-1930s was also the period of the introduction of sound which lasted, contrary to received wisdom, nearly a decade in the Soviet Union.[121] Moreover, the coincidence of sound film with the shift from the limited free market situation of NEP to a » command economy « and the transition from a limited pluralistic public sphere to a cultural revolution complicates the retrospective understanding of sound cinema in the Soviet Union.

Probably one of the first statements on the sound film by filmmakers anywhere in the world (not just in the Soviet Union) came from Eisenstein, Alexandrov and Pudovkin. They published their » Manifesto on Sound Film « (› Zayavka ‹) first in German as » Achtung! Goldgrube! Gedanken über die Zukunft des Hörfilms « on 28 July 1928 in the trade paper *Lichtbild-Bühne*. It was subsequently published on 5 August 1928 in the magazine *Zizn' iskusstva* (› The Life of Art ‹) and in December 1928 in English[122], long before any of them had actually seen a sound film. Quite significantly, they greeted the new technology with cautious enthusiasm and referred to it as » [o]ur cherished dreams «[123]. They continued with a number of qualifications about the proper use of sound and pointed out the danger that a purely illustrative use of sound might have in » dramas of high culture «. More importantly, the three filmmakers saw sound technology as » an organic escape for cinema's cultural avant-garde from a whole series of blind alleys which have appeared inescapable «. The blind alleys are identified as the inter-title (and its integration into the image) and explanatory sequences. These issues were particularly pertinent in the other two centres of the European avant-garde: in Germany where the title-less film DER LETZTE MANN (GER 1924, F.W. Murnau, THE LAST LAUGH) and other experiments in a similar vein had caused a considerable stir[124] and in France where impressionist filmmaking had refined the art of the insert and close-up and subjective sequences illustrating mental states. Even though the text was not absolutely clear on these matters it seems that overt complexity and *raffinesse* was seen by Soviet filmmakers as the main problem of the avant-garde. They also addressed the question of internationality and claim that a contrapuntal use of sound would not imprison » the sound film ... within national markets ..., but will provide an even greater opportunity than before of speeding the idea contained in a film throughout the whole globe, preserving its world-wide viability. « Rejected outright was the use of dialogue for advancing the plot of the film. Even though sound film developed quite differently, some of the ideas were used for several years. DEZERTIR (SU 1933, Vsevolod Pudovkin), for example, was still employing written inter-titles to explain details about the ongoing strike while sound is used contrapuntally, for example, in the confrontations between the striking dock workers and the police. Whereas in comparable films from the same period, sound is employed in a Brechtian fashion to illustrate the divergent positions of the social democrats and communists like in KUHLE WAMPE ODER WEM GEHÖRT DIE WELT? (GER 1932, Slatan Dudow).

Sound film in the Soviet Union was introduced within the context of the first Five-Year-Plan (1928-32), which stressed the development of heavy industry. In its accompanying move towards centralisation and huge production centres, the plan » gave a new propaganda job to the comparatively light film industry, and geared film-making to the basic industrial programme. «[125] Filmmaking became a sector of heavy industry, a similar development as in the West where huge electrical companies (General Electric, Western Electric, AEG, Siemens & Halske, Philips) offered the capital stimulus necessary for the film industry to revert swiftly to sound. In the Soviet Union as well as in the West, it was the industry at large that supported the film sector in achieving sound in a fairly short period of time. One of the first applications of the Soviet sound system, PLAN VELIKIKH RABOT (SU 1929/30, Abram Room, › Plan for Great Works ‹), which was completely post-synchronised with sound effects, music and voice-over agit-prop statements, dealt with the achievements of the Five-Year-Plan. The film presents an allegory or *mise-en-abyme* of the introduction of sound film as its technological novelty value (sound) is made possible through that which is the subject of the film itself. Similarly Dziga Vertov's first sound film ENTU-ZIAZM: SINFONIJA DONBASSA (SU 1930) portrays a variety of industries concerned with the Five-Year-Plan, while Aleksandr Dovshenko's first sound film, IVAN (SU 1932), focuses on the construction of the great Dnjepr Dam, which also stresses the industrialisation of the agrarian countryside. Many early sound films were directly or indirectly concerned with issues pertinent to the forced industrialisation process included in the Five-Year-Plan: ZEMLJA ZAZDET (SU 1930, Juri Raizman, › The Earth Thirsts ‹) and ODNA (SU 1931, Grigori Kozintsev / Leonid Trauberg, › Alone ‹) deal with regional developments while Esfir Shub's KSE – KOMSOMOL, SEF ELEKTRIFIKACII (SU 1932, › Komsomol, Patron of Electrification ‹) is concerned with one of the key measures in the industrialisation and electrification of this enormous country.[126] The first sound films in the Soviet Union can therefore be seen as allegories of their own production process and the industrial development in general.

The introduction of sound not only coincided with the efforts of building up the heavy industry within the framework of the first Five-Year-Plan, it also arrived roughly at the same time as the introduction of the Stalinist dogma of Socialist Realism. Thus, sound and realism happened to grow stronger simultaneously, even if nothing in fact necessitates this connection between sound film and a realist agenda. In fact, early sound films such as ENTUZIAZM and DEZER-TIR have a very experimental approach to using sound, which consciously refrains from realistic sound effects. The reason for the shift to realism has to be located elsewhere and cannot be detected in some inherent characteristic of sound film. In fact, Socialist Realism is very different from the critical realism of bourgeois art in the second half of the 19th century and it is much closer to the revolutionary films of the 1920s than commonly assumed. The collective heroes of the » Russenfilme « were not replaced by individualised and internally rounded characters that would adhere to ideals of psychological verisimilitude, but these larger-than-life heroes were individualised versions of the collective protagonists of 1920s cinema. A film like Sergei Eisenstein's ALEXANDER NEVSKI (SU 1937) makes this dialectic between the individual and the collective clear in the way that individuals are juxtaposed with or framed by the masses. The title character Nevski remains a poorly developed Socialist idea while the dramatic conflicts are found in the supporting characters. In fact, individuals in films of this period are often just stand-ins for the collective agent of history. Similar observations could be made for CHAPAEV (SU 1934, Georgii & Sergei Vasilev) and the Maxim-trilogy of Leonid Trauberg and Grigorij Kozintsev (IUNOST' MAKSIMA, SU 1934-35, › The Youth of Maxim ‹; VOZVRASHCHENIE MAKSIMA, SU 1937, › The Return of Maxim ‹; VYBORGSKAIA STORONA, SU 1939 › The Vyborg Side ‹).[127]

Two arguments in favour of traditional narratives with recognisable heroes as identification figures were advanced in the Soviet Union at that time: One was polemically directed against experimentation (formalism) and the lack of popularity of montage cinema with audiences, the other was more intricate and was designed to promote the Soviet planned economy. While the former was inherently populist and remained a staple of polemic attacks throughout the 1930s, the latter is more interesting as it points towards a theoretical concept behind Socialist Realism. This argument for a more realistic film style in general was to present the Soviet achievements to the spectators. Foreign films which exhibited a bourgeois lifestyle in alluring images remained popular with Soviet audiences despite progress in Soviet production processes. Many of the homemade montage films were hailed as great artistic achievements, yet they did not elicit enthusiastic responses from the audience, while the more traditional Soviet films by directors such as Iakov Protazanov were popular, but did not meet the demands of the political functionaries. Thus, to counter the popularity of the lush foreign films, realism was promoted as an advertising possibility for the Soviet way of life. In a wider perspective, this is a logical shift in avant-garde positions in the arts: At a time when the communist economy and society had been firmly established, at a time when a certain stability had been achieved (at least in the sector of basic necessities), culture no longer had to fulfil the function of presenting a future ideal to be achieved. The arts could now provide an image of Soviet life, so that the spectators could recognise the achievements made by socialism. The deferral into a far-away future typical of the 1920s gave way to a very different kind of cultural policy which promoted the Soviet chic.

5.8 Vanishing Point: From Imaginary Projections to Literal Purges

Back in the USSR
Don't know how lucky you are
The Beatles (1968)

The trips Soviet filmmakers took to the West inaugurated a period of intensive travel activities. Only briefly after this exchange set in, trips in the opposite direction – from East to West – began. Many journalists had travelled to the Soviet Union in the years following the revolution, reporting on the state of this huge experiment. Filmmaking contacts – in the sense of working abroad or presenting films and lecturing – only began seriously in the late 1920s. Naturally, Moscow was for Western filmmakers what Berlin was to the Soviets: landing pad, gateway and network node. One of the first directors to come to the Soviet Union with his films was Joris Ivens who departed for Moscow on 13 January 1930 where he stayed in Sergei Eisenstein's apartment and was shown around by Pera Attasheva.[128] After two weeks in the capital, he travelled around the country presenting his films (and some of his *Filmliga* colleagues' films) in various Russian cities, but also in the Ukraine, Georgia and Armenia. He received two commissions for non-fiction films on this trip: one from the builder's union for a film about the construction of a dam, the second from Sovkino on a topic that was to be decided later. Ivens returned on 6 April to Amsterdam with every intention on returning to the Soviet Union as soon as possible. For both Ivens and the Soviet Union the trip proved successful: Ivens sold copies of his films to Sovkino's distribution arm and he was commissioned to return to the young country not as a visitor, but as a » film worker «. Much to the advantage of the Soviet Union, Ivens had turned from a sympathetic observer to an ardent propagandist of the communist cause. Back in the Netherlands, he toured worker's clubs, gave interviews and did everything he could to support the Soviet Union. Some of his friends poked fun at him by calling him » Boris Ivens « after his conversion. The prospect of films by Joris Ivens (and other established Western directors) must have thrilled the functionaries in the Soviet film industry as these filmmakers had an established following and often distribution contacts as well which meant that those productions could be both commercially viable and ideologically pleasing – the marriage of these two elements had been the focus of discussions throughout the 1920s.

Ivens' second trip began on 9 October 1931 and he stayed for more than a year making KOMSOMOL (SU 1932-33, › Song of Heroes ‹) in Magnitogorsk where Ernst May from Frankfurt and Mart Stam and Johan Niegeman from the Netherlands worked as architects at the same time. Ivens contracted Hanns Eisler for the music and Sergei Tretiakov for the lyrics of the film. Ivens' trip belongs to a series of invitations issued by *Mezhrabpom'* and other institutions not limited to film directors – besides Ivens, also avant-garde filmmakers Hans Richter and Walter Ruttmann, writers Belá Balázs, Friedrich Wolf and Egon Erwin Kisch, composer Hanns Eisler and theater director Erwin Piscator were asked to work in the Soviet Union. Piscator accepted the invitation in September 1930 after he found himself in a difficult financial position in Berlin when his theatres filed for bankruptcy and a new start seemed difficult due to the generally strained economic situation. Piscator left Germany on 10 April 1931 with his close collaborator Otto Katz who stayed behind in Moscow to work as a production manager for *Mezhrabpom'*.[129] The production of Vosstanie rybakov / Der Aufstand der Fischer (SU/GER, 1931-1934), based on Anna Seghers novel, turned into a labyrinthine nightmare full of accidents, misunderstandings, personal over-sensitivity, and political cabals.[130] Planned originally in two language versions (Russian and German), the shooting was interrupted several times until the film finally premiered on 5 October 1934 in Moscow, more than three years after the shooting started.[131] The German version had been abandoned in the meantime and *Mezhrabpom'* was attacked in the increasingly tense atmosphere for inviting film workers who never finished their Soviet projects.[132]

Ivens made a third trip to the Soviet Union, staying from April 1934 to January 1936 where he worked on a film about the Saar vote, prepared a new version of Misère au Borinage (BE 1933/34, Joris Ivens/Henri Storck) and collaborated with Gustav von Wangenheim on Borzy (SU 1935/36, › Fighter ‹). However, he failed to finish a new film not unlike some of the other invitees.[133] Richter's unfinished film Metall (SU 1931-33) was conceived as a complimentary piece to Pudovkin's Dezertir – while the former was to deal with a strike and a subsequent visit by Hamburg dock workers to the Soviet Union. Richter's film, scripted by Friedrich Wolf, should have done the same with Berlin metal workers from the borough of Henningsdorf.[134] In May 1931, Wolf travelled to the Soviet Union, in June Richter followed – the crew for Metall spent a beautiful, yet unproductive summer in Odessa. Evidence points to frictions between *Mezhrabpom'* (Francesco Misano, the head of production, and Otto Katz, Piscator's long-time collaborator and production manager) and the Russians. Another artist commissioned to do a project was the Hungarian-German writer Belá Balázs who arrived in 1931 in Moscow where he made Tisza Garit (SU 1933/34) about the short-lived Hungarian communist episode. But the film was suppressed by the authorities and is nowadays considered lost.[135]

Jacques Feyder who had earned a reputation in avant-garde circles with Visages des enfants (FR 1923-25) and Les nouveaux messieurs (FR 1928) had already been invited in 1928 to make a film in the Soviet Union[136] – instead

Feyder chose to go to Hollywood on the invitation of M-G-M from where he returned disillusioned in 1931, like many other avant-garde artists. An invitation was also offered to Luis Buñuel in the winter of 1931-32[137] and reissued by Louis Aragon in December 1932.[138] Buñuel's project was based on a script to be written by André Gide based on his novel *Les caves du Vatican* (1914). Even though Gide politely declined, in February 1935, Buñuel was still contemplating the possibility of making a film in the Soviet Union.[139]

A last wave of co-operation can be discerned around 1935-36 when the worst purges where just commencing. At least 19 of the film *émigrés* from Germany were shot or died in the Gulag, at least seven were sent to prison.[140] The most important event of the German emigration to the Soviet Union was certainly the production of Borzy (SU 1935-36, Gustav von Wangenheim, FIGHTER), based on the Nazi court case against Georgi Dimitrov following the fire in the Berlin Reichstag in 1933.[141] In January 1936, Max Ophüls went to the Soviet Union where he spent two months auditioning film projects while also helping to promote Borzy. In the spring of 1936, Ernst Lubitsch also came to the Soviet Union from Hollywood just as William Dieterle did one year later, all hoping to find work at Sumjacki's » Hollywood on the Krimean «. More important was the ComIntern policy of the popular front, which with the outbreak of the Spanish Civil War in 1936, the official communist policy reverted to a collaboration with left-wing liberals who were not self-proclaimed communists.[142]

If this is going to be more than just a regurgitation of biographical data, we have to consider the facts on a structural level. What made these symmetrically mirrored journeys from East to West and from West to East possible and desirable for both parties involved? Perhaps more importantly, why did they either produce works that never succeeded within the canon of avant-garde classics (KOMSOMOL, DEZERTIR, BORZY) or abandoned projects after a considerable amount of time and energy had been devoted to them? It seems that several paradoxes inherent in the avant-garde of the 1920s resurfaced here. For once, politics returned with a vengeance as the Western filmmakers were inexperienced in dealing with the Soviet public sphere, which was considerably different from its Western counterpart. Ideological debates were fierce and as the decade progressed the danger of intellectual isolation or unemployment turned into a life-threatening situation when someone was suddenly suspiciously unreliable by the authorities. While Peter Wollen's theory of » two avant-gardes «[143] (one oriented towards formal abstraction, the other towards political activism) might be overstated for the 1920s (on which side do we put Eisenstein or Ivens before the arrival of sound?), the 1930s certainly witnessed a split of the avant-garde into various directions. It is interesting to note that no French or British activists were invited; one reason may have been that these two countries still offered considerable room for left-wing activities, thus making the uncertain trip to Moscow unnecessary. Moreover, the French filmmakers leaned towards a commercial art cinema while the German and Dutch activists had considerable experience with an industrial environment and commissioned film work. The artists and technicians ultimately came from Germany, the Netherlands, Hungary and other countries. Another reason is found in the official policy of the ComIntern, which proclaimed a united front against the fascists, but dealing with Soviet authorities remained complicated. The gap between official rhetoric and the gritty day-to-day dealings often proved to be unbridgeable. And, last but not least, these Western filmmakers came at a time when the working conditions were deteriorating for everybody in the Soviet Union as Stalinist restructuring was in full swing. Thus, one has to remember that *Mezhrabpom'* was viewed by many as a remnant from the NEP period and was itself under fire. Part of that pressure was passed onto the visitors who often were either ignorant of the general development of the Soviet film industry or had an inadequate grasp of the Russian language and cultural politics to be able to understand (their own role in) the events.

5.9 Conclusion

> *In Russian film the notion of art,*
> *as it exists in Europe, is overcome.*
> Hans Richter (1930)[144]

Traditional views of the Soviet cinema that started to develop when Soviet films were first encountered in the 1920s and 1930s often resort to two models which dominated the 1920s and 1930s respectively and which still have currency today: revolutionary, formally innovative and modernist cinema – the » good « object – was followed by reactionary, formally conservative and classicist film – the » bad « object. That the transition between the two phases could be short-circuited with the introduction of sound only intensified the attraction of this model. Ian Christie has described and problematised the over-simplified historiography of these two phases:

> Soviet cinema … was first constructed as an › idealised other ‹ in relation to its western counterpart. And when that opposition was made redundant by the sweeping changes in western cinema after the introduction of sound, the still struggling › industrialised ‹ Soviet cinema of the mid-1930s was rejected as inferior to both Hollywood and the emerging documentary movements of Britain and America. Thus a new interpretive model emerged: that of a state propaganda machine, ruthlessly subordinating artistry and non-conformity to its philistine needs. Essentially this remains the domi-

nant western model, continuing to colour the perception of contemporary Soviet cinema.[145]

I hope I have also contributed to the breaking apart of this binary dichotomy, which does neither decade justice. By employing a different frame of references, this period gives a somewhat different image from the traditional film historical account.

As I have argued, much of the avant-garde spirit of the wave of the » Russen-filme « derived from the specific circumstances under which they were produced and received: While the official government doctrine at the time of their making proclaimed that the socialist society was still evolving and as the economic system reverted back to a market economy in the mid-1920s, the arts were obliged to fulfil the function of depicting an ideal, a state that had to be achieved because the present could not yet live up to the high expectations. Even though many of the films dealt with revolutionary events in the past, the manner in which individuals or groups were presented was firmly anchored in the future. Future socialist people were presented in the revolutionary cinema classics, while the films took place in the past. They showed the revolution (a historical event) as it would be seen by subsequent generations, anticipating the future. This was a denial of historicity, which resulted from the scientific logic of historical-materialist progression. The Soviet Union believed it was moving rapidly towards a socialist society that would mark the end of history. The films manifested this in the past (the time of change) and in the future (the end result of this change, thus the end of history) simultaneously. As a side effect, this double movement disregarded the messiness of the present and it is no coincidence that the films most fiercely attacked were films that dealt with contemporary problems of Soviet life. In a paradoxical movement, the revolutionary past was depicted in a way that evoked a future yet to be achieved. This double movement away from the present is typical of the avant-garde: the temporal slippage into the past and future is a unifying element for all the avant-garde activities. The paradoxes of the avant-garde are simultaneously central elements of their constitution, yet also the reason for their (cyclical) demise. It was especially during the NEP period that the projection of the imaginary future into an imaginary past played an immense role because the economy had so obviously not yet achieved what it was supposed to – moving forward, looking back. This utopian ideal was the legacy of montage cinema that had solidified into a static monument that the following epoch had to deal with.

The 1930s, in many respects reversed the situation of the 1920s: social development was declared redundant, and socialism had officially arrived. If historical progress had indeed come to an end because history has run its logical course through revolution, construction of socialism and ossification (this was the official doctrine of the Stalinist 1930s), then art could only deal with the present because historical time has coagulated into a perpetual now. This is especially true for the hero who suddenly cannot develop any further, but has to behave from an elevated position of conclusion and achievement as in CHAPAEV (SU 1934, Georgii & Sergei Vasilev), in Leonid Trauberg and Grigorij Kozintsev's MAXIM trilogy (SU 1934-39) or in Sergei Eisenstein's return to filmmaking ALEKSANDR NEVSKY (SU 1938). The idea of the avant-garde becomes meaningless once historical development is declared over. Art cannot be at the forefront of a development if a final and static situation has been reached.

While the constructivists were, on the one hand, constructing a new world and new consciousness in their art, they were, on the other hand, very destructive in their desire to burn down museums, to shatter the traditional arts completely, not just to reinvent under another guise but to get rid of it completely. This resulted in the Stalinist era which produced the Stachanov movement and the heroes of Socialist Realism like Capaev who would change the world through pure acts of will because – according to Marx – consciousness determines being. In this context, Boris Groys has pointed out the importance of the figure of the parasite:

> The figure of the › parasite ‹ so important to the mythology of the Stalin era is at bottom not realistically motivated, just as the superhuman and creative potential of the › positive hero ‹. ... The positive and negative heroes of the Stalin era are two faces of the previous demiurgic practice of the avant-garde. Both exceed the reality created and destroyed by themselves, and also the struggle between them does not happen in reality, but beyond its limitations: reality is the only stake in this game.[146]

The flipside of the constructivist ethos of change are the Stalinist purges. If a pure act of will could change things for the better, then a negative thought could also lead to a change for the worse. In this logic, which developed out of the avant-garde idea of overcoming the distinction between life and art, any act of criticism, even within the confines of art, was logically seen as sabotage because it had a negative influence on reality. If everything becomes art, then the category itself becomes meaningless because it no longer holds any discriminatory energy. The purges in the beginning were not directed against the avant-garde movement, but their own cynical and murderous consequences were consistent in a way with 1920s avant-garde ideology. Thus, one could see the 1930s as a logical progression of 1920s avant-garde idea(l)s brought to their natural conclusion and the Soviet Union was once more the place where the avant-garde experiment was carried out to its most radical extremes.

6 Melodies Across the Oceans – The Intersection of Documentary and Avant-garde

> *To the retrospective mind, the end of a year that gave us Stuttgart,*
> *La Sarraz, as banners to the avant garde – that strange platoon*
> *forever marking time – that saw the dawn of montage consciousness,*
> *not altogether unlike the angry weal of an insect sting, and sent or promised*
> *a thousand and one mixed blessings, talkies überall; needs some recapitulation,*
> *some winnowing thoughts to shape its varying developments for future benefit.*
> Kenneth MacPherson (1929)[1]

The year 1929, the mid-point between World War One and Two, is pivotal for several film historical trajectories that intersect and compete in astounding ways. In June 1929, Hans Richter curated an extensive program of avant-garde films to accompany a film and photo exhibition in Stuttgart, the *Film- und Fotoausstellung (FiFo)* organised by the *Deutsche Werkbund*, with personal appearances by luminaries such as Dziga Vertov. In September of that same year, the *crème de la crème* of the European film avant-garde met in an old castle in Switzerland near La Sarraz for the *Congres International du Cinéma Indépendent (CICI)*, which entered the history books as » the first film festival « and » the most important film event on Swiss soil «. The year 1929 is crucial not only for the avant-garde, but also for the introduction of sound film in Europe. In summer 1929, a deadlock between the US and European film industries had effectively frozen the wiring of cinemas for sound and the further dissemination of sound film in most major European markets.[2] The talks between the two blocks failed and the film industry approached the season 1929-30 with gloomy feelings. The avant-garde seemed to be on the verge of a leap into a brighter future while the film industry was haunted by an imminent sense of crisis. Strangely enough, only a year later this situation had been completely reversed with the industry reaping huge profits and the avant-garde falling apart at the follow-up meeting to La Sarraz, which took place in December 1930 in Brussels.

This year was also pivotal for the development of the avant-garde and documentary film. I will focus in this chapter on two films which I position as partly antagonistic, partly complimentary to one another, but which nevertheless take the discourses regarding the avant-garde, the industry and the documentary in new and unexpected directions. The films are Walter Ruttmann's MELODIE DER WELT (GER 1929) and John Grierson's DRIFTERS (GB 1929). Other films from this key year similarly walk the line between fact and fiction, between experiment and mainstream, between silence and sound, between documentary and avant-garde such as Dziga Vertov's CELOVEK S KINOAPPARATOM (SU 1929), Jean Vigo's A PROPOS DE NICE (FR 1929) or Robert Siodmak's MENSCHEN AM SONNTAG (GER 1929). I have chosen DRIFTERS and MELODIE DER WELT because both point backwards and forwards in many different ways and they occupy key turning points in film history where the avant-garde and the documentary occupied a common platform. They mark a moment of intersection in film history where the film avant-garde rubbed shoulders with the documentary in a contradictory manner around issues such as abstraction and realism, independence and commission, fiction and non-fiction, colonialism and the other.

6.1　Melodie der Welt and Drifters: Models for What?

> [T]he documentary film was … created … in Europe,
> around 1927. It was part of the avant-garde movement,
> to give film artistic and educational values.
> Joris Ivens (1939)[3]

As different as John Grierson's DRIFTERS and Walter Ruttmann's MELODIE DER WELT might appear at first glance, the two films nevertheless share a lot of common ground, starting with the subject matter. Both films trace the journey of a single ship, recording and presenting sights and events from this voyage. Both films have an innovative approach to new forms of perception and expression, which are characterised by formal experimentation, public relations and social concern. Note how a description of DRIFTERS fits MELODIE DER WELT equally well when substituting title and name of the director

> [The film] dispenses with any psychological interplay between characters and instead treats ordinary actions as dramatic in themselves. The film is both an abstract depiction of objective reality and a poetic treatment of reality. [The director] treats nature, industry and humans as abstract material, lingering on the shapes and patterns they create. [The film] is also rhythmic in that drama is created through editing juxtapositions and tempo. These elements conform to the poetic, rhythmic and visual cinema that [the director] advocated in his writings.[4]

This statement is equally valid for both films because both operate inside the parameters and characteristics of what alternative film making practice was in 1929. Paramount was the rejection of conventional dramatic and narrative structure (» psychological interplay «) while the aim was to uncover some underlying truth. In fact, it was rather opposition (to the film industry, to ordinary narrative etc.) than an agreed upon aesthetic or political program that kept the avant-garde together for a few crucial years. But how was it possible that two such different figures, Grierson who is normally considered the » father « of the British Documentary Movement and Ruttmann, the » fallen angel « of German experimental film, made films at the same time that share so much common ground? In order to understand this coincidence, this intersection, it is necessary to move backward and forward in time simultaneously. Only by widening the temporal context can we achieve a deeper understanding of the forces that shaped both filmmakers and films. To start with, both characters should be located in their context of origin, a task that will stress the different approaches to the cinema that Grierson and Ruttmann stand for, making their 1929 congruence all the more surprising.

Walter Ruttmann had possibly reached the peak of his reputation in 1929.[5] He came out of the generation that had gravitated from painting to filmmaking in the early 1920s (other representatives in Germany were Viking Eggeling and Hans Richter) and built up a reputation on the strength of his four abstract animation films, OPUS I-IV (GER 1921-1925). His cross-section film BERLIN. DIE SINFONIE DER GROSSSTADT (GER 1927), was met with enthusiasm in Germany and abroad, inaugurating the genre of the city symphony, which flourished for some time around 1930.[6] This film presents a portrait of the city as a » day in the life « or » slice of life «, a day from early in the morning until night, from the surrounding rural area to the bustling city centre. The film shows glimpses of work and play, technology and entertainment, wealth and poverty without portraying a human protagonist in the conventional way. BERLIN was produced by the German branch of the Hollywood major Fox, the production was supervised by cameraman Karl Freund, and the idea came from writer Carl Mayer.[7] Ruttmann subsequently worked on an early sound experiment for the emerging German radio system (DEUTSCHER RUNDFUNK / TÖNENDE WELLE, GER 1928) before being commissioned by the shipping company Hapag (Hamburg-Amerikanische Packetfahrt Actiengesellschaft) and the hardware company Tobis (Tonbild-Syndikat AG) to oversee the montage and post-synchronisation of the raw material shot by a crew aboard the Hapag vessel *Resolute* during a trip around the world. Ruttmann was confronted with approximately 16,000 metres of exposed film stock which he had to select and arrange into little more than 1,100 meters (the length of the finished film). The audiovisual round the world trip was fused by Ruttmann into MELODIE DER WELT, one of the first German sound films, which premiered on 12 March 1929 in Berlin.[8] The film stylistically follows BERLIN. DIE SINFONIE DER GROSSSTADT by rhythmically editing the material together according to formal principles of musical phraseology. The material, framed by a (fictional) story of a sailor (Iwan Kowal-Samborski) and his girlfriend (Renée Stobrawa), is arranged in three parts dealing with the life and

cultures of different places; it is not a chronological account of the ship's itinerary. After MELODIE DER WELT Ruttmann went to Paris where he collaborated
with Abel Gance on the flawed catastrophe film LA FIN DU MONDE (FR 1930),
then on to Italy where he made a semi-fictional film of the steel work(er)s in
Terni, ACCIAIO (IT 1933) before returning to Germany where he continued to
make films about cities, industry and steel works for the Nazi government until
his death in 1941.

While Ruttmann's MELODIE DER WELT is often seen as the beginning of the
end of the avant-garde movement as sound was introduced, John Grierson's
DRIFTERS is normally considered the origin of the British documentary movement of the 1930s and 1940s.[9] The Scotsman Grierson had studied sociology at
Glasgow University and he had been conducting research in the United States
on the social effects of the cinema. Upon his return to England in 1927, Grierson,
also an active member of the *Film Society* in London, sought employment within
film circles and approached Stephen Tallents, secretary of the recently established (in 1926) Empire Marketing Board (EMB). This government institution
was the public relations arm of the ministry overseeing the British Empire,
which sought to foster trade, exchange and well-being within this global network. His first film, DRIFTERS (which is also the only film he signed as director
without a collaborator – later he was mainly a supervisor and producer) is a
promotional film for herring fishing in the North Sea and was commissioned as
the first film of the newly formed EMB film department. It was shot in the summer of 1928 and Grierson and his later wife Margaret Taylor edited the roughly
10,000 feet of rushes (circa 3,000 meters) down to 3,631 feet (circa 1,100 meters)
in winter 1928–29. The finished film was presented to the EMB Film Committee
in the summer of 1929 and had its premiere at the London Film Society on 10
November 1929. Incidentally (or not quite so incidentally, we will come back to
this) the film premiered alongside Sergei Eisenstein's BRONENOSEZ POTEMKIN
(SU 1925) which Grierson himself had prepared for its English release and Walt
Disney's THE BARN DANCE (US 1929). Grierson was able to build on the strength
of the public success of this film and was able to establish a film unit of considerable importance. He thus became the godfather of the British documentary
movement (under the auspices of the Empire Marketing Board and the General
Post Office) before going to Canada and the United States on the eve of World
War II.

While film history situates Grierson firmly in the genealogy of the documentary, Ruttmann belongs to the avant-garde, two schools of filmmaking normally
quite different. But then again, when one looks closely at the labels that film
history has placed on filmmaking practice in the late 1920s, a measure of overlap emerges. In a way the avant-garde provided a kind of Rorschach test in
which most observers would recognise what s/he was interested in because the

avant-garde marked a moment of overlap and intersection. Their open film form was hailed as an achievement and the films that adhered most strictly to this open form were canonised as classics of the avant-garde movement. It is thus striking – and here is my point of departure – how both DRIFTERS and MELODIE DER WELT, which both occupy pivotal positions in the respective film-maker's careers – can be described with the same brief text quoted above and can both be inserted into an avant-garde as well as a documentary tradition. Yet, before examining the two films more closely we need to look back a bit into the history of non-fiction and documentary film in order to understand » the instability of the documentary and the avant-garde «, at least until the arrival of sound. This genealogical sketch will provide some issues that will become pertinent when we return to these two films.

6.2   On the Threshold: An Invention of a Tradition

In a surprisingly short time, › documentary ‹ has become
transformed from a mere word into a sentence –
almost a life sentence for all those who happen
to be making films from natural material.
Andrew Buchanan (1933)[10]

Defining a documentary film has never been an easy task: The definition has political as well as social and cultural implications. One potential way to dodge the notoriously difficult question of » What is documentary? «, thus moving away from a quasi-ontological definition towards a more pragmatic approach, would be to look at examples of films which have been termed documentary and what features have been singled out to demarcate the (fuzzy) boundaries of this genre. The line between non-fiction and documentary is a highly contested one, especially in early cinema. Many historians of the documentary have returned to the earliest days of cinema to locate the origin of the documentary. In a famous gesture, François Truffaut cut film history in half (and effectively French-ised it): documentary film begins with the Lumière brothers, fictional film with Georges Méliès.[11] Addressing this initial divide, Bill Nichols has raised the question of why – following this story of mythical origins – it has taken 30 years for the documentary to be named and to acquire its form and to ascend to its » rightful « place.[12] While John Grierson, in a by now classical argument, saw the films of Robert Flaherty as the first documentary films[13], other suggestions have been put forward more recently: Martin Loiperdinger, for instance, has located the birth of the documentary in World War I propaganda[14], while Charles Musser instead opted to insist that the documentary's ancestry and genealogy appeared long before the cinema emerged, with the 18th and 19th century magic lantern lecture.[15] Moreover, the booming studies of Early Cinema has seriously questioned this simplistic dichotomy of Méliès vs. Lumière, introducing the more neutral and highly useful distinction between fiction (everything that is staged for the camera) and non-fiction (in which the pro-filmic event is assumed to have taken place the same way but without a camera being present).[16] From this vantage point of early cinema, Tom Gunning has asked why historians of documentaries have persistently ignored the pre-classical period, a time in which non-fiction filmmaking in its various guises was the dominant form of screen practice. Conventionally, historians of the documentary locate the beginning of their subject at the time when fiction film was becoming dominant in the 1920s.[17]

Traditional film history has it that Robert Flaherty single-handedly brought the documentary genre into existence. More recently, scholars working on the documentary have questioned this myth of origin. One argument that has been used against Flaherty's films is the fact that he was convincing and persuading the subjects of his films to re-enact scenes that were far removed from their actual lives. In what is possibly the most (in)famous scene from NANOOK OF THE NORTH (US 1922), the Eskimos stage a dangerous kind of walrus hunt that their culture had abandoned generations ago. While this might be explained as a necessary limitation of any filmmaking practice what appears more crucial to me is the absence of historical time. What Flaherty's films present are timeless bubbles in which Polynesians, Inuits and Aran Islanders leading a life they have always lived and will always live. Because (temporal) change or development (which differs from a cyclical pattern) is absent from his films, it is difficult to see Flaherty's work as documentary filmmaking. If we follow Grierson's definition of a documentary as » the creative treatment of actuality «, then Flaherty's films are certainly not actuality and while they may be treatments, it is not actuality they are treating (they are creative, however). A certain measure of change – and therefore history – is absolutely necessary for a film to be classified as a documentary in the contemporary sense. Flaherty's films also lack a sense of public responsibility and purposefulness, which became an important facet of the documentary for Grierson as a public reformer. In fact, when Flaherty worked for Grierson on INDUSTRIAL BRITAIN (GB 1931), he focused, much to Grierson's dismay, almost exclusively on arts and crafts, ignoring industry, machines and issues of modernisation. It's easy to see why this was the only film Flaherty made in the Grierson circle.

It is my contention that the documentary is a highly unstable entity and that a textual definition of the documentary alone does not suffice for a proper delineation of the conditions that justify its existence. A documentary needs a number of contextual factors for it to be stable. Let me illustrate this by glancing back into the history of the documentary. In his classical history of the docu-mentary film, Erik Barnouw passes through a pantheon of great men who have advanced the art and science of documentary film. His chapters have program-matic titles like: prophet, explorer, reporter, painter, advocate, bugler, prosecu-tor, poet, chronicler, promoter, observer, catalyst, guerrilla.[18] At the same time that these romantic notions of man of (and in) action are deeply problematic in different ways, they also point out that the non-fiction film can also be inte-grated into many other fields and discourses. » Prophet « deals with inventors and their quasi-religious zeal, thus opening up the genealogy of non-fiction into the archaeology of technology. » Explorer « with its extensive discussions of the feats and adventures of Robert Flaherty, on the one hand, opens up the films to a reading across ethnography, but on the other, it also situates Flaherty's move-ments and actions within the force field of colonialism and imperialism (not to mention the fictional dimension of the staged scenes). » Reporter « concentrates on how in Dziga Vertov's work the non-fiction film is related to the printed press, but also to the popular genre of reportage and thus opens the genealogy up to the newsreel, journalism and propaganda. The list could go on, but what Barnouw (involuntarily) uncovers here is that the early documentary as a genre is an unstable entity at least until the introduction of sound because what passes for » realistic « or » authentic « is subject to constant shifts and changes in the public eye. The necessary condition for the documentary as a genre is not, as commonly assumed, the depiction of the outside world » as it really is « (in the Rankean sense), but the fortuitous intersection of different developments in the late 1920s that brought the documentary as we know it into existence.

Barnouw's categories demonstrate the contiguity of non-fictional filmmaking to other discourses and the instability of the documentary until the 1930s. My point is not to argue that Grierson's DRIFTERS is the first documentary, that would just replace one dogma with another, but to show the fragility of the documentary as a film form, at least until 1930, possibly until after World War Two. Grierson's achievement was to eclectically construct a film style (he freely borrowed from Flaherty, Soviet montage cinema, abstract film) to borrow an organisational form from the avant-garde (*Medienverbund*) and to transpose it onto governmental institutions (thus breaking away from other, more fragile or precarious forms of dependence), thereby creating a relatively stable context that was able to generate a canon and a definition of the documentary in the 1930s. The instability of the documentary is shared in many respects by avant-garde filmmaking, which was adjacent to advertising and non-fiction, to com-mercial art cinema and political propaganda in the interwar period. The various film forms (not genres in the sense of Western, detective film etc.) need a some-what stable context of production and exhibition in order to find their shape. This instability can be located in all of the contextual sectors of cinema: funding (state or private companies, film industry or patrons?), style (closer to the avant-garde or to classical film style?), address (giving the audience identification possibilities or turning to abstraction?), distribution and exhibition pattern (using commercial channels or those of educational film? screened as part of commercial cinema programs or in special events?), even length (short, medium or feature length) and format (35 or 16mm, silent or sound?). Thus, the problem of locating an » origin « for the documentary has as much to do with the instability of institutions as with transformations in film style, as with changes in exhibition and reception. It is all these entities and factors one has to examine in turn in order to understand how avant-garde and documentary intersected, but also differentiated into different film forms.

6.3   The Index, the Narrative, the Fragment and the Persuasion of the Masses

> ... what documentary film history sought to deny was not simply
> an overly aesthetic lineage but the radically transformative potential
> of film pursued by a large segment of the international avant-garde.
> ... [A] wave of documentary activity takes shape at the point when
> cinema comes into the direct service of various, already active
> efforts to build national identity during the 1920s and 1930s.
> Bill Nichols (2001)[19]

Bill Nichols locates the documentary at the crucial intersection of four elements: » photographic realism, narrative structure, and modernist fragmentation – along with a new emphasis on the rhetoric of social persuasion «[20]. Let me offer a quick survey of Nichols's categories because the two films I will be dealing with could serve as a test case for his model. Nichols starts off by pointing out » a false division between the avant-garde and documentary that obscures their necessary proximity «.[21] It was John Grierson who » tamed « modernist fragmentation to social(-democratic) ends, thus covering the distance between DRIFTERS to POTEMKIN. By stressing documentary film's social responsibility, another link that was equally important in the formation of the genre fades away, namely the common genealogy that the documentary shares with the radical avant-garde. At their heart and origin, both the avant-garde and the documentary share the deep-seated desire to change the world. However, they just differed in the both the means and goals pursued.

Nichols isolates four elements that constitute the adequate conditions for a film to be labelled documentary. The first element, the indexicality of the photographic image, is not the exclusive property of the documentary, but is a » necessary if not sufficient condition for the appearance of documentary film. «[22] The indexical nature was exploited before and after in non-documentary films. Narrative, the second element, is conventionally connected with fiction, not with documentary. However, as Hayden White and others have pointed out, narrative imbues historical time with meaning because time without narrative is simply duration. In documentary, a typical structure of conflict-resolution is used, even if the protagonist is an impersonal agent such as a river or a city. For Nichols, the avant-garde contributed a third element: » ... representational techniques and a social context conducive to a documentary movement [that] affirmed the close proximity of modernist exploration and documentary address «[23]. In documentaries, reality is constructed and authored, not simply recorded. » It was precisely the power of the *combination* of the indexical representations of the documentary image and the radical juxtapositions of time and space allowed by montage that drew many avant-garde artists to film. «[24] The fourth element, rhetorical strategies, can also be called the » educational impulse «: the will to change film as a medium and the will to change the world as this transformative impulse is a key feature of the avant-garde. However, this can again also head in other directions: » Like the other three elements, rhetoric does not necessarily lead to documentary film. As a persuasive strategy it also supports overt propaganda, all advertising, and some forms of journalism. «[25]

Nichols, rightly shying away from essentialist notions such as » birth « or » origin «, locates what he terms » documentary's historical moment « in the second half of the 1920s. Documentary's » moment « first emerges in the Soviet Union while Grierson is the key figure in translating the Soviet experiments to a British context. The more radical attempts at change are turned into issues of nationality and citizenship, transforming the revolutionary constructivist spirit into a social-conservative reformism: » Grierson's commitment to government and corporate sponsorship as the only viable means of institutional support required an act of separation from the more radical potentialities of the modernist avant-garde and the particular example of the Soviet cinema «.[26] Thus, revolutionary energy is turned into a citizen's duty and the imaginary (and publicly stated) genealogy of the documentary is transposed into an act of hagiography from Vertov and Eisenstein to Flaherty. Consequently, Nichols objects to Flaherty being referred to as the godfather of documentary because he » lacked ... the orator's sense of social persuasiveness ... Flaherty had the right sense of drama and conflict but the wrong sense of modernity «.[27] In fact, Nichols sees the shift to Flaherty as an evasive action and claims that Grierson's celebration of Flaherty was meant to deflect attention away from the Soviet example. The acknowledgement of a communist influence would have caused him trouble with his corporate and state sponsors and thus he deferred the function of an

» origin « to Flaherty when he really meant Eisenstein and the Soviet school of filmmaking.

Now, while I am very much in agreement with Nichols and while I consider his article to be one of the most important contributions to the study of documentary film in recent time, I would name one more crucial element: the coming of sound. Sound as technology and as medium, on the one hand, gave an easier handle to persuasive strategies, on the other hand, it increased the national sentiments connected to cinema. A rhetorical discourse was easier with sound as it usually required an amount of language that would be too tedious as inter-titles. Spoken language also increased the notions of nationality connected to cinema.[28] My focus on John Grierson's DRIFTERS and Walter Ruttmann's MELODIE DER WELT is meant to show two different reactions to synchronised sound film (even though DRIFTERS is silent) that is paradigmatic of the wider issues that were at stake in this period of media transition.

With Bill Nichols' categories in mind, let us return to the two films that straddle the boundary of silent and sound film, of documentary and avant-garde, of commissioned and independent film. By examining the four categories proposed we can get a clearer sense of how the films position themselves in relation to the trends and lines of flight relevant to that key year of 1929 in which both were produced. Both DRIFTERS and MELODIE DER WELT clearly partake of the sense of realism and indexicality offered by the photographic camera image, Nichols' first category. Both revel in spectacular sights and present the spectator with a variety of attractive images that must have been unknown to most contemporary spectators. Ruttmann proudly presents us with faraway and exotic places, with strange looking buildings, musical instruments and diversions, with customs and types of entertainment from cultures and places still largely unknown to Westerners at that time. Grierson's film, despite being » closer to home «, exhibits a similar added value offered by the indexical. The thorough and detailed presentation of a fishing boat's trip offers plenty of spectacular sights such as the fish that are caught in the net underwater or the storm during the hauling in of the nets. Despite their differences, both films clearly indulge in the indexical power of the photographic image in reproducing sights and events that must have been unknown and fascinating to most spectators.

In terms of narrative, Nichols' second category, both DRIFTERS and MELODIE DER WELT present a highly structured texture with much more internal coherence than the views or travelogues of earlier times. Both films consist of three parts. The first part of Ruttmann's film deals with architecture, traffic, religion, and war; the second part shows images of children, sailing and rowing, hunting and agriculture, and sports; while the third part is concerned with women, languages, food, dance, music, theatre, entertainment and work.[29] A similar tripartite structure can be found in Grierson's film: the narration presents two consecutive days and the intervening night. On the first day, the ship goes out to sea and casts its nets. At night the sailors eat and rest while the true drama unfolds underwater as the fish get caught up in the nets, and the next day presents the hauling in of the nets and the bustling atmosphere of the harbour where the catch is sold. Both films therefore try to make sense of the spectacular images by means of a recognisable structure, i.e., narration. The style of narrative in both films is more radical than one finds in most documentaries: neither in DRIFTERS nor in MELODIE DER WELT do we have a human protagonist in the conventional sense. Now, while this is not unusual for many of the documentaries that deal with issues that cannot be portrayed through a psychological portrait, the films under investigation here are special insofar as we never get acquainted with any of the persons shown in the films. Both films radicalise the modernist impulse of the avant-garde, which is directed against conventional and melodramatic narrative centred on characters. Yet, both films still present a recognisable three-act division not altogether untypical of classical narrative. Thus, it is the mediation of modernist abstraction through narrative structure that characterises both films.

Probably the most important feature of both films is what Nichols has termed » modernist fragmentation «, i.e., the degree to which those films employ aesthetic and formal devices introduced by the avant-garde. In Ruttmann's MELODIE DER WELT the transitions between sections and the organisation within appear to be heavily based on formal criteria of similarity of line, shape, form and movement, also preoccupations of his earlier abstract films from the first half of the 1920s. The opening of Ruttmann's previous film BERLIN, DIE SINFONIE DER GROSSSTADT (GER 1926/27) already offered abstract moving shapes that transformed into glimpses caught from a train window as the train approaches a big city, thus marking a transition from pure abstraction to more concrete representations. Ruttmann was fond of recognising abstract patterns in photographically produced images. Some examples from MELODIE DER WELT might clarify this: the architecture section, the first section after the prologue with the departure of the ship, begins when a sailor climbing up a ladder to the top of the mast is inter-cut first with a man and then with an ape climbing up a palm tree. The structure of the palm tree's trunk is, after a closer shot, then likened to a pillar which has a similar look and texture, at least in the photographic images. This process of replacement via metonymy and metaphor takes place mainly on a formal level and is less concerned with a semantic relationship, but instead with parallels in terms of surface appearance. The transition from the agriculture section to the sports section moves from a rice paddy in a high angle shot to a stadium seen from a similar perspective, which in their terrace structure and use of slow movement (water in the rice paddies, people in the stadium), resembles the field structurally. The sports section ends with planes performing loops in formation followed by a shot of seagulls, both filmed against the sky, thus giving the images a very similar visual impression. The seagulls, in turn, lead back to the ship before the next thematic section commences. It is this chain of images – planes and seagulls flying in the sky marking a metaphorical substitution while the seagulls lead to the ship through their metonymical contiguity – that characterises Ruttmann's film. This is a typical stylistic trend that was pioneered in *Neue Sachlichkeit*. Photography in particular displays an obsession with natural phenomena that – at a specific angle and at a various proximities of closeness (distant or close-up) – resemble human-made structures. Typical proponents of this technique in the second half of the 1920s were Karl Bloßfeldt[30] and Albrecht Renger-Patzsch[31] who visually likened grass to columns or cacti to religious buildings in Egypt. Even though external reality is used as raw material in this approach, it is nevertheless not representational reality we see on the screen, but a specific form of aesthetic abstraction.[32] Accepting the objective nature of perception as a formal given also describes Grierson's style very accurately. Both Ruttmann and Grierson adopted the concrete representation of outside reality as the starting point for aesthetic abstraction. These modernist elements – which should not just be limited to fragmentation as a specific technique – were shared by many artists in circa 1930.

Ruttmann often breaks up continuous action by inter-cutting disparate material, yet there is always a relation to be found: ever more rapid and closer shots of traffic (cars, trams, pedestrians, carriages) with its accompanying noise on the soundtrack are mixed with shots of an African banging on a drum. The similarity is here provided by sound as the drum produces a very similar sound as the city noise. In another instance, a man dressed in traditional Japanese attire is shooting an arrow with a longbow, which is then inter-cut with Africans throwing spears and arrows at a target. In a way this is the reverse of a Kuleshov effect because spectators are first led to believe that they are seeing a match-on-action cut from the shooter to the target, but upon seeing the Africans throwing a spear followed by another arrow hitting the same target, this relationship breaks down. The repeated series of the bowman and the target only reinforces the doubts about the spatial and causal contiguity of these two shots. The film foregrounds the artificial nature of the spatial coupling of two consecutive shots which would conventionally be understood as presenting contiguous spaces. Shattering conventionalised illusion was seen as a radical political weapon in avant-garde circles. In fact, Ruttmann practically never employs a shot-reverse shot pattern in a classical way. Two similar activities are often mixed such as when we see an Asian family serving and eating a meal, which is inter-cut with people from other cultures filling their plates with food and eating. While this hints at a resemblance – an imagined unity that must have appealed to Ruttmann's avant-garde sensibility – it also breaks up the action itself into its constituent parts. Isolating smaller parts has been a preoccupation of the classical avant-garde as much as proclaiming the unity of life and art, the ultimate aim of avant-garde activity. However, MELODIE DER WELT also hints at the incompatibility of these two objectives.

Despite its simple story, which could easily be told in a classical style, DRIFTERS employs a number of modernist techniques and estranging elements. The film starts off in a relatively slow tempo, at least in montage speed as the ship is prepared and leaves the harbour. The first intense sequence depicts the labour of casting the nets. The film rhythmically puts the working men together, but often just presents activities – a knot being made, a rope runs through a winch, a buoy lands on the water, a net falls into the sea – without identifying a human protagonist as the agent of the action. Grierson thus presents work as something impersonal or at least de-personalised, devoid of a human agent. On the one hand, this depersonalised style creates an ideal or exemplary representation: DRIFTERS does not present any one specific ship with any one specific group of sailors (we never learn the boat's name nor the name of any of the fishermen), but it is one ship that represents the countless other boats (we sometimes get short glimpses of a large number of other fishing boats that hint at this hidden multitude this one boat represents) and one trip that represents the countless trips of countless other boats. On the other hand, Grierson presents a kind of Marxist version of labour under the conditions of modernity in the way the fishermen on the ship are neither individualised as they would in a humanistic argument nor are they intimately related with their occupation as is the case with master craftsmen. Even the dinner scene consists of shots of the table with reaching hands interspersed with shots of men coming down the stairs with cutaways before we see the face, leaving out any distinguishing marks. Eating and social activity becomes a part of the fisherman's job like mending nets or shaking the nets to free the fish.

While the fishermen sleep at night, the film presents the drama of the sea in one of the most impressive sequences of the film. Congers and catfish take advantage of the herring already trapped in the net and feed on the catch. These impressive submarine images were shot in a tank at the Plymouth Marine Biological Research Station.[33] This underwater drama is the most obvious evidence that the trip is much less unified than it appears at first because the film was shot in many different places and only assembled at the editing table. The bird scenes were shot in one place, the ship's cabin was a constructed set, and when their fishing trips were unsuccessful, Grierson's team even bought loads of herring that would be placed into the nets by hand and subsequently hauled out of the water to give the impression that the catch was bountiful.[34] Grierson learned Kuleshov's important lesson from his Soviet montage films: shots executed in different places and different times could be combined to create the illusion of a unified filmic space.

The counterpart to the casting of the nets – and in some sense even more climactic as a storm is brewing and the sea is heavy – is the hauling in of nets full of fish, which have to be shaken from the nets into the hold. The repetitiveness of this activity is stressed by a long series of shots that mirror the laborious and monotonous nature of the work. Afterwards, the ship returns to port and the modern machinery of selling and transporting the fish to other places is presented. In the market we see the auctioneer with a bell in his hand, but we never get a proper shot of his face. Again, Grierson abstracts from any concrete character, instead opting for a style in which the function of individuals overrides their individuality. The film achieves a very symmetrical structure of two days and the intervening night, with the impressive shots of the fish functioning simultaneously as a division between casting and hauling, but also in its natural drama as a climax.

In Ruttmann's film, activities and people are often likened to animals. Children playing tag are inter-cut with pigeons on Venice's St. Mark's square and a sumo wrestler looking angrily into the camera as he gets ready for his match is followed by a shot of a tiger hissing at the spectator. A scene of a violent fight between two men is inter-cut with battering rams colliding at full speed. This parallelism is also employed on the soundtrack: In the language section, we see two men in Arabic-style attire in front of what appears to be a mosque in a heated argument. They are literally going at each other's throats while on the soundtrack we hear the barking of dogs. This technique is somewhat reminiscent of Eisenstein's intellectual montage in which he comments on certain screen actions by cutting to extra-diegetic material. Transposing this idea to sound and therefore creating a sound juxtaposition could have been directly taken from Eisenstein's, Alexandrov and Pudovkin's manifesto on sound film with which Ruttmann was surely familiar.[35] In the war section, images of battles, soldiers and military machinery accompanied by battle noises is contrasted twice with a woman emitting a stark scream and subsequently even more starkly with a cemetery and an almost inaudible wind blowing on the soundtrack. There is no such instance of extraneous reference or stark juxtaposition in DRIFTERS, which is very sparse and almost laconically minimalist in the way we neither get to know any of the fishermen nor are we presented any film material from outside of the herring fishing business. The views of the fishermen's villages are the only instances of a reality that exists outside of the context of the fishing and they have a very precise function: to show that their old homes are the only remnants of a past way of life that has otherwise changed completely for the fishermen. The fishermen occupy a functional position, much like the steamboat and the nets: They are necessary for the job of fishing, but are also utterly replaceable and therefore not interesting as individuals. The distance between Grierson and Flaherty, his self-proclaimed idol, becomes very clear here: Flaherty would have chosen a family or a family-like group, thereby providing personal identification to the audience, and have them re-enact a traditional way of fishing and living that they only know from their forefathers' stories. The single worker is replaceable just like a cog in a machine and the relationship of the worker to his work is equally impersonal – one could read Grierson's film as a scathing attack on the alienation of the worker working under the conditions of modernity, but again, Grierson is also celebrating the machine-like precision and the functional perfection of the fishing business.

Let me return to Nichols' fourth necessary element for the emergence of the documentary: a sense of social persuasion. Here we can begin to see how Grierson diverges from Ruttmann. So far we have seen some stylistic and narrative differences, but no fundamental incongruity between the two films. However, what MELODIE DER WELT seems to lack is a clear sense of (social or political) purpose. In its disinterestedness towards the materials from different cultures, it scans the shots for parallelisms, similarities and structural repetitions without attempting to create a clear sense of the forces of history shaping the lives and cultures of the people depicted. By contrast, DRIFTERS makes it very clear in the beginning that it is concerned with herring fishing under the conditions of modernity. The very first title immediately after the opening credits and before we have seen any image of fishermen or fish reads: » The herring fishing has changed. Its story was once an idyll of brown sails and village harbours – its story is now an epic of steam and steel. « This is immediately followed by the second title: » Fishermen still have their homes in the old-time villages – but they go down, for each season, to the labour of a modern industry. « Contrary to what Ruttmann does – seeing formal similarities everywhere – and contrary to what Flaherty would have done – presenting an unchanging and a-historical timeless way of fishing – Grierson consciously chooses to present fishing not as a romantic endeavour, but as a modern industry. He announces change in the first sentence and then juxtaposes a time already in the past (» an idyll of brown sails and village harbours «) to a present state (» an epic of steam and steel «) – and in the second title he underlines this temporal structure by contrasting » old-time villages « with a » modern industry «. The film opens up an horizon of expectation that draws the audience's attention into an historical mood. And even though we do not see, hear or read a lot about the older ways of fishing, the film properly opens with images of traditional villages. This is how the film reinforces the contrast with what the rest of the film will show, namely the modern business of fishing. In this opening – and we should remind ourselves that the first couple of minutes of a film are always decisive – the emphasis is firmly put on the transformative nature of modernity. Even though the film's main body does not particularly stress this contrast between tradition and modernity, it nevertheless remains » an epic of steam and steel « as it merely presents the modern business of fishing and does not even refer back to something like » the good old times «.

What Ruttmann achieves with his parallelisms between different cultures, people, animals and activities is that he conjures up an imaginary » harmony of the world «.[36] Everything is in sync and the artistic task is to track down the hidden resonances and bring them to light. Despite this conscious take on similarity and the connections being thus forged around the globe, the film nevertheless very seldom makes any deeper connections. While in the final section DRIFTERS shows how the fish are sold, stored and shipped, thus linking the fishing industry to a much larger context of the globalised food industry, MELODIE, with all its visual links, remains very much on the surface of things. While similarities are found almost everywhere within the film, Ruttmann does not expose any structural dependencies. His concentration on formal similarity and the absence of structural dependencies shows that Ruttmann's film refers back to the styles and structures of the silent avant-garde film, much like Pudovkin's DEZERTIR in the early 1930s imitates the silent Soviet montage film long after the paradigm had shifted elsewhere. DRIFTERS, meanwhile, borrowed freely from silent cinema, but it also looked forward as it inaugurated a film style that would become one of the most influential styles. However, Ruttmann's main model remains the Soviet montage film. His turn from abstraction (OPUS I-IV) to a more concrete external reality – BERLIN marks the transition point – coincides with the triumph of POTEMKIN in Berlin and a wider cultural shift from abstraction to a highly codified form of realism as it was promoted in the *Neue Sachlichkeit*.[37] Even though it was an early sound film, MELODIE DER WELT followed the model of Soviet silent montage cinema in its rapid pace and style of editing. In a way, Ruttmann became a victim of his own success with BERLIN, which was an international hit not only on the avant-garde circuit, but also in regular cinemas. The ensuing boom of city symphonies must have confirmed his belief that he was on the right track with his cross-section and his montage style based on formal similarity. Quite logically, MELODIE DER WELT stylistically attempts to transpose this style to the sound film and to thematically transfer it to the world.

Grierson was similarly influenced by Soviet revolutionary cinema, but he insisted on giving it a somewhat different inflection when he » tamed « the frantic style and toned down the fast cutting to a style that is outwardly located somewhere between montage and classical cinema. Even though Grierson's film is silent, his style was already anticipating sound film. Grierson's true achievement, however, probably lies in the process of combining different models into his own style, in his ability to adapt and adjust. Grierson was not an innovator himself, but a brilliant moderator. From Flaherty he borrowed storytelling and drama, from the Soviets the clash of images and stark juxtapositions in montage, from the French a certain lyricism that can is evidenced only occasionally in DRIFTERS (in the night scenes with the fish in the net), but appears more convincingly in later films that emerged from his filmmaking unit and the ones he supervised such as SONG OF CEYLON (GB 1934-35, Basil Wright), COAL FACE (GB 1936, Alberto Cavalcanti), and NIGHT MAIL (GB 1936, Harry Watt / Basil Wright). Meanwhile from journalism, he borrowed the idea of public relations and persuasion, and from sociology the idea of constructing a public consensus on specific topics.

Let me summarise the results of my analysis so far. Both DRIFTERS and MELODIE DER WELT appear very similar at first glance, but also upon closer examination. Both revel in the indexical capacity of the photographic image when presenting spectacular scenes, both use a strict and codified narrative pattern and both employ stylistic elements typical of modernist aesthetics, like a fragmentation or abstraction of concrete reality. The two films only begin to differ in relation to rhetorical strategies when DRIFTERS reveals a clearer sense of social responsibility, historicity and modern public relations; while MELODIE DER WELT, by contrast, focuses much more on the formal and aesthetic aspects typical of a depoliticised and aestheticised version of *Neue Sachlichkeit*. I believe that in contextualising filmmaking we should now turn to the contexts of the two films in order to better understand where they come from and what they attempt to achieve. We see most clearly how Ruttmann and Grierson both come out of the avant-garde, when we look at the production policies and exhibition strategies that eventually progress in different directions.

6.4 Authenticity and Modernity: The Politics of Dependency

> *Nothing seems now more significant of the period than that, at a time so crucial, there was no eager sponsorship for world thinking in a country which still pretended to world leadership. ... In the light of events, how much on the right lines Tallents was and how blind were the people who defeated his great concept! For documentary the effect was important.*
> John Grierson (1942)[38]

By the sheer power of habit and having been quoted so often, Grierson's famous definition of the documentary as » the creative treatment of actuality «[39] has lost some of its paradoxical edge.[40] For Grierson, the claim of reality differed from the treatment of the » phenomena «; while the real denoted a more abstract (and in some sense a » more real «) reality that went beyond the actual object itself. The phenomenon constituted the surface for Grierson. Meanwhile, the perceivable and recordable data and material at hand could be examined to access the real, however, one should remain careful not to mix it up with the » real « itself. Thus, actual raw (non-fiction) material had to be treated (shot, selected, ordered, edited, narrated, voiced over) in creative ways in order to reach a deeper truth that lay beneath the surface of things. Modern media like film thus offered the means to gain access to this deeper truth hidden behind the appearance of things. However far apart Ruttmann and Grierson were in their filmmaking practices, in their theoretical texts, in their political affiliations and their choice of subjects, they did share this idea of aiming to uncover a truth that lies beneath or beyond a single image. Both used non-fiction material (in contrast, for example, to most Russian montage cinema), both were interested in the social aspects of modernisation (unlike Flaherty), both subordinated the representation of people to some deeper truth that they wanted to uncover. Furthermore, the idea of structuring non-fiction material into a coherent whole using a rhetorical strategy for a specific political or social end lies at the heart of the documentary film in a Griersonian tradition; but, this description also fits MELODIE DER WELT and most of Ruttmann's other work.

One of the crucial issues for the avant-garde and the independent cinema movement was the question of independence, or rather, the question from whom dependency was acceptable because true independence was not realistic. Consequently, neither DRIFTERS nor MELODIE DER WELT emerged from a vacuum of disinterested aesthetic creation. Ruttmann's film was jointly produced by the shipping line Hapag and the film syndicate Tobis-Klangfilm, which in turn, was to a large extent backed by the German electrical industry (Siemens & Halske, AEG). These are hardly the backers one would expect from somebody who at the time was considered to be one of the central figures of the European alternative cinema movement, being invited to foreign countries by workers' film club and various opposition circles. Hapag, the Hamburg-Amerika Linie[41], was an instrumental part of the German effort to rule the seas (and lands) worldwide. Founded in the mid-19th century to carry emigrants to the United States, its long-time director Albert Ballin had already realised by the turn of the century that the company's future was in tourism. Hapag took the logical step and was one of the first companies to move into the field of sea cruises and picturesque sea tours. The modernisation (read: mediatisation) on board was only a logical next step with the addition of luxury service, newspapers and cinemas on board.[42] Soon after World War One, which temporarily marked the end of German super power ambitions, Hapag moved from the receiving end of the film industry to the production side: between 1922 and 1931, at least 31 films were made under the auspices of Hapag. The majority of these films were brief travel films which advertised its tour destinations and the luxuries one would find aboard their huge ships. But, Hapag got even more ambitious: In 1924 the first four-reeler was produced to document a trip from Hamburg to New York (MIT DER HAPAG VON HAMBURG NACH NEW YORK) and a 1926 feature-length film that presented the sights and wonders of the United States (AMERIKA, DAS LAND DER UNBEGRENZTEN MÖGLICHKEITEN), which tied in with the popular vogue of *Amerikanismus*, the fascination in the 1920s with all things American,[43] while also referring to the then-popular genre of the travel-adventure film. At roughly the same time, an agreement with Ufa was struck, giving the film company access to the short non-fiction subjects that Hapag had produced while the on-board cinemas provided an additional outlet for Ufa films.[44] But Hapag's biggest success in terms of publicity was going to be MELODIE DER WELT, in this context, a product of Hapag's self-image as a company investing in modernisation and technological progress while also touching on issues of colonialism and imperialism.

While Hapag was in the business of transportation and tourism, Tobis-Klangfilm was a technology and electrical company. This German-Dutch-Swiss joint venture, had a surprisingly experimental approach to filmmaking in the early years of 1928-30[45]: The French branch hired René Clair and his brother Henri Chomette, both key figures from the French ciné-clubs of the mid-1920s. Meanwhile, the German company Tobis placed their bets on Ruttmann, *eminence gris* of the abstract film, and Alexis Granowsky, Soviet *émigré* and experimental theatre director, who also produced the film program for the modernist new music festival at Baden-Baden. This strategy of consciously seeking out and employing avant-garde artists in the early sound period had a triple function: First, the company hoped that the films would relatively easily cross national borders, banking on the fact that the avant-garde in the second half of the 1920s was decidedly *international*. The avant-garde had demonstrated their experience in addressing a transnational audience. This was all the more important as foreign films met resistance in many countries because sound films increased (via spoken dialogue) the national limitations present in a film. As Tobis – with its headquarters in Amsterdam and studios in Berlin, Paris, and London, later also in Madrid, Vienna and Lisbon[46] – saw itself as a decidedly European venture, this strategy appeared quite logical. Second, the film industry turned to these filmmakers as a kind of *Research & Development* department. The industry expected the avant-garde to produce prototypes that could subsequently go into serial production. Thus, Tobis approached them because of their *innovative potential*. The success of Clair's films seems to come from his attempt to create a production line: a successful prototype, SOUS LES TOITS DE PARIS (FR 1929/30), which was not just copied in France by Clair and others (LE MILLION, FR 1930; À NOUS LA LIBERTÉ, FR 1931), but also in Portugal with A CANÇÃO DE LISBOA

(PT 1933, José Augusto Cottinelli Telmo).[47] And third, one crucial difference between the Tobis, Ufa and other large studios, has to do with the origin and identity of Tobis, which was in the business of technology, not film production and exhibition. Tobis emerged from an innovative and experimental initiative where inventors turned to film production. Ufa, by contrast, was a production company which had to cope with new technological developments in order to defend its position. The *constructivist* spirit of the avant-garde is much closer to an *engineering* triple jump of » problem – insight – solution « than to the sentimental stories of the film industry. To summarise: The corporate culture of Tobis was certainly closer to the avant-garde spirit of innovation and experiment than to the conservative corporate culture of Ufa. Similar thoughts must have animated Philips in this same period of time as they commissioned Joris Ivens, Hans Richter and George Pal to produce advertisements and image films.[48]

While MELODIE DER WELT emerged from the heart of the industry, John Grierson coordinated and led the activities of a group of young filmmakers employed by the British government and other semi-official institutions while simultaneously accepting commissions from the industry. Grierson, in fact, actively sought out the state and private companies as sponsors and was well aware of the precarious position that experimental-minded filmmakers found themselves in:

> Indeed, it is a curious comment on our art that the only freedom given to directors since has also been by propagandist groups: by Shell, the B.B.C., the Ministry of Labour, the Ceylon Government, the Gas Light and Coke Co., and by certain shipping, creosoting and radio firms in Europe. It is, of course, a relative freedom only, for State propaganda has its own ideological limits. This, however, can be said for it: the freshness and even the difficulty of its material drives the director to new forms and rich perspectives.[49]

A distant, but still discernible echo of Joris Ivens' statement on the documentary as avant-garde film can be heard in Grierson's plea for industry commissions despite the political differences between the conservative reformer Grierson and the radical revolutionary Ivens. In a 1931 article, Ivens argued that to work within the film industry was like slavery while industrial and commissioned films provided relatively more freedom because the filmmaker only had to deal with cinema outsiders.[50] Grierson, in this vein, thus consciously sought out sponsors for his films. He never made a film for the film industry preferring instead to work towards the creation of an organisation that did not need these structures. In keeping with avant-garde attempts to create a vertically integrated formation, the Griersonian institutions were not just concerned with producing films, but also ventured into distribution and exhibition, publishing and theorising, lecturing and teaching. Grierson had once avidly observed the shortcomings and successes of the 1920s avant-garde screening circles. He learnt his aesthetic lesson from the various films screened in the *Film Society* and he realised the necessity of vertical integration to remain functional over a longer period of time. Yet, he must have understood the problematic nature of the dependency on the film industry. Grierson therefore created a wholly autonomous film unit in which he only had to report to his superiors at regular intervals instead of having to discuss every single decision.

6.5 Exotic Adventures and Social Engineering

> *One will continue to provide the audience with*
> *foreign countries, so it does not notice anything at home.*
> Siegfried Kracauer (1929)[51]

In 1929, a young critic and aspiring filmmaker who had just finished his first medium-length film complained about the state of cinema in general and about the way reality was treated in particular:

> Apart from the work of the Russians, the cinema has done very little for the world of the genuine. There was Flaherty with NANOOK and MOANA. Then Schoedsack and Cooper with CHANG, and in between some excellent travel films like ARCTIC SKIES, STELLA POLARIS and VOYAGE AU CONGO. But in all these natural films the cinema has, for the sake of an easy romance, gone primitive. No one, to my knowledge, has gone forth on a wild expedition to the coal mines of Durham, or adventured under banners of publicity to Wolverhampton. No one for that matter has taken a tuppenny ride to Silvertown.[52]

The author of this text is none other than John Grierson writing for the magazine *The Clarion*. His charge that the cinema » has gone primitive « is a double reproach as it refers to the exotic subjects to which he objected, but more importantly, also to the style of filmmaking which still used models that had changed very little since the beginning of cinema. The attraction of the travel films is to be found less in their documentary value and more in their presentation of amazing feats (like stunts) and overwhelming sights and sites.[53] The travel-adventure film in certain ways exhibits the concerns of the cinema of attraction that was continued by the avant-garde filmmakers.[54] In this respect, the documentary was a turn away from earlier filmmaking practices, but also away from the avant-garde tendency to lead non-fiction towards a classical film style with its emphasis on psychological or social motivation, continuity editing, a coherent time-space frame and an overall dramaturgy.

Until recently, film history has been largely oblivious to the fact that one of the most popular genres of the 1920s was in fact the expedition film, presenting trips to exotic places, be it Africa, Asia, Latin America or the Arctic circle. The genre of the » expedition film « or » travel adventure film « provides an important element for the emerging documentary film and was a popular genre for short, but also for feature-length films throughout the 1920s. Very few of these films are remembered (and archived) by film history, even though only a brief glance at the specialised press and cinema programs of the time just prior to the introduction of sound demonstrates the ubiquity of this genre. Exotic and expedition films form a broad development throughout the silent era.[55] While some have claimed that these were early documentaries, not only did they resort to staging scenes for pictorial, nostalgic or colonialist purposes, but after 1930 many of the key protagonists stopped contributing to the developing documentary: Robert Flaherty's trajectory from Nanook of the North (US 1922) through Moana (US 1926) and White Shadows in the South Sea (US 1928, with W.S. Van Dyke) to Tabu (US 1930/31, with F.W. Murnau)[56] is similar to that of Merian C. Cooper's and Ernest B. Schoedsack's development from Grass (US 1925) through Chang: A Drama of the Wilderness (US 1927) to King Kong (US 1933). Their development involved an increased fictionalisation in which the exotic and the unknown formed a picturesque backdrop for the adventure or love story. The increasing popularisation, as well as the increasing production costs forced the explorer-filmmakers to choose either the direction of fictionalised accounts of journeys that adhered more strictly to fiction models or the alternative route taken by many avant-garde artists. This route was perhaps most successfully and most consequently realised by John Grierson, and led a trend toward industry sponsorship or government funding. While Americans like Flaherty or the Schoedsack/Cooper team opted for larger productions, often under the banner of Hollywood studios, filmmakers in Europe turned instead to industry for support, preferably steel or automobile manufacturers, but also electrical or chemical companies, a niche they shared with the avant-garde. Many companies like the car manufacturer Citroën or the steel magnate Stinnes financed expeditions which were set up as media events and the journeys not only resulted in films, but also in newspaper reports, books, theatre productions and other media products.[57]

Not coincidentally, a number of those working in the exotic adventure film genre were the same people we encountered in various avant-garde circles. Two protagonists from the mountain film genre emerged from the encounter of exploring, mountaineering, experimentation and fiction – avant-garde activists in 1930 considered Arnold Fanck as their ally. Meanwhile, Leni Riefenstahl graduated from experimental dance into Fanck's magic mountains and on her directorial debut Das blaue Licht, she collaborated with Béla Balázs as screen-

writer.[58] That the popularity of the genre was not lost on contemporary observers is visible in a parody on expedition films made by the avant-garde filmmaker and a founding member of the London *Film Society* Adrian Brunel,
whose CROSSING THE GREAT SAGRADA (GB 1924) produced by a » Mr. Spoof «,
was called a » great voyageogue « and was, in fact, a parody of contemporary
travel films consisting mainly of found footage from exotic and expedition
films. [59] The Stinnes clan demonstrated their fascination for a different kind of
cinema when they financed Abel Gance's disastrous NAPOLEON adventure before Clairenore Stinnes filmed her own car trip in CLAIRENORE STINNES – IM
AUTO DURCH ZWEI WELTEN (GER 1929). Marc Allégret and André Gide who
certainly also belong to this avant-garde tradition, however, also made the expedition film VOYAGE AU CONGO. In France, Andrè Sauvage not only co-directed
LA CROISIÈRE JAUNE with Léon Poirier, he also made mountain climbing films
that were screened in the specialised avant-garde cinemas and ÉTUDES SUR
PARIS (FR 1929), one of the many cinematic city symphonies of the French capital.[60] Even Ivor Montagu, key figure of the London *Film Society*, ventured into
the travel genre with » WINGS OVER EVEREST, a survey of the 1933 flying expedition financed by the flamboyantly patriotic Lady Houston «[61] These films often
simultaneously portrayed the geography and the filmmaker. In this way, Flaherty's NANOOK OF THE NORTH (US 1922) does fit into this genre of travel-adventure films. The French fur company Revillon Frères financed the film and so this
commission also documented the company's reach – and Flaherty's filmmaking
style mirrors the magical hunting capabilities projected onto Nanook. After all,
expedition filmmaking is not unlike hunting, as it creates an allegorical relationship between Flaherty and his subject in this case.[62]

And indeed, MELODIE DER WELT also fits into this field of discourse, as the
film depends on stereotypes from the popular genre of the exotic expedition
film. The official film brochure claimed that its goal was to discover the unifying
idea of a shipping line that circumnavigates the entire globe:

> to find the common element, the underlying idea of a shipping company encompass-
> ing the globe. When the sword is resting, research and economy are getting together.
> The human being blossoms under the warm beams of peace. But is not the cause of
> strive only the misunderstanding of others? Lack of knowledge produces hatred, un-
> derstanding creates love.[63]

Despite its avowed goal of world peace, the notion of subjugating the entire
world first to the eye of the camera, then to the Ruttmannesque montage is basically colonialist at heart. All of the processes, things and humans are subjected
to one master principle. In a universalising gesture that links the accessibility of
mass culture with the Eurocentrism of touristic ethnography, Ruttmann first
manages to transform a city into a symphony, and then transforms the whole

world into a melody. Ruttmann himself has argued that film as a medium needs a unifying concept for its immanent structure: » The film, consisting of different artistic and technical elements, can only have a filmic film if it, like a great symphonic composition, unites all contrapuntual, optical and acoustic rules in its score. «[64] This essentialising view of the medium was typical of the modernist avant-garde of the 1920s; the thrust was to fit disparate parts together to create a homogeneous whole, to subjugate the whole world to one formal principle. However, even the cinematic globetrotters of the time considered this gesture of totality already cast by colonialism.

If we follow this thought and consider Ruttmann a » Kulturfilmer «, in the sense of the Ufa *Kulturfilm* department[65], then Ruttmann could be considered a consequence of Germany's belated and forced modernisation that began in the late 19th century. If we consider Ruttmann within this (national) context of exaggerated imperial ambition and in terms of industrial development and colonialism, then Grierson makes for an interesting comparison. The Empire Marketing Board where Grierson first found employment was set up to support the global connections of the British Empire. Brian Winston has described this set-up as a colonial enterprise:

> Grierson's first major job was an attempt to › sell ‹ the British Empire, by establishing a film production programme at the Empire Marketing Board (EMB). The Empire was becoming at that time an object of derision to much progressive opinion. Only some engaged in the ... search for › national efficiency ‹ continued to embrace imperialism as a species of necessary reform of › backward ‹ societies. ... [I]t is far from being an accident that the documentary film in the service of the selling of the Empire (albeit unfortunately at exactly the moment of its formal disappearance) was Grierson's initial supposedly radical › social purpose ‹ in the cinema.[66]

Again we are confronted with Grierson and Ruttmann: Both of them considered film a means for achieving other goals, not a purpose in itself; seen in this perspective both were more modernisers than modernists. Thus, the reproach of being overtly formalist that has often been levelled against Ruttmann becomes obsolete as his formal obsession becomes the way to deal with the social implication of increasing modernisation.

Grierson's particular achievement was not any specific film or aesthetic program per se, but rather the machinery that he constructed around the films. He was not only just a filmmaker and supervisor of other people's films, his unit also achieved the establishment of government support (lobbying), the training of a relatively large group of filmmakers (teaching), the stabilisation of a core group of workers, the acquisition of industry sponsorship, the construction of a circuit of non-theatrical distribution, the establishment of magazines and of a critical tradition. In short, Grierson (used as shorthand for the documentary film movement) succeeded in coupling aesthetic preoccupations (film as art) with an instrumental use of cinema (education, reform, propaganda), thus creating a new kind of cinema (in terms of production methods as well as formal features) and a new kind of public (distribution and exhibition patterns, theoretical framework). In this sense, Grierson in fact succeeded in completely restructuring the cinema not only in aesthetic terms, but also in their institutional aspects, a field that had previously been occupied by the avant-garde.

If we follow the lead of the concept » engineer « we can also see why Robert Flaherty – adopted into the documentary movement by Grierson as his imaginary father – has always held such a precarious position and has sometimes even been rejected by the keepers of the documentary tradition: Flaherty was a totally romantic individual, utterly uninterested in social engineering or the living conditions of the working masses or the conditions of modern society in general. The negative view of Western influence and civilisation in WHITE SHADOWS IN THE SOUTH SEAS (US 1928, W.S. van Dyke / Robert Flaherty) is a case in point. The film presents the denigration of a Tahitian community via its contacts with Western traders. Flaherty was fascinated with the atavistic, even a-historical, struggle between man (and I am deliberately using the male gender here) and nature. This struggle was hard to find in industrialised countries, so Flaherty had to travel to the remote corners of the globe in order to find people and vistas not tainted too much by modernity's transformative powers.[67] However, Flaherty's project is only imaginable within the framework of another deeply modern concept, i.e., colonialism:

> Flaherty's was to be largely an imperial film-making career. It was to be almost entirely spent in the far-flung corners of empire or domestic backwaters, in the pay of governments or exploitative commercial interests. The mystery is how untainted by this is his reputation – as if the cinema were too puny, its pantheon too insecure, to support the vicissitudes suffered by other imperial artists – Kipling, say. Flaherty's explorer stance, although remarked on, is deemed to be without import. It is not even defended (as is Riefenstahl's fascism); it is ignored. No mistake must be made about this imperialism, though, for Flaherty was not a man to rise above his time.[68]

Thus, it seems difficult to escape modernity and modernisation when one thinks about the documentary, not least of all because the technology itself is a true product of that period. Flaherty tried to dodge these issues by going to faraway places, but he never truly succeeded because both his commission and his technology always ended up betraying him in his efforts to portray an imaginary state of innocence.

Ruttmann's purpose was inseparable from his artistic and social experiments; thus it is no coincidence that, over the course of his career, he returned at certain times to films belonging to the tradition of public health education, social engineering and eugenics.[69] In 1926, he made the promotional film DER AUFSTIEG for the exhibition GeSoLei (Gesundheitspflege, Soziale Fürsorge, Leibesübungen – health care, social welfare, physical exercise) to try to educate the population to lead a healthier life style. In 1931, Ruttmann produced the feature-length FEIND IM BLUT, and educational film about the dangers of venereal disease, while his very last film dealt with the dangers and prevention of cancer, EIN FILM GEGEN DIE VOLKSKRANKHEIT KREBS (GER 1941). In this perspective, Rutt-mann was not, as he is often been portrayed, an artist of the cross-section and a proponent of *Neue Sachlichkeit*, but more of a social reformer, public health edu-cator and social engineer.

6.6 Locating the Avant-garde in its (National) Context

> *The documentary film is a kind of microscope which helps us*
> *to perceive aspects of reality which we would not perceive without it.*
> *In a documentary film, in a scientific film life appears in its thousand details,*
> *in its processes, in everything that the eye normally cannot see.*
> Germaine Dulac (1925)[70]

The program has become a focus of film-historical investigation, especially in the study of early cinema,[71] however, the avant-garde is also a fruitful field when one considers the contexts in which various films have been screened.[72] Since films are partly determined by their context, it is necessary to look at var-ious facets: My discussion of modernity and production policy was intended to uncover the open and Ruttmann and Grierson's hidden dependencies, while the argument regarding the exotic in relation to cinema locates their filmic practices within certain generic and stylistic frameworks of the 1920s. The following re-marks about the screening context are meant to specify how contemporary spectators made sense of the two films.

The premiere of MELODIE DER WELT was of national significance for at least two reasons: Ruttmann had, by virtue of his international success with BERLIN, graduated from an avant-garde outsider into one of the most celebrated innova-tors in German film. Second, the film was one of the first German sound films to be completed and screened as conflicts with the US industry were mounting and the press coverage was enormous. The film was anticipated with an equal measure of hope, pride and fear. Weeks before the press was anxiously awaiting the upcoming » historical day «[73] and the premiere itself promised to have » every sign of an event « and with *tout Berlin* in attendance.[74] The show began with an opening speech by Hapag director Wilhelm Cuno (and German chan-cellor during the inflationary period of 1922-23), which was filmed and projected in order to demonstrate the new sound system (even though he was present in person and could have given the speech himself).[75] After the show, Hapag and Cuno invited the audience at the premiere to a reception at the hotel *Esplanade*, one of Berlin's best hotels. It was less an artistic or cultural event, and more a social and political one that surpassed many other film premieres and the reviews were full of superlatives:

> Only seldomly has the world city Berlin seen a social event of such style. The driving up of cars for this eagerly awaited premiere was of such a manner that the police had to redirect the traffic everywhere around Nollendorfplatz. The theatre itself offered a festive attire as even an opera gala can seldomly boast. The most representative society of the Imperial capitol, including the most marked heads of economy, politics and press, were in attendance.[76]

The intersection of politics, the economy and art in MELODIE DER WELT turned it into such an important event comparable to the biggest German premieres in Weimar film culture. The struggle against the American sound system and the joint efforts of Hapag and Tobis, backed by the large electronic companies, turned the film into a national event. It is ironic to note that the film fostered very few successors, in aesthetic terms, who were willing to carry on Ruttmann's frantic montage style.

By contrast, DRIFTERS premiered in the classic and solemn surroundings of alternative British film culture, the London *Film Society*. In this case, it is quite ironic that Grierson's film, now considered to be a prototype for a very fruitful branch of filmmaking, premiered in a marginal and somewhat ghettoised context whereas Ruttmann's film was an important social event, but, by contrast, has had very few, if any, obvious emulators and epigones. DRIFTERS was shown alongside THE FALL OF THE HOUSE OF USHER (US 1926-28, Melville Webber / J.S. Watson Jr.), an amateur production from the US,[77] Walt Disney's THE BARN DANCE (US 1929) and Eisenstein's POTEMKIN.[78] The context of Disney and Eisenstein appear quite significant in retrospect. Grierson himself had prepared Eisenstein's film for its British release and I have argued that Grierson consciously downplayed the influence of Soviet revolutionary cinema on the British documentary movement in order to moderate it outwardly. What Grierson took from the avant-garde was not only a tamed version of its energy and revolutionary force, but also the realisation that winning the state as a patron guarantees a steady production and output. Disney's animation on the other hand had fascinated intellectuals and filmmakers from the very beginning. Like Chaplin and the music hall, animation proved to be one of those cultural expressions where modernism and modernity met in a fruitful way. Animation fascinated both the mass audience and the intellectuals.[79]

Grierson's achievement can be seen in the context of a British » alternative film culture « on the verge of making a leap into the mainstream. The *Film Society* and the journal *Close Up*, the two crucial institutions and tastemakers, had both advocated improving British cinema for some time. British films either were considered dull and patriotic or as derivative of innovative Soviet, German or French films. Both options – the traditional and conservative British films and the copies of foreign models – were rejected by the key figures influenced by modernism's movement towards medium specificity. What was being requested was an adaptation of those leading international movements to a British context. Grierson was able to reconcile Britishness with a measure of modernist experimentation to arrive at a film style and media concept that found both backers in government institutions and a general audience. Grierson's program can be summed up as: » evolution as opposed to revolution, moderation as opposed to radicalism, and a commitment to mapping out areas of modern Britain overlooked within the commercial cinema «.[80] He was capable of winning the support of the intellectual tastemakers, which meant media and government support. Grierson came at the right moment for the British public, managing to combine several trends into his own unique blend of filmmaking: experimental in form, borrowing the montage methods from the Soviets, abstraction from *absoluter Film* and *cinéma pur* and a certain poetic style from the French, very British in its subject matter and all couched within topics of industrialisation and the negotiations of modernity for the general public. But, as we have already noted, the logic and logistics of production and distribution were borrowed from the avant-garde – a model that proved to be crucial in creating a steady foundation.

6.7 Conclusion

> *To demonstrate the identity of the artistic and scientific*
> *uses of photography which heretofore usually were separated*
> *will be one of the revolutionary functions of the film.*
> Walter Benjamin (1936)[81]

When we look at Grierson's and Ruttmann's filmmaking with a more abstract eye they appear quite similar: both were opposed to the commercial film industry, both used non-fiction material and had an abstract and poetic sense of montage in which the underlying truth would shine up through the surface of things which hid it from direct view. Both were fascinated by the exotic as much as by the quotidian, both were visionaries striving for a different kind of cinema. Both graduated from their own national cinema culture and came to wider prominence; in this process, both developed influential models for making films, but also for funding, for institutional support and for the creation of a steady support network.

The crucial difference between these two key figures lies in their institutional ramifications, their media strategies as one might call them. Ruttmann – even though he rhetorically called for artistic collaboration and a constructivist ethics – remained a lonesome artist-activist in the romantic vein, while Grierson had a very clear sense of how to negotiate and manipulate a public sphere and how to operate inside a bureaucracy. Grierson's greatest feat was not an artistic achievement in itself, but rather in the media concept that he developed, the institutional support he garnered and the longevity of his institution. Grierson found a niche that he expanded into a veritable organisation in which he could work on his media concept which needed the state (or state-affiliated institutions) as a reference point. Even though Ruttmann also finally turned to the state (in Nazi Germany) for support he did not develop a concept of how to collaborate and how to create a certain measure of freedom within the system of state or industry commissions. Grierson, it could be argued, was in a certain sense a successor to the 1920s avant-garde, which had attempted to develop alternative ways of producing, distributing and exhibiting cinema. Grierson's various film units worked on a concept of how to integrate certain ideas and theories of propaganda, social control, change and reform into a filmmaking practice. He was capable of gaining support for his concept of media activism, while Ruttmann failed to construct his own support network. This at least partly explains Ruttmann's willingness to work for the Nazis because they had a very specific idea of what cinema was. They easily integrated a talent like Ruttmann's and kept him on a tight leash. Ruttmann simply had no real strategy of how to deal with the context in which he was working. As a result of his collaboration, film history has labelled him a » traitor « who abandoned his leftist circles to work for the Nazis. The Griersonian movement, by contrast, was thoroughly » on the right side « and played a decisive role in launching a new genre, changing public opinion about cinema, winning a world war and altering film culture as a whole.

I have tried to avoid auteuristic arguments and purely aesthetic approaches because I believe that the avant-garde viewed itself more as a radical socio-political revolutionary movement than as purveyors of an aesthetic style. Even though Grierson diverged in important respects from the avant-garde, his approach with a closely-knit unit of practitioners clearly targeted idiosyncrasies, original creation and overstated individualism was similar. By adapting and modulating the avant-garde's goals, Grierson's group was able to overcome many of the tensions that had riddled the avant-garde. The source of energy and inspiration for the avant-garde is neither located in one creative genius nor in a collective of varied temperaments, but rather in technological, economic, social, and cultural ruptures and tectonic shocks that create fissures and crevices in the smooth surfaces on and in which the avant-garde was able to thrive for a short while. The avant-garde responded to the widespread existential feeling during the period between the two world wars that the modern world had nothing left to offer humankind. The activists were highly susceptible to seismic shifts and vibrations as they sought a way to deal with drastic changes in society. As a consequence, they were often absorbed or co-opted into larger political movements like communism and fascism. Grierson's radicalism is evident in his clear and conscious realisation that there was no way out of the dependency impasse, so the most reputable compromise was to work under the auspices of various state institutions. Grierson immediately laid out all his cards on the table by admitting his own dependency on support in very name of the institution.

What remains to be discussed here is the issue of sound. While MELODIE DER WELT, one of the first feature-length sound films in Germany, put sound to innovative use it also cast a nostalgic glance back to the heyday of the silent film avant-garde in both its structure and style. It superimposed the structure of Ruttmann's » city symphonies « over a trip around the world by presenting groups of images via their semantic similarity and, within a particular section, he utilised structural similarity for the film's rhythms and rhymes.

DRIFTERS, on the other hand, was silent, but looked forward to one option of how alternative film culture could transform itself (and by forces outside of its sphere of influence) in the 1930s. Grierson's film dealt with how modernity had reshaped the traditional occupation of fishermen. His film exhibits neither romantic longing for the lost traditions of the fisherman nor does it use experimentation as a structural feature for the mere sake of experimentation itself. Juxtaposition and unusual editing have a very clear effect in DRIFTERS as the entire structure of the film is subordinated to a rhetorical idea. I am aware that this is retrospective reasoning using knowledge unavailable in 1929, but I believe that this moment focuses several plot branches and developments into a singular moment that allows us to untangle the often complicated motions, coincidences and decisions. One could therefore – counter-factually, but also logically – claim that MELODIE DER WELT is a silent film with sound while DRIFTERS, by comparison, is a sound film which is silent.

Conclusion – Bridging the Gaps, Connecting the Dots

> POTEMKIN *is that rarity, a hugely successful film. …*
> *This film is ideologically concrete, correctly calculated*
> *in every detail like a bridge arch. The more forceful one*
> *hits it, the more beautifully it resounds. Only upon rattling*
> *one's gloved fingers upon it does one not hear or move anything.*
> Walter Benjamin (1927)[1]

Upon our return from this extensive tour that highlighted some of the features of the European avant-garde what remains to be done in the concluding remarks is to bridge the gap between the historiographic past and the current situation of film and media studies. By connecting some of the dots that delineate the field I hope to integrate this research into a bigger pattern and the wider context of film history. It is via two historicising detours that I want to approach the significance of my results beyond the confines of the historical avant-garde. On the one hand, I want to redraw some of the labyrinthine trajectories of avant-garde ideas and the activists involved in order to show how influential the avant-garde eventually became and, on the other hand, I want to turn my attention towards a specific instance that can serve as a case study for my argument: the international film festival circuit.

When the international archivists of the *Fédération Internationale des Archives du Film* (FIAF), an organisation founded as a result of the functional differentiation of avant-garde energies in 1938 (as argued in chapter three), met in Brighton in 1978 to re-examine the early cinema of the years 1900-06 it was in a sober and serious spirit of study. They did not anticipate that this meeting would provide *the* decisive inspiration for the study of early cinema that still proves to be one of the most fruitful fields in film studies today. In the following year, 1979, the FIAF conference took place in Lausanne and was devoted to a rediscovery of the international avant-garde of the interwar period. This time the spirits were exuberant, the atmosphere (self-)celebratory.[2] But this meeting did not give rise to a revisionist consideration of the avant-garde in any way comparable to what early cinema had experienced after Brighton. The Lausanne-meeting, fifty years on from La Sarraz, had a feeling similar to the high hopes of 1929, but seems to have led nowhere in terms of generating new research and scholarship. The classic approaches that centred on the works of art and organised along biographical lines still prevail(ed). Why are the myths and legends connected to the film avant-garde so strong? Why did Lausanne » fail « where

Brighton » succeeded « (if we can talk about failure and success in those terms)?
One reason might be, as I suggested in the introduction, that the recycling of the
style of the historical avant-garde by post-modern art in the 1980s, largely ignorant of the larger concerns of the revolutionary movements and social transformations, made a neutral perspective on the highly politicised 1920s and
1930s impossible. The artists and activists in the 1920s had to cope with a radically changed situation: the appearance of a bipolar world that overrode many
other concerns until 1989. It was only after the breakdown of the binary world
system that a novel perspective on the historical avant-garde was possible.

However, the avant-garde culture of the interbellum did not vanish or go
completely underground, it just shifted its terrain after World War Two. The
energy flows that had ebbed between the cities of modernism and generated so
much activity before World War Two shifted after 1945 from the imaginary axis
Paris-Berlin-Moscow to the axis across the Atlantic, more specifically in the case
of film, to the connection between New York and Paris.[3] The United States was
possibly the most avid receiver of European avant-garde culture of the interwar
period: Hans Richter and Oskar Fischinger, Man Ray and George Pal, Marcel
Duchamp and Alexander Hackenschmied (Hammid), René Clair and Jean Renoir, Luis Buñuel and Iris Barry, Siegfried Kracauer and Jay Leyda – all these
activists from an earlier period found temporary or permanent refuge in the
US. Through their work and their legacies they planted the seeds that would
grow and prosper into the independent or alternative movements that came
into existence in various places around the United States, most notably in New
York and San Francisco.

The history of *Cinema 16*, a New York-based film society, is a case in point.[4]
The club was established in 1947 by Amos Vogel, Austrian *émigré*, who followed the example set by the European networks in the interwar period. When
Vogel started screening films that would not find an outlet elsewhere it was not
with a long-running film club in mind. The successful screenings soon developed into a membership society, the biggest of its kind in the United States in
the 1950s. A magazine followed suit, as did a distribution network when the
society opened chapters in different places. These activities spun off into the
New York Film Festival, the first of its kind in the US, which was founded and
run by Vogel (with Richard Roud) from the 1960s onwards and which con-
tinues to this day as an important showcase for alternative, independent and
avant-garde cinema culture.[5] *Cinema 16* succeeded in building an audience
which not only watched avant-garde films in the narrow sense of the work, but
Vogel and his collaborators also screened educational, political, scientific and
documentary films demonstrating once again the broad approach of avant-
garde cinema culture. In fact, *Cinema 16* was killed by its own success as it
paved the way for the screening of foreign art house movies on American

screens, and helped stir the first flames of the New American Cinema of the 1950s and 1960s, which developed into the foundation for the circuit of repertoire cinemas.

Another field where the twisted energy streams of the interwar avant-garde emerge is in the genealogy of film studies. One important figure of the London avant-garde screening circle *Film Society* was Iris Barry who relocated to New York in the early 1930s. New York increasingly has been a major node for the traffic in ideas, people and institutional energy since the 1930s. Barry not only helped Siegfried Kracauer and Luis Buñuel at crucial moments in their lives, she also found and hired Jay Leyda, another prodigal child of the European interwar avant-garde, who studied and worked with Eisenstein in the mid-1930s in the Soviet Union. Leyda, along with Annette Michelson, established the film studies department at New York University, one of the most influential in the world, while also being instrumental in giving the field in general a better reputation through his history of the Russian cinema and his study of the compilation film.[6] Michelson and her magazine *October*, aptly named after Eisenstein's revolutionary epic, became a crucial factor in bridging the gap between the European revolutionary art movements of the 1920s and 1930s and the post-war American avant-garde around Ken Jacobs and P. Adam Sitney, Stan Brakhage and Andy Warhol. Here, the aforementioned Amos Vogel as well as another European émigré, Jonas Mekas, deserve at least brief mention as both were running important institutions for the circulation of the European avant-garde to a US audience. *October* must be given credit in at least two other respects regarding the dissemination of avant-garde energy: *October* partly inaugurated and greatly supported the revival of Soviet cinema and theory in an American academic context in the 1970s and 1980s[7] while also supporting the fledging study of early cinema. Not coincidentally then, three of Michelson's and Leyda's students at NYU have been at the forefront of this field that has been prospering for the past 25 years (since the meeting in Brighton). I am thinking here of Noël Burch, Tom Gunning and Charles Musser, all with a marked interest in the avant-garde and renowned as eminent scholars of early cinema.[8] The bridge that Tom Gunning constructed between early cinema and the avant-garde in his classic article on the cinema of attractions is far from arbitrary and implicitly points out a genealogy of film studies and of the avant-garde when read through the overlapping and intersecting trajectories of people and institutions.[9]

Besides the transatlantic current that gave rise to film studies as an established field, the mobile, dynamic and free-floating energy of the avant-garde helped to implement film festivals and art houses. The event culture of Stuttgart, Baden-Baden and La Sarraz gave rise to the international festival circuit, the archival impulse created archives in major cities across the globe and also

the international network connecting them (*FIAF*) while the avant-garde cinemas *Studio des Ursulines*, *Studio 28*, *Theatre du Vieux Colombier*, *De Uitkijk* and
Kamera gave rise to a parallel system of production, distribution and exhibition
that was institutionalised after World War Two and is commonly known as art
cinema.[10] Film education and media studies were inspired by the vocational
impulse developed in avant-garde circles. Film, books and magazines are still
inspired by classic examples from the 1920 and 1930s, many of which continue
to be reprinted in new editions for students of film like the texts of Arnheim,
Balázs, Delluc, Dulac, Eisenstein, Grierson, Kracauer, Pudovkin, Richter, Rotha,
Vertov and others who still form part of the film studies curriculum. I hope that
I have shown that the production of films was only one element in a much
wider strategy to change cinema culture: teaching and publishing, screenings
and discussions, distribution and theory formation, invention and adaptation
were all part of the avant-garde conception: » those who change the cinema will
change the world «. Since cinema was then understood in its widest possible
sense, as discourse, *dispositif*, practice and cultural formation, this avant-garde
is still with us, perhaps even more so than it has been for a very long time. It is
only when we look back at the European avant-garde cinema from today's vantage point that we realise its pervasive influence. This is one way in which the
title *Moving Forward, Looking Back* relates to the vertiginous pathways of the
avant-garde.

Another possibility in illustrating the long-term effects that the avant-garde
has had on film culture in general is to look at film festivals.[11] What turned the
film festivals into such a successful concept, one could argue, in contrast to the
avant-garde, was its ability to tap into many different discourses at many different levels. Whereas the avant-garde attempted to invent everything from
scratch – they seldom accepted such elements as ready-made audience bases,
imported aesthetic concepts or pre-fabricated discourses. This is quite the contrary for film festivals: In terms of finance and organisation, they utilised political, tourist and economic institutions that would support the festival in terms of
organisation. Festivals, in regard to the specialised needs of the film industry,
are able to provide local showcases for international products (test screenings
so to speak) while also providing a trade fair audience of potential buyers. At
the same time, festivals also connect into existing networks of cultural value: By
bringing together filmmakers and critics and by presenting numerous novel
works the festival also caters to the artistic-cultural side of filmmaking. On a
local level it caters to the spectators' desires to attend a media event while internationally it also has to sustain itself as a destination at a specific time (Locarno
in August has definite advantages here over Rotterdam in January). The film
festival does not need to produce the discourses that it thrives on, it just has to
remember all the different constituencies that it tries to cater to: not too much

Hollywood because then the quality press turns up its nose, not too little because then the tabloids and TV stations don't show up (which, in turn, might
endanger sponsorship possibilities); enough tickets for the industry (because
they pay the most), but also enough for the international press (you don't want
unfavourable results) and for the local audience (or the local politicians might
reconsider their financial investment). Of course, this is already difficult
enough, but it shows how the discourses cannibalise the film festivals while in
turn also being cannibalised by the festivals. It also reveals their mutual dependency and the film festival can thus be seen as a nodal point in a complex and
ever-changing network.

The case for the avant-garde was quite the contrary; it ultimately aspired to
overcome and abolish itself because it wanted to do away with traditional art.
By refusing to accept the institutions of bourgeois art, by trying to dispose of
these, the avant-garde at once evoked a mythical past in which art was an integral part of life as well as a future in which the barriers between art and life had
been torn down. However, this characteristic, double movement that skips the
present, was not aimed at a restorative reconstruction of a mythical past, but
wanted to bracket the tensions and contradictions of modernity in order to
solve them on another level and in another time. Working with modern technology meant accepting the given reality and including and redeeming it within
the avant-garde, which – as the activists believed – prefigured a future society
and constituted a test run for the art yet to come. This was the specific contribution of the avant-garde working in reproductive media: to self-reflexively address through its very means of expression the conditions of modernity that
had brought it into existence in the first place. If we consider the avant-garde as
a self-deconstructing myth, as an attempt to modernise and update the antique,
pre-modern hero in a Hegelian sense who transcends himself, then the avant-
garde is indeed heroic in the way that it did what it (thinks it) had to do because
their deeds ultimately made their own existence superfluous. By anticipating a
future order, by presenting a utopian promise, the avant-garde also robs itself of
its own place in that future society because the avant-garde had to exceed all of
the limits imposed by the present society in order to make the future come true.
It is this heroic act – sacrificing itself by attempting to destroy its very own
foundation upon which it stood because annihilating the present was necessary
for the realisation of the future – that hurls the avant-garde out of the realm of
the modern. This concept of heroism and the pre-modern at which I also meant
to hint with the title *Moving Forward, Looking Back* offers another perspective on
the results of the study.

There is widespread agreement in sociology circles that the most prominent
feature of modern societies is » functional differentiation «.[12] The avant-garde,
was squarely a part of modernity and attempted to do away with it. By concep-

tualising their activities as a totality, the avant-garde wanted to overcome functional differentiation and specialisation. But it was precisely functional differentiation that came back with a vengeance once it became clear that the high promises of the avant-garde were not achievable in the near future. The
developments of the 1930s demonstrate how a broad movement yielded many
results, but failed in its ultimate goal of restructuring art and society. Still, many
of its notions survived and prevailed: One can interpret Grierson's genealogical
reference to Flaherty as a displacement in order to cover up his debt to the Soviet revolutionary cinema because he could not openly acknowledge the Soviet
influence in the 1930s and 1940s. Thus, Flaherty served as a deflection against
the possibility of being accused of communist sympathies. The perspective proposed here opens up another avenue: Flaherty's exclusive concentration on pre-
modern social formations camouflages the avant-garde's heroic attempt to overcome the specialisation of modern times with a similarly heroic totality. The
paradoxical Soviet situation in which art had the function of illustrating the future paradise mirrors the situation in which the past is evoked toward the realisation of a future state. The utopian aspiration towards a total cinema, the
various teaching activities as well as the attempts at restructuring exhibition
and distribution, and the examples that I have discussed work towards a wholeness and totality that was directed against functional differentiation. Yet, it is
exactly this specialisation that provided the true achievements of the avant-
garde that have been preserved (archives, film history, film theory, vocational
training etc.). The avant-garde was riddled and haunted by unsolvable, indeed
dialectical, paradoxes.

Even though the avant-garde is often seen as something that ultimately
failed, one can also conceptualise the development that set in around 1929 as
the ultimate triumph: it did not bring about a transformation of the kind it had
hoped for (i.e., a social, political and cultural revolution), but it clearly had a
visible impact in many different areas. The avant-garde achieved the naturalisa-
tion of the documentary as a genre and the foundation of film archives in various countries, it helped introduce large-scale government support for cinema
in virtually all European countries, it was decisive in the establishment of film
theory as a field of its own, and it stimulated the emergence of art house cinemas. The cultural acceptance of cinema as an artistic form and cultural force
leads us invariably back to the avant-garde and its wide-ranging activities.
Thus, what counts as a defeat from one perspective, can be rephrased as a success story when using a different focus.

Inevitably, I have had to be very broad at times, mapping a terrain where there
is still much leeway to drill deeper holes than I have been able to do in this
work. The relationship of the avant-garde to the various amateur movements in

the 1930s or a closer look at the links between the emerging documentary and the self-differentiating avant-garde seem viable research projects and interesting topics to follow up on. Moreover, the various conceptions of employing the cinema to rally support, propagate (political) opinions and agitate for specific causes that different nation-states instituted over the course of the 1930s and 1940s closely relates to concerns first articulated within the framework of the avant-garde. It may be time to comparatively explore the use of film and the cinema not only in fascist-totalitarian countries as different as Germany, Italy or Portugal, which all used film as a heavily state-controlled propaganda instrument, but also in liberal reform governments such as France during the *front populaire*, Britain and Sweden in the 1930s and the United States during the New Deal, where democracies attempted to employ film as a means of persuasion and education, while assessing both practices in relation to the engagement of media in Stalinist Soviet Union.

As far as the wider implications of this study are concerned, I hope to have also contributed to putting Europe more firmly on the map of cinema history. While Europe has often been conceptualised as a rather disconnected accumulation of national cinematographies or as a series of national new waves that succeeded one another from the late 1940s (Neo-Realism) until the 1970s (New German Cinema), I have attempted to create a conceptualisation of Europe not as a series of distinct national territories, but as a unified (even though highly heterogeneous) space in which energy flows stagnate and re-distribute themselves regardless of national frontiers. In a way, the alternative network proposed here was the shadow of the power of the big corporations. While the vertically integrated German major Ufa was arguably the most important European company from 1919 to 1945, it was complemented by the avant-garde – both were stuck in an antagonistic stance towards each other, but both also needed the other: not only as a means of differentiation and to be able » to make a distinction « in a Luhmannian sense of double contingency, but moreover in a dialectical relationship in which Ufa (and some other big companies such as Tobis or Gaumont-Franco-Film-Aubert) provided the avant-garde with (direct and indirect) commissions while, in turn, the avant-garde delivered prototypes and innovations that the industry sometimes adapted and sometimes discarded.

In the epitaph to this epilogue I have quoted Walter Benjamin's comparison of Sergei Eisenstein's film POTEMKIN to a perfectly constructed bridge that resonates beautifully upon being struck. I hope that I have not only used the avant-garde as a resonance board and percussion instrument by listening to the still fresh and original sound material 80 years later. I hope that I have been able to use the bridge in another and much more obvious way – to cross a gap or a divide between the historicity of the canonical avant-garde and my present *situatedness* within institutional and professional parameters. However, since the avant-garde could not connect two dots with a straight line, this bridge is far from explored and exhausted. It supports more research and it will sound louder and more beautifully the more scholars and students, film archivists and media-activists dare to walk across it and make it resonate. Only upon rattling one's gloved fingers upon it does one not move or hear anything.

Notes

Notes Introduction

1. Walter Benjamin: »Erwiderung an Oscar A.H. Schmitz«. In: W.B.: *Gesammelte Schriften. II.2.* Frankfurt am Main: Suhrkamp 1977: 751-755, here 752. [»Die technischen Revolutionen – das sind die Bruchstellen der Kunstentwicklung, an denen die Tendenzen je und je,freiliegend sozusagen, zum Vorschein kommen.In jeder neuen technischen Revolution wird die Tendenz aus einem sehr verborgenen Element der Kunst wie von selber zum manifesten. Und damit wären wir dann endlich beim Film. «, my trans.]

2. Niklas Luhmann: *Die Kunst der Gesellschaft.* Frankfurt am Main: Suhrkamp 1995: 198f. Walter Benjamin: »Über den Begriff der Geschichte«. In: W.B.: *Gesammelte Schriften. I.2.* Frankfurt am Main: Suhrkamp 1977: 691-704, here 697f. For a thorough discussion of both images see 1.5.

3. A series of Benjamin's texts from the second half of the 1920s onwards implicitly or explicitly illustrate this position. See as central examples »Das Kunstwerk im Zeitalter seiner technischen Reproduzierbarkeit«. (written 1935/36) In: W.B.: *Gesammelte Schriften. I.2.* Frankfurt am Main: Suhrkamp 1977: 471-508; »Der Sürrealismus. Die letzte Momentaufnahme der europäischen Intelligenz«. (written 1928/29) In: W.B.: *Gesammelte Schriften. II.1.* Frankfurt am Main: Suhrkamp 1977: 295-310; »Der Erzähler. Betrachtungen zum Werk Nikolai Lesskows«. (written 1928-35) In: W.B.: *Gesammelte Schriften. II.2.* Frankfurt am Main: Suhrkamp 1977: 438-465; »Der Autor als Produzent«. (lecture given in Paris 27 April 1934) In: W.B.: *Gesammelte Schriften. II.2.* Frankfurt am Main: Suhrkamp 1977: 683-701; »Zur Lage der russischen Filmkunst«. In: W.B.: *Gesammelte Schriften. II.2.* Frankfurt am Main: Suhrkamp 1977: 747-751; »Erwiderung an Oscar A.H. Schmitz«. (both written 1927). In: W.B.: *Gesammelte Schriften. II.2.* Frankfurt am Main: Suhrkamp 1977: 751-755. See also the series of texts on Bertolt Brecht and the unfinished *Passagenwerk.*

4. My understanding of the avant-garde relies to a large extent on Peter Bürger's ideas as elaborated in: *Theorie der Avantgarde.* Frankfurt am Main: Suhrkamp 1974. (Eng.: *Theory of the Avant-garde.* Manchester: Manchester University Press 1984). I will discuss the notion of avant-garde in relation to the cinema of around 1930 in detail in chapter two.

5. Walter Benjamin: »Der Autor als Produzent«. (lecture, Paris 27 April 1934). In: W. B.: *Gesammelte Schriften. II.2.* Frankfurt am Main: Suhrkamp 1977: 683-701, here 692. [»...[E]inen Produktionsapparat zu beliefern, ohne ihn – nach Maßgabe des Möglichen – zu verändern, [stellt] selbst dann ein höchst anfechtbares Verfahren dar ..., wenn die Stoffe, mit denen dieser Apparat beliefert wird, revolutionärer Natur scheinen. «, trans. Anna Bostock, *Understanding Brecht*: 93f.]

6. Ibid.: 693. [» [E]rst die Überwindung jener Kompetenzen im Prozeß der geistigen Produktion, welche, der bürgerlichen Auffassung zufolge, dessen Ordnung bilden, macht diese Produktion politisch tauglich; und zwar müssen die Kompetenzschranken von bei-den Produktivkräften, die sie zu trennen errichtet waren, vereint gebrochen werden. «, trans. Anna Bostock, *Understanding Brecht*: 95]

7. See Lotte H. Eisner: » Avantgarde – Achtung! «. In: *Film-Kurier*, vol. 10, no. 126, 26.5.1928. [» Bleibt die Avantgarde nicht Privileg der wirklich mutigen Vorkämpfer, so besteht die Gefahr, dass sie bald ein großer Träger vorwärtskriechender Heerhaufen wird. ... Die Avantgarde muß in ihren eigenen Reihen sondieren. Sich von Mitläufern und Konjunktursüchtigen befreien, die ihrer Sache schaden. ... Die Avantgarde muß sehen, daß sie wirklich Avantgarde bleibt. Sie muß verstehen, wo ihre Freunde sind, und Kritik aus den eigenen Reihen annehmen. Sonst wird sie trotz ihres Namens zu einer Angelegenheit von gestern. «, my trans.]

8. I detail these developments in chapter three.

9. For more on these terms, see Thomas Elsaesser: » Moderne und Modernisierung. Der deutsche Film der dreißiger Jahre «. In: *montage/av*, vol. 3, no. 2, 1994: 23-40; see also Thomas Elsaesser: *Das Weimarer Kino – aufgeklärt und doppelbödig*. Berlin: Vorwerk 8 1999: passim.

10. Benjamin, Erwiderung, op. cit.: 753. [» ...die wichtigen, elementaren Fortschritte der Kunst sind weder neuer Inhalt noch neue Form – die Revolution der Technik geht beiden voran. «, my trans.]

11. Andreas Huyssen: » The Hidden Dialectic: Avantgarde – Technology – Mass Culture «. In: A.H.: *After the Great Divide: Modernism, Mass Culture, Postmodernism*. Bloomington and Indianapolis, IN: Indiana University Press 1986: 3-15, here 3.

12. The term » historical avant-garde « for the movements of Dada, Surrealism and Constructivism was coined by Peter Bürger in his seminal study *Theorie der Avantgarde*. Frankfurt am Main: Suhrkamp 1974. (Eng.: *Theory of the Avant-garde*. Manchester: Manchester University Press 1984).

Notes Chapter I

1. Andreas Huyssen: » The Hidden Dialectic: Avantgarde – Technology – Mass Culture «. First published in Kathleen Woodward (ed.): *The Myths of Information: Technology and Postindustrial Culture*. Madison, WI: Coda Press 1980: 151-164. Reprinted in and quoted after: Andreas Huyssen: *After the Great Divide: Modernism, Mass Culture, Postmodernism*. Bloomington and Indianapolis: Indiana University Press 1986: 3-15, here 9.

2. Saskia Sassen: *The Global City: New York, London, Tokyo*. Princeton, NJ: Princeton University Press 1991.

3. See Peter Wollen: » Viking Eggeling «. In: P. Wollen: *Paris Hollywood: Writings on Film*. London, New York: Verso 2002: 39-54. See also the book-length study Louise O'Konor: *Viking Eggeling 1880-1925. Artist and Filmmaker*. Stockholm: Almquist & Wiksell 1971.

4. See, for a useful introductory description, Malcolm Bradbury: » The Cities of Modernism «. In: Malcolm Bradbury, James McFarlane (eds.): *Modernism 1890-1930*. Harmondsworth: Penguin 1991: 96-103.

5. Alan Williams: » Historical and Theoretical Issues in the Coming of Recorded Sound to the Cinema «. In: Rick Altman (ed.): *Sound Theory, Sound Practice*. New York, London: Routledge 1992: 126-137, here 126.

6. See Harald Jossé: *Die Entstehung des Tonfilms. Beitrag zu einer faktenorientierten Mediengeschichtsschreibung*. Freiburg, München: Alber 1984, and Wolfgang Mühl-Benninghaus: *Das Ringen um den Tonfilm. Strategien der Elektro- und Filmindustrie in den 20er und 30er Jahren*. Düsseldorf: Droste 1999. For English-language overviews see also Douglas Gomery: » Tri-Ergon, Tobis Klangfilm, and the Coming of Sound «. In: *Cinema Journal*, vol. 16, (1976): 51-61 and Douglas Gomery: » Economic Struggle and Hollywood Imperialism: Europe Converts to Sound «. In: *Yale French Studies*, no. 60 (1980): 80-93. The classic (and by now somewhat dated) works in this field are Harry M. Geduld: *The Birth of the Talkies: From Edison to Jolson*. Bloomington, IN and London: Indiana University Press 1975 and Alexander Walker: *The Shattered Silents: How the Talkies Came to Stay*. London: Elm Tree 1978.

7. See Karel Dibbets: *Sprekende films. De komst van de geluidsfilm in Nederland 1928-1933*. Amsterdam: Cramwinckel 1993.

8. See, for a thorough study, Donald Crafton: *The Talkies. American Cinema's Transition to Sound 1926-1931*. New York: Charles Scribner's Sons 1997, and for a more popular account Scott Eyman: *The Speed of Sound: Hollywood and the Talkie Revolution*. New York: Simon & Schuster 1997. See for a comparative perspective Charles O'Brien: *Cinema's Conversion to Sound: Technology and Film Style in France and the US*. Bloomington, IN: Indiana University Press 2005.

9. See Christien Belaygue (ed.): *Le passage du muet au parlant*. Toulouse: Cinémathèque de Toulouse 1988; Michele Canosa (ed.): *L'Immagine Acustica. Dal muto al sonoro: gli anni della transizione in Europa*. Ancona: Transeuropa 1992. (Cinegrafie 2/5); Martin Barnier: *En route vers le parlant. Histoire d'une évolution technologique, économique et esthéthique du cinéma (1926-1934)*. Liège (BE): Éditions du Céfal 2002. (Histoire du Cinéma / Collection Travaux & Thèses) and Corinna Müller: *Vom Stummfilm zum Tonfilm*. München: Wilhelm Fink 2003.

10. Cda [= Chris Darke]: » Avant-garde Cinema in Europe «. In: Ginette Vincendeau (ed.): *Encyclopedia of European Cinema*. London / New York: Cassell, British Film Institute / Facts on File 1995: 25

11. The term *cinema pur* was used in the French discourse in the 1920s to describe the free montage of photographically created images according to laws of music or formal logic (films by Henri Chomette, Germaine Dulac, Jean Epstein and others) while *absoluter Film* was employed in the mid-1920s in Germany to denote the abstract and non-figurative animations of Viking Eggeling, Hans Richter and Walter Ruttmann.

12. I will examine the role of the Soviet Union in the European film avant-garde in more detail in my chapter on the » Vanishing Point Soviet Union «.

13. David Bordwell, Janet Staiger, Kristin Thompson: *The Classical Hollywood Cinema: Film Style & Mode of Production to 1960*. London: Routledge 1985: 301.

14. Alan Williams: » Historical and Theoretical Issues in the Coming of Recorded Sound to the Cinema «. In: Rick Altman (ed.): *Sound Theory, Sound Practice*. New York, London: Routledge 1992: 126-137, here 128.

15. Andrew Higson: » The Limiting Imagination of National Cinema «. In: Mette Hjort, Scott MacKenzie (eds.): *Film & Nation*. London and New York: Routledge 2000: 63-74, here 66.

16. Darrell Davis has, along very similar revisionist lines, examined Western scholarship of Japanese film in which he also distinguishes three successive stages, which he labels reflectionist, dialogic, and contamination. See Darrell William Davis: » Reigniting Japanese Tradition with *Hana-Bi* «. In: *Cinema Journal* 40, no. 4 (Summer 2001): 58-79.

17. See Benedict Anderson: *Imagined Communities: Reflections on the Origin and Spread of Nationalism*. London: Verso 1983; Anthony Smith: *Theories of Nationalism*. London: Duckworth 1983; Anthony D. Smith: *The Ethnic Origins of Nations*. Oxford: Blackwell 1986; Anthony D. Smith: *National Identity*. London: Penguin / Reno, NV: University of Nevada Press 1991; Anthony D. Smith: *Nationalism and Modernism*. London, New York: Routledge 1998; and Eric J. Hobsbawm: *Nations and Nationalism since 1780: Programme, Myth, Reality*. Cambridge: Cambridge University Press 1990.

18. Homi K. Bhabha: *Nation and Narration*. London: Routledge 1990; Homi K. Bhabha: *The Location of Culture*. London, New York: Routledge 1994; Edward W. Said: *Orientalism: Western Conceptions of the Orient*. London: Routledge & Kegan Paul 1978; Terry Eagleton, Fredric Jameson, Edward Said (eds.): *Nationalism, Colonialism and Literature*. Minneapolis: University of Minnesota Press 1990. For an application of some of the issues on the cinema see the influential book by Hamid Naficy: *An Accented Cinema: Exilic and Diasporic Filmmaking*. Princeton, NJ, Oxford: Princeton University Press 2001.

19. Important contributions to this debate in the last 20 years are Thomas Elsaesser: » Images for England (and Scotland, Ireland, Wales...) «. In: *Monthly Film Bulletin*, vol. 51, no. 608, September 1984: 267-269; Thomas Elsaesser: » Chronicle of a Death Retold: Hyper, Retro, or Counter-Cinema «. In: *Monthly Film Bulletin*, vol. 54, no. 641, June 1987: 164-167; Thomas Elsaesser: » The Idea of National Cinema «. (» De competitie met Hollywood «). In: *Skrien* 186, October/November 1992; Thomas Elsaesser: » InpersoNations: National Cinema, Historical Imaginaries «. In: T.E.: *European Cinema: Face to Face with Hollywood*. Amsterdam: Amsterdam University Press 2005: 57-81; Thomas Elsaesser: » German Cinema in the 1990s «. In: Thomas Elsaesser, Michael Wedel (eds.): *The BFI Companion to German Cinema*. London: British Film Institute 1999; Stephen Crofts: » Reconceptualising National Cinema/s «. In: *Quarterly Review of Film and Video*, vol. 14, no. 3, 1993: 49-67; Stephen Crofts: » Concepts of National Cinema «. In: John Hill, Pamela Church Gibson (eds.): *The Oxford Guide to Film Studies*. Oxford: Oxford University Press 1998: 385-394; Andrew Higson: » The Concept of National Cinema «. In: *Screen*, vol. 30, no. 4, Autumn 1989: 36-46; Andrew Higson: » The Instability of the National «. In: Justine Ashby, Andrew Higson (eds.): *British Cinema, Past and Present*. London, New York: Routledge 2000: 35-47. Two well-selected and edited anthologies also testify to the increasing significance of this field: see Mette Hjort, Scott MacKenzie (eds.): *Cinema & Nation*. London, New York: Routledge 2000, and Alan Williams: *Film and Nationalism*. New

Brunswick, NJ and London: Rutgers University Press 2002. (Rutgers Depth of Field Series).

20. See Richard Abel: *French Cinema: The First Wave, 1915-1929*. Princeton, NJ: Princeton University Press 1984: 251f.; Richard Abel: » *Cinégraphie* and the Search for Specificity «. In: R.A.: *French Film Theory and Criticism, 1907-1939: A History/Anthology. I: 1907-1929*. Princeton, NJ: Princeton University Press 1988: 194-223, here 198; Christophe Gauthier: *La passion du cinéma. Cinéphiles, Ciné-Clubs et salles specialisées à Paris de 1920 à 1929*. Paris: École nationale de Chartres / AFRHC 1999 : 57. See Kristin Thompson: » Dr. Caligari at the Folies-Bergère, or, The Successes of an Early Avant-Garde Film «. In: Mike Budd (ed.): *The Cabinet of Dr. Caligari. Texts, Contexts, Histories*. New Brunswick, NJ and London: Rutgers University Press 1990: 121-169, on the French reception of CALIGARI see 149-156.

21. Malcolm Bradbury: » The Cities of Modernism «. In: Malcolm Bradbury, James McFarlane (eds.): *Modernism 1890-1930*. Harmondsworth: Penguin 1991: 96-103, here 96.

22. Thomas Elsaesser: *Filmgeschichte und frühes Kino. Archäologie eines Medienwandels*. München: edition text + kritik 2002: 305. [» Ein konsequent archäologischer Ansatz müsste deshalb nicht nur die Reichweite der Fragen, die man für relevant erachtet, vergrößern, sondern noch einmal den Ansatzpunkt der Fragestellung verändern und die eigenen historiografischen Prämissen infrage stellen; beispielsweise indem man die Diskontinuitäten mitbedenkt, die so genannten Sackgassen und die Möglichkeit einer erstaunlichen Andersartigkeit der Vergangenheit. « , my trans.]

23. On the *New Film History* see Thomas Elsaesser: » The New Film History «. In: *Sight and Sound*, vol. 55, no. 4, Autumn 1986: 246-251 for a concise introduction. See for a book-length discussion Robert C. Allen, Douglas Gomery: *Film History: Theory and Practice*. New York: Knopf 1985. A critical evaluation is provided by Paul Kusters: » New Film History. Grundzüge einer neuen Filmgeschichtswissenschaft «. In: *montage/av*, vol. 5, no. 1, 1996: 39-60.

24. For more recent overviews and re-evaluations see the special section on » Film History, or a Baedeker Guide to the Historical Turn « edited by Sumiko Higashi in: *Cinema Journal*, vol. 44, no. 1, Fall 2004: 94-143. See also Thomas Elsaesser: » Writing and Rewriting Film History: Terms of a Debate «. In: *Cinéma et cie.*, no. 1, Fall 2001: 24-33.

25. Rick Altman has suggested a more general model of crisis historiography that could also be subsumed under these archaeological approaches. See Rick Altman: » Penser l'histoire (du cinéma) autrement : un modèle de crise «. In: *Vingtième siécle*, no. 46, 1995: 65-74.

26. On the cultural, technological and political pitfalls of dubbing see Nataša Ďurovičová: » Local Ghosts: Dubbing Bodies in Early Sound Cinema «. In: Anna Antonini (ed.): *Il film e i suoi multipli. Film and Its Multiples*. Udine: Forum 2003: 83-98.

27. See especially his *The Archaeology of Knowledge & The Discourse on Language*. New York: Pantheon 1972.

28. See *Discipline and Punish: The Birth of the Prison*. Harmondsworth: Penguin 1977.

29. See *The Order of Things: An Archaeology of the Human Sciences*. London: Tavistock 1970.

30. See *Madness and Civilisation: A History of Insanity in the Age of Reason*. New York: Random House 1965.

31. See *The Birth of the Clinic: An Archaeology of Medical Perception*. London: Tavistock 1973.

32. See Thomas Elsaesser: *Filmgeschichte und frühes Kino. Archäologie eines Medienwandels*. München: edition text + kritik 2002. See Siegfried Zielinski: *Archäologie der Medien*. Reinbek: Rowohlt 2002. See also Wolfgang Ernst: » Der medienarchäologische Blick «. In: Harro Segeberg (ed.): *Die Medien und ihre Technik. Theorien – Modelle – Geschichte*. Marburg: Schüren 2004: 28-42. For an evaluation of Elsaesser's position see Leonardo Quaresima: » Sherlock Holmes und das marokkanische Wadi «. In: *Kintop – Jahrbuch zur Erforschung des frühen Films. Vol. 12: Theorien zum frühen Kino*. Frankfurt am Main and Basel: Stroemfeld / Roter Stern 2003: 165-170.

33. Wolfgang Ernst: » Der medienarchäologische Blick «. In: Harro Segeberg (ed.): *Die Medien und ihre Technik. Theorien – Modelle – Geschichte*. Marburg: Schüren 2004: 28-42, here 32. [» ...das Artefakt zunächst nur in seiner Gegebenheit, also: als datum, als Daten zu beschreiben, quasi als Monument stehenzulassen, statt es (wie in der Operation der Historiker) sogleich zum Dokument oder zur Illustration einer dahinterstehenden Geschichte zu machen «, my trans.]

34. See Thomas Elsaesser: *Filmgeschichte und frühes Kino. Archäologie eines Medienwandels*. München: edition text + kritik 2002. See also Thomas Elsaesser: » Early Film History and Multi-Media: An Archaeology of Possible Futures? «. In: Wendy Chung (ed.): *The Archaeology of Multimedia*. New York: Routledge 2003.

35. See as a methodological primer Niklas Luhmann: *Soziale Systeme. Grundriß einer allgemeinen Theorie*. Frankfurt am Main: Suhrkamp 1984, for a general overview see Niklas Luhmann: *Die Gesellschaft der Gesellschaft*. Frankfurt am Main: Suhrkamp 1998, and for a study of the art system Niklas Luhmann: *Die Kunst der Gesellschaft*. Frankfurt am Main: Suhrkamp 1995.

36. Niklas Luhmann: *Soziale Systeme. Grundriß einer allgemeinen Theorie*. Frankfurt am Main: Suhrkamp 1984: 59. [» Selbstreferentielle Systeme haben keine andere Form für Umweltkontakte als Selbstkontakte «, my trans.]

37. Stephen C. Foster: » Hans Richter: Prophet of Modernism «. In: Stephen C. Foster (ed.): *Hans Richter: Activism, Modernism, and the Avantgarde*. Cambridge, MA and London: MIT Press 1998. (In collaboration with the University of Iowa Museum of Art, Iowa City): 2-15, here 3.

38. See, for good overviews Robert Stam: *Film Theory: An Introduction*. Oxford: Blackwell 2000, and Francesco Casetti: *Teorie del cinema (1945-1990)*. Milano: Bompiani 1993; Eng.: *Theories of Cinema, 1945-1995*. Austin, TX: University of Texas Press 1999. See, for collections of early texts, Helmut H. Diederichs (ed.): *Geschichte der Filmtheorie. Kunsttheoretische Texte von Méliès bis Arnheim*. Frankfurt am Main: Suhrkamp 2004 and Richard Abel: *French Film Theory and Criticism, 1907-1939. A History/ Anthology. I: 1907-1929. II: 1929-1939*. Princeton, NJ: Princeton University Press 1988.

39. See Francesco Bono et al. (eds.): *La Filmliga olandesa (1927-1933). Avanguardia, critica, organizzazione del cinema*. Bologna: Commune di Bologna 1991. and Nico de Klerk, Ruud Visschedijk(eds.): *Het gaat om de film! Een nieuwe geschiedenis van de Nederlandsche Filmliga 1927-1933*. Amsterdam: Bas Lubberhuizen / Filmmuseum 1999. For the Dutch Filmliga, see Christophe Gauthier: *La Passion du cinéma. Cinéphiles, ciné-clubs et salles spécialisées à Paris de 1920 à 1929*. Paris: Association Française de Recherche sur l'Histoire du Cinéma / Ecole des Chartres 1999 for the Parisian cinephiles of the pre-sound era, see Jamie Sexton: *The British Film Societies*. Norwich:

University of East Anglia 2001 (unpublished Ph.D. thesis) for the activities of the British Film Societies.

40. See Jan Heijs (ed.): *Filmliga 1927-1931*. Nijmegen: SUN 1982 for the Dutch *Filmliga*, see James Donald, Anne Friedberg, Laura Marcus (eds.): *Close Up, 1927-1933. Cinema and Modernism*. London: Cassell 1998 for a valuable annotated selection of *Close Up*, see the complete reprint of the magazine in 10 volumes Nendeln (Liechtenstein): Kraus Reprint 1969, see Richard Weber (ed.): *Film und Volk. Organ des Volksfilmverbandes. Februar 1928-März 1930*. Köln: Verlag Gaehme, Henke 1975 for *Film und Volk*, see Rolf Henke, Richard Weber (eds.): *Arbeiterbühne und Film. Zentralorgan des Arbeiter-Theater-Bundes Deutschlands e.V. Juni 1930-Juni 1931*. Cologne: Verlag Gaehme, Henke 1974 for *Arbeiterbühne und Film*.

41. See Paul Hammond: *The Shadow and Its Shadow: Surrealist Writings on the Cinema*. Edinburgh: Polygon 1991; Standish Lawder: *The Cubist Cinema*. New York: New York University Press 1975, Inez Hedges: *Languages of Revolt: Dada and Surrealist Literature and Film*. Durham, NC: Duke University Press 1983; Rudolf E. Kuenzli (ed.): *Dada and Surrealist Film*. New York: Willis, Locker and Owens 1987; and Thomas Elsaesser: » Dada/Kino? Die Avantgarde und das frühe Filmerlebnis «. In: T.E.: *Filmgeschichte und frühes Kino. Archäologie eines Medienwandels*. München: edition text + kritik 2002: 250-277.

42. See Angelika Leitner, Uwe Nitschke (eds.): *Der deutsche Avant-Garde Film der 20er Jahre*. München: Goethe-Institut 1989 and Christine Noll Brinckmann: » Experimentalfilm, 1920-1990. Einzelgänge und Schübe «. In: Wolfgang Jacobsen, Anton Kaes, Hans Helmut Prinzler (eds.): *Geschichte des deutschen Films*. Stuttgart, Weimar: J.B. Metzler 1993: 417-450 and Anne Hoormann: *Lichtspiele. Zur Medienreflexion der Avantgarde in der Weimarer Republik*. Munich: Wilhelm Fink 2003 on the German avant-garde film; see Nicole Brenez, Christian Lebrat (eds.): *Jeune, dure et pure! Une histoire du cinéma d'avant-garde et expérimental en France*. Milano / Paris: Mazzotta / Cinéma-thèque française 2001 and Oliver Fahle: *Jenseits des Bildes. Poetik des französischen Films der zwanziger Jahre*. Mainz: Bender 2000 on the French avant-garde. See Michael O'Pray (ed.): *The British Avant-Garde Film 1936-1995*. Luton: Arts Council / John Libbey 1996, for the British avant-garde.

43. See Jeanpaul Goergen (ed.): *Walter Ruttmann. Eine Dokumentation*. Berlin: Freunde der Deutschen Kinemathek 1989 and Leonardo Quaresima (ed.): *Walter Ruttmann. Cinema, pittura, ars acustica*. Calliano: Manfrini 1994 for Walter Ruttmann, see Herbert Gehr, Marion von Hofacker (eds.): *Hans Richter. Malerei und Film*. Frankfurt am Main: Deutsches Filmmuseum 1989, Stephen C. Foster (ed.): *Hans Richter: Activism, Modernism and the Avant-Garde*. Boston, MA: MIT Press 1998 and Jeanpaul Goergen, Angelika Hoch, Erika Gregor, Ulrich Gregor (eds.): *Hans Richter. Film ist Rhythmus*. Berlin: Freunde der Kinemathek 2003 for Hans Richter, see Joris Ivens: *The Camera and I*. Berlin/DDR: Seven Seas Publishers 1969, Joris Ivens, Robert Destanque: *Joris Ivens ou la mémoire d'un regard*. Paris: Éditions BFB 1982; Hans Schoots: *Gevaarlijk leven. Een biografie van Joris Ivens*. Amsterdam: Jan Mets 1995. (English edition: *Living Dangerously: A Biography of Joris Ivens*. Amsterdam: Amsterdam University Press 2000); and Kees Bakker (ed.): *Joris Ivens and the Documentary Context*. Amsterdam: Amsterdam University Press 1999; for Joris Ivens; see Prosper Hillairet (ed.): *Germaine Dulac. Ecrits sur le cinéma (1919-1937)*. Paris : Éditions Expérimental 1994; and Sabine Nessel, Heide Schlüpmann, Stefanie Schulte Strathaus (eds.): *L'Invitation au*

voyage. Germaine Dulac. Berlin: Freunde der Deutschen Kinemathek 2002. (Kinemathek 93) for Germaine Dulac, see Jean Epstein: *Écrits sur le cinéma, 1921-1953. Édition chronologique. I: 1921-1947. II: 1946-1953.* (2 vols.) Paris: Seghers 1974; 1975; Jacques Aumont (ed.): *Jean Epstein. Cinéaste, poète, philosophe.* Paris: Cinémathèque française 1998 ; for Jean Epstein; see Joseph Zsuffa: *Béla Balázs. The Man and the Artist.* Berkeley, CA et al.: University of California Press 1987; Hanno Loewy: » Die Geister des Films. Balázs' Berliner Aufbrüche im Kontext «. In: Béla Balázs: *Der Geist des Films.* Frankfurt am Main: Suhrkamp 2001. (originally Halle/Saale: Wilhelm Knapp 1930): 171-230; Helmut H. Diederichs: » › Ihr müßt etwas von guter Filmkunst verstehen ‹ Béla Balázs als Filmtheoretiker und Medienpädagoge «. In: Béla Balázs: *Der sichtbare Mensch, oder die Kultur des Films.* Frankfurt am Main: Suhrkamp 2001. (originally Wien, Leipzig: Deutsch-Österreichischer Verlag 1924): 115-147; and Hanno Loewy: *Béla Balázs – Märchen, Ritual und Film.* Berlin: Vorwerk 8 2003; for Béla Balázs, see Hilmar Hoffmann, Walter Schobert (eds.): *Optische Poesie. Oskar Fischinger – Leben und Werk.* Frankfurt am Main: Deutsches Filmmuseum 1993. (Kinematograph 9) for Oskar Fischinger, see Michael Omasta (ed.): *Tribute to Sasha. Das filmische Werk von Alexander Hammid. Regie, Kamera, Schnitt und Kritiker.* Wien: Synema 2002 for Alexander Hackenschmied / Hammid.

44. See Roger Manvell (ed.): *Experiment in the Film.* London: Grey Walls Press 1948; Parker Tyler: *Underground Film. A Critical History.* New York: Grove Press 1969; David Curtis: *Experimental Cinema: A Fifty-Year Evolution.* London: Studio Vista 1971; Jean Mitry: *Le cinéma expérimental. Histoire et perspectives.* Paris: Seghers 1974; Hans Scheugl, Ernst Schmidt: *Eine Subgeschichte des Films.* Frankfurt am Main: Suhrkamp 1974; Birgit Hein, Wulf Herzogenrath (eds.): *Film als Film. 1910 bis heute.* Köln: Kölnischer Kunstverein 1977; P. Adams Sitney (ed.): *The Avant-Garde Film: A Reader of Theory and Criticism.* New York: New York University Press Anthology 1978; Phillip Drummond (ed.): *Film as Film: Formal Experiment in Film, 1910-1975.* London: Hayward Gallery 1979; Ingo Petzke: *Das Experimentalfilm-Handbuch.* Frankfurt am Main: Deutsches Filmmuseum 1989; Peter Weiss: *Avantgarde Film.* Frankfurt am Main: Suhrkamp 1995 (originally Swedish 1956); Paolo Bertetto, Sergio Toffetti (eds.): *Cinema d'avanguardia in Europa. Dalle origini al 1945.* Torino: Il Castoro 1996; A.L. Rees: *A History of Experimental Film and Video: From the Canonical Avant-Garde to Contemporary British Practice.* London: British Film Institute 1999.

45. See Tom Gunning: » Ontmoetingen in verduisterde ruimten. De alternatieve programmering van de Nederlandsche Filmliga «. In: Nico de Klerk and Ruud Visschedijk (eds.): *Het gaat om de film! Een nieuwe geschiedenis van de Nederlandsche Filmliga 1927-1933.* Amsterdam: Bas Lubberhuizen / Filmmuseum 1999: 218.

46. The term » avant-garde « had currency in the 1920s and 1930s: The German trade daily *Film-Kurier* in 1928 introduced, as part of its weekend edition, a special on » Die Avantgarde « which ran for several months and demonstrates the currency of the term (and of the movement) in the late 1920s. Richard Abel has gathered a substantial number of contemporary articles from France which address the avant-garde as a focus (and term) of interest. See Richard Abel (ed.): *French Film Theory and Criticism, 1907-1939. A History/Anthology, vol. 1: 1907-1929.* Princeton, NJ: Princeton University Press 1988: 319-436 (especially part 4, » The Great Debates « on the years 1925-29). See also the texts by activists such as Ruttmann, Richter or Dulac who applied the term frequently in the 1920s and 1930s. Ruttmann's texts can be

found in Jeanpaul Goergen (ed.): *Walter Ruttmann. Eine Dokumentation*. Berlin: Freunde der Deutschen Kinemathek 1989, Richter's in Jeanpaul Goergen, Angelika Hoch, Erika Gregor, Ulrich Gregor (eds.): *Hans Richter. Film ist Rhythmus*. Berlin: Freunde der Kinemathek 2003 and Dulac's in Prosper Hillairet (ed.): *Germaine Dulac. Ecrits sur le cinéma (1919-1937)*. Paris : Éditions Expérimental 1994.

47. Alan Williams: » Historical and Theoretical Issues in the Coming of Recorded Sound to the Cinema «. In: Rick Altman (ed.): *Sound Theory, Sound Practice*. New York, London: Routledge 1992: 126-137, here 136.

48. See my discussion in chapter four on the event culture of the avant-garde.

49. See the presentation by Petr Szczepanik: » Czech Industrial Film of the 1930s and Bat'a «. Paper given at *Films at Work. International Industrial Film Workshop*, Bibliothek des Ruhrgebiets, Bochum, 9-10 December 2004. See moreover the website aimed at a resuscitation of the old industrial town www.zlinbata.com.

50. Niklas Luhmann: *Die Kunst der Gesellschaft*. Frankfurt am Main: Suhrkamp 1995: 198f. [» Das, was sich merkwürdigerweise Avantgarde nennt, hat diese rückblickende Bestimmungsweise ins Extrem getrieben – wie Ruderer, die nur sehen, woher sie kommen, und das Ziel ihrer Fahrt im Rücken haben. «, my trans.]

51. Walter Benjamin: » Über den Begriff der Geschichte «. In: W.B.: *Gesammelte Schriften*. *I.2*. Frankfurt am Main: Suhrkamp 1977: 691-704, here 697f. [» Er hat das Antlitz der Vergangenheit zugewendet. Wo eine Kette von Begebenheiten vor *uns* erscheint, da sieht *er* eine einzige Katastrophe, die unablässig Trümmer auf Trümmer häuft und sie ihm vor die Füße schleudert. Er möchte wohl verweilen, die Toten wecken und das Zerschlagene zusammenfügen. Aber ein Sturm weht vom Paradiese her, der sich in seinen Flügeln verfangen hat und so stark ist, dass der Engel sie nicht mehr schließen kann. Dieser Sturm treibt ihn unaufhaltsam in die Zukunft, der er den Rücken kehrt, während der Trümmerhaufen vor ihm zum Himmel wächst. Das, was wir Fortschritt nennen, ist *dieser* Sturm. «, trans. Harry Zohn, *Illuminations*: 257f.]

Notes Chapter 2

1.   Walter Benjamin: » Aus dem Brecht-Kommentar «. In: W.B.: *Gesammelte Schriften*. *Band II.2*. Frankfurt am Main: Suhrkamp 1977: 506. [» Das Neue [an Brechts Schaffen] ist, daß diese Stellen in ihrer ganzen Wichtigkeit hervortreten, der Dichter um ihretwillen sich von seinem › Werke ‹ beurlaubt und, wie ein Ingenieur in der Wüste mit Petroleumbohrungen anfängt, in der Wüste der Gegenwart an genau berechneten Punkten seine Tätigkeit aufnimmt. Solche Stellen sind hier das Theater, die Anekdote, das Radio – andere werden später in Angriff genommen werden. «, trans. Anna Bostock]

2.   The idea of the *Medienverbund* in connection to the interwar avant-garde has been proposed by Thomas Elsaesser in his study on the *Bund » Das Neue Frankfurt «*. See Thomas Elsaesser: » Die Stadt von Morgen: Filme zum Bauen und Wohnen in der Weimarer Republik «. In: Klaus Kreimeier, Antje Ehmann, Jeanpaul Goergen

(Hrsg.): *Geschichte des dokumentarischen Films in Deutschland. Band 2: Weimarer Republik 1918-1933*. Stuttgart: Reclam 2005: 381-409.

3.   See below for more on the constructivist logic of the avant-garde.

4.   Ej. [=Ernst Jäger]: » Berlins Filmproduktion braucht ein Film-Studio. Aber es muß unter Aufsicht der Industrie arbeiten «. In: *Film-Kurier*, vol. 9, no. 255, 28.10.1927. [» Hoffentlich gelingt es, die Ziele der Gesellschaft mit den Zielen der Industrie zu verbinden. Was nütze sonst alle Modernität, wenn sie ein Spielzeug der Experimentler bleibt. Die Filmfabrikation von heute muß für den Film von morgen gewonnen werden. ... Deshalb sind an der Avantgarde der Experimentler alle Filmproduktionsstätten der Erde gleich interessiert. Die Einsichtigen wissen es. Und sie müssen nun veranlaßt werden, die Avantgarde der schöpferisch Bemühten als ihre Vorhut anzuerkennen, ebenso wie die Techniker und Theoretiker des neuen Films wissen müssen, daß sie für die heutige Industrie arbeiten, und daß ihre Versuche und Erfahrungen sobald sie praktische Ergebnisse gezeitigt haben, für die gegenwärtige Filmfabrikation verwertbar gemacht werden müssen. «, my trans.]

5.   Oswald Blakeston in: *Commercial Art*, vol. 10: 65. Quoted in Deke Dusinberre: » The Other Avantgardes «. In: Philip Drummond et al. (eds.): *Film as Film: Formal Experiment in Film 1910-1975*. London: Hayward Gallery 1979: 53-58, here 54.

6.   Hans Richter: » Avant-Garde Film in Germany «. In: Roger Manvell (ed.): *Experiment in the Film*. London: Grey Walls Press 1949: 219-233, here 227.

7.   An echo of this position can be detected in the ironic comment by Todd Solondz – normally considered to be an American independent filmmaker – who, upon being confronted with this label remarked that the only truly independent filmmaker in the United States is Steven Spielberg who has the money and power to basically produce and distribute any film he wants to.

8.   This problem has persisted into the present-day; although, many experimental filmmakers can nowadays make a living through lecturing, commissions and scholarships from art foundations or teaching positions at art school – a different kind of dependency.

9.   As far as names are concerned, for consistency I have chosen: Walter (instead of Walther) Ruttmann as he himself dropped the » h « because it appeared more sober and modern to him. Alexander Hackenschmied changed his name to Hammid in the United States – I will stick to his original name since, during the time under consideration, he was known as Hackenschmied.

10. For a detailed account of Richter's film DIE NEUE WOHNUNG, see Andres Janser, Arthur Ruegg: *Hans Richter: New Living. Architecture, Film, Space*. Baden: Lars Müller 2001.

11. Ironically, the German administration did not accept BERLIN as a quota filler for a foreign fiction film, arguing that it was a » Kulturfilm «, an educational film. See Herbert Ihering: » Gegen den Paragraphengeist der behördlichen Kontingentschützer. Die Behörde erzwingt den Filmkitsch «. In: *Film-Kurier*, vol. 9, no. 213, 9.9.1927.

12. In fact, Richter and Eggeling first considered transferring their scroll paintings to film when a banker friend of Richter's father offered them money, which they instead used to write and print their manifesto *Universelle Sprache*, which in turn helped them to secure the assistance of Ufa.

13. One of the first public presentations of OPUS I (1919) took place in Munich in the screening rooms of the Emelka. The company involved in its production and/or dis-

tribution was the so-called » Neue Kinematographische Gesellschaft «, which was a company owned by Emelka. See L. Adelt: » Optische Symphonie «. In: *Film-Kurier*, vol. 3, no. 295, 19.12.1921.

14. William Moritz: » Oskar Fischinger «. In: Herbert Gehr (ed.): *Optische Poesie. Oskar Fischinger – Leben und Werk*. Frankfurt am Main: Deutsches Filmmuseum 1993. (Kinematograph 9): 7-80, here 18f.

15. See Michal Bregant: » Alexander Hammid's Czech Years: Space and Time of His Early Films «. In: Michael Omasta (ed.): *Tribute to Sasha. Das filmische Werk von Alexander Hammid. Regie, Kamera, Schnitt und Kritiker*. Vienna: Synema 2002: 21-41. An overview was presented by Petr Szczepanik: » Czech Industrial Film of the 1930s and Bata «. Presentation on 9 December 2004 at the conference *Filme, die arbeiten. Internationale Tagung zum Industriefilm / Films at Work. International Industrial Film Workshop*. Bibliothek des Ruhrgebiets, Bochum: Ruhr-Universität Bochum, Insitut für Medienwissenschaft. 9–10.12.2004.

16. Tom Gunning: » Ontmoetingen in verduisterde ruimten. De alternatieve programmering van de Nederlandsche Filmliga «. In: Nico de Klerk, Ruud Visschedijk (eds.): *Het gaat om de film! Een nieuwe geschiedenis van de Nederlandsche Filmliga 1927-1933*. Amsterdam: Bas Lubberhuizen / Filmmuseum 1999: 217-263, here 226.

17. A classic study tracing the outlines of the transitions from an aristocratic form of governance to a bourgeois public sphere with free circulation of discourse and art on a capitalist market is Jürgen Habermas: *Strukturwandel der Öffentlichkeit. Untersuchung zu einer Kategorie der bürgerlichen Gesellschaft*. Neuwied: Luchterhand 1962. A different account of the path to autonomy of the arts (under the name of autopoeisis and functional differentiation) is sketched in Niklas Luhmann: *Die Kunst der Gesellschaft*. Frankfurt am Main: Suhrkamp 1995. A canonised case study on the appearance of the novel is Ian Watt: *The Rise of the Novel*. London: Chatto & Windus 1957. More generally on the visual arts, see Arnold Hauser: *Sozialgeschichte der Kunst und Literatur*. Munich 1969.

18. Walter Ruttmann: » Der isolierte Künstler «. In: *Filmtechnik*, 25 May 1929. Reprinted in and quoted from: Jeanpaul Goergen (ed.): *Walter Ruttmann. Eine Dokumentation*. Berlin: Freunde der Deutschen Kinemathek 1989: 86. [» Denkbar wäre die Versöhnung und Ausbalancierung von Kunst und Geschäft durch einen außerhalb stehenden Machtfaktor: durch einen Mäzen oder den Staat. Aber Mäzene existieren nur noch in Märchenbüchern oder zur Propagierung einer Diva und der Staat scheint – wenigstens in unseren kapitalistischen Ländern – an diesem Problem vorläufig gänzlich uninteressiert zu sein. Bleibt also die Initiative der Kunst. Wer aber repräsentiert die Kunst für den Film? In Frankreich, vielleicht auch in Holland und anderswo besteht die Möglichkeit des Zusammenschlusses, der Einheitsfront derer, die Kunst wollen und Kunst für nützlich halten. Man nennt das › Avantgarde ‹, hat Kenntnis genommen von ihrem Vorhandensein und rechnet bis zu einem gewissen Grade mit ihr, weil sie Beweise dafür erbracht hat, daß Nachfrage besteht. ... Dieser anderswo erzielte Erfolg ist aber ... in Deutschland nicht einfach zu imitieren. ... So bleibt für uns nur die Hoffnung auf die Persönlichkeit, die stark genug ist, alle Kompromisse zu riskieren, ohne sich zu degradieren; auf die Persönlichkeit, die elastisch genug ist, sich bis ins Hauptquartier des Gegners durchzuschwindeln – um ihn zu überzeugen. « «, my trans.]

19. Laura Vichi: *Henri Storck. De l'avant-garde au documentaire social*. Crisnée (BE): Édi-
     tions Yellow Now 2002: 11f. [» Une question en particulier avait alimenté les discus-
     sions et suscité des prises de positions opposées, celle de la définition même de › cin-
     éma indépendant ‹; la plupart des congressistes, parmi lesquels Moussinac, Richter,
     Balázs, Ruttmann et Eisenstein, reconnaissaient le caractère illusoire d'une indépen-
     dance absolue et attribuaient l'épithète à un cinéma affranchi des lois de l'indus-
     trie. «, my trans.]

20. Julien J. London: » Entretiens: Victor Trivas nous a parlé du cinéma-art et du cin-
     éma-industrie «. In: *Ciné-Comoedia*, no. 2138, 12.1.1933. German translation reprin-
     ted in and quoted after Jeanpaul Goergen (ed.): *Victor Trivas*. Hamburg, Berlin: Cine-
     Graph, Stiftung Deutsche Kinemathek 1996; 6-8, here 7. [» Ich kann mir kein
     unabhängiges Kino vorstellen. Film ist ein industrielles Produkt, das seinen Weg zu
     den Konsumenten finden muß. Für sie werden die Filme gemacht – sie müssen da-
     her vor allem der Masse zugänglich sein. Falls nicht, so wurde das Ziel sowohl vom
     gesellschaftlichen als auch vom kommerziellen Gesichtspunkt aus verfehlt. Der Re-
     gisseur muß sich bemühen, die wirkliche Verbindung zwischen sich und dem Pub-
     likum zu finden. Verheerende Abhängigkeiten sind solche, die für jedermann gel-
     ten... «, my trans.]

21. See anon: » Moritz Seelers Filmstudie «. In: *Film-Kurier*, vol. 11, no. 166, 15.7.1929.
     For production background, biographical information, and contemporary texts see
     Wolfgang Jacobsen, Hans Helmut Prinzler (eds.): *Siodmak Bros. Berlin – Paris – Lon-
     don – Hollywood*. Berlin: Argon 1998: passim. For a report on future film plans of
     Seeler see » Nachwuchs? Bitte! «. In: *Film-Kurier*, vol. 12, no. 111, 18.5.1930.

22. For examples from this debate about the centralised » film studio « see anon.: » Der
     deutsche Film fordert vom Staat «. In: *Film-Kurier*, vol. 10, no. 197, 18.8.1928; anon.:
     » Eine der Republik würdige Aufgabe: Wo bleibt das Film-Experimental-Studio? «.
     In: *Film-Kurier*, vol. 10, no. 274, 16.11.1928; Hans Richter: » Filmstudio – Industrie –
     Staat «. In: *Film-Kurier*, vol. 10, no. 280, 24.11.1928; Erik Reger: » Avantgarde-De-
     batte: Von außen besehen «. In: *Film-Kurier*, vol. 10, no. 280, 24.11.1928.

23. See anon.: » Der absolute Film braucht die Industrie. Ein Gespräch mit Hans Rich-
     ter «. In: *Film-Kurier*, vol. 11, no. 6, 5.1.1929.

24. See Patricia Zimmermann: *Reel Families: A Social History of Amateur Film*. Blooming-
     ton, IN: Indiana University Press 1995, for a history of amateur film in the United
     States. For two collection of articles see Nancy Kapstein (ed.): *Rencontres autour des
     inedits. Jubilee Book. Essays on Amateur Film*. Charleroi (BE): Association Européenne
     Inédits / European Association Inedits 1997 and *Film History*, vol. 15, no. 2, 2003
     (special issue » Small Gauge and Amateur Film «, edited by Melinda Stone and Dan
     Streible). See for a case study of Switzerland Alexandra Schneider: *Die Stars sind wir.
     Heimkino als filmische Praxis*. Marburg: Schüren 2004. (Zürcher Filmstudien 9).

25. See Walter Benjamin's lecture » Der Autor als Produzent « for an explanation of this
     position. In: W.B.: *Gesammelte Schriften. II.2*. Frankfurt am Main: Suhrkamp 1977:
     683-701.

26. See the manifesto » Het gaat om de film « in: Jan Heijs (ed.): *Filmliga 1927-1931*. (rep-
     rint of magazine published by the *Filmliga*). Nijmegen: SUN 1982: 34. [» Eens op de
     honderd keer zien wij: de film. Voor de rest zien wij: bioscoop. «]

27. There are other reasons (gender, sexual orientation) that also played into this conflict. See Naomi Green: » Artaud and Film: A Reconsideration «. In: *Cinema Journal*, vol. 23, no. 4, Summer 1984: 28-40.

28. Germaine Dulac: » Le cinéma d'avant-garde «. In : Henri Fescourt (ed.): *Le Cinéma des origines à nos jours*. Paris Éditions du Cygne 1932 : 357-364. Reprinted in and quoted from Prosper Hillairet (ed.): *Germaine Dulac. Ecrits sur le cinéma (1919-1937)*. Paris : Éditions Expérimental 1994: 182-190, here 182f. [» L'industrie du cinéma produit les films commerciaux, c'est-à-dire les films composés avec le souci de toucher la grande masse, et les films mercantiles. Il faut entendre par films mercantiles ceux qui, se soumettant à toutes les concessions, poursuivent un simple but financier et par films commerciaux ceux qui, s'emparant au mieux de l'expression et de la technique cinématographiques, produisent parfois des œuvres intéressantes tout en visant des gains justifiés. C'est alors l'union de l'industrie et de l'art. Du cinéma commercial sort l'oeuvre totale, le film équilibré pour lequel l'industrie et l'avant-garde, séparées en deux camps travaillent. Généralement, l'industrie ne s'attache pas, avec zèle, à l'apport artistique; dans un élan opposé, le considère seul. D'où antagonisme. ... L'avant-garde et le cinéma commercial, soit l'art et l'industrie du film, forment un tout inséparable. Mais l'avant-garde nécessaire à l'évolution a contre elle la majorité du public et la totalité des éditeurs. «, my trans.]

29. anon.: » Experimente sind Geschäfte «. In: *Film-Kurier*, vol. 10, no. 101, 28.4.1928. (special » Die Avant-Garde «). [» Experimente sind Geschäfte, so paradox es klingt. ... Findet man etwas, das des Wagens wert erscheint, dann heißt es durchsetzen. À la longue sind wertvolle Anregungen bisher immer durchgegangen. Weiterkommen ist nur möglich durch Ausprobieren neuer Wege. Denn gerade bei einer Massenkunst wie der Film ist die Gefahr einer Erstarrung gefährlich. «, my trans.]

30. A wide context of popular entertainment, of mass-circulated media, and of new modes of spectatorship around 1900 can be found in the seminal anthology Leo Charney, Vanessa R. Schwartz: *Cinema and the Invention of Modern Life*. Berkeley, CA: University of California Press 1995.

31. Joris Ivens: » Quelques réflections sur les documentaires d'avant-garde «. In: *La revue des vivants*, No. 10, 1931: 518-520. English translation reprinted in and quoted after: » Notes on the Avant-garde Documentary Film «. In: Kees Bakker (ed.): *Joris Ivens and the Documentary Context*. Amsterdam: Amsterdam University Press 1999: 224226, here 224.

32. The *locus classicus* for the concept » paratext « in relation to literature is Gérard Genette: *Seuils*. Paris: Éditions du Seuil 1987. (Eng.: *Paratexts: Thresholds of Interpretation*. Cambridge: Cambridge University Press 1997). See, on special forms related to the cinema such as the film trailer Vinzenz Hediger: *Verführung zum Film. Der amerikanische Kinotrailer seit 1912*. Marburg: Schüren 2001 and on the poster Wolfgang Beilenhoff, Martin Heller (eds.): *Das Filmplakat*. Zurich, Berlin, New York: Scalo 1995.

33. For a concise and good (albeit already somewhat dated) introduction to this discussion, see Judith Mayne: *Cinema and Spectatorship*. London, New York: Routledge 1993.

34. See chapter three on film societies and ciné-clubs.

35. Only the post-World War II avant-garde worked directly on the film material, scratching and painting directly on the celluloid, eliminating the photographical process altogether.

36. See Béla Balázs: *Der sichtbare Mensch, oder die Kultur des Films*. Wien, Leipzig: Deutsch-Österreichischer Verlag 1924. (reprint Frankfurt am Main: Suhrkamp 2001), Béla Balázs: *Der Geist des Films*. Halle an der Saale: Wilhelm Knapp 1930. (reprint Frankfurt am Main: Suhrkamp 2001) and Rudolf Arnheim: *Film als Kunst*. Berlin: Rowohlt 1932. (reprint Frankfurt am Main: Suhrkamp 2002).

37. For an attempt to understand the » absoluter Film « as a movement, see Holger Wilmesmeier: *Deutsche Avantgarde und Film. Die Filmmatinee » Der absolute Film « 3. und 10. Mai 1925*. Münster, Hamburg: Lit Verlag 1993.

38. It is not absolutely certain which of Richter's RHYTHMUS-films was shown and if that film was shown at both matinees. See Wilmesmeier, absolute Film, op. cit., 17-30.

39. See chapter three on film societies for more on the *Gesellschaft » Neuer Film «*.

40. Walter Ruttmann: » Die › absolute ‹ Mode «. In: *Filmkurier*, no. 30, 3 February 1928. Reprinted in and quoted after: Jeanpaul Goergen (ed.): *Walter Ruttmann. Eine Dokumentation*. Berlin: Freunde der Deutschen Kinemathek 1989: 82. [» Es konnte offenbar nicht ausbleiben: Der › absolute ‹ Film, den man vor Jahren, als ich seine ersten Proben zeigte, teils fanatisch begrüßte, teils gönnerhaft als Outsidertum belächelte, ist Mode geworden. Eine Ebbe der allgemeinen Filmproduktion ist Anlaß, den absoluten Film als Evangelium zu propagieren. Die Unklarheit über sein Wesen ist der Propaganda nur günstig. Was ist ein absoluter Film? Ein Film, bei dem man sich nicht darauf verläßt, daß aus der Praxis des Filmemachens heraus sich Kunst entwickeln möge, sondern bei dem die Theorie, die überzeugte Vorstellung von autonomer Filmkunst am Anfang steht – die Gewißheit a priori: » So und nur so sind die ästhetischen Gesetze des Films. « Natürlich wäre es an sich erfreulich, wenn Künstler die Routiniers verdrängen. Aber – meint man es gut mit dem Film, wenn man zu eifrig auf seine künstlerische Reinigung drängt? Versteht man ihn richtig, wenn man ihm z.B. das Schicksal der absoluten Musik wünscht? Soll er in schlecht besuchte Konzertsäle abwandern, sich klösterlich destillieren für eine kleine Gemeinde ästhetisch Anspruchsvoller, die über die › Reinheit ‹ seiner Struktur wachen? Doch wo er [der absolute Film, MH] sich als Selbstzweck und -ziel gebärdet, gleitet er automatisch in die Rumpelkammern des l'art pour l'art hinein, aus denen gerade der Film uns erlöst hat. «, my trans.]

41. See Siegfried Kracauer: » Wir schaffens «. In: *Frankfurter Zeitung*, 17.11.11927. Reprinted in S.K.: *Von Caligari zu Hitler. Eine psychologische Geschichte des deutschen Films*. Frankfurt am Main: Suhrkamp 1979: 404f. See also ibid.: 192-198.

42. See chapter four on the discursive formations for more on Baden-Baden.

43. Tom Gunning: » Ontmoetingen in verduisterde ruimten. De alternatieve programmering van de Nederlandsche Filmliga «. In: Linssen, Céline; Schoots, Hans; Gunning, Tom: *Het gaat om de film! Een nieuwe geschiedenis van de Nederlandsche Filmliga 1927-1933*. Amsterdam: Bas Lubberhuizen / Filmmuseum 1999: 217-263, here 252. [» De Filmliga was niet alleen opgericht om films te draaien die elders zelden te zien waren, maar ook om nieuwe manieren van filmkijken te ontdekken en te onderrichten. In wezen sprak hieruit een minachting voor eenvoudige narratieve uitgangspunten. De Liga programmeerde wel veel verhalende films, maar lanceerde ook een frontale aanval op de hegemonie van de verhalende film zoals die door de klassieke Hollywood-speelfilm werd vertegenwoordigd. Zij bood een gevarieerde keuze aan alternatieven. De abstracte films, de zwaar politieke en meestal weinig

psychologische sovjetfilms, de absurdistische melange van dadaïstische en surrea-
listische films, de visuele associaties en het symbolisme van de Franse impressionis-
ten, de dynamische beelden uit het alledaagse leven in de stadsymfonieën en in
andere documentaires – in al deze vormen werden organisatieprincipes gezocht die
afstand namen van het conventionele, rond personages opgebouwde verhaal.
Nieuwe vormen van film eisten een nieuw publiek, en de Filmliga-programma's
moesten de oude gewoonten in het kijken naar film doorbreken om een nieuw besef
van filmkunst op te bouwen. «, my trans.]

44. See for the program » Die Stuttgarter Sondervorführungen der Werkbundausstellung › Film und Foto ‹ «. In: *Lichtbild-Bühne*, vol. 22, no. 145, 19.6.1929. See, for an
annotated reconstruction of the program, Helma Schleif (ed.): *Stationen der Moderne
im Film. Vol. 1: FiFo. Film- und Fotoausstellung Stuttgart 1929. Rekonstruktion des Filmprogramms.* Berlin: Freunde der Deutschen Kinemathek 1988.

45. For classical accounts of the aesthetic and cultural style of *Neue Sachlichkeit* see John
Willett: *The New Sobriety.* New York: Pantheon 1978, and Helmut Lethen: *Verhaltenslehren der Kälte. Lebensversuche zwischen den Kriegen.* Frankfurt am Main: Suhrkamp
1994.

46. Tom Gunning: » Ontmoetingen in verduisterde ruimten. De alternatieve programmering van de Nederlandsche Filmliga «. In: Linssen, Céline; Schoots, Hans; Gunning, Tom: *Het gaat om de film! Een nieuwe geschiedenis van de Nederlandsche Filmliga
1927-1933.* Amsterdam: Bas Lubberhuizen / Filmmuseum 1999: 217-263, here 232.
[» Hier zien we ... een theoretische tegenstelling waarbij in praktijk verschillende
filmstijlen een dialectische relatie aangaan, in plaats van elkaar uit te sluiten. Voor
een deel wordt dit begrijpelijk wanneer we ons realiseren dat deze ogenschijnlijk
botsende technieken beide tegenover de commerciële speelfilm staan. «, my trans.]

47. For more on Painlevé see Andy Masaki Bellows, Marina McDougall (eds.): *Science Is
Fiction: The Films of Jean Painlevé.* Cambridge, MA and London: The MIT Press 2000.

48. Cf. László Moholy-Nagy: *The New Vision and Abstract of an Artist*: New York: George
Wittenborn 1947. (orig. German as *Von Material zu Architektur* 1928, orig. English
1930). For more on Moholy-Nagy see Jan Sahli: *Filmische Sinneserweiterung. László
Moholy-Nagys Filmwerk und Theorie.* Marburg: Schüren 2006. (Zürcher Filmstudien).

49. Walter Benjamin: » Das Kunstwerk im Zeitalter seiner technischen Reproduzierbarkeit « (Dritte Fassung). In: W.B.: *Gesammelte Schriften. Band I.2.* Frankfurt am Main:
Suhrkamp 1977: 471-508, here 499. [» Es wird eine der revolutionären Funktionen
des Films sein, die künstlerische und die wissenschaftliche Verwertung der Photographie, die vordem meist auseinander fielen, als identisch erkennbar zu machen. «,
trans. Harry Zohn, *Illuminations*: 236].

50. See Ian Aitken: *Film and Reform: John Grierson and the Documentary Film Movement.*
London, New York: Routledge 1990 for a detailed discussion of the background and
influences upon Grierson. See also Ian Aitken: *European Film Theory and Cinema: An
Introduction.* Edinburgh: Edinburgh University Press 2001 (chapter 7 on realism) for
a more concise overview. See, for a study of Grierson's film theory, Patrick Hörl:
*Film als Fenster zur Welt. Eine Untersuchung des filmtheoretischen Denkens von John
Grierson.* Konstanz: UVK Medien Ölschläger 1996.

51. Ian Aitken: *European Film Theory and Cinema: An Introduction.* Edinburgh: Edinburgh
University Press 2001: 165.

52. For more on the distinction between modernism and modernisation and a detailed discussion of Grierson, see chapter six on the emergence of the documentary.

53. See chapter five on the » Vanishing Point Soviet Union « for more details.

54. For filmmaking during the *front populaire* period, see Goffredo Fofi: » The Cinema of the Popular Front in France (1934-38) «. In: *Screen*, vol. 13, no. 4, Winter 1972/73: 5-57; Ginette Vincendeau, Keith Reader (eds.): *La vie est à nous: French Cinema of the Popular Front 1935-1938*. London: British Film Institute 1986; Geneviève Guillaume-Grimaud: *Le cinema du front populaire*. Paris: Lherminier 1986; Jonathan Buchsbaum: *Cinema engage. Film in the Popular Front*. Urbana, IL: University of Illinois Press 1988. On films from the Spanish civil war inside and outside Spain see Marjorie A. Valleau: *The Spanish Civil War in American and European Films*. Ann Arbor, MI: UMI Research Press 1982; Román Gubern: *La guerra de España en la pantalla (1936-1939). De la propaganda a la historia*. Madrid : Filmoteca Española 1986; Wolfgang Martin Hamdorf: *Zwischen » No Pasaran! « und » Arriba Espana! «. Film und Propaganda im Spanischen Bürgerkrieg*. Münster: MakS Publikationen 1991.

55. See Hans-Michael Bock, Jürgen Berger (eds.): *Photo: Casparius. Filmgeschichte in Berlin. Berlin um 1930*. Berlin: Stiftung Deutsche Kinemathek 1978 and Erika Wottrich (ed.): *M wie Nebenzal*. München: edition text + kritik 2002; both books contain documents and texts on the case. For Brecht's perspective see Bertolt Brecht: *Der Dreigroschenprozess*. In: Bertolt Brecht: *Gesammelte Werke. Band 18: Schriften zur Literatur und Kunst I*. Frankfurt am Main: Suhrkamp 1967: 139-209. [first published 1931]

56. For a collection of annotated source material, see Harry M. Geduld, Ronald Gottesman (eds.): *Sergei Eisenstein and Upton Sinclair: The Making and Unmaking of › Que viva Mexico! ‹*. Bloomington, IN and London: Indiana University Press 1970.

57. See, for a general history of surrealism largely from Breton's perspective, Maurice Nadeau: *Histoire du Surréalisme*. Paris: Éditions du Seuil 1945, see also for Buñuel's reasons to resign from the group Paul Hammond: » To the Paradise of Pitfalls «. In: Maria Casanova (ed.): *Tierra sin pan. Luis Buñuel y los nuevos caminos de las vanguardias*. Valencia: Institut Valencià d'Art Modern 1999 : 211-217.

58. Laszlo Moholy-Nagy: » Produktion – Reproduktion «. In: *De Stijl*, vol. 5, no. 7, July 1922: 98-100. Reprinted in and quoted after: *Laszlo Moholy-Nagy. Fotogramme 1922-1943*. Munich, Paris and London: Schirmer/Mosel 1996: 28-29. [» Da vor allem die Produktion (produktive Gestaltung) dem menschlichen Aufbau dient, müssen wir versuchen, die bisher nur für Reproduktionszwecke angewandten Apparate (Mittel) auch zu produktiven Zwecken zu erweitern. «, my trans.]

59. I am aware that I am using the term modernism here to designate what some theorists (like Fredric Jameson) call high modernism. Yet, I find the latter term unrewarding and hard to define; therefore I refrain from using it and employ modernism to refer to artistic production from (roughly) 1900 to 1960, which challenged the dominant institutions of art and traditional manners of expression.

60. Thomas Elsaesser: *Weimar Cinema and After: Germany's Historical Imaginary*. London, New York: Routledge 2000: 390.

61. I am aware that the surrealists also shared some preoccupations with constructivists such as a fascination for the city, an investigation into chance encounters; and, more generally speaking, an interest in social aspects of modern life.

62. Hans Schoots: *Living Dangerously: A Biography of Joris Ivens*. Amsterdam: Amsterdam University Press 2000: 41.

63. Joris Ivens: » Quelques réflections sur les documentaires d'avant-garde «. In: *La re-
     vue des vivants*, no. 10, 1931: 518-520. Reprinted translation in and quoted from:
     » Notes on the Avant-garde Documentary Film «. In: Kees Bakker (ed.): *Joris Ivens
     and the Documentary Context*. Amsterdam: Amsterdam University Press 1999: 224-
     226, here 224.

64. Ivens: » Quelques réflections sur les documentaires d'avant-garde «. 1931. Reprinted
     translation in and quoted from: Bakker (ed.), *Documentary Context*: 224-226, here
     224f.

65. I have borrowed this list from Lev Manovich's essay » Avant-garde as Software «
     (http://www.manovich.net/docs/avantgarde_as_software.doc) in which he draws
     extensive parallels between the constructivist avant-garde of the 1920s and develop-
     ments in new media in the 1990s. Even though I do not share all of Manovich's
     conclusions, which sometimes appear like technological determinism, I still find
     this article useful in giving a historical perspective on new media as well as a con-
     temporary perspective on the canonical avant-garde.

66. See Herbert Molderings: » Lichtjahre eines Lebens. Das Fotogramm in der Ästhetik
     Laszlo Moholy-Nagys «. In: Museum Folkwang (ed.): *Lászlo Moholy-Nagy: Foto-
     gramme 1922-1943*. Munich, Paris and London: Schirmer/Mosel 1996: 8-17.

67. For the strategies of Tobis after the introduction of sound, see Malte Hagener: » Un-
     ter den Dächern der Tobis. Nationale Märkte und europäische Strategien «. In: Jan
     Distelmeyer (Red.): *Tonfilmfrieden/Tonfilmkrieg. Die Geschichte der Tobis vom Technik-
     Syndikat zum Staatskonzern*. München: edition text + kritik 2003: 51-64.

68. S. Palsma [= Paul Schuitema]: » Foto als wapen in de klassestrijd «. In: *Links Richten*,
     February 1933. Reprinted in and quoted after: Flip Bool: » Paul Schuitema und Piet
     Zwart. Die Neue Typografie und die Neue Fotografie im Dienste der Industrie und
     des politischen Kampfes «. In: Stanislaus von Moos, Chris Smeenk (eds.): *Avantgarde
     und Industrie*. Delft: Delft University Press 1983: 121-134, here 122. [» Es ist dumm zu
     glauben, es genüge, ein Proletarier zu sein, um im Klassenkampf mit Waffen umge-
     hen zu können. Klassenbewusster proletarischer Kampf bedeutet Üben und
     schließlich Beherrschen der Waffen im Klassenkampf. Das Training des proletar-
     ischen Fotokorrespondenten muss sich in erster Linie auf die praktische Handha-
     bung seines Apparates beziehen und erst an zweiter Stelle auf das Studium der
     Suggestion. Keine Romantik, keine Kunst, sondern sachliche, grell suggestive Pro-
     paganda: Taktisch auf den Klassenkampf, technisch auf das Fach ausgerichtet. «,
     my trans.]

69. Bool, » Schuitema und Zwart «, op. cit.: 124. [» Die Reklame bot ihnen [Schuitema
     and Zwart] die Gelegenheit, eine aktive Rolle innerhalb des Produktionsprozesses
     zu spielen ... und ihre Theorien einer zeitgenössischen Formgestaltung einem Mas-
     senpublikum mittels modernster Produktionsmethoden vor Augen zu führen. «, my
     trans.]

70. Lev Manovich: » Avant-garde as Software «, op. cit.: 8.

71. I have elaborated the role of the Soviet Union within the imaginary geography of
     the avant-garde in more detail in the chapter » Vanishing Point Soviet Union «.

72. Walter Ruttmann: » Technik und Film «. In: Leo Kestenberg (ed.): *Kunst und Technik*.
     Berlin 1930: 327. Reprinted in and quoted from: Jeanpaul Goergen: *Walter Ruttmann.
     Eine Dokumentation*. Berlin: Freunde der Deutschen Kinemathek 1989, S. 87-88. A
     discussion of this quote and Ruttmann's position in detail can be found in Thomas

Elsaesser, Malte Hagener: »Walter Ruttmann. 1929«. In: Stefan Andriopoulos, Bernhard Dotzler (eds.): *1929. Beiträge zur Archäologie der Medien*. Frankfurt/Main: Suhrkamp 2002: 316–349. [»So überrascht vor allen Dingen an [der Filmi]ndustrie bei einem Vergleich mit anderen Industrien und Fabrikationszweigen das vollkommene Fehlen des Laboratoriums. ... Und doch wäre gerade das Laboratorium für den Film der Nährboden, auf dem er sich aus sich selbst heraus ... entwickeln und befestigen könnte. ... Es wäre nicht etwa die Aufgabe dieses Laboratoriums, die Verbesserung und Erweiterung der Apparaturen zu studieren. ... Wohl aber müsste hier eine Versuchs- und Untersuchungswerkstätte geschaffen werden, in der das Ausdrucksmittel Film von allen Seite ... auf seine Entwicklungsmöglichkeiten geprüft wird. «, my trans.]

73.   See Flip Bool: »Paul Schuitema und Piet Zwart. Die Neue Typografie und die Neue Fotografie im Dienste der Industrie und des politischen Kampfes«. In: Stanislaus von Moos, Chris Smeenk (eds.): *Avantgarde und Industrie*. Delft: Delft University Press 1983: 121-134, for a case study on a photographer between political and commercial assignments.

74.   Thomas Elsaesser: *Weimar Cinema and After: Germany's Historical Imaginary*. London, New York: Routledge 2000: 402f.

75.   Actually, the third largest laboratory in the 1930s was Nazi-Germany, which drew upon artistic figureheads such as Leni Riefenstahl and Walter Ruttmann. See Thomas Elsaesser, Malte Hagener: »Walter Ruttmann. 1929«. In: Stefan Andriopoulos, Bernhard Dotzler (eds.): *1929. Beiträge zur Archäologie der Medien*. Frankfurt am Main: Suhrkamp 2002: 316-349.

76.   Lev Manovich: »Avant-garde as Software«: 8. (http://www.manovich.net/docs/ avantgarde_as_software.doc).

77.   Paul Schuitema in Heinz Rasch, Bodo Rasch (eds.): *Gefesselter Blick*. 1930. Reprinted in and quoted after Flip Bool: »Paul Schuitema und Piet Zwart. Die Neue Typografie und die Neue Fotografie im Dienste der Industrie und des politischen Kampfes«. In: Stanislaus von Moos, Chris Smeenk (eds.): *Avantgarde und Industrie*. Delft: Delft University Press 1983: 121-134, here 124; [»der entwerfer ist kein zeichner, sondern organisator der optischen faktoren. seine arbeit soll nicht handarbeitlich sein; sondern soll sich beschränken auf notieren, gruppieren und technisch organisieren. «, my trans.]

78.   Peter Bürger: *Theorie der Avantgarde*. Frankfurt am Main: Suhrkamp 1974: 29. [»Die Avantgarde wendet sich gegen beides – gegen den Distributionsapparat, dem das Kunstwerk unterworfen ist, und gegen den mit dem Begriff der Autonomie beschriebenen Status der Kunst in der bürgerlichen Gesellschaft. «, my trans.]

79.   For more on the Weimar art cinema between commercialism, cultural value and modernisation, see Thomas Elsaesser: *Weimar Cinema and After: Germany's Historical Imaginary*. London and New York: Routledge 2000.

80.   In this respect, Hollywood could have been different because a former avant-gardist like Slavko Vorkapich was only used for a very circumscribed technique: montage sequences in which stylistic influences from the avant-garde are noticeable. For Slavko Vorkapich see Don Whittemore, Philip Alan Cecchettini: *Passport to Hollywood: Film Immigrants Anthology*. New York et al. : McGraw-Hill 1976: 432f. See also the special section in *Monthly Film Bulletin*, vol. 48, no. 572, September 1981: 185-190.

81. Charles Boost: *Van Ciné-Club tot Filmhuis. Tien jaren die de filmindustrie deden wankelen*. Amsterdam: Meulenhoff 1979: 42. [» ...ondanks de ijver, inspanning en toewijding van een inventieve avant-garde, zijn de grote en blijvende impulsen in het proces dat leidde tot de erkenning van de film als kunstvorm, uitgegaan van opdrachten die met particuliere subsidie of in industrieel verband tot stand kwamen. In de jaren tussen 1920 en 1930 hebben drie films een dominerende rol gespeeld in de bewustmaking bij het bioscooppubliek, daarbij inbegrepen de filmcritici en de theoretici, van mogelijkheden en potenties die in het nieuwe medium aanwezig waren. Zowel DAS KABINETT DES DR. CALIGARI als POTEMKIN en LA PASSION DE JEANNE D'ARC zijn in hun tijd en ver daarna eye-openers geweest, schokkende films die niet pasten binnen het raam van de toen gangbare filmproduktie, maar revoluties veroorzaakten in kijkgewoontes, bestaande definities omverwierpen en in een korte tijd (de vertoningstijd) veel duidelijk maakten van wat vaag begrepen werd of bevestigden wat tot dan vage vermoeden waren. «, my trans.]

82. Thomas Elsaesser: » » Dada/Cinema? «. In: Rudolf E. Kuenzli (ed.): *Dada and Surrealist Film*. New York: Willis, Locker and Owens 1987: 13-27, here 19.

83. Tom Gunning has discussed the affinity between early cinema and avant-garde film in his seminal article: » The Cinema of Attractions: Early Film, Its Spectator and the Avant-Garde «. In: Thomas Elsaesser (ed.): *Early Cinema: Space – Frame – Narrative*. London: BFI 1990: 56-62.

84. A. Kraszna-Krausz: » Exhibition in Stuttgart, June, 1929, and Its Effects «. In: *Close Up*, vol. 5, no. 6, December 1929: 455-464, here 463.

85. Catalogue edited by Cesar Domela for exhibition at the Kunstgewerbemuseum Berlin quoted in: Bool, » Schuitema und Zwart «, op. cit.: 125. [» Wichtigster Verwendungsbereich der Fotomontage ist die Propaganda, kommerziell wie auch politisch. «, my trans.]

86. André Stufkens: » The Song of Movement. Joris Ivens's First Films and the Cycle of the Avant-garde «. In: Kees Bakker (ed): *Joris Ivens and the Documentary Context*. Amsterdam: Amsterdam University Press 1999: 46-71, here 66.

87. Gunning, » Ontmoetingen... «, op. cit.: 254. [» laat zien dat het onmogelijk is de visuele ervaring van een moderne structuur te scheiden van het object zelf. «, my trans.]

88. The developments in the German film industry around the coming of sound points to a high level of awareness of these issues not only in the circles of the avant-garde, but also in the industry at large: The commercial cinema is in a somewhat different, yet also similar fashion staging its own *mise-en-abyme* in films such as UND NELSON SPIELT (GER 1928-29, Hans Conradi), DAS LIED IST AUS (GER 1930, Geza von Bolvary), DAS CABINET DES DR. LARIFARI (GER 1930, Robert Wohlmuth), DIE GROSSE SEHNSUCHT (GER 1930, István Székely), DER SCHUSS IM TONFILMATELIER (GER 1930, Alfred Zeisler), WIR SCHALTEN UM AUF HOLLYWOOD (GER 1931, Frank Reicher), DAS LIED EINER NACHT (GER 1932, Anatol Litvak), DIE VERLIEBTE FIRMA (GER 1932, Max Ophüls), ICH BEI TAG UND DU BEI NACHT (GER 1932, Ludwig Berger). For some of the issues concerning the industry, see the essays collected in Malte Hagener, Jan Hans (eds.): *Als die Filme singen lernten. Innovation und Tradition im Musikfilm 1928-1938*. München: edition text + kritik 1999. For the self-reflexive wave in early German sound films see Jörg Schweinitz: » › Wie im Kino! ‹. Die autothematische Welle im frühen Tonfilm. Figurationen des Selbstreflexiven «. In: Thomas Koebner,

Norbert Grob, Bernd Kiefer (eds.): *Diesseits der › Dämonischen Leinwand ‹*. München: edition text + kritik 2003: 373-392.

89. Andreas Huyssen: » The Hidden Dialectic: Avantgarde – Technology – Mass Culture «. First published in Kathleen Woodward (ed.): *The Myths of Information: Technology and Postindustrial Culture*. Madison, WI: Coda Press 1980: 151-164. Reprinted in and quoted after: Andreas Huyssen: *After the Great Divide: Modernism, Mass Culture, Postmodernism*. Bloomington and Indianapolis: Indiana University Press 1986: 3-15, here 11.

90. I am aware that most avant-garde movements tried to work in different genres and formats and consciously attempted to break down the barriers between the various art forms; however, disciplinary limitations within the academy have largely confined studies to a concentration of one art form with occasional asides about others.

91. See, for the basic operation of making a distinction and observation, Niklas Luhmann: *Soziale Systeme. Grundriß einer allgemeinen Theorie*. Frankfurt am Main: Suhrkamp 1984: 242-285 and Niklas Luhmann: *Die Kunst der Gesellschaft*. Frankfurt am Main: Suhrkamp 1995: 92-164.

92. Seen from this perspective, my four aporias are also closely related to the » three As « proposed by Thomas Elsaesser in relation to the commissioned industrial film – » Auftraggeber, Anlass, Adressat « (commissioning body, occasion, expected audience / address). See Thomas Elsaesser: » Die Stadt von Morgen: Filme zum Bauen und Wohnen in der Weimarer Republik «. In: Klaus Kreimeier, Antje Ehmann, Jeanpaul Goergen (Hrsg.): *Geschichte des dokumentarischen Films in Deutschland. Band 2: Weimarer Republik 1918-1933*. Stuttgart: Reclam 2005: 381-409.

Notes Chapter 3

1. Bertolt Brecht, Slatan Dudow, Georg M. Höllering, Kaspar, Ernst Ottwald, Robert Scharfenberg: » Tonfilm › Kuhle Wampe oder Wem gehört die Welt? «. In: Bertolt Brecht: *Gesammelte Werke. Vol. 18: Schriften zur Literatur und Kunst I*. Frankfurt am Main: Suhrkamp 1967: 210-212. [» Selbstverständlich kostet uns die Organisierung der Arbeit weit mehr Mühe als die (künstlerische) Arbeit selber, das heißt, wir kamen immer mehr dazu, die Organisation für einen wesentlichen Teil der künstlerischen Arbeit zu halten. Es war das nur möglich, weil die Arbeit als ganze eine politische war. «, my trans.]

2. This phrase simultaneously refers to Richard Abel's book on the early French avantgarde: *French Cinema: The First Wave 1915-1929*. Princeton, NJ: Princeton University Press 1984, while it also ties the activists of the 1920s to the later generation of the *Nouvelle Vague*.

3. A similar program was formulated by Tom Gunning in an essay on the programming policy of the Dutch *Filmliga*. See Tom Gunning: » Ontmoetingen in verduisterde ruimten. De alternatieve programmering van de Nederlandsche Filmliga «. In: Nico de Klerk, Ruud Visschedijk (eds.): *Het gaat om de film! Een nieuwe geschiedenis van de Nederlandsche Filmliga 1927-1933*. Amsterdam: Bas Lubberhuizen / Filmmuseum 1999: 217-263.

4. See, for some examples of research on alternative movements in the United States, Bill Nichols: » The American Photo League «. In: *Screen*, no. 13, Winter 1972/73: 108-115; Russell Campbell: » Film and Photo League. Radical Cinema in the 30s «. In: *Jump Cut*, no. 14, March 1977: 23-33 ; William Alexander: *Film on the Left: American Documentary Film from 1931 to 1942*. Princeton, NJ: Princeton University Press 1981; Russell Campbell: *Cinema Strikes Back: Radical Filmmaking in the United States 1930-1942*. Ann Arbor: UMI Research Press 1982; Jan-Christopher Horak: *Lovers of Cinema: The First American Film Avant-Garde 1919-1945*. Madison, WI: Wisconsin University Press 1995; Bruce Posner (ed.): *Unseen Cinema: Early American Avant-Garde Film 1893-1941*. New York: Anthology Film Archive 2001; presentation by John M. Frankfurt on » Constructing Cinephilia: Theatre Design and the Little Cinema Movement « at the SCMS annual conference, 6 March 2003, Minneapolis.

5. See, for English-language accounts of the Japanese film avant-garde, Noël Burch: *To the Distant Observer: Form and Meaning in the Japanese Cinema*. Berkeley, CA: University of California Press 1979: 123-139; James Peterson: » A War of Utter Rebellion: Kinugasa's PAGE OF MADNESS and the Japanese Avant-Garde of the 1920s «. In: *Cinema Journal*, vol. 29, no. 1, Fall 1989: 36-53; William O. Gardner: » New Perceptions: Kinugasa Teinosuke's Films and Japanese Modernism «. In: *Cinema Journal*, vol. 43, no. 3, 2004: 59-78. For a German-language account see Mariann Lewinsky: *Eine verrückte Seite. Stummfilm und filmische Avantgarde in Japan*. Zurich: Chronos 1997: passim, see on the context of the avant-garde in Japan and on the influence of European experimental films 136-174.

6. Charles de Vesme: » Éditorial «. In: *Le Journal du Ciné-Club*, no. 1, Jan. 1920. Quoted after: Pierre Lherminier: » Présentation : › Le Journal du Ciné-Club ‹ et › Cinéa ‹, 1920-1923 «. In: Louis Delluc: *Ecrits cinématographiques II: Cinéma & Cie.* (edited by Pierre Lherminier). Paris: Cinémathèque Française 1986: 287-295, here 287. [» Les passionnés du cinématographe se comptent par dizaines de millions, appartenant à tout le pays, à toutes les classes, depuis les plus intellectuelles jusqu'à celles dont la culture est plus rudimentaire. «, my trans.]

7. Thomas Elsaesser: » Realität zeigen: Der frühe Film im Zeichen Lumières «. In: Ursula von Keitz, Kay Hoffmann (eds.): *Die Einübung des dokumentarischen Blicks. Fiction Film und Non Fiction Film zwischen Wahrheitsanspruch und expressiver Sachlichkeit 1895-1945*. Marburg: Schüren 2001: 27-50, hier 28. [» [B]ei der Überlegung, was denn eigentlich Kino sei, bleibt manche Selbstverständlichkeit auf der Strecke. Ist es eine Reihe von Fotografien, die Bewegungsabläufe festhält, oder sind es Bilder, gezeichnet oder fotografiert, die mechanisch angetrieben werden, um den Eindruck kontinuierlicher Bewegung zu erwecken? ...] Ist es das projizierte Bild oder die Vorführung lebender Bilder vor einem zahlenden Publikum? ...] Es gibt ...] mindestens ...] zwei Dutzend ...] Anwärter. «, my trans.]

8. And indeed, the only book length academic study on the subject deals with Paris in the 1920s. See Christophe Gauthier: *La Passion du cinéma. Cinéphiles, ciné-clubs et salles spécialisées à Paris de 1920 à 1929*. Paris: Association Française de Recherche sur l'Histoire du Cinéma / Ecole des Chartres 1999.

9. See Gauthier, *passion*: 14-16 (» Prologue: La premiére séance «).

10. See » annexe no. 2: Le premier › Ciné-Club de France ‹ et les › Matinées de *Cinéa* ‹. In : Gauthier, *passion* : 344f.

11. See Richard Abel: » *Cinégraphie* and the Search for Specificity «. In: R.A.: *French Film Theory and Criticism, 1907-1939. A History/Anthology. I: 1907-1929.* Princeton, NJ: Princeton University Press 1988: 194-223, here 198.

12. See Steve Neale: » Art Cinema as Institution «. In: *Screen*, vol. 22, no. 1 (Spring 1981): 11-39; Charles Boost: *Van Ciné-Club tot Filmhuis. Tien jaren die de filmindustrie deden wankelen.* Amsterdam: Meulenhoff 1979. (Grote cineasten).

13. See, for example, the writings of Louis Delluc: *Ecrits cinématographiques. 3 Vols. I: Le Cinéma et les Cinéastes. II: Cinéma et Cie. III: Drames de Cinéma.* (edited by Pierre Lherminier). Paris: Cinémathèque Française 1985; 1986; 1990 or Béla Balázs : *Der sichtbare Mensch, oder die Kultur des Films.* Frankfurt am Main: Suhrkamp 2001. (originally Vienna, Leipzig: Deutsch-Österreichischer Verlag 1924).

14. Even the protagonists of the second wave of cinephilia, the *Nouvelle Vague,* temporarily connected criticism to filmmaking. Most of them ended their theoretical and critical engagement once they established themselves as filmmakers. The possible exception here is Jean-Luc Godard who retained an avant-garde stance in his strategic interventions in public debates, in his changes of material and his overall partisan stance even after he had firmly established himself as a filmmaker.

15. See Richard Abel: *French Cinema. The First Wave, 1915-1929.* Princeton, NJ: Princeton University Press 1984: 264.

16. See Christophe Gauthier: *La Passion du cinéma. Cinéphiles, ciné-clubs et salles spécialisées à Paris de 1920 à 1929.* Paris: Association Française de Recherche sur l'Histoire du Cinéma / Ecole des Chartres 1999: 74-79. See also Richard Abel: *French Cinema. The First Wave, 1915-1929.* Princeton, NJ: Princeton University Press 1984: 252-257.

17. For a contemporary overview of the Parisian screening situation see Jean Lenauer: » The Cinema in Paris «. In: *Close Up*, vol. 3, no. 6, December 1928.

18. Ian Christie: » The avant-gardes and European cinema before 1930 «. In: Hill, Gibson, *Film Studies*, 1998: 449f.

19. For memories and eye witness accounts of the British Film Society see Jen Samson: » The Film Society, 1925-1939 «. In: Charles Barr (ed.): *All Our Yesterdays. 90 Years of British Cinema.* London: BFI 1986: 306-313; Peter Wollen, Alan Lovell, Sam Rohdie: » Interview with Ivor Montagu «. In: *Screen*, vol. 13, no. 3, autumn 1972: 71-113; Ivor Montagu: » Old Man's Mumble. Reflections on a Semi-Centenary «. In: *Sight & Sound*, Autumn 1975: 222; and, for the Progressive Film Institute, see Bert Hogenkamp: » Interview met Ivor Montagu over het Progressive Film Institute «. In: *Skrien*, no. 51, July-Aug. 1975: 25-33. For an unauthorised reprint of the programs accompanying the screenings see *The Film Society Programmes, 1925-1939.* New York: Arno Press 1972. For a thorough historiographic overview of this period in Great Britain see Jamie Sexton: *The Emergence of an Alternative Film Culture in Inter-War Britain.* Norwich: University of East Anglia 2001 [Unpublished PhD thesis] and his article » The Film Society and the creation of an alternative film culture in Britain in the 1920s «. In: Andrew Higson (ed.): *Young and Innocent? The Cinema in Britain, 1896-1930.* Exeter: University of Exeter Press 2002. See also the autobiographies by Ivor Montagu: *The Youngest Son. An Autobiography.* London: Lawrence and Wishart 1970, and by another key figure, Adrian Brunel: *Nice Work. The Story of Thirty Years in British Film Production.* London: Forbes Robertson 1949: 112-116.

20. Adrian Brunel: *Nice Work The Story of Thirty Years in British Film Production.* London: Forbes Robertson 1949: 114.

21. Quoted in Montagu, Old Man's Mumble, op. cit., 1975: 220.

22. For an account of the activities of Brunel & Montagu (punningly called Brunel & Montage) see Adrian Brunel: *Nice Work The Story of Thirty Years in British Film Production*. London: Forbes Robertson 1949: 117-124.

23. Wollen, Lovell, Rohdie, Interview with Montagu, op. cit.: 71.

24. On the history of the Filmliga see Nico de Klerk, Ruud Visschedijk (eds.): *Het gaat om de film! Een nieuwe geschiedenis van de Nederlandsche Filmliga 1927-1933*. Amsterdam: Bas Lubberhuizen / Filmmuseum 1999. For a complete reprint of their magazine see Jan Heijs (ed.): *Filmliga 1927-1931*. Nijmegen: SUN 1982.

25. See the manifesto » Het gaat om de film «. In: *Filmliga*, no. 1, September 1927. [» Eens op de honderd keep zien wij: de film. Voor de rest zien wij: bioscoop. «, my trans.]

26. See Temple Willcox: » Soviet Films, Censorship and the British Government: A Matter of the Public Interest «. In: *Historical Journal of Film, Radio and Television*, vol. 10, no. 3, 1990: 275-292, here 275.

27. For film activities in Germany on the left of the political spectrum see Willi Lüdecke: *Der Film in Agitation und Propaganda der revolutionären deutschen Arbeiterbewegung (1919–1933)*. Berlin: Oberbaumverlag 1973; Gertraude Kühn, Karl Tümmler, Walter Wimmer (eds.): *Film und revolutionäre Arbeiterbewegung in Deutschland 1918-1932*. (2 vols.). Berlin/DDR: Henschel 1975; Jürgen Berger et al. (eds.): *Erobert den Film! Proletariat und Film in der Weimarer Republik*. Berlin: Neue Gesellschaft für Bildende Künste 1977; Bruce Murray: *Film and the German Left in the Weimar Republic. From » Caligari « to » Kuhle Wampe «*. Austin, TX: University of Texas Press 1990; Stattkino Berlin e.V.: *Revolutionärer Film in Deutschland (1918-1933)*. Berlin: Stattarchiv 1996.

28. See the documents reprinted in Kühn et al., *Film und revolutionäre Arbeiterbewegung*, op. cit., vol. 2: 203-207.

29. For more on Willi Münzenberg – who also makes a notable appearance in Peter Weiss' *Ästhetik des Widerstands* – see Babette Gross: *Willi Münzenberg. Eine politische Biografie*. Leipzig: Forum Verlag 1991 and Stephen Koch: *Double Lives: Stalin, Willi Münzenberg and the Seduction of the Intellectuals*. New York: Enigma 1994. (revised and updated edition 2004); see also Helmut Gruber: » Willi Münzenberg's German Communist Propaganda Empire, 1921-1933 «. In: *Journal of Modern History*, no. 38, vol. 3 (1966): 278-297; Rolf Surmann: *Die Münzenberg-Legende. Zur Publizistik der revolutionären deutschen Arbeiterbewegung, 1921-1933*. Köln: Prometh 1982.

30. Berger, *Erobert*, 1977: 16.

31. See Stattkino, *Revolutionärer Film*, op. cit.: 10.

32. See for the activities of the SPD on the film sector David Welsh: » The Proletarian Cinema and the Weimar Republic «. In: *Historical Journal of Film, Radio and Television*, vol. 1, no. 1, 1981: 3-18.

33. Willy Achsel: » Eine Anregung «. In: *Film-Kurier*, vol. 5, no. 101, 2.5.1923. [» Die Quintessenz der Propaganda muß in der Forderung gipfeln: Sorgt dafür, daß das Publikum in der Gesamtheit immer höhere Ansprüche stellt und geht selbst oft ins Kino, dann wird der Kitsch immer mehr verschwinden. Das Publikum bekommt letzten Endes immer das vorgesetzt, wonach es verlangt. «, my trans.]

34. For a detailed account of the organisation of the travels of ambulant cinema programs see » Rundschreiben der KPD zur Aktivierung der revolutionären Filmpropaganda «. Reprinted in and quoted after: Kühn et al., *Film und revolutionäre Arbei-*

terbewegung, vol. 2, 1975: 213-217. See moreover my chapter » Vanishing point Soviet Union «.

35. The program was repeated at least once, in Hanover on 28 May 1925, organised by the Kestner-Gesellschaft. See TTO [= Thomas Tode]: entry Wilfried Basse. In: Hans-Michael Bock (ed.): *CineGraph – Lexikon zum deutschsprachigen Film.* München: edition text + kritik 1984ff.: inst. 29, 15.8.1997.

36. For a detailed contextualisation of this event see the micro-study by Holger Wilmesmeier: *Deutsche Avantgarde und Film. Die Filmmatinee » Der absolute Film «. (3. und 10. Mai 1925).* Münster, Hamburg: Lit Verlag 1993. Wilmesmeier has collected an impressive wealth of material, yet many of his conclusions are debatable.

37. Edgar Beyfuß, A. Kossowsky: *Das Kulturfilmbuch.* Berlin: Carl P. Chryselins'scher Verlag 1924.

38. In fact, the society had already been announced in late 1927, see *Film-Kurier,* vol. 9, no. 252, 25.10.1927, but seems to have been inactive until January 1928 even though in November its first program was announced: » *Die erste Matinee der Gesellschaft Neuer Film wird bereits in der letzten Novemberwoche stattfinden. Ort der Veranstaltung wird voraussichtlich ein von der Ufa zur Verfügung gestelltes Theater sein.* « (*Film-Kurier,* vol. 9, no. 265, 9.11.1927) Announced are scenes by Léger, Picasso [sic], Cavalcanti, Eggeling, Ruttmann and music by Hindemith and Bergier.

39. See Thomas Tode: » Hans Richter «. In: *CineGraph – Lexikon zum deutschsprachigen Film.* Inst. 35. München: edition text + kritik 2001. See also Stattkino, *Revolutionärer Film,* 1996: 15. For a review in the trade press see Hans Feld: » Drei absolute Filme «. In: *Film-Kurier,* vol. 10, no. 14, 16.1.1928.

40. See Hans Feld: » Die Gesellschaft › Neuer Film ‹ stellt sich vor «. In: *Film-Kurier,* vol. 10, no. 44, 20.2.1928.

41. Hans Richter: *Köpfe und Hinterköpfe.* Zürich: Verlag Die Arche 1967: 145. [» In ganz Europa war man inzwischen sehr avantgardefilmbewußt geworden. ... Zwischen Paris, Holland und Berlin kam ein internationaler Austausch von Filmen, Personen und Artikeln in Schwung. Da meine Filme alle im » Studio des Ursulines « liefen, auch in Holland gezeigt wurden, fühlte ich mich nicht nur dazugehörig, sondern auch verantwortlich, in Deutschland etwas für unsere Europa-Bewegung zu tun. ...] So gründeten wir [Karl Freund, Guido Bagier und ich] 1926/27 die Gesellschaft » Neuer Film «. «, my trans.]

42. See Kr. [= Siegfried Kracauer]: » Abstrakter Film. Zur Vorführung der Gesellschaft Neuer Film «. In: *Frankfurter Zeitung,* no. 195, 13.3.1928. Reprinted in Siegfried Kracauer: *Werke. Band 6.2: Kleine Schriften zum Film 1928-1931.* Frankfurt am Main: Suhrkamp 2004: 46-49. See also anon.: » Gesellschaft › Neuer Film ‹ in Frankfurt «. In: *Film-Kurier,* vol. 10, no. 60, 9.3.1928.

43. Editor: » Het eerste Ligajaar «. In: *Filmliga,* no. 12, August 1928: 12.

44. For an overview of Bagier's biography, see kun [= Karin Unfried]: entry Guido Bagier. In: Hans-Michael Bock (ed.): *CineGraph – Lexikon zum deutschsprachigen Film.* München: edition text + kritik 1984ff.: installment 36, 15.5.2002.

45. See anon.: » Gesellschaft › Neuer Film ‹ aufgelöst? «. In: *Film-Kurier,* vol. 10, no. 153, 28.6.1928.

46. O.B. [= Oswell Blakeston]: » Interview with Carl Freund «. In: *Close Up,* vol. 4, no. 1, Jan. 1929: 58-61, here 59.

47. See the January 1928 letter where prominent politicians, scientists and artists are asked to join. In: Heinrich-Mann-Archiv, Mappe Volks-Film-Verband, Akademie der Künste. Reprinted in: Kühn et al., *Film und revolutionäre Arbeiterbewegung*, vol. 2, 1975: 238. Members of the board of directors included Mann, Käthe Kollwitz, Alfons Goldschmidt, Erwin Piscator, Max Deri, Leonhard Frank, Franz Höllering, and Rudolf Schwarzkopf. See the list in the first issue of *Film und Volk*, 1. Heft, Februar/März 1928: n.p.

48. » Volksfilmverband. Gründungsaufruf vom Januar 1928 «. In: Archiv Akademie der Künste, Heinrich-Mann-Archiv, Mappe Volks-Film-Verband. Reprinted in and quoted after: Stattkino, *Revolutionärer Film*, op. cit.: 14. [» Wir wollen und verlangen keine verstiegenen Experimente. Wir haben keinen in Ästhetik und Literatur befangenen Bildungsfimmel. Wir wissen, daß das Kino in erster Reihe eine Stätte der Entspannung und Unterhaltung sein will und sein soll. Aber wir glauben, daß » Unterhaltung « nicht gleichbedeutend ist mit » Schund «, daß » Entspannung « nicht dasselbe ist, wie » geistige Armut «. Gegen den künstlerischen Schund, gegen die geistige Armut und nicht zuletzt auch gegen die politische und soziale Reaktion, die nur allzuoft der heutigen Filmproduktion den Stempel aufdrückt, richtet sich unser Kampf, damit der Film zu dem werde, was er sein könnte und sein sollte: Ein Mittel zur Verbreitung von Wissen, Aufklärung und Bildung, Kenntnissen, Gedanken, Ideen – ein Mittel der Völker-Verständigung und Versöhnung – ein lebendiger, wirkender Faktor des alltäglichen wie des geistigen und künstlerischen Lebens! «, my trans.]

49. The VFV is thus not an initiative of the KPD as claimed by Karl Tümmler in: » Zur Geschichte des Volksfilmverbandes «. In: *Filmwissenschaftliche Mitteilungen*, no. 5, 1964: 1224f. See also the refutation in Richard Weber: » Der Volksfilmverband. Von einer bürgerlichen Bündnisorganisation zur proletarischen Kulturorganisation «. In: *Film und Volk. Organ des Volksfilmverbandes. Februar 1928-März 1930*. Köln: Verlag Gaehme, Henke 1975: 12.

50. Richter is only mentioned once in a list of participants at La Sarraz (*Film und Volk*, vol. 2. no. 8, October 1929: 3). Given Richter's status at the time as one of the key figures in Germany this is surprising and can only be explained as the rivalry that existed between the various organisations. Karl Freund is mentioned once (*Film und Volk*, vol. 1, no. 2, April 1928: 12) in an essay on DIE ABENTEUER EINES ZEHNMARKSCHEINS (GER 1926, Berthold Viertel).

51. See part 2.1 on » The Aporias of the Avant-garde « and Walter Ruttmann: » Die › absolute ‹ Mode «. In: *Filmkurier*, no. 30, 3 February 1928. Reprinted in and quoted from: Jeanpaul Goergen (ed.): *Walter Ruttmann. Eine Dokumentation*. Berlin: Freunde der Deutschen Kinemathek 1989: 82.

52. The Film Society: » Programme. The First Performance at 2:30 P.M., on Sunday, October 25th, 1925. at the New Gallery Kinema, Regent Street «. In: Council of the London Film Society (ed.): *The Film Society Programmes 1925-1939*. New York: Arno Press 1972.

53. See Christophe Gauthier: *La Passion du cinéma. Cinéphiles, ciné-clubs et salles spécialisées à Paris de 1920 à 1929*. Paris: Association Française de Recherche sur l'Histoire du Cinéma / Ecole des Chartres 1999 : 81-102 for an account of the birth of film history and of the creation of a canon of classical films.

54. Anon.: » Die bedrohte Pariser Avant-Garde «. In: *Film-Kurier*, vol. 10, no. 119/120, 19.5.1928.

55. See for some detailed numbers the statistics accompanying some of Montagu's reflections; » Extra List for Statisticophiles «. In: *Sight & Sound*. autumn 1975: 224.

56. It was this economic threshold built into the Film Society membership fee that contributed to the foundation of workers' film clubs around 1929, see below.

57. I am aware that » commercial art cinema « is a term that is not contemporary to the interwar period, but a concept that emerged in the 1960s. I am using the expression in the sense that has been suggested by Thomas Elsaesser: *Weimar Cinema and After. Germany's Historical Imaginary.* London, New York: Routledge 2000: passim.

58. Menno ter Braak: *Cinema Militans.* Utrecht: De Gemeenschap 1929.

59. See Gunning, Ontmoetingen, op. cit., 1999: 242.

60. See *Berliner Volkszeitung*, vol. 76, no. 89, 22.2.1928; as quoted by Tümmler, » Geschichte «, op. cit.: 1229.

61. Both speeches were reprinted in the magazine of the society. See Béla Balázs: » Der Film arbeitet für uns! «. In: *Film und Volk*, no. 1, March 1928: 6-8; Heinrich Mann: » Film und Volk «. In: *Film und Volk*, no. 2, April 1928: 4-6.

62. See Thomas Tode: » Albrecht Viktor Blum «. In: *CineGraph – Lexikon zum deutschsprachigen Film.* Inst. 29 (15.8.1997). München: edition text + kritik 1984ff.: B2f.

63. See for a review of the event Bernard von Brentano: » Volksverband für Filmkunst «. In: *Frankfurter Zeitung*, no. 159, 28.2.1928.

64. See the programmatic statement by Rudolf Schwarzkopf, general secretary of the VFV: » Unser Ziel und unser Weg. « In: *Film und Volk*, 1. Heft, März 1928: 4f.

65. Letter from Rudolf Schwarzkopf to Heinrich Mann, dated March 30th, 1928. In: Archiv Akademie der Künste, Heinrich-Mann-Archiv, Mappe Volks-Film-Verband, Briefwechsel. Reprinted in and quoted after: Kühn et al., *Film und revolutionäre Arbeiterbewegung*, op. cit., vol. 2: 244f. [» unangenehme und schädliche Polemik. ...] Überhaupt wollen wir in nächster Zeit mehr im stillen werben und wirken, und erst an die breite Öffentlichkeit herantreten, wenn unsere Vorbereitungen entsprechend weit gediehen sein werden. «, my trans.]

66. See the open letter by the *Volksfilmverband*: » Der Verband will ins Kino «. In: *Film-Kurier*, vol. 10, no. 296, 13.12.1928.

67. See –e– : » Russische Film-Matinee. Die Künstler sprechen «. In: *Lichtbild-Bühne*, vol. 22, no. 11, 14.1.1929. [» Gut gewählte und geschnittene Teile «, my trans.]

68. anon : » Die Wunder des Films. Sondervorstellung des Volks-Film-Verbandes im Tauentzienpalast «. In: *Lichtbild-Bühne*, vol. 22, no. 29, 4.2.1929. [» [um] dem Publikum einen Einblick in die so vielseitige Materie der Filmherstellung zu geben to give the public an insight into the varied materials of film production. «, my trans.]

69. Rudolf Arnheim : » Erich von Stroheim in der Kamera «. In: *Das Stachelschwein*, no. 8, August 1928: 50-53; reprinted in and quoted after R.A.: *Kritiken und Aufsätze zum Film.* (Edited by Helmut H. Diederichs). Frankfurt am Main: Fischer 1979: 204-208, here 205. [» Der liebe Gott möge den Ungläubigen ein sichtbarlich Zeichen geben und der » Kamera « ein ganzseitiges Inserat an seinem Himmel spendieren, damit das Publikum in Scharen herbeiströme. «, my trans.]

70. See Jeander: » Les ciné-clubs «. In: Marcel Defosse (ed.): *Le cinéma par ceux qui le font.* Paris: Fayard 1949; Vincent Pinel: *Introduction au ciné-club. Histoire, théorie, et pratique du ciné-club en France.* Paris: Éditions ouvrières 1964; Léon Moussinac: » Les amis de

Spartacus «. In: *Cinéma 74. Le guide du spectateur*, no. 189, July-Aug. 1974: 73f.; Maurice Pelinq: » A la conquête du public populaire (Naissance des ciné-clubs. Le Mouvement Spartacus) « In: *Jeune cinéma*, no. 131, December 1980/January 1981 and Timothy Barnard: » From Impressionism to Communism: Léon Moussinac's Technics of the Cinema, 1921-1933. « In: *Framework: The Journal of Cinema and Media*, no. 42, 2000 and Gauthier, *passion*, op. cit.: 169-181.

71. Léon Moussinac: » Les amis de Spartacus «. In: *Cinéma 74. Le guide du spectateur*, no. 189, July-Aug 1974: 73. [» tous les films, nouveaux ou anciens, interdits ou non, exprimant des beautés ou des vérités techniques, artistiques, idéologiques ou éducatives «, my trans.]

72. Anon.: » Les Amis de Spartacus «. In: *La Cinématographie française*, vol. 10, no. 489, 17.3.1928: 20.

73. Richard Abel: *French Cinema. The First Wave, 1915-1929*. Princeton, NJ: Princeton University Press 1984: 266f.

74. Ibid.: 272.

75. See » Ein neues Avantgardekino in Paris «. In: *Film-Kurier*, vol. 12, no. 256, 29.10.1930.

76. See anon.: » Hausse in Avantgarde-Kinos in Paris. Werden sich 17 Theater halten «. In: *Film-Kurier*, vol. 14, no. 278, 25.11.1932.

77. See anon: » Krise der Avantgarde-Kinos «. In: *Film-Kurier*, vol. 15, no. 24, 27.1.1933.

78. See Bert Hogenkamp: » Interview met Ivor Montagu over het Progressive Film Institute «. In: *Skrien*, no. 51, Jul-Aug 1975: 25-33.

79. See Hogenkamp, Bond, op. cit.: 22. See more on the connection between Grierson, Soviet cinema and the evolution of the documentary in chapters five and six on the Soviet Union and on the documentary.

80. See Gerry Turvey: » › That insatiable body ‹. Ivor Montagu's confrontation with British film censorship «. In: *Journal of Popular British Cinema*, vol. 3, 2000: 31-44.

81. See Peter Wollen's seminal article » The Two Avant-Gardes «. In: P.W.: *Readings and Writings. Semiotic Counter-Strategies*. London: Verso 1982.

82. A detailed account of the activities of workers' film societies in England can be found in Bert Hogenkamp: *Deadly Parallels: Film and the Left in Britain, 1929-1939*. London: Lawrence & Wishart 1986. See, for an earlier overview of similar material, Bert Hogenkamp: » Film and the Workers' Movement in Britain, 1929-39 «. In: *Sight & Sound*, vol. 45, no. 2, Spring 1976: 68-76.

83. See Wollen, Lovell, Rohdie, Interview with Montagu, op. cit.: 91; 94f.

84. Hogenkamp, Interview met Montagu, op. cit.: 26.

85. See » › Kamera ‹ bleibt Reprisenkino «. In: *Kinematograph*, vol. 23, no. 49, 27.2.1929.

86. See » › Kamera ‹ informiert über Eckardt-Konflikt. Kurs der Kamera bleibt. Erhebliche Verbindlichkeiten der Gesellschaft für den guten Film «. In: *Film-Kurier*, vol. 14, no. 86, 12.4.1932 and » Filmkräche jenseits der Filmindustrie. Wieder Kamerakonflikt. Die Antwort der Gesellschaft «. In: *Film-Kurier*, vol. 14, no. 89, 15.4.1932

87. On the Frankfurt opening see Kr.: » Volksverband für Filmkunst «. In: *Frankfurter Zeitung*, no. 325, 1.5.1928. Reprinted in and quoted after Siegfried Kracauer: *Werke. Band 6.2. Kleine Schriften zum Film 1928-1931*. Frankfurt am Main: Suhrkamp 2004: 71-73.

88. Letter from Rudolf Schwarzkopf to Heinrich Mann, dated 30 March 1928. In: Archiv Akademie der Künste, Heinrich-Mann-Archiv, Mappe Volks-Film-Verband, Brief-

wechsel. Reprinted in and quoted after: Kühn et al., *Film und revolutionäre Arbeiterbewegung*, op. cit., vol. 2: 244f.

89. See Rudolf Schwarzkopf: » Unser Ziel und unser Weg «. In: *Film und Volk*, vol. 1, no. 1, March 1929: 5.

90. Anon.: » In eigener Sache! (Volks-Film-Verband) «. In: *Film und Volk*, vol. 2, no. 9/10, November 1929: 4. [» Keine hochtrabenden Produktionspläne – sondern Umstellung auf praktisch realisierbare Pläne, Verstärkung der Arbeit unter den werktätigen Filmfreunden, aktiverer Kampf gegen Filmreaktion und Filmschund, die gerade jetzt in Hochkunjunktur stehen. «, my trans.]

91. See, for an example of the public debate in Hamburg, Hans-Michael Bock: » › Brüder zum Licht! ‹ Kino, Film und Arbeiterbewegung «. In: Skrentny, Werner (ed.): *Vorwärts – und nicht vergessen. Arbeiterkultur in Hamburg um 1930*. Hamburg: Projektgruppe Arbeiterkultur Hamburg 1982: 312ff.

92. Arthur Hollitscher: » Volksfilm und Volksbühne «. In: *Film und Volk*, vol. 1, no. 2, April 1928: 7f. [» …ja es kam sogar gelegentlich zu gemeinsamen Beratungen mit den Vertretern der Gewerkschaften und der Bildungsausschüsse der SPD. – bald aber versank alles im bewußten lethargischen Schlaf… «, my trans.]

93. See » Mitteilungen des Volksverbandes für Filmkunst «. In: *Film und Volk*, vol. 1, no. 2, April 1928: 22f. [» Der » Volksverband für Filmkunst « ist links gerichtet, aber parteipolitisch neutral. Er will die Volksbewegung gegen den schlechten, unwahren und reaktionären Film zusammenfassen. Diese Volksbewegung schließt alle fortschrittlichen Elemente ein, einerlei welcher politischen Partei sie angehören. «, my trans.]

94. See Willy Haas: » Der Volksverband für Filmkunst «. In: *Film-Kurier*, vol. 10, no. 52, 29.2.1928.

95. See » Eine deutsche Liga für unabhängigen Film «. In: *Film-Kurier*, vol. 12, no. 115, 15.5.1930. The board consisted of Dr. Blumenthal, Dr. Feld, Dr. Flesch, Werner Graeff, Paul Hindemith, Arthur Hollitscher, Dr. Marianoff, Mies van der Rohe, Asta Nielsen, Carl Nierendorf, Lotte Reiniger, Hans Richter, Walter Ruttmann.

96. See » Avant Garde-Studio in München «. In: *Kinematograph*, vol. 24, no. 109, 12.5.1930.

97. For activities in Munich see » Konsolidierung des künstlerischen Schaffens? Film-Vorträge in der Münchener Universität «. In: *Film-Kurier*, vol. 12, no. 112, 12.5.1930; » Verbandsleben: Die Liga in München «. In: *Film-Kurier*, vol. 12, no. 122, 23.5.1930; » Münchener Liga für unabhängigen Film «. In: *Kinematograph*, vol. 24, no. 119, 23.5.1930; » Werbeabend der Film-Liga in München «. In: *Film-Kurier*, vol. 12, no. 126, 28.5.1930.

98. See » Die erste Veranstaltung der Film-Liga «. In: *Film-Kurier*, vol. 12, no. 256, 29.10.1930. For a report and review of the evening see L.H.E. [=Lotte H. Eisner]: » Film-Kritik. 1. Matinee der Liga für unabhängigen Film «. In: *Film-Kurier*, vol. 12, no. 272, 17.11.1930.

99. See Hans-Michael Bock, Jürgen Berger (eds.): *Photo: Casparius. Filmgeschichte in Berlin. Berlin um 1930*. Berlin: Stiftung Deutsche Kinemathek 1978 and Erika Wottrich (ed.): *M wie Nebenzal*. Munich: edition text + kritik 2002; both books contain documents and texts on the case. For Brecht's perspective see Bertolt Brecht: *Der Dreigroschenprozess*. In: Bertolt Brecht: *Gesammelte Werke. Band 18: Schriften zur Literatur und Kunst I*. Frankfurt am Main: Suhrkamp 1967: 139-209 [first published 1931].

100. Thomas Tode: » Hans Richter «. In: *CineGraph – Lexikon zum deutschsprachigen Film*. Inst. 35. München: edition text + kritik 2001: B8. [» in kleinem Rahmen entwickelt sie sich zu einer kritischen Besucherorganisation mit intelligenten Programmen und einem bescheidenen Vertriebssystem mit Ligafilmen «, my trans.]

101. See Bryher: » What Can I Do «. In: *Close Up*, vol. 2, no. 3, March 1928: 21-25; Bryher: » What Can I Do (II) «. In: *Close Up*, vol. 2, no. 5, May 1928: 32-37; Bryher: » How I Would Start a Film Club «. In: *Close Up*, vol. 2, no. 6, June 1928.

102. S. Nestriepke: *Wege zu neuer Filmkultur*. Berlin: Verlag der Volksbühne 1927.

103. Jan-Christopher Horak: » Entwicklung einer visuellen Sprache im Stummfilm «. In: Ute Eskildsen, Jan-Christopher Horak (eds.): *Film und Foto der Zwanziger Jahre. Eine Betrachtung der Internationalen Werkbundausstellung » Film und Foto « 1929*. Stuttgart: Gerd Hatje 1979: 38-60, here 55.

104. See the overview given by Carl Vincent of production and exhibition activities in the alternative sector in: *Close Up*, vol. 5, no. 4, October 1929: 264-271.

105. See » Un nouveau › Club du Cinéma ‹ à Ostende «. In: *La Cinématographique Française*, vol. 10, no. 493, 10.4.1928: 15.

106. Richard Abel: *French Cinema: The First Wave, 1915-1929*. Princeton, NJ: Princeton University Press 1984: 264.

107. In 1934 several societies are reported for Belgium. See Ludo Patris: » The Film Abroad: Activity in Belgium «. In: *Cinema Quaterly*, vol. 2, no. 4, Summer 1934: 233f.

108. See Philip Mosley: *Split Screen: Belgian Cinema and Cultural Identity*. Albany, NY: State University of New York Press 2001: 40-41; 58-59; and Bert Hogenkamp, Rik Stallaerts: » Pain noir et film nitrate: le mouvement ouvrier socialiste belge et le cinéma durant l'entre deux guerres «. In: *Revue Belge du Cinéma*, no. 15, Spring 1986.

109. The detailed facts in the following abstract on the Swiss situation uses material mainly from Andres Janser: » Es kommt der gute Film. Zu den Anfängen der Filmclubs in Zürich «. In: Vinzenz Hediger, Jan Sahli, Alexandra Schneider, Margrit Tröhler (eds.): *Home Stories. Neue Studien zu Film und Kino in der Schweiz / Nouvelles approches du cinéma et du film en Suisse*. Marburg: Schüren 2001: 55-69. See also Hervé Dumont: *Geschichte des Schweizer Films*. Lausanne: Schweizer Filmarchiv / Cinémathèque Suisse 1987: passim, and, for a comparative perspective from Basel, Kaspar Birkhäuser: » Fünfzig Jahre im Dienste der Filmbesucher und des guten Films. Le Bon Film Basel 1931-1981 «. In: Le Bon Film (ed.): *50 Jahre Le Bon Film*. Basel: Le Bon Film 1981.

110. See the regular reports in *Close Up*, e.g. the first announcement in vol. 2, no. 4, April 1928: 52f. See also for reports on further activities Freddy Chevalley: » Le film à Genève «. In: *Close Up*, vol. 3, no. 4, October 1928: 52-55; Freddy Chevalley: » Chine – Machines – Electricite «. In: *Close Up*, vol. 4, no. 3, March 1929: 85-88; Freddy Chevalley: » Man Ray – Ruttmann – L. Reiniger «. In: *Close Up*, vol. 4, no. 6, June 1929: 88-91; Freddy Chevalley: » Sur les écrans genèvois «. In: *Close Up*, vol. 5, no. 3, September 1929: 225-228.

111. See, for a detailed analysis of this film Andres Janser, Arthur Ruegg: *Die neue Wohnung – Architektur / Film / Raum*. Baden: Lars Müller 2001.

112. See Bert Hogenkamp: » Critical Dialogue: Workers' Film in Europe «. In: *Jump Cut*, no. 19, Dec 1978: 36-37.

113. See Christel Henry: » Le mouvement › cineclubista ‹ au Portugal entre 1945 et 1959 «. In: *Estudos do Século XX*, no. 1, 2001: 241-276, here 243f.

114. On the films of the Themersons, see the special section in *Pix*, no. 1, Winter 1993/94: 67-122. See especially A.L. Rees: » The Themersons and the Polish Avant-garde. Warsaw – Paris – London «: 86-101.

115. See Frank Bren: *World Cinema. 1: Poland*. London: Flicks Books 1986: 22f.; Marek Haltof: *Polish National Cinema*. New York, Oxford: Berghahn 2002: 37-40; Wladyslaw Banaszkiewicz et al.: *La cinématographie Polonaise*. Warsaw: Éditions » Polonia « 1962: 108f.

116. See Michal Bregant: » Le cinéma d'avant-garde: entre le reve et l'utopie «. In: Eva Zaoralova, Jean-Loup Passek (eds.): *Le Cinéma Tcheque et Slovaque*. Paris: Éditions du Centre Pompidou 1996: 74-83.

117. For an overview of Zlín and Bat'a see the website: www.zlinbata.com.

118. I am thankful to Petr Szczepanik who made a large amount of material on the Czech context available. I can by no means do justice here to the complexity of the material.

119. Walter Benjamin: » Der Sürrealismus «. In: *Die literarische Welt*, vol. 5, no. 5, 1.2.1929: 3f. and vol. 5, no. 6, 8.2.1929: 4 and 15 & vol. 5, no. 7, 15.2.1929: 7f. Reprinted in and quoted after Walter Benjamin: *Gesammelte Schriften. II.1*. Frankfurt am Main: Suhrkamp 1977: 295-310, here 296. [» Es gibt in solchen [Avantgarde-]Bewegungen immer einen Augenblick, da die ursprüngliche Spannung des Geheimbundes im sachlichen, profanen Kampf um Macht und Herrschaft explodieren oder als öffentliche Manifestation zerfallen und sich transformieren muß. «, trans. Edmund Jephcott, *One Way Street*: 226]

120. See the book-length study on the emergence and development of art-house cinemas by Barbara Wilinsky: *Sure Seaters: The Emergence of the Art House Cinema*. Minneapolis, London: University of Minnesota Press 2001. See also presentation by John M. Frankfurt on » Constructing Cinephilia: Theatre Design and the Little Cinema Movement « at the SCMS annual conference, 6 March 2003 in Minneapolis.

121. Anon.: » Filmer aus Opposition. Avantgarde und Filmgeschäft «. In: *Film-Kurier*, vol. 11, no. 117, 24.7.1929. [» Bedenklich, daß unsere Avantgarde so sichtlich Inzucht der Ideen treibt. Die starken Talente bleiben aus, die Schulen blühen. Einer stiehlt's vom andern. Daß Karuselle sich drehen, auf Rummelplätzen Typen wimmeln – wie oft hat's das Auge erfahren. Welche Umwege, welcher Formenballast wird da für nichts ersonnen. ... Bei uns quetscht man sich ein paar Experimente für Eingeweihte, für Höchstgebildete ab. Die Snobgarde filmt. «, my trans.]

122. Robert Herring: » Twelve Rules for the Amateur, or How to Make Money, Though Honest «. In: *Close Up*, vol. 4, no. 5, May 1929: 22-27.

123. See Norman Wilson: » The Spectator «. In: *Cinema Quarterly*, vol. 1, no. 1, autumn 1932, 3-6, here 3.

124. See, for an overview of the amateur societies in London, Orlton West: » Bits and Pieces «. In: *Close Up*, vol. 5, no. 3, September 1929: 231-233.

125. See, for a report from this event, R. Bond: » The Amateur Convention «. In: *Close Up*, vol. 5, no. 6, December 1929: 479-483.

126. I have sketched this development in Malte Hagener: » Unter den Dächern der Tobis. Nationale Märkte und europäische Strategien «. In: Jan Distelmeyer (ed.): *Tonfilmfrieden/Tonfilmkrieg. Die Geschichte der Tobis vom Technik-Syndikat zum Staatskonzern*. München: edition text + kritik 2003: 51-64.

127. See » Ein internationales Büro der niederländischen Filmliga «. In: *Film-Kurier*, vol. 14, no. 129, 3.6.1932 and » Nederlandsche Filmliga Bulletin «. In: *Cinema Quaterly*, vol. 1, no. 2, winter 1932.

128. See advertisement in *Cinema Quarterly*, vol. 1, no. 4, summer 1933: 194.

129. See, as an example for London, hfr.: » Der Schrei nach dem Repertoire-Theater. Die Theater der guten Filme in England «. In: *Lichtbildbühne*, vol. 22, no. 81, 5.4.1929.

130. Ej. [=Ernst Jäger]: » Berlins Filmproduktion braucht ein Film-Studio. Aber es muß unter Aufsicht der Industrie arbeiten «. In: *Film-Kurier*, vol. 9, no. 255, 28.10.1927. [» Genau wie man sich eines Tages zusammenfinden wird, um einen gemeinsamen Export der deutschen Filmfabrikate ins Ausland in die Hand zu nehmen, genau so werden sich die maßgebenden Firmen vereinen, um eine Stelle zu finanzieren, die zum Nutzen der gesamten Fabrikation unter Aufsicht der Industrie und für die Industrie Filmexperimente macht. «, my trans.]

131. Anon.: » Eine der Republik würdige Aufgabe: Wo bleibt das Film-Experimental-Studio? «. In: *Film-Kurier*, vol. 10, no. 274, 16.11.1928.

132. Ian Aitken: *Film and Reform: John Grierson and the Documentary Film Movement*. London, New York: Routledge 1990: 1.

133. See Penelope Houston: *Keepers of the Frame: The Film Archives*. London: British Film Institute 1994: 21f.

134. For a contemporary evaluation of the newly founded institution see R.S. Lambert: » The British Film Institute «. In: *Cinema Quarterly*, vol. 1, no. 4, summer 1933.

135. Montagu, Old Man's Mumble, op. cit.: 247.

136. Mats Björkin, Pelle Snickars: » 1923-1933. Production, Reception and Cultural Significance of Swedish Non-fiction Films «. In: Peter Zimmermann, Kay Hoffmann (eds.): *Triumph der Bilder. Kultur- und Dokumentarfilme vor 1945 im internationalen Vergleich*. Konstanz: UVK Verlagsgesellschaft 2003: 272-290, here 281.

137. Anon.: » Der deutsche Film fordert vom Staat «. In: *Film-Kurier*, vol. 10, no. 197, 18.8.1928.

138. Iris Barry: » Hunting the Film in Germany «. In: *The American-German Review*, vol. 3, no. 4, June 1937. Quoted after Martin Loiperdinger: » Riefenstahls Parteitagsfilme zwischen Bergfilm und Kriegswochenschau «. In: *Filmblatt*, vol. 8., no. 21, Winter/ Spring 2003: 12-28, here 15.

139. Walter Ruttmann: » Von kommender Filmkunst. Was die Avantgarde vom kommenden Jahr erhofft «. In: *Film-Kurier*, vol. 10, no. 1, 1.1.1928. [» [Der Staat] könnte z.B. damit beginnen, ein Filmarchiv zu errichten. Er würde so ein Mittel schaffen, jene wenigen wichtigen Filme, die an der 100prozentigen Erfolgsnotwendigkeit scheiterten, überhaupt wieder zugänglich zu machen. Wäre erst einmal eine Heimat für diese Waisenkinder gegründet, so würde sich automatisch das zugehörige Publikum um sie grupppieren, vorausgesetzt, daß mit dem Archiv eine entsprechende Aufführungsmöglichkeit verbunden würde. Das wäre der zweite wichtige Schritt und würde bedeuten: Die Errichtung des Staatskinos. «, my trans.]

140. See Raymond Borde: *Les Cinémathèques*. Paris: Éditions L'Age d'Homme 1983: 30-34. See also Penelope Houston: *Keepers of the Frame: The Film Archives*. London: British Film Institute 1994: 10-12. Matuszewski's text is reprinted in English in *Film History*, vol. 7, 1995.

141. Richard Abel: *French Cinema. The First Wave, 1915-1929*. Princeton, NJ: Princeton University Press 1984: 249.

142. Anon. [Kenneth MacPherson?]: » Comment and Review «. In: *Close Up*, vol. 1, no. 1, July 1927: 51-55, here 54.

143. See for a historiographic account of the rediscovery of Méliès Roland Cosandey: » L'inescamotable escamoteur: Méliès, der unsterbliche Zauberkünstler «. In: Stefan Andriopoulos, Bernhard Dotzler (eds.): *1929. Beiträge zur Archäologie der Medien*. Frankfurt am Main: Suhrkamp 2002: 370-388.

144. See, for the special issue on Méliès: *La revue du cinéma*, vol. 1, no. 4, 15 October 1929. See for a report of the screenings that took place on 16 December 1929 *La revue du cinéma*, vol. 2, no. 6, 1 Jan. 1930: 72.

145. Examples are given in Wolfgang Mühl-Benninghaus: *Das Ringen um den Tonfilm. Strategien der Elektro- und Filmindustrie in den 20er und 30er Jahren*. Düsseldorf: Droste 1999: 154f.

146. On Iris Barry in general, see Margareta Akerman (ed.): *Remembering Iris Barry*. New York: Museum of Modern Art 1980. For a reprint of the original MOMA plans, see John E. Abbott, Iris Barry: » An outline of a project for founding the film library of the Museum of Modern Art «. In: *Film History*, vol. 7, 1995: 325-335.On Barry's early film criticism, see Haidee Wasson: » Writing the Cinema into Daily Life; Iris Barry and the Emergence of British Film Criticism in the 1920s «. In: Andrew Higson: *Young and Innocent? The Cinema in Britain, 1896-1930*. Exeter: University of Exeter Press 2002: 321-337. See also, for a contextual history of the preservatory impulse in film until the mid-1930s in the United States, Peter DeCherney: *Imagining the Archive: Film Collection in America Before MoMA*. New York: New York University 2001 [unpublished Ph.D. thesis].

147. François Truffaut: » Foreword «. In: Richard Roud: *A Passion for Films: Henri Langlois and the Cinémathèque Française*. London: Secker & Warburg 1983: XII

148. There are two English-language accounts of Henri Langlois's life and work, Richard Roud: *A Passion for Films: Henri Langlois and the Cinémathèque Française*. London: Secker & Warburg 1983 and Glenn Myrent, Georges P. Langlois: *Henri Langlois: First Citizen of the Cinema*. New York: Twayne 1995. In French see Patrick Olmeta: *La Cinémathèque française de 1936 à nos jours*. Paris: CNRS 2000. See also Raymond Borde: *Les Cinémathèques*. Paris: Éditions L'Age d'Homme 1983.

149. See Raymond Borde, Pierre Guibbert: » Sur la naissance du la Cinémathèque Française. La parole est à Jean Mitry «. In: *Archives (Institut Jean Vigo / Cinémathèque de Toulouse)*, vol. 7, Oct. 1987: 1-12.

150. See, on Albatros within the context of the French cinema, François Albera: *Albatros. Des Russes à Paris 1919-1929*. Milano and Paris: Mazzotta / Cinémathèque française 1995.

151. Roud, *Passion*, op.cit.: 9f.

152. See » Vita Germaine Dulac «. In: Nessel, Schlüpmann, Schulte Strathaus (eds.), *Dulac*, 2002: 117-120.

153. For a concise history of the *Reichsfilmarchiv*, see Hans Barkhausen: » Zur Geschichte des ehemaligen Reichsfilmarchivs «. In: Günter Moltmann, Karl Friedrich Reimers (eds.): *Zeitgeschichte im Film- und Tondokument. 17 historische, pädagogische und sozialwissenschaftliche Beiträge*. Göttingen, Zürich, Frankfurt: Musterschmidt 1970: 241-250.

154. For Hensel's film work before 1933, see the filmography in Thomas Hanna-Daoud: *Die NSDAP und der Film bis zur Machtergreifung*. Köln, Weimar, Wien: Böhlau 1996.

155. A new perspective on Dulac was offered by a retrospective in the autumn of 2002 in Frankfurt and Berlin accompanied by a solid publication comprising documents and critical evaluations. See Sabine Nessel, Heide Schlüpmann, Stefanie Schulte Strathaus (eds.): *Germaine Dulac*. Berlin: Freunde der Kinemathek 2002. (Kinemathek 93). For a reevaluation of Dulac's life and work see also the Ph.D. work-in-progress by Tami Williams; see, for an abstract, Tami Williams: » Beyond Impressions: Germaine Dulac (1882-1942), Her Life and Films, from Aesthetics to Politics «. In: *Cinéma & Cie*. no. 2, Spring 2003: 156f. See also Williams's contributions to *1895* (June and October 2001) and her analysis » Germaine Dulac, du figuratif à l'abstraction «.In: Nicole Brenez, Christian Lebrat (eds.): *Jeune, Dure et Pure! Une histoire du cinéma d'avant-garde et expérimental en France*. Paris / Milano: Cinémathèque Française / Mazzota 2001: 78-82. Dulac's writings are collected in Prosper Hillairet (ed.): *Germaine Dulac: Écrits sur le cinéma (1919-1937)*. Paris: Éditions Expérimental 1994.

156. See Ré Soupault: *Frauenporträts aus dem » Quartier reserve « in Tunis*. Heidelberg: Das Wunderhorn 2001.

157. For a thorough discussion of the Porten film and a general evaluation of the compilation film, see A. [=Andor] Kraszna-Krausz: » The Querschnittsfilm «. In: *Close Up*, vol. 3, no. 5, November 1928: 25-34.

158. Claude Vermorel in *Pous Vous*, no. 292, 21.6.1934. [» C'est grâce à elle que les programmes de France-Actualités ont cette objectivité, cette honnêteté, ces choix heureux que nous avons déjà signalés «, my trans.]

159. See Raymond Borde, Pierre Guibbert: » › Le cinéma au service de l'histoire ‹ (1935). Un film retrouvé de Germaine Dulac «. In: *Archives (Institut Jean Vigo / Cinémathèque de Toulouse)*, vol. 44/45, Nov./Dec. 1991: 1-20.

160. I discuss Shub's filmmaking in chapter five within the context of the Soviet cinema.

161. Germaine Dulac: » Le cinéma d'avant-garde «. In: Henri Fescourt (ed.): *Le Cinéma des origines à nos jours*. Paris: Éditions du Cygne 1932. Reprinted in and quoted after Prosper Hillairet (ed.): *Germaine Dulac. Ecrits sur le cinéma (1919-1937)*. Paris : Éditions Expérimental 1994: 182-190, here 182. [» Le film d'avant-garde ne s'adresse pas au simple plaisir de la foule. Il est à la fois, plus égoïste et plus altruiste. Egoïste, puisque manifestation personnelle d'une pensée pure ; altruiste, puisque dégagé de tout souci autre que le progrès. Le film d'avant-garde d'inspiration sincére a cette qualité primordiale de contenir en germe sous une apparence parfois inaccessible, les découvertes susceptibles d'acheminer les films vers la forme cinématographique des temps futurs. L'avant-garde naît, à la fois, de la critique du présent et de la prescience de l'avenir. «, my trans.]

Notes Chapter 4

1. René Clair: » Le cinématographe contre l'esprit «, written in 1927. Reprinted in and quoted after: René Clair: *Réflexion faite. Notes pour servir à l'histoire de l'art cinématographique de 1920 à 1950*. Paris: Gallimard 1951: 133. [» L'avant-garde, c'est la curiosité d'esprit appliquée à un domaine où les découvertes à faire restent nombreuses et passionnantes. «, my trans.]

2.   H.R. [=Herbert Read]: » The Cinema Library «. In: *Cinema Quaterly*, vol. 1, no. 1, autumn 1932: 62f.

3.   See Ute Schneider: » Artikulationsort Zeitschrift «. In: Heinz Ludwig Arnold (ed.): *Aufbruch ins 20. Jahrhundert. Über Avantgarden*. Munich: edition text + kritik 2001. (text + kritik Sonderband IX/01): 171-181.

4.   The postwar avant-garde has compellingly taken up this issue , especially militant Third World filmmakers with battle cries like » imperfect cinema « (see Julio García Espinosa: » Towards an Imperfect Cinema «. In: Michael Chanan (ed.): *Twenty-five Years of the New Latin American Cinema*. London: British Film Institute / Channel Four 1983. [Originally published in Spanish as » Por un cine imperfecto « in 1970]) and » aesthetics of hunger « (see Glauber Rocha: » An Aesthetics of Hunger «. In: Randal Johnson, Robert Stam (eds.): *Brazilian Cinema*. New Brunswick, NJ: Associated University Presses 1982. [originally published in Portuguese as » Estética da fome « in 1965]) See, for discussions of » Third Cinema « in general, Teshome Gabriel: *Third Cinema in the Third World: The Aesthetics of Liberation*. Ann Arbor, MI: University of Michigan Research Press 1982, Paul Willemen: *Questions of Third Cinema*. London: British Film Institute 1989.

5.   See Toke van Helmond: » » Un journal est un monsieur «. Arthur Lehning und seine Internationale Revue i 10. « and Kees van Wijk: » Avantgarde in der Zwischenkriegszeit. Betrachtungen über die Internationale Revue i 10«. Both in: Hubertus Gaßner, Karlheinz Kopanski, Karin Stengel (eds.): *Die Konstruktion der Utopie. Ästhetische Avantgarde und politische Utopie in den 20er Jahren*. Marburg: Jonas Verlag 1992. (documenta Archiv): 89-104; 105-123. See also the reprint: *Internationale Revue i 10*. Nendeln-Liechtenstein 1979. (Kraus-Reprint) and the bibliography in Gaßner et al., op. cit.: 104.

6.   See Ines Lindner: » Demontage in *documents* «. In: Stefan Andriopoulos, Bernhard J. Dotzler (eds.): *1929. Beiträge zur Archäologie der Medien*. Frankfurt am Main: Suhrkamp 2002: 110-131.

7.   See Sabine Nessel, Heide Schlüpmann, Stefanie Schulte Strathaus (eds.): *L'Invitation au voyage. Germaine Dulac*. Berlin: Freunde der Deutschen Kinemathek 2002: 29, fn 6; see also » Vita Germaine Dulac «. In: ibid.: 117ff.

8.   *Cinema Quarterly*, vol. 3, no. 1, autumn 1934: 55.

9.   Council of the London Film Society (ed.): *The Film Society Programmes 1925-39*. Reprint. New York: Arno Press 1972.

10. See chapter three for a thorough discussion of the political stance of the London *Film Society*.

11. For overviews of the various publication organs in France see the introductions to the different sections in Richard Abel: *French Film Theory and Criticism, 1907-1939. A History/Anthology. I: 1907-1929. II: 1929-1939*. Princeton, NJ: Princeton University Press 1988.

12. See Belá Balázs: *Der sichtbare Mensch oder Die Kultur des Films*. Wien, Leipzig: Deutsch-Österreichischer Verlag 1924; Edgar Beyfuss (ed.): *Das Kulturfilmbuch*. Berlin: Carl P. Chryselius'scher Verlag 1924; Willi Münzenberg: *Erobert den Film! Winke aus der Praxis proletarischer Filmpropaganda*. Berlin: Neuer Deutscher Verlag 1925.

13. See Georges Michel Coissac: *Histoire du cinématographie. De ses origines à nos jours*. Paris: Éditions Cinéopse / Librairie Gauthier-Villars & Cie. 1925 ; Léon Moussinac: *Naissance du cinéma*. Paris: J. Povolozky 1925; Henri Fescourt, Jean-Louis Bouquet:

L'Idée et l'écran. Opinions sur le cinéma. Paris: Haberschill et Sergent 1925-26; Iris Barry: *Let's Go to the Pictures.* London: Chatto & Windus 1925.

14. Pierre Marchand, René Weinstein,: *L'art dans la Russie nouvelle: Le cinéma (1917-1926).* Paris: Rider 1927; Léon Moussinac: *Le cinéma sovietique.* Paris: Gallimard 1928; Alfred Kerr: *Russische Filmkunst.* Berlin: Ernst Pollak 1927; Winifred Bryher: *Film Problems of Soviet Russia.* London: POOL 1929.

15. Lion Feuchtwanger has given brilliant portrait of such conservative angst in the face of the power of montage cinema in his novel *Erfolg.* See the chapter » Panzerkreuzer Orlow « (Berlin: Aufbau 1993: 533-538).

16. Hans Richter: *Filmgegner von heute – Filmfreunde von morgen.* Berlin: Verlag Hermann Reckendorff 1929; Werner Graeff: *Es kommt der neue Photograph!* Berlin: Verlag Hermann Reckendorff 1929; Léon Moussinac: *Panoramique du cinéma.* Paris: Au sens pareil 1929 ; Menno ter Braak: *Cinema Militans.* Utrecht: De Gemeenschap 1929; Paul Rotha: *The Film Till Now: A Survey of the Cinema.* London: Jonathan Cape 1930.

17. Guido Bagier: *Der kommende Film. Eine Abrechnung und eine Hoffnung. Was war? Was ist? Was wird?* Stuttgart, Berlin, Leipzig: Deutsche Verlags-Anstalt 1928; Rudolf Arnheim: *Film als Kunst.* Berlin: Rowohlt 1932; Béla Balázs: *Der Geist des Films.* Halle an der Saale: Wilhelm Knapp 1930; C.A. Lejeune: *Cinema.* London: Alexander Macklehose 1931; Ilja Ehrenburg: *Die Traumfabrik. Chronik des Films.* Berlin: Malik 1931.

18. Vsevolod Pudovkin: *Filmregie und Filmmanuskript.* Berlin: Verlag der » Lichtbildbühne « 1928; Vsevolod Pudovkin: *On Film Technique: Three Essays and an Address.* London: Victor Gollancz 1929. [expanded English edition: V.I. Pudovkin: *Film Technique: Five Essays and Two Addresses.* London: George Newnes 1933. (Translated by Ivor Montagu)]; Sergei Eisenstein: *Der Kampf um die Erde.* Berlin 1929. [Contains OLD AND NEW-scenario and Eisenstein's preface » Drehbuch? Nein: Kinonovelle! «].

19. Quoting –r.: » Film vom Bauhaus «. In: *Film-Kurier,* vol. 8, no. 290, 11.12.1926. [» [Zweck des Bauhauses] ist die geistige, handwerkliche und technische Durchbildung schöpferisch begabter Menschen zur bildnerischen Gestaltungsarbeit, besonders für den Bau und die Durchführung praktischer Versuchsarbeit, besonders für Hausbau und Hauseinrichtung, sowie die Entwicklung von Modelltypen für Industrie und Handwerk. «, my trans.]

20. I have discussed the Soviet film school here and again in chapter five » Vanishing Point Soviet Union «.

21. See Christophe Gauthier: *La Passion du cinéma. Cinéphiles, ciné-clubs et salles spécialisées à Paris de 1920 à 1929.* Paris: Association Française de Recherche sur l'Histoire du Cinéma / Ecole des Chartres 1999 : annexe no. 6 : Programme des conférences du Musée Galliera (Mai-Octobre 1924), 356f. See Richard Abel: *French Cinema: The First Wave, 1915-1929.* Princeton, NJ: Princeton University Press 1984: 254f.

22. See Christophe Gauthier: *La Passion du cinéma. Cinéphiles, ciné-clubs et salles spécialisées à Paris de 1920 à 1929.* Paris: Association Française de Recherche sur l'Histoire du Cinéma / Ecole des Chartres 1999: 123, 136f. See also Richard Abel: *French Cinema: The First Wave, 1915-1929.* Princeton, NJ: Princeton University Press 1984: 256f.

23. On teaching at the *Bauhaus* in general, see Rainer K. Wick: *Teaching at the Bauhaus.* Ostfildern-Ruit: Hatje Crantz 2000 and Rainer K. Wick: *Bauhaus-Pädagogik.* Köln: DuMont 1994, and Silvia Verena Schmidt: » Experiment und Methode – Unterricht am Bauhaus «. In: Burkhard Leismann (ed.): *Das Bauhaus. Gestaltung für ein modernes Leben.* Köln: Wienand 1994: 65-90.

24. See anon.: » Der Künstler gehört in die Industrie! Ein Gespräch mit Professor L. Moholy-Nagy, Dessau-Berlin «. In: *Film-Kurier*, vol. 10, no. 283, 28.11.1928.

25. The program is described as the » Nurmi-Film «, WACHSENDE KRISTALLE, and parts of the » Humboldt-film « (E. Paulick). See –r.: » Film vom Bauhaus «. In: *Film-Kurier*, vol. 8, no. 290, 11.12.1926.

26. László Moholy-Nagy: *Malerei Fotografie Film*. Munich: Langen 1925. (Bauhaus-Bücher 8).

27. Klaus Lippert: » Bauhaus et cinématographie «. In: *Travelling*, no. 56-57, Spring 1980: 42-51, here 43.

28. l. moholy-nagy: » film im bauhaus. eine erwiderung «. In: *Film-Kurier*, vol. 8, no. 296, 18.12.1926. [» meine, unsere kraftausgabe wird form in anregungen, vorschlägen, plänen, » manuskripten «, theorien. sache der anderen, sagen wir der industrie, wäre es, die kraftausgabe nach der andern seite auf sich zu nehmen: nämlich die mittel zur verfügung zu stellen, da, wo man etwas zu erwarten hat. zu erwarten, da liegt die aufgabe der unterstützenden faktoren, da, wo schon » bewiesen « wurde, ist keine aufgabe mehr zu lösen. «, my trans.]

29. See Karin Wilhelm: » Das Bauhaus. Architektur und Design «. In: Monika Wagner (ed.): *Moderne Kunst. Das Funkkolleg zum Verständnis der Gegenwartskunst. Vol. 2*. Reinbek: Rowohlt 1991: 424-442.

30. Herbert Molderings: » Lichtjahre eines Lebens. Das Fotogramm in der Ästhetik Laszlo Moholy-Nagys «. In: *Laszlo Moholy-Nagy. Fotogramme 1922-1943*. Munich, Paris and London: Schirmer/Mosel 1996: 8-17, here 14f. [» 1929 forderte er die Verantwortlichen in Staat und Kommune auf, von den » überlebten Malerakademien « Abstand zu nehmen und an ihrer Stelle » Lichtstudios « zu gründen, in denen Lehrer und Studierende das seiner Meinung nach modernste Gestaltungsmittel der Gegenwart erforschen und meistern lernen könnten. Acht Jahre später kam er in seinem Londoner Exil erneut auf diesen Vorschlag zurück. Inzwischen war der Name, den die neue Lehranstalt haben sollte, anspruchsvoller geworden: » Academy of Light « sollte sie heißen. 1939 schließlich führte er in die Arbeit im » Lichtatelier « als Pflichtkursus für jeden Studierenden an der von ihm in Chicago gegründeten » School of Design « ein. «, my trans.]

31. Hans Richter: *Köpfe und Hinterköpfe*. Zürich: Verlag Die Arche 1967: 136. [» Ivor Montagu ... hatte Eisenstein eingeladen, ein paar Vorträge in der von Montagu geleiteten Film-Society in London zu halten. (Mich bat er, dort einen Workshop-Kurs zu geben.) Derweil wollte Montagu versuchen, für Eisenstein ein Hollywood-Engagement abzuschließen, um ihm endlich eine angemessene Produktionsmöglichkeit auch außerhalb der Sowjetunion zu geben. Die Vortragsabende fanden unter intensivster Beteiligung aller derer statt, die sich später einen Namen in der britischen Filmproduktion, besonders in der Dokumentarfilm-Produktion machten. «, my trans.]

32. See anon.: » Der große Regisseur über Regietechnik: Eisenstein-Kolleg in London «. In: *Lichtbild-Bühne*, vol. 22, no. 271, 13.11.1929.

33. Julia Winckler: » Gespräch mit Wolfgang Suschitzky, Fotograf und Kameramann. Geführt in seiner Wohnung in Maida Vale, London, am 15. Dezember 2001, 22. März 2002, 17. Mai 2002 «. In: Claus-Dieter Krohn et al.: *Exilforschung. Film und Fotografie*. Munich: edition text + kritik 2003: 254-279, here 269f. [» Beide wollten lehren, glaube ich. Grierson war ein Akademiker und umgab sich mit Leuten aus Cam-

bridge und Oxford. Er hatte nur sehr wenige Vorkenntnisse über Film und lernte alles, was er über Film wusste, in der praktischen Erfahrung. ... Grierson und Rotha wollten die Menschen in diesem Land über Armut und über Medizin und Gesundheit aufklären. Rotha schrieb mehrere Bücher. ... Er war ein Filmtheoretiker. Er schrieb zum Beispiel über russische Filme, die hier in England fast gänzlich unbekannt waren, weil sie zensiert wurden. Wir hatten aber die Möglichkeit, manche Filme von Vertov, Pudovkin und Eisenstein in privaten Vorstellungen zu sehen. Es gab einen Filmklub und ein Kino in Regent Street, die importierte russische Filme zeigten. «, my trans.]

34. John Grierson: » The E.M.B. Unit «. In: Jack C. Ellis: *John Grierson: Life, Contributions, Influence*. Carbondale, Edwardsville, IL: Southern Illinois University Press 2000: 36.

35. See » Mitteilungen des Volksverbandes für Filmkunst: Film-Seminar «. In: *Film und Volk*, vol. 1, no. 1, Feb.-March 1928: 32.

36. See Marianne Mildenberger: *Film und Projektion auf der Bühne*. Emsdetten: Lechte 1961.

37. See TTO [=Thomas Tode]: entry Erwin Piscator. In: Hans-Michael Bock (ed.): *Cinegraph. Lexikon zum deutschsprachigen Film*. Munich: edition text + kritik 1984ff., installment 33, 15.5.2000.

38. For more on Piscator's school see da.: » Regeneration des Theaters vom Film her. Unterredung mit Erwin Piscator«. In: *Lichtbild-Bühne*, vol. 22, no. 148, 22.6.1929, and anon.: » Die Schule der Piscatorbühne. Das Schuljahr beginnt am 10. September «. In: *Lichtbild-Bühne*, vol. 22, no. 205, 28.8.1929.

39. Sabine Nessel, Heide Schlüpmann, Stefanie Schulte Strathaus (eds.): *L'Invitation au voyage. Germaine Dulac*. Berlin: Freunde der Deutschen Kinemathek 2002: 28f.

40. Vance Kepley, Jr.: » The Kuleshov workshop «. In: *Iris*, vol. 4, no. 1, 1986: 5-23, here 6.

41. An autobiographical account of the school is given by Alexandra Chochlowa: » Die erste Staatliche Filmschule «. In: Wladimir Sabrodin, Karin Meßlinger (eds.): *Amazonen der Avantgarde im Film*. Berlin: Freunde der Deutschen Kinemathek / Deutsche Guggenheim 1999: 27-32. The text is translated from Chochlowa's autobiography (Moscow 1975).

42. Vance Kepley, Jr.: » Building a National Cinema: Soviet Film Education, 1918-1934 «. In: *Wide Angle*, vol. 9, no. 3, 1987: 5-19, here 5.

43. For a critical view of GTK see Denise J. Youngblood: *Soviet Cinema in the Silent Era, 1918-1935*. Ann Arbor, MI: UMI Research Press 1985: 63ff.

44. Vance Kepley, Jr.: » The Kuleshov workshop«. In: *Iris*, vol. 4, no. 1, 1986: 5-23, here 12.

45. Vance Kepley, Jr.: » The Kuleshov workshop«. In: *Iris*, vol. 4, no. 1, 1986: 5-23, here 19ff.

46. For more on the birth of the historicist movement from the spirit of the avant-garde and the functional differentiation see chapter three on the film societies.

47. Freddy Chevalley: » Pour la defense du cinéma artistique «. In: *Close Up*, vol. 5, no. 4, October 1929: 304-306, here 305f. [» ...à La Sarraz c'est d'armement qu'il est question, armement rapide et minutieux, mobilisation générale de toutes les unités agissantes, préparation de plans de campagne définis en vue d'assurer au film artistique sa place au soleil et aux gourmets des salles obsures un régal, au moins, par semaine. «, my trans.]

48. See Christophe Gauthier: *La passion du cinéma. Cinéphiles, Ciné-Clubs et salles speciali-sées à Paris de 1920 à 1929.* Paris: École nationale de Chartres / AFRHC 1999 : 72-74 on the *Salon d'automne,* 74-76 on *L'art dans le cinéma français.* See also Richard Abel: *French Cinema: The First Wave, 1915-1929.* Princeton, NJ: Princeton University Press1984: 252f.

49. See Oliver Fahle: *Jenseits des Bildes. Poetik des französischen Films der zwanziger Jahre.* Mainz: Bender 2000.

50. See Wolfgang Mühl-Benninghaus: *Das Ringen um den Tonfilm. Strategien der Elektro- und Filmindustrie in den 20er und 30er Jahren.* Düsseldorf: Droste 1999: 207f.

51. For a production history of the film, see Andres Janser: » New Living: A Model Film? Hans Richter's Werkbund Film: Between Commissioned Work and Poetry on Film «. In: Andres Janser, Arthur Rüegg: *Hans Richter. New Living. Architecture. Film. Space.* Baden (CH): Lars Müller 2001.

52. On Vertov's film in the context of Constructivism, see Vlada Petrić: *Constructivism in Film; The Man with the Movie Camera. A Cinematic Analysis.* Cambridge et al.: Cambridge University Press 1987.

53. For an examination of the discourses surrounding hypnosis, the control of the body in relation to the cinema, especially CALIGARI, see Stefan Andriopoulos: *Besessene Körper. Hypnose, Körperschaften und die Erfindung des Kinos.* Munich: Wilhelm Fink 2000.

54. See, for the multiplicity of DAS CABINET DES DR. CALIGARI and an interpretation of the film along these lines, Thomas Elsaesser: » Caligari's Family: Expressionism, Frame Tales and Master-Narratives «. In: T.E.: *Weimar Cinema and After: Germany's Historical Imaginary.* London, New York: Routledge 2000: 61-105.

55. Rudolf Arnheim: » Dr. Caligari redivivus «. In: *Das Stachelschwein,* vol. 19, October 1925: 47-48. Reprinted in: R.A.: *Kritiken und Aufsätze zum Film.* (edited by Helmut H. Diederichs). Frankfurt am Main: Fischer 1979: 177f.

56. For a report on this exhibition, see *Close Up,* vol. 2, no. 5, May 1928: 75-77.

57. See Karel Dibbets: *Sprekende films. De komst van de geluidsfilm in Nederland 1928-1933.* Amsterdam: Cramwinckel 1993: 40-43.

58. A. Kraszna-Krausz: » Exhibition in Stuttgart, June, 1929, and Its Effects «. In: *Close Up,* vol. 5, no. 6, December 1929: 455-464, here 455.

59. For a description of the 1927-festival at Baden-Baden from the perspective of the mechanisation of sound synchronisation see Michael Wedel: » Vom Synchronismus zur Synchronisation. Carl Robert Blum und der frühe Tonfilm «. In: Joachim Polzer (ed.): *Aufstieg und Untergang des Tonfilms. Die Zukunft des Kinos: 24p?* Potsdam: Polzer 2002: 97-112, here 104f.

60. See Bradford Smith: » Hans Richter und das Baden-Badener Musikfestival «. In: Gehr, Hofacker, *Richter.* 1989: 24-29.

61. See, for a short description of the 1928 festival, Michael Wedel: » Vom Synchronis- mus zur Synchronisation. Carl Robert Blum und der frühe Tonfilm «. In: Joachim Polzer (ed.): *Aufstieg und Untergang des Tonfilms. Die Zukunft des Kinos: 24p?* Pots- dam: Polzer 2002: 105f.

62. For an archaeological overview of the 1929 program, see Hans-Christian von Herr- mann: » Psychotechnik versus Elektronik. Kunst und Medien beim Baden-Badener Kammermusikfest 1929 «. In: Andriopoulos, Stefan; Dotzler, Bernhard (eds.): *1929. Beiträge zur Archäologie der Medien.* Frankfurt am Main: Suhrkamp 2002: 253-267. See

also Sebastian Klotz: » Der Lindberghflug von Brecht • Hindemith • Weill (1929) als Rundfunkproblem «. In: Andriopoulos, Stefan; Dotzler, Bernhard (eds.): *1929. Beiträge zur Archäologie der Medien*. Frankfurt am Main: Suhrkamp 2002: 268-287.

63. See, for example, the frequent announcements and reports in the cinema trade press which would not have been interested in a specialised modernist music festival without its cross-over potential: *Lichtbild-Bühne*, vol. 22, no. 146, 20.6.1929; » Tonfilme auf der Baden-Badener Musikfestwoche «. In: *Lichtbild-Bühne*, vol. 22, no. 152, 27.6.1929; » Neue Tobis-Filme «. In: *Lichtbild-Bühne*, vol. 22, no. 163, 10.7.1929; » Erfolgreiche deutsche Musikfilme. Baden-Baden als Anreger. Musikfilme der Tobis zum Kammermusikfest «. In: *Film-Kurier*, vol. 11, no. 174, 24.7.1929; » Die Tonfilme für Baden-Baden. Eine Vorschau «. In: *Lichtbild-Bühne*, vol. 22, no. 178, 27.7.1929.

64. Hans Richter, lecture, p. 4. Manuscript in art historical archive Getty Center for the History of Art and Humanities, Los Angeles. Quoted by: Bradford Smith: » Hans Richter und das Baden-Badener Musikfestival «. In: Gehr, Hofacker, *Richter*. 1989: 26. [» besonders beachtenswert, daß die deutsche Tonfilm-Produktion, die Tobis, anläßlich der Baden-Badener Musikfestspiele am 25. Juli eine Anzahl von Tonfilmen vorbereitet hat, die dem Tonfilm als künstlerischem Problem gerecht werden. «, my trans.]

65. See for an account of the cooperation between director and composer Walter Gronostay: » Zum Kammer-Musikfest in Baden-Baden. Der Komponist kommentiert: Zur Musik des Tonfilms ALLES DREHT SICH, ALLES BEWEGT SICH «. In: *Film-Kurier*, vol. 11, no. 176, 26.7.1929.

66. Hans Richter: *Filmgegner von heute – Filmfreunde von morgen*. Berlin: Hermann Reckendorf 1929: 117. Quoted after the reprint Zürich: Hans Rohr 1968. (Filmwissenschaftliche Studientexte 2). [» Der Ton kann Geräusch, Klang oder gesprochenes Wort sein – aber sinnvoll wird er im Film erst dadurch, daß er seinen Platz in einem künstlerischen Gesamtplan erhält. «, my trans.]

67. A context for this exhibition with a discussion of the status of photography, of previous exhibitions and of the general discourse around photography is provided by Ute Eskildsen: » Fotokunst statt Kunstphotographie. Die Durchsetzung des fotografischen Mediums in Deutschland 1920-1933 «. In: Ute Eskildsen, Jan-Christopher Horak (eds.): *Film und Foto der Zwanziger Jahre*. Stuttgart: Gerd Hatje 1979: 8-25.

68. See » Film und Photo [sic] Stuttgart 1929. Zur kommenden Werkbund-Ausstellung «. In: *Lichtbild-Bühne*, vol. 22, no. 42, 19.2.1929; announcement in *Close Up*, vol. 4, no. 2, February 1929: 93f.; » Film und Foto Stuttgart «. In: *Kinematograph*, vol. 23, no. 53, 4.3.1929; » Das Ausland und › Film und Foto ‹. Die Stuttgarter Werkbundausstellung «. In: *Lichtbild-Bühne*, vol. 22, no. 57, 8.3.1929; hs.: » Ausland und Ausstellung › Film und Photo [sic] ‹ «. In: *Lichtbild-Bühne*, vol. 22, no. 91, 17.4.1929; anon.: » The Stuttgart exhibition «. In: *Close Up*, vol. 4, no. 4, April 1929: 40-41.

69. See for contemporary reports ha.: » Film und Photo [sic] Stuttgart 1929. Eröffnung der Internationalen Werkbund-Ausstellung «. In: *Lichtbildbühne*, vol. 22, no. 119/120, 19.5.1929; anon.: » Ausstellung › Film und Photo ‹ [sic] in Stuttgart eröffnet «. In: *Film-Kurier*, vol. 11, no. 120, 21.5.1929; ha: » Stärkstes Interesse für Film und Foto «. In: *Lichtbildbühne*, vol. 22, no. 131, 3.6.1929; A. [=Andor] Kraszna-Krausz: » Exhibition in Stuttgart, June, 1929, and Its Effects «. In: *Close Up*, vol. 5, no. 6, December 1929: 455-464.

70. See the catalogue *Internationale Ausstellung des Deutschen Werkbunds Film und Foto*. Stuttgart 1929. (Reprint Stuttgart 1979). See also the reconstruction Ute Eskildsen, Jan-Christopher Horak (eds.): *Film und Foto der Zwanziger Jahre*. Stuttgart: Gerd Hatje 1979 and Inka Graeve: » Internationale Ausstellung des Deutschen Werkbunds Film und Foto «. In: Michael Bollé, Eva Züchner, Gesine Asmus (eds.): *Stationen der Moderne. Die bedeutenden Kunstausstellungen des 20. Jahrhunderts in Deutschland*. Berlin: Berlinische Galerie / Nicolai 1988: 236-273.

71. For the program, see wh.: » Die Stuttgarter Sondervorführungen der Werkbundausstellung Film und Photo [*sic*] «. In: *Lichtbildbühne*, vol. 22, no. 145, 19.6.1929 and ad.: » Die Avantgarde im Stuttgarter Programm. Donnerstag – Beginn der Filmschau «. In: *Film-Kurier*, vol. 11, no. 139, 13.6.1929.

72. See the annotated reconstruction of the film program in Helma Schleif (ed.): *Stationen der Moderne im Film I: FiFo – Film- und Fotoausstellung Stuttgart 1929*. Berlin: Freunde der Deutschen Kinemathek 1988.

73. Jan-Christopher Horak: » Entwicklung einer visuellen Sprache im Stummfilm «. In: Ute Eskildsen, Jan-Christopher Horak (eds.): *Film und Foto der Zwanziger Jahre. Eine Betrachtung der Internationalen Werkbundausstellung » Film und Foto « 1929*. Stuttgart: Gerd Hatje 1979: 38-60, here 49.

74. See *Film-Kurier*, vol. 11, no. 136, 10.6.1929. For a summary of the opening speeches see Rudolf Schand: » Film und Foto: Ehrentage des stummen Films «. In: *Film-Kurier*, vol. 11, no. 141, 15.6.1929.

75. See » › Avantgarde ‹ in Stuttgart «. In: *Lichtbild-Bühne*, vol. 22, no. 147, 21.6.1929.

76. See, for an example from Munich, glk.: » Die Avantgardisten in München «. In: *Lichtbild-Bühne*, vol. 22, no. 197, 19.8.1929; Walter Jerven: » Vorführung der Münchner Filmfestwochen: Avant-Garde-Filme «. In: *Film-Kurier*, vol. 11, no. 193, 15.8.1929.

77. See » Film, Photo, Filmphoto «. In: *Lichtbild-Bühne*, vol. 22, no. 263, 4.11.1929.

78. See » Stuttgarter › Film und Foto ‹-Ausstellung in Berlin «. In: *Lichtbild-Bühne*, vol. 22, no. 238, 5.10.1929.

79. See » › Der gute Film ‹ «. In: *Lichtbild-Bühne*, vol. 22, no. 247, 16.10.1929 and » Berliner Sondervorführung guter Filme «. In: *Film-Kurier*, vol. 11, no. 241, 10.10.1929.

80. On accounts and documentation of the La Sarraz meeting see Freddy Buache: » Le cinéma indépendant et d'avant-garde à la fin du muet «. In: *Travelling. Cahiers de la Cinémathèque Suisse*, no. 55, (été 1979) and no. 56/57, (printemps 1980); Roland Cosandey and Thomas Tode: » Le 1er congrès international du cinéma indépendant. La Sarraz, Septembre 1929 «. In: *Archives, Perpignan*, no. 84 (April 2000): 1-30; and Helma Schleif: *Stationen der Moderne im Film. II. Texte, Manifeste, Pamphlete*. Berlin: Freunde der Kinemathek 1989: 200-219; a detailed bibliography can be found in Thomas Tode: » Auswahlbibliographie zu La Sarraz «. In: *Filmblatt*, no. 11, autumn 1999, 31-33.

81. For cautious evaluations from the film trade press see anon.: » Filmtagung in der Schweiz. Ein bedeutsames Meeting «. In: *Film-Kurier*, vol. 11, no. 206, 30.8.1929 and Paul Medina: » Das Fazit der Schweizer Filmtagung «. In: *Film-Kurier*, vol. 11, no. 219, 14.9.1929.

82. For an account concentrating on Ruttmann's trajectory see Thomas Elsaesser, Malte Hagener: » Walter Ruttmann: 1929 «. In: Stefan Andriopoulos, Bernhard Dotzler

(eds.): *1929. Beiträge zur Archäologie der Medien*. Frankfurt am Main: Suhrkamp 2002: 317-349.

83. See Jean Lenauer: » The Independent Cinema Congress «. In: *Close Up*, vol. 5, no. 4, October 1929: 306-308; see also Freddy Chevalley: » Pour la defense du cinéma artistique «. In: *Close Up*, vol. 5, no. 4, October 1929: 304-306.

84. See » Bemerkenswerte Tagung. Die Avantgarde in Brüssel. Der 2. Kongreß des Cinéma Indépendant «. In: *Film-Kurier*, vol. 12, no. 243, 14.10.1930.

85. For a detailed account of the Brussels meeting see Laura Vichi: » Un point de départ: le Congrès international du cinéma indépendant de Bruxelles «. In: Laura Vichi: *Henri Storck. De l'avant-garde au documentaire social*. Crisnée (BE): Éditions Yellow Now 2002: 11–21.

86. See » Die Avantgarde tagt in Brüssel. Bemerkenswerte Filmvorführungen «. In: *Film-Kurier*, vol. 12, no. 283, 1.12.1930. Originally from Germany also Béla Balázs and G. W. Pabst were invited. See » Die Avantgarde. Deutschlands Vertreter auf dem Brüsseler Kongreß «. In: *Film-Kurier*, vol. 12, no. 256, 29.10.1930.

87. See » 1931: Kongreß der Avantgarde. In Berlin Maitagung der Filmkünstler «. In: *Film-Kurier*, vol. 12, no. 304, 27.12.1930.

88. This exchange was triggered by Béla Balázs' talk at an association of cameramen in Berlin on 9 June 1926. The text was published as » Produktive und reproduktive Filmkunst «. In: *Filmtechnik*, no. 12, 12.6.1926: 234f. Reprinted in B.B.: *Schriften zum Film. Vol. 2: Der Geist des Films. Kritiken und Aufsätze 1926-1931*. (edited by Helmut H. Diederichs and Wolfgang Gersch). Munich / Berlin (Ost) / Budapest: Hanser / Henschel / Akademie 1984. The article was translated into Russian as » O budushchem fil'my «. In: *Kino*, 6.7.1926. Sergei Eisenstein responded polemically to Balázs' contention that the cameraman was the most important part in the film production process. His response was published in two parts as » O pozitsii Bela Balasha «. In: *Kino*, 20.7.1926 and » Bela zabyvaet nozhnitsy «. In: *Kino*, 16.8.1926. In German published as: » Béla vergisst die Schere «. Reprinted in Helmut H. Diederichs (ed.): *Geschichte der Filmtheorie. Kunsttheoretische Texte von Méliès bis Arnheim*. Frankfurt am Main: Suhrkamp 2004: 257-264.

89. See S. Kracauer: » Wir schaffens «. In: *Frankfurter Zeitung*, no. 856, 17.11.1927. Reprinted in S.K.: *Werke 6.1. Kleine Schriften zum Film 1921-1927*. Frankfurt am Main: Suhrkamp 2004: 411-413; S. Kracauer: » Tonbildfilm. Zur Vorführung im Frankfurter Gloria-Palast «. In: *Frankfurter Zeitung*, no. 766, 12.10.1928. Reprinted in S.K.: *Werke 6.2. Kleine Schriften zum Film 1928-1931*. Frankfurt am Main: Suhrkamp 2004: 122-125; see also Siegfried Kracauer: *Von Caligari zu Hitler. Eine psychologische Geschichte des deutschen Films*. Frankfurt am Main: Suhrkamp 1979: 192-198; see also for a more general criticism of the avant-garde Siegfried Kracauer: *Theorie des Films. Die Errettung der äußeren Wirklichkeit*. Frankfurt am Main 1985: 237-258.

90. S. Kracauer: » Der Mann mit dem Kinoapparat. Ein neuer russischer Film «. In: *Frankfurter Zeitung*, no. 369, 19.5.1929. Reprinted in S.K.: *Werke 6.2. Kleine Schriften zum Film 1928-1931*. Frankfurt am Main: Suhrkamp 2004: 247-251, here 248. [» Während aber seine [Ruttmanns, MH] Assoziationen rein formal sind – er scheint sich auch in seinen Tonbildfilmen mit äußerlichen, unerhellten Verknüpfungen zu begnügen –, gewinnt Wertow [sic] durch die Montage dem Zusammenhang der Wirklichkeitssplitter einen Sinn ab. Ruttmann gibt ein Nebeneinander, ohne es aufzuklären; Wertow interpretiert es, indem er es darstellt. «, my trans.]

91. I have presented these internal contradictions of the avant-garde in more detail in part 2.1 *The Aporias of the Avant-garde.*

92. See chapter six on the intersection of the documentary and the avant-garde with state institutions for further details.

93. Laura Vichi: *Henri Storck. De l'avant-garde au documentaire social.* Crisnée (BE): Éditions Yellow Now 2002: 181. [» [L]a présence de Germaine Dulac, directrice d'une des plus grandes maisons de production françaises, Gaumont-Franco-Film-Aubert (GFFA), qui soutint la génération des cinéastes des années trente, était emblématique de la jonction avec le cinéma commercial. C'est là [à Bruxelles, MH], en effet, qu'elle recrute Vigo pour la réalisation de TARIS (1931) ainsi que [Henri] Storck, choisi comme assistant de Pierre Billon au Studio des Buttes-Chaumont. «, my trans.]

94. Rudolf Arnheim: »Kino von hinten«. In: *Das Stachelschwein,* no. 6, 1.6.1927: 63. Quoted after Rudolf Arnheim: *Kritiken und Aufsätze zum Film.* (Edited by Helmut H. Diederichs). Frankfurt am Main: Fischer 1979: 309. [» [D]ie Modernsten haben uns ja schon angedroht, nächstens mit Scheinwerfern reflektorische Spiele an den Himmel zu werfen, statt zu malen und zu zeichnen. Dieser Lichtkegel ist vielleicht ein graphisches Blatt aus dem Buche der zukünftigen Kunstgeschichte. «, my trans.]

95. See, as an early example of this approach the curious mixture of illustrations, scientific study, and adventure serial, C.W. Ceram: *Eine Archäologie des Kinos.* Reinbek: Rowohlt 1965.

96. André Bazin: » Le mythe du cinéma total «. In: André Bazin: *Qu'est-ce que le cinéma? I: Ontologie et Langage.* Paris: Les éditions du Cerf 1958. (7e art): 21-26, here 25. [» C'est celui du réalisme intégral, d'une recréation du monde à son image, une image sur laquelle ne péserait pas l'hypothèque de la liberté d'interprétation de l'artiste ni l'irreversibilité du temps. Si le cinéma au berceau n'eut pas tous les attributs du cinéma total de demain, ce fut donc bien à son corps défendant et seulement parce que ses fées étaient techniquement impuissantes à l'en doter en dépit de leurs désirs. «, my trans.]

97. See part two of Miriam Hansen: *Babel and Babylon: Spectatorship in American Silent Film.* Cambridge, MA: Harvard University Press 1991: 127-241.

98. Valérie Peseux: *Abel Gance (1889-1981). L'innovation artistique et technique du › triptyque ‹, de la › perspective sonore ‹ et de la Polyvision.* Perpignan: Institut Jean Vigo 2001. (Archives 87 – April 2001): 2. [» Dès cette epoque j'avais compris la nécessité de s'évader des limites ordinaires de l'écran. Le cinéma muet était arrivé aux limites extrêmes de ses enseignements. Pour ma part, j'essayais de les dépasser. ... Le triptyque avait le mérite d'enrichir l'alphabet. «, my trans.]

99. Jean Mauclaire: » Studio 28 «. In: *Photo-Ciné,* no. 10, Jan. 1928: n.p. [» La véritable raison du Studio 28 étant d'être un laboratoire du film, il ne comportera pas un orchestre animé de mouvements ascensionnels, une seule chose importe: la cabine de projection photographique, et l'écran, qui d'une seule pièce, s'étendra sur neuf mètres de largeur formant une vaste fresque murale au fond de la salle. ... Le Studio 28 est donc la seule salle à Paris où une cabine triptyque est installée d'une manière permanente et toutes les recherches faites sur cette invention y seront poursuivies par l'inventeur même: Abel Gance. «, my trans.]

100. See Bert Hogenkamp: » J.C. Mol en Multifilm: wetenschap – film – bedrijf «. In: B.H.: *De Nederlandse documentaire film 1920-1940*. Utrecht: Audiovisueel Archief van de Stichting Film en Wetenschap / Amsterdam: Van Gennep 1988: 96-108, here 97.
101. Jean Mauclaire: » Studio 28 «. In: *Photo-Ciné*, no. 10, Jan. 1928: n.p. [» Les possibilités du triptyque sont plus vastes encore, permettant l'orchestration des images, le triptyque tuera l'orchestre. Aussi n'emploierons-nous qu'une musique mécanique, concession nécessaire pour préparer la transition trop brusque. Mais un jour très proche les salles ne posséderont qu'un écran et qu'une cabine. Le cinéma suffit à lui-même. Le cinéma est une force qui se rit de ses adversaires. «, my trans.]
102. See chapter five on the visits of Soviet filmmakers to the West.
103. Hans Richter: *Köpfe und Hinterköpfe*. Zürich: Verlag Die Arche 1967: 159. [» Wir besuchten gemeinsam die Premiere von Abel Gances NAPOLÉON im Ufapalast am Zoo. So deprimierend und dumm der Monsterfilm METROPOLIS vorher an derselben Stelle ausgesehen hatte, so großartig und intelligent offenbarte sich NAPOLÉON. «]
104. Ibid.: 160. [» Was ich machen möchte? Einen Film in Schnee und Eis, aber nicht nur auf drei Leinwände vorn auf der Bühne, sondern überall projizierend. An der Decke, an den Seiten und selbst im Rücken des Publikums. Es soll mit dem Helden frieren und sich mit ihm am Feuer wärmen, während draußen die hungrigen Wölfe um uns immer engere Kreise ziehen. Die rohen, gefrorenen Fische zerreißen wir mit den Zähnen, und die erfrorenen Gesichter werden mit Schnee abgerieben. Das Publikum zittert, friert, kommt wieder zu sich, fühlt sich, fast erfroren, als Held. «, my trans.]
105. Steven Philip Kramer, James Michael Walsh: *Abel Gance*. Boston: Twayne 1978. (Twayne's Theatrical Arts Series): 67.
106. An interesting case of comparison would be HIGH TREASON (GB 1929, Maurice Elvey) in terms of content as well as its position between silent and sound cinema. The film deals with attempts by women's groups to disarm nations. It was shot as a silent film and – during the transition – sound was added to increase the market value of the film. See Kenton Bamford: *Distorted Images: British National Identity and Film in the 1920s*. London, New York: I.B. Tauris 1999: 169.
107. A special number of *Archives* is devoted to these technical experiments of Gance. See Valérie Peseux: *Abel Gance (1889-1981). L'innovation artistique et technique du › triptyque ‹, de la › perspective sonore ‹ et de la Polyvision*. Perpignan: Institut Jean Vigo 2001. (Archives 87 – Avril 2001).
108. For a genealogy of Imax in popular cinema (wide-screen, 3-D), see Tana Wollen: » The Bigger the Better. From CinemaScope to Imax «. In: Philip Hayward, Tana Wollen (eds.): *Future Visions: New Technologies of the Screen*. London: BFI Publishing 1993: 10-30. For more recent contextualisations of ride films and surround systems, see Constance Balides: » Immersion in the Virtual Ornament: Contemporary › Movie Ride ‹ Films « and Angela Ndalianis: » Architectures of the Senses: Neo-Baroque Entertainment Spectacles «. Both in David Thorburn, Henry Jenkins (eds.): *Rethinking Media Change: The Aesthetics of Transition*. Cambridge, MA, London: The MIT Press 2003: 315-336 and 355-373.
109. The relationship between auditorium space and screen space could form a basis for a rewriting of film history, which would factor in many contextual factors that are

ignored by classical film theory. See Thomas Elsaesser: *Filmgeschichte und frühes Kino. Archäologie eines Medienwandels*. Munich: edition text + kritik 2002: passim.

110. Peter Wollen: » Viking Eggeling «. In: P.W.: *Paris Hollywood: Writings on Film*. London, New York: Verso 2002: 39-54, here 53.

111. See, for an overview of international developments, Sara Selwood: » Farblichtmusik und abstrakter Film «. In: Karin v. Maur (Hrsg.): *Vom Klang der Bilder. Die Musik in der Kunst des 20. Jahrhunderts*. Munich: Prestel 1985: 414-421. For a detailed account of this strand of the avant-garde, yet limited to the German situation see Anne Hoormann: *Lichtspiele. Zur Medienreflexion der Avantgarde in der Weimarer Republik*. Munich: Wilhelm Fink 2003.

112. Malcolm Le Grice: » German Abstract Film in the Twenties «. In: Philip Drummond et al. (Eds.): *Film as Film; Formal Experiment in Film 1910-1975*. London: Hayward Gallery 1979: 30-35, here 30.

113. Alexander László: *Die Farblichtmusik*. Leipzig: Breitkopf & Härtel 1925.

114. See for a contemporary overview Adrian Bernard Klein: *Colour Music: The Art of Light*. London: Lockwood 1926.

115. William Moritz: » Oskar Fischinger «. In: Herbert Gehr (ed.): *Optische Poesie. Oskar Fischinger – Leben und Werk*. Frankfurt am Main: Deutsches Filmmuseum 1993. (Kinematograph 9): 7-80, here 13.

116. Esther Leslie: *Hollywood Flatlands. Animation, Critical Theory and the Avant-Garde*. London, New York: Verso 2002: 283.

117. See R.C. Dale: *The Films of René Clair: 2 Vols. I: Exposition and Analysis. II: Documentation*. Metuchen, NJ, London: Scarecrow Press 1986: 29-42 (vol. I), 22-27 (vol. II).

118. See, for a contemporary account, E. Goldey: » Le film dans les mises en scène d'Erwin Piscator «. In: *La revue du cinéma*, vol. 2, no. 7, 1. February 1930: 47-58.

119. See Thomas Tode: entry » Erwin Piscator «. In: Hans-Michael Bock (ed.): *CineGraph. Lexikon zum deutschsprachigen Film*. Munich: edition text + kritik 1984ff.: installment 33, 15.5.2000.

120. See, for a contemporary overview, E. Hellmund-Waldow: » Combinaison le film et la scène «. In: *Close Up*, vol. 2, no. 4, April 1928: 23-30.

121. For a geneaology of this development from a formalist perspective, see Wulf Herzogenrath: » Light-play and Kinetic Theatre as Parallels to Absolute Film «. In: Philip Drummond et al. (Eds.): *Film as Film: Formal Experiment in Film 1910-1975*. London: Hayward Gallery 1979: 22-26.

122. Gene Youngblood: *Expanded Cinema*. London: Studio Vista 1970.

123. For Bill Nichols LICHTSPIEL: SCHWARZ WEISS GRAU falls into the category of the » poetic documentary «. See Bill Nichols: *Introduction to Documentary*. Bloomington and Indianapolis: Indiana University Press 2002: 103.

124. For an interpretation of Moholy-Nagy as a constructivist see Jan-Christopher Horak: » László Moholy-Nagy: The Constructivist Urge «. In Jan-Christopher Horak: *Making Images Move. Photographers and the Avant-Garde Cinema*. Washington, DC and London: Smithsonian Institution Press 1997: 109-135.

125. André Bazin: » Le mythe du cinéma total «. In: André Bazin: *Qu'est-ce que le cinéma? I: Ontologie et Langage*. Paris: Les éditions du Cerf 1958. (7e art): 21-26, here 26. [» Les fanatiques, les maniaques, les pionniers désintéressés, capables comme Bernard Palissy de brûler leurs meubles pour quelques secondes d'images tremblotantes, ne sont ni des industriels ni des savants mais des possédés de leur imagination. Si le

cinéma est né, c'est de la convergence de leur obsession; c'est-à-dire d'un mythe, celui du cinéma total. «, my trans.]

126. Loren Cocking: » Ever-Expanding Cinema: The Films of Alexander Hammid and Francis Thompson «. In: Michael Omasta (ed.): *Tribute to Sasha. Das filmische Werk von Alexander Hammid. Regie, Kamera, Schnitt und Kritiker*. Wien: Synema 2002 : 99-116.

127. Peter Bürger: *Theorie der Avantgarde*. Frankfurt am Main: Suhrkamp 1974: 35. [» Das Zusammenfallen von Institution und Gehalten enthüllt die gesellschaftliche Funktionslosigkeit als Wesen der Kunst in der bürgerlichen Gesellschaft und fordert damit die Selbstkritik der Kunst heraus. Es ist das Verdienst der historischen Avantgarde- bewegungen, diese Selbstkritik praktisch geleistet zu haben. «, my trans.]

Notes Chapter 5

1. Michael Hardt, Antonio Negri: *Empire*. Cambridge, MA and London: Harvard University Press 2000: 176.

2. Boris Groys: » The Birth of Socialist Realism from the Spirit of the Russian Avant-Garde «. In: John E. Bowlt, Olga Matich (eds.): *Laboratory of Dreams: The Russian Avant-garde and Cultural Experiment*. Stanford, CA: Stanford University Press 1996: 193-218, here 210.

3. Josef von Sternberg: *Fun in a Chinese Laundry*. San Francisco, CA: Mercury House 1988 (1965): 319.

4. The best overview of these internal debates can be found in Denise J. Youngblood: *Soviet Cinema in the Silent Era, 1918-1935*. Ann Arbor, MI: UMI Research Press 1985: passim. The entertainment-enlightenment question is treated in more detail in chapter 2 of Denise J. Youngblood: *Movies for the Masses: Popular Cinema and Soviet Society in the 1920s*. Cambridge: Cambridge University Press 1992: 35-49.

5. For a discussion on the distinction between the acted vs. the non-acted film as a basic category of Soviet film culture, see » Sergei Eisenstein vs. Dziga Vertov «. In: *Skrien*, no. 33, March/April 1973: 3-9.

6. Jay Leyda: *Kino: A History of the Russian and Soviet Film*. London: George Allen Cinema and Soviet Society, 1917-1953. *Cambridge: Cambridge University Press 1992: 32.*

8. For more on the so-called » Cibrario affair « and the early years of the re-organisation of the Soviet film industry, see Jay Leyda: *Kino: A History of the Russian and Soviet Film*. London: George Allen The Red Screen: Politics, Society, Art in Soviet Cinema. *London, New York: Routledge 1992: 19-41.*

9. Jekaterina Chochlowa: » Es gibt ein Land Film, die Bewohner sind Deutsche. Deutsche Filme in Sowjetrußland «. In: Oksana Bulgakowa (ed.): *Die ungewöhnlichen Abenteuer des Dr. Mabuse im Lande der Bolschewiki. Das Buch zur Filmreihe » Moskau – Berlin «*. Berlin: Freunde der Deutschen Kinemathek 1995: 159-164, here 159. See also Kristin Thompson: » Government Policies and Practical Necessities in the Soviet Cinema of the 1920s «. In: Anna Lawton (ed.): *The Red Screen: Politics, Society, Art in Soviet Cinema*. London, New York: Routledge 1992: 19-41.

10. On the circulation of foreign films in 1920s Russia, see Vance Kepley and Jr., Betty Kepley: » Foreign Films on Soviet Screens, 1921-1935 «. In: *Quarterly Review of Film Studies*, vol. 4, no. 4, Fall 1979: 429-442.

11. See Peter Kenez: *Cinema and Soviet Society, 1917-1953*. Cambridge: Cambridge University Press 1992: 72.

12. On the development of the Soviet industry from the Revolution until the end of the NEP see Vance Kepley, Jr.: » The origins of Soviet cinema: a study in industry development «. In: Richard Taylor, Ian Christie (eds.): *Inside the Film Factory: New Approaches to Russian and Soviet Cinema*. London and New York: Routledge 1991: 60-79.

13. The NEP also had the more immediate effect of starting up all the various sectors of the film industry. On the development of the cinema sector under NEP see the chapter » Reconstruction « in Jay Leyda: *Kino: A History of the Russian and Soviet Film*. London: George Allen & Unwin 1960: 155-169.

14. For a detailed account of this crucial period in Soviet film history see Eberhard Nembach: *Stalins Filmpolitik. Der Umbau der sowjetischen Filmindustrie 1929 bis 1938*. St. Augustin: Gardez! Verlag 2001. (Filmstudien 17).

15. See chapter two on the aporias of the avant-garde for a detailed discussion.

16. Peter Kenez: *Cinema and Soviet Society, 1917–1953*. Cambridge: Cambridge University Press 1992: 78.

17. Victor Skhlovski: » Po powodu kartiny Esfir Schub «. In: *Lef*, no. 8-9, 1927: 32-54, here 53. [reprinted in and quoted after Janina Urussowa: *Das neue Moskau. Die Stadt der Sowjets im Film 1917-1941*. Köln, Weimar, Wien: Böhlau 2004: 26.] [» Die Sache ist die, dass damals der Sozialismus als ein Vorschuss verwirklicht wurde. Die Luft der Freiheit und nicht die Notwendigkeit, eine paradoxe Vorahnung der Zukunft ersetzte damals in Piter das Fett, das Brennholz und war die Atmosphäre überhaupt. ... Wir flogen auf einer eisernen Kugel aus der Vergangenheit in die Zukunft – und die Gravitation existierte nicht mehr, wie in der Kugel von Jules Verne. «, my trans.]

18. Janina Urussowa: *Das neue Moskau. Die Stadt der Sowjets im Film 1917-1941*. Köln, Weimar, Wien: Böhlau 2004: 28. [» Die gleichzeitige Präsenz der Vergangenheit und der Zukunft im heimatlosen Alltag der jungen sowjetischen Gesellschaft war für das erste postrevolutionäre Jahrzehnt charakteristisch... «, my trans.]

19. See chapter 4 on the discourses of the avant-garde.

20. See François Albera: » Formzerstörung und Transparenz – Glass House, vom Filmprojekt zum Film als Projekt «. In: Oksana Bulgakowa (ed.): *Eisenstein und Deutschland. Texte – Dokumente – Briefe*. Berlin: Akademie der Künste / Henschel 1998: 123-142.

21. Jay Leyda: *Kino: A History of the Russian and Soviet Film*. London: George Allen & Unwin 1960: 175.

22. A good account of the re-editing practice for home distribution, but also for export is Yuri Tsivian: » The Wise and Wicked Game: Re-editing and Soviet Film Culture of the 1920s «. In: *Film History*, vol. 8, no. 3, 1996: 327-343.

23. On this work see Jekatarina Chochlowa: » Die erste Filmarbeit Sergej Eisensteins. Die Ummontage des › Dr. Mabuse, der Spieler ‹ von Fritz Lang «. In: Oksana Bulgakowa: *Eisenstein und Deutschland. Texte – Dokumente – Briefe*. Berlin: Akademie der Künste / Henschel 1998: 115-122.

24. Yuri Tsivian: » The Wise and Wicked Game: Re-editing and Soviet Film Culture of the 1920s «. In: *Film History*, vol. 8, no. 3, 1996: 336.

25. For the FEKS-strategies borrowed from popular culture see Oksana Bulgakowa: » Das Phänomen FEKS: › Boulevardisierung ‹ der Avantgarde «. In: *montage/AV*, vol. 2, no. 1, 1993: 94-115. On FEKS in general see Bernadette Poliwoda: *FEKS – Fabrik des exzentrischen Schauspielers. Vom Exzentrismus zur Poetik des Films in der frühen Sowjetkultur.* München: Verlag Otto Sagner 1994 and Oksana Bulgakowa: *FEKS. Die Fabrik des exzentrischen Schauspielers.* Berlin: PotemkinPress 1996.

26. For the significance of the music hall to the Italian and Russian futurists as well as some relationships between classical avant-garde and popular entertainment media see Wanda Strauven: » The Meaning of the Music-Hall: From the Italian Futurism to the Soviet Avant-garde «. In: *Cinéma , no. 4, Spring 2004: 119-134.*

27. See the examples in Evgenij Margolit: » Der sowjetische Stummfilm und der frühe Tonfilm «. In: Christine Engel (ed.): *Geschichte des sowjetischen und russischen Films.* Stuttgart, Weimar: Metzler 1999: 17-67, here 23f.

28. Boris Groys: *Gesamtkunstwerk Stalin. Die gespaltene Kultur in der Sowjetunion.* München, Wien: Carl Hanser 1988: 8. [» Die Neuorganisation der Welt nach ästhetischen Prinzipien ist im Westen mehrfach vorgeschlagen und sogar erprobt worden, zum erstenmal wirklich gelungen ist sie jedoch in Rußland. «, my trans.]

29. In one of these discussions in the intellectual magazine *Novij Lef* Vertov's films were stigmatised as » acted « and compared unfavourably to Esfir Shub's compilation films. See the documents in Ian Christie, Richard Taylor (eds.): *The Film Factory: Russian and Soviet Cinema in Documents, 1896-1939.* London: Routledge & Kegan Paul 1988. See also my discussion of Shub below.

30. Denise J. Youngblood: *Soviet Cinema in the Silent Era, 1918-1935.* Ann Arbor, MI: UMI Research Press 1985: XIIIf.

31. An account of the making of these films can be found in the chapter » Anniversary Year « in Jay Leyda: *Kino: A History of the Russian and Soviet Film.* London: George Allen October. *London: British Film Institute 2002.*

32. One could see a large part of the cinema policy of the Soviet government up to the early 1930s as an attempt at » nation building « in the sense that Benedict Anderson has used it. See B.A. *Imagined Communities: Reflections on the Origin and Spread of Nationalism.* London: Verso 1983.

33. Of course it is possible to group the films of the 1920s into genres as has been done for example by Denise J. Youngblood: *Movies for the Masses: Popular Cinema and So-viet Society in the 1920s.* Cambridge: Cambridge University Press 1992: 33. Even she, however, has had to include » revolutionary « as a genre (she sees it as a substitute for the action-adventure film of the Western cinema) to accommodate those films that do not fit into other categories. According to Youngblood, the » revolutionary « genre accounts for 17-20% of the Soviet production 1924-29, and 11-14% in the period 1930-33.

34. See Erik Barnouw: *Documentary: A History of the Non-Fiction Film.* Oxford: Oxford University Press 19932: 66f.

35. Erik Barnouw: *Documentary: A History of the Non-Fiction Film.* Oxford: Oxford University Press 19932: 69ff.

36. See my chapter on the documentary for the codification of this genre.

37. See for Vertov's formative years (1917-25) Seth R. Feldman: *Evolution of Style in the Early Works of Dziga Vertov with a New Appendix.* New York: Arno Press 1977.

38. Annette Michelson: » The Kinetic Icon and the Work of Mourning: Prolegomena to the Analysis of a Textual System «. In: Anna Lawton (ed.): *The Red Screen: Politics, Society, Art in Soviet Cinema*. London, New York: Routledge 1992: 113-131.

39. See chapter two on the aporias of the avant-garde for a discussion of the question around in/dependence.

40. See chapter three on the distribution and exhibition network for a more detailed account.

41. Peter Kenez: *Cinema and Soviet Society, 1917-1953*. Cambridge: Cambridge University Press 1992: 54.

42. See Walter Ruttmann: » Der isolierte Künstler «. In: *Filmtechnik*, 25.5.1929. Reprinted in Jeanpaul Goergen: *Walter Ruttmann. Eine Dokumentation*. Berlin West: Freunde der Deutschen Kinemathek 1989: 85f. See chapter two for a discussion of this text.

43. Walter Benjamin: » Der Erzähler «. In: W.B.: *Gesammelte Schriften. Vol. II.2*. Frankfurt am Main: Suhrkamp 1977: 438-465, here 451. (first published 1936). [» Jedwede Untersuchung einer bestimmten epischen Form hat es mit dem Verhältnis zu tun, in dem diese Form zur Geschichtsschreibung steht. «, trans. Harry Zohn, *Illuminations*: 95]

44. Vlada Petrić: » Esther Shub: Cinema Is My Life «. In: *Quarterly Review of Film Studies*, vol. 3, no. 4, Fall 1978: 430.

45. Esfir Shub: *Krupnym planom*. Moscow 1959: 90f. Translated in and quoted after Jay Leyda: *Films Beget Films. Compilation Films from Propaganda to Drama*. London: George Allen & Unwin 1964: 24.

46. For a contemporary account of this style of filmmaking see A. [=Andor] Kraszna-Krausz: » The Querschnittsfilm «. In: *Close Up*, vol. 3, no. 5, November 1928: 25-34.

47. Esfir Shub: » LEF i kino. Stenogramma soveshchaniya «. In: *Novyi Lef*, no. 11/12, November/December 1927, 58-59. Translated in and quoted in Taylor, Christie (eds.), *Film Factory*, op. cit.: 185f.

48. See Regine Halter: » Esther Schub: Ihre Bedeutung für die Entwicklung des Dokumentarfilms «. In: *Frauen , no. 9, Oktober 1976: 34-44, here 36*.

49. Dziga Vertov: » V poryadke predlozheniya. « In: *Pravda*, 24.July 1926, 6. Translated in and quoted after Taylor, Christie (eds.), *Film Factory*, op. cit.: 150f.

50. Esfir Shub: » Fabrikatsiya faktov «. (The Manufacture of Facts) In: *Kino*, no. 41, 1926. Translated in and quoted after Taylor, Christie (eds.), *Film Factory*, op. cit.: 152.

51. Viktor Shklovsky: » Kuda shagaet Dziga Vertov? « (» Where is Dziga Vertov Striding? «). In: Taylor, Christie, *Film Factory*, op. cit.: 151f.

52. Mikhail Yampolsky: » Reality at Second Hand «. In: Historical Journal of Film, Radio and Television, vol. 11, no. 2, 1991: 161-171, here 164.

53. Mikhail Yampolsky: » Reality at Second Hand «. In: Historical Journal of Film, Radio and Television, vol. 11, no. 2, 1991: 161-171, here 165.

54. For the » angel of history « see Walter Benjamin: » Über den Begriff der Geschichte «. In: W.B.: *Gesammelte Schriften. I.2*. Frankfurt am Main: Suhrkamp 1977: 691-704; for a discussion of the image in relation to the avant-garde see part 1.6.

55. Walter Benjamin: » Zur Lage der russischen Filmkunst «. In: W.B.: *Gesammelte Schriften II.2*. Frankfurt am Main 1977: 747-751, here 747. [» Die Spitzenleistungen der russischen Filmindustrie bekommt man in Berlin bequemer zu sehen als in Moskau. «, my trans.]

56. See Helmut Kresse: » Internationale Arbeiterhilfe und Film in der Weimarer Republik «. In: Horst Knietzsch (ed.): *Prisma 7. Film- und Fernseh-Almanach*. Berlin/DDR: Henschel 1976: 240-261, here 240.

57. Jay Leyda: *Kino: A History of the Russian and Soviet Film*. London: George Allen & Unwin 1960: 157.

58. For the activities of the IAH and Soviet films circulating in Germany and Europe, see Helmut Kresse: » Internationale Arbeiterhilfe und Film in der Weimarer Republik «. In: Horst Knietzsch (ed.): *Prisma 7. Film- und Fernseh-Almanach*. Berlin/DDR: Henschel 1976: 240-261; David Welsh: » The Proletarian Cinema and the Weimar Republic «. In: *Historical Journal of Film, Radio and Television*, vol. 1, no. 1, March 1981: 3-18; Vance Kepley, Jr.: » The Workers' International Relief and the Cinema of the Left 1921-1935 «. In: *Cinema Journal*, vol. 23, no. 1, Fall 1983: 7-23; Denise Hartsough: » Soviet Film Distribution and Exhibition in Germany, 1921-1933 «. In: *Historical Journal of Film, Radio and Television*, vol. 5, no. 2, 1985: 131-148; Bruce Murray: *Film and the German Left in the Weimar Republic. From Caligari to Kuhle Wampe*. Austin, TX: University of Texas Press 1990: passim.

59. See Kristin Thompson: » Government Policies and Practical Necessities in the Soviet Cinema of the 1920s «. In: Anna Lawton (ed.): *The Red Screen: Politics, Society, Art in Soviet Cinema*. London, New York: Routledge 1992: 19-41. See also Oksana Bulgakowa: » Russische Filme in Berlin «. In: Oksana Bulgakowa (ed.): *Die ungewöhnlichen Abenteuer des Dr. Mabuse im Lande der Bolschewiki. Das Buch zur Filmreihe » Moskau – Berlin «*. Berlin: Freunde der Deutschen Kinemathek 1995: 81-114, 82 on POLIKUSH-KA.

60. See » Bildertransfer: Deutsch-russischer Filmexport und -import «. In: Oksana Bulgakowa (ed.): *Die ungewöhnlichen Abenteuer des Dr. Mabuse im Lande der Bolschewiki. Das Buch zur Filmreihe » Moskau – Berlin «*. Berlin: Freunde der Deutschen Kinemathek 1995: 277-292.

61. Kristin Thompson: » Government Policies and Practical Necessities in the Soviet Cinema of the 1920s «. In: Anna Lawton (ed.): *The Red Screen: Politics, Society, Art in Soviet Cinema*. London, New York: Routledge 1992: 35.

62. For an overview of the Prometheus from an East German perspective, see Gerd Meier: » Materialien zur Geschichte der Prometheus Film-Verleih und Vertriebs GmbH. 1926-1932 « (8 parts). In: *Deutsche Filmkunst*, vol. 10, no. 1-8, 1962: 12-16; 57-60; 97-99; 137-140; 177-180; 221-224; 275-277; 310-312.

63. Denise Hartsough: » Soviet Film Distribution and Exhibition in Germany, 1921-1933 «. In: *Historical Journal of Film, Radio and Television*, vol. 5, no. 2, 1985: 136.

64. The IAH had its own distribution, Weltfilm and Prometheus; its production arm, Prometheus and Mezhrabpom; and even controlled its own cinema, the *Filmstern*, Berlin (Große Frankfurter Straße 28).

65. Vance Kepley, Jr.: » The Workers' International Relief and the Cinema of the Left 1921-1935 «. In: *Cinema Journal*, vol. 23, no. 1, Fall 1983: 13.

66. For more on Mezhrabpom see the exhibition catalogue Aïcha Kherroubi (ed.): *Le studio Mejrabpom ou l'aventure du cinéma privé au pays des bolcheviks*. Paris: La documentation française 1996. This book contains a detailed filmography of Mezhrabpom, compiled by Valérie Posner (pp. 145-192). See also Oksana Bulgakowa: » Der Fall Meshrabpom « and » Meshrabpom. Dokumente « (edited by Jekaterina Chochlowa). In: Oksana Bulgakowa (ed.): *Die ungewöhnlichen Abenteuer des Dr. Mabuse*

im Lande der Bolschewiki. Das Buch zur Filmreihe » Moskau – Berlin «. Berlin: Freunde der Deutschen Kinemathek 1995: 185-193.

67. For more on this ill-fated collaboration between Friedrich Wolf and Hans Richter see Heide Schönemann: » Hans Richter und Friedrich Wolf im Mashrabpom-Programm «. In: Jeanpaul Goergen et al. (eds.): *Hans Richter. Film ist Rhythmus*. Berlin: Freunde der Deutschen Kinemathek 2003: 115-122.

68. In fact, the production of Kuleshov's film was only made possible after the assistant head of Goskino, Kosman, made a shopping trip to Berlin for cameras, equipment and raw stock in September 1923. See Kristin Thompson: » Government Policies and Practical Necessities in the Soviet Cinema of the 1920s «. In: Anna Lawton (ed.): *The Red Screen: Politics, Society, Art in Soviet Cinema*. London, New York: Routledge 1992: 34.

69. A reply to the challenge inherent in this film could be seen in Ernst Lubitsch's NI-NOTCHKA (1939) in which a textbook communist is turned into a capitalist by consumerism and romantic love in Paris.

70. Vance Kepley, Jr.: » Mr. Kuleshov in the Land of the Modernists «. In: Anna Lawton (ed.): *The Red Screen: Politics, Society, Art in Soviet Cinema*. London, New York: Routledge 1992: 132-147, here 133.

71. On the reception of the film see Richard Taylor: *The Battleship Potemkin: The Film Companion*. London and New York: I.B. Tauris 2000: 65-127.

72. Other examples from the fringes of the avant-garde during this same period are DAS CABINET DES DR. CALIGARI (GER 1919/20, Robert Wiene), which returned triumphantly from Paris after having broken the French ban against German films, and SOUS LES TOITS DE PARIS (FR 1929/30, René Clair) which was hailed by German critics and was only subsequently embraced in Paris. It is as if recognition abroad adds extra cache to the film that is then transported back to the country of origin where innovation had originally met with criticism. These » prodigal son « films that were accepted only into the » imagined community « of nationhood after having gained recognition from an equally » imagined other « abroad would make for an interesting case study.

73. On Meisel in general and the POTEMKIN-music in particular, see Werner Sudendorf (ed.): *Der Stummfilmmusiker Edmund Meisel*. Frankfurt am Main: Deutsches Filmmuseum 1984.

74. Richard Taylor: *The Battleship Potemkin: The Film Companion*. London, New York: I.B. Tauris 2000: 112.

75. Evgenij Margolit: » Der sowjetische Stummfilm und der frühe Tonfilm «. In: Christine Engel (ed.): *Geschichte des sowjetischen und russischen Films*. Stuttgart, Weimar: Metzler 1999: 17-67, here 39.

76. See Temple Willcox: » Soviet Films, Censorship and the British Government: A Matter of Public Interest «. In: *Historical Journal of Film, Radio and Television*, vol. 10, no. 3, 1990: 275-292.

77. See François Albera: » La réception du cinéma soviétique en France, dans les années 1920-1930 «. In: Aïcha Kherroubi (ed.): *Le studio Mejrabpom ou l'aventure du cinéma privé au pays des bolcheviks*. Paris: La documentation française 1996: 117-126. See also Léon Moussinac : » Les Ciné-Clubs et l'explosion du POTEMKINE «. Reprinted as annexe no. 1 in Christophe Gauthier : *La Passion du cinéma. Cinéphiles, ciné-clubs et salles spécialisées à Paris de 1920 à 1929*. Paris : École des Chartes 1999 : 340-343.

78. See Oksana Bulgakowa: *Sergej Eisenstein. Eine Biographie.* Berlin: Potemkin Press 1997: 86.

79. See Bert Hogenkamp: » Interview met Ralph Bond «. In: *Skrien,* 51, Jul-Aug 1975: 21-24, here 21. See also Bill Nichols: » Documentary Film and the Modernist Avant-Garde «. In: *Critical Inquiry,* no. 27, Summer 2001: 580-610. See chapter six on the intersection of the documentary and the avant-garde for more details.

80. See Léon Moussinac: *Le cinéma sovietique.* Paris: Gallimard 1928: 187.

81. Jay Leyda: *Kino: A History of the Russian and Soviet Film.* London: George Allen & Unwin 1960: 201, 252.

82. Dziga Vertov: Diary entry of 12 April 1926. See Dziga Vertov: *Tagebücher, Arbeitshefte.* (edited by Thomas Tode and Alexandra Gramatke) Konstanz: UVK Medien 2000: 12.

83. Standish Lawder: » Eisenstein and Constructivism «. In: P. Adams Sitney (ed.): *The Essential Cinema.* New York: New York University Press 1975: 65.

84. See » Daten und Anmerkungen zu Pudowkins Leben « In: Wsewolod Pudowkin: *Die Zeit in Großaufnahme. Erinnerungen/Aufsätze/Werkstattnotizen.* (edited by Tatjana Sapasnik and Adi Petrowitsch). Berlin/DDR: Henschel 1983: 608ff.

85. See Bert Hogenkamp: » De russen komen! Poedowkin, Eisenstein en Wertow in Nederland «. In: *Skrien,* no. 144, Nov/Dec 1985: 46-49.

86. See Hans Schoots: *Gevaarlijk leven. Een biografie van Joris Ivens.* Amsterdam: Jan Mets 1995: 82f.

87. See –e–: Russische Film-Matinee. Die Künstler sprechen «. In: *Lichtbild-Bühne,* vol. 22, no. 11, 14.1.1929.

88. See for example *Lichtbild-Bühne,* vol. 22, no. 7, 9.1.1929 and *Lichtbild-Bühne,* vol. 22, no. 8, 10.1.1929; see also for a sympathetic portrait Hans Wollenberg: » Pudowkin, der Mensch «. In: *Lichtbild-Bühne,* vol. 22, no. 5, 7.1.1929.

89. See Thomas Tode: » Bio-Filmographie «. In: Dziga Vertov: *Tagebücher, Arbeitshefte.* (edited by Thomas Tode and Alexandra Gramatke) Konstanz: UVK Medien 2000: 200-244, here 227ff.

90. See, for reviews of this event, da.: » Theorie des ungestellten Films «. In: *Lichtbildbühne,* vol. 22, no. 138, 11.6.1929 and –d.: » Russische Avantgarde im Phoebus-Palast «. In: *Film-Kurier,* vol. 11, no. 136, 106.1929.

91. See on the Frankfurt-event anon. [Siegfried Kracauer]: » Wertoff in Frankfurt «. In: *Frankfurter Zeitung,* no. 456, 21.6.1929. Reprinted in Siegfried Kracauer: *Werke. Band 6.2. Kleine Schriften zum Film 1928-1931.* Frankfurt am Main: Suhrkamp 2004: 258f., and Benno Reifenberg: » Für wen sieht das Kinoauge «. In: *Frankfurter Zeitung,* no. 466, 25.6.1929. See also anon.: » Kinoauge in Frankfurt am Main «. In: *Film-Kurier,* vol. 11, no. 148, 24.6.1929.

92. See h.s.: » Noch einmal › Film und Foto ‹ «. In: *Lichtbild-Bühne,* vol. 22, no. 156, 2.7.1929.

93. For Vertov's German tour see Thomas Tode: » Ein Russe projiziert in die Planetariumskuppel. Dsiga Wertows Reise nach Deutschland «. In: Oksana Bulgakowa (ed.): *Die ungewöhnlichen Abenteuer des Dr. Mabuse im Lande der Bolschewiki. Das Buch zur Filmreihe* » Moskau – Berlin «. Berlin: Freunde der Deutschen Kinemathek 1995: 143-151.

94. On Vertov's Parisian stay, see Thomas Tode: » Un Soviétique escalade la Tour Eiffel: Dziga Vertov à Paris «. In: *Cinémathèque,* no. 5, printemps 1994: 68-85.

95. See –d.: » Dsiga Werthoff fährt nach Rußland «. In: *Film-Kurier*, vol. 13, no. 296, 18.12. 1931.

96. See Tode, Vertov, 230ff.

97. Thorold Dickinson, Catherine de la Roche: *Soviet Cinema*. London: Falcon Press 1948.

98. Handwritten note signed by Chaplin reprinted in Dziga Vertov: *Tagebücher, Arbeitshefte*. (edited by Thomas Tode and Alexandra Gramatke) Konstanz: UVK Medien 2000: 23.

99. See Bert Hogenkamp: » De russen komen! Poedowkin, Eisenstein en Wertow in Nederland «. In: *Skrien*, no. 144, Nov./Dec. 1985: 46-49.

100. Eisenstein wrote kept a journal about this trip to Berlin, which was first published as » Germanskaya kinematografiya. Iz putevykh vpechatlenii «. In: *Westnik rabotnikow iskusstw*, no. 10, October 1926: 8-9. English as » The German Cinema. A Traveller's Impression «. In: S.M. Eisenstein: *Selected Works: Volume I: Writings, 1922-34*. (edited by Richard Taylor). London: British Film Institute / Bloomington and Indiana: Indiana University Press 1988: 85-88.

101. Eisenstein's characterisation of Lang is that of Kuleshov » well fed over a period of time «.

102. See Ronald Bergan: *Sergei Eisenstein: A Life in Conflict*. London: Little, Brown and Company 1997: 122-125.

103. See Oksana Bulgakowa: *Sergej Eisenstein. Eine Biographie*. Berlin: PotemkinPress 1997: 107ff.

104. Jay Leyda: *Kino: A History of the Russian and Soviet Film*. London: George Allen & Unwin 1960: 269.

105. For a critical portrait of Eisenstein as a talented artist subjugated by a political system on the occasion of this premiere, see » Begegnung mit Eisenstein « in the (rightwing) journal *Kinematograph*, vol. 23, no. 202, 30.8.1929.

106. On Eisenstein's stay in Switzerland and on the production of FRAUENNOT – FRAUENGLÜCK, see François Albera: » Eisenstein en Suisse. Premiers materiaux «. In: *Travelling*, no. 48, Winter 1976: 89–119.

107. See Bert Hogenkamp: » De russen komen! Poedowkin, Eisenstein en Wertow in Nederland «. In: *Skrien*, no. 144, Nov./Dec. 1985: 46-49.

108. See Ronald Bergan: *Sergei Eisenstein: A Life in Conflict*. London: Little, Brown and Company 1997: 155-171. See also Oksana Bulgakowa: *Sergej Eisenstein. Eine Biographie*. Berlin: PotemkinPress 1997: 118-133.

109. See Rotislaw Jurenjew: » Unter fremden Himmeln. Zum 80. Geburtstag von Sergej Eisenstein «. In: *Film und Fernsehen*, no. 1, 1978: 29.

110. See Samuel Brody: » Paris Hears Eisenstein «. In: *Close Up*, vol. 6, no. 4, April 1930 for a contemporary account of that event.

111. For a detailed and annotated collection of material on the production see Harry M. Geduld, Ronald Gottesman (eds.): *Sergei Eisenstein and Upton Sinclair: The Making and Unmaking of › Que viva Mexico! ‹*. Bloomington, IN and London: Indiana University Press 1970.

112. George O. Liber: *Alexander Dovzhenko: A Life in Soviet Film*. London: BFI 2002: 120.

113. François Albera, Roland Cosandey (eds.): *Boris Barnet. Ecrits – Documents – Etudes – Filmographie*. Locarno: Festival international du film 1985: 11-28.

114. Similar reasons, advantageous both to the artist and to the home country, can be found in the travels of Iranian directors such as Abbas Kiarostami or Jafar Panahi.

115. Jay Leyda: *Kino: A History of the Russian and Soviet Film*. London: George Allen & Unwin 1960: 211.

116. Peter Wollen, Alan Lovell, Sam Rohdie: » Interview with Ivor Montagu «. In: *Screen*, vol. 13, no. 3 (Autumn 1972): 71-113, here 93.

117. See the list in Denise J. Youngblood: *Movies for the Masses: Popular Cinema and Soviet Society in the 1920s*. Cambridge: Cambridge University Press 1992: 25.

118. For a detailed account of the 1928 party conference and its aftermath see Denise J. Youngblood: *Soviet Cinema in the Silent Era*. Ann Arbor, MI: UMI Research Press 1985: 157-187.

119. For a general overview of the developments under Stalin in the Soviet Union, see Eberhard Nembach: *Stalins Filmpolitik. Der Umbau der sowjetischen Filmindustrie 1929 bis 1938*. St. Augustin: Gardez! Verlag 2001. For an overview of the role that Sumjackij played in the Soviet cinema of the 1930s, see Richard Taylor: » Boris Shumyatsky and the Soviet Cinema in the 1930s: Ideology as Mass Entertainment «. In: *Historical Journal of Film, Radio and Television*, vol. 6, no. 1, 1986: 43-64.

120. See Denise J. Youngblood: *Soviet Cinema in the Silent Era*. Ann Arbor, MI: UMI Research Press 1985: 230ff.

121. See Ian Christie: » Soviet Cinema: Making Sense of Sound. A Revised Historiography «. In: *Screen*, vol. 23, no. 2, July-Aug. 1982: 34-49.

122. See *Close Up*, vol. 3, no. 4, October 1928: 10-13.

123. Sergei Eisenstein, Vsevolod Pudovkin, Grigori Alexandrov: » Statement on Sound «. In: Eisenstein, S.M.: *Selected Works. Volume I: Writings, 1922-34*. (edited by Richard Taylor). London: British Film Institute / Bloomington, IN: Indiana University Press 1988: 113f., here 113.

124. For an account of films without titles in 1920s Germany and the accompanying discussion, see Irmbert Schenk: » › Titelloser Film ‹ im deutschen Kino der Zwanziger Jahre «. In: Francesco Pitassio, Leonardo Quaresima (eds.): *Scrittura e immagine. La didascalia nel cinema muto / Writing and Image. Titles in Silent Cinema*. Udine: Forum 1998: 225-246.

125. Jay Leyda: *Kino: A History of the Russian and Soviet Film*. London: George Allen & Unwin 1960: 278.

126. A number of short experimental sound films likewise deal with industrialisation and electrification within the Five-Year-Plan. See Ian Christie: » Soviet Cinema: Making Sense of Sound. A Revised Historiography «. In: *Screen*, vol. 23, no. 2, July-August 1982: 34-49.

127. See Evgenij Margolit: » Der sowjetische Stummfilm und der frühe Tonfilm «. In: Christine Engel (ed.): *Geschichte des sowjetischen und russischen Films*. Stuttgart, Weimar: Metzler 1999: 17-67, here 65f.

128. See Hans Schoots: *Gevaarlijk leven. Een biografie van Joris Ivens*. Amsterdam: Jan Mets 1995: 83-89.

129. See TTO [= Thomas Tode]: entry » Erwin Piscator – Regisseur «. In: Hans-Michael Bock (ed.): *CineGraph – Lexikon zum deutschsprachigen Film*. München: edition text + kritik 1984ff.: inst. 33, 15.5.2000. On Otto Katz see Marcus G. Patka: » › Columbus Discovered America, and I Discovered Hollywood ‹. Otto Katz und die Hollywood Anti-Nazi League «. In: *Filmexil*, no. 17, 2003: 44-65.

130. See, for a collection of Piscator's letter from the Black Sea where the shooting took place, Hermann Haarmann (ed.): *Erwin Piscator am Schwarzen Meer. Briefe, Erinnerungen, Photos.* Berlin: Bostelmann & Siebenhaar 2002.

131. See Rainhard May, Hendrik Jackson (eds.): *Filme für die Volksfront. Erwin Piscator, Gustav von Wangenheim, Friedrich Wolf – antifaschistische Filmemacher im sowjetischen Exil.* Berlin: Stattkino 2001.

132. On the strained relationship between Piscator and Mezhrabpom see Peter Diezel: » Im ständigen Dissens. Erwin Piscator und die Meshrabpom-Film-Gesellschaft «. In: *Filmexil*, no. 20, 2004: 39-56.

133. See the chapter » Op dood spoor (1934-1936) «. In: Hans Schoots: *Gevaarlijk leven. Een biografie van Joris Ivens.* Amsterdam: Jan Mets 1995: 136-151.

134. See Heide Schönemann: » Hans Richter und Friedrich Wolf im Meshrabpom-Programm «. In: Jeanpaul Goergen, Angelika Hoch, Erika Gregor, Ulrich Gregor (eds.): *Hans Richter. Film ist Rhythmus.* Berlin: Freunde der Deutschen Kinemathek 2003: 115-122.

135. See Joseph Zsuffa: *Béla Balázs. The Man and the Artist.* Berkeley, CA et al.: University of California Press 1987. See also Hanno Loewy: *Béla Balázs – Märchen, Ritual und Film.* Berlin: Vorwerk 8 2003: 379-396.

136. See *Film-Kurier*, vol. 10, no. 283, 28.11.1928.

137. See the letter by Luis Buñuel to Charles de Noailles on 27 January 1932, reprinted in Jean-Michel Bouhours, Nathalie Schoeller (eds.): *L'Âge d'or. Correspondance Luis Buñuel – Charles de Noailles. Lettres et Documents (1929-1976).* Paris : Les Cahiers du Musée nationale de l'art moderne 1993: 150.

138. See the letter reprinted in Yasha David (ed.): *Buñuel. Auge des Jahrhunderts.* Bonn: Kunst- und Ausstellungshalle der Bundesrepublik Deutschland 1994: 316. The letter is incorrectly dated December 1934 (it should be December 1932).

139. See Paul Hammond: » To the Paradise of Pitfalls «. In: Maria Casanova (ed.): *Tierra sin pan. Luis Buñuel y los nuevos caminos de las vanguardias.* Valencia: Institut Valencià d'Art Modern 1999 : 211-217.

140. See Günter Agde: » Neue Einblicke in alte Hoffnungen. Filmexil in der UdSSR 1933-1945 «. In: *Filmexil*, no. 20, 2004: 4-16.

141. For an archeological account of the film and its production circumstances, those involved in the making and their fates see Günter Agde: *Kämpfer. Biographie eines Films und seiner Macher.* Berlin: Das Neue Berlin 2001.

142. Helmut G. Asper: *Max Ophüls. Eine Biographie.* Berlin: Bertz 1998: 323-331.

143. Peter Wollen: » The Two Avant-Gardes «. In: P.W.: *Readings and Writings: Semiotic Counter-Strategies.* London: Verso 1982: 92-104.

144. Hans Richter: Der moderne Film «. Lecture given on 16 February 1930 to the Filmliga Amsterdam. Reprinted in and quoted after: *Filmliga*, vol. 3, no. 6, March 1930: 75. [» Im russischen Film ist der Begriff der Kunst, wie er in Europa gilt, überwunden. «, my trans.]

145. Ian Christie: » Introduction: Soviet cinema: a heritage and its history «. In: Ian Christie, Richard Taylor (eds.): *The Film Factory: Russian and Soviet Cinema in Documents, 1896-1939.* London: Routledge & Kegan Paul 1988: 3.

146. For a more detailed discussion of this » rhetoric of possibility «, see Boris Groys: *Gesamtkunstwerk Stalin. Die gespaltene Kultur in der Sowjetunion.* München, Wien: Carl Hanser 1988: 66ff, quote 68 and 69. [» Die für die Mythologie der Stalinzeit so

wichtige Figur des › Schädlings‹ ist im Grunde auf keine Weise › realistisch ‹ motiviert, genausowenig wie die übermenschliche schöpferische Potenz des › positiven Helden‹. … Der positive und der negative Held der Stalinzeit sind die zwei Gesichter der ihr vorangegangenen demiurgischen Praxis der Avantgarde, beide übersteigen die von ihnen geschaffene und zerstörte Wirklichkeit, und auch der Kampf zwischen ihnen spielt sich nicht auf dem Boden der Wirklichkeit ab, sondern jenseits ihrer Grenzen: die Wirklichkeit ist nur der Einsatz in diesem Spiel. «, my trans.]

Notes Chapter 6

1. Kenneth MacPherson: » As Is «. In: *Close Up*, vol. 5, no. 6, Dec. 1929: 447.
2. Still the best account of the introduction of sound in Europe can be found in Karel Dibbets: *Sprekende films. De komst van de geluidsfilm in Nederland 1928-1933*. Amsterdam: Cramwinckel 1993. Other useful studies include Harald Jossé: *Die Entstehung des Tonfilms. Beitrag zu einer faktenorientierten Mediengeschichtsschreibung*. Freiburg, Munich: Alber 1984 and Wolfgang Mühl-Benninghaus: *Das Ringen um den Tonfilm. Strategien der Elektro- und Filmindustrie in den 20er und 30er Jahren*. Düsseldorf: Droste 1999.
3. Joris Ivens: » Documentary: Subjectivity and Montage «. Lecture at the Museum of Modern Art, New York, December 13, 1939. Reprinted in and quoted after Kees Bakker (ed.): *Joris Ivens and the Documentary Context*. Amsterdam: Amsterdam University Press 1999: 250-260, here 250.
4. Jamie Sexton: *The Emergence of an Alternative Film Culture in Inter-War Britain*. Norwich: University of East Anglia 2001 [Unpublished Ph.D. thesis]: 180.
5. The most thorough collection of texts and documents on the life and work of Walter Ruttmann is Jeanpaul Goergen: *Walter Ruttmann. Eine Dokumentation*. Berlin: Freunde der Kinemathek 1989. Other books on Ruttmann's career are Adrianus van Domburg: *Walter Ruttmann en het beginsel*. Purmerend: Nederlands Filminstituut 1956 and Leonardo Quaresima (ed.): *Walter Ruttmann. Cinema, pittura, ars acustica*. Calliano: Manfrini 1994.
6. See William Uricchio: *Ruttmann's Berlin and the City Film to 1930*. New York: New York University 1982 [Unpublished Ph.D. thesis].
7. In fact, painter-filmmaker Laszlo Moholy-Nagy claimed that he had already written a scenario dealing with the chaotic images of a metropolis in 1921, but the film was never produced. The idea is reproduced in *Film-Kurier*, vol. 7, no. 109, 9.5.1925. After Ruttmann's film came out, Moholy-Nagy indirectly complained about the theft of his idea. See LMN: » film im bauhaus. eine erwiderung «. In: *Film-Kurier*, vol. 8, no. 296, 18.12.1926.
8. MELODIE DER WELT is often labeled the first German sound film, but this claim raises complicated issues of what is meant when we talk about a » sound film «, and what constitutes the » German-ness « of the film, and finally the distinction between short, medium-length and feature-length film (as the film with a running time of under 50 minutes too short for today's definition of » feature length «). For these reasons I have opted for a more cautious formulation.

9.   There is an abundance of material on Grierson and the documentary movement. For an positive overview of his biography and activities, see Forsyth Hardy: *John Grierson: A Documentary Biography.* London: Faber and Faber 1979. A somewhat more critical approach is taken by Jack C. Ellis: *John Grierson: Life, Contributions, Influence.* Carbondale, IL: Southern Illinois University Press 2000. On the documentary film movement, see Elizabeth Sussex: *The Rise and Fall of British Documentary: The Story of the Film Movement Founded by John Grierson.* Berkeley, CA: University of California Press 1975 and Paul Swann: *The British Documentary Film Movement, 1926-1946.* Cambridge: Cambridge University Press 1989. For a study of the theoretical, philosophical and intellectual foundations of the movement, see Ian Aitken: *Film and Reform: John Grierson and the Documentary Film Movement.* London: Routledge 1990. On a critical reassessment, see Brian Winston: *Claiming the Real: The Documentary Film Revisited.* London: British Film Institute 1995.

10. Andrew Buchanan: » Director's Notebook «. In: *Cinema Quarterly,* vol. 1, no. 3, Spring 1933: 163.

11. For a productive discussion of how to deal with this distinction see Thomas Elsaesser: » Realität zeigen: Der frühe Film im Zeichen Lumières «. In: Ursula von Keitz, Kay Hoffmann (eds.): *Die Einübung des dokumentarischen Blicks. Fiction Film und Non Fiction Film zwischen Wahrheitsanspruch und expressiver Sachlichkeit 1895-1945.* Marburg: Schüren 2001: 27-50.

12. Bill Nichols: » Documentary Film and the Modernist Avant-Garde «. In: *Critical Inquiry* 27 (Summer 2001): 580-610, here 583-5.

13. See John Grierson: » Directors of the 'Thirties « and » First Principles of Documentary «. In: Forsyth Hardy (ed.): *Grierson on Documentary.* Berkeley, CA: University of California Press 1966: 38-58, especially 55ff. and 78-89, especially 80f.

14. See Martin Loiperdinger: » World War I Propaganda and the Birth of Documentary «. In: Daan Hertogs, Nico de Klerk (eds.): *Uncharted Territory: Essays on Early Non-Fiction Film.* Amsterdam: Nederlands Filmmuseum 1998: 25-31.

15. Charles Musser: » The Silent Film: Documentary «. In: Geoffrey Nowell-Smith: *The Oxford History of World Cinema.* Oxford: Oxford University Press 1996: 86-95. Musser basically claims that early non-fiction films » had › documentary value ‹ but did not necessarily function within › the documentary tradition ‹ « (88), here borrowing Grierson's expression of » documentary value «.

16. See, for example, the essays collected in two volumes by the Amsterdam film museum, Daan Hertogs, Nico de Klerk (eds.): *Nonfiction from the Teens.* Amsterdam: Nederlands Filmmuseum 1994, Daan Hertogs and Nico de Klerk (eds.): *Uncharted Territory: Essays on Early Nonfiction Film.* Amsterdam: Nederlands Filmmuseum 1997. See also the essays collected in two volumes of the year book *KinTop.* Frank Kessler, Sabine Lenk, Martin Loiperdinger (eds.): *KinTop 4: Anfänge des dokumentarischen Films.* Basel, Frankfurt am Main: Stroemfeld/Roter Stern 1995. and Frank Kessler, Sabine Kenk, Martin Loiperdinger (eds.): *KinTop 5: Aktualitäten.* Basel, Frankfurt am Main: Stroemfeld/Roter Stern 1996.

17. Tom Gunning: » A Quarter of a Century Later: Is Early Cinema Still Early? «. In: Frank Kessler, Sabine Lenk, Martin Loiperdinger (eds.): *KINtop 12: Theorien zum frühen Kino.* Frankfurt am Main, Basel: Stroemfeld / Roter Stern 2003: 17-31.

18. Erik Barnouw: *Documentary: A History of the Non-Fiction Film.* Oxford: Oxford University Press 1993².

19. Bill Nichols: » Documentary Film and the Modernist Avant-Garde «. In: *Critical Inquiry* 27 (Summer 2001): 580-610, here 582.
20. Ibid.: 582.
21. Ibid.: 581.
22. Ibid.: 589.
23. Ibid.: 591f.
24. Ibid.: 595, italics in original.
25. Ibid.: 599.
26. Ibid.: 600.
27. Ibid.: 600f.
28. See Petr Szczepanik: » Undoing the National: Representing International Space in 1930s Czechoslovak Multiple-Language Versions «. In: *Cinema & Cie. International Film Studies Journal*, no. 4, Spring 2004: 55-65.
29. The title for the first act announces » Ausfahrt in die Welt / Ihre Bauten / Ihre Strassen / Ihre Gottesverehrung / Ihr Kriegslärm «, the title for the second act is missing, while the third act deals with » Morgen der Frau / Sprachen der Welt / Mahlzeiten / Tanz und Musik / Schauspiel-Rummel / Arbeit und Heimkehr «.
30. Karl Bloßfeldt: *Urformen der Kunst. Photographische Pflanzenbilder.* (edited with an introduction by Karl Nierendorff). Berlin: Ernst Wasmuth n.y. [1928]. See also Walter Benjamin: » Kleine Geschichte der Photographie «. In: W.B.: *Gesammelte Schriften. II.1.* Frankfurt am Main: Suhrkamp 1977: 368-385, here 372.
31. See Albert Renger-Patzsch: *Die Welt ist schön.* Munich: Kurt Wolff 1928.
32. Hermann Kappelhoff: » Eine neue Gegenständlichkeit. Die Bildidee der Neuen Sachlichkeit und der Film «. In: Thomas Koebner, Norbert Grob, Bernd Kiefer (eds.): *Jenseits der › Dämonischen Leinwand. Neue Perspektiven auf das späte Weimarer Kino.* Munich: edition text + kritik 2003: 119-138.
33. Forsyth Hardy: *John Grierson: A Documentary Biography.* London: Faber and Faber 1979: 52.
34. See Forsyth Hardy: *John Grierson: A Documentary Biography.* London: Faber and Faber 1979: 51f. However, these staged scenes of the catch proved unsatisfactory, so the film crew stayed on until they were lucky enough to witness a real big catch.
35. The article was first published in Russian in: *Zhizn iskusstva*, no. 32, 1928: 4-5, and in German as » Achtung! Goldgrube! Gedanken über die Zukunft des Hörfilms « on 28 July 1928 in the trade paper *Lichtbildbühne*, an article with which Ruttmann was surely familiar. In English it was published as » The Sound Film. A Statement from U.S.S.R. «. In *Close Up*, vol. 3, no. 4, October 1928: 10-13.
36. On the unity and harmony of the world, see Holger Wilmesmeier: » Die Einheit der Welt. Harmonisierung von Natur und Technik im Geiste des Übermenschen – eine ikonographische und rhetorische Spurensuche «. In: *Das kalte Bild. Neue Studien zum NS-Propagandafilm.* Marburg: Schüren 1996. (Augen-Blick. Marburger Hefte zur Medienwissenschaft; Heft 22): 6-38.
37. For a description of different forms of *Neue Sachlichkeit* and realism in relation to film, see Norbert M. Schmitz: » Zwischen › Neuem Sehen ‹ und › Neuer Sachlichkeit ‹. Der Einfluß der Kunstphotographie auf den Film der zwanziger Jahre «. In: Michael Esser (ed.): *Gleißende Schatten. Kamerapioniere der zwanziger Jahre.* Berlin: Henschel 1994: 79-94.

38. John Grierson: » The Documentary Idea: 1942 «. In: Forsyth Hardy (ed.): *Grierson on Documentary*. Berkeley, CA: University of California Press 1966: 181.

39. As quoted by Forsyth Hardy in his edited volume of Grierson writings: *Grierson on Documentary*. Berkeley, CA: University of California Press 1966: 13.

40. See Brian Winston: *Claiming the Real: The Documentary Film Revisited*. London: British Film Institute 1995, part 1.

41. The company's original name was *Hamburg-Amerikanische Packetfahrt Actiengesellschaft*, established in 1847. On the history of the company, see Susanne Wiborg, Klaus Wiborg: *1847-1997. Unser Feld ist die Welt*. Hamburg: Hapag-Lloyd 1997.

42. My account of the Hapag's engagement in film activities relies on Michael Töteberg: » Die Sehnsucht unserer Zeit. Exotik und Tourismus: Die Reisefilme der Hapag «. Unpublished manuscript.

43. A useful study examining the German view of the US before 1920 is Deniz Göktürk: *Künstler, Cowboys, Ingenieure. Kultur- und mediengeschichtliche Studien zu deutschen Amerika-Texten 1912-1920*. Munich: Wilhelm Fink 1997.

44. Ufa-Vorstandsprotokolle, protocol no. 209 from the meeting on 12 December 1927.

45. Another example of the intersection of industry and avant-garde during the early sound period: In March 1930 René Clair and Sergei Eisenstein were sharing the large studio at the complex in Epinay; Clair was finishing work on SOUS LES TOITS DE PARIS (1929/30) while Eisenstein, Grigorij Alexandrov and Eduard Tissé shot ROMANCE SENTIMENTALE. See anon.: » Eisenstein macht seinen ersten Tonfilm. Besuch bei der französischen Tobis «. In: *Film-Kurier*, no. 65, 15.3.1930.

46. For a detailed discussion of the European dimension of Tobis, see Malte Hagener: » Unter den Dächern der Tobis. Nationale Märkte und europäische Strategien «. In: Jan Distelmeyer (ed.): *Tonfilmfrieden/Tonfilmkrieg. Die Geschichte der Tobis vom Technik-Syndikat zum Staatskonzern*. Munich: edition text + kritik 2003: 51-64.

47. See the thorough filmography of Tobis for some production cycles, Hans-Michael Bock, Wiebke Annkatrin Mosel, Ingrun Spazier (eds.): *Die Tobis 1928-1945. Eine kommentierte Filmographie*. Munich: edition text + kritik 2003.

48. This does not imply that Tobis was an experimental company, however, Tobis's openness towards innovation from 1928 until early 1930 is astonishing when compared to other production firms facing similar problems. See also Thomas Elsaesser, Malte Hagener: » Walter Ruttmann: 1929 «. In: Stefan Andriopoulos, Bernhard Dotzler (eds.): *1929. Beiträge zur Archäologie der Medien*. Frankfurt am Main: Suhrkamp 2002, S. 316-349.

49. John Grierson: » Summary and Survey: 1935 «. In: *Grierson on Documentary*. (Edited with an introduction by Forsyth Hardy). London: Collins 1946, 102-120, here 114.

50. See the text Joris Ivens: » Quelques réflections sur les documentaires d'avant-garde «. In: *La revue des vivants*, no. 10, 1931: 518-520. Reprinted translation in and quoted from: » Notes on the Avant-garde Documentary Film «. In: Kees Bakker (ed.): *Joris Ivens and the Documentary Context*. Amsterdam: Amsterdam University Press 1999: 224-226.

51. S. Kracauer: » Exotische Filme «. In: *Frankfurter Zeitung*, no. 390, 28.5.1929. Reprinted in S.K.: *Werke 6.2. Kleine Schriften zum Film 1928-1931*. Frankfurt am Main: Suhrkamp 2004: 251-254, here 253. [» Man wird auch weiterhin dem Publikum fremde Länder vorsetzen, damit es im eigenen nichts merkt. «, my trans.]

52. John Grierson in: *The Clarion*, August 1929. Reprinted in and quoted in Forsyth Hardy (ed.): *John Grierson on the Movies*. London, Boston, MA: Faber & Faber 1981: 28-31, here 30.

53. Cf. Nico de Klerk: » The Moment of Screening. What Non-Fiction Films Can Do «. In: Peter Zimmermann, Kay Hoffmann (eds.): *Triumph der Bilder. Kultur- und Dokumentarfilme vor 1945 im internationalen Vergleich*. Konstanz: UVK 2003: 291-301.

54. The *locus classicus* of the convergence of early cinema is Tom Gunning: » The Cinema of Attractions: Early Film, Its Spectator and the Avant-Garde «. In: Thomas Elsaesser (ed.): *Early Cinema: Space, Frame, Narrative*. London: BFI 1990: 56-62.

55. An overview of Germany is provided by the essays collected in Jörg Schöning (ed.): *Triviale Tropen. Exotische Reise- und Abenteuerfilme aus Deutschland, 1919-1939*. Munich: edition text + kritik 1997.

56. Flaherty's return to the » documentary impulse « was due to Grierson's insistence that Flaherty work for his Film Unit; it was thus Grierson's » invention of a tradition « (and his move away from Soviet film practice that effectively silenced this important source of inspiration) that put Flaherty firmly on the map of documentary filmmaking as we know it today.

57. An early example of this exotic *Medienverbund*, which dates back to the 19th century and also points forward to the experience economy of the late 20th century is provided by the Hagenbeck-Umlauff-family in Hamburg. See Hilke Thode-Arora: *Für fünfzig Pfennig um die Welt. Die Hagenbeckschen Völkerschauen*. Frankfurt and New York: Campus 1989. A typical proponent from the 1920s is Colin Ross. See Bodo-Michael Baumunk: » Ein Pfadfinder der Geopolitik. Colin Ross und seine Reisefilme «. In: Jörg Schöning: *Triviale Tropen. Exotische Reise- und Abenteuerfilme aus Deutschland, 1919–1939*. Munich: edition text + kritik 1997: 84-94.

58. See Rainer Rother: *Leni Riefenstahl. Die Verführung des Talents*. Munich: Wilhelm Heyne 2002: 20-44; see Lutz Kinkel: *Die Scheinwerferin. Leni Riefenstahl und das » Dritte Reich «*. Hamburg, Wien: Europa-Verlag 2002: 10-44 on her career pre-1933; see Jürgen Trimborn: *Riefenstahl. Eine deutsche Karriere. Biographie*. Berlin: Aufbau-Verlag 2002: 36-60 on her dance career, 61-100 on her acting career with Fanck, 102-122 on her directorial debut DAS BLAUE LICHT.

59. See, for the director's account, Adrian Brunel: » Experiments in Ultra-Cheap Cinematography «. In: *Close Up*, vol. 3, no. 4, October 1928: 43-46. See also Jamie Sexton: » Parody on the Fringes. Adrian Brunel, Minority Film Culture and the Art of Deconstruction «. In: Alan Burton, Laraine Porter (eds.): *Pimple, Pranks and Pratfalls: British Film Comedy Before 1930*. Trowbridge: Flicks Books 2000.

60. For more on the life and work of André Sauvage see Philippe Esnault: » André Sauvage, cinéaste maudit «. In: *La revue du cinéma*, no. 394, May 1984: 92-94; Philippe Esnault: » Sauvages «. In: *Cinématographe*, no. 112, July 1985: 63-67; Dominique Païni, Eric LeRoy : » Les archives du film (CNC) : la collection André Sauvage «. In: *Cinémathèque*, no. 2, Nov. 1992 : 124-129; Alain Virmaux: » Cinémemoire 96: Deux mécomptes (A. Sauvage et J. Duvivier) «. In: *Jeune cinéma*, no. 244, summer 1997: 53f.

61. Geoff Brown: » Table Tennis over Everest. Ivor Montagu will be eighty on 23 April. « In: *Sight & Sound*, Spring 1984: 98.

62. See William Rothman: » The Filmmaker as Hunter: Robert Flaherty's NANOOK OF THE NORTH «. In: Barry Keith Grant, Jeannette Sloniowski (eds.): *Documenting the*

Documentary: Close Readings of Documentary Film and Video. Detroit, MI: Wayne State University Press 1998. (Contemporary Film and Television Series): 23-39.

63. Heinrich Mutzenbecher: *Melodie der Welt. ein Präludium zum ersten deutschen Tonfilm.* Hamburg: Hapag [1929], 2. [» die Zusammenfassung zu finden, die Idee, der eine den Erdball umspannende Schiffahrtslinie dient. Wenn das Schwert ruht, reichen sich Forschung und Wirtschaft die Hand. Der Mensch blüht auf unter den wärmenden Strahlen des Friedens. Ist aber nicht Wurzel des Streites so oft nur Mißverstehen des anderen? Unkenntnis wirkt Haß, Verständnis wirkt Liebe. «, my trans.]

64. Walter Ruttmann: » Auch Eisen kann Filmstar sein. S. Pfannkuch im Gespräch mit Walter Ruttmann «. Undated newspaper clipping, Ruttmann archive, Filmmuseum Frankfurt. Reprinted in and quoted after: Jeanpaul Goergen: *Walter Ruttmann. Eine Dokumentation.* Berlin: Freunde der Kinemathek 1989, 92f. [» Der Film, der sich aus verschiedenartigsten künstlerischen und technischen Elementen zusammensetzt, wird immer nur ein filmischer Film sein, wenn er wie eine große symphonische Dichtung alle kontrapunktischen, optischen und akustischen Gesetze in seiner Partitur vereinigt. «, my trans.]

65. Michael Töteberg offers a useful introduction: » Wie werde ich stark. Die Kulturfilm-Abteilung «. In: Hans-Michael Bock, Michael Töteberg (eds.): *Das Ufa-Buch.* Frankfurt am Main: Zweitausendeins 1992, 64-67.

66. Brian Winston: *Claiming the Real: The Documentary Film Revisited.* London: British Film Institute 1995, 33f.

67. Indeed, Flaherty did not only travel in space, but he also urged the subjects of his films to time travel. Thus, for NANOOK OF THE NORTH and for MAN FOR ARAN he had the portrayed people re-enact the ways they used to dress, hunt and live many years ago.

68. Brian Winston: *Claiming the Real: The Documentary Film Revisited.* London: British Film Institute 1995, 20.

69. For films of the Weimar Republic dealing with sex education and exploitation see Malte Hagener (ed.): *Geschlecht in Fesseln. Sexualität zwischen Aufklärung und Ausbeutung im Weimarer Kino.* Munich: edition text + kritik 2000.

70. Germaine Dulac: » L'essence du cinéma: L'idée visuelle «. In: *Les cahiers du mois,* no. 16/17, 1925. Reprinted in and quoted after Prosper Hillairet (ed.): *Germaine Dulac. Ecrits sur le cinéma (1919-1937).* Paris: Éditions Expérimental 1994: 62-67, here 65. [» ...les films documentaires nous le montrent comme une forme de microscope grâce auquel nous percevons dans le domaine réel ce que nous ne percevrions pas sans lui. Dans un documentaire, dans un film scientifique, la vie nous apparaît avec ses mille détails, son évolution, tout ce que l'œil ne peut suivre ordinairement., my trans.]

71. See, for a collection of essays on this format, Frank Kessler, Sabine Lenk, Martin Loiperdinger (eds.): *Kintop. Jahrbuch zur Erforschung des frühen Films. 11: Kinematographen-Programme.* Frankfurt am Main, Basel: Stroemfeld/Roter Stern 2002. See, for a crucial case study that contains numerous examples, Ivo Blom: *Jean Desmet and the Early Dutch Film Trade.* Amsterdam: Amsterdam University Press 2003. See, for a more theoretically inclined discussion, Thomas Elsaesser: *Filmgeschichte und frühes Kino. Archäologie eines Medienwandels.* Munich: edition text + kritik 2002: passim, especially chapter 3 (» Wie der frühe Film zum Erzählkino wurde «): 69-93.

72. For a consideration of the specific screening and programming strategies of the Dutch *Filmliga*, see Tom Gunning: »Ontmoetingen in verduisterde ruimten. De alternatieve programmering van de Nederlandsche Filmliga«. In: Nico de Klerk, Ruud Visschedijk (eds.): *Het gaat om de film! Een nieuwe geschiedenis van de Nederlandsche Filmliga 1927-1933*. Amsterdam: Bas Lubberhuizen / Filmmuseum 1999: 217-263. See also my »Programming Attractions. Avant-garde Exhibition Practice in the 1920s and 1930s«. In: Wanda Strauven (eds.): *The Cinema of Attractions Reloaded*. Amsterdam: Amsterdam University Press 2006. (Film Culture in Transition): 265-279.

73. Anon.: »Historischer Tag des deutschen Tonfilms: Uraufführung ›Melodie der Welt‹«. In: *Film-Kurier*, vol. 11, no. 60, 9.3.1929.

74. See the lead article »Der Film der Hapag. Der Ruttmann-Film im Mozartsaal«. In: *Film-Kurier*, vol. 11, no. 63, 13.3.1929.

75. This speech is missing in the existing prints of MELODIE DER WELT.

76. anon: »›Melodie der Welt‹«. In: *Lichtbild-Bühne*, 13.3.1929. See also anon.: »Die ›Melodie der Welt‹. Grundsätzliches zum ersten großen deutschen Tonfilm«. In: *Kinematograph*, vol. 23, no. 61, 13.3.1929. [»Selten hat die Weltstadt Berlin ein gesellschaftliches Ereignis derartigen Stils erlebt. Die Auffahrt der Autos zu dieser mit höchster Aufmerksamkeit erwarteten Premiere war derart, daß die Polizei in der Umgebung des Nollendorfplatzes umfassende Verkehrsumleitungen vornehmen mußte. Das Theater selbst bot ein festliches Bild, wie man es selbst bei einer Gala-Oper selten gesehen hat. Die repräsentativste Gesellschaft der Reichshauptstadt, darunter die markantesten Köpfe der Wirtschaft, der Politik, der Presse, hatten sich eingefunden.«, my trans.]

77. See Bruce Posner (ed.): *Unseen Cinema: Early American Avant-Garde Film 1893-1941*. New York: Anthology Film Archive 2001: 113-130.

78. See *The Film Society Programme. (Fifth Season). The 33rd Performance*. Sunday, November 10th, 1929 at 2.30 P.M. at the Tivoli Palace, Strand. Reprinted in Council of the London Film Society (ed.): *The Film Society Programmes 1925-1939*. New York: Arno Press 1972: 128-131.

79. See Esther Leslie: *Hollywood Flatlands: Animation, Critical Theory and the Avant-Garde*. London, New York: Verso 2002.

80. This development is sketched in Jamie Sexton: »Grierson's Machines: DRIFTERS, the Documentary Film Movement and the Negotiation of Modernity«. In: *Canadian Journal of Film Studies / Revue canadienne d'études cinématographiques*, vol. 11, no. 1, Spring 2002: 40-59, quoted on page 54.

81. Walter Benjamin: »Das Kunstwerk im Zeitalter seiner technischen Reproduzierbarkeit« (Dritte Fassung). In: W.B.: *Gesammelte Schriften. Band I.2*. Frankfurt am M: Suhrkamp 1977: 471-508, here 499. [»Es wird eine der revolutionären Funktionen des Films sein, die Künstlerische und die wissenschaftliche Verwertung der Photographie, die vor dem meist anseinander fielen, als identisch erkennbar zu machen.«]

Notes Conclusion

1. Walter Benjamin: » Erwiderung an Oscar A.H. Schmitz «. In: W.B.: *Gesammelte Schriften. II.2.* Frankfurt am Main: Suhrkamp 1977: 751-755, here 755. [» POTEMKIN ist ein großer, selten geglückter Film. … Dieser Film aber ist ideologisch ausbetoniert, richtig in allen Einzelheiten kalkuliert wie ein Brückenbogen. Je kräftiger die Schläge darauf niedersausen, desto schöner dröhnt er. Nur wer mit behandschuhten Fingerchen daran rüttelt, der hört und bewegt nichts. «, my trans.]

2. See Roland Cosandey: » On Borderline «. In: *Afterimage*, no. 12, autumn 1985: 66-85. See for photos of the 1979-meeting Freddy Buache (ed.): » *Le cinéma indépendant et d'avant-garde à la fin du muet. Le Congrès de La Sarraz (1929) et présentation des films projetés au Symposium de Lausanne (1-4 juin 1979) organisé à l'occasion du Congrès annuel de la Fédération Internationale des Archives du Film (FIAF) à Lausanne du 30 mai au 1er juin 1979* «. In: *Travelling*, no. 55, summer 1979.

3. For a genealogical sketch of cinephilia see Thomas Elsaesser: » Cinephilia or the Uses of Disenchantment «. In: Marijke de Valck, Malte Hagener (eds.): *Cinephilia: Movies, Love and Memory.* Amsterdam: Amsterdam University Press 2005: 27-43.

4. See Paul Cronin's film: FILM AS A SUBVERSIVE ART: AMOS VOGEL AND CINEMA 16 (GB 2003) screened at the Berlin Film Festival 2004; see also the recent collection by Scott MacDonald: » Cinema 16: Documents Towards a History of the Film Society «. In: *Wide Angle*, vol. 19, no. 1: 3-48; see also Vogel's own statements in *Film As a Subversive Art.* New York: Random House 1974.

5. See the presentation by Rahul Hamid: » Establishing the New York Film Festival «. At: *Cinephilia: A Symposium*, New York University, February 22-23, 2002. Richard Roud in turn, the co-director of the New York Film Festival, has written the first English language biography of Henri Langlois, one of the » fathers « of the archival movement who had his first contacts with the cinema in the ciné-clubs of the 1920s and 1930s. There are many such circular relations to be found. See Richard Roud: *A Passion for Films: Henri Langlois and the Cinémathèque Française.* London: Secker & Warburg 1983.

6. See Jay Leyda: *Kino: A History of the Russian and Soviet Film.* London: George Allen & Unwin 1960 and *Films Beget Films: Compilation Films from Propaganda to Drama.* London: George Allen & Unwin 1964.

7. Annette Michelson, besides editing books on Warhol and Oshima and publishing countless articles, edited a book of the collected writings of Vertov in English. See Annette Michelson (ed.): *Kino-Eye: The Writings of Dziga Vertov.* Berkeley, CA: University of California Press 1984.

8. See the personal reminiscences of Charles Musser: » Noël Burch, *Film Practice* und das Studium des frühen Kinos – eine persönliche Erinnerung «. In: Frank Kessler, Sabine Lenk, Martin Loiperdinger (eds.): *KINtop 12: Theorien zum frühen Kino.* Frankfurt am Main and Basel: Stroemfeld / Roter Stern 2003: 87-90 and, especially for the notion of » revalorization « and a critical comparison of the positions occupied by Burch, Gunning and Musser, see Charles Musser: » Historiographic Method and the Study of Early Cinema «. In: *Cinema Journal*, vol. 44, no. 1, Fall 2004: 101-107. Tom Gunning has actually pointed out the importance of Jay Leyda's biography as

a » missing link « and bridge between different developments and trends in cinema and politics; personal conversation, Bremen 22 Jan. 2006.

9. Tom Gunning: » The Cinema of Attractions: Early Film, Its Spectator and the Avant-Garde «. In: *Wide Angle*, vol. 8, no. 3/4, 1986. Reprinted in Thomas Elsaesser (ed.): *Early Cinema: Space, Frame, Narrative*. London: BFI 1990: 56-62.

10. For a study of the American post-war art houses see Barbara Wilinsky: *Sure Seaters: The Emergence of the Art House Cinema*. Minneapolis and London: University of Minnesota Press 2001.

11. See for a thorough study of the different layers relevant to a film festival Marijke de Valck: *Film Festivals: History and Theory of a European Phenomenon That Became a Global Network*. Amsterdam: ASCA 2006.

12. This can be traced back to Georg Simmel and Emile Durkheim. See, for more recent overviews, for example, Jeffrey C. Alexander, Paul Colomy (eds.): *Differentiation Theory and Social Change: Comparative and Historical Perspectives*. New York: Columbia University Press 1990. See, for a perspective from systems theory, Niklas Luhmann: *Die Kunst der Gesellschaft*. Frankfurt am Main: Suhrkamp 1995: 215ff.

Bibliography

Magazines Used

Avant-garde Magazines

Arbeiterbühne und Film. Zentralorgan des Arbeiter-Theater-Bundes Deutschlands (GER, June 1930-June 1931).

Cinema Quarterly (GB 1932-35; thereafter incorporated into *World Film News*, first 3 issues edited by Hans Feld, thereafter edited by Marion A. Grierson).

Close Up (CH/GB 1927-1933) edited by Kenneth Mac Pherson, La Territet (CH).

Experimental Cinema (US 1930-1934, five issues, edited by David Platt and Lewis Jacobs)

Film Art: Review of the Advanceguard Cinema (GB, first number published as *Film* in 1933, thereafter *Film Art*, edited by Mr. B. Vivian Braun).

Filmliga (NL 1927-1931).

Film und Volk. Organ des Volksfilmverbandes (GER February 1928-March 1930).

Revue du cinéma (FR 1928-31, edited by Jean Georges Auriol, Robert Aron).

Sight and Sound (GB 1932-).

World Film News (GB 1936-38; incorporating *Cinema Quarterly*).

General Film Magazines

Cinématographie Française (FR)
Ciné-Miroir (FR)
Film-Kurier (GER)
Der Kinematograph (GER)
Lichtbildbühne (GER)
Pour Vous (FR)
Reichsfilmblatt (GER)

Articles and Books

Abbott, John E.; Barry, Iris: » An outline of a project for founding the film library of the Museum of Modern Art «. In: *Film History*, vol. 7, 1995: 325-335.

Abel, Richard: *French Cinema: The First Wave 1915-1929*. Princeton, NJ: Princeton University Press 1984.

Abel, Richard: » On the Threshold of French Film Theory and Criticism, 1915-1919 «. In: *Cinema Journal*, vol. 25, no. 1, Fall 1985: 12-33.

Abel, Richard: *French Film Theory and Criticism, 1907-1939: A History/Anthology. I: 1907-1929. II: 1929-1939.* (2 vols.) Princeton, NJ: Princeton University Press 1988.

Abel, Richard: » *Cinégraphie* and the Search for Specificity «. In: R.A.: *French Film Theory and Criticism, 1907-1939: A History/Anthology. I: 1907-1929.* Princeton, NJ: Princeton University Press 1988: 194-223

Abel, Richard; Altman, Rick (eds.): *The Sounds of Early Cinema*. Bloomington, IN: Indiana University Press 2001.

Adkins, Helen: » Erste Russische Kunstausstellung «. In: Michael Bollé, Eva Züchner, Gesine Asmus (eds.): *Stationen der Moderne. Die bedeutenden Kunstausstellungen des 20. Jahrhunderts in Deutschland*. Berlin: Berlinische Galerie / Nicolai 1988: 184-215.

Agde, Günter: *Kämpfer. Biographie eines Films und seiner Macher*. Berlin: Das Neue Berlin 2001.

Agde, Günter: » Neue Einblicke in alte Hoffnungen. Filmexil in der UdSSR 1933-1945 «. In: *Filmexil*, no. 20, 2004: 4-16.

Aitken, Ian: *Film and Reform: John Grierson and the Documentary Film Movement*. London, New York: Routledge 1990. (Cinema and Society).

Aitken, Ian: *European Film Theory and Cinema: An Introduction*. Edinburgh: Edinburgh University Press 2001.

Akerman, Margareta (ed.): *Remembering Iris Barry*. New York: The Museum of Modern Art 1980.

Albera, François: » Eisenstein en Suisse. Premiers materiaux «. In: *Travelling*, no. 48, Winter 1976: 89-119.

Albera, François: *Albatros. Des russes à Paris 1919-1929*. Paris: Cinémathèque Française 1995.

Albera, François: » La réception du cinéma soviétique en France, dans les années 1920-1930 «. In: Aïcha Kherroubi (ed.): *Le studio Mejrabpom ou l'aventure du cinéma privé au pays des bolcheviks*. Paris: La documentation française 1996: 117-126.

Albera, François: » Formzerstörung und Transparenz – Glass House, vom Filmprojekt zum Film als Projekt «. In: Oksana Bulgakowa (ed.): *Eisenstein und Deutschland. Texte – Dokumente – Briefe*. Berlin: Akademie der Künste / Henschel 1998: 123-142.

Albera, François: *Avanguardie*. Milano: Il Castoro 2004. (Le dighe).

Albera, François; Cosandey, Roland (eds.): *Boris Barnet. Ecrits – Documents – Etudes – Filmographie*. Locarno: Festival international du film 1985.

Alexander, William: *Film on the Left: American Documentary Film from 1931 to 1942*. Princeton, NJ: Princeton University Press 1981.

Allen, Robert C.; Gomery, Douglas: *Film History: Theory and Practice*. New York: Knopf 1985.

Altman, Rick (ed.): *Sound Theory, Sound Practice*. New York, London: Routledge 1992. (AFI Film Reader).

Altman, Rick: » Penser l'histoire (du cinéma) autrement : un modèle de crise «. In: *Vingtième siècle*, no. 46, 1995: 65-74.

Anderson, Benedict: *Imagined Communities: Reflections on the Origin and Spread of Nationalism*. London: Verso 1983.

Andriopoulos, Stefan: *Besessene Körper. Hypnose, Körperschaften und die Erfindung des Kinos*. München: Wilhelm Fink 2000.

Andriopoulos, Stefan; Dotzler, Bernhard (eds.): *1929. Beiträge zur Archäologie der Medien*. Frankfurt am Main: Suhrkamp 2002. (stw 1579).

anon.: » Sergei Eisenstein vs. Dziga Vertov «. In: *Skrien*, no. 33, Maart/April 1973: 3-9.

Anstey, Edgar: » Paul Rotha and Thorold Dickinson «. In: *Sight & Sound*, Summer 1984: 194f.

Arnheim, Rudolf: *Film als Kunst*. Berlin: Rowohlt 1932. [reprint Frankfurt am Main: Suhrkamp 2002. (stw 1553)]

Arnheim, Rudolf: *Kritiken und Aufsätze zum Film*. (edited by Helmut H. Diederichs). Frankfurt am Main: Fischer 1979.

Arnheim, Rudolf: *Die Seele in der Silberschicht. Medientheoretische Texte. Photographie – Film – Rundfunk*. Frankfurt am Main: Suhrkamp 2004. (stw 1654)

Arnold, Heinz Ludwig (ed.): *Aufbruch ins 20. Jahrhundert. Über Avantgarden*. München: edition text + kritik 2001. (text + kritik Sonderband IX/01).

Ashby, Justine; Higson, Andrew (eds.): *British Cinema, Past and Present*. London, New York: Routledge 2000.

Asper, Helmut G.: *Max Ophüls. Eine Biographie*. Berlin: Bertz 1998.

Aumont, Jacques (ed.): *Jean Epstein. Cinéaste, poète, philosophe*. Paris: Cinémathèque française – Musée du cinéma 1998. (Conférences du Collège d'histoire de l'art cinématographique).

Aurich, Rolf; Jacobsen, Wolfgang (eds.): *Werkstatt Film. Selbstverständnis und Visionen von Filmleuten der zwanziger Jahre*. München: edition text + kritik 1998.

Bagier, Guido: *Der kommende Film. Eine Abrechnung und eine Hoffnung. Was war? Was ist? Was wird?* Stuttgart, Berlin, Leipzig: Deutsche Verlags-Anstalt 1928.

Bakker, Kees (ed.): *Joris Ivens and the Documentary Context*. Amsterdam: Amsterdam University Press 1999. (Film Culture in Transition).

Balázs, Béla: *Der Geist des Films*. Frankfurt am Main: Suhrkamp 2001. (originally Halle/Saale: Wilhelm Knapp 1930).

Balázs, Béla: *Der sichtbare Mensch, oder die Kultur des Films*. Frankfurt am Main: Suhrkamp 2001. (originally Wien, Leipzig: Deutsch-Österreichischer Verlag 1924).

Balides, Constance: » Immersion in the Virtual Ornament: Contemporary › Movie Ride ‹ Films «. In: David Thorburn, Henry Jenkins (eds.): *Rethinking Media Change: The Aesthetics of Transition*. Cambridge, MA and London: The MIT Press 2003: 315-336.

Bamford, Kenton: *Distorted Images: British National Identity and Film in the 1920s*. London, New York: I.B. Tauris 1999. (Cinema and Society).

Banaszkiewicz, Wladyslaw; et al.: *La cinématographie Polonaise*. Warsaw: Éditions » Polonia « 1962.

Barkhausen, Hans: » Zur Geschichte des ehemaligen Reichsfilmarchivs «. In: Günter Moltmann, Karl Friedrich Reimers (eds.): *Zeitgeschichte im Film- und Tondokument. 17 historische, pädagogische und sozialwissenschaftliche Beiträge*. Göttingen, Zürich, Frankfurt: Musterschmidt 1970: 241-250.

Barnard, Timothy: » From Impressionism to Communism: Léon Moussinac's Technics of the Cinema, 1921-1933 «. In: *Framework: The Journal of Cinema and Media*, no.42, 2000. Online at http://www.frameworkonline.com/42tb.htm, visited 6.2.2003.

Barnier, Martin: *En route vers le parlant. Histoire d'une évolution technologique, économique et esthéthique du cinéma (1926-1934)*. Liège (BE): Éditions du Céfal 2002. (Histoire du Cinéma / Collection Travaux & Thèses).

Barnouw, Erik: *Documentary: A History of the Non-Fiction Film*. Oxford: Oxford University Press 1993[2].

Barr, Charles (ed.): *All Our Yesterdays: 90 Years of British Cinema*. London: British Film Insitute 1986.

Barry, Iris: *Let's Go to the Pictures*. London: Chatto & Windus 1925.

Barsam, Richard Meran: *Nonfiction Film: A Critical History*. Bloomington, Indianapolis, IN: Indiana University Press 1992. (Revised and expanded edition).

Baumunk, Bodo-Michael: » Ein Pfadfinder der Geopolitik. Colin Ross und seine Reisefilme «. In: Jörg Schöning: *Triviale Tropen. Exotische Reise- und Abenteuerfilme aus Deutschland, 1919-1939*. München: edition text + kritik 1997: 84-94.

Bazin, André: » Le mythe du cinéma total «. In: André Bazin: *Qu'est-ce que le cinéma? I: Ontologie et Langage*. Paris: Les éditions du Cerf 1958. (7e art): 21-26.

Becker, Wieland; Petzold, Volker: *Tarkowski trifft King Kong. Geschichte der Filmklubbewegung der DDR*. Berlin: Vistas 2001.

Beeren, Wim; Bloem, Marja; Mignot, Dorine (eds.): *De grote utopie. Russische Avantgarde 1915-1932 / The Great Utopia: Russian Avant-garde 1915-1932 / Die grosse Utopie. Russische Avant-Garde 1915-1932*. Amsterdam: Stedelijk Museum 1992.

Beilenhoff, Wolfgang; Heller, Martin (eds.): *Das Filmplakat*. Zurich, Berlin and New York: Scalo 1995.

Belaygue, Christien (ed.): *Le passage du muet au parlant*. Toulouse: Cinémathèque de Toulouse 1988.

Bellows, Andy Masaki; McDougall, Marina (eds.): *Science Is Fiction: The Films of Jean Painlevé*. Cambridge, MA and London: MIT Press 2000.

Benjamin, Walter: *Gesammelte Schriften*. (Rolf Tiedemann and Herrmann Schweppenhäuser (eds.)). Frankfurt am Main: Suhrkamp 1977.

Benjamin, Walter: *Illuminations: Essays and Reflections*. (trans. by Harry Zohn, introduced by Hannah Arendt). New York: Schocken 1969.

Benjamin, Walter: *Understanding Brecht*. (trans. by Anna Bostock, introduced by Stanley Mitchell). London, New York: Verso 1973.

Benjamin, Walter: *One Way Street and Other Writings*. (trans. by Edmund Jephcott and Kingsley Shorter, introduced by Susan Sontag). London, New York: Verso 1985.

Bergan, Ronald: *Sergei Eisenstein: A Life in Conflict*. London: Little, Brown and Company 1997.

Berger, Jürgen; Garner, Curt; Gregor, Erika; Gregor, Ulrich; Ross, Heiner; Stooss, Toni (eds.): *Erobert den Film! Proletariat und Film in der Weimarer Republik*. Berlin: Neue Gesellschaft für Bildende Künste 1977. (Materialien zur Filmgeschichte 7).

Bernstein, Matthew: »Visual Style and Spatial Articulation in BERLIN, SYMPHONY OF A CITY«. In: *Journal of Film and Video*, vol. 36, no. 4, Fall 1984: 5-12.

Bertetto, Paolo; Toffetti, Sergio (eds.): *Cinema d'avanguardia in Europa. Dalle origini al 1945*. Torino: Il Castoro 1996.

Beyfuß, Edgar; Kossowsky, A. (eds.): *Das Kulturfilmbuch*. Berlin: Carl P. Chryselins'scher Verlag 1924.

Bhabha, Homi K. (ed.): *Nation and Narration*. London: Routledge 1990.

Bhabha, Homi K.: *The Location of Culture*. London, New York: Routledge 1994.

Bigsby, Christopher (ed.): *Superculture.* London: Elek 1975.

Birkhäuser, Kaspar: »Fünfzig Jahre im Dienste der Filmbesucher und des guten Films. Le Bon Film Basel 1931-1981«. In: Le Bon Film (ed.): *50 Jahre Le Bon Film*. Basel: Le Bon Film 1981.

Björkin, Mats; Snickars, Pelle: »1923-1933. Production, Reception and Cultural Significance of Swedish Non-fiction Films«. In: Zimmermann, Peter; Hoffmann, Kay (eds.): *Triumph der Bilder. Kultur- und Dokumentarfilme vor 1945 im internationalen Vergleich*. Konstanz: UVK Verlagsgesellschaft 2003: 272-290.

Blom, Ivo: *Jean Desmet and the Early Dutch Film Trade*. Amsterdam: Amsterdam University Press 2003.

Bloßfeldt, Karl: *Urformen der Kunst. Photographische Pflanzenbilder*. (edited with an introduction by Karl Nierendorff). Berlin: Ernst Wasmuth n.y. [1928].

Bock, Hans-Michael; Berger, Jürgen (eds.): *Photo: Casparius. Filmgeschichte in Berlin. Berlin um 1930*. Berlin: Stiftung Deutsche Kinemathek 1978.

Bock, Hans-Michael: »›Brüder zum Licht!‹ Kino, Film und Arbeiterbewegung «. In: Werner Skrentny (ed.): *Vorwärts – und nicht vergessen. Arbeiterkultur in Hamburg um 1930*. Hamburg: Projektgruppe Arbeiterkultur Hamburg 1982: 298-316.

Bock, Hans-Michael (ed.): *CineGraph – Lexikon zum deutschsprachigen Film*. München: edition text + kritik 1984ff.

Bock, Hans-Michael; Töteberg, Michael (eds.): *Das Ufa-Buch*. Frankfurt am Main: Zweitausendeins 1992.

Bock, Hans-Michael; Mosel, Wiebke Annkatrin; Spazier, Ingrun (eds.): *Die Tobis 1928-1945. Eine kommentierte Filmographie*. Munich: edition text + kritik 2003.

Bono, Francesco; et al. (eds.): *La Filmliga olandesa (1927-1933). Avanguardia, critica, organizzazione del cinema*. Bologna: Commune di Bologna 1991. (Giornate internazzionali di studio e documentazione sul cinema 4).

Bool, Flip: » Paul Schuitema und Piet Zwart. Die Neue Typografie und die Neue Fotografie im Dienste der Industrie und des politischen Kampfes «. In: Stanislaus von Moos, Chris Smeenk (eds.): *Avantgarde und Industrie*. Delft: Delft University Press 1983: 121-134.

Boost, Charles: *Van Ciné-Club tot Filmhuis. Tien jaren die de filmindustrie deden wankelen*. Amsterdam: Meulenhoff 1979. (Grote cineasten).

Borde, Raymond: *Les Cinémathèques*. Paris: Éditions L'Age d'Homme 1983. (Cinéma Vivant).

Borde, Raymond; Guibbert, Pierre: » Sur la naissance du la Cinémathèque Française. La parole est à Jean Mitry «. In: *Archives (Institut Jean Vigo / Cinémathèque de Toulouse)*, vol. 7, Oct. 1987: 1-12.

Borde, Raymond; Guibbert, Pierre: »› Le cinéma au service de l'histoire ‹ (1935). Un film retrouvé de Germaine Dulac «. In: *Archives (Institut Jean Vigo / Cinémathèque de Toulouse)*, vol. 44/45, Nov/Dec 1991: 1-20.

Bordwell, David: » The Idea of Montage in Soviet Art and Film «. In: *Cinema Journal*, vol. 11, no. 2, Spring 1972: 9-17.

Bordwell, David: » The Musical Analogy «. In: *Yale French Studies*, no. 60, 1980: 141-146.

Bordwell, David: *Narration in the Fiction Film*. Madison, WI and London: University of Wisconsin Press / Methuen 1985.

Bordwell, David; Staiger, Janet; Thompson, Kristin: *The Classical Hollywood Cinema: Film Style & Mode of Production to 1960*. London: Routledge 1985.

Bordwell, David; Thompson, Kristin: *Film History: An Introduction*. New York et al.: McGraw-Hill 1994.

Bouhours, Jean-Michel; Schoeller, Nathalie (eds.): *L'Âge d'or. Correspondance Luis Buñuel – Charles de Noailles. Lettres et Documents (1929-1976)*. Paris : Les Cahiers du Musée nationale de l'art moderne 1993.

Bovier, François: » Pool Production: logique de la modernité «. In: Maria Tortajada, François Albera (eds.): *Cinéma suisse: nouvelles approches. Histoire – Esthétique – Critique – Thèmes – Matériaux*. Lausanne: Éditions Payot 2000: 73-87.

Bradbury, Malcolm: » The Cities of Modernism «. In: Malcolm Bradbury, James McFarlane (eds): *Modernism 1890-1930*. Harmondsworth: Penguin 1976: 96-103.

Bradbury, Malcolm; McFarlane, James (eds.): *Modernism 1890-1930*. Harmondsworth: Penguin 1976.

Bregant, Michal: » Alexander Hammid's Czech Years. Space and Time of His Early Films «. In: Michael Omasta (ed.): *Tribute to Sasha. Das filmische Werk von Alexander Hammid. Regie, Kamera, Schnitt und Kritiker*. Wien: Synema 2002: 21-41.

Brenez, Nicole ; Lebrat, Christian (eds.): *Jeune, dure et pure! Une histoire du cinéma d'avant-garde et expérimental en France*. Milano / Paris: Mazzotta / Cinémathèque française 2001.

Brinckmann, Christine Noll: » Experimentalfilm, 1920-1990. Einzelgänge und Schübe «. In: Wolfgang Jacobsen, Anton Kaes, Hans Helmut Prinzler (eds.): *Geschichte des deutschen Films*. Stuttgart, Weimar: J.B. Metzler 1993: 417-450

Brinckmann, Christine N.: » › Abstraktion ‹ und › Einfühlung ‹ im frühen deutschen Avantgardefilm «. In: Harro Segeberg (ed.): *Die Perfektionierung des Scheins. Das Kino der Weimarer Republik im Kontext der Künste*. Munich: Wilhelm Fink Verlag 2000: 111-140.

Bregant, Michal: » Le cinéma d'avant-garde : entre le reve et l'utopie «. In: Eva Zaoralova, Jean-Loup Passek (eds.): *Le Cinéma Tcheque et Slovaque*. Paris: Éditions du Centre Pompidou 1996 : 74-83.

Bren, Frank: *World Cinema: 1: Poland*. London: Flicks Books 1986.

Brenez, Nicole; Lebrat, Christian (eds.): *Jeune, Dure et Pure! Une histoire du cinéma d'avant-garde et expérimental en France*. Paris / Milano: Cinémathèque Française / Mazzota 2001.

Brown, Geoff: » Table Tennis over Everest. Ivor Montagu will be eighty on 23 April. « In: *Sight & Sound*, Spring 1984: 98.

Brunel, Adrian: *Nice Work: The Story of Thirty Years in British Film Production*. London: Forbes Robertson 1949.

Bryher, Winifred: *Film Problems of Soviet Russia*. London: POOL 1929.

Buache, Freddy: » Le cinéma indépendant et d'avant-garde à la fin du muet «. In: *Travelling. Cahiers de la Cinémathèque Suisse*, no. 55, summer 1979 and no. 56/57, spring 1980.

Buchsbaum, Jonathan: *Cinema Engage: Film in the Popular Front*. Urbana, IL: University of Illinois Press 1988.

Budd, Mike (ed.): *The Cabinet of Dr. Caligari: Texts, Contexts, Histories*. New Brunswick, London: Rutgers University Press 1990.

Bulgakowa, Oksana: » Das Phänomen FEKS: › Boulevardisierung ‹ der Avantgarde «. In: *montage/AV*, vol. 2, no. 1, 1993: 94-115.

Bulgakowa, Oksana (Hg.): *Die ungewöhnlichen Abenteuer des Dr. Mabuse im Lande der Bolschewiki. Das Buch zur Filmreihe » Moskau – Berlin «*. Berlin: Freunde der Deutschen Kinemathek 1995.

Bulgakowa, Oksana: » Russische Filme in Berlin «. In: Oksana Bulgakowa (ed.): *Die ungewöhnlichen Abenteuer des Dr. Mabuse im Lande der Bolschewiki. Das Buch zur Filmreihe » Moskau – Berlin «*. Berlin: Freunde der Deutschen Kinemathek 1995: 81-114.

Bulgakowa, Oksana: » Der Fall Meshrabpom «. In: Oksana Bulgakowa (ed.): *Die ungewöhnlichen Abenteuer des Dr. Mabuse im Lande der Bolschewiki. Das Buch zur Filmreihe » Moskau – Berlin «*. Berlin: Freunde der Deutschen Kinemathek 1995: 185-193.

Bulgakowa, Oksana: *FEKS. Die Fabrik des exzentrischen Schauspielers*. Berlin: PotemkinPress 1996.

Bulgakowa, Oksana: *Sergej Eisenstein. Eine Biographie*. Berlin: PotemkinPress 1997.

Bulgakowa, Oksana (ed.): *Eisenstein und Deutschland. Texte – Dokumente – Briefe*. Berlin: Akademie der Künste / Henschel 1998.

Burch, Noël: *To the Distant Observer: Form and Meaning in the Japanese Cinema*. Berkeley, CA: University of California Press 1979.

Bürger, Peter: *Theorie der Avantgarde*. Frankfurt am Main: Suhrkamp 1974 (edition suhrkamp 727). (eng.: *Theory of the Avant-garde*. Manchester: Manchester University Press 1984).

Campbell, Russell: » Film and Photo League. Radical Cinema in the 30's «. In: *Jump Cut*, no. 14, March 1977: 23-33.

Campbell, Russell: *Cinema Strikes Back: Radical Filmmaking in the United States 1930-1942*. Ann Arbor, MI: UMI Research Press 1982. (Studies in Cinema 20).

Canosa, Michele (ed.): *L'Immagine Acustica. Dal muto al sonoro: gli anni della transizione in Europa*. Ancona: Transeuropa 1992. (Cinegrafie 2/5).

Casanova, Maria (ed.): *Tierra sin pan. Luis Buñuel y los nuevos caminos de las vanguardias*. Valencia: Institut Valencià d'Art Modern 1999.

Casetti, Francesco: *Teorie del cinema (1945-1990)*. Milano: Bompiani 1993. (engl.: *Theories of Cinema, 1945-1995*. Austin, TX: University of Texas Press 1999).

Ceram, C.W.: *Eine Archäologie des Kinos*. Reinbek: Rowohlt 1965.

Chanan, Michael (ed.): *Twenty-five Years of the New Latin American Cinema*. London: British Film Institute / Channel Four 1983.

Chochlowa, Jekatarina: » Es gibt ein Land Film, die Bewohner sind Deutsche. Deutsche Filme in Sowjetrußland «. In: Oksana Bulgakowa (ed.): *Die ungewöhnlichen Abenteuer des Dr. Mabuse im Lande der Bolschewiki. Das Buch zur Filmreihe » Moskau – Berlin «*. Berlin: Freunde der Deutschen Kinemathek 1995: 159-164.

Chochlowa, Jekatarina: » Die erste Filmarbeit Sergej Eisensteins. Die Ummontage des › Dr. Mabuse, der Spieler ‹ von Fritz Lang «. In: Oksana Bulgakowa: *Eisenstein und Deutschland. Texte – Dokumente – Briefe*. Berlin: Akademie der Künste / Henschel 1998: 115-122.

Christie, Ian: » French Avant-garde Film in the Twenties: from › Specificity ‹ to Surrealism «. In: Philip Drummond et al. (eds.):*Film as Film: Formal Experiment in Film 1910-1975*. London: Hayward Gallery 1979: 37-45.

Christie, Ian: » Soviet Cinema: Making Sense of Sound. A Revised Historiography «. In: *Screen*, vol. 23, no. 2, July-Aug. 1982: 34-49.

Christie, Ian; Taylor, Richard (eds.): *The Film Factory: Russian and Soviet Cinema in Documents, 1896-1939*. London: Routledge & Kegan Paul 1988.

Christie, Ian: » The avant-gardes and European cinema before 1930 «. In: John Hill, Pamela Church Gibson (eds.): *The Oxford Guide to Film Studies*. Oxford et al.: Oxford University Press 1998: 449-454.

Close Up. Territet (CH). Complete reprint in 10 volumes Nendeln (Liechtenstein): Kraus Reprint 1969.

Coissac, Georges Michel: *Histoire du cinématographie. De ses origines à nos jours*. Paris: Éditions Cinéopse / Librairie Gauthier-Villars & Cie. 1925.

Cory, Mark E.: » Soundplay: The Polyphonous Tradition of German Radio Art «. In: Douglas Kahn, Gregory Whitehead (eds.) *Wireless Imagination: Sound, Radio and the Avant-Garde*. Cambridge, MA, London: The MIT Press 1992: 331-371.

Cosandey, Roland: » On Borderline «. In: *Afterimage*, no. 12, autumn 1985: 66-85.

Cosandey, Roland; Tode, Thomas: » Le 1er congrès international du cinéma indépendant. La Sarraz, Septembre 1929 «. In: *Archives (Perpignan)*, no. 84, April 2000: 1-30.

Cosandey, Roland: » L'inescamotable escamoteur: Méliès, der unsterbliche Zauberkünstler «. In: Stefan Andriopoulos, Bernhard Dotzler (eds.): *1929. Beiträge zur Archäologie der Medien*. Frankfurt am Main: Suhrkamp 2002: 370-388.

Council of the London Film Society (ed.): *The Film Society Programmes 1925-1939*. New York: Arno Press 1972.

Crafton, Donald: *The Talkies: American Cinema's Transition to Sound 1926-1931*. New York: Charles Scribner's Sons 1997. (History of the American Cinema 4).

Crofts, Stephen: » Reconceptualising National Cinema/s «. In: *Quaterly Review of Film and Video*, vol. 14, no. 3, 1993: 49-67.

Crofts, Stephen: » Concepts of National Cinema «. In: John Hill, Pamela Church Gibson (eds.): *The Oxford Guide to Film Studies*. Oxford: Oxford University Press 1998: 385-394.

Curtis, David: *Experimental Cinema: A Fifty-Year Evolution*. London: Studio Vista 1971.

Dale, R.C.: *The Films of René Clair: 2 Vols. I: Exposition and Analysis. II: Documentation*. Metuchen, NJ, London: Scarecrow Press 1986.

Davis, Darrell William (2001): » Reigniting Japanese Tradition with *Hana-Bi* «. In: *Cinema Journal 40*, No. 4, Summer: 58-79.

David, Yasha (ed.): *Buñuel. Auge des Jahrhunderts*. Bonn: Kunst- und Ausstellungshalle der Bundesrepublik Deutschland 1994.

DeCherney, Peter: *Imagining the Archive: Film Collection in America Before MoMA*. New York: New York University 2001. [unpublished Ph.D. thesis].

De Klerk, Nico; Visschedijk, Ruud (eds.): *Het gaat om de film! Een nieuwe geschiedenis van de Nederlandsche Filmliga 1927-1933*. Amsterdam: Bas Lubberhuizen / Filmmuseum 1999.

De Klerk, Nico: » The Moment of Screening. What Non-Fiction Films Can Do «. In: Peter Zimmermann, Kay Hoffmann (eds.): *Triumph der Bilder. Kultur- und Dokumentarfilme vor 1945 im internationalen Vergleich*. Konstanz: UVK 2003: 291-301.

Delluc, Louis: *Ecrits cinématographiques. 3 Vols. I: Le Cinéma et les Cinéastes. II: Cinéma et Cie. III: Drames de Cinéma*. (edited by Pierre Lherminier). Paris: Cinémathèque Française 1985; 1986; 1990.

De Pina, Luís: *História do cinema português*. Mem Martins: Publicações Europa-América 1986. (Colecção saber).

De Valck, Marijke: *Film Festivals: History and Theory of a European Phenomenon That Became a Global Network*. Amsterdam: ASCA 2006.

Dibbets, Karel: *Sprekende films. De komst van de geluidsfilm in Nederland 1928-1933*. Amsterdam: Cramwinckel 1993.

Dickinson, Thorold; Roche, Catherine de la: *Soviet Cinema*. London: Falcon Press 1948. (National Cinema).

Diederichs, Helmut H.: »› Ihr müßt etwas von guter Filmkunst verstehen ‹ Béla Balázs als Filmtheoretiker und Medienpädagoge «. In: Béla Balázs: *Der sichtbare Mensch, oder die Kultur des Films*. Frankfurt am Main: Suhrkamp 2001: 115-147

Diederichs, Helmut H. (ed.): *Geschichte der Filmtheorie. Kunsttheoretische Texte von Méliès bis Arnheim*. Frankfurt am Main: Suhrkamp 2004. (stw 1652).

Diezel, Peter: » Im ständigen Dissens. Erwin Piscator und die Meshrabpom-Film-Gesellschaft «. In: *Filmexil*, no. 20, 2004: 39-56.

Dillmann-Kühn, Claudia (Hrsg.): *Sergej Eisenstein im Kontext der russischen Avantgarde 1920-1925*. Frankfurt am Main: Deutsches Filmmuseum 1992. (Kinematograph 8).

Distelmeyer, Jan (ed.): *Tonfilmfrieden/Tonfilmkrieg. Die Geschichte der Tobis vom Technik-Syndikat zum Staatskonzern*. Munich: edition text + kritik 2003. (Ein CineGraph Buch).

Donald, James; Friedberg, Anne; Marcus, Laura (eds.): *Close Up, 1927-1933: Cinema and Modernism*. London: Cassell 1998.

Dozoretz, Wendy: » Dulac versus Artaud «. In: *Wide Angle*, vol. 3, no. 1, 1979: 46-53.

Drubek-Meyer, Natascha; Murašov, Jurij (eds.): *Apparatur und Rhapsodie. Zu den Filmen des Dziga Vertov*. Frankfurt am Main et al.: Peter Lang 2000. (Berliner Slawistische Arbeiten).

Drummond, Philip ; et al. (eds.): *Film as Film: Formal Experiment in Film 1910-1975*. London: Hayward Gallery 1979.

Dumont, Hervé: *Geschichte des Schweizer Films. Spielfilme 1896-1965*. Lausanne: Cinémathèque Suisse 1987.

Ďurovičová, Nataša: » Local Ghosts: Dubbing Bodies in Early Sound Cinema «. In: Anna Antonini (ed.): *Il film e i suoi multipli. Film and Its Multiples*. Udine: Forum 2003: 83-98.

Dusinberre, Deke: » The Other Avantgardes «. In: Philip Drummond et al. (eds.): *Film as Film: Formal Experiment in Film 1910-1975*. London: Hayward Gallery 1979: 53-58.

Eagleton, Terry; Jameson, Fredric; Said, Edward (eds.): *Nationalism, Colonialism and Literature*. Minnesota: University of Minnesota Press 1990.

Ehrenburg, Ilja: *Die Traumfabrik. Chronik des Films*. Berlin: Malik 1931.

Eisenstein, S.M.: *Selected Works: Volume I: Writings, 1922-34*. (edited by Richard Taylor). London: British Film Institute / Bloomington and Indiana: Indiana University Press 1988.

Eisler, Hanns; [Adorno, Theodor]: *Komposition für den Film*. Berlin: Henschel 1948.

Ellis, Jack C.: *John Grierson: Life, Contributions, Influence*. Carbondale, IL: Southern Illinois University Press 2000.

Elsaesser, Thomas: » Two Decades in Another Country. Hollywood and the Cinephiles «. In: Christopher Bigsby (ed.): *Superculture*. London: Elek 1975: 199-216.

Elsaesser, Thomas: » Images for England (and Scotland, Ireland, Wales...) «. In: *Monthly Film Bulletin*, vol. 51, no. 608, September 1984: 267-269.

Elsaesser, Thomas: » The New Film History «. In: *Sight and Sound*, vol. 55, no. 4, Autumn 1986: 246-251.

Elsaesser, Thomas: » Chronicle of a Death Retold: Hyper, Retro, or Counter-Cinema «. In: *Monthly Film Bulletin*, vol. 54, no. 641, June 1987: 164-167.

Elsaesser, Thomas: » The Idea of National Cinema «. (» De competitie met Hollywood «). In: *Skrien* 186, October/November 1992. Reprinted in English translation in T.E.: *European Cinema: Face to Face with Hollywood*. Amsterdam: Amsterdam University Press.

Elsaesser, Thomas: » Moderne und Modernisierung. Der deutsche Film der dreißiger Jahre «. In: *montage/av*, vol. 3, no. 2, 1994: 23-40.

Elsaesser, Thomas: » Über den Nutzen der Enttäuschung. Filmkritik zwischen Cinephilie und Nekrophilie «. In: Irmbert Schenk (ed.): *Filmkritik. Bestandsaufnahmen und Perspektiven*. Marburg: Schüren 1998: 91-114.

Elsaesser, Thomas: » Dada/Cinema? «. In: Rudolf E. Kuenzli (ed.): *Dada and Surrealist Film*. New York: Willis, Locker and Owens 1987: 13-27.

Elsaesser, Thomas: » German Cinema in the 1990s «. In: Thomas Elsaesser, Michael Wedel (eds.): *The BFI Companion to German Cinema*. London: British Film Institute 1999.

Elsaesser, Thomas: *Weimar Cinema and After: Germany's Historical Imaginary*. London, New York: Routledge 2000. (German: *Das Weimarer Kino – aufgeklärt und doppelbödig*. Berlin: Vorwerk 8 1999.)

Elsaesser, Thomas: » Writing and Rewriting Film History: Terms of a Debate «. In: *Cinéma et cie.*, no. 1, Fall 2001: 24-33.

Elsaesser, Thomas: » Realität zeigen: Der frühe Film im Zeichen Lumières «. In: Ursula von Keitz, Kay Hoffmann (eds.): *Die Einübung des dokumentarischen Blicks. Fiction Film und Non Fiction Film zwischen Wahrheitsanspruch und expressiver Sachlichkeit 1895-1945*. Marburg: Schüren 2001: 27-50.

Elsaesser, Thomas: *Filmgeschichte und frühes Kino. Archäologie eines Medienwandels*. Munich: edition text + kritik 2002.

Elsaesser, Thomas: » Early Film History and Multi-Media: An Archaeology of Possible Futures? «. In: Wendy Chung (ed.): *The Archaeology of Multimedia*. London, New York: Routledge 2003.

Elsaesser, Thomas: » Cinephilia or the Uses of Disentchantment «. In: Marijke de Valck, Malte Hagener (eds.) : *Cinephilia: Movies, Love and Memory*. Amsterdam: Amsterdam University Press 2005: 27-43.

Elsaesser, Thomas: » Die Stadt von Morgen: Filme zum Bauen und Wohnen in der Weimarer Republik «. In: Klaus Kreimeier, Antje Ehmann, Jeanpaul Goergen (Hrsg.): *Geschichte des dokumentarischen Films in Deutschland. Band 2: Weimarer Republik 1918-1933*. Stuttgart: Reclam 2005: 381-409.

Elsaesser, Thomas: »InpersoNations: National Cinema, Historical Imaginaries«. In: T.E.: *European Cinema: Face to Face with Hollywood*. Amsterdam: Amsterdam University Press 2005: 57-81.

Elsaesser, Thomas; Hagener, Malte: »Walter Ruttmann: 1929«. In: Stefan Andriopoulos, Bernhard Dotzler (eds.): *1929. Beiträge zur Archäologie der Medien*. Frankfurt am Main: Suhrkamp 2002: 316-349.

Engel, Christine (ed.): *Geschichte des sowjetischen und russischen Films*. Stuttgart, Weimar: Metzler 1999.

Epstein, Jean: *Écrits sur le cinéma, 1921-1953. Édition chronologique. I: 1921-1947. II: 1946-1953.* (2 vols.) Paris: Seghers 1974; 1975. (Cinéma club).

Ernst, Wolfgang: »Der medienarchäologische Blick«. In: Harro Segeberg (ed.): *Die Medien und ihre Technik. Theorien – Modelle – Geschichte*. Marburg: Schüren 2004: 28-42.

Eskildsen, Ute; Horak, Jan-Christopher (eds.): *Film und Foto der Zwanziger Jahre. Eine Betrachtung der Internationalen Werkbundausstellung »Film und Foto« 1929*. Stuttgart: Gerd Hatje 1979.

Esnault, Philippe: »André Sauvage, cinéaste maudit«. In: *La revue du cinéma*, no. 394, May 1984: 92-94.

Esnault, Philippe: »Sauvages«. In: *Cinématographe*, no. 112, July 1985: 63-67.

Espinosa, Julio García: »Towards an Imperfect Cinema«. In: Michael Chanan (ed.): *Twenty-five Years of the New Latin American Cinema*. London: British Film Institute / Channel Four 1983. [originally published in Spanish as »Por un cine imperfecto« in 1970]

Eyman, Scott: *The Speed of Sound: Hollywood and the Talkie Revolution*. New York: Simon & Schuster 1997.

Fahle, Oliver: *Jenseits des Bildes: Poetik des französischen Films der zwanziger Jahre*. Mainz: Bender 2000.

Feldman, Seth R.: *Evolution of Style in the Early Works of Dziga Vertov with a New Appendix*. New York: Arno Press 1977. (Dissertation on Film).

Feldman, Seth: »›Peace between Man and Machine‹. Dziga Vertov's THE MAN WITH A MOVIE CAMERA«. In: Barry Keith Grant, Jeannette Sloniowski (eds.): *Documenting the Documentary: Close Readings of Documentary Film and Video*. Detroit, MI: Wayne State University Press 1998: 40-54.

Fescourt, Henri; Bouquet, Jean-Louis: *L'Idée et l'écran. Opinions sur le cinéma*. Paris: Haberschill et Sergent 1925-26.

Flitterman-Lewis, Sandy: *To Desire Differently: Feminism and the French Cinema*. Urbana, Chicago, IL: University of Illinois Press 1990.

Fofi, Goffredo: »The Cinema of the Popular Front in France (1934-38)«. In: *Screen*, vol. 13, no. 4, Winter 1972/73: 5-57.

Ford, Charles (ed.): *Jacques Feyder. Présentation. Choix de textes. Filmographie. Illustrations*. Paris: Éditions Seghers 1973. (Cinéma d'aujourd'hui 75).

Foster, Stephen C. (ed.): *Hans Richter: Activism, Modernism, and the Avantgarde*. Cambridge, MA, London: The MIT· Press 1998. (in collaboration with the University of Iowa Museum of Art, Iowa City).

Foster, Stephen C.: » Hans Richter: Prophet of Modernism «. In: Stephen C. Foster (ed.): *Hans Richter: Activism, Modernism, and the Avantgarde*. Cambridge, MA, London: The MIT Press 1998: 2-15.

Foucault, Michel: *Madness and Civilisation: A History of Insanity in the Age of Reason*. New York: Random House 1965.

Foucault, Michel: *The Order of Things: An Archaeology of the Human Sciences*. London: Tavistock 1970.

Foucault, Michel: *The Archaeology of Knowledge & The Discourse on Language*. New York: Pantheon 1972.

Foucault, Michel: *The Birth of the Clinic: An Archaeology of Medical Perception*. London: Tavistock 1973.

Foucault, Michel: *Discipline and Punish: The Birth of the Prison*. Harmondsworth: Penguin 1977.

Frey, Reiner: » Geschichten von jenen, die versuchten die laufenden Bilder wieder einzufangen – die Anfänge der Zuschauerfilmkritik in Deutschland, das Beispiel Arbeiterbühne und Film (1930/31) «. In: *Filmfaust*, no. 19, June 1980: 8-16.

Friedberg, Anne: » Gemeinsame Tagträume: Eine psychoanalytische Film-Affäre – Pabst, Sachs und das Filmjournal *Close Up* «. In: Gottfried Schlemmer, Bernhard Riff, Georg Haberl (ed.): *G.W. Pabst*. Münster: MakS Publikationen 1990: 36-62.

Gabriel, Teshome: *Third Cinema in the Third World: The Aesthetics of Liberation*. Ann Arbor, MI: University of Michigan Research Press 1982.

Gardner, William O.: » New Perceptions: Kinugasa Teinosuke's Films and Japanese Modernism «. In: *Cinema Journal*, vol. 43, no. 3, 2004: 59-78.

Gaßner, Hubertus; Kopanski, Karlheinz; Stengel, Karin (eds.): *Die Konstruktion der Utopie. Ästhetische Avantgarde und politische Utopie in den 20er Jahren*. Marburg: Jonas Verlag 1992. (documenta Archiv)

Gauthier, Christophe: *La Passion du cinéma. Cinéphiles, ciné-clubs et salles spécialisées à Paris de 1920 à 1929*. Paris: Association Française de Recherche sur l'Histoire du Cinéma / Ecole des Chartes 1999.

Gauthier, Guy: » Die › vier Winde ‹ des französischen Dokumentarfilms. Seine Entwicklung zwischen den beiden Weltkriegen «. In: Peter Zimmermann, Kay Hoffmann (eds.): *Triumph der Bilder. Kultur- und Dokumentarfilme vor 1945 im internationalen Vergleich*. Konstanz: UVK 2003: 189-202.

Geduld, Harry M.; Gottesman, Ronald (eds.): *Sergei Eisenstein and Upton Sinclair: The Making and Unmaking of › Que viva Mexico! ‹*. Bloomington, IN and London: Indiana University Press 1970.

Geduld, Harry M.: *The Birth of the Talkies: From Edison to Jolson*. Bloomington, IN, London: Indiana University Press 1975.

Gehr, Herbert; von Hofacker, Marion (eds.): *Hans Richter. Malerei und Film*. Frankfurt am Main: Deutsches Filmmuseum 1989. (Kinematograph 5).

Gehr, Herbert (ed.): *Optische Poesie. Oskar Fischinger – Leben und Werk*. Frankfurt am Main: Deutsches Filmmuseum 1993. (Kinematograph 9).

Genette, Gérard: *Seuils*. Paris: Éditions du Seuil 1987. (Collection poétique). [engl.: *Paratexts. Thresholds of Interpretation*. Cambridge: Cambridge University Press 1997].

Goergen, Jeanpaul (ed.): *Walter Ruttmann. Eine Dokumentation*. Berlin: Freunde der Deutschen Kinemathek 1989.

Goergen, Jeanpaul: *Walter Ruttmanns Tonmontagen als Ars Acustica*. Siegen: MuK 1994. (Massenmedien und Kommunikation 89).

Goergen, Jeanpaul (ed.): *Victor Trivas*. Hamburg / Berlin: CineGraph – Hamburgisches Centrum für Filmforschung e.V. / Stiftung Deutsche Kinemathek / CineGraph Babelsberg – Brandenburgisches Centrum für Filmforschung e. V. 1996. (FilmMaterialien 9).

Goergen, Jeanpaul: » Lebenswahrheit im Musikfilm. René Clairs SOUS LES TOITS DE PARIS «. In: Malte Hagener, Jan Hans (eds.): *Als die Filme singen lernten. Innovation und Tradition im Musikfilm 1928-1938*. Munich: edition text + kritik 1999: 72-85.

Goergen, Jeanpaul; Hoch, Angelika; Gregor, Erika; Gregor, Ulrich (eds.): *Hans Richter. Film ist Rhythmus*. Berlin: Freunde der Deutschen Kinemathek 2003. (Kinemathek 95).

Goergen, Jeanpaul: » Dokumentarischer Idealbeweis «. In: *Filmblatt*, vol. 8, no. 23, Autumn/Winter 2003: 10-14.

Goergen, Jeanpaul: » Filmreise und Reisefilm. AMERIKA, DAS LAND DER UNBEGRENZTEN MÖGLICHKEITEN (1926). In: *Filmblatt*, vol. 9, no. 24, Spring/Summer 2004: 48-51.

Göktürk, Deniz: *Künstler, Cowboys, Ingenieure. Kultur- und mediengeschichtliche Studien zu deutschen Amerika-Texten 1912-1920*. Munich: Wilhelm Fink 1997.

Gomery, Douglas: » Tri-Ergon, Tobis Klangfilm, and the Coming of Sound «. In: *Cinema Journal*, vol. 16, 1976: 51-61

Gomery, Douglas: » Economic Struggle and Hollywood Imperialism: Europe Converts to Sound «. In: *Yale French Studies*, no. 60, 1980: 80-93.

Graeff, Werner: *Es kommt der neue Fotograf!* Berlin: Hermann Reckendorf 1929.

Graeve, Inka: » Internationale Ausstellung des Deutschen Werkbunds Film und Foto «. In: Michael Bollé, Eva Züchner, Gesine Asmus (eds.): *Stationen der*

Moderne. Die bedeutenden Kunstausstellungen des 20. Jahrhunderts in Deutsch-land. Berlin: Berlinische Galerie / Nicolai 1988: 236-273.

Grant, Barry Keith; Sloniowski, Jeannette (eds.): *Documenting the Documentary: Close Readings of Documentary Film and Video*. Detroit, MI: Wayne State University Press 1998. (Contemporary Film and Television Series).

Green, Christopher: »Painting and Architecture: Léger's Modern Classicism and the International avant-garde«. In: C.G.: *Léger and the Avant-garde*. New Haven and London: Yale University Press 1976: 286-309.

Greene, Naomi: »Artaud and Film: A Reconsideration«. In: *Cinema Journal*, vol. 23, no. 4, Summer 1984: 28-40.

Grottle Strebel, Elizabeth: »Le droit à la libre critique et le process Moussinac – Sapène (1928)«. In: *Travelling*, no. 43, March 1975: 17-19.

Groys, Boris: *Gesamtkunstwerk Stalin. Die gespaltene Kultur in der Sowjetunion*. Munich, Wien: Carl Hanser 1988. (Edition Akzente).

Gubern, Román : *La guerra de España en la pantalla (1936-1939). De la propaganda a la historia*. Madrid : Filmoteca Española 1986. (Filmoteca Española 2).

Guillaume-Grimaud, Geneviève: *Le cinema du front populaire*. Paris: Lherminier 1986. (Le cinéma et son histoire).

Gunning, Tom: »The Cinema of Attractions: Early Film, Its Spectator and the Avant-Garde«. In: *Wide Angle*, vol. 8, no. 3/4, 1986. Reprinted in Thomas Elsaesser (ed.): *Early Cinema: Space, Frame, Narrative*. London: BFI 1990: 56-62.

Gunning, Tom: »Ontmoetingen in verduisterde ruimten. De alternatieve programmering van de Nederlandsche Filmliga«. In: Nico de Klerk, Ruud Visschedijk (eds.): *Het gaat om de film! Een nieuwe geschiedenis van de Nederlandsche Filmliga 1927-1933*. Amsterdam: Bas Lubberhuizen / Filmmuseum 1999: 217-263.

Gunning, Tom: »A Quarter of a Century Later: Is Early Cinema Still Early?«. In: Frank Kessler, Sabine Lenk, Martin Loiperdinger (eds.): *KINtop 12: Theorien zum frühen Kino*. Frankfurt am Main, Basel: Stroemfeld / Roter Stern 2003: 17-31.

Haarmann, Hermann (ed.): *Erwin Piscator am Schwarzen Meer. Briefe, Erinnerungen, Photos*. Berlin: Bostelmann & Siebenhaar 2002.

Hagener, Malte; Hans, Jan (eds.): *Als die Filme singen lernten. Innovation und Tradition im Musikfilm 1928-1938*. Munich: edition text + kritik 1999. (Ein Cine-Graph Buch).

Hagener, Malte (ed.): *Geschlecht in Fesseln. Sexualität zwischen Aufklärung und Ausbeutung im Weimarer Kino*. Munich: edition text + kritik 2000. (Ein Cine-Graph Buch).

Hagener, Malte: »Nationale Filmproduktion und Exil: Zur Produktion und Rezeption des Films GADO BRAVO«. In: Malte Hagener, Wolfgang Jacobsen,

Heike Klapdor (Red.): *Exil in Portugal. Filmexil 16/2002*. Munich: edition text + kritik 2002: 50-69.

Hagener, Malte: » Unter den Dächern der Tobis. Nationale Märkte und europäische Strategien «. In: Jan Distelmeyer (ed.): *Tonfilmfrieden/Tonfilmkrieg. Die Geschichte der Tobis vom Technik-Syndikat zum Staatskonzern*. Munich: edition text + kritik 2003: 51-64.

Hagener, Malte: » Programming Attractions. Avant-garde Exhibition Practice in the 1920s and 1930s «. In: Wanda Strauven (eds.): *The Cinema of Attractions Reloaded*. Amsterdam: Amsterdam University Press 2006. (Film Culture in Transition): 265-279.

Halter, Regine: » Esther Schub: Ihre Bedeutung für die Entwicklung des Dokumentarfilms «. In: *Frauen & Film*, no. 9, October 1976: 34-44.

Haltof, Marek: *Polish National Cinema*. New York, Oxford: Berghahn 2002.

Hamdorf, Wolfgang Martin: *Zwischen » No Pasaran! « und » Arriba Espana! «. Film und Propaganda im Spanischen Bürgerkrieg*. Münster: MakS Publikationen 1991. (Film- und Fernsehwissenschaftliche Arbeiten).

Hammond, Paul: *The Shadow and Its Shadow: Surrealist Writings on the Cinema*. Edinburgh: Polygon 1991.

Hanna-Daoud, Thomas: *Die NSDAP und der Film bis zur Machtergreifung*. Köln, Weimar, Wien: Böhlau 1996. (Medien in Geschichte und Gegenwart).

Hansen, Miriam: *Babel and Babylon: Spectatorship in American Silent Film*. Cambridge, MA: Harvard University Press 1991.

Hardt, Michael; Negri, Antonio: *Empire*. Cambridge, MA, London: Harvard University Press 2000.

Hardy, Forsyth (ed.): *Grierson on Documentary*. Berkeley, CA: University of California Press 1966.

Hardy, Forsyth: *John Grierson: A Documentary Biography*. London: Faber and Faber 1979.

Hardy, Forsyth (ed.): *John Grierson on the Movies*. London, Boston, MA: Faber & Faber 1981.

Hartsough, Denise: » Soviet Film Distribution and Exhibition in Germany, 1921-1933 «. In: *Historical Journal of Film, Radio and Television*, vol. 5, no. 2, 1985: 131-148.

Haus, Andreas: » Moholy-Nagy: Sinnlichkeit und Industrie «. In: Stanislaus von Moos, Chris Smeenk (eds.): *Avantgarde und Industrie*. Delft: Delft University Press 1983.

Hayward, Philip; Wollen, Tana (eds.): *Future Visions: New Technologies of the Screen*. London: BFI Publishing 1993.

Hedges, Inez: *Languages of Revolt: Dada and Surrealist Literature and Film*. Durham, NC: Duke University Press 1983.

Hediger, Vinzenz: *Verführung zum Film. Der amerikanische Kinotrailer seit 1912.* Marburg: Schüren 2001. (Zürcher Filmstudien 5).

Hediger, Vinzenz; Sahli, Jan; Schneider, Alexandra; Tröhler, Margrit (eds.): *Home Stories. Neue Studien zu Film und Kino in der Schweiz / Nouvelles approches du cinéma et du film en Suisse.* Marburg: Schüren 2001. (Zürcher Filmstudien 4).

Heijs, Jan (ed.): *Filmliga 1927-1931.* (reprint of magazine published by the *Filmliga*). Nijmegen: SUN 1982.

Hein, Birgit; Herzogenrath, Wulf (eds.): *Film als Film. 1910 bis heute.* Köln: Kölnischer Kunstverein 1977.

Heller, Heinz-B.: » Dokumentarfilm als transitorisches Genre «. In: Ursula von Keitz, Kay Hoffmann (eds.): *Die Einübung des dokumentarischen Blicks.* Fiction Film *und* Non Fiction Film *zwischen Wahrheitsanspruch und expressiver Sachlichkeit 1895-1945.* Marburg: Schüren 2001: 15-26.

Helmstetter, Rudolf: » László Moholy-Nagy. Versachlichung des Lichts, Verhaltenslehre jenseits der Kälte «. In: Ursula von Keitz, Kay Hoffmann (eds.): *Die Einübung des dokumentarischen Blicks.* Fiction Film *und* Non Fiction Film *zwischen Wahrheitsanspruch und expressiver Sachlichkeit 1895-1945.* Marburg: Schüren 2001: 123-146.

Henke, Rolf; Weber, Richard (eds.): *Arbeiterbühne und Film. Zentralorgan des Arbeiter-Theater-Bundes Deutschlands e.V. Juni 1930-Juni 1931.* (Complete reprint of the magazine). Köln: Verlag Gaehme, Henke 1974. (Kulturpolitische Dokumente der revolutionären Arbeiterbewegung).

Henry, Christel: » Le mouvement › cineclubista‹ au Portugal entre 1945 et 1959 «. In: *Estudos do Século XX,* no. 1, 2001: 241-276.

Hercher, Jutta; Hemmleb, Maria: » Dokument und Konstruktion. Zur Filmarbeit von Ella Bergmann-Michel «. In: *Frauen und Film,* no. 49, December 1990: 106-118.

Hertogs, Daan; Klerk, Nico de (eds.): *Nonfiction from the Teens.* Amsterdam: Nederlands Filmmuseum 1994.

Hertogs, Daan; Klerk, Nico de (eds.): *Uncharted Territory: Essays on Early Nonfiction Film.* Amsterdam: Nederlands Filmmuseum 1997.

Hervo, Brigitte: » Zuschauerfilmkritik Anfang der 30er Jahre in Frankreich «. In: *Filmfaust,* no. 20, November 1980: 35-45.

Herzogenrath, Wulf: » Light-play and Kinetic Theatre as Parallels to Absolute Film «. In: Philip Drummond et al. (eds.):*Film as Film: Formal Experiment in Film 1910-1975.* London: Hayward Gallery 1979: 22-26.

Higson, Andrew: » The Concept of National Cinema «. In: *Screen,* vol. 30, no. 4, Autumn 1989: 36-46.

Higson, Andrew: » The Instability of the National «. In: Justine Ashby, Andrew Higson (eds.): *British Cinema, Past and Present*. London, New York: Routledge 2000: 35-47.

Higson, Andrew: » The Limiting Imagination of National Cinema «. In: Mette Hjort, Scott MacKenzie (eds.): *Film & Nation*. London, New York: Routledge 2000: 63-74.

Higson, Andrew (ed.): *Young and Innocent? The Cinema in Britain, 1896-1930*. Exeter: University of Exeter Press 2002. (Exeter Studies in Film History).

Hill, John; Gibson, Pamela Church (eds.): *The Oxford Guide to Film Studies*. Oxford et al.: Oxford University Press 1998.

Hillairet, Prosper (ed.): *Germaine Dulac. Ecrits sur le cinéma (1919-1937)*. Paris : Éditions Expérimental 1994.

Hjort, Mette; MacKenzie, Scott (eds.): *Cinema & Nation*. London, New York: Routledge 2000,

Hobsbawm, Eric J.: *Nations and Nationalism since 1780: Programme, Myth, Reality*. Cambridge: Cambridge University Press 1990.

Hoffmann, Kay; Keitz, Ursula von (eds.): *Die Einübung des dokumentarischen Blicks. Fiction Film und Non Fiction Film zwischen Wahrheitsanspruch und expressiver Sachlichkeit 1895-1945*. Marburg: Schüren 2001.

Hogenkamp, Bert: » Interview met Ralph Bond «. In: *Skrien*, no. 51, July-Aug. 1975: 21-24.

Hogenkamp, Bert: » Interview met Ivor Montagu over het Progressive Film Institute «. In: *Skrien*, no. 51, Jul-Aug 1975: 25-33.

Hogenkamp, Bert: » Film and the Workers' Movement in Britain, 1929-39 «. In: *Sight & Sound*, vol. 45, no. 2, Spring 1976: 68-76.

Hogenkamp, Bert: » Critical Dialogue: Workers' Film in Europe «. In: *Jump Cut*, no. 19, Dec 1978: 36-37.

Hogenkamp, Bert: » De russen komen! Poedowkin, Eisenstein en Wertow in Nederland «. In: *Skrien*, no. 144, Nov/Dec 1985: 46-49.

Hogenkamp, Bert: *Deadly Parallels: Film and the Left in Britain, 1929-1939*. London: Lawrence & Wishart 1986.

Hogenkamp, Bert; Stallaerts, Rik: » Pain noir et film nitrate: le mouvement ouvrier socialiste belge et le cinéma durant l'entre deux guerres «. In: *Revue Belge du Cinéma*, no. 15, Spring 1986.

Hogenkamp, Bert: » J.C. Mol en Multifilm: wetenschap – film – bedrijf «. In: B. H.: *De Nederlandse documentaire film 1920-1940*. Utrecht: Audiovisueel Archief van de Stichting Film en Wetenschap / Amsterdam: Van Gennep 1988: 96-108.

Hoormann, Anne: *Lichtspiele. Zur Medienreflexion der Avantgarde in der Weimarer Republik*. Munich: Wilhelm Fink 2003.

Horak, Jan-Christopher: » Entwicklung einer visuellen Sprache im Stummfilm «. In: Ute Eskildsen, Jan-Christopher Horak (eds.): *Film und Foto der Zwanziger Jahre. Eine Betrachtung der Internationalen Werkbundausstellung » Film und Foto «* 1929. Stuttgart: Gerd Hatje 1979: 38-60.

Horak, Jan-Christopher (ed.): *Lovers of Cinema: The First American Film Avant-Garde 1919-1945.* Madison, WI: University of Wisconsin Press 1995.

Horak, Jan-Christopher: *Making Images Move: Photographers and the Avant-Garde Cinema.* Washington, London: Smithsonian Institution Press 1997. (Smithsonian Studies in the History of Film and Television).

Hörl, Patrick: *Film als Fenster zur Welt. Eine Untersuchung des filmtheoretischen Denkens von John Grierson.* Konstanz: UVK Medien Ölschläger 1996. (kommunikation audiovisuell 20).

Houston, Penelope: *Keepers of the Frame: The Film Archives.* London: British Film Institute 1994.

Huyssen, Andreas: *After the Great Divide: Modernism, Mass Culture, Postmodernism.* Bloomington and Indianapolis: Indiana University Press 1986.

Ivens, Joris: » Quelques réflections sur les documentaires d'avant-garde «. In: *La revue des vivants,* no. 10, 1931: 518-520. Reprinted translation » Notes on the Avant-garde Documentary Film « in: Kees Bakker (ed.): *Joris Ivens and the Documentary Context.* Amsterdam: Amsterdam University Press 1999: 224-226.

Ivens, Joris: *The Camera and I.* Berlin/DDR: Seven Seas Publishers 1969.

Ivens, Joris; Destanque, Robert: *Joris Ivens ou la mémoire d'un regard.* Paris: Éditions BFB 1982.

Izod, John; Kilborn, Richard; with Hibberd, Matthew (eds.): *From Grierson to the Docu-Soap: Breaking the Boundaries.* Luton: University of Luton Press 2000.

Jacobsen, Wolfgang; Prinzler, Hans Helmut (eds.): *Siodmak Bros: Berlin – Paris – London – Hollywood.* Berlin: Argon 1998.

Janser, Andres; Ruegg, Arthur: *Hans Richter: New Living, Architecture, Film, Space.* Baden: Lars Müller 2001.

Janser, Andres: » Es kommt der gute Film. Zu den Anfängen der Filmclubs in Zürich «. In: Hediger et al.: *Home Stories,* 2001: 55-69.

Jeander: » Les ciné-clubs «. In: Marcel Defosse (ed.): *Le cinéma par ceux qui le font.* Paris: Fayard 1949.

Jones, Stephen G.: *The British Labour Movement and Film, 1918-1939.* London: Routledge & Kegan Paul 1987.

Johnson, Randal; Stam, Robert (eds.): *Brazilian Cinema.* New Brunswick, NJ: Associated University Presses 1982.

Jossé, Harald: *Die Entstehung des Tonfilms. Beitrag zu einer faktenorientierten Mediengeschichtsschreibung*. Freiburg, Munich: Karl Alber 1984. (Alber-Broschur Kommunikation 13).

Jurenjew, Rotislaw: » Unter fremden Himmeln. Zum 80. Geburtstag von Sergej Eisenstein «. In: *Film und Fernsehen*, no. 1, 1978: 26-31.

Kappelhoff, Hermann: » Eine neue Gegenständlichkeit. Die Bildidee der Neuen Sachlichkeit und der Film «. In: Thomas Koebner, Norbert Grob, Bernd Kiefer (eds.): *Jenseits der › Dämonischen Leinwand. Neue Perspektiven auf das späte Weimarer Kino*. Munich: edition text + kritik 2003: 119-138.

Kenez, Peter: *Cinema and Soviet Society, 1917-1953*. Cambridge: Cambridge University Press 1992.

Kepley, Jr., Vance; Kepley, Betty: » Foreign Films on Soviet Screens, 1921-1935 «. In: *Quaterly Review of Film Studies*, vol. 4, no. 4, Fall 1979: 429-442.

Kepley, Jr., Vance: » The Workers' International Relief and the Cinema of the Left 1921-1935 «. In: *Cinema Journal*, vol. 23, no. 1, Fall 1983: 7-23.

Kepley, Jr., Vance: » The Kuleshov workshop «. In: *Iris*, vol. 4, no. 1, 1986: 5-23.

Kepley, Jr., Vance: » Building a National Cinema: Soviet Film Education, 1918-1934 «. In: *Wide Angle*, vol. 9, no. 3, 1987: 5-19.

Kepley, Jr., Vance: » The origins of Soviet cinema: a study in industry development «. In: Richard Taylor, Ian Christie (eds.): *Inside the Film Factory: New Approaches to Russian and Soviet Cinema*. London, New York: Routledge 1991: 60-79.

Kepley, Jr., Vance: » Mr. Kuleshov in the Land of the Modernists «. In: Anna Lawton (ed.): *The Red Screen: Politics, Society, Art in Soviet Cinema*. London, New York: Routledge 1992: 132-147.

Kerr, Alfred: *Russische Filmkunst*. Berlin: Ernst Pollak 1927.

Kessler, Frank; Lenk, Sabine; Loiperdinger, Martin (eds.): *Kintop. Jahrbuch zur Erforschung des frühen Films. 11: Kinematographen-Programme*. Frankfurt am Main, Basel: Stroemfeld/Roter Stern 2002.

Kessler, Frank; Lenk, Sabine; Loiperdinger, Martin (eds.): *KINtop. Jahrbuch zur Erforschung des frühen Films. 12: Theorien zum frühen Kino*. Frankfurt am Main, Basel: Stroemfeld / Roter Stern 2003.

Kherroubi, Aïcha (ed.): *Le studio Mejrabpom ou l'aventure du cinéma privé au pays des bolcheviks*. Paris: La documentation française 1996. (Les dossiers du musée d'Orsay 59).

Kinkel, Lutz: *Die Scheinwerferin. Leni Riefenstahl und das » Dritte Reich «*. Hamburg and Vienna: Europa-Verlag 2002.

Klein, Adrian Bernard: *Colour Music: The Art of Light*. London: Lockwood 1926.

Klejman, Naum: » › Nationales ‹, › Internationales ‹ und die sowjetische Filmavantgarde «. In: Ryszard Stanislawski, Christoph Brockhaus (eds.): *Europa,*

Europa. Das Jahrhundert der Avantgarde in Mittel- und Osteuropa. Bonn: Kunst- und Ausstellungshalle 1994: 161-168.

Klingeman, William K.: *1929: The Year of the Great Crash.* New York 1989.

Klotz, Sebastian: » Der Lindberghflug von Brecht • Hindemith • Weill (1929) als Rundfunkproblem «. In: Stefan Andriopoulos, Bernhard Dotzler (eds.): *1929. Beiträge zur Archäologie der Medien.* Frankfurt am Main: Suhrkamp 2002: 268-287.

Koch, Stephen: *Double Lives: Stalin, Willi Münzenberg and the Seduction of the Intellectuals.* New York: Enigma 1994. (revised and updated edition 2004).

Koebner, Thomas; Grob, Norbert; Kiefer, Bernd (eds.): *Diesseits der › Dämonischen Leinwand ‹. Neue Perspektiven auf das späte Weimarer Kino.* Munich: edition text + kritik 2003.

Kracauer; Siegfried: *Von Caligari zu Hitler. Eine psychologische Geschichte des deutschen Films.* Frankfurt am Main: Suhrkamp 1979. [orig.: *From Caligari to Hitler: A Psychological History of the German Film.* Princeton, PA: Princeton University Press 1947]

Kracauer; Siegfried: *Theorie des Films. Die Errettung der äußeren Wirklichkeit.* Frankfurt am Main 1985. (= Werke. Band 3). [orig.: *Theory of Film: The Redemption of Physical Reality.* New York: Oxford University Press 1960]

Kracauer, Siegfried: *Werke. Band 6: Kleine Schriften zum Film 1921-1961.* 3 vols. (edited by Inka Mülder-Bach). Frankfurt am Main: Suhrkamp 2004.

Kreimeier, Klaus: » Mechanik, Waffen und Haudegen überall. Expeditionsfilme: das bewaffnete Auge des Ethnografen «. In: Jörg Schöning (ed.): *Triviale Tropen. Exotische Reise- und Abenteuerfilme aus Deutschland, 1919-1939.* Munich: edition text + kritik 1997, 47-61.

Kresse, Helmut: » Internationale Arbeiterhilfe und Film in der Weimarer Republik «. In: Horst Knietzsch (ed.): *Prisma 7. Film- und Fernseh-Almanach.* Berlin/DDR: Henschel 1976: 240-261.

Krohn, Claus-Dieter; Rotermund, Erwin; Winckler, Lutz; Wojak, Irmtrud; Koepke, Wulf im Auftrag der Gesellschaft für Exilforschung / Society for Exile Studies (eds.): *Exilforschung. Ein internationales Jahrbuch. Film und Fotografie.* Munich: edition text + kritik 2003. (Band 21).

Kuenzli, Rudolf E.: *Dada and Surrealist Film.* New York: Willis, Locker and Owens 1987.

Kühn, Gertraude; Tümmler, Karl; Wimmer, Walter (eds.): *Film und revolutionäre Arbeiterbewegung in Deutschland 1918-1932. Dokumente und Materialien zur Entwicklung der Filmpolitik der revolutionären Arbeiterbewegung und zu den Anfängen der sozialischen Filmkunst in Deutschland.* (2 Vols.) Berlin/DDR: Henschel 1975. (Film – Funk – Fernsehen).

Kusters, Paul: » New Film History. Grundzüge einer neuen Filmgeschichtswissenschaft «. In: *montage/av,* vol. 5, no. 1, 1996: 39-60.

László, Alexander: *Die Farblichtmusik*. Leipzig: Breitkopf & Härtel 1925.

Lawder, Standish: *The Cubist Cinema*. New York: New York University Press 1975.

Lawder, Standish: » Eisenstein and Constructivism «. In: P. Adams Sitney (ed.): *The Essential Cinema*. New York: New York University Press 1975.

Lawton, Anna (ed.): *The Red Screen: Politics, Society, Art in Soviet Cinema*. London, New York: Routledge 1992.

Leitner, Angelika; Nitschke, Uwe (eds.): *Der deutsche Avant-Garde Film der 20er Jahre*. Munich: Goethe-Institut 1989.

Lejeune, C.A.: *Cinema*. London: Alexander Macklehose 1931.

Leslie, Esther: *Hollywood Flatlands: Animation, Critical Theory and the Avant-Garde*. London, New York: Verso 2002.

Lethen, Helmut: *Verhaltenslehren der Kälte. Lebensversuche zwischen den Kriegen*. Frankfurt am Main: Suhrkamp 1994.

Lewinsky, Mariann: *Eine verrückte Seite. Stummfilm und filmische Avantgarde in Japan*. Zürich: Chronos 1997. (Zürcher Filmstudien 2).

Leyda, Jay: *Kino: A History of the Russian and Soviet Film*. London: George Allen & Unwin 1960.

Leyda, Jay: *Films Beget Films: Compilation Films from Propaganda to Drama*. London: George Allen & Unwin 1964.

Liber, George O.: *Alexander Dovzhenko: A Life in Soviet Film*. London: BFI 2002.

Lindner, Ines: » Demontage in *documents* «. In: Stefan Andriopoulos, Bernhard J. Dotzler (eds.): *1929. Beiträge zur Archäologie der Medien*. Frankfurt am Main: Suhrkamp 2002: 110-131.

Loewy, Hanno: » Die Geister des Films. Balázs' Berliner Aufbrüche im Kontext «. In: Béla Balázs: *Der Geist des Films*. Frankfurt am Main: Suhrkamp 2001: 171-230.

Loewy, Hanno: *Béla Balázs – Märchen, Ritual und Film*. Berlin: Vorwerk 8 2003.

Loewy, Hanno: » Zwischen Utopie und Initiation. Béla Balázs' Versuche über die visuelle Kultur des Films «. In: Thomas Koebner (ed.): *Jenseits der › Dämonischen Leinwand ‹*. Munich: edition text + kritik 2003: 139-167.

Loiperdinger, Martin: » Riefenstahls Parteitagsfilme zwischen Bergfilm und Kriegswochenschau «. In: *Filmblatt*, vol. 8., no. 21, Winter/Spring 2003: 12-28.

Lüdecke, Willi: *Der Film in Agitation und Propaganda der revolutionären deutschen Arbeiterbewegung (1919-1933)*. Berlin: Oberbaumverlag 1973. (Materialistische Wissenschaft 7)

Luhmann, Niklas: *Soziale Systeme. Grundriß einer allgemeinen Theorie*. Frankfurt am Main: Suhrkamp 1984. (stw 666).

Luhmann, Niklas: *Die Kunst der Gesellschaft*. Frankfurt am Main: Suhrkamp 1995. (stw 1303).

Luhmann, Niklas: *Die Gesellschaft der Gesellschaft*. Frankfurt am Main: Suhrkamp 1998. (stw 1360).

MacDonald, Scott: »Cinema 16: Documents Towards a History of the Film Society«. In: *Wide Angle*, vol. 19, no. 1: 3-48.

Manovich, Lev: »Avant-garde as Software«. Online at: http://www.manovich. net/docs/avantgarde_as_software.doc (September 28, 2002; 2pm).

Manvell, Roger (ed.): *Experiment in the Film*. London: Grey Walls Press 1948.

Marchand, Pierre; Weinstein, René: *L'art dans la Russie nouvelle: Le cinéma (1917-1926)*. Paris: Rider 1927.

Margolit, Evgenij: »Der sowjetische Stummfilm und der frühe Tonfilm«. In: Christine Engel (ed.): *Geschichte des sowjetischen und russischen Films*. Stuttgart, Weimar: Metzler 1999: 17-67.

May, Rainhard; Jackson, Hendrik (eds.): *Filme für die Volksfront. Erwin Piscator, Gustav von Wangenheim, Friedrich Wolf – antifaschistische Filmemacher im sowjetischen Exil*. Berlin: Stattkino 2001.

Medvedkin, Alexander: »Interview«. In: Richard Taylor, Ian Christie (eds.): *Inside the Film Factory: New Approaches to Russian and Soviet Cinema*. London and New York: Routledge 1991: 165-175.

Meier, Gerd: »Materialien zur Geschichte der Prometheus Film-Verleih und Vertriebs GmbH. 1926-1932« (8 parts). In: *Deutsche Filmkunst*, vol. 10, no. 1-8, 1962: 12-16; 57-60; 97-99; 137-140; 177-180; 221-224; 275-277; 310-312.

Michelson, Annette: *Kino-Eye: The Writings of Dziga Vertov*. Berkeley, CA: University of California Press 1984.

Michelson, Annette: »The Kinetic Icon and the Work of Mourning: Prolegomena to the Analysis of a Textual System«. In: Anna Lawton (ed.): *The Red Screen: Politics, Society, Art in Soviet Cinema*. London, New York: Routledge 1992: 113-131.

Mierau, Fritz (ed.): *Russen in Berlin. Literatur – Malerei – Theater – Film, 1918-1933*. Leipzig: Reclam 1991[3].

Mildenberger, Marianne: *Film und Projektion auf der Bühne*. Emsdetten: Lechte 1961.

Mitry, Jean: *Le cinéma expérimental. Histoire et perspectives*. Paris: Seghers 1974.

Montagu, Ivor: »Old Man's Mumble. Reflections on a Semi-Centenary«. In: *Sight & Sound*, autumn 1975: 220-224, 227.

Moholy-Nagy, László: *The New Vision and Abstract of an Artist*. New York: George Wittenborn 1947. (orig. German as *Vom Material zu Architektur* 1928, orig. English 1930).

Molderings, Herbert: »Lichtjahre eines Lebens. Das Fotogramm in der Ästhetik Laszlo Moholy-Nagys«. In: Museum Folkwang (ed.): *László Moholy-Nagy: Fotogramme 1922-1943*. Munich, Paris, London: Schirmer/Mosel 1996: 8-17.

Montagu, Ivor: *With Eisenstein in Hollywood: A Chapter in Autobiography*. New York/ Berlin/DDR: International Publishers / Seven Seas 1968.

Montagu, Ivor: The Youngest Son. An Autobiography. London: Lawrence and Wishart 1970.

Montagu, Ivor: » Old Man's Mumble. Reflections on a Semi-Centenary «. In: *Sight & Sound*, Autumn 1975: 220-224, 247.

Moos, Stanislaus von; Smeenk, Chris (eds.): *Avantgarde und Industrie*. Delft: Delft University Press 1983.

Moussinac, Léon: *Naissance du cinéma*. Paris: J. Povolozky 1925.

Moussinac, Léon: *Le cinéma sovietique*. Paris: Gallimard 1928. (Les documents bleues).

Moussinac, Léon: *Panoramique du cinéma*. Paris: Au sens pareil 1929.

Moussinac, Léon: » Les Amis de Spartacus «. In : *Cinéma 74*, no. 189, July-Aug 1974: 73-74.

Mosley, Philip: *Split Screen: Belgian Cinema and Cultural Identity*. Albany, NY: State University of New York Press 2001.

Mühl-Benninghaus, Wolfgang: *Das Ringen um den Tonfilm. Strategien der Elektro- und Filmindustrie in den 20er und 30er Jahren*. Düsseldorf: Droste 1999. (Schriften des Bundesarchivs 54)

Müller, Corinna: *Vom Stummfilm zum Tonfilm*. Munich: Wilhelm Fink 2003.

Münzenberg, Willi: *Erobert den Film! Winke aus der Praxis proletarischer Filmpropaganda*. Berlin: Neuer Deutscher Verlag 1925.

Murray, Bruce: *Film and the German Left in the Weimar Republic: From » Caligari « to » Kuhle Wampe «*. Austin, TX: University of Texas Press 1990.

Musser, Charles: » The Silent Film: Documentary «. In: Geoffrey Nowell-Smith: *The Oxford History of World Cinema*. Oxford: Oxford University Press 1996: 86-95.

Musser, Charles: » Noël Burch, *Film Practice* und das Studium des frühen Kinos – eine persönliche Erinnerung «. In: Frank Kessler, Sabine Lenk, Martin Loiperdinger (eds.): *KINtop 12: Theorien zum frühen Kino*. Frankfurt am Main, Basel: Stroemfeld / Roter Stern 2003: 87-90.

Musser, Charles: » Historiographic Method and the Study of Early Cinema «. In: *Cinema Journal*, vol. 44, no. 1, Fall 2004: 101-107.

Mutzenbecher, Heinrich: *Melodie der Welt. ein Präludium zum ersten deutschen Tonfilm*. Hamburg: Hapag n.y. [1929].

Myrent, Glenn ; Langlois, Georges P.: *Henri Langlois: First Citizen of the Cinema*. New York: Twayne 1995. (Twayne's Filmmakers).

Nadeau, Maurice: *Histoire du Surréalisme*. Paris: Éditions du Seuil 1945.

Naficy, Hamid: *An Accented Cinema: Exilic and Diasporic Filmmaking*. Princeton and Oxford: Princeton University Press 2001.

Ndalianis, Angela: » Architectures of the Senses: Neo-Baroque Entertainment Spectacles «. Both in David Thorburn, Henry Jenkins (eds.): *Rethinking Media Change: The Aesthetics of Transition*. Cambridge, MA, London: The MIT Press 2003: 355-373.

Neale, Steve: » Art Cinema as Institution «. In: *Screen*, vol. 22, no. 1, Spring 1981: 11-39.

Nembach, Eberhard: *Stalins Filmpolitik. Der Umbau der sowjetischen Filmindustrie 1929 bis 1938*. St. Augustin: Gardez! Verlag 2001. (Filmstudien 17).

Nessel, Sabine; Schlüpmann, Heide; Schulte Strathaus, Stefanie (eds.): *Germaine Dulac*. Berlin: Freunde der Kinemathek 2002. (Kinemathek 93).

Nestriepke, S.: *Wege zu neuer Filmkultur*. Berlin: Verlag der Volksbühne 1927.

Nichols, Bill: » The American Photo League «. In: *Screen*, no. 13, Winter 1972/73: 108-115.

Nichols, Bill: » Eisenstein's Strike and the Genealogy of Documentary «. In: Bill Nichols: *Blurred Boundaries: Questions of Meaning in Contemporary Culture*. Bloomington, Indianapolis: Indiana University Press 1994: 107-116.

Nichols, Bill: » The Documentary and the Turn from Modernism «. In: Kees Bakker (ed.): *Joris Ivens and the Documentary Context*. Amsterdam: Amsterdam University Press 1999: 142-159.

Nichols, Bill: » Documentary Film and the Modernist Avant-Garde «. In: *Critical Inquiry*, no. 27, Summer 2001: 580-610.

Nichols, Bill: *Introduction to Documentary*. Bloomington and Indianapolis: Indiana University Press 2002.

Nowell-Smith, Geoffrey: *The Oxford History of World Cinema*. Oxford: Oxford University Press 1996.

O'Brien, Charles: *Cinema's Conversion to Sound: Technology and Film Style in France and the US*. Bloomington, IN: Indiana University Press 2005.

O'Konor, Louise: *Viking Eggeling 1880-1925: Artist and Filmmaker*. Stockholm: Almquist & Wiksell 1971.

O'Pray, Michael (ed.): *The British Avant-Garde Film 1936-1995*. Luton: Arts Council / John Libbey 1996.

Olmeta, Patrick: *La Cinémathèque française de 1936 à nos jours*. Paris: CNRS 2000.

Omasta, Michael (ed.): *Tribute to Sasha. Das filmische Werk von Alexander Hammid. Regie, Kamera, Schnitt und Kritiker*. Wien: Synema 2002.

Otto, Daniel: *Filmwirtschaft und schwerindustrielle Unternehmensstrategie in der Weimarer Republik. Das Beispiel der Westi-Gesellschaft von Hugo Stinnes*. Bochum: Ruhr-Universität 1993. [Unveröffentlichte Diplomarbeit]

Païni, Dominique; LeRoy, Eric: » Les archives du film (CNC): la collection André Sauvage «. In: *Cinémathèque*, no. 2, Nov. 1992: 124-129.

Patka, Marcus G.: » › Columbus Discovered America, and I Discovered Hollywood ‹. Otto Katz und die Hollywood Anti-Nazi League «. In: *Filmexil*, no. 17, 2003: 44-65.

Pelinq, Maurice: » Naissance des ciné-clubs. (1. Louis Delluc ou l'invention des Ciné-clubs. 2. Les ciné-clubs au service du 7e art. 3. A la conquête du public populaire) « In: *Jeune cinéma*, no. 126, 127, 131, April-May 1980, June 1980, Dec-Jan 1980-81: 1-5, 1-6, 1-7.

Peterson, James: » A War of Utter Rebellion: Kinugasa's PAGE OF MADNESS and the Japanese Avant-Garde of the 1920s «. In: *Cinema Journal*, vol. 29, no. 1, Fall 1989: 36-53.

Petrić, Vlada: » Esther Shub: Cinema Is My Life «. In: *Quaterly Review of Film Studies*, vol. 3, no. 4, Fall 1978: 429-456.

Petrić, Vlada: *Constructivism in Film: The Man with the Movie Camera. A Cinematic Analysis*. Cambridge et al.: Cambridge University Press 1987. (Cambridge Studies in Film).

Petrie, Duncan; Kruger, Robert (eds.): *A Paul Rotha Reader*. Exeter: University of Exeter Press 1999.

Petzke, Ingo: *Das Experimentalfilm-Handbuch*. Frankfurt am Main: Deutsches Filmmuseum 1989.

Pinel, Vincent: *Introduction au ciné-club. Histoire, théorie, et pratique du ciné-club en France*. Paris: Éditions ouvrières 1964.

Poliwoda, Bernadette: *FEKS – Fabrik des exzentrischen Schauspielers. Vom Exzentrismus zur Poetik des Films in der frühen Sowjetkultur*. Munich: Verlag Otto Sagner 1994. (Slavistische Beiträge 312).

Polzer, Joachim (ed.): *Aufstieg und Untergang des Tonfilms. Die Zukunft des Kinos: 24p?* Potsdam: Polzer 2002. (Weltwunder der Kinematographie. Beiträge zu einer Kulturgeschichte der Filmtechnik; 6).

Posner, Bruce (ed.): *Unseen Cinema: Early American Avant-Garde Film 1893-1941*. New York: Anthology Film Archive 2001.

Pudowkin, Wsewolod: *Die Zeit in Großaufnahme. Erinnerungen/Aufsätze/Werkstattnotizen*. (edited by Tatjana Sapasnik and Adi Petrowitsch). Berlin/DDR: Henschel 1983.

Quaresima, Leonardo (ed.): *Walter Ruttmann: Cinema, pittura, ars acustica*. Calliano: Manfrini 1994.

Quaresima, Leonardo: » Sherlock Holmes und das marokkanische Wadi «. In: *Kintop – Jahrbuch zur Erforschung des frühen Films. Vol. 12: Theorien zum frühen Kino*. Frankfurt am Main, Basel: Stroemfeld / Roter Stern 2003: 165-170.

Rees, A.L.: *A History of Experimental Film and Video: From the Canonical Avant-Garde to Contemporary British Practice*. London: British Film Institute 1999.

Rees, A.L.: » The Themersons and the Polish Avant-garde. Warsaw – Paris – London «. In: *Pix*, no. 1, Winter 1993/94: 86-101.

Renger-Patzsch, Albert: *Die Welt ist schön*. Munich: Kurt Wolff 1928.

Reynolds, Siân: » Germaine Dulac and French documentary film making in the 1930s «. In: John Izod, Richard Kilborn (eds.): *From Grierson to the Docu-Soap: Breaking the Boundaries*. Luton: University of Luton Press 2000: 71-81.

Richter, Hans: *Filmgegner von heute – Filmfreunde von morgen*. Berlin: Hermann Reckendorf 1929. Reprint Zürich: Hans Rohr 1968. (Filmwissenschaftliche Studientexte 2).

Richter, Hans: » Avant-Garde Film in Germany «. In: Roger Manvell (ed.): *Experiment in the Film*. London: The Grey Walls Press 1949: 219-233.

Richter, Hans: *Köpfe und Hinterköpfe*. Zürich: Verlag Die Arche 1967.

Rocha, Glauber: » An Aesthetics of Hunger «. In: Randal Johnson, Robert Stam (eds.): *Brazilian Cinema*. New Brunswick, NJ: Associated University Presses 1982. [originally published in Portuguese as » Estética da fome « in 1965]

Rotha, Paul: *The Film Till Now: A Survey of the Cinema*. London: Jonathan Cape 1930.

Rotha, Paul: *Celluloid: The Film To-Day*. London: Longmans 1933.

Rother, Rainer: *Leni Riefenstahl. Die Verführung des Talents*. Munich: Wilhelm Heyne 2002.

Rothman, William: » The Filmmaker as Hunter. Robert Flaherty's NANOOK OF THE NORTH «. In: Barry Keith Grant, Jeannette Sloniowski (eds.): *Documenting the Documentary: Close Readings of Documentary Film and Video*. Detroit, MI: Wayne State University Press 1998: 23-39.

Roud, Richard: *A Passion for Films: Henri Langlois and the Cinémathèque Française*. London: Secker & Warburg 1983.

Roura, Pierre: » L'edition cinématographique en Espagne dans l'années 20 «. In: *Archives (Institut Jean Vigo / Cinémathèque de Toulouse)*, no. 13, avril 1988 : 1-12.

Sabrodin, Wladimir; Meßlinger, Karin (eds.): *Amazonen der Avantgarde im Film*. Berlin: Freunde der Deutschen Kinemathek / Deutsche Guggenheim 1999. (Kinemathek 90).

Sahli, Jan: *Filmische Sinneserweiterung. László Moholy-Nagys Filmwerk und Theorie*. Marburg: Schüren 2006. (Zürcher Filmstudien 14).

Said, Edward W.: *Orientalism: Western Conceptions of the Orient*. London: Routledge & Kegan Paul 1978.

Salt, Barry: *Film Style & Technology: History & Analysis*. London: Starwood 1992².

Samson, Jen: » The Film Society, 1925-1939 «. In: Charles Barr (ed.): *All Our Yesterdays: 90 Years of British Cinema*. London: BFI 1986: 306-313.

Sandro, Paul: » Parodic Narration in ENTR'ACTE «. In: *Film Criticism*, vol. 4, no. 1, Fall 1979: 44-55.

Sassen, Saskia: *The Global City: New York, London, Tokyo*. Princeton, NJ: Princeton University Press 1991.

Schenk, Irmbert: »›Politische Linke‹ versus ›Ästhetische Linke‹. Zum Richtungsstreit der Zeitschrift ›Filmkritik‹ in den 60er Jahren«. In: Irmbert Schenk (ed.): *Filmkritik. Bestandsaufnahme und Perspektiven*. Marburg: Schüren 1998: 43-73.

Schenk, Irmbert (ed.): *Filmkritik. Bestandsaufnahmen und Perspektiven*. Marburg: Schüren 1998.

Schenk, Irmbert: »›Titelloser Film‹ im deutschen Kino der Zwanziger Jahre«. In: Francesco, Pitassio, Leonardo Quaresima (eds.): *Scrittura e immagine. La didascalia nel cinema muto / Writing and Image: Titles in Silent Cinema*. Udine: Forum 1998: 225-246.

Scheugl, Hans; Schmidt Jr., Ernst : *Eine Subgeschichte des Films. Lexikon des Avantgarde-, Experimental- und Undergroundfilms*. 2 vols. Frankfurt am Main: Suhrkamp 1974. (edition suhrkamp 471).

Schlegel, Hans-Joachim: »Die Utopie der universellen Synthese. Zu Konzept und Schicksal ost- und mitteleuropäischer Filmavantgarden«. In: Ryszard Stanislawski, Christoph Brockhaus (eds.): *Europa, Europa. Das Jahrhundert der Avantgarde in Mittel- und Osteuropa*. Bonn: Kunst- und Ausstellungshalle 1994: 149-160.

Schleif, Helma: *Stationen der Moderne im Film. I. Film und Foto. Eine Ausstellung des Deutschen Werkbunds, Stuttgart 1929. Rekonstruktion des Filmprogramms. II. Texte, Manifeste, Pamphlete*. (2 Vols.) Berlin: Freunde der Kinemathek 1988; 1989.

Schlemmer, Gottfried; Riff, Bernhard; Haberl, Georg (ed.): *G.W. Pabst*. Münster: MakS Publikationen 1990. (Schriften der Gesellschaft für Filmtheorie).

Schmitz, Norbert M.: »Zwischen ›Neuem Sehen‹ und ›Neuer Sachlichkeit‹. Der Einfluß der Kunstphotographie auf den Film der zwanziger Jahre«. In: Michael Esser (Red.): *Gleißende Schatten. Kamerapioniere der zwanziger Jahre*. Berlin: Henschel 1994: 79-94.

Schmitz, Norbert M.: »Der Film der Neuen Sachlichkeit. Auf der Suche nach der medialen Authentizität«. In: Ursula von Keitz, Kay Hoffmann (eds.): *Die Einübung des dokumentarischen Blicks. Fiction Film und Non Fiction Film zwischen Wahrheitsanspruch und expressiver Sachlichkeit 1895-1945*. Marburg: Schüren 2001: 147-168.

Schneider, Alexandra: »Autosonntag (CH 1930). Eine Filmsafari im Klöntal«. In: Hediger, Vinzenz; Sahli, Jan; Schneider, Alexandra; Tröhler, Margrit (eds.): *Home Stories. Neue Studien zu Film und Kino in der Schweiz / Nouvelles approches du cinéma et du film en Suisse*. Marburg: Schüren 2001. (Zürcher Filmstudien 4): 83-99.

Schneider, Alexandra: *Die Stars sind wir. Heimkino als filmische Praxis*. Marburg: Schüren 2004. (Zürcher Filmstudien 9).

Schneider, Ute: » Artikulationsort Zeitschrift «. In: Heinz Ludwig Arnold (ed.): *Aufbruch ins 20. Jahrhundert. Über Avantgarden*. Munich: edition text + kritik 2001: 171-181.

Schönemann, Heide: » Hans Richter und Friedrich Wolf im Mashrabpom-Programm «. In: Jeanpaul Goergen et al. (eds.): *Hans Richter. Film ist Rhythmus*. Berlin: Freunde der Deutschen Kinemathek 2003: 115-122.

Schöning, Jörg (ed.): *Fantaisies russes. Russische Filmmacher in Berlin und Paris 1920-1930*. Munich: edition text + kritik 1995. (Ein CineGraph-Buch).

Schöning, Jörg: *Triviale Tropen. Exotische Reise- und Abenteuerfilme aus Deutschland, 1919-1939*. Munich: edition text + kritik 1997. (Ein CineGraph-Buch).

Schoots, Hans: *Gevaarlijk leven. Een biografie van Joris Ivens*. Amsterdam: Jan Mets 1995. (English: *Living Dangerously; A Biography of Joris Ivens*. Amsterdam: Amsterdam University Press 2000. (Film Culture in Transition).).

Schultz, Klaus (ed.): *Deutsche Kammermusik Baden-Baden 1927-1929. Texte, Bilder, Programme*. Baden-Baden: Südwestfunk / Theater Baden-Baden 1977.

Schweinitz, Jörg: » › Wie im Kino! ‹. Die autothematische Welle im frühen Tonfilm. Figurationen des Selbstreflexiven «. In: Thomas Koebner, Norbert Grob, Bernd Kiefer (eds.): *Diesseits der › Dämonischen Leinwand ‹*. Munich: edition text + kritik 2003: 373-392.

Segeberg, Harro (ed.): *Die Perfektionierung des Scheins. Das Kino der Weimarer Republik im Kontext der Künste*. Munich: Wilhelm Fink Verlag 2000. (Mediengeschichte des Films 3).

Segeberg, Harro (ed.): *Die Medien und ihre Technik. Theorien – Modelle – Geschichte*. Marburg: Schüren 2004. (Schriftenreihe der Gesellschaft für Medienwissenschaft 11).

Selwood, Sara: » Farblichtmusik und abstrakter Film «. In: Karin v. Maur (Hrsg.): *Vom Klang der Bilder. Die Musik in der Kunst des 20. Jahrhunderts*. Munich: Prestel 1985: 414-421.

Sexton, Jamie: » Parody on the Fringes. Adrian Brunel, Minority Film Culture and the Art of Deconstruction «. In: Alan Burton, Laraine Porter (eds.): *Pimple, Pranks and Pratfalls: British Film Comedy Before 1930*. Trowbridge: Flicks Books 2000.

Sexton, Jamie: *The Emergence of an Alternative Film Culture in Inter-War Britain*. Norwich: University of East Anglia 2001. [Unpublished PhD thesis]

Sexton, Jamie: » The Film Society and the creation of an alternative film culture in Britain in the 1920s «. In: Andrew Higson (ed.): *Young and Innocent? The Cinema in Britain, 1896-1930*. Exeter: University of Exeter Press 2002: 291-305.

Sexton, Jamie: » Grierson's Machines: DRIFTERS, the Documentary Film Movement and the Negotiation of Modernity «. In: *Canadian Journal of Film Studies*

/ *Revue canadienne d'études cinématographiques*, vol. 11, no. 1, Spring 2002: 40-59.

Sichel, Kim: *Avantgarde als Abenteuer. Leben und Werk der Fotografin Germaine Krull*. Munich: Schirmer/Mosel 1999.

Sitney, P. Adams (ed.): *The Avant-Garde Film: A Reader of Theory and Criticism*. New York: New York University Press Anthology 1978.

Skrentny, Werner (ed.): *Vorwärts – und nicht vergessen. Arbeiterkultur in Hamburg um 1930*. Hamburg: Projektgruppe Arbeiterkultur Hamburg 1982.

Smith, Anthony D.: *Theories of Nationalism*. London: Duckworth 1983.

Smith, Anthony D.: *The Ethnic Origins of Nations*. Oxford: Blackwell 1986;

Smith, Anthony D.: *National Identity*. London: Penguin / Reno, NV: University of Nevada Press 1991.

Smith, Anthony D.: *Nationalism and Modernism*. London, New York: Routledge 1998.

Sorensen, Janet: » Lef, Eisenstein, and the Politics of Form «. In: *Film Criticism*, vol. 19, no. 2, Winter 1994/95: 55-74.

Soupault, Ré: *Frauenporträts aus dem » Quartier reserve « in Tunis*. Heidelberg: Das Wunderhorn 2001.

Stam, Robert: *Film Theory: An Introduction*. Oxford: Blackwell 2000.

Stattkino Berlin e.V.: *Revolutionärer Film in Deutschland (1918-1933)*. Berlin: Stattarchiv 1996.

Strauven, Wanda: » The Meaning of the Music-Hall: From the Italian Futurism to the Soviet Avant-garde «. In: *Cinéma & Cie.*, no. 4, Spring 2004: 119-134.

Stufkens, André: » The Song of Movement. Joris Ivens's First Films and the Cycle of the Avant-garde «. In: Kees Bakker (ed.): *Joris Ivens and the Documentary Context*. Amsterdam: Amsterdam University Press 1999: 46-71.

Sudendorf, Werner (ed.): Der Stummfilmmusiker Edmund Meisel. Frankfurt am Main: Deutsches Filmmuseum 1984. (Kinematograph 1)

Sussex, Elizabeth: *The Rise and Fall of British Documentary: The Story of the Film Movement Founded by John Grierson*. Berkeley, CA: University of California Press 1975.

Swann, Paul: » John Grierson and the G.P.O. Film Unit, 1933-1939 «. In: *Historical Journal of Film, Radio and Television*, vol. 3, no. 1, 1983: 19-34.

Swann, Paul: *The British Documentary Film Movement, 1926-1946*. Cambridge: Cambridge University Press 1989.

Szczepanik, Petr: » Undoing the National: Representing International Space in 1930s Czechoslovak Multiple-Language Versions «. In: *Cinema & Cie: International Film Studies Journal* (special issue on » Multiple and Multiple-Language Versions « edited by Nataša Ďurovičá), no. 4, Spring 2004: 55-65.

Szczepanik, Petr: » Czech Industrial Film of the 1930s and Bat'a «. Presentation on 9 December 2004 at the conference *Filme, die arbeiten. Internationale Tagung zum Industriefilm / Films at Work. International Industrial Film Workshop*. Bibliothek des Ruhrgebiets, Bochum / Ruhr-Universität Bochum, Institut für Medienwissenschaft. 9.-10.12.2004.

Taylor, Richard; Christie, Ian (eds.): *The Film Factory: Russian and Soviet Cinema in Documents 1896-1939*. London: Routledge & Kegan Paul 1988.

Taylor, Richard: *The Battleship Potemkin: The Film Companion*. London, New York: I.B. Tauris 2000. (KINOfiles Film Companion 1).

Taylor, Richard: » Boris Shumyatsky and the Soviet Cinema in the 1930s: Ideology as Mass Entertainment «. In: *Historical Journal of Film, Radio and Television*, vol. 6, no. 1, 1986: 43-64.

Taylor, Richard: » Ideology and Popular Culture in Soviet Cinema: THE KISS OF MARY PICKFORD «. In: Anna Lawton (ed.): *The Red Screen: Politics, Society, Art in Soviet Cinema*. London, New York: Routledge 1992: 42-65.

Taylor, Richard: *The Battleship Potemkin: The Film Companion*. London and New York: I.B. Tauris 2000. (Kino: The Russian Cinema Series).

Taylor, Richard: *October*. London: British Film Institute 2002. (BFI Film Classics).

Taylor, Richard; Christie, Ian (eds.): *Inside the Film Factory: New Approaches to Russian and Soviet Cinema*. London and New York: Routledge 1991.

ter Braak, Menno: *Cinema Militans*. Utrecht: De Gemeenschap 1929. (Reprint Utrecht: Reflex 1980).

Thode-Arora, Hilke: *Für fünfzig Pfennig um die Welt. Die Hagenbeckschen Völkerschauen*. Frankfurt, New York: Campus 1989.

Thompson, Kristin: » The Ermolieff Group in Paris: Exile, Impressionism, Internationalism «. In: *Griffithiana*, no. 35/36, October 1989: 50-57.

Thompson, Kristin: » Dr. Caligari at the Folies-Bergère, or, The Successes of an Early Avant-Garde Film «. In: Mike Budd (ed.): *The Cabinet of Dr. Caligari: Texts, Contexts, Histories*. New Brunswick, London: Rutgers University Press 1990: 121-169.

Thompson, Kristin: » Government Policies and Practical Necessities in the Soviet Cinema of the 1920s «. In: Anna Lawton (ed.): *The Red Screen: Politics, Society, Art in Soviet Cinema*. London, New York: Routledge 1992: 19-41.

Thompson, Kristin: » Early Alternatives to the Hollywood Mode of Production. Implications for Europe's Avantgardes «. In: *Film History* vol 5, 1993: 386-404.

Thorburn, David; Jenkins, Henry (eds.): *Rethinking Media Change: The Aesthetics of Transition*. Cambridge, MA, London: The MIT Press 2003. (Media in Transition).

Timmer, Petra: *Avant-garde en commercie. Een nabeschouwing bij Metz & Co – de creativen jaren*. Amsterdam: Vrije Universiteit 2000. [Unpublished Ph.D. thesis]

Tode, Thomas: » Un Soviétique escalade la Tour Eiffel: Dziga Vertov à Paris «. In: *Cinémathèque*, no. 5, printemps 1994: 68-85.

Tode, Thomas: » Ein Russe projiziert in die Planetariumskuppel. Dsiga Wertows Reise nach Deutschland 1929 «. In: Bulgakowa (Hg.): *ungewöhnlichen Abenteuer*, 1995: 143-158.

Tode, Thomas: » Albrecht Viktor Blum «. In: Hans-Michael Bock (ed.): *CineGraph – Lexikon zum deutschsprachigen Film*. Munich: edition text + kritik 1984ff.: inst. 29 (15.8.1997).

Tode, Thomas: » Ella Bergmann-Michel «. In: Hans-Michael Bock (ed.): *CineGraph – Lexikon zum deutschsprachigen Film*. Munich: edition text + kritik 1984ff.: inst. 30 (15.6.1998).

Tode, Thomas: » Auswahlbibliographie zu La Sarraz «. In: *Filmblatt*, no. 11, autumn 1999, 31-33.

Tode, Thomas: » Hans Richter «. In: Hans-Michael Bock (ed.): *CineGraph – Lexikon zum deutschsprachigen Film*. Munich: edition text + kritik 1984ff.: inst. 35 (15.10.2001).

Toeplitz, Jerzy: *Geschichte des Films. Band 2: 1928-1933*. Berlin/DDR: Henschel 1979.

Tortajada, Maria; Albera, François (eds.): *Cinéma suisse: nouvelles approches. Histoire – Esthétique – Critique – Thèmes – Matériaux*. Lausanne: Éditions Payot 2000. (Cinéma).

Töteberg, Michael: » Wie werde ich stark. Die Kulturfilm-Abteilung «. In: Hans-Michael Bock, Michael Töteberg (eds.): *Das Ufa-Buch*. Frankfurt am Main: Zweitausendeins 1992: 64-67.

Töteberg, Michael: » Die Sehnsucht unserer Zeit. Exotik und Tourismus: Die Reisefilme der Hapag «. Unpublished manuscript n.y. [1996]

Trimborn, Jürgen: *Riefenstahl. Eine deutsche Karriere. Biographie*. Berlin: Aufbau-Verlag 2002.

Tsivian, Yuri: » The Wise and Wicked Game: Re-editing and Soviet Film Culture of the 1920s «. In: *Film History*, vol. 8, no. 3, 1996: 327-343.

Tümmler, Karl: » Zur Geschichte des Volksfilmverbandes «. In: *Filmwissenschaftliche Mitteilungen*, no. 5, 1964: 1224-1251.

Turvey, Gerry : » › That insatiable body ‹. Ivor Montagu's confrontation with British film censorship «. In: *Journal of Popular British Cinema*, vol. 3, 2000: 31-44.

Tyler, Parker: *Underground Film: A Critical History*. New York: Grove Press 1969.

Uricchio, William: *Ruttmann's Berlin and the City Film to 1930*. New York: New York University 1982. [Unpublished PhD thesis]

Urussowa, Janina: *Das neue Moskau. Die Stadt der Sowjets im Film 1917-1941*. Köln, Weimar, Wien: Böhlau 2004.

Valleau, Marjorie A.: *The Spanish Civil War in American and European Films*. Ann Arbor, MI: UMI Research Press 1982. (Studies in Cinema 18).

Van Domburg, Adrianus: *Walter Ruttmann en het beginsel*. Purmerend: Nederlands Filminstituut 1956.

Van Wert, William: » Germaine Dulac: First Feminist Filmmaker «. In: *Women & Film*, vol. 1, no. 5-6, 1974: 55-61, 102-103

Vertov, Dziga: *Tagebücher, Arbeitshefte*. (edited by Thomas Tode and Alexandra Gramatke) Konstanz: UVK Medien 2000. (Close Up – Schriften aus dem Haus des Dokumentarfilms 14).

Vichi, Laura: » Un point de départ: le Congrès international du cinéma indépendant de Bruxelles «. In: Laura Vichi: *Henri Storck. De l'avant-garde au documentaire social*. Crisnée (BE): Éditions Yellow Now 2002: 11-21.

Vichi, Laura: *Henri Storck. De l'avant-garde au documentaire social*. Crisnée (BE): Éditions Yellow Now 2002.

Vincendeau, Ginette ; Reader, Keith (eds.): *La vie est à nous. French Cinema of the Popular Front 1935-1938*. London: British Film Institute 1986. (NFT Dossier 3).

Vincendeau, Ginette (ed.): *Encyclopedia of European Cinema*. London and New York: Cassell, British Film Institute / Facts on File 1995.

Virmaux, Alain: » Cinémemoire 96: Deux mécomptes (A. Sauvage et J. Duvivier) «. In: *Jeune cinéma*, no. 244, summer 1997 : 53f.

Vogel, Amos: *Film As a Subversive Art*. New York: Random House 1974.

von Herrmann, Hans-Christian: » Psychotechnik versus Elektronik. Kunst und Medien beim Baden-Badener Kammermusikfest 1929 «. In: Stefan Andriopoulos, Bernhard Dotzler (eds.): *1929. Beiträge zur Archäologie der Medien*. Frankfurt am Main: Suhrkamp 2002: 253-267.

von Keitz, Ursula; Hoffmann, Kay (eds.): *Die Einübung des dokumentarischen Blicks. Fiction Film und Non Fiction Film zwischen Wahrheitsanspruch und expressiver Sachlichkeit 1895-1945*. Marburg: Schüren 2001. (Schriften der Friedrich-Wilhelm-Murnau-Gesellschaft 7).

Vonderau, Patrick: » Kulturelle Landmarken. Reisen in den hohen Norden (1930-1939) «. In: *Filmblatt*, vol. 9, no. 24, Spring/Summer 2004: 52-55.

Walker, Alexander: *The Shattered Silents: How the Talkies Came to Stay*. London: Elm Tree 1978.

Wasson, Haidee: » Writing the Cinema into Daily Life. Iris Barry and the Emergence of British Film Criticism in the 1920s «. In: Andrew Higson (ed.): *Young and Innocent? The Cinema in Britain, 1896-1930*. Exeter: University of Exeter Press 2002: 321-337.

Weber, Richard (ed.): *Film und Volk. Organ des Volksfilmverbandes. Februar 1928-März 1930*. (Complete reprint of the magazine). Köln: Verlag Gaehme, Henke 1975. (Kulturpolitische Dokumente der revolutionären Arbeiterbewegung).

Weber, Richard: » Der Volksfilmverband. Von einer bürgerlichen Bündnisorganisation zur proletarischen Kulturorganisation «. In: *Film und Volk. Organ des Volksfilmverbandes. Februar 1928-März 1930.* Köln: Verlag Gaehme, Henke 1975: 5-27.

Wedel, Michael: » Vom Synchronismus zur Synchronisation. Carl Robert Blum und der frühe Tonfilm «. In: Joachim Polzer (ed.): *Aufstieg und Untergang des Tonfilms. Die Zukunft des Kinos: 24p?* Potsdam: Polzer 2002: 97-112.

Weiss, Peter: *Avantgarde Film.* Frankfurt am Main: Suhrkamp 1995. (edition suhrkamp – neue folge 444). (orig. Swedish 1956).

Welsh, David: » The Proletarian Cinema and the Weimar Republic «. In: *Historical Journal of Film, Radio and Television,* vol. 1, no. 1, 1981: 3-18.

Whittemore, Don; Cecchettini, Philip Alan: *Passport to Hollywood: Film Immigrants Anthology.* New York et al.: Mc Graw-Hill 1976.

Wiborg, Susanne; Wiborg, Klaus: *1847-1997. Unser Feld ist die Welt.* Hamburg: Hamburger Abendblatt / Axel-Springer Verlag 1997.

Wichner, Ernest; Wiesner, Herbert; Dittrich, Lutz (eds.): *1929. Ein Jahr im Fokus der Zeit.* Berlin: Literaturhaus 2001.

Wick, Rainer K.: *Teaching at the Bauhaus.* Ostfildern-Ruit: Hatje Crantz 2000

Wick, Rainer K.: *Bauhaus-Pädagogik.* Köln: DuMont 1994. (DuMont Dokumente).

Wilinsky, Barbara: *Sure Seaters: The Emergence of the Art House Cinema.* Minneapolis, London: University of Minnesota Press 2001.

Willcox, Temple: » Soviet Films, Censorship and the British Government: A Matter of the Public Interest «. In: *Historical Journal of Film, Radio and Television,* vol. 10, no. 3, 1990: 275-292.

Willemen, Paul: *Questions of Third Cinema.* London: British Film Institute 1989.

Willemen, Paul: *Looks and Frictions: Essays in Cultural Studies and Film Theory.* London: British Film Institute 1994.

Willemen, Paul: » Photogénie and Epstein «. In: P.W.: *Looks and Frictions: Essays in Cultural Studies and Film Theory.* London: British Film Institute 1994: 124-133.

Willemen, Paul: » Through the Glass Darkly: Cinephilia Reconsidered «. In: P. W.: *Looks and Frictions: Essays in Cultural Studies and Film Theory.* London: British Film Institute 1994: 223-257.

Willett, John: *The New Sobriety.* New York: Pantheon 1978.

Williams, Alan: » Historical and Theoretical Issues in the Coming of Recorded Sound to the Cinema «. In: Rick Altman (ed.): *Sound Theory, Sound Practice.* New York, London: Routledge 1992: 126-137.

Williams, Alan: *Film and Nationalism.* New Brunswick, NJ and London: Rutgers University Press 2002. (Rutgers Depth of Field Series).

Williams, Tami: » Beyond Impressions: Germaine Dulac (1882-1942), Her Life and Films, from Aesthetics to Politics «. In: *Cinéma & Cie.*, no. 2, Spring 2003: 156f.

Williams, Tami: » Germaine Dulac, du figuratif à l'abstraction «. In: Brenez, Nicole; Lebrat, Christian (eds.): *Jeune, Dure et Pure! Une histoire du cinéma d'avant-garde et expérimental en France*. Paris and Milano: Cinémathèque Française / Mazzota 2001: 78-82.

Wilmesmeier, Holger: *Deutsche Avantgarde und Film. Die Filmmatinee » Der absolute Film«. (3. und 10. Mai 1925)*. Münster and Hamburg: Lit Verlag 1993. (Kunstgeschichte 25).

Wilmesmeier, Holger: » Stahlsport. Avantgarde und Faschismus am Beispiel von Walter Ruttmanns ACCIAIO «. In: *Filmdienst*, vol. XLVIII, no. 11, 23 May 1995: 14-16.

Wilmesmeier, Holger: » Die Einheit der Welt. Harmonisierung von Natur und Technik im Geiste des Übermenschen – eine ikonographische und rhetorische Spurensuche «. In: *Das kalte Bild. Neue Studien zum NS-Propagandafilm*. Marburg: Schüren 1996. (Augen-Blick. Marburger Hefte zur Medienwissenschaft; Heft 22): 6-38.

Winckler, Julia: » Gespräch mit Wolfgang Suschitzky, Fotograf und Kameramann. Geführt in seiner Wohnung in Maida Vale, London, am 15. Dezember 2001, 22. März 2002, 17. Mai 2002 «. In: Claus-Dieter Krohn, Erwin Rotermund, Lutz Winckler, Irmtrud Wojak, Wulf Koepke im Auftrag der Gesellschaft für Exilforschung / Society for Exile Studies (eds.): *Exilforschung. Ein internationales Jahrbuch. Film und Fotografie*. Munich: edition text + kritik 2003. (Band 21): 254-279.

Winston, Brian: *Claiming the Real: The Documentary Film Revisited*. London: British Film Institute 1995.

Wollen, Peter; Lovell, Alan; Rohdie, Sam: » Interview with Ivor Montagu «. In: *Screen*, vol. 13, no. 3, Autumn 1972: 71-113.

Wollen, Peter: *Readings and Writings: Semiotic Counter-Strategies*. London: Verso 1982.

Wollen, Peter: » Art in Revolution «. In: P.W.: *Readings and Writings: Semiotic Counter-Strategies*. London: Verso 1982: 65-78.

Wollen, Peter: » The Two Avant-Gardes «. In: P.W.: *Readings and Writings: Semiotic Counter-Strategies*. London: Verso 1982: 92-104.

Wollen, Peter: *Raiding the Icebox: Reflections on Twentieth-Century Culture*. Bloomington, Indianapolis, IN: Indiana University Press 1993.

Wollen, Peter: » Out of the Past: Fashion / Orientalism / The Body «. In: P.W.: *Raiding the Icebox: Reflections on Twentieth-Century Culture*. Bloomington and Indianapolis, IN: Indiana University Press 1993: 1-34.

Wollen, Peter: » Modern Times: Cinema / Americanism / The Robot «. In: P.W.: *Raiding the Icebox: Reflections on Twentieth-Century Culture*. Bloomington and Indianapolis, IN: Indiana University Press 1993: 35-71.

Wollen, Peter: *Paris Hollywood: Writings on Film*. London, New York: Verso 2002.

Wollen, Peter: » Viking Eggeling «. In: P.W.: *Paris Hollywood: Writings on Film*. London and New York: Verso 2002: 39-54.

Wollen, Tana: » The Bigger the Better. From CinemaScope to Imax «. In: Philip Hayward, Tana Wollen (eds.): *Future Visions: New Technologies of the Screen*. London: BFI Publishing 1993: 10-30.

Wottrich, Erika (ed.): *M wie Nebenzal. Nero-Filmproduktion zwischen Europa und Hollywood*. Munich: edition text + kritik 2002. (Ein CineGraph Buch).

Yampolsky, Mikhail: » Reality at Second Hand «. In: *Historical Journal of Film, Radio and Television*, vol. 11, no. 2, 1991: 161-171.

Youngblood, Denise J.: *Soviet Cinema in the Silent Era, 1918-1935*. Ann Arbor, MI: UMI Research Press 1985. (Studies in Cinema 35).

Youngblood, Denise J.: *Movies for the Masses: Popular Cinema and Soviet Society in the 1920s*. Cambridge: Cambridge University Press 1992.

Zaoralova, Eva ; Passek, Jean-Loup (eds.): *Le Cinéma Tcheque et Slovaque*. Paris: Éditions du Centre Pompidou 1996. (Cinéma / Pluriel).

Zielinski, Siegfried: *Archäologie der Medien*. Reinbek: Rowohlt 2002. (rowohlts enzyklopädie 55649).

Zimmermann, Peter; Hoffmann, Kay (eds.): *Triumph der Bilder. Kultur- und Dokumentarfilme vor 1945 im internationalen Vergleich*. Konstanz: UVK Verlagsgesellschaft 2003. (Close Up. Schriften aus dem Haus des Dokumentarfilms. Europäisches Medienforum, Stuttgart 16).

Zsuffa, Joseph: *Béla Balázs: The Man and the Artist*. Berkeley, CA et al.: University of California Press 1987.

Zurhake, Monika: *Filmische Realitätsaneignung. Ein Beitrag zur Filmtheorie, mit Analysen von Filmen Viking Eggelings und Hans Richters*. Heidelberg: Carl Winter Universitätsverlag 1982. (Reihe Siegen – Beiträge zur Literatur- und Sprachwissenschaft 36).

Filmography

À NOUS LA LIBERTÉ (FR 1931, René Clair, › Freedom for Us ‹)

ACCIAIO (IT 1933, Walter Ruttmann)

AELITA (SU 1924, Iakov Protazanov)

L'ÂGE D'OR (FR 1930, Luis Buñuel / Salvador Dalí, › The Golden Age ‹)

ALEXANDER NEVSKI (SU 1937, Sergei Eisenstein)

ALLES DREHT SICH, ALLES BEWEGT SICH (GER 1929, Hans Richter, › Everything Turns, Everything Revolves ‹)

APROPOS DE NICE (FR 1929-30, Jean Vigo, › On the Subject of Nice ‹)

ARCHITEKTURKONGRESS ATHEN (GER 1933, László Moholy-Nagy, › Architecture Congress Athens ‹)

L'ATALANTE (FR 1933-34, Jean Vigo)

DER AUFSTIEG (GER 1926, Walter Ruttmann, › The Ascent ‹);

AUTOUR DE L'ARGENT (FR 1928, Jean Dréville, › Around L'ARGENT ‹)

AZBUKA KINOMONTAZHA (SU 1926, › The ABC of Film Editing ‹)

BALLET MECHANIQUE (FR 1924, Fernand Léger / Dudley Murphy, › Mechanical Ballet ‹)

THE BARN DANCE (US 1929, Walt Disney)

BAUEN UND WOHNEN (GER 1928, Hans Richter, › Building and Dwelling ‹)

BERLIN, DIE SINFONIE DER GROSSSTADT (GER 1926-27, Walter Ruttmann, › Berlin, Symphony of a Big City ‹)

BERLINER STILLLEBEN (GER 1930, László Moholy-Nagy, › Berlin Still Life ‹)

BEZIN LUG (SU 1936, Sergej Eisenstein, › Bezhin-Meadow ‹)

BEZÚL ELNÁ PROCHÁZKA (1930, Alexander Hackenschmied, › Aimless Walk ‹)

BORDERLINE (CH 1930, Kenneth MacPherson)

BORZY (SU 1935-36, Gustav von Wangenheim, › Fighter ‹)

LE BRASIER ARDENT (FR 1923, Ivan Mosjoukine / Alexandre Volkoff, › Blazing Embers ‹)

BRONENOSEZ » POTEMKIN « (SU 1925, Sergei Eisenstein, › Battleship Potemkin ‹)

DE BRUG (NL 1928, Joris Ivens, › The Bridge ‹)

DAS CABINET DES DR. CALIGARI (GER 1919-20, Robert Wiene, › The Cabinet of Dr. Caligari ‹)

A CANÇÃO DE LISBOA (PT 1933, José Augusto Cottinelli Telmo, › The Song of Lisbon ‹)

CARMEN (FR 1926, Jacques Feyder)

CELOVEK S KINOAPPARATOM (SU 1929, Dziga Vertov, › The Man with the Movie Camera ‹)

CHAMPION CHARLIE (US 1916, Charlie Chaplin)

CHANG: A DRAMA OF THE WILDERNESS (1927, Merian C. Cooper / Ernest B. Schoedsack)

CHAPAEV (SU 1934, Georgii & Sergei Vasilev)

UN CHAPEAU DE PAILLE D'ITALIE (FR 1927, René Clair, › An Italian Straw Hat ‹)

CHICAGO (US 1927, Frank Urson)

UN CHIEN ANDALOU (FR 1928, Luis Buñuel / Salvador Dalí, › An Andalusian Dog ‹)

LA CHUTE DE LA MAISON USHER (FR 1928, Jean Epstein, › The Fall of the House of Usher ‹)

LE CINÉMA AU SERVICE DE L'HISTOIRE (FR 1935, Germaine Dulac, › Cinema in the Service of History ‹)

THE CIRCUS (US 1926-28, Charlie Chaplin)

CLAIRENORE STINNES – IM AUTO DURCH ZWEI WELTEN (GER 1929, Clairenore Stinnes, › Clairenore Stinnes – By Car through Two Worlds ‹)

COAL FACE (GB 1936, Alberto Cavalcanti)

LA COQUILLE ET LE CLERGYMAN (FR 1927, Germaine Dulac, › The Shell and the Clergyman ‹)

CREOSOTE (NL 1931, Joris Ivens)

LA CROISIÈRE JAUNE (FR 1934, Léon Poirier / André Sauvage, › The Yellow Cruise ‹)

LA CROISIÈRE NOIRE (FR 1926, Léon Poirier, › The Black Cruise ‹)

CROSSING THE GREAT SAGRADA (GB 1924, Adrian Brunel)

DIE DAME MIT DER MASKE (GER 1928, Wilhelm Thiele, › The Lady with the Mask ‹)

DEIN SCHICKSAL (GER 1928, Ernö Metzner, › Your Destiny ‹)

DEUTSCHE WELLE – TÖNENDER RUNDFUNK (GER 1928, Walter Ruttmann, › German Wave – Sounding Radio ‹)

DEZERTIR (SU 1933, Vsevolod Pudovkin, › Deserter ‹)

DOURO, FAINA FLUVIAL (PT 1931, Manoel de Oliveira, › Working on the Douro River ‹)

DR. MABUSE, DER SPIELER (GER 1921-22, Fritz Lang, › Dr. Mabuse, the Gambler ‹)

DIE 3-GROSCHEN-OPER (GER 1930, G.W. Pabst, › The Three –Penny Opera ‹)

DRIFTERS (GB 1929, John Grierson)

DURCH AFRIKA IM AUTOMOBIL (AT 1929, › By Car through Africa ‹)

EMAK BAKIA (FR 1927, Man Ray)

ENTR'ACTE (FR 1924, René Clair / Francis Picabia, › Interlude ‹)

ENTUZIAZM: SINFONIJA DONBASSA (SU 1930, Dziga Vertov, › Enthusiasm: Don-bass Symphony ‹)

DIE EROBERUNG DES HIMMELS (CH 1938, Hans Richter, › The Conquest of Hea-ven ‹)

L'ETOILE DE MER (FR 1928, Man Ray, › The Sea Urchin ‹)

ÉTUDES SUR PARIS (1929, Andrè Sauvage, › Studies of Paris ‹)

EUROPA RADIO (NL 1931, Hans Richter)

EVERYDAY (GB 1929-1975, Hans Richter)

THE FALL OF THE HOUSE OF USHER (US 1926-28, Melville Webber / J.S. Watson Jr.)

FALSCHMÜNZER / SALAMANDRA (GER/SU 1929, Grigori Roschal, SALAMANDER)

FANTASIA (US 1940, Walt Disney)

FAUST (GER 1926, F.W. Murnau)

FEIND IM BLUT (CH 1931, Walter Ruttmann, › Enemy in the Blood ‹)

EIN FEIERTAG IN HESSEN-NASSAU / HITLERS BRAUNE SOLDATEN KOMMEN (GER 1931, Frank Hensel, › A Holiday in Hesse-Nassau ‹ / › Hitler's Brown Soldiers Are Coming ‹)

FELIX THE CAT AT THE CIRCUS (US 1926)

FEU MATHIAS PASCAL (FR 1924, Marcel L'Herbier, › The Late Mathias Pascal ‹)

EIN FILM GEGEN DIE VOLKSKRANKHEIT KREBS (GER 1941, Walter Ruttmann, › A Film Against the Widespread Disease Cancer ‹)

FILMSTUDIE (GER 1928, Hans Richter, › Film Study ‹)

LA FIN DU MONDE (FR 1930, Abel Gance, › The End of the World ‹)

DIE FRAU IM MOND (GER 1928-29, Fritz Lang, › Woman in the Moon ‹)

FRAUENNOT – FRAUENGLÜCK (CH 1930, Sergei Eisenstein /Grigorij Alexandrov, › Women's Misery, Women's Happiness ‹)

FREIES VOLK (GER 1925, Martin Berger, › Free People ‹)

FREUDLOSE GASSE (GER 1925, G.W. Pabst, › Joyless Street ‹)

LA GLACE À TROIS FACE (FR 1927, Jean Epstein, › The Three-Sided Mirror ‹)

GOLOD... GOLOD... GOLOD (SU 1921, Vladimir Gardin / Vsevolod Pudovkin, › Hunger, Hunger, Hunger ‹)

GRASS (US 1925, Merian C. Cooper / Ernest B. Schoedsack)

GROSSSTADTZIGEUNER (GER 1932, László Moholy-Nagy, › Big City Gipsies ‹)

LA GUERRE ENTRE LE FILM INDÉPÉNDANT ET LE FILM INDUSTRIEL / TEMPÊTE SUR LA SARRAZ (CH 1929, Sergei Eisenstein et al., › The War between Indepen-dent and Commercial Film ‹ / › The Storming of La Sarraz ‹)

HALLELUJAH (US 1929, King Vidor)

HALLO EVERYBODY (NL 1933, Hans Richter)

HEIEN (NL 1929, Joris Ivens)

HENNY PORTEN – LEBEN UND LAUFBAHN EINER FILMKÜNSTLERIN (GER 1928, Oskar Kalbus, › Henny Porten – Life and Career of a Film Artist ‹)

HIGH TREASON (GB 1929, Maurice Elvey)

HITLERS KAMPF UM DEUTSCHLAND (GER 1932, Frank Hensel, › Hitler's Struggle for Germany ‹)

L'HORLOGE (FR 1924, Marcel Silver, › The Watch ‹)

HOW BRONCHO BILLY LEFT BEAR COUNTRY (US 1912)

IMPRESSIONEN VOM ALTEN MARSEILLER HAFEN (GER 1929, László Moholy-Nagy, › Impressions of the Old Marseille Port ‹)

INDUSTRIAL BRITAIN (GB 1931, Robert Flaherty / John Grierson)

INFLATION (GER 1928, Hans Richter)

IUNOST' MAKSIMA (SU 1934-35, Leonid Trauberg / Grigorij Kozintsev, › The Youth of Maxim ‹)

IVAN (SU 1932, Aleksandr Dovshenko)

J'ACCUSE (FR 1918, Abel Gance, › I Accuse ‹)

JEUX DES REFLETS ET LE LA VITESSE (FR 1925, Henri Chomette, › Play of Reflections and Velocity ‹)

KEAN (FR 1923, Aleksandr Volkov)

KING KONG (US 1933, Merian C. Cooper / Ernest B. Schoedsack)

KINOGLAZ (SU 1920, Dziga Vertov, › Cinema Eye ‹)

KIPHO-FILM (GER 1925, Guido Seeber)

KOMSOMOL (SU 1932-33, Joris Ivens, › Song of Heroes ‹)

KONEC SANKT-PETERBURGA (SU 1926, Vsevolod Pudovkin, › The End of St. Petersburg ‹)

KSE – KOMSOMOL, SEF ELEKTRIFIKACII (SU 1932, Esfir Shub, › Komsomol, Patron of Electrification ‹)

KUHLE WAMPE, ODER WEM GEHÖRT DIE WELT (GER 1932, Slatan Dudow, › Kuhle Wampe, or to whom belongs the world? ‹)

DER LEBENDE LEICHNAM / SHIWOI TRUP (GER/SU 1929, Fedor Ozep, › The Living Corpse ‹)

DER LETZTE MANN (GER 1924, F.W. Murnau, › The Last Laugh ‹)

LICHTSPIEL SCHWARZ-WEISS-GRAU (GER 1931-32, László Moholy-Nagy, › Light Play Black – White – Grey ‹)

DIE LIEBE DER JEANNE NEY (GER 1927, G.W. Pabst, › The Love of Jeanne Ney ‹)

DAS LIED VOM LEBEN (GER 1930, Alexis Granowsky, › The Song of Life ‹)

THE LIFE AND DEATH OF 9413 – A HOLLYWOOD EXTRA (US 1927, Robert Florey)
LE LION DES MOGOLS (FR 1924, Jean Epstein, › The Lion of Mongolia ‹)
LOHNBUCHHALTER KREMKE (GER 1930, Marie Harder, › Wages Clerk Kremke ‹)

M (GER 1930-31, Fritz Lang)
MATJ (SU 1926, Vsevolod Pudovkin, › Mother ‹)
MEDWESHJA SWADBA (SU 1925, Konstantin Eggert, › The Bear's Wedding ‹)
MEHANIKA GOLOVNOGO MOZGA (SU 1925, Vsevolod Pudovkin, › Mechanics of the Brain ‹)
MELODIE DER WELT (GER 1928-29, Walter Ruttmann, › Melody of the World ‹)
MENSCHEN AM SONNTAG (GER 1929, Robert Siodmak et al., › People on Sunday ‹)
METROPOLIS (GER 1925-26, Fritz Lang)
LE MILLION (FR 1930, René Clair, › The Million ‹)
MIMOSA LA DERNIÈRE GRISETTE (FR 1906, Leonce Perret, › Mimosa, the Last Grisette ‹)
MISÈRE AU BORINAGE (BE 1933-34, Joris Ivens/Henri Storck, › Misery at Borinage ‹)
MISS MEND. PRIKLJUCENIJA TREH REPORTEROV (SU 1926, Fedor Ozep / Boris Barnet, › Miss Mend ‹)
MIT ELLY BEINHORN ZU DEN DEUTSCHEN IN SÜDWEST-AFRIKA (GER 1933, Elly Beinhorn, › With Elly Beinhorn to the Germans in Southwest Africa ‹)
MOANA (US 1926, Robert Flaherty)
MOSKVA V OKTJABRE (SU 1927, Boris Barnet, › Moscow in October ‹)
LES MYSTÈRES DU CHÂTEAU DE DÉ (FR 1929, › The Mystery of the Chateau of the Dice ‹)

NA KROSNOM FRONTE (SU 1920, Lev Kuleshov, › On the Red Front ‹)
NA PRAŽSKÉM HRAD (1932, Alexander Hackenschmied, › Prague Castle ‹)
NANOOK OF THE NORTH (US 1922, Robert Flaherty)
NAPOLÉON (FR 1925-27, Abel Gance)
NEOBYCHAINIYE PRIKLUCHENIYA MISTERA VESTA V STRANYE BOLSHEVIKOV (SU 1924, Lev Kuleshov, › The Extraordinary Adventures of Mr. West in the Land of the Bolsheviks ‹)
DIE NEUE WOHNUNG (CH 1930, Hans Richter, › New Living ‹)
NEW ARCHITECTURE AT THE LONDON ZOO (GB 1936, László Moholy-Nagy)
DIE NIBELUNGEN (GER 1922-24, Fritz Lang)
NIGHT MAIL (GB 1936, Harry Watt & Basil Wright)
NOSFERATU – EINE SYMPHONIE DES GRAUENS (GER 1921, F.W. Murnau, › Nosferatu, a Symphony of Terror ‹)
LES NOUVEAUX MESSIEURS (FR 1928, Jacques Feyder, › The New Gentlemen ‹)

Novyj Vavilon (SU 1929, Grigorij Kozincev & Leonid Trauberg, › The New Babylon ‹)

Oblomok Imperii (SU 1929, Fridrih Ermler, › Fragment of an Empire ‹)
Odinnadcatyj. Hronika (SU 1927, Dziga Vertov, › The Eleventh Year ‹)
Odna (SU 1931, Grigori Kozintsev / Leonid Trauberg, › Alone ‹)
Okraina (1933, Boris Barnet, › Outskirts ‹)
Oktjabr' (SU 1927, Sergej Eisenstein, › Ten Days That Shook the Earth ‹ / › October ‹)
Opus I-IV (GER 1919/1921/1924/1925, Walter Ruttmann)

Padenie dinastii Romanovyh (SU 1927, Esfir Shub, › The Fall of the Romanoff Dynasty ‹)
Pamir, das Tal des Todes (GER/SU 1929, Vladimir Snejderov, › Pamir, the Valley of Death ‹)
Paris qui dort (FR 1923-24, René Clair, › Paris Is Sleeping ‹)
La Passion de Jeanne d'Arc (FR 1928, Carl Theodor Dreyer, › The Passion of Joan of Arc ‹)
La Petite Marchande d'Allumettes (FR 1927-28, Jean Renoir, › The Little Match Girl ‹)
La p'tite Lili (FR 1927-28, Alberto Cavalcanti, › Little Lili ‹)
Philips Radio (NL 1931, Joris Ivens)
Photogénies (FR 1924, Jean Epstein)
Plan velikikh rabot (SU 1929-30, Abram Room, › Plan for Great Works ‹)
Polikushka (SU 1919-20, Alexander Sanin)
Potomok Cingis-hana (SU 1928, Vsevolod Pudovkin, › Storm over Asia ‹ / › The Heir of Tschingis Khan ‹)
Potselui Meri Pikford (SU 1927, Sergei Komarov, › The Kiss of Mary Pickford ‹)
La première traversée du Sahara en autochenilles (FR 1923, Paul Castelnau, › The First Crossing of the Sahara with a Caterpillar Vehicle ‹)

Que viva Mexico (US 1930-32, Sergej Eisenstein)

Regen (NL 1929, › Rain ‹)
Rennsymphonie (GER 1928, Hans Richter, › Race Symphony ‹)
Rhythmus 23 (GER 1923-1925, Hans Richter, › Rhythm 23 ‹)
Romance Sentimentale (FR 1929, Grigorij Alexandrov, › Sentimental Romance ‹)
Rossija Nikolaja II i Lev Tolstoj (SU 1928, Esfir Shub, › Czar Nikolaus II. and Leo Tolstoi ‹)

LA ROUE (FR 1920-22, Abel Gance, › The Wheel ‹)
RUND UM DIE LIEBE (GER 1929, Oskar Kalbus, › Around Love ‹)

LE SANG D'UN POÈTE (FR 1930, Jean Cocteau, › The Blood of a Poet ‹)
DIE SCHMIEDE (GER 1924, Martin Berger, › The Forge ‹)
SILNICE ZPÍVÁ (CZ 1937, Alexander Hackenschmied et al., › The Highway Sings ‹)
SIX ET DEMI-ONZE (FR 1927, Jean Epstein, › 6 1/2 x 11 ‹)
SOL' SVANETII (SU 1930, Mikhail Kalatozonov, › Salt for Svanetia ‹)
SONG OF CEYLON (GB 1934-35, Basil Wright)
SOS EISBERG (GER 1932-33, Arnold Fanck, › SOS Iceberg ‹)
LA SOURIANTE MADAME BEUDET (FR 1923, Germaine Dulac, › The Smiling Madame Beudet ‹)
SOUS LES TOITS DE PARIS (FR 1929-30, René Clair, › Under the Roofs of Paris ‹)
SPRECHENDER FILM (GER 1927, Guido Bagier, › Talking Film ‹)
STAROE I NOVOE / GENERAL'NAJA LINIJA (SU 1926-29, Sergei Eisenstein, › The Old and the New ‹ / › The General Line ‹)
STÜRME ÜBER DEM MONTBLANC (GER 1930, Arnold Fanck, › Storm Over Montblanc ‹)
SUNNYSIDE (US 1921, Charlie Chaplin)
SYMPHONIE DIAGONALE (GER 1923-1924, Viking Eggeling)

TABU (US 1930-31, F.W. Murnau / Robert Flaherty)
LA TERRE DE FEU (FR 1927, › Country of Fire ‹)
TIERRA SIN PAN / LAS HURDAS (ES 1932, Luis Buñuel, › Land without Bread ‹)
TISZA GARIT (SU 1933-34, Béla Bálasz)
LA TRAVERSÉ DU GRÉPON / L'ASCENSION DU GRÉPON (FR 1923, André Sauvage, › The Ascent of the Grepon ‹)
TRET'JA MESCANSKAJA (SU 1927, › Bed and Sofa ‹ / › Third Meshchanskaia Street ‹)
TRI PESNI O LENIN (SU 1934, Dziga Vertov, › Three Songs for Lenin ‹)
TRIUMPH DES WILLENS (GER 1934-35, Leni Riefenstahl, › Triumph of the Will ‹)
TURKSIB (SU 1929, Victor Turin)
TYPICAL BUDGET (GB 1925, Adrian Brunel)

UIT HET RIJK DER KRISTALLEN (NL 1927, J.C. Mol, › From the Empire of Crystals ‹)

VARIETÉ (GER 1925, E.A. Dupont)
VELIKIJ PUT' (SU 1927, Esfir Shub, › The Great Way ‹)
DIE VERRUFENEN (GER 1925, Gerhard Lamprecht, › The Disreputables ‹)

LA VIE SOUS-MARINE (FR 1927, Jean Painlevé, › Underwater Life ‹)

VISAGES DES ENFANTS (FR 1923-25, Jacques Feyder, › Children's Faces ‹)

VORMITTAGS-SPUK (GER 1927-28, › Ghosts before Breakfast ‹)

VOSSTANIE RYBAKOV / DER AUFSTAND DER FISCHER (SU/GER, 1931-1934, Erwin Piscator, › The Fishermen's Uprising ‹)

VOYAGE AU CONGO (FR 1927, Marc Allégret, › Journey to the Congo ‹)

VOZVRASHCHENIE MAKSIMA (SU 1937, Leonid Trauberg / Grigorij Kozintsev, › The Return of Maxim ‹)

VYBORGSKAIA STORONA (SU 1939, Leonid Trauberg / Grigorij Kozintsev, › The Vyborg Side ‹)

WACHSFIGURENKABINETT (1923, Paul Leni, › Wax Works ‹)

WAS WIR WOLLEN – WAS WIR NICHT WOLLEN (GER 1928, Béla Balázs, Albrecht Viktor Blum, › What We Want – What we Don't Want ‹)

WEGE ZU KRAFT UND SCHÖNHEIT (GER 1924-25, Wilhelm Prager, › Ways to Strength and Beauty ‹)

DIE WEISSE HÖLLE VOM PIZ PALÜ (GER 1929, Arnold Fanck, › The White Hell of Pitz Palü ‹)

WHITE SHADOWS IN THE SOUTH SEA (US 1928, Robert Flaherty / W.S. Van Dyke)

DAS WIEDERGEFUNDENE PARADIES (GER 1925, Walter Ruttmann, › Paradise Regained ‹)

WIJ BOUWEN (NL 1929, Joris Ivens, › We Are Building ‹)

WING BEAT (CH 1927, H.D.)

WINGS OVER EVEREST (GB 1934, Geoffrey Farkas / Ivor Montagu)

DAS WUNDER (GER 1922, Walter Ruttmann, › The Miracle ‹)

DIE WUNDER DES FILMS (GER 1928, Edgar Beyfuß, › The Miracles of Film ‹)

ZEITBERICHT – ZEITGESICHT (GER 1928, Ernst Angel / Albrecht Viktor Blum, › Report of the Times – Faces of the Times ‹)

ZEMLJA (SU 1930, Aleksandr Dovzenko, › Earth ‹)

ZEMLJA W PLENU (SU 1928, Fedor Ozep, › The Yellow Pass ‹)

ZEMLJA ZAZDET (SU 1930, Juri Raizman, › The Earth Thirsts ‹)

ZERO DE CONDUITE (FR 1933, Jean Vigo, › Zero for Conduct ‹)

ZUIDERSEE (NL 1930, Joris Ivens)

DER ZWEIGROSCHEN-ZAUBER (GER 1929, Hans Richter, › The Two-Penny Magic ‹)

Index of Names

Index of Film Titles

Index of Subjects

Film Culture in Transition

General Editor: *Thomas Elsaesser*

Thomas Elsaesser, Robert Kievit and Jan Simons (eds.)
Double Trouble: Chiem van Houweninge on Writing and Filming, 1994
ISBN paperback 978 90 5356 025 9

Thomas Elsaesser, Jan Simons and Lucette Bronk (eds.)
Writing for the Medium: Television in Transition, 1994
ISBN paperback 978 90 5356 054 9

Karel Dibbets and Bert Hogenkamp (eds.)
Film and the First World War, 1994
ISBN paperback 978 90 5356 064 8

Warren Buckland (ed.)
The Film Spectator: From Sign to Mind, 1995
ISBN paperback 978 90 5356 131 7; ISBN hardcover 978 90 5356 170 6

Egil Törnqvist
Between Stage and Screen: Ingmar Bergman Directs, 1996
ISBN paperback 978 90 5356 137 9; ISBN hardcover 978 90 5356 171 3

Thomas Elsaesser (ed.)
A Second Life: German Cinema's First Decades, 1996
ISBN paperback 978 90 5356 172 0; ISBN hardcover 978 90 5356 183 6

Thomas Elsaesser
Fassbinder's Germany: History Identity Subject, 1996
ISBN paperback 978 90 5356 059 4; ISBN hardcover 978 90 5356 184 3

Thomas Elsaesser and Kay Hoffmann (eds.)
Cinema Futures: Cain, Abel or Cable? The Screen Arts in the Digital Age, 1998
ISBN paperback 978 90 5356 282 6; ISBN hardcover 978 90 5356 312 0

Siegfried Zielinski
Audiovisions: Cinema and Television as Entr'Actes in History, 1999
ISBN paperback 978 90 5356 313 7; ISBN hardcover 978 90 5356 303 8

Kees Bakker (ed.)
Joris Ivens and the Documentary Context, 1999
ISBN paperback 978 90 5356 389 2; ISBN hardcover 978 90 5356 425 7

Egil Törnqvist
Ibsen, Strindberg and the Intimate Theatre: Studies in TV Presentation, 1999
ISBN paperback 978 90 5356 350 2; ISBN hardcover 978 90 5356 371 7

Michael Temple and James S. Williams (eds.)
The Cinema Alone: Essays on the Work of Jean-Luc Godard 1985-2000, 2000
ISBN paperback 978 90 5356 455 4; ISBN hardcover 978 90 5356 456 1

Patricia Pisters and Catherine M. Lord (eds.)
Micropolitics of Media Culture: Reading the Rhizomes of Deleuze and Guattari, 2001
ISBN paperback 978 90 5356 472 1; ISBN hardcover 978 90 5356 473 8

William van der Heide
Malaysian Cinema, Asian Film: Border Crossings and National Cultures, 2002
ISBN paperback 978 90 5356 519 3; ISBN hardcover 978 90 5356 580 3

Bernadette Kester
Film Front Weimar: Representations of the First World War in German Films of the Weimar Period (1919-1933), 2002
ISBN paperback 978 90 5356 597 1; ISBN hardcover 978 90 5356 598 8

Richard Allen and Malcolm Turvey (eds.)
Camera Obscura, Camera Lucida: Essays in Honor of Annette Michelson, 2003
ISBN paperback 978 90 5356 494 3

Ivo Blom
Jean Desmet and the Early Dutch Film Trade, 2003
ISBN paperback 978 90 5356 463 9; ISBN hardcover 978 90 5356 570 4

Alastair Phillips
City of Darkness, City of Light: Émigré Filmmakers in Paris 1929-1939, 2003
ISBN paperback 978 90 5356 634 3; ISBN hardcover 978 90 5356 633 6

Thomas Elsaesser, Alexander Horwath and Noel King (eds.)
The Last Great American Picture Show: New Hollywood Cinema in the 1970s, 2004
ISBN paperback 978 90 5356 631 2; ISBN hardcover 978 905356 493 6

Thomas Elsaesser (ed.)
Harun Farocki: Working on the Sight-Lines, 2004
ISBN paperback 978 90 5356 635 0; ISBN hardcover 978 90 5356 636 7

Kristin Thompson
Herr Lubitsch Goes to Hollywood: German and American Film after World War I, 2005
ISBN paperback 978 90 5356 708 1; ISBN hardcover 978 90 5356 709 8

Marijke de Valck and Malte Hagener (eds.)
Cinephilia: Movies, Love and Memory, 2005
ISBN paperback 978 90 5356 768 5; ISBN hardcover 978 90 5356 769 2

Thomas Elsaesser
European Cinema: Face to Face with Hollywood, 2005
ISBN paperback 978 90 5356 594 0; ISBN hardcover 978 90 5356 602 2

Michael Walker
Hitchcock's Motifs, 2005
ISBN paperback 978 90 5356 772 2; ISBN hardcover 978 90 5356 773 9

Nanna Verhoeff
The West in Early Cinema: After the Beginning, 2006
ISBN paperback 978 90 5356 831 6; ISBN hardcover 978 90 5356 832 3

Anat Zanger
Film Remakes as Ritual and Disguise: From Carmen to Ripley, 2006
ISBN paperback 978 90 5356 784 5; ISBN hardcover 978 90 5356 785 2

Wanda Strauven
The Cinema of Attractions Reloaded, 2006
ISBN paperback 978 90 5356 944 3; ISBN hardcover 978 90 5356 945 0